World Food Security

Also by D. John Shaw

D. John Shaw (*author*)
THE UN WORLD FOOD PROGRAMME AND THE DEVELOPMENT OF FOOD AID

D. John Shaw (*author*)
SIR HANS SINGER
The Life and Work of a Development Economist

D. John Shaw (*editor*)
INTERNATIONAL DEVELOPMENT COOPERATION
Selected Essays by H.W. Singer on Aid and the United Nations System

D. John Shaw and Edward Clay (*editors*)
WORLD FOOD AID
Experiences of Recipients and Donors

Helene Delisle and D. John Shaw (*editors*)
THE QUEST FOR FOOD SECURITY IN THE TWENTY-FIRST CENTURY

D. John Shaw and H.W. Singer (*authors*)
A FUTURE FOOD AID REGIME: IMPLICATIONS OF THE FINAL ACT OF THE GATT
URUGUAY ROUND

Edward Clay and D. John Shaw (*editors*)
POVERTY, DEVELOPMENT AND FOOD
Essays in Honour of H.W. Singer on his 75th Birthday

D. John Shaw (*author*)
THE WORLD FOOD PROGRAMME AND EMERGENCY RELIEF

D. John Shaw and H.W. Singer (*editors*)
FOOD POLICY, FOOD AID AND ECONOMIC ADJUSTMENT

J.P. Greaves and D. John Shaw (*editors*)
FOOD AID AND THE WELL-BEING OF CHILDREN IN THE DEVELOPING WORLD

World Food Security

A History since 1945

D. John Shaw

© D. John Shaw 2007
Softcover reprint of the hardcover 1st edition 2007 978-0-230-55355-2

All rights reserved. No reproduction, copy or transmission of this
publication may be made without written permission.

No paragraph of this publication may be reproduced, copied or transmitted
save with written permission or in accordance with the provisions of the
Copyright, Designs and Patents Act 1988, or under the terms of any licence
permitting limited copying issued by the Copyright Licensing Agency,
90 Tottenham Court Road, London W1T 4LP.

Any person who does any unauthorized act in relation to this publication
may be liable to criminal prosecution and civil claims for damages.

The author has asserted his right to be identified
as the author of this work in accordance with the Copyright,
Designs and Patents Act 1988.

First published 2007 by
PALGRAVE MACMILLAN
Houndmills, Basingstoke, Hampshire RG21 6XS and
175 Fifth Avenue, New York, N.Y. 10010
Companies and representatives throughout the world

PALGRAVE MACMILLAN is the global academic imprint of the Palgrave
Macmillan division of St. Martin's Press, LLC and of Palgrave Macmillan Ltd.
Macmillan® is a registered trademark in the United States, United Kingdom
and other countries. Palgrave is a registered trademark in the European
Union and other countries.

ISBN 978-1-349-36333-9   ISBN 978-0-230-58978-0 (eBook)
DOI 10.1057/9780230589780

This book is printed on paper suitable for recycling and made from fully
managed and sustained forest sources. Logging, pulping and manufacturing
processes are expected to conform to the environmental regulations of the
country of origin.

A catalogue record for this book is available from the British Library.

Library of Congress Cataloging-in-Publication Data
Shaw, D. John.
  World food security: a history since 1945 / D. John Shaw.
     p. cm.
  Includes bibliographical references and index.
  1. Food supply—History. 2. Food relief—International
cooperation—History. 3. Agricultural assistance—History.
  4. Economic development—History. 5. Hunger—Prevention—History.
  I. Title.
HD9000.5.S425 2007
338.1'9—dc22   2007023190

Transferred to Digital Printing in 2014

This book is dedicated to the memory of Professor Sir Hans Singer, friend and mentor for over forty years, who died during the final stages of this history at the age of 95, and who devoted his long and productive life to addressing the problems of developing countries.

Contents

List of Tables, Figures and Annexes	ix
Preface	x
Acknowledgements	xv
List of Abbreviations	xviii

Part I 1945–70. Early Attempts: FAO's Pioneering Work

1	FAO's Origins	3
2	Food Surpluses: Historical Background	12
3	World Food Board Proposal	15
4	International Commodity Clearing House	32
5	A World Food Reserve	37
6	National Food Reserves in Developing Countries	58
7	International Commodity Agreements	65
8	Freedom from Hunger Campaign	77
9	The Development of Food Aid	85

Part II 1970–90. The World Food Crisis of the 1970s and its Aftermath

10	World Food Crisis	115
11	World Food Conference 1974	121
12	International Undertaking on World Food Security	150
13	An International Grain Reserves System	155
14	International Emergency Food Reserve	159
15	Global Information and Early Warning System	163
16	International Trade, Stability and Agricultural Adjustment	165
17	World Food Council	167
18	ILO World Employment Conference, 1976	222
19	Food Entitlement	230

viii *Contents*

20	Pragmatism and Politics	235
21	World Bank Perspective	259
22	Food Subsidies	264

Part III   The 1990s and Beyond: International Conferences

23	International Development Strategy for the 1990s	271
24	International Conferences	274
25	World Summit for Children, 1990	279
26	UN Conference on Environment and Development, 1992	286
27	International Conference on Water and the Environment, 1992	299
28	International Conference on Nutrition, 1992	304
29	World Conference on Human Rights, 1993	313
30	World Conference on Overcoming Global Hunger, 1993	318
31	International Conference on Population and Development, 1994	321
32	World Summit for Social Development, 1995	328
33	A 2020 Vision for Food, Agriculture and the Environment, 1995	334
34	Fourth World Conference on Women, 1995	340
35	World Food Summit, 1996	347
36	World Agricultural Trade: WTO and the Doha Ministerial Declaration, 2001	361
37	UN Millennium Summit, 2000	364
38	International Conference on Financing for Development, 2002	369
39	World Summit, 2005	375

Part IV   Assessment. The Graveyard of Aspirations

40	Redefining the Concept of Food Security	383
41	Dimensions of Poverty and Food Insecurity	387
42	Future Action	432

Notes	462
Bibliography	476
Index	496

List of Tables, Figures and Annexes

Tables

3.1	Cereals: World exports and prices, 1910–50	19
10.1	World cereal supplies, 1971/72 to 1973/74	116
10.2	Changes in export prices of selected agricultural commodities, 1971–74	117
17.1	World Food Council and the World Food Security situation	171
41.1	Undernutrition in the developing world, 1979–81 to 2000–02	389
41.2	The effects of protein-energy malnutrition on preschool children, 1980–2005	390
41.3	Population affected by micro-nutrient malnutrition (millions), 2001/2004	391
41.4	Numbers of people living below $1 and $2 a day, 1981–2001	417

Figures

17.1	United Nations bodies with an interest in food and nutrition security	207
40.1	The broad concept of food and nutrition security: the eye of the storm	384
41.1	A classification of hungry people	395
42.1	Possible impacts of climate change on growth and development	448

Annexes

9.1	Guidelines and Criteria for Food Aid	109
11.1	Resolutions adopted by the World Food Conference	149
14.1	Modalities for the Operation of the International Emergency Food Reserve	161
17.1	World Food Council Presidents and Executive Directors	221
24.1	International Conferences: 1990–2005	277
37.1	Millennium development goals and targets	366

Preface

It is an appalling fact that in this globalizing world of increasing prosperity, in which the richest tenth own 85 per cent of the world's assets, just under one billion people subsist on less than one dollar a day, 2.8 billion on less than two dollars a day, and 850 million suffer from undernourishment in dehumanizing, abject poverty. Almost 200 million children under five years of age are underweight due to lack of food and one child dies every 5 seconds from hunger and related causes. Hunger and malnutrition kill more people every year than AIDS, malaria and tuberculosis combined, and more people die from hunger than in wars. At the centre of this human tragedy is food insecurity, inability to access the safe and nutritious food necessary for a healthy and active life. World leaders and international bodies have many times made a commitment, and have acknowledged that there are sufficient resources and know-how, to end hunger and poverty. This scourge is not only morally unacceptable but is a serious impediment to equitable and sustainable economic and social development, and to world peace. This history is about what attempts have been made over the past sixty years to address this problem in what I have come to call 'the graveyard of aspirations'.

My interest in the concept of food security, and of the consequences of its antithesis, food insecurity that dominate the lives and livelihoods of hungry poor people and households was kindled during my undergraduate and post-graduate field research in such diverse places as Western Ireland, Morocco, Bosnia and Croatia. It continued during my time as senior lecturer in rural economy at the University of Khartoum, Sudan (1959–66), when I was also a consultant to the Food and Agriculture Organization of the United Nations (FAO), the World Bank and the United Nations World Food Programme (WFP). This involved visits to a number of countries in North Africa and the Middle East and sub-Saharan Africa. My interest and concern were strengthened further when I was employed by WFP at its headquarters in Rome, Italy (1967–94) first as senior evaluation officer, then as senior economist and head of the Policy Unit in the Office of the Executive Director, then as economic adviser, and finally as chief of WFP's Policy Affairs Service. During this time, I visited many countries in Asia and Africa and liaised with a number of the UN organizations concerned with issues related to food security. Located WFP's headquarters in Rome, I was also able to consult the papers and documents on the early pioneering work of FAO on food and nutrition security in its archives and library, many of which have long been forgotten, and follow closely discussions in FAO's principal committees.

This rich experience convinced me of the need for an historical account of attempts to set up some form of world food security arrangement since the Second World War (1939–45) and the establishment of FAO as the first United Nations specialized agency after the war ended. This is the first comprehensive account of the numerous attempts that have been made over the past sixty years. I felt that a comprehensive history was necessary not only to show the many ways in which attempts have been made to achieve world food and nutrition security unfolded, and the sequence in which they occurred, but also why they did not succeed, and what lessons can be drawn for the future. I also felt that such a history was necessary as a point of reference for all those individuals and institutions interested and involved in achieving food security for all who come at the subject from many and diverse perspectives and specialities. As such, it contains material that appears in the public domain for the first time: the account of FAO's early pioneering work; a comprehensive account of the work of the World Food Council that was set up after the world food crisis of the early 1970s and the 1974 World Food Conference to coordinate the work of the UN system of organizations interested and engaged in food security issues; and the compounding effect of the sequence of international conferences that were held in the 1990s, culminating in the World Summit of 2005.

My history is divided into four parts. The first three parts give the history of the quest for world food security as it unfolded chronologically. The final part gives the current status for world malnutrition and hunger seen from the various dimensions of poverty and an assessment of effects of various attempts to overcome these scourges in what I have called the 'graveyard of aspirations'. These developments are set against the background of the evolving concepts of development theory and practice and major changes in the evolution of the global food system. Part I (1945–70) begins with the creation of FAO in response to President Roosevelt's call for 'freedom from want' and the emergence of the new science of nutrition, and the need, as FAO's constitution put it, 'to ensure humanity's freedom from hunger'. The first director-general of FAO, Sir John (later Lord) Boyd Orr of the United Kingdom, who proposed the establishment of a World Food Board as a marriage of nutrition, health, agriculture, trade and industry, is described in detail and remains one of the boldest and most imaginative plans for international action to achieve world food security.

The proposal, and a similar one on an International Commodity Clearing House, was not approved. When it became clear that the major industrialized countries, particularly the United States and the United Kingdom, were not prepared to see some form the world food security arrangement set up under the multilateral control of a United Nations body, the FAO secretariat kept the goal of world food security alive through a series of seminal pioneering studies, reports and proposals throughout the 1950s. These included: the establishment of a World Food Reserve to meet food emergencies, control excessive price fluctuations, and constructively use accumulating food surpluses; the drafting of Principles of Surplus Disposal to ensure their use to support development and to avoid any negative effects on domestic agricultural production in developing countries and on international trade; the creation of national and regional food reserves in developing countries; and different types of international commodity agreements.

An entirely different approach was adopted when the first FAO director-general from a developing country, the highly respected B. R. Sen from India, was elected xii *Preface*

in 1957. He was no less committed to making the elimination of hunger the central focus of the work of his organization but, given the continuing opposition of the major industrialized countries to any multilaterally controlled world food security arrangement, he realized that a new approach was necessary. He therefore launched a worldwide Freedom from Hunger Campaign to arose public awareness through education and information, which was designed to bring pressure to bare of governments to take action. One positive outcome was the development of food aid as a resource not only to meet food emergencies caused by natural and manmade disasters but also activities to foster economic and social development in the developing countries, which led to the establishment of the World Food Programme, the food aid arm of the United Nations system.

The second part of the history (1970–90) begins with the worst world food crisis to occur in modern times at the beginning of the 1970s. This led to the UN World Food Conference of 1974, which is described in detail to show the attitudes of the world leading powers, especially the United States, that led to the adoption of 20 substantive resolutions by the conference to eradicate world hunger and malnutrition. There follows a description of the action taken on some of the more prominent resolutions including: the International Undertaking on World Food Security; an international grain reserve system; an International Emergency Food Reserve; a General Information and Early Warning System to predict and forestall food emergencies; and international trade, stability and agricultural adjustment. The first comprehensive account of the work of the World Food Council that was set up to coordinated the activities of the UN bodies concerned with world food security is given, including the reasons for its demise in 1993. The ILO employment conference of 1976 is also described, including the concept of 'basic needs', which encompassed food security. The concept of food 'entitlement' originated by Amartya Sen, who was to receive the Nobel Prize in Economics, is then described as yet another approach to achieve food security.

The election of a new FAO director-general, Edouard Saouma, a Maronite Christian from the Lebanon, in 1976, who remained in office for the next eighteen years, ushered in a period of pragmatism and politics in the search for world food security. Like his predecessors, he saw food security as the central focus of the work of his organization. Pragmatically, he continued work started before he assumed office, including on: FAO's General Information and Early Warning System; preparations for large-scale and acute food shortages; a Food Security Assistance Scheme; a Special Action Programme for the Prevention of Food Losses (some countries suffered up to 20 per cent of food losses after harvest); and expansion of national and regional food storage facilities. Critically, in 1983, he revised FAO's concept of world food security by adding to the two pillars of increased food production and stability of food supplies, the third pillar of access to food by the poor, no doubt influences by Sen's concept of food entitlement. This differentiated the world food problem from the world food security problem and brought in issues that went beyond FAO's mandate. To obtain a perspective of the future dimensions of world food security, he continued the publication of FAO's world food surveys and converted work started on an Indicative World Plan for Agricultural Development into a study of World Agriculture: towards the year 2000. He also proposed a Plan of Action on World Food Security and a World Food Security Compact, which once again brought him into conflict with the leading industrialized countries who continued to resist any attempts to establish multilateral world food security arrangements beyond their control. In the meantime, a World Bank perspective on world food security issues was presented in a seminal study in 1986, which constructively distinguished between transitory and chronic food security, and called for different policies and programmes in their solution. Two years later, the International Food Policy Research Institute (IFPRI) published the results of its ten-year research programme on the costs and benefits of food subsidies in developing countries, and the policy options that they offered in providing food security.

Part III of the history (the 1990s and beyond) describes the series of international conferences that took place during the 1990s that relate to world food security, and the resolutions, goals and targets they adopted, in the order in which they occurred on: children, the environment, water resources, nutrition, human rights, overcoming global hunger, population, social development, food, agriculture and the environment, women, food security, and agricultural trade. By bringing these conferences together in one place, and describing their outcomes, the full range and diversity of the commitments made can more clearly be seen. The series of conferences ended with the Millennium Summit at the United Nations in 2000 at which world leaders agreed to specific millennium development goals and targets, which included halving the proportion of the world's population whose income is less than a \$1 a day and who suffered from hunger. The summit was followed by an International Conference on Financing for Development in 2002, at which commitments were made to provide the resources necessary to reach the millennium development goals, and by a World Summit at the United Nations in 2005 at which world leaders reiterated their commitment to achieve the goals set at the 2000 summit.

The final part of the history assesses the effects of attempts to achieve world food security. It recognizes the importance of locating the discussion in changing food policy and in the ebb and flow of the general discussion about development policy, including: the markedly changing views about agriculture, from the negative to the positive, in the 1960s; the shift in attention from economic growth to basic needs in the 1970s; the focus on structural change in the 1980s; the dominance of poverty and human development concerns of the 1990s; and the emphasis on reaching agreed millennium development goals since 2000. At the same time, national and international food systems have evolved markedly with the effects of increasing commercialization, industrialization, urbanization, and the emergence of the supermarket food economy and expanding world agricultural trade. A broader concept of world food security has also emerged in the light of these developments and the series of international conferences held in the 1990s.

The current status of the various dimensions of poverty is given in terms of food and nutrition insecurity, including: the grotesque paradox of the growth of obesity in the developed countries as a major killer when many continue to suffer

xiv *Preface*

and die from malnutrition and hunger in developing world; population growth; the income factor; the state of the world's children; the quest for education for all; employment, productivity and poverty reduction; and international trade. The dangerous division and lack of agreement, particularly between the United States and Europe, on the key issues of: genetically modified crops and food; climate change; globalization; as well as the breakdown of multilateral negotiations on liberalizing world trade are outlined as they can have a major impact on future world food security. The history ends with a call for leadership and coordinated and cohesive action to achieve the millennium development goals, including halving the proportion of the world's population living in abject and dehumanizing poverty and hunger, not only as a moral imperative but for the sake of just and equitable world economic and social development, and peace.

Much of the material contained in this history appears in the public domain for the first time, or has long since been forgotten. I hope this account will serve as a point of reference for all those interested and involved in world food security issues and concerns in organizations of the UN system, bilateral aid agencies and NGOs, and academia and the general public, who come to the subject from many different perspectives and disciplines.

My collection of documents and papers used in the writing of this history has been deposited in the British Library of Development Studies at the University of Sussex, UK.

D. John Shaw

Acknowledgements

This history has been a long time in the making and involved much research, travel, visits to archives and libraries, and interviewing and corresponding with people prominent in the quest for world food and nutrition security. Without their co-operation, it would not have been possible to have given many of the details contained in this book, some of which are revealed publicly for the first time. In many ways, this book is an outcome of the generosity of their time, opinions and recollections, and their collaboration in collecting and searching through a great deal of historical and archival material. I hope that I have adequately conveyed my sense of indebtedness to them and, particularly, that they feel that the final product repays my gratitude for all the help they gave me.

I begin my debts of gratitude with Professor Sir Hans Singer, to whom this history is dedicated. My friend and mentor for over forty years, he died at the age of 95 as this history was being completed. He devoted his long and productive life to the service of developing countries, as shown in my biography, *Sir Hans Singer. The Life and Work of a Development Economist* (Palgrave Macmillan, 2002). Senator George McGovern, who has devoted much of his long and distinguished public service to addressing the problem of world hunger, helped me considerable through an interview with him, personal correspondence and material, and access to his papers at the Seeley G. Mudd Manuscripts Library at Princeton University. Amongst other things, he played a leading role in the constructive use of food aid as the first director of the United States Food for Peace programme and special assistant to President John F. Kennedy, and played a key part in the establishment of the United Nations World Food Programme (WFP), as shown in my *The UN World Food Programme and the Development of Food Aid* (Palgrave Macmillan, 2001). He also served as United States Ambassador to the United Nations food and agricultural agencies in Rome, Italy and is now WFP Goodwill Ambassador.

I have benefited greatly from the co-operation, friendship and encouragement of many colleagues, particularly, Professor Sir Richard Jolly, formerly director of the Institute of Development Studies (IDS) at the University of Sussex, UK, UNICEF deputy executive director, principal co-ordinator and architect of the UNDP annual *Human Development Report*, chair of the UN Standing Committee on Nutrition, and chair of the Water Supply and Sanitation Collaborative Council, and now co-director of the *United Nations Intellectual History Project* (UNIHP) and honorary professorial fellow at IDS; Simon Maxwell, director, Edward Clay, senior research associate, Margaret Cornell, associate editor and Joanna Adcock, production, *Development Policy Review*, at the Overseas Development Institute, London; John Mellor of John Mellor Associates, Inc., a former director general of the International Food Policy Research Institute (IFPRI) in Washington, DC; and

xv

xvi *Acknowledgements*

Professor John Toye, a former IDS director, now at the Department of International Development, Queen Elizabeth House, Oxford University.

Sartaj Aziz gave me copies of the position papers he prepared for the 1974 World Food Conference when he was director of FAO's Commodities and Trade Division and one of the deputy secretaries-general of the conference that were to have an important bearing on the proposals presented to the conference and its eventual outcomes. I also benefited from him in subsequent discussions on the conference. The secretariat of the World Food Council gave me a complete set of the Council's documentation and papers when it was disbanded in 1993. Uwe Kracht, who served in the secretariat of the World Food Council (WFC) as senior economist from 1976 to 1986 and as chief of Policy Development and Analysis from 1986 to 1993, and is now co-ordinator, World Alliance for Nutrition and Human Rights and external research associate, International Project on the Right to Food in Development, reviewed the section in the book on the WFC and its work. Louis Emmerij, who, as director of ILO's World Employment Programme and secretary general of the ILO World Employment Conference in 1976, and now a co-director of the UNIHP, was one of the architects of the basic needs concept, provided me with his personal recollection of the origin of the concept and the background and outcomes of the conference. Rajul Pandya-Porch and Djhoanna Cruz of IFPRI provided me with publications and documents produced by that institute.

For their co-operation in guiding me through the vast amount of historical and archival material and publications referred to in preparing this book, I would like to record my sincere appreciate to the staffs of: the FAO Archives and Library in Rome; the United Nations Archives and Records Centre and the Dag Hammarskjold Library at the United Nations in New York; the John Fitzgerald Kennedy Presidential Library in Boston, MA; the Lyndon Baines Johnson Presidential Library in Austin, Texas; the Library of Congress in Washington, DC; the National Archives in College Park, Maryland; National Agricultural Library in Beltsville, Maryland; the Hubert H. Humphrey Institute of Public Affairs, University of Minnesota, Minneapolis, Minnesota; the Hubert H. Humphrey Collection, Minnesota Historical Society, St. Paul, Minnesota; the Seeley G. Mudd Manuscripts Library and the Harvey S. Firestone Memorial Library, Princeton University, New Jersey; the Walter William Fondren Library, Rice University, Houston, Texas; the British Library, London; the British Library of Development Studies and the Library of the Institute of Development Studies, University of Sussex, United Kingdom.

The UN World Food Programme gave me permission to reproduce the world hunger map as a cover image. Blackwell Publishing and the Production Manager gave me permission to use my articles and book reviews that have appeared in the journals *Development Policy Review* and the *Canadian Journal of Development Studies* respectively. The Food and Agriculture Organization of the United Nations (FAO) gave me permission to publish Tables 3.1, 10.1 and 17.2. The United Nations gave me permission to publish Table 10.2. Shaohua Chen and Martin Ravallion of the World Bank gave me permission to publish Table 41.4. The

United Nations Development Programme (UNDP) gave me permission to publish Figure 41.1. Cambridge University Press gave me permission to publish Figure 42.1. I am grateful to Uwe Kracht and Manfred Schulz for permission to quote from the book they edited on *Food Security and Nutrition. The Global Challenge* (1999).

Last, but far from being least, I owe much to my wife, Ileana, and my son and daughter, David and Elizabeth, for their support and encouragement, to Julia Botsford for her technical computer guidance, and to Elaine Johnson, who prepared the tables and figures that appear in this book.

I am grateful to Palgrave Macmillan, and particularly Amanda Hamilton, economics publisher and Alec Dubber, economics editorial assistant, and to Geetha Naren, project manager at Integra-India for the expeditious way in which this book was published.

I alone am responsible for the views expressed in this book and for any shortcomings therein.

D. John Shaw

List of Abbreviations

ACC	Administrative Committee on Coordination (UN)
ASEAN	Association of South-East Asian Nations
BSFF	Buffer Stock Financing Facility (IMF)
CCC	Commodity Credit Corporation (US)
CCP	Committee on Commodity Problems (FAO)
CFF	Compensatory Financing Facility (IMF)
CFS	Committee on World Food Security (FAO)
CGIAR	Consultative Group on International Agricultural Research
CIS	Commonwealth of Independent States (former USSR)
CSD	Consultative Subcommittee on Surplus Disposal (FAO)
ECLA	Economic Commission for Latin America (UN)
ECOSOC	Economic and Social Council of the United Nations
EEC	European Economic Community (now European Union)
EFA	Education for All
EPTA	Expanded Programme of Technical Assistance of the UN
EU	European Union
FAC	Food Aid Convention
FAO	Food and Agriculture Organization of the United Nations
FFHC	Freedom from Hunger Campaign (FAO)
FIVIMS	Food Insecurity and Vulnerability Information and Mapping Systems
FPC	Food priority countries
FSAS	Food Security Assistance Scheme (FAO)
G7	Group of seven leading industrialized countries (Canada, France, Germany, Italy, Japan, United Kingdom, United States)
G8	G7 plus Russian Federation
G77	Group of non-aliened developing countries
GATT	General Agreement on Tariffs and Trade
GDP	Gross Domestic Product
GIEWS	General Information and Early Warning System (FAO)
GNP	Gross National Product
IAEA	International Atomic Energy Agency
Habitat	UN Centre for Human Settlements
IBRD	International Bank for Reconstruction and Development (World Bank)
ICCH	International Commodity Clearing House
ICN	International Conference on Nutrition
ICPD	International Conference on Population and Development

IDA	International Development Association (World Bank)
IEFR	International Emergency Food Reserve
IFAD	International Fund for Agricultural Development
IFAP	International Federation of Agricultural Producers
IFPRI	International Food Policy Research Institute
IGC	International Grains Council
ILO	International Labour Organization
IMF	International Monetary Fund
INSTRAW	International Research and Training Institute for the Advancement of Women
ITO	International Trade Organization
IUWFS	International Undertaking on World Food Security
IWA	International Wheat Agreement
IWC	International Wheat Council (now International Grains Council)
IWP	Indicative World Plan for World Agriculture (FAO)
MDGs	Millennium development goals
OPEC	Organization of Oil Exporting Countries
SADCC	Southern Africa Development Conference
SCN	UN Standing Committee on Nutrition
SDR	Special Drawing Rights (IMF)
SELA	Latin American Economic System
SUNFED	Special United Nations Fund for Economic Development
TAB	Technical Assistance Board of the UN
TCP	Technical Cooperation Programme (FAO)
UDHA	Universal Declaration in Human Rights
UK	United Kingdom
US	United States
UN	United Nations
UNCTAD	United Nations Conference on Trade and Development
UNCTC	UN Commission on Transnational Corporations
UNDHA	UN Department for Humanitarian Affairs
UNDP	United Nations Development Programme
UNESCO	United Nations Education, Scientific and Cultural Organization
UNFPA	United Nations Population Fund
UNHCR	UN High Commissioner for Refugees
UNICEF	United Nations Children's Fund
UNRRA	United Nations Relief and Rehabilitation Administration
UNRWA	UN Relief and Works Agency
UNEP	United Nations Environment Programme
UNSO	UN Sudano-Sahelian Office
USDA	United States Department of Agriculture
UN/WIDER	United Nations University World Institute for Development Economic Research
VAM	Vulnerability Analysis and Mapping (WFP)
WFB	World Food Board

WFC	World Food Council
WFCF	World Food Capital Fund
WFP	World Food Programme (UN)
WFR	World Food Reserve
WFS	World Food Summit 1996
WMO	World Meteorological Organization
WHO	World Health Organization
WSSCC	Water Supply and Sanitation Collaborative Council
WSSD	World Summit on Sustainable Development
WTO	World Trade Organization

Part I

1945–70. Early Attempts: FAO's Pioneering Work

> And he gave it for his opinion, that whoever could make two ears of corn or two blades of grass to grow upon a spot of ground where only one grew before, would deserve better of mankind, and do more essential service to his country, than the whole race of politicians put together.
>
> *Jonathan Swift, Gulliver's Travels.*
> *Voyage to Brobdingnag, ch. 7*

ensuring humanity's freedom from hunger

Preamble to FAO's Constitution

people ask for bread and we give them pamphlets

Sir John (later Lord) Boyd Orr,
FAO's first Director-General (1945–48)

hunger has a unique universal appeal. Nothing touches the consciousness as much as hunger. It brings into man's immediate consciousness the social injustices and inequalities, the divisions between man and man that encrust social structures everywhere

B. R. Sen, FAO Director-General (1957–67)

1
FAO's Origins

The United Nations Conference on Food and Agriculture, convened by President Franklin D. Roosevelt at Hot Springs, Virginia, USA in May/June 1943, during the Second World War, led to the creation of the Food and Agriculture Organization of the United Nations (FAO). In his State of the Union address on 6 January 1941, before the United States entered the war, President Roosevelt had identified 'four essential freedoms': freedom of speech; of worship; from want; and from fear – 'everywhere in the world' (Rosenman, 1950). FAO's founding conference was organized 'to consider the goal of freedom from want in relation to food and agriculture'. It was recognized that 'freedom from want means a secure, an adequate, and a suitable supply of food for every man' (FAO, 1943). The conference was strongly influenced by the 'new science' of nutrition and its importance for health and well-being, already recognized by the League of Nations before the Second World War (see below). Its ultimate objective was defined as insuring 'an abundant supply of the right kinds of food for all mankind', hence the importance of dietary standards as a guide for agricultural and economic policies concerned with improving the diet and health of the world's population. The work of the conference emphasized 'the fundamental interdependence of the consumer and the producer'. All inhabitants of the earth were consumers. At the time, more than two-thirds of adults were also food producers.

The bold declaration adopted at the conference stated:

> This Conference, meeting in the midst of the greatest war ever waged, in full confidence of victory, has considered the world problems of food and agriculture and declares its belief that the goal of freedom from want of food, suitable and adequate for the health and strength of all peoples can be achieved.

The first task the declaration identified after winning of the war was to deliver millions of people from tyranny and hunger. Thereafter, a concerted effort was needed to 'win and maintain freedom from fear and freedom from want. The one cannot be achieved without the other'. But, the declaration also stated: 'There has never been enough food for the health of all people'. Food production had to be 'greatly expanded', for which 'we now have the knowledge of the means

4   1945–70. Early Attempts: FAO's Pioneering Work

by which this can be done'. It required 'imagination and firm will' on the part of governments and people to make use of that knowledge.

The declaration recognized that

> The first cause of malnutrition and hunger is poverty. It is useless to produce more food unless men and nations provide the markets to absorb it. There must be an expansion of the whole world economy to provide the purchasing power sufficient to maintain an adequate diet for all. With full employment in all countries, enlarged industrial production, the absence of exploitation, an increasing flow of trade within and between countries, an orderly management of domestic and international investment and currencies, and sustained internal and international economic equilibrium, the food which is produced can be made available to all people.

The primary responsibility for ensuring that people had the food needed for life and health lay with each nation. But each nation could fully achieve that goal only if all work together. The declaration ended:

> The first steps towards freedom from want of food must not await the final solution of all other problems. Each advance made in one field will strengthen and quicken advance in all others. Work already begun must be continued. Once the war has been won decisive steps can be taken. We must make ready now.

It became clear at an early stage of the conference that there was general agreement that a permanent organization in the field of food and agriculture should be established. It was also agreed that the organization should act as a centre of information and advice on both agricultural and nutritional questions, and that it should maintain a service of international statistics. The conference recommended the establishment of an Interim Commission in Washington, DC to draw up a detailed plan for the permanent organization for the approval of governments and authorities represented at the conference.

After two and a half years of preparatory work by the Interim Commission, FAO was established at the first FAO Conference in Quebec, Canada in October 1945 and Sir John Boyd Orr, 'that brave persistent Scottish prophet, that pioneer in nutrition, that indefatigable researcher, that prophet of greater human welfare', was elected as its first director-general (FAO, 1945). An executive committee of 15 members was also elected. Washington, DC was designated as the temporary seat of FAO but it was agreed that the permanent location should be at the United Nations on the understanding that that would also be the location of ECOSOC. Eventually, ECOSOC was placed in Geneva, Switzerland and FAO was located in Rome, Italy, where it inherited the library of the International Institute of Agriculture.

In his address to the conference after his election, Boyd Orr gave an indication of the vision of the 'great world scheme' he had for FAO, He noted that in the past forty years, science had advanced more than it did in the previous two thousand years to 'let loose new forces into the world'. He added:

> those forces cannot be bottled up; they must either be harnessed to serve the ends of mankind, or they will break loose in a riot of destruction. How those forces are used will affect all nations equally. The world is now so small that any war will be a world war; and prosperity must be a world prosperity. Governments realize this, and they are, therefore, attempting to set up world organizations which will enable those powers of science to be applied on a world scale. It is very fitting ... that FAO should be the first of these organizations. It deals with the primary products of land and sea; it deals with food – the primary necessity of life.

He went on:

> Each nation has accepted the responsibility ... to provide, as far as possible, food and a health standard for all peoples. . . . But something new has arisen. All the governments have agreed to cooperate in a great world food scheme, which will bring freedom from want to all men, irrespective of race and colour. . . . If the nations of the world are going to get together to feed the people of the world, they must increase the production of the most important foods. In many cases that production must more than double. This will bring prosperity to agriculture ... [which] must overflow into other businesses and into world trade. But ... we do these things not because they will bring prosperity, but because they are right ... if we put first things first, and do the things which we know to be right, a great many social, economic and political difficulties will disappear. . . . You say it is a dream. Then, it is the business of FAO to make that dream come true. . . . I am almost tempted to say that if this Organization succeeds it will perform a miracle. Well, we are living in a day of miracles.

The need for some form of multilateral world food security arrangement had already been recognized by the League of Nations before the Second World War to rationalize food production, supply and trade for the benefit of both producers and consumers, in both developing as well as developed countries. Attention was focused on two basic concerns: first, to reconcile the interests of producers and consumers by protecting them from uncontrolled fluctuations in world agricultural production and prices; and secondly, to use constructively agricultural output in excess of commercial market demand (the so-called agricultural 'surpluses') to assist economic and social development in developing countries *without* creating disincentive to their domestic agricultural production or disruption to local or international trade. This vision of world food security that re-emerged at the creation of FAO has remained a constant, if flicking, light.

In the 1920s, the preoccupation with post-war recovery and the impact of a rather short lived boom and slump, followed by a new era of prosperity (which in the views of many was expected to last much longer than it did), provided relatively little incentive for intergovernmental action on international commodity

6   *1945–70. Early Attempts: FAO's Pioneering Work*

problems, although there were some, mainly producers', agreements. In the early 1930s, on the other hand, the disastrous effects of the Great Depression on consumer purchasing power and on the incomes of primary producers, underlined the need for some form of intergovernmental arrangement for staple foodstuffs. At the same time, the results of important new advances in the science of nutrition were widely propagated. This led to the discovery that the incidence of chronic malnutrition, with harmful effects on health, was widespread, even in relatively high-income countries, and particularly among children and other vulnerable groups. Following the Great Depression, when markets for staple foods were glutted and producers faced ruin, the growing recognition of the widespread character of nutritional deficiencies strengthened the conviction that there was something wrong with the recurring manifestations of 'poverty in the midst of plenty' and that solutions should be sought through the selective expansion of food consumption rather than through the curtailment of output that had been previously practiced. Furthermore, the basic cure of under-consumption had to be seen in the promotion of measures designed to raise the real incomes of needy people.

In the early 1930s, Yugoslavia proposed that in view of the importance of food for health, the Health Division of the League of Nations should disseminate information about the food position in representative countries of the world. Its report was the first introduction of the world food problem into the international political arena.[1] Dr. Frank Boudreau, head of the League's Health Division, with Drs. Aykroyd and Bennet, visited a number of countries and submitted a report on *Nutrition and Public Health* (1935), which showed that there was an acute food shortage in the poor countries, the first account of the extent of hunger and malnutrition in the world. Discussions held on nutrition policies in the Assembly of the League of Nations were based on some important pioneering efforts that had helped to prepare the ground and led to further practical progress. These endeavours marked the beginnings of co-ordinated nutrition policies in a number of countries. Meanwhile, the hardships caused by the unprecedented slump of the early 1930s, and fears of their recurrence, led governments to adopt national price and production controls for foodstuffs and other agricultural products in exporting countries, coupled with trade restrictions in importing countries. At the same time, there was also growing interest in the regulation of world trade in foodstuffs and other staple products through intergovernmental action.

The ILO, in a comprehensive report on intergovernmental commodity control agreements, stated that 'although there was a marked tendency for raw material control schemes to develop before the great depression, intergovernmental schemes have developed during the years since the depression' (ILO, 1943). In essence, the inter-war agreements for foodstuffs were based on quotas as well as the operation of buffer stocks. The possibility of organizing international buffer stocks as part of international control arrangements was first discussed more thoroughly only in 1937 by the League of Nations Committee on the Study of the Problems of Raw Materials. To sum up, the main trends of thought and action developed during the 1930s were: first, the beginning of national nutrition policies based on the spread of newer knowledge of nutrition and promoted by international co-operation; second, and partly in conflict with the first, the growth of market rigidities, national price and production controls, and trade restrictions; and third, growing interest in intergovernmental commodity arrangements.

No action was taken on the League of Nations nutrition report until 1935 when the subject was raised again in the Assembly of the League by Stanley Bruce, formerly Prime Minister of Australia, and by then Viscount Bruce of Melbourne and High Commissioner for Australia in London. Bruce had attended the World Monetary and Economic Conference in London in 1932–33 when, as a result of the economic crisis, and the shrinkage of international trade, widespread unemployment occurred in both Europe and the United States. The only remedies that were being applied were tariff barriers and other measures to *restrict* the production of food and other goods in order to raise prices. Bruce uttered the solemn warning that 'an economic system which restricted the production and distribution of the things that the majority of mankind urgently needed was one that could not endure'. He predicted disaster unless measures were taken to develop the potential wealth of the world in a rapidly expanding world economy. Bruce proposed at the League of Nations that committees should be set up to find out how much more food was needed and what means might be taken to get nations to cooperate in a world food plan based on human needs.

As a result, a three-day debate took place in the Assembly of the League of Nations during which it was argued that increasing food production to meet human needs would bring prosperity to agriculture, which would overflow into industry, and bring about the needed expansion of the world economy, through what Bruce described as 'the marriage of health and agriculture'. This new conception of considering food in all its relationships to health, economics and politics, roused considerable enthusiasm. It was decided to consider ways and means of applying this new idea in practice. An international committee of physiologists, including Americans and Russians, was appointed to report on the food needed for health. An 'International Standard of Food Requirements' was agreed upon, which gave an indication of the amount of food needed throughout the world. A 'mixed committee' of leading authorities on nutrition, agriculture and economics was then appointed to examine and make recommendations on every aspect of the food problem, including production, transport and trade. This committee of 20 members brought out a report on the benefits from developing the world's food supplies. A conference was called to consider what action to take to implement its recommendations. Bruce and others sent the following telegram to Boyd Orr with whom the subject had been discussed: 'Dear Brother Orr, this day we have lit a candle which, by the Grace of God's grace, will never be put out' (a reference to a speech made by Hugh Latimer when he and another Protestant were burned at the stake) (Boyd Orr, 1966, p. 119).

At the committee which had been charged to draw up the standard diet needed for health, Boyd Orr sat between the American and Russian delegates. He found that both 'co-operated harmoniously' in preparing the report. When it was received, the League of Nations Assembly decided to set up another committee

8   *1945–70. Early Attempts: FAO's Pioneering Work*

of financiers, economists, business men and scientists to work out the economic advantages of a world food policy. The final report on *The Relation of Health, Agriculture and Economic Policy*, published by the League in 1937, indicated the lines along which the expansion of the world economy could most easily begin. It was declared a best-seller by *The New York Times* (Boyd Orr, 1966, p. 120). Walter Elliot and Earl De La Warr, respectively Minister and Under-Secretary for Agriculture in the United Kingdom, saw that the food problem of a 'glut' followed by a fall in food prices paid to farmers was one of under-consumption rather than over-production. In 1938, 22 nations, including the United States and Russia, met in conference to arrange how this new world food policy could be carried out. But the outbreak of the Second World War in 1939 brought this promising development to an end. The view was expressed that if the League of Nations had devoted more time to social and economic problems than to politics, it might have succeeded in eliminating the causes of war.

The conference at Hot Springs in 1943 was attended by some of those who had taken part in the League of Nations work and debates on nutrition and food security. They discussed the League's work with both President Roosevelt and Vice-President Henry Wallace, and suggested that as food was, in Roosevelt's language, 'the first want of man', a world food policy would be the best way to begin to fulfil the promise of freedom from want for all people that was previously made in the *Atlantic Charter*, signed by President Roosevelt and Prime Minister Churchill in August 1941 (Freidel, 1990, pp. 387–8).

Out of this historical background emerged FAO. Of all the personalities involved, Frank McDougall is especially linked with the founding of FAO (Boerma, 1968; Phillips, 1981). Born in the United Kingdom, he became a fruit grower in Australia and then economic adviser to Lord Bruce, the Australian High Commissioner in London. MacDougall had shown a keen interest in the work of Boyd Orr on human nutrition and had frequently visited his research institute in Scotland, and had kept Lord Bruce informed. He was enormously impressed by the new knowledge of nutrition that developed between the two world wars. He was equally impressed by the paradox of the emergence of food surpluses during the depression of the 1930s alongside hunger and malnutrition not only in the developing countries but also among the unemployed, children and old people in the most economically advanced countries. His conviction that these two 'evils' should cancel each other out was crystallized in his phrase 'the marriage of food and agriculture'. He succeeded in inducing the League of Nations to set up an international committee on nutrition. He wrote a memorandum on *The Agricultural and Health Problem* in 1935, which served as a first step towards bringing before the League the findings of nutritionists indicating that a large proprtion of the world's population did not get enough of the right sort of food, and the view that food production should be expanded to meet nutritional requirements, rather than restricted (Phillips, 1981). But his greatest success was when he sold the idea of an international agency to combat hunger to President Franklin D. Roosevelt, which led to the Hot Springs conference.

The recommendations for approval at the Hot Springs conference called for national and international action under three main headings: consumption levels and requirements; expansion of production and adaptation to consumer needs; and facilitation and improvement of distribution. They advocated the use of international commodity arrangements as a means for promoting stability and orderly development. It was also recommended that 'adequate reserves should be maintained to meet all consumption needs' and that 'provision should be made, when applicable, for the orderly disposal of surpluses'. The report of the conference distinguished three types of 'functional disorders' in international commodity distribution: short-term fluctuations in prices; disorders concomitant of general cyclical depressions; and disorders that were structural modifications in relations between existing productive capacity and the need of society for certain commodities or groups of commodities. The conference unanimous agreed that 'the world after the war should follow a bold policy of economic expansion instead of the timid regime of scarcity which characterized the 1930s'. Different views were expressed on the nature of international commodity regulations. Some delegates envisaged future arrangements chiefly for the establishment and operation of buffer stocks. But it was not possible to reach agreement concerning the part to be allotted to quantitative regulation for both short-term fluctuations and long-term disequilibrium. In a resolution summing up the conclusions of the conference, it was recommended that international commodity arrangements should be so designed as to promote 'the expansion of an orderly world economy'. A 'body of broad principles' should be agreed upon, which should include fair prices for both consumers and producers.

At the first session of the FAO Conference, held in Quebec City, Canada from 16 October to 1 November 1945, attended by representatives of 44 countries, FAO's constitution was approved by which member nations 'being determined to promote the common welfare' pledged 'to work separately and collectively' for the purposes of FAO, which were defined as

- raising levels of nutrition and standards of living of the peoples under their respective jurisdictions;
- securing improvements in the efficiency of the production and distribution of all food and agricultural products;
- bettering the condition of rural populations; and thus
- contributing toward an expanding world economy [and ensuring humanity's freedom from hunger] (FAO, 1945).[2]

The constitution also set out, clearly and explicitly, the functions of FAO:

- The organization was to 'collect, analyze, interpret and disseminate' information relating to 'nutrition, food and agriculture'.
- It was to 'promote and, where appropriate, recommend national and international action' concerning:

  (a) scientific, technological, social, and economic research relating to nutrition, food and agriculture;

10   *1945–70. Early Attempts: FAO's Pioneering Work*

(b) the improvement of education and administration, relating to nutrition, food and agriculture, and the spread of public knowledge of nutritional and agricultural science and practice;

(c) the conservation of natural resources and the adoption of improved methods of agricultural production;

(d) the improvement of the processing, marketing and distribution of food and agricultural products;

(e) the adoption of policies for the provision of adequate agricultural credit, national and international and

(f) the adoption of international policies with respect to agricultural commodity arrangements.

- It was also to

(a) furnish such technical assistance as governments may request;

(b) organize, in cooperation with the governments concerned, such missions as may be needed to assist them to fulfil the obligations arising from their acceptance of the recommendations of the United Nations Conference on Food and Agriculture and of FAO's constitution; and

(c) generally to take all necessary and appropriate action to implement the purposes of FAO.

Like the other specialized agencies of the UN system, FAO was to have its own budget based on assessed, not voluntary, contributions from its member states. These contributions were augmented by resources from the UN Technical Assistance Board (TAB), later the Expanded Programme of Technical Assistance (EPTA) and the UN Special Fund (SF). EPTA and the SF were amalgamated in 1965 to form the United Nations Development Programme (UNDP). Trust funds were also deposited by donor governments in FAO for special projects and programmes that they wished the organization to implement.

The Quebec conference discussed both problem of food shortages and the possible recurrence of food surpluses that had existed before the war. Concerning shortages, it foreshadowed the need for an internationally representative body to allocate scarce supplies. As to surpluses, it prophesized the need for national agricultural adjustment programmes, framed in the light of international review and consultation, and advocated international commodity agreements and special international measures for wider food distribution. The conference also recommended that 'adequate reserves should be maintained to meet all consumption needs' and that 'provision should be made, when applicable, for the orderly disposal of surpluses'. Taken together, 'these recommendations constituted a surprisingly accurate forecast of what the world would need in the post-war decade' (Yates, 1955, p. 76).

Intent on achieving the long-term objective of improving overall food intake, the conference at Hot Springs had recommended that 'adequate reserves should be maintained to meet all consumption needs' and that 'provision should be made, when applicable, for the orderly disposal of surpluses'. It went into some detail about 'functional disorders' in the world distribution of food but had little to say about planning for emergencies. This reflected the broad approach taken at the time. Intent upon the long-term objective of improving overall food consumption, the conference gave little attention to accidental (but recurring) disruptions in supplies that required emergency assistance. The urgent task of providing the war-ravaged countries of Europe and Asia with food and other essential relief goods was addressed at another conference held in Washington, DC in November 1943, which led to the establishment of the United Nations Relief and Rehabilitation Administration (UNRRA) (Woodbridge, 1950).

The spirit of international solidarity among allied nations during the war, which led to the creation of the United Nations in 1945 and the other UN specialized agencies, including the International Monetary Fund (IMF) and the International Bank for Reconstruction and Development (IBRD), started to unravel by the time of the first FAO conference in Quebec, Canada in 1945 as the major economic powers returned to self-centred national policies and preference for bilateral as opposed to multilateral arrangements. Their intentions were clearly expressed. FAO was to keep off the short-term food crisis and commercial and commodity policies and concentrate on long-term issues of nutrition, production and national distribution. The course of subsequent events, and the personality of the first FAO director-general, Sir (later Lord) John Boyd Orr, called for different action. The world food situation rapidly worsened and the agencies involved in handling it, including the UNRRA, were blamed at the UN General Assembly in February 1947. UNRRA was disbanded and Boyd Orr announced that FAO was willing to take over its role and accept responsibility for mobilizing world resources to meet the crisis. He proposed calling a conference, which took place in Washington, DC in May 1947, for which FAO prepared a survey showing the expected severity of the food situation. This resulted in the establishment of an International Emergency Council (later Committee), which was eventually absorbed into FAO as its Distribution Division. At the same time, Boyd Orr was requested to submit to the next FAO conference in Copenhagen, Denmark proposals for dealing with the long-term problems, including the risk of accumulating surpluses.

2
Food Surpluses: Historical Background

Even before the First World War (1914–18), there were a number of instances when surpluses of agricultural products arose beyond market demand. Governments intervened to protect farmers' incomes and to provide food aid to needy countries. The first major food aid operations evolved from the special post-war relief credits voted by the US Congress for the period between the signing of the Armistice in 1918 that marked the end of the First World War and the signing of the Treaty of Versailles in 1919, and then for the so-called reconstruction period in Europe from 1919 to 1926, when a total of 6.23 million tons of food was shipped. The importance of this US initiative lay not only in the quantity of relief provided. It established the precedent for operations of this type involving prominent personalities, the most significant being President Herbert Hoover, and brought a general realization of the value of food aid as a politically stabilizing factor (Singer, Wood and Jennings, 1987).

Agricultural surplus problems after the Second World War (1939–45) had their genesis in the 1920s and 1930s. With the end of the special credits for agriculture in 1926, and with the United States still producing considerable surpluses of cereals, moves were made to formalize the type of food aid arrangement started in 1896 by the US Department of Agriculture. During this period, incomes from agriculture fell drastically, in absolute terms as well as in relation to that of other sectors of the national economies. Governments everywhere intervened to bolster farm income. In the exporting countries, intervention usually took the form of government or quasi-government marketing boards with monopoly powers. In the importing countries, it mainly took the form of new devices for the control and redistribution of imports, such as quotas, regulations and preferential and bilateral trade arrangements. Government interventions in the importing countries had the effect of stimulating domestic production and of reducing the demand for imports of some agricultural products. But interventions in the exporting countries did not, in general, lead to a reduction in exportable supplies. Thus, in the late 1920s, excess stocks started to accumulate and world prices fell to very low levels.

In the United States, the largest exporter of farm products, the establishment of the Federal Farm Board in 1929 marked the first time that the US Government intervened directly to influence the prices of export crops. Legislation aimed at raising farm prices through government loans to agricultural cooperatives failed in its objectives largely because of worldwide depression, associated with declining prices, and because there was no provision for the control of production. Production control was accepted for the first time in the United States with the passage of the Agricultural Adjustment Act of 1933. Control was based on the area planted rather than supply limitation. As production efficiency increased with the introduction of new technology and modern farming methods, the effect of restricting the area planted was partially or fully offset. Under an amendment to the 1933 act, a Grain Stabilization Board was established to provide direct subsidies for agricultural exports. In addition, a Commodity Credit Corporation (CCC) was created to buy and sell agricultural commodities and make loans to farmers. The CCC became the vehicle for managing agricultural surpluses and the basis for the first structured US food aid programmes drawing from the mounting food surpluses. The scope of the CCC was widened by an amendment to the Agricultural Adjustment Act in 1935, which authorized its use of customs revenues to subsidize agricultural exports and encourage domestic production. The outbreak of the Second World War in 1939 led eventually to the passing of the Lend-Lease Act of 1941 (signed before US entry into the war in December of that year). Under this act, some $6 billion of agricultural products were shipped to the Allied powers.

Although not on the same scale, similar developments took place in other industrialized countries as surpluses accumulated and disposal programmes were operated. These operated largely within a network of associated states or communities, such as the British Commonwealth, the French Community, the Portuguese overseas territories, and the Belgian, German and Italian overseas territories.

During the Second World War, government attempts to control farm output were reversed, especially in North America, and every effort was made to increase food production. In the United States, price support was increased on basic food crops and introduced, for the first time, on animal products. The continuation of incentives in the United States after the war, and of price support in Canada, together with advancing technology, led to the accumulation of large surpluses, especially of wheat and dairy products, during the 1950s. Price support was introduced and maintained to ensure a reasonable income for farming communities not to increase production, although this was its effect. After the Second World War, the United States continued essentially the same price support policies that had been developed during the war. From time to time, the support levels were lowered and area planting restrictions reintroduced for the principal crops but production continued to increase. The concept of supply management was introduced to adjust supply to domestic and foreign needs for some major food crops and food grains with some effect, but not for dairy products, leading to serious surplus problems. Following President Hoover's example after the First World War, a European Recovery Programme, more popularly known as the Marshall Plan (named after its originator, George Marshall, Secretary of State in President Truman's administration) resulted in the largest transfer of bilateral aid in history. Of the total aid package of $13.5 billion supplied between 1948 and 1953, about a quarter was committed in food, feed and fertilizer.

14 1945–70. Early Attempts: FAO's Pioneering Work

In Canada, agricultural price support legislation was introduced in 1944 for the protection of farmers against a post-war price decline, such as occurred after the First World War. In 1959, the Canadian Government found that support for certain lines of production contributed to increased production and new programmes were introduced involving deficiency payments to farmers. Since wheat produced in the main producing area was marketed through a government agency, the Canadian Wheat Board, it did not qualify for support. For dairy products, there was no limitation on production in the price support programme.

Other post-war policies varied from country to country. Initially, the main emphasis was on expanding agricultural production to avoid hunger or inflation. Later, emphasis was placed on such factors as the need to reduce imports because of the dollar gap, as in Western Europe, or to maximize foreign exchange availabilities for the purchase of capital goods, as in Latin America, the Near East and the Far East. As supplies became more plentiful, greater attention was paid, especially in Western Europe and Japan, to improving and safeguarding the economic position of farmers. This involved income protection and various measures of price and income support, and led to subsidized exports. Eventually, during the early 1950s, especially in some Western European countries, increasing attention was given to problems of surplus production in some agricultural commodities.

3
World Food Board Proposal

When FAO was established in 1945, it was assumed that with the aid of the temporary organizations dealing with food, nations would be able to cope with the emergencies arising after the end of hostilities and that reasonable conditions would soon be established in which FAO could start its work. But the food situation continued to deteriorate. In February 1946, the UN General Assembly called on governments and international organizations concerned with food and agriculture to make 'special efforts'. FAO's response was to convene a 'Special Meeting on Urgent Food Problems', which met in Washington, DC in May 1946. While primarily concerned with the immediate problems of emergency food supplies, the meeting also called for 'longer term machinery to deal with certain practical international problems connected therewith' and requested the director-general of FAO:

> to submit to the Conference of FAO at its next session [in Copenhagen, Denmark in September 1946] a survey of existing and proposed international organizations designed to meet long-term problems concerned with the production, distribution, and consumption of food and agricultural products, including the risk of accumulating surpluses; [and]
> to make proposals to the Conference on any extension of the functions of existing organizations or any new organizations which the survey may indicate as necessary.

Out of this request came the opportunity for Boyd Orr to realize the 'dreams and miracles' he had spoken about in this address at the first FAO Conference in Quebec City after his election as FAO director-general, and his proposal for a 'World Food Board' (WFB) (FAO, 1946a). It is difficult now to appreciate the full impact the experiences of the previous three decades had had on Body Orr and his FAO staff when drafting the WFB proposal. The triple impact in North America and Europe of dramatically falling agricultural prices and incomes, the general economic slump, and the rapid rise in large-scale unemployment had created widespread depression and mass poverty. The political drift both to the right and the left in search for solutions had led to the New Deal and isolationism in the

16   *1945–70. Early Attempts: FAO's Pioneering Work*

United States and to extreme nationalism and fascism in Europe, which eventually led to a war resulting in the greatest loss of life and physical destruction in human history. Out of this terrible experience came the spirit of hope and optimism expressed in the *Atlantic Charter* of 1941, the *Declaration of the United Nations* of 1942, and the conference in San Francisco in 1945 that established the United Nations, and adopted the UN *Charter*, which proclaimed, among other things:

> We the people of the United Nations determined . . . to reaffirm faith in fundamental human rights, in the dignity and worth of the human person, in the equal rights of man and women and of nations large and small, and . . . to promote social progress and better standards of life in larger freedom . . . and for these ends . . . to employ international machinery for the promotion of the economic and social advancement of all people. (*Charter of the United Nations*, 24 June 1945, San Francisco, USA)

As a student of biology, a doctor of medicine, a practicing farmer and a researcher who had spent much time trying to improve the nutrition of poor people in the depressed areas of the United Kingdom, Boyd Orr was convinced that food should be considered as something much more than merely a tradable commodity. He also thought that: 'If the nations cannot agree on a food program affecting the welfare of people everywhere, there is little hope of their reaching agreement on anything' (Hambridge, 1955, p. 67). Being a farmer, its trade aspects he appreciated shrewdly enough, as his attention to prices showed. But as a medical man and researcher, he saw food as the prime necessity of life itself. He felt that ways should be found to feed all people adequately, even if it could not always be done at a profit. To him, civilization had a profound moral obligation to provide food for the hungry poor, just as it had to provide them with medical care. He believed that the WFB proposal, or something like it, was necessary not only to galvanize expanded production and industrial development, and start what he liked to refer to as 'the upward spiral of prosperity', but also to solve the problem of surpluses, the nightmare of agriculture during the economic depression of the 1930s.

On a personal level, no doubt Boyd Orr still carried with him memories of his nutrition work in Britain in the 1920s and 1930s at the Rowett Research Institute in Animal Nutrition, where he was its first director, during which time he travelled extensively visiting research institutions in many parts of the world, at the Duthiue Experimental Farm, in Scotland, and during the war years when he was intimately involved in wartime food policy in the United Kingdom, all admirably described in his autobiography *As I Recall* (Boyd Orr, 1966). He undertook a series of tests among schoolchildren in Scotland in 1926/27, which showed that given additional milk their rate of growth increased by over 20 per cent. This led to the provision of free milk to school children in the United Kingdom, which was maintained during and after the Second World War, and gave rise to Winston Churchill's famous statement: 'There is no finer investment than putting milk in babies'. He was also involved in a pioneering survey, *Food, Health and Income*, into the adequacy of diet in relation to income in Britain in the 1930s (Boyd Orr, 1936).

The importance of the subject had been increased by measures taken to support agriculture during the economic depression of the 1930s. Some measures were designed to raise the price of foodstuffs to a level remunerative to the producer by limiting the amounts marketed. He considered that while it was desirable to make agriculture prosperous, it was equally desirable to ensure that the food supply of a nation was sufficient for health and available at a price within the reach of the poorest. He felt that the necessity for reconciling the interests of agriculture and public health raised questions of the utmost importance on government measures affecting the food supply.

A review of the status of health of people in different income groups suggested that as income increased disease and death-rates decreased, children grew more quickly, adult stature was greater and general health and physique improved. He concluded that the results, if accepted, raised important economic and political questions. One problem was that they were not all within the sphere of any single department of government, or, by extension, any single agency. This was what was called the 'new knowledge of nutrition', which showed that there could be significant improvement in the health and physique of a nation, coming at the same time when the power of producing food increased markedly, created an entirely new situation, which demanded 'economic statesmanship'. The prominence given to this new social problem at the Assembly of the League of Nations showed, in his opinion, that it was occupying the attention of all civilized countries.

In making the case for the WFB, given his background and experience, it is understandable why Boyd Orr chose to embrace the wider interrelationships between nutrition, health and agriculture with industry and trade. These interrelationships are set out in some detail here not only because it shows the thinking of the time but also, more importantly, because they explain why the dimensions of the WFB proposal were cast so wide. First, the relationship between nutrition, health and agriculture, which the League of Nations had earlier examined. FAO's first world food survey of 1946 estimated that 1 billion people consumed less than 2250 calories a day. (By contrast, average intake per person in the United Kingdom was 2750 calories even with acute food shortages.) But calorie intake did not tell the full story. A diet sufficient for health should contain animal products, fruit and vegetables. These supplied calories at much higher cost but were rich in constituents necessary for health. Food consumption depended on purchasing power. As family income rose, the consumption of more expensive foods increased. And food consumption directly correlated with health. As diet deteriorated in quality, health and physical ability declined and length of life decreased. Although these facts had been stated at length many times in the past, it was considered necessary to repeat them again as they were fundamental to the long-term problems of food and agriculture.

It was difficult to estimate accurately how much the production of each of the main foodstuffs would need to be increased to provide adequate food for the world's population because for a number of countries statistics were absent or unreliable. It was known, however, that even in the wealthiest countries in pre-war days between 20 and 30 per cent of the population did not have enough of the more expensive foods essential for health. The first problem of production, therefore, was how to get sufficient food not only to feed the expanding world population but also to feed people better. The advance of agricultural science and technology had enabled more food to be produced with less labour. But the rapid increase in population in certain countries posed a serious political problem, and full weight had to be given to its bearing on food production. The limiting factor was not the physical capacity to produce enough food but the ability of nations to bring about the complex economic adjustments necessary to make adequate production and distribution possible. The application of science and technology while solving the problem of production at the same time created its own problems. Industrialization should take place if unemployment and under-employment in agriculture were to be avoided. The net result would then be an increase in the numbers fully employed and to enlarge the world's total wealth.

The problems of food producers varied with the type of agriculture. In developing countries, food was produced on very small holdings cultivated by obsolete methods. The problem here was one of providing profitable employment in other industries and of education in modern methods of cultivation. Underlying this problem was that of providing the needed capital equipment. In countries where modern agricultural science and technology had been applied, the main problem was finding a continuous market at a remunerative price. A relatively small excess of supply over demand was followed by a big drop in prices, as occurred in the late 1920s. On the other hand, a relatively small excess in economic demand over supply was followed by a big increase in prices. This was dramatically demonstrated in times of war, when prices had to be controlled to prevent an excessive rise. Besides these cyclical movements, there were weekly and monthly oscillations in prices. In nine out of the ten years in the decade between 1928 and 1938, the price of wheat on the world market fluctuated by 70 per cent. These fluctuations were described as 'the bane of agricultural producers'. It was recognized that the wide variation in the prices prevailing in different countries made it difficult to agree on a common price for the world market. But this was essential to ensure that there was a world market for exportable surpluses at stable prices. It had long been recognized that primary producers did not get a fair share of the world's total wealth commensurate with the proportion they created.[3] This was not only a social injustice. It was an economic problem because the low purchasing power of food producers was a limiting factor in the market for industrial products. Conversely, limitation on industrial prosperity, and hence of the purchasing power of industrial producers, limited the markets for agricultural products (Table 3.1).

To add to the complexity, the future state of human nutrition and the prosperity of agriculture were also interdependent with the volume of trade. A long-term food and agriculture policy had therefore not only to reconcile the interests of consumers and producers but also the interests of agriculture and trade. The crux of the question was at which end of the chain should we begin? Food could be treated as a normal tradable commodity but it was also an essential of life.

Table 3.1 Cereals: World exports and prices, 1910–50

Year	Absolute Values						Year-to-Year Fluctuations					
	Volume			Price			Volume			Price		
	Wheat Flour	Maize	Rice	Wheat Flour	Maize	Rice	Wheat Flour	Maize	Rice	Wheat Flour	Maize	Rice
	Thousand m. tons			C. c. bu	US. C/bu.	$/m.t.	per cent					
1910	19 400	5 900	...	96.6	53	...	8	5	...	−5	−11	...
11	19 200	5 900	...	100.8	71	...	−1	0	...	4	34	...
12	19 400	8 500	...	89.4	53	...	1	44	...	−13	−34	...
13	22 500	8 200	...	89.4	70	...	16	−4	...	0	32	...
14	17 700	6 300	...	132.4	70	...	−27	−30	...	48	0	...
15	17 100	6 600	...	113.3	79	...	−4	5	...	−17	13	...
16	18 500	5 600	...	205.6	111	...	8	−18	...	81	41	...
17	14 800	2 700	...	221.0	163	...	−25	−107	...	7	47	...
18	14 000	2 000	...	224.1	162	...	−6	−35	...	1	−1	...
19	18 200	2 800	...	217.6	159	...	30	40	...	−3	−2	...
20	21 000	5 700	3 000	205.7	62	77.2	15	104	...	−6	−156	...
21	21 700	7 900	4 700	127.0	55.1	61.4	3	39	57	−62	−13	−26
22	21 000	7 800	5 000	111.0	73.4	65.3	−3	−1	6	−17	33	6
23	21 300	5 900	5 200	107.0	87.7	53.1	1	−32	4	−4	19	−23
24	24 500	7 100	5 500	169.0	106.4	55.0	15	20	6	58	21	4
25	21 400	6 500	6 400	151.0	74.7	68.6	−14	−9	16	12	−42	25
26	22 100	8 100	6 300	146.0	86.7	69.5	3	25	−2	−3	16	1
27	25 000	11 600	7 000	146.0	101.0	70.4	13	43	11	0	16	1
28	26 200	9 000	6 300	124.0	92.5	69.2	5	−29	−11	−18	−9	−2
29	24 200	7 700	5 800	124.0	83.2	66.9	−8	−17	−9	0	−11	−3
30	21 700	8 100	6 000	64.0	59.6	68.4	−12	5	3	−94	−40	2
31	24 500	12 100	7 400	60.0	35.6	30.0	13	49	23	−7	−67	−128

Table 3.1 Continued

Year	Absolute Values						Year-to-Year Fluctuations					
	Volume			Price			Volume			Price		
	Wheat Flour	Maize	Rice	Wheat Flour	Maize	Rice	Wheat Flour	Maize	Rice	Wheat Flour	Maize	Rice
	Thousand m. tons			C. c. bu	US. C/bu.	$/m.t.	per cent					
32	20 900	10 600	8 100	54.0	35.4	18.3	−17	−14	9	−11	−1	−64
33	19 100	8 300	7 500	68.0	52.0	19.4	−9	−28	−8	26	47	6
34	17 900	8 300	9 000	82.0	86.3	17.2	−7	0	20	21	66	−13
35	17 400	9 500	8 800	85.0	74.6	14.1	−3	14	−2	4	−16	−22
36	16 900	10 600	8 200	123.0	121.0	17.1	−3	12	−7	45	62	21
37	16 900	12 900	7 500	132.0	57.0	16.3	0	22	−9	7	−112	−5
38	17 600	8 900	7 600	62.0	48.9	18.0	4	−45	1	−113	17	10
39	20 300	6 700	8 800	76.0	54.0	17.3	15	−33	16	23	10	−4
40	15 300	4 500	...	74.0	67.3	...	−33	−49	...	−3	25	...
41	13 700	1 800	...	77.0	80.0	...	−12	−150	...	4	19	...
42	10 600	900	...	95.0	91.0	...	−29	−100	...	23	14	...
43	13 200	600	...	123.0	114.3	...	25	−50	...	29	26	...
44	17 800	1 000	...	144.0	115.2	...	35	67	...	17	1	...
45	22 600	1 200	1 100	175.0	194.0	...	27	20	...	22	68	...
46	20 400	3 200	2 400	244.0	180.0	83	−11	167	18	39	−8	...
47	24 205	6 200	2 800	288.0	233.0	142	19	94	17	18	29	71
48	26 101	4 900	3 900	226.0	138.0	140	8	−27	39	−27	−69	−1
49	26 000	5 800	4 100	219.0	130.0	121	0	18	5	−3	−6	−16
50	21 200	4 600	4 250	212.0	173.0	102	−23	−26	4	−3	33	−19

... Not available

Source: FAO (1956)

The provision of food should therefore not be dependent solely on the interest of trade. On the contrary, trade should be considered as a means of bringing sufficient food and other necessities for a full life within the reach of people. The starting point for policy depended on what the aim was. If the welfare of people was the objective, the provision of food, the first essential of life, should be the first goal. Beginning with food had the advantage of affording a definite and limited objective. Taking into account dietary habits, the amount of food needed for health could be estimated. (A preliminary survey had been made by FAO and targets set up as a first step for improved nutrition in the first world food survey of 1946.) The two viewpoints, one concerned primarily with trade and the other with adequate food supplies, were different aspects of the same objective, which was 'prosperity'. Trade sought outlets for commodities in new and enlarged markets, which were often hard to find. Setting improved nutrition as a goal provided enormous new markets, not limited to food alone. It also furnished a motivation that had profound human appeal.

The case for a WFB also spelled out the economic advantages of a world food policy based on human needs. If each government undertook to raise the level of nutrition of its people up to the health standard, as member nations agreed to do in accepting FAO's constitution, and adjusted its agricultural policy to that end, there would need to be an expansion of food supplies, even in the best fed countries. The additional food production required was so great that it could hardly be attained, unless production were progressively co-ordinated on a world scale. With such co-ordination, many countries would find it advantageous to diversify farming and concentrate on the more perishable foods of special value to health, leaving a larger proportion of such foods as wheat and sugar, which were easily stored and transported, to be grown in areas that were best adapted to their production. This expansion of agriculture would accelerate the development of mechanization and expand the market for agricultural equipment of all kinds, for fertilizers, and for facilities for storing and transporting food. In the developing countries, there was also need for machinery for irrigation, flood control, land reclamation and drainage. Providing the capital equipment for the great expansion needed in the future development of agriculture would help to keep the wheels of industry turning and to provide full employment. Prosperity in agriculture would also increase the demand for consumer goods among agricultural producers, who outnumbered those in all other industries combined.

It was acknowledged that the 'vast enterprise' of providing food for health for all people was beset with difficulties requiring international collaboration but the difficulties were not so great as those encountered and overcome in winning the war. The end result would be, described in language that had a particular resonance for the time: 'instead of being death and the destruction of real wealth, would be life, enrichment of man's greatest asset – the soil, and economic prosperity, which is one of the essentials of a permanent peace'. If this reasoning were valid, a world food policy based on human needs would provide a programme for agriculture and direct trade along the lines that should be followed not only to achieve prosperity but to attain 'the great humanitarian ends proclaimed by the leading statesmen of

22   *1945–70. Early Attempts: FAO's Pioneering Work*

the United Nations during the war as the fruits of victory to which the people of the world might look forward'.

The natural resources and the knowledge required to produce the food needed and with which to set off an upward spiral of economic expansion were available. But food could not be distributed and consumed by the people who needed it unless purchasing power increased as rapidly as production. There were two aspects to this problem, the national and the international. While developed countries had taken various steps to bridge the gap between the price of food adequate for health and the purchasing power of families, developing countries, and those devastated by war, were unable to make food sufficient for health available for the whole population. It was advocated that the needed development of agriculture and industry should be put on a business footing through the supply of capital equipment on terms involving deferred payments and long-term credits to give the countries concerned time to repay. These financial arrangements should be made for an approved programme of development which would lead to the development of all the natural resources of a country to enable it to repay by exports. From whatever sources the funds were obtained, certain principles should be kept in mind in financing a world food policy. The immediate credit-worthiness of the borrowing country should not always be the primary test. In some transactions, it may be desirable to forgo interest for a period of years while the effects of the programme, in terms of increasing capacity to render a country self-supporting, made themselves felt. It may also be necessary to defer the beginning of gradual amortization, and introduce an element of flexibility by making the credit terms, or the extent of debt service, subject to indices of growth within a country and equilibrium in the external balance of payments. Such a proposal had been put forward by the League of Nations Committee on Economic Depressions. In addition to credits for development purposes, it was recommended that a fund should be provided to finance arrangements for countries in great nutritional need to purchase the agricultural surpluses of other nations on special terms.[4] It was noted that such surpluses might otherwise paralyze any price stabilizing operations and bring ruin to farmers. A third type of financing could be connected with price stabilizing operations.

But, if approved, how would the proposed WFB be implemented? Would it be done by expanding the functions of existing organizations or by the setting up a new body? For a long time, there had been efforts to set up international commodity organizations. International agreements had been concluded for sugar, rubber, tea and certain minerals. Most of them were quota agreements based on the allocation among members of shares in the world markets. These agreements were the 'children of the depression', when the view was held that world markets were limited and incapable of much expansion. They were inevitably restrictive in character and did not counteract business cycle fluctuations. And they lacked any overall agency to co-ordinate their activities. During the Second World War, further developments took place along the same lines. An Inter-American Coffee Agreement began operations in 1940. An International Wheat Council composed of Argentina, Australia, Canada, the United Kingdom and the United States, was established in 1942. Other governments with a major interest in wheat were invited to join its deliberations and to revise the draft an international wheat agreement for submission to an international wheat conference. The governments of Australia, New Zealand, South Africa and the United Kingdom established a Joint Organization in 1946 to undertake the marketing of accumulated wool surpluses. And there had been international study and discussion concerning the feasibility of an international cotton agreement. All existing and projected commodity councils suffered from two important defects arising from the same cause, the need for a more comprehensive organization. First, each commodity was considered in isolation. Second, they lacked the financial resources to enable them to hold stocks, bring stability to existing markets and develop new markets.

During the war, determined to realize in peace the ideals of freedom and human welfare for which they had fought, the *Declaration of the United Nations* signed in January 1942 by 26 governments provided the vision of the United Nations organization and a number of what were called UN 'specialized agencies' to fulfil the promises of Roosevelt's 'four freedoms'. By its constitution, FAO was created to make studies and recommendations for developments in the whole field of food and agriculture, forestry and fisheries, and to stimulate and foster the international co-operation necessary to carry them out. Its technical advisory services were concerned with a wide range of scientific, economic and statistical problems that underlay improved production and better distribution. The International Bank for Reconstruction and Development (IBRD) was established by the UN to assist in providing part of the large investment needed for agricultural and industrial development. Development could proceed rapidly only on a basis of improved education and health services, for which UNESCO and WHO had been set up, and satisfactory and full employment, for which ECOSOC and ILO had general international responsibility. One of the functions of the International Monetary Fund (IMF) was to assist in alleviating the balance of payments difficulties of member countries, which in itself was a major contribution toward mitigating international trade difficulties.

In addition, an International Trade Organization (ITO) had been proposed, which contemplated international machinery for encouraging progressive reduction of trade barriers, the elimination of restrictive business practices and action in the field of commodity policy. Apart from the IBRD and the IMF, which were designed to facilitate the solution of financial problems at the international level, the functions of the other UN specialized agencies were limited almost entirely to the accumulation and interpretation of facts and to make recommendations. Neither singly nor in combination were they able to take measures to translate their recommendations fully into action. The research and advisory functions of FAO were necessary and could accomplish a great deal in achieving the elimination of famine and chronic hunger and the attainment of prosperity and stability for primary producers. But there was a vitally important gap. No UN agency had the requisite authority and funds for carrying out co-ordinated international action where it was needed. In the discussions of world issues, it had been repeatedly emphasized that nations should act together if major economic

24 *1945–70. Early Attempts: FAO's Pioneering Work*

and social problems were to be solved. But they could not act together without adequate international machinery. Provision had been made for joint consultation but not for putting the results of such consultation into effect.

Against this background, it was recommended that a 'WFB' should be established with the necessary authority and funds to tackle the long-term problems of world food security. The proposed WFB, which would act through commodity committees, might be established as a new international agency or FAO's constitution might be altered to enable it to set up the WFB. There were drawbacks to having a multiplicity of international agencies acting in the same field. If FAO could establish the proposed WFB, it could be appointed by the FAO Conference, which, it was hoped, ultimately would include representatives of all countries, including those of the Soviet Union. But as the actions of the WFB would involve broad problems of world economics and finance, it would be necessary to include representatives of other international organizations such as the IBRD, ECOSOC and the proposed ITO.

According to Boyd Orr's proposal, the WFB would have four functions:

- stabilization of prices of agricultural commodities on the world markets, including provision of the necessary funds for stabilizing operations;
- establishment of a world food reserve adequate for any emergency that might arise through crop failure in any part of the world;
- provision of funds for financing the disposal of surplus agricultural products on special terms to countries that needed them; and
- co-operation with organizations concerned with international credits for industrial and agricultural development, and with trade and commodity policy, in order that their common ends might be more quickly and effectively achieved (FAO, 1946b).

For agricultural price stabilization, the WFB, operating through its commodity committees, would have power to hold stocks of each of the important commodities, in line with principles previously put forward by the League of Nations and other bodies. The WFB would undertake the investigations necessary to determine what world prices would call forth the quantities that could be marketed. It would announce a minimum and maximum price and would undertake to buy into its stocks when the world price falls below the declared minimum price and sell from its stocks when the world price exceeds the maximum. It was recognized that care would be needed to commence operations at the correct moment and to choose an appropriate world price. The WFB would need a revolving fund to operate such a plan. For safety, the normal stocks held by the WFB would represent six to twelve months' trade, the amounts varying with different commodities. In determining the contributions made to the fund, the relative benefits derived from the stabilizing operations by exporting and importing, developed and developing, countries, would need to be carefully weighed.

Since the WFB would normally be buying at its minimum and selling at its maximum price, it was considered that the Board would earn enough to cover the costs of storage. On occasion, the WFB might have to hold very much larger stocks than in normal times. These extra holdings would be financed by borrowing on the market against its commodity assets. Such operations would be greatest in times of depression when funds would be available at advantageous rates. It was envisaged that producers of livestock products and other perishables not suited to long-term stock holding would find their markets stabilized by the buffer stocks operations on feed grains and other items and enlarged through nutritional policies concurrently developed. Certain livestock products capable of being stored for long periods would be included directly in the buffer stock operations. The danger of competitive export subsidization was recognized, which could destroy the international stock holding programme. In such cases, schedules of export quotas could be negotiated between governments until new markets were developed. This contingency had been recognized and provided for in a similar way in the US proposal for an ITO.

The overall objective of WFB operations would be to ensure that sufficient food was produced and distributed to bring the consumption of all people up to a health standard. It was considered that the need for additional food was so great that if human requirements were translated into economic demand, there would be no question of surpluses of basic foods, which previously had been regarded as inevitable and, which if permitted to re-emerge might overwhelm the WFB. The basic problem was seen as one of increasing purchasing power of people who were unable to obtain sufficient food for their needs. The WFB should, therefore, be able to divert unmarketable surpluses to these consumers and arrange for financing the cost of selling at prices that they could afford.

The proposed WFB was considered to be neither a revolutionary nor a new idea. It merely synthesized many national and international measures and brought them together in one organization, which had the machinery and funds to correlate them and take executive action to carry out an adequate world food policy. The proposal warned that there were really only two alternatives: co-operation for mutual benefit; or a drift back to nationalistic policies leading to economic conflict 'that might well be the prelude to a third world war that will end our civilization'.

The proposal that was submitted to the second session of the FAO Conference in Copenhagen, Denmark in September 1946 suggested that if approved in principle, the next step should be the appointment of a committee to work out the details and prepare a specific plan for setting up the WFB. The committee would be requested to complete its report by the end of December 1946. Boyd Orr explained that under normal conditions governments would have had more time to consider the far-reaching WFB proposal, which was submitted to them within six months of FAO being set up. But it was thought that delay would reduce the chance of its acceptance. The fear was that the promise of the *Atlantic Charter* that Roosevelt and Churchill had signed in 1941, of the 'New and Better World' that Roosevelt sought, of 'the fuller life, the true and great inheritance of the common man' that Churchill envisaged, 'the relegation of poverty to the limbo of the past' that Ernest Bevin, a member of Churchill's UK war cabinet, foresaw, and other similar high hopes, 'would be quickly forgotten' (Boyd Orr and Lubbock, 1953, p. 94).

26 *1945–70. Early Attempts: FAO's Pioneering Work*

The WFB proposal was described as 'one of the boldest and most imaginative plans for international action ever put forward' (Sinha, 1976). Boyd Orr was a passionate and tireless advocate of the WFB approach to the world's food and economic problems – and to world peace. 'If the nations cannot agree on a food programme affecting the welfare of the people everywhere', he said many times, 'there is little hope of their reaching an agreement on anything else'. If, on the other hand, they agreed to co-operate in bold measures, 'the people will have hope that the resources of the earth will be developed to provide adequate food, clothing, and shelter.... Hope for tomorrow will make them better able to bear the hardships of today' (Boyd Orr and Lubbock, 1953).

His 'bold aim' was discussed in an appropriately impressive location at the second FAO conference in Copenhagen, Denmark in September 1946. The Danes had turned over a large part of the Rigsdagen, that portion of Christiansborg Castle where the Danish Parliament met, for the conference. (They were also hoping that FAO, which was temporarily located in Washington, DC, would make its permanent headquarters in Copenhagen.) At the start of the conference, the feeling seemed to be on the side of Boyd Orr's proposals. The head of UNRRA made a rousing speech before a plenary session. Generally favourable statements came from a number of delegates. The debate was opened by the leader of the United States delegation, Norris E. Dodd, then US Undersecretary of Agriculture who later became director-general of FAO after Boyd Orr. Dodd served as chairman of the conference commission that dealt with the broad subject of world food policy. He said that his government gave general approval to the proposals and to the setting up of a commission to work out the plan in greater detail, adding:

I believe... farmers generally can have fair prices and the world can have better nutrition but we will have to devise better methods... to make it possible.... The solution to this problem will be essential to securing lasting peace and greater wellbeing. We in the United States therefore strongly favour the general objectives laid down by Sir John Boyd Orr. (FAO, 1946b)

The British Minister of Food, John Strachey, quoted the epitaph, 'Here lies the body of Farmer Pete, who starved from growing too much wheat'. He said that no one wanted to see that situation occur again, but did not say that his government was prepared to co-operate. The chairman of the committee that actually considered Boyd Orr's proposal, (Herbert Broadley, a member of the UK delegation), summed up the prevailing opinion when he said:

This Conference... accepts the general objectives of the proposal.... It does not say... that a World Food Board shall be set up forthwith. What it does say is that there is a necessity for international machinery for achieving those objectives.

So the WFB proposal was approved in principle, with no country dissenting, and it was decided to set up a commission as Boyd Orr had requested. But from the foundation of FAO, there had been a great deal of opposition to any centralized, multilateral world food security setup. The idea of buffer stocks, designed essentially as a commodity-holding operation to stabilize prices, had come up at the Hot Springs conference, where it was politely shelved. While some producer groups strongly favoured this approach, others were fearful of it, and trade interests were in general strongly opposed.

Later, when writing his memoirs, Boyd Orr stated that the 'first opposition' to the proposed WFB came from Will Clayton of the US government who was trying to organize the ITO with the aim of lowering tariffs and better regulating world trade. Clayton urged Boyd Orr to withdraw his proposal. Boyd Orr argued that the WFB need not conflict with the ITO: on the contrary, they would complement each other. But Boyd Orr placed opposition to his proposal mainly on the two major powers at the time, the United States and the United Kingdom. He wrote

> Britain and America were not prepared to give either funds or authority to an organization over which they had not got full control. Britain might have lost her advantage of cheap food imports, while the US thought that she could do better for herself as a world power through bilateral aid to other countries. This is an understandable attitude for these national governments to adopt. Indeed, to have decided otherwise might appear to their people as a dereliction of duty. (Boyd Orr and Lubbock, 1953, p. 57)

In order that the search for an acceptable approach to the problem might continue, the conference established a 'Preparatory Commission on World Food Proposals'. The commission was requested to examine not only Boyd Orr's ideas but also any others that seemed pertinent. Sixteen governments were appointed as members of the commission.[5] Boyd Orr nominated Stanley Bruce of Australia as its chairman. The commission met in Washington, DC in October 1946 and continued working until the end of January the following year. By then, as Boyd Orr explained, 'the political atmosphere had changed' The US government was not prepared to give either funds or authority to any international organization over which it did not have full control. With the US refusing to co-operate, the United Kingdom not favourable to the idea, and the Soviet Union 'cynically suspicious', it was not possible to proceed with the WFB proposal.

The commission did not favour the creation of a WFB (FAO, 1946b). But it emphasized that the traumatic experience of the inter-war years, the collapse of agricultural prices, and the consequent misery of the farming communities in several grain surplus countries caused by over-production, at a time when millions were starving in other parts of the world, had laid bare the weaknesses of the traditional methods of unregulated production and marketing of foodstuffs. With state regulation of prices and trade in several countries in order to maintain farm incomes and food supplies to consumers at reasonable prices, the commission noted that the international market in agricultural products was by no mean a 'free' market in the traditional sense.

28   1945–70. Early Attempts: FAO's Pioneering Work

The commission felt that 'only by consultation and co-operation between governments can reasonable stability of agricultural prices be achieved'. It recommended that 'for many commodities, the most satisfactory method would be inter-governmental commodity arrangements and agreements'. It further emphasized that commodity arrangements

> should be motivated by genuine multilateral considerations. They should all of them meet three requirements: first, they should contribute towards stabilization of agricultural prices at levels fair to producers and consumers alike; secondly, they should, so far as possible, avoid restriction of production and should stimulate an expansion of consumption and an improvement of nutrition and thirdly, they should encourage, consistently with considerations relevant to the national economy of each country, shifts of production to areas in which the commodities can be most economically and effectively produced.

The commission undertook an exhaustive examination of basic economic and technical questions related to the production and distribution of agricultural products. Its report is remarkable for the fact that most, if not all, of the features of the world food security proposals for the next twenty years were present in the commission's recommendations. The most elaborate part of the commission's report dealt with the definitions and concepts of stocks and reserves. It envisaged three types: working stocks, famine reserves and price-stabilization reserves. Working stocks as defined by the commission included: pipeline (normal shipping and distribution) requirements, a reserve against crop fluctuations, and, for importing countries, a reserve against fluctuations in import supply, or for exporting countries, a reserve to help maintain export markets. According to the commission, the decision concerning the size of the working stock should be the responsibility of individual countries.

For essential foodstuffs, the commission recommended the creation of a 'famine reserve'. The commission's report stated:

> A famine reserve should be created as soon as the supply position made it possible to do so. This was regarded as necessary, particularly for bread grains and rice. It was proposed that such a reserve should be held nationally by exporting and importing countries for use nationally and internationally under agreed conditions. The amount of reserve to be carried by each member was to be decided for each commodity by international agreement. Each member was to bear the cost of carrying its own share, but the distribution among members of the aggregate burden was to be equitable, both as to carrying stocks and as to any loss which might be incurred in distribution to famine areas. Contributions were to be made in kind, as far as feasible.

For counteracting seasonal and cyclical price fluctuations, the commission recommended the creation of a price stabilization reserve or buffer stock. The commission favoured the idea that 'the stocks should be nationally held, but administered under internationally agreed rules', This, they regarded, was 'the only practical alternative', since 'many important governments are unlikely to accept the obligation of making large financial contributions to an international Price Stabilization Reserve'.

In the end, the commission's suggestions met with no more success than Body Orr's WFB proposal. As a later FAO director-general, Addeke Boerma, put it, they were rejected not on grounds of technical feasibility or logistical difficulties, which were not even discussed, but on political and ideological grounds (Boerma, 1975). In place of a WFB, the commission proposed that FAO establish a 'World Food Council', or 'Council of FAO', with a membership of 18 nations. This would replace the original FAO Executive Committee comprised of persons chosen solely for their individual competence, the drawback being that they did not speak officially for their governments and hence could not provide an authoritative direction for FAO. The proposal for an FAO Council was approved[6] and has remained in being until today. Meeting between sessions of the FAO Conference, the Council would not only be concerned with the work of FAO in general but would espe-cially keep the world food situation under continuous review and, when neces-sary, would promptly call emergency needs to the attention of governments, a matter of considerable importance since the post-war food emergency situation still continued.

The commission also addressed the concern of the recurrence of surpluses in some of the high-producing countries, particularly the United States, stimulated by the war effort during the Second World War. Two approaches were identified. Development and modernization of agriculture and industry should be speeded up, which would increase purchasing power and stimulated international trade. And intergovernmental commodity arrangements designed to keep the prices of agricultural products sufficiently stable to assure continued production, including limited reserves (buffer stocks) of certain commodities that were especially subject to extreme price fluctuations. While Boyd Orr thought production and trade logic-ally belonged together in the same organization since they interacted, the Prepar-atory Commission separated them. FAO would be the production stimulator. Trade arrangements would be in the hands of separate commodity organizations (like the International Wheat Council) with which FAO might be rather loosely related, at least pending the establishment of the proposed ITO.

At the International Monetary Conference held at Bretton Woods, New Hamp-shire in the United States in 1944, three 'pillars' for a new world economic structure were proposed by John Maynard Keynes, the eminent economist and leader of the British delegation, and modified by the United States delegation (Moggridge, 1992; Skidelsky, 2000). The first pillar became the IMF. The second pillar was the IBRD. The third pillar was to be the ITO. Keynes was a strong believer in the stabilization of primary commodity prices, which was to be one of the main functions of the ITO. At one point, Keynes combined his proposals for a world central bank and world currency with his proposals for commodity price stabil-ization by suggesting a world currency based on 30 primary commodities rather than gold, dollars or special drawing rights (SDRs). This would have stabilized the

30 1945–70. Early Attempts: FAO's Pioneering Work

average price of the 30 commodities included. Successfully negotiated at a UN conference in Havana, Cuba in 1948, the ITO's charter included a set of rules and procedures for the conclusion and operation of international commodity agreements (UN, 1948b). Pending the ratification of the ITO's charter, ECOSOC requested the UN secretary-general to appoint an Interim Co-ordinating Committee for International Commodity Arrangements to facilitate intergovernmental consultation or action in this field. In the committee's work, less importance was attributed to the use of commodity agreements in connection with persistent 'burdensome surpluses' and more attention was paid to the avoidance of excessive fluctuations, however caused, in commodity prices. Instability, it was pointed out, could be caused by shortage as well as surpluses, a view shared by the FAO Conference and other FAO bodies. In 1954, ECOSOC decided to establish a Commission for International Commodity Trade and to transfer to it some of the general commodity review functions of the interim co-ordinating committee. But the ITO was never ratified. It became a victim of hostility in the US Congress during the communist witch-hunt conducted by Senator Joseph McCarthy. In place of the ITO came the General Agreement on Tariffs and Trade (GATT), which was replaced by the World Trade Organization (WTO) in 1995. The key function of commodity price stabilization was not included among the functions of either the GATT or the WTO, to the disadvantage particularly of developing countries.

Like Boyd Orr, the Preparatory Commission emphasized that the basis of all intergovernmental arrangements should be an expansion of consumption, not restriction of production. Thus, it vigorously endorsed the idea of making surpluses available to needy countries at special prices for approved nutrition-improvement programmes. It also proposed that the FAO Conference should undertake a more elaborate annual review of the world food and agricultural situation, acting as a kind of world food parliament through which governments would co-operate in shaping policies, plans and programmes. In addition, the commission advocated larger investments, both national and international, in agricultural development and urged much more active work by other UN bodies, particularly ECOSOC, in stimulating industrial development. It also undertook a number of studies of individual commodities and made recommendations. In the case of wheat, for example, it outlined guiding principles for an international wheat agreement, which were useful later when the first post-war international wheat agreement was being negotiated. In the case of rice, the commission recommended an international conference in Southeast Asia, the first move toward setting up the International Rice Commission.

Boyd Orr made the best of the commission's recommendations. He certainly hoped that the proposed FAO Council would become a dynamic and influential body. But he was bitterly disappointed over the failure of his original proposals to win endorsement. He therefore made up his mind to resign as director-general of FAO. He agreed to continue in office until his successor was appointed in 1948. He believed strongly in the technical assistance work of FAO and felt that world food and agricultural production could be significantly increased if farmers could only apply on a wide scale what was already known. But he was impatient: 'when people ask for bread and we give them pamphlets'. After all, he had come up with the motto for FAO, *Fiat Panis* ('let there be bread'), which has remained to this day. Driven by an intense desire to right wrongs and help make the world a better place to live in, he thought in terms of a big plan, a bold idea, to solve the world food security problem. When it did not work out that way, his interests and energies turned increasingly to the cause of world government. In recognition of his contributions to world peace through FAO and in other ways, he was awarded the Nobel Peace Prize in 1949 (Boyd Orr, 1949) and was elevated to the British peerage as Lord Boyd Orr in the same year.

4
International Commodity Clearing House

The departure of Boyd Orr did not signal the end of his ambitious proposal and the problems they were designed to overcome. It was obvious that his bold aim was metaphorically and politically 'a bridge too far' but as a platform for venting the desires of many governments, especially the poorer and smaller ones, it was invaluable. And the issues it raised were to be addressed for many years to come. Therefore, it was understandable that the next director-general of FAO, Norris E. Dodd from the United States (1948–53), who had strongly supported the WFB proposal at the Copenhagen conference in 1946, should seek to salvage what he considered to be some of its more acceptable elements. The opportunity presented itself when the FAO Council, which met in Paris in June 1949, requested the FAO director-general to report on the underlying causes of emerging commodity trade problems and present recommendations for possible action by governments. A group experts was appointed, with John B. Conliffe of the University of California as chairman, 'to propose measures for promoting the balanced expansion of world trade in agricultural products', in order to assist the FAO director-general make his recommendations, no doubt taking the experience of what had happened to the WFB proposal into account.

The global food supply situation had gradually improved since the proposal for a WFB was first introduced. The world food situation had again become characterized by surpluses of certain commodities, particularly in the dollar area, though supplies in other parts of the world were still only barely sufficient or even scarce. It became apparent that food import needs existed that could not be met from available stocks for lack of foreign exchange in food-deficit countries. The immediate problem was diagnosed as an accumulation of surpluses in hard currency countries (principally the US dollar area) while countries with weak inconvertible currencies found it difficult to import food on commercial terms.

This led to the expert group's proposal for a kind of barter scheme, called an International Commodity Clearing House (ICCH), as a public corporation with an authorized capital fund equivalent to $5 billion, as an operating organization and action arm of FAO, with the following functions:

International Commodity Clearing House 33

- purchase, subject to certain provisions, of stocks of commodities in surplus supply;
- negotiate sales in inconvertible currencies in order to assist in maintaining the flow of trade during periods of exchange disequilibrium, such payments being guaranteed by the buying countries against losses from exchange depreciation;
- sales at special prices to countries in need, under strictly defined conditions of use, for example, for relief purposes, special nutritional programmes, or development projects;
- hold stocks acquired in periods of surplus as a reserve to protect the interests of consumers in periods of shortage;
- negotiate bilateral or multilateral trading agreements or exchanges of commodities on a barter basis;
- co-ordinate the negotiation and administration of international commodity arrangements, pending further decisions on intergovernmental machinery for these purposes; and
- organize consultations between governments and other institutions in respect of commodity policies and arrangements, and the uses of land and other national resources, in order to meet the changing structures of world demand and supply.

The ICCH would start with a revolving fund, contributed by member countries in proportion to national income, with each country contributing in its own currency. Additional contributions could be called upon for specific transactions, which would be earmarked for use in the contributing countries to buy commodities that were declared to be in surplus.

The ICCH's authorized capital fund would be provided by national quotas based on the national incomes of the member countries and payable in the currencies of the supplying countries. Two methods could be used to dispose of surpluses. Under one method, the purchasing country could buy from the exporting country through the ICCH with soft currency at the full market price. The exporting country would then use the soft currency to buy products in the purchasing country or, alternatively, the money would be held in the credit of the selling country until world economic conditions improved enough to convert it into hard currency. Under the other method, the purchasing country would buy in hard currency at less than the market value. These cut-price sales would be made only under special circumstances to countries in need and for strictly defined uses, such as relief, nutrition-improvement programmes, or feeding workers employed on development projects. Such arrangements were considered to be of a temporary nature to help countries during the period of economic distress pending wider economic expansion and improvement in world trade. But there were also to be longer-term functions of the ICCH. To prevent extreme price declines, the organization could buy and store certain commodities when world market prices fell below an agreed level and sold in periods of rising prices to protect against extreme increases. The ICCH might also negotiate and administer international commodity agreements, pending the establishment of the proposed ITO, which, as noted above, was never ratified.

As with the WFB proposal, the ICCH was not approved by FAO member nations. But the stumbling block of hard currency shortages was bypassed when the United States initiated substantial food aid programmes under its Public Law 480 in 1948. Thereafter, and for almost twenty years, a system emerged whereby security rested almost entirely on the stockholding policies of the major food exporting countries, policies that were the by-product of domestic agricultural policies and associated price and income support programmes. As we saw above, a number of the features of the proposed ICCH were already incorporated in United States food export and food aid policies and programmes before the Second World War. These included the operations of an Export-Import Bank set up in 1934 to promote US exports by providing loans at concessional rates to foreign governments and businesses for the purchase of US commodities. A Grains Stabilization Board was established to finance exports. And a Commodity Credit Corporation (CCC) was set up to manage releases from the increasing government food stocks for food aid and subsidized exports, thereby stabilizing, supporting and protecting farm income and prices in the US. The Second World War gave a further boost to food surpluses and stock held by the federal government in the United States. Under the Lend-Lease Act of 1941, some $6 billion of agricultural products were provided to European allies. The Surplus Act of 1944 and the Agricultural Act of 1949 authorized the CCC to sell stockpiled surplus commodities on the international market at below market price. Surpluses were also made available for disaster relief under special legislation. This legislation included the sale of US agricultural commodities for local currencies.

As we also saw above, at the end of the Second World War, the US came to the aid of war-ravaged Europe in a massive reconstruction effort involving the largest bilateral aid programme in world history, popularly known as the Marshall Plan. It proved to be a boon for US domestic agriculture by providing a guaranteed export market for US farm output at the very time when high levels of peacetime production were resumed. But the combination of the farm price support systems instituted in the 1930s and explosion in the scale and pace of technological advance in US agriculture led to ever-increasing surpluses as supply outstripped domestic and international demand. This created enormous food stocks in government inventories, draining financial reserves, and leading to heated debates in the US Congress on how to resolve the problem. At the same time, under section 550 of the Mutual Security Act of 1951, the idea was introduced of stimulating the disposal of US agricultural surpluses by offering to sell them to interested countries for local currency. The purpose was to facilitate the export of US products, and create new and enlarge existing markets, while helping to ease the balance of payments difficulties of developing countries.

The 1949 FAO Conference rejected the ICCH proposals outright. Several objections were raised. It was felt that the accumulated debts in soft currency under the scheme, which would eventually have to be paid by food-deficit countries in the form of exports, would be a burden that would tend to delay rather than hasten their recovery. And payment for food bought at reduced prices would further reduce the small hard-currency reserves of the deficit countries.

Transactions under the ICCH would tend to interfere with normal trade. And the proposed buffer stock operations were open to the same objections as those of the WFB proposals. In essence, it was evident that key major countries were still not prepared to entrust to a multilateral organization over which they had no control with such potent functions as the management of a world food security arrangement no matter how urgent it was or how it was shaped.

As to the continuation of surpluses arising through currency difficulties, the FAO Conference saw no remedy. For those arising from other causes, it recommended a more vigorous use of the Interim Co-ordinating Committee for International Commodity Arrangements, an institutional remnant of the ITO that never came into being. However, the FAO Conference did establish a purely advisory Committee on Commodity Problems (CCP), to function under the FAO Council, initially to provide advice on surplus problems arising out of balance-of-payments difficulties, which was later extended to review all commodity problems. The CCP continues to function today. In 1952, the CCP was requested to examine the feasibility of establishing an emergency food reserve to be available promptly to countries threatened by famine. Three possibilities were suggested: a stock of food owned by an international agency; a central fund administered by an international agency for the purchase and distribution of emergency food; and emergency food stocks held by national governments for international use. While the central fund idea was generally preferred, no further action was taken at that time. Action was taken, however, on another issue.

Attention was turned to the problems arising from the disposal of agricultural surpluses especially as the United States government sought to export on special terms part of the large stocks that had accumulated under its control. The CCP recommended that two steps be taken. First, the establishment of a set of principles, a code of conduct, to govern the disposal of agricultural surpluses (see below). Second, the establishment of a permanent committee, to be known as the Consultative Subcommittee on Surplus Disposal (CSD), as a subcommittee of the CCP, to monitor continuously the impact of surplus disposal on agricultural production and international trade. The CSD was established in Washington, DC in 1954. It has continued to function to the present time and reports to the FAO Council through the CCP.

While attempts to set up some form of world food security arrangement during the first decade of FAO did not succeed, the FAO secretariat continued to keep the issues alive through a series of seminal pioneering studies and reports throughout the 1950s. These publications helped to clarify the issues involved, attempted to facilitate the evolution of an international code of conduct, and constantly sought out new approached for bringing governments together to get something done. Experience had shown that it was not possible to obtain approval for a wide-ranging or comprehensive proposal. Instead, there might be better chance of advancement if individual issues, or components of a world food security arrangement, were addressed separately. While many in the FAO secretariat took part in this work, two individuals stood out, Gerda Blau, who eventually became director of FAO's Commodities and Trade Division, and Mordecai Ezekiel, director of FAO's

Economic Division and previously one of the authors of President Roosevelt's New Deal. A number of resolutions were adopted by the FAO Council and Conference on issues relating to world food security and passed on to ECOSOC and the UN General Assembly for action, which led to nothing or to calls for further studies (FAO, 1973). The main reason for lack of progress was the continued reluctance of governments in developed countries, especially the US and the UK, to approve measures that might weaken their national initiatives and powers of control. The climate of opinion was against multilateral action in operational fields as distinct from advisory or information-providing roles.

5
A World Food Reserve

The need for some form of international management of global food reserves was not forgotten. The first half of the 1950s witnessed 'a long and at times agitated phase' of international activity on this subject (FAO, 1975). Responding to ECOSOC and the UN General Assembly resolutions regarding the problem of food in times of emergency, procedures were evolved under the leadership of the FAO director-general: to investigate threats of localized famine; initiate intergovernmental consultations; and bring about 'prompt, concerted and effective assistance'. At the same time, in a resolution passed by the UN General Assembly in 1954,[7] FAO was requested to conduct an in-depth study of the then popular concept of a 'world food reserve' (WFR) (FAO, 1956).

Mobilization of resources to meet an emergency was seen at the time as 'the hard core' of the food security problem. It was noted, however, that this raised difficulties depending on the global food stocks situation when a disaster struck. With plentiful stocks, as was the case during the 1950s and 1960s, the main problem was to finance, and guarantee in advance (and on agreed conditions), the speedy delivery to disaster-stricken areas of the relatively small portion of total available stocks that were required for emergency relief. Hence, a group of experts convened in the early 1950s dismissed the case for an emergency food reserve physically established in advance and gave preference to an international relief fund for the purchase of relief supplies as and when needed. Other suggestions included contingent national pledges in kind to be activated in emergencies.

The drastic rundown of world food stocks clearly raised different issues. Procurement for emergency operations would come into direct competition with effective commercial demand. In such circumstances, it was considered that no famine relief fund was likely to command resources sufficient to secure, at short notice, the quantities required without triggering a rise in market prices, which would further reduce the fund's purchasing power. In any case, both approaches – a physically established world food reserve and an international relief fund – proved equally unacceptable to governments, and the FAO Conference took no action on any of the many alternative proposal presented to it in 1953.

38   *1945–70. Early Attempts: FAO's Pioneering Work*

The idea of a world food reserve was revived in 1954–55 when the UN General Assembly requested the UN secretary-general to invite FAO to prepare

> a factual and comprehensive report on what has been done and is being done [regarding]: (a) the feasibility of establishing a world food reserve within the framework of the United Nations, [and] (b) the feasibility of such a reserve acting as an institution which could contribute to relieve emergency situations and to counteract excessive price fluctuations.

In making its request, the UN General Assembly resolution noted that 'no factual report has been made dealing comprehensively with '[these subjects]' and expressed 'its appreciation of the valuable work being done in these fields by the Food and Agriculture Organization'.

The resolution referred to the need for national and international action to meet four main objectives:

- raise low levels of food production and consumption and fight chronic malnutrition;
- relieve famine and other emergency situations;
- counteract excessive price fluctuations; and
- promote the rational disposal of intermittent agricultural surpluses.

The resolution was prompted by a proposal, presented by the Government of Costa Rica, which called for 'the establishment of an organ capable of fulfilling all the functions of a "World Food Reserve"'.[8] In introducing these proposals, reference was made to the proposal for a WFB, and to the activities of the CCP and other FAO organs. While commending the efforts made, the Government of Costa Rica concluded that, in view of the serious food distribution problems that still remained, the establishment of a WFR called for renewed consideration 'at the highest international level'. The Costa Rican proposal did not give any details regarding the structure, method of operation, or international character of the proposed WFR, preferring that these matters should be determined by the UN General Assembly.

In the ensuing debate, while different views were expressed on methods, there was widespread agreement on the objectives of a WFR listed by Costa Rica, and on the need for their continued promotion through national and international action. Discussion ranged over a wide front, touching on the need for improved food supply and better nutritional standards, the harmful effect of excessive price fluctuation, the importance of famine prevention, and the nature and functions of food reserves. The functions of the proposed WFR were remarkably close to those of the proposed WFB that was not approved. A similar proposal was made in a bipartisan draft resolution placed before the US Senate in March 1955.[9] This called on the US president to promote, through the UN and other appropriate international channels, negotiations on the establishment of a 'World Food Bank' which, by issuing loans of foods and fibres, could help promote a series of objectives similar to those of the WFB proposal.

Fighting chronic malnutrition

As the requested FAO report revealed, a common factor underlying these proposals was the revolt against 'poverty in the midst of plenty'. This led to a series of basic questions that were often repeated in the international debate. If supplies in some parts of the world exceeded requirements, why, it was asked, cannot those supplies be used to relieve hunger and starvation in other parts where nutrition levels were low and famine threatened? Moreover, why should crop fluctuations due to the vagaries of weather and other factors influencing the short-run movements of supply and demand be allowed to lead to rapid alternations of glut and scarcity, accompanied by even more erratic and sharp fluctuations in the movements of food prices? Why, in a world which was becoming 'richer and smaller than it had ever been', could not all those evils be met and discrepancies of supply and demand be bridged in space and time through the operation of an international food reserve?

The FAO report considered that 'there can be little doubt' about the importance and desirability of the main objectives of a WFR. However, it also recognized that as regards the methods of achieving those objectives, the answers were not always as simple as might appear at first sight, nor could they always be found in the direction that at first might seem the most obvious. Some answers had not been found. On others, informed opinion differed. In several major respects, however, the answers were clear and the call for action urgent. It was of great practical importance that the issues were understood as widely as possible. Otherwise, there was the danger that well-meant, but wrongly directed, efforts would lead to unnecessary frustration and delay progress in fields where the need for action was both urgent and clearly defined. The report recognized that FAO itself, in its early plans for a WFB, 'did not perhaps pay sufficient heed to the crucial need for clarity of concepts as a basis for action'. While the basic issues remained to be solved, a good deal of further thinking had been done, and some practical experience gained, since the WFB was first proposed in 1946.

The FAO report attempted to explain both the relationships and the differences in approach required for dealing with each of the four issues listed in the UN General Assembly resolution, with special reference to the scope and limitations of food reserve operations. In addressing the background to the problems, the report showed the serious and widespread character of under-nutrition and malnutrition in many parts of the world.[10] It concluded that the main cause was poverty and that the main cure against poverty was economic development. More needed to be done to promote economic development. It was not possible, however, to cure the world's chronic malnutrition through the establishment of a WFR that operated on a self-financing basis and, at the same time, acted as a world buffer pool, for two main reasons. First, malnutrition was a chronic problem the main cause of which was lack of consumers' purchasing power. Food distribution to poor consumers would have to be subsidized on a continuing basis, which would deplete the resources of a WFR unless they were constantly replenished or the cost of food subsidies were paid for, at least in part, out of income derived from the additional development that extra food supplies would help to finance.

40   *1945–70. Early Attempts: FAO's Pioneering Work*

The dedication of surplus food stocks to development purposes, either in the form of additional 'food capital' through the creation of a 'World Food Capital Fund', which could be linked with, or form an additional part of, the propose Special United Nations Fund for Economic Development (SUNFED),[11] or through other channels, would have to be seen in the wider context of the fight against chronic poverty and the promotion of economic development through organized international assistance. Second, the international use of food supplies to fight chronic malnutrition required methods that were almost entirely distinct from, and largely incompatible with, the types of operation that a WFR would have to perform for price stabilization purposes.

On the other hand, a number of benefits could be derived from the establishment of national reserves in developing countries, including: insurance against famine and other emergencies; protection against the effects of excessive and erratic fluctuations in the prices of staple foods; and provision of some 'elbow room' in national planning for economic development. But, paradoxically, the need for such reserves was greatest, and the ability to maintain them lowest, in the very countries that were suffering from chronic malnutrition. These considerations pointed to possibilities of international food surplus being used in the wider context of economic assistance, taking into account the *Principles of Surplus Disposal* recommended by FAO (see below). It was easier to plan multipurpose reserves on a national basis than on an international scale. The same international pool of foodstuffs could not simultaneously serve the two different purposes of counteracting market instability and relieving famine or chronic poverty. The former would require something like a 'world market stabilization fund' or buffer pool, which might be replenished by something like a 'world food capital fund'.

Famine and other emergency relief

The report noted the close link between chronic malnutrition and famine in the sense that the latter was most likely to occur, and reach drastic proportions, in countries where normal food supplies were precariously low. It drew an analogy with the state of health stating that 'just as critical illness differed from lingering sickness, so does famine differ from chronic malnutrition in that it is not only more acutely serious but also lesser in incidence, more localized, intermittent, and unpredictable'. This marked, perhaps for the first time, the important distinction between chronic and transitory food insecurity, which was later revived in a seminal World Bank study in 1986 (World Bank, 1986), with critical policy and operational implications (see below).[12]

In the great famines of history, people depended for food on the crops produced by themselves, or at no great distance from their homes. Crops failed, usually because of drought, and the people starved. There were no reserves in store, no means of transporting food in sufficient amounts from elsewhere, and no administrative organization for procuring or distributing food to relieve famine.[13] While steps had been taken to respond quickly and effectively in times of famine, the report acknowledged that much more still remained to be done. It listed the main requirements as follows:

Before the event:

- build up health and physical resistance;
- national food stocks of adequate composition and scale;
- adequate storage facilities and location of stocks with a view to relief strategy;
- develop effective administration, distribution, and transport facilities;
- efficient apparatus for early detection.

In the case of emergency:

- speed of relief operations;
- immediate availability of funds for financing relief supplies;
- adequate economic controls to prevent speculation and hoarding and to provide for priority needs.

The main responsibility for most of these aspects rested with national governments. Effective advanced provision for supplementary international action, if needed, should also be made to ensure that disasters were averted or mitigated. International aid could also help governments in needy countries in strengthening their own defences and preparedness against future emergencies.[14]

A world emergency food reserve

The two main aspects covered in post-war intergovernmental studies and resolutions on international famine relief were (a) procedures for detection and appeal; and (b) the possibility of creating a world emergency food reserve to be drawn on when international assistance was requested. In defining a situation in which international relief would be called for, the UN and FAO distinguished between causes and circumstances. A UN General Assembly resolution of 1952, which called for the establishment of procedures to deal with famine emergencies arising from natural causes, referred to 'emergency famines . . . created by crop failure due to plague, drought, flood, blight, volcanic eruptions, earthquakes and similar accidents of a natural character' (UN, 1952a). The UN secretary-general, in a report to ECOSOC in the same year, commented that famine emergencies arising from the aftermath of war and civil disturbances were excluded from the resolution. The FAO Conference and Council endorsed these definitions in principle but suggested some degree of flexibility in applying them, as in situations where an emergency was exacerbated by the lethal combination of war and natural causes such as drought. A working party was appointed by the FAO Council in 1952 'to study and explore suitable ways and means whereby an emergency food reserve can be established and made available promptly to member states threatened or affected by serious food shortages or famine' (FAO, 1951).[15]

The working party concluded that it would be advantageous to reconsider the definition based on further study of the origin of famines and of the relative importance of different causes. Regarding the definition of circumstances requiring international relief action, since famine was most likely to occur in countries where there was much chronic under-nourishment, it might at first sight appear difficult to define the criteria for distinguishing between famine and chronic under-nourishment. Neither physiological nor economic criteria would be sufficient in themselves, or in combination, to define the circumstances requiring international emergency relief action. The working party noted that through the operation of the Indian Famine Code, a distinction was made between chronic malnutrition and emergency famine by common sense administrative methods.[16] It suggested that the Indian example should be adopted in calling for international relief action and that full account should also be taken of the criteria contained in the UN secretary-general's report to ECOSOC of 1952 including: the probable degree of shortage of food supplies in relation to the usual consumption if the affected population; the area and number of people likely to be affected; the probably duration of the emergency; the extent to which the government concerned was dealing, and could deal, with the situation through its own resources; the effects of the famine in fields other than food; and the consequences of the famine on economic and social conditions in the country (UN, 1952b). Other factors included: the internal transport facilities available; the administrative machinery for distributing food; and the effectiveness of controls to prevent excessive food price rises and hoarding, and panic. The report concluded that, 'It is only in the light of considerations of the character [of the situation] that the gravity of the emergency can be judged and the need assessed'. Taking all these factors into account, the working party put forward the following definition of famine as appropriate for the purpose of assessing the need for international action:

It is a food situation in which there are clear indications, *based on careful and impartial study*, (emphasis added) that serious catastrophe and extensive suffering will occur if international assistance is not rendered (FAO, 1952a)

The definition implied that the government of the threatened country had taken all the internal measures that were its duty and responsibility in such circumstances. The definition was accepted by the FAO Council and Conference.

Machinery for the detection of, and appeals for, emergency famines were discussed and approved by the UN, ECOSOC and the FAO Conference. These stressed the importance of early warning and continuous surveillance of an impending disaster. FAO was given primary responsibility for ascertaining the nature, scope and probable duration of impending food shortages and famine, making emergency reports, and advising the UN secretary-general of the need for international action (UN, 1952b). The machinery for invoking international emergency aid through FAO was first brought into play in 1952 in response to a request from the Government of Yugoslavia resulting from drought.

In 1951, the FAO Conference asked the FAO Council 'to study and explore suitable ways and means whereby an emergency food reserve can be established and made available promptly to Member States threatened or affected by serious food shortages or famine'. Studies were undertaken with the help of two successive expert groups (FAO, 1951). The main conclusions to emerge from these studies may be summarized as follows. Technical and financial obstacles rather than inadequate physical world food supplies were the main difficulties in relieving emergencies caused by natural disasters. The requirements for meeting even a major famine emergency would constitute but 'a very small fraction' of the volume of world exportable food supplies. The main problem, therefore, was to finance, organize and guarantee in advance, and on agreed conditions, the speedy delivery to famine-stricken areas of that small portion of total available stocks required for emergency relief.

The working group considered three basic alternatives for the establishment of an emergency famine reserve: (a) an internationally owned emergency food reserve; (b) an internationally owned emergency relief fund and (c) nationally owned emergency stocks. On the basis of its general conclusions, the working group was of the view that the desired objective of utmost speed and flexibility of relief operations could best be met through the establishment of an 'International Relief Fund'. The fund should have sufficient financial resources for the purchase of relief supplies as and where needed rather than through the creation of an internationally owned 'Emergency Food Reserve' physically established in advance.[17] In favouring a fund rather than a reserve, it was pointed out that the latter would not be sufficiently flexible and that the wrong kinds of food might be held in the wrong places. On the other hand, a fund would allow the speedy provision of aid through the purchase of the required commodities close to where the emergency occurred. In addition, the creation of internationally owned stocks might cause political difficulties in determining the strategic points where stores should be held, in responding to relief needs, and in creating the required central administrative structure, which would be considerably greater than that needed for the management of a fund.

The FAO studies were also guided by the consideration that in a humanitarian relief scheme, every effort should be made to accept and use different kinds of contributions, in terms of cash, commodities or facilities such as shipping, however small. Consideration was therefore given to an alternative plan of 'nationally owned emergency stocks'. Under this plan, contributing governments would agree to set aside from their own supplies, or procure in advance at their own expense, specified quantities and types of emergency food stocks. These reserves would be owned by the governments concerned who would take full responsibility for maintaining and storing them on a standby basis. Such an arrangement might be better than an emergency fund or reserve in that it would be administratively simpler, would not require clearing requirements, would not involve currency complications, and the physical size of the reserve could be guaranteed. Despite these apparent advantages, the working group concluded that an international relief scheme based solely on nationally owned or earmarked stocks would not be sufficiently flexible to make the most of relief resources in cases of emergency. Among the potential difficulties that such an arrangement would

44 1945–70. Early Attempts: FAO's Pioneering Work

entail were the complications in working out a scale of contributions on the basis of agreed criteria, replenishment and location of stocks, and an administrative mechanism that would require an international authority to ensure some central control.

In an effort to combine the workability of a permanent relief fund with the acceptance of contributions in kind, the FAO Council decided that a group of experts should be appointed to explore the problem further.[18] The group proposed the establishment of what was called the 'Plan of the Three Circles' (FAO, 1953). The 'three circles' of the plan consisted of

(a) an inner circle of financial contributors to provide the nucleus of the plan and to constitute a relief fund based on renewable financial contributions on an agreed scale;
(b) a second circle of contributions in kind, which provided an additional reserve; and
(c) an outer circle of *ad hoc* participants and financial contributors to its administrative expenses, but without any other advance commitments.

The group recommended that a 'FAO Famine Unit' should be established to administer the proposed plan with a budget of 'not less than $150,000' to be drawn from FAO regular budget. Although the plan was found to be technically sound by the FAO Council and Conference in 1953, it was not pursued. Further steps depended on the attitude of governments concerning the need for action and on the prospects for their contributions in money and kind to an international pool for emergency purposes. Insufficient support was obtained on either count and so no action was taken.

Counteracting excessive price fluctuations

The other main objective referred to in the UN General Assembly's resolution concerning the establishment of a world food reserve was that of counteracting excessive price fluctuations. This was described in the FAO report as 'a large subject and a very important one'. It therefore felt that it might come as a surprise that 'in sharp contrast' to the number of proposals that had been put forward for the operation of international commodity stabilization reserves, or buffer stocks, 'the history of the world since the days of Joseph yields no peacetime examples of any such reserves ever having been operated on an international scale for any foodstuffs, or group of foodstuffs'.[19] (A relatively small tin buffer stock managed by producers operated in the 1930s was the only international buffer stock ever established for any primary product.) Therefore, as there was no previous experience to draw on, the report turned to the nature and causes of price fluctuations for agricultural products. Short-term movements in the prices of primary products, and particularly agricultural commodities, if left entirely to the free play of market forces, 'tend to be excessive and harmful to the long-term interests of both producers and consumers'.

The fundamental reason for this was that 'owing to the low short-term elasticities of demand and supply, even small changes in the balance of production and consumption tend to be associated with large variations in prices'. Short-term price movements may be the cause of a fresh disturbance of the balance of production and consumption in a later period 'owing to the slowness of production responses to price changes'. In markets where wide price fluctuations were common, the behaviour of stocks 'may tend to exaggerate the instability of prices even further, owing to the perverse influence of speculative stock movements' (FAO, 1952b). Smoothing excessive short-term price fluctuations was not only in the interest of both producers and consumers but also in the wider interest of world economic stability generally.

Price instability had a major adverse impact on developing countries whose economies depended in large measure on receipts from the export sales of one or a few primary products. It could also have adverse effects on the economies of importing countries and may cause disturbingly large variations in the balance of payments, and on the living standards of consumers everywhere. Concerning what constituted 'excessive' price instability, the FAO report quoted from the report of a group of UN experts (UN, 1953). 'Excessive' referred to both the frequency and amplitude of price fluctuations. The encouragement of a better allocation of economic resources, which was the desirable result of price changes, should be achieved without violent instability. If prices had to change by 15 per cent or 20 per cent from year to year in order to achieve minor allocations in resource allocation, this would raise serious doubt about the effectiveness of this method of securing a desirable allocation.

The destabilizing influence of speculative stock movements was seen as having a particular effect in causing the high degree of instability of primary commodity prices. They often tended to amplify changes in supply and demand in the market and to the 'perverse influence of expectations' that may make traders sell when prices were falling and add to their stock in a rising market. The marginal character of import requirements for some primary products, especially foodstuffs, was an additional destabilizing influence on international commodity prices. Many importing countries produced at home a large part of their total food requirements, relying on imports for the remainder. Small changes in total consumption or domestic production could lead to variations in their import requirements. On the side of exporters, on the other hand, the proportions of exports to production of both foodstuffs and raw materials were large for a number of major exporting countries and their dependence on exports receipts was correspondingly great. While exporters of raw materials were therefore likely to suffer most from changes in industrial activity and particularly in the output of capital goods that often were much more pronounced than changes in economic activity generally, the exporters of foodstuffs, though catering for a more stable level of world consumption, were affected particularly by the marginal character of their trade. In addition, there was the influence of national price-support and price-fixing measures and export subsidies that had a perverse effect on world market prices and rendered the world market far from being free.[20]

Against this background, what part could a WFR play in counteracting excessive price fluctuations on the assumption of separate international buffer stocks for each of a range of eligible food commodities, internationally owned and controlled, and with balanced representation of producer and consumer interests? Buffer stocks would operate by absorbing supplies in times of abundance and releasing them in times of scarcity. They attempted to prevent or moderate excessive price fluctuations by buying commodities when prices are relatively low and selling them when prices are relatively high. The general idea of maintaining world commodity buffer stocks that would carry productive resources from periods of relative abundance to periods of scarcity was 'an essentially sound one'. But the situation was rather different concerning the feasibility of combining, in one WFR, the functions of providing emergency relief, fighting chronic malnutrition, and stabilizing prices with their conflicting calls for the disbursement of resources from a common pool of resources, which needed continuous replenishment.

In analyzing the effects of buffer stock operations, the report found that the larger a buffer stock's resources, the more would be its controlling influence on prices, provided that prices were allowed to respond freely to supply/demand changes in a given market, and provided that there were no other stockholders or market operators who were even more powerful financially than the international buffer stock. They could dominate the market by countering the buffer stock's moves, as could be done, for example, by some strong national stockholding agency. A buffer stock would be a 'highly unsuitable instrument for influencing longer-term trends in supply, demand or prices'. It might be 'a very suitable instrument', however, for provoking or preventing short-term price changes through additions to, or withdrawals from, the supplies available in the market. It may also be 'particularly suitable' for counteracting the destabilizing influence of short-term speculative stock movements.

Through its steadying effect on prices, a buffer stock could also help to lessen the short-term disturbing influence on annual crop production plans which might be caused, despite low price-elasticities, by large and sudden variations in prices. A buffer stock could, in addition, help in smoothing out the effects on the market of large variations in crop yields or other short-term supply changes due to factors beyond producers' control. However, it would not necessarily have a stabilizing effect on producers' income because without any counteracting buffer or control operation an extra large supply on the market would tend to depress prices and thus stimulate sales. A short crop would have the opposite effect.

The report noted that buffer stocks had a number of important advantages over other techniques of international commodity stabilization. The two main types of multilateral commodity stabilization arrangements other than buffer stocks were international quota agreements and multilateral long-term contracts. Quotas tended to freeze the geographical pattern of production and could lead to unnecessary unemployment of resources. It was better to stockpile a commodity in times of reduced demand than to limit production. Only where surpluses could not be dealt with by stockholding, and where the price mechanism would restore a balance between supply and demand only 'painfully and slowly' should restriction of output be considered (UN, 1951). Moreover, a quota scheme could not be expected to function effectively unless all major exporters were prepared to participate in its operation. An international buffer stock, on the other hand, could work effectively even with a more limited membership, provided it could commend sufficient resources for influencing the market in the desired direction. The same argument applied to a multilateral long-term contractual arrangement but they carried the risk of generating the so-called 'cobweb effect' of a succession of larger-than-necessary short-term changes in output and consumption, which might be overcome by combining them with buffer stocks.

The 'outstanding advantages' of a buffer stock were in its basic function of carrying forward from times of abundance to times of scarcity the services of available productive resources. This argument acquired additional strength insofar as the fluctuations which prompted a buffer stock's operations that were part and parcel of fluctuations of trade generally. The risk of 'magnified failure' was one of the main drawbacks of the more ambitious commodity stabilization plans in multicommodity arrangements through one master agreement for a large group of primary food and non-food products. Mention was made of the long-standing proposal for a 'Composite Commodity Reserve', which aimed at stabilizing the average price level of a basket of primary commodities by means of international buffer stock operations.[21] The report concluded that some of these proposals 'may deserve further study'.

Despite these significant potential advantages, no buffer stock arrangements were in operation. This was because they carried with them some practical limitations. A buffer stock commodity had to be storable, fairly homogeneous, and capable of a high degree of standardization. It should be traded in an international market of sufficient importance, and sufficient inherent instability, to justify the operation of an international buffer pool. Market prices should be free to respond to additions to, and withdrawals from, the supply available in the market. No one government should have a commanding share of market supplies or dominate purchases. And demand for the commodity concerned should not be influenced predominantly by a substitute commodity or commodities outside the buffer pool. The requirement of 'storability' implied a reasonably high value in relation to bulk, thus ruling out commodities with high storage costs per unit, and fair keeping qualities, to avoid excessive costs of frequent rotation or of insurance against deterioration.

Given the technology available by the beginning of the 1950s, a list of about a dozen food commodities, accounting for about 10–12 per cent of world trade, 'represented the maximum range of foodstuffs that might be considered eligible for buffer stock operations'. This list could be reduced further by other difficulties. FAO studies had shown the technical difficulties for establishing international buffer stock arrangements in rice and sugar, for example, and the rather tight world supply situation made it difficult to build up an initial stock reserve in cocoa. Substitution created difficulties for coarse grains and some oils. And for several commodities, notably wheat, major producers had their own national

48   1945–70. Early Attempts: FAO's Pioneering Work

stockholding policies, which they might be reluctant to internationalize by transferring their stocks to a world buffer pool. In addition, there were significant financial and management problems to overcome, problems of individual commodity bargaining, and lack of guarantees for securing stability in terms of real purchasing power and not merely in monetary terms.

The difficulties, although complex and considerable, were not insurmountable. But because of the lack of political support shown so far for the far-reaching institutional changes that would be involved in adopting even the more modest versions of arrangements for reducing excessive price fluctuation, 'their adoption cannot at this stage be regarded as being within the realms of practical politics'. Six points were made for improving the technical, economic and political conditions for concluding international buffer stock arrangements:

- lessening the technical obstacles through national and international action to improve standardization of grades, contracts and other market practices;
- reducing the range of trading risks against which insurance was sought by means of international bargaining by co-ordinated development of national stabilization measures, adoption of liberal national stockholding policies and acceptance of a code of international behaviour;
- further close study of the effectiveness of alternative types of stabilization techniques *in terms of the different types of risks* (original emphasis) against which insurance was sought on the international plane;
- better insight into the possible conflict between some existing national policies and international stock arrangements;
- setting realistic expectations for international commodity agreements such as the operation of international buffer stocks and not expect them to solve too many problems; and
- better understanding of the complicated technical, economic, and political issues involved.

Food surpluses and their possible uses

The fourth main objective of a WFR referred to in the UN General Assembly resolution was to 'promote the rational disposal of intermittent agricultural surpluses'. The FAO secretariat had been forced to address the issue of the disposal of agricultural surpluses with the growth of large food stocks, particularly in the United States, and pressures to release them (FAO, 1964). Wheat stocks in the four major exporting countries (United States, Canada, Argentina and Australia) had reached over 34 million metric tons by 1955 and were to grow to over 58 million tons in 1961. Stocks of coarse grains (barley, oats, maize, sorghum and rye) in the United States and Canada alone were 32 million metric tons in 1955 and increased to almost 82 million metric tons in 1961. In addition, there were accumulating stocks of rice, dairy products, vegetable oils and oil seeds, cotton and coffee.

This called for the need to establish some kind of 'code of conduct' to avoid the potential disruptive effects of surplus disposal on agricultural production and trade. The explosion in the scale and pace of technological advance in US agriculture, and government support programmes enacted to help farming communities through the years of economic depression of the 1930s, led to ever-increasing surpluses as supply outstripped domestic and international commercial demand (Benedict and Bauer, 1960, pp. 60–1). Hoping that the problem would go away, the US Congress and the White House adopted *ad hoc* measures, which, in reality, supported high levels of production long after changes in post-war demand for US farm products had indicated the need for a major adjustment in national agricultural policies. It was at this point that a mixture of political, economic, social and humanitarian objectives was fused in fashioning the US food aid programme largely in the form that we know it today (Austin and Wallerstein, 1978; Ruttan, 1996).

In the late 1940s, the United States faced new economic and political challenges as European countries began to emerge from the devastation of war and rebuild their economies. Despite persistent imbalance between agricultural production and demand, leading to huge surpluses, US farmers had benefited from a large and growing overseas market and a considerable food aid programme. Now, new challenges were emerging. European agricultural production began to rebound and demand for US farm commodities declined as competition increased and the need for a large US food aid programme in Europe receded. However, the US farm price support system instituted in the 1930s remained largely in place, and the impact of new technologies helped create enormous food stocks in government-held inventories, draining financial reserves, and leading to heated political debate about how to resolve the problem.

At the same time, the United States emerged as the world's pre-eminent, free-market, economic power, facing the Soviet Union in what became known as the Cold War. This brought new global political leadership and responsibility. The United States began to assume a more vigorous role in world affairs, including the all-consuming interest in halting and containing the spread of Communism, particularly in poor, developing countries. One way to secure the allegiance of such countries was to provide economic assistance, including, and especially, food aid. The rationale of prominent political leaders was that countries receiving US aid were more likely to be US allies. And if they received US food aid, they would eventually become commercial markets for US agricultural commodities as their economies developed. Food for war and food for peace became the order of the day (Wallerstein, 1980). At the same time, a large-scale food aid programme would relieve the economic pressures of mounting food stocks held by the government at the taxpayers' expense, and avoid the necessity for awkward domestic agricultural reform measures and their political consequences.

Out of this mixture of conflicting economic, social, humanitarian, political and foreign policy motives came the historic Agricultural Trade Development and Assistance Act of 1954, which became widely know by its number, Public Law (PL) 480 (US, 1964a; Baker, 1979, pp. 107; Epstein, 1987). This marked the beginning of a systematic attempt to utilize US agricultural surpluses along lines tentatively laid down in section 550 of the Mutual Security Act of 1951. The act institutional-ized and provided the legal framework for the US food aid programme basically in

50 *1945–70. Early Attempts: FAO's Pioneering Work*

a form that has largely endured almost to the present day. PL 480 finally marked recognition that the paradox of US surplus food production alongside hunger and malnutrition in the world could no longer be considered to be isolated and temporary occurrences. It established a relationship between US domestic agricultural and foreign policy interests and external assistance that shaped the country's food aid policies and programmes. And, critically, it sparked a rapid growth in US food aid in addition to its export enhancement programmes.

At the beginning, PL 480 contained three, what were called, 'titles'. A fourth title was added in 1959. Title I (the largest of the four outlets) provided programme food aid on concessional credit terms, which was sold in recipient countries for local (inconvertible) currency. With the agreement of recipient governments, the proceeds could be used for a number of purposes: the development of new markets for US agricultural commodities on a mutually benefiting basis; purchase of strategic and critical materials; procurement of military equipment; financing the purchase of goods and services from other friendly countries; promotion of balanced economic development and trade among nations; payment of US obligations abroad; loans to promote multilateral trade and economic development; and financing international educational exchange. In negotiating agreements under this title, 'reasonable precautions' were to be taken to safeguard the usual markets of the United States and to ensure that world agricultural commodity prices would not be 'unduly disrupted'. Private trade channels were to be used to the maximum extent practicable. Special consideration was to be given to developing and expanding sustained market demand for US agricultural products. Resale or trans-shipment of commodities to other countries or use for other than domestic purposes was prohibited. And maximum opportunity to purchase US surplus agricultural commodities was to be afforded. Title II authorized grants of food commodities to provide emergency assistance to meet famine and other urgent relief requirements through voluntary relief agencies and intergovernmental organizations. Title III provided for barter agreements and for donations through private voluntary agencies. And Title IV authorized the sale of surplus commodities under long-term dollar credits to foreign governments, which was amended in 1962 to extend credits to private commercial trade. Between 1954 and 1963, total food aid assistance under PL 480 increased to reach $10.7 million, 28 per cent of all US agricultural exports.

The main purpose of the US Government in initiating the PL 480 programme was said to be to move into foreign outlets part of its growing stockpile of agricultural products that had accumulated under its price support policy. Initially, a considerable part of total PL 480 shipments went to the more economically developed countries, such as Italy and Japan, but as time went on the main emphasis was placed on local currency sales and grants to meet food needs as assist economic development in the less developed countries, such as Brazil, India and Pakistan. At the same time, more emphasis was placed on the use of surpluses for the alleviation of hunger in the less well-nourished nations of the world. PL 480 operations were conducted through bilateral agreements between the US and the recipient countries. At the beginning, these agreements were of one year duration. In 1956, a three-year agreement was concluded with Brazil. Subsequently, four-year agreements were signed with India in 1960 and Pakistan in 1961. These long-term agreements involved the introduction of an element of planning on the part of both the US and the recipient country but contained a clause limiting supplies to commodities in surplus in the US at the time of shipment.

These developments intensified interest in the FAO secretariat to establish some form of 'guiding principles' to safeguard agricultural production in the developing countries and international trade from the potential adverse effects of large-scale food aid programmes, while seeking to obtain the potential benefits that could be obtained in food-aid recipient countries, and an institutional arrangement to monitor their impact. Two path breaking studies were undertaken to address both these issues (Blau, 1954; FAO, 1955a). The first study, on the *Disposal of Agricultural Surpluses*, attempted to list the 'rather baffling' variety of methods that had been devised on different occasions for dealing with surplus stocks, under three main headings:

- holding or segregation of stocks;
- possible methods for expanding consumption; and
- restricting new supply.

Concerning stock holding or segregation, the FAO study concluded that liberal and wisely managed governmental stockholdings were important, even essential, elements of a balanced economy. The segregation of surplus stocks into new reserves for special purposes could help in relieving the immediate pressure of supplies but would not provide an enduring solution. It could be of help, however, as a transitional measure facilitating adjustment.

The study listed an impressive array of possible methods of expanding consumption the national and international uses of agricultural surpluses grouped under two categories. The first involved measures to expand markets without concessions on prices and sales. The second gave examples of sales on concessional prices or special terms to some identified market sectors, with special safeguards in the interests of competing sellers. Under the first category, examples were given of education or publicity campaigns, the development of new uses, the discouragement or restriction of the use of competing products, the reduction of distribution margins, and measures to raise the general purchasing power through full employment policies, development programmes, credits and income redistribution, and raising importers' external purchasing power through the provision of loans and the liberalization of exporter's import policies. Under the second category, sales of special terms to specific market sectors, examples were given of special feeding programmes for children and other vulnerable and low-income groups, emergency relief programmes, export subsidies, sales against importers' currencies and barter deals. Restricting new supply could be achieved by restricting output or the crop area planted, destruction in growth or unharvested crops, through disincentives by taxation or lower support prices or market quotas, and by creating output variation by other means.

Another positive potential was that agricultural surpluses could be provided to finance economic development in developing countries. A pilot investigation was conducted in India by an FAO team from its economic, agricultural and nutrition divisions under the leadership of Mordecai Ezekiel (FAO, 1955a) The study used an early version of what later became known as the 'two-gap model', a foreign exchange gap and a food gap, to simulate the effects of food aid.[22] The results of the study exceeded expectation (FAO, 1985a, p. ix). They showed in detail how the enormous capital represented by food surpluses could be used to finance a general expansion of investment programmes. Specific projects were set out as illustrations of where food aid could be distributed in kind, such as education programmes, milk marketing schemes, and food-for-work projects involving additional labour, as in road building, irrigation works, and reforestation and soil erosion control. Examples were also given of how developing countries might use their own domestic food surpluses for self-help, community development programmes.

The study concluded that if food was used to put under-employed labour to work in building infrastructure, it could contribute as much as one-fourth of the investment costs. To give an indication of the possible magnitudes involved, it was estimated that assistance to the individual projects identified added up to an average annual additional investment of $135 million, absorbing $73 million of surplus products on an average over four years. It could also ease the foreign exchange gap resulting from the lag in responsiveness of domestic agricultural supply to rising demand in the initial stages of development. Recognizing the limitations of these approaches, the study also explored the preconditions for avoiding damaging side effects on domestic agricultural production and on trade.

The originality of the study was twofold. There was a systematic distinction between the use of food surpluses for individual development projects and for general development programmes. And the emphasis was on the use of surpluses as an addition to the capital resources of a low-income country for financing its economic development, and not from the negative viewpoint of disposing of burdensome surpluses of high-income countries. Critically, the study also provided a rationale for the 'marriage of convenience' between surplus disposal and development assistance at the very time that the US food aid programme was being institutionalized through the enactment of Public Law 480 (Rattan, 1996, p. 185).

Ezekiel conveyed the results of the Indian pilot study to the academic community at an International Wheat Surplus Utilization Conference at South Dakota State College in Brookings, South Dakata in 1958 (Attiga et al., 1958).[23] The holding of the conference was itself an indication of the serious situation that had been reached regarding wheat stocks in the United States. Since the Second World War, American agriculture had been characterized by what was called a 'structural imbalance' between its productive performance and the ability to sell its total output at prices high enough to bring it fair returns on its human and physical investments. This situation made it necessary for the government to initiate various price-support measures designed to maintain adequate returns to farmers regardless of the actual supply and demand situation in the free market.

At the time of the conference in 1958, US agricultural surpluses represented a total inventory of over $7 billion. To give some idea of the magnitude of these surpluses, it was noted that total investment of India's second five-year plan was less than $11 billion. Judging from all available data and experienced observations, the structural imbalance in US agriculture was likely to continue for 'the next 5–10 years'. While US agriculture was characterized by an excessive productive capacity, much of the developing world was suffering from insufficient agricultural production to meet its needs, even at the existing level of economic activity. At the same time, there was a substantial amount of unemployment on both rural and urban areas. This 'surplus' labour represented total waste of a valuable and highly perishable productive resource as well as a social problem creating 'persistent and, at times, dangerous pressures'. The central question with which the conference was concerned was whether it was feasible to use the substantial food surpluses produced in North America in a way that would utilize the surplus labour in the developing countries in the development of social overhead facilities and improvements and thereby contribute to economic growth.

Ezekiel gave the global (not only United States) dimension of the problem by quoting from the report of the FAO Group on Grains (FAO, 1958a). Grain production, trade and consumption trends, and appraisal of factors underlying them, indicated that surpluses, or the persistence of production in excess of effective demand, 'may now be considered as a chronic feature of the present world grain economy'. The heart of the problem was seen to lie in the level of price or income guarantees to grain producers in many exporting as well as importing countries. These guarantees, combined with other aspects of national agricultural policies, if maintained substantially unchanged, would continue, together with technological advance, to stimulate output year by year larger than could be absorbed by normal effective demand. Independent measures of surplus disposal might therefore assume 'a semi-permanent character', thereby affecting an increasing part of international grain trade, thereby adding to the marketing difficulties experienced by exporting countries.

The Indian pilot study had shown that the idea of using surpluses to aid economic development is 'very simple'. Developing countries needed capital to finance their economic development. Stored food was capital that could help in speeding up the rate of economic development. However, there were two fundamental conditions. First, under-employment or unemployment among people to be put to work. Second, the need to have projects that are planned and ready to go that would put buying power in the hands of the workers. Surpluses could help provide more money to spend without causing inflation. But there were limitations to the use of surpluses. One was that when people get more money they do not spend it all on food. Another was that development projects do not start producing right away. A third was that additional capital was needed for other demands that can not all be met with surpluses.

The Indian pilot study also led to some general conclusions about the use of surpluses for financing economic development. First, the market basket of surplus products should be as broad as possible and should include more than just grains. Second, if a country has unused industrial capacity that can be put to work through increased employment, it can offset some of its own expenditures by its own increased production. Third, a long period of commitments was needed for supplies of surplus products. And, to cover increased development expenditures without inflation, it was necessary to provide some cash as well as surplus commodities. Additional foreign financing was needed in addition to surpluses.

These possible uses of agricultural surpluses gave rise to the idea of the creation of a World Food Capital Fund (WFCF), an international fund composed of surplus food stocks either as a stand alone fund or as an additional part of the proposed SUNFED. The main purpose of a WFCF would be to provide assistance for the economic development of developing countries. Such a fund should not be regarded as a substitute for, but as an addition to, other forms of financing. It should be composed of as wide a market basket of foods habitually consumed in potential recipient countries. Stocks owned by the fund would remain in the country of origin and marked for use by the fund. Continuity of the fund's resources should be assured. And if assistance from the fund was made available in the form of long-term loans rather than outright grants, supplies should be delivered to recipient countries at prices not higher than the corresponding domestic prices in those countries. The fund's resources could be used not only for financing the expansion or acceleration of investment programmes in developing countries but also for building up national reserves to serve various purposes. They might also provide emergency relief for which replenishment provisions would have to be made. It would not be possible to combine the non-self-liquidating functions of the fund, operating within the framework of international economic assistance, with the use of the same capital resources for the very different functions of self-financing world buffer stocks for stabilization purposes. The joint administration of such diverse arrangements by one single international agency, 'while not perhaps entirely beyond the realms of administrative possibilities', would be 'a very difficult thing to do', and might lead to frustration in over-complicated and competing objectives. For these reasons, it was considered advisable to keep them separate.

FAO principles of surplus disposal

Recognition of the potential positive uses of agricultural surpluses and their potential negative effects on agricultural production and trade, together with the continued accumulation of surplus stocks in major producing countries led to the formulation of the FAO *Principles of Surplus Disposal* (Blau, 1954; FAO, 1954b). A FAO study distinguished between the common usage of 'surplus' as 'that which remains when use or need is satisfied' (Webster) and its economic meaning, which distinguished between 'the intrinsic usefulness of goods (i.e., their capacity for satisfying needs) as against effective demand (i.e., the potential consumer's ability and willingness to buy these goods at given prices and on given conditions of sale'. Supplies of commodities could, therefore, be in 'excess' or 'surplus' even though the needs of potential consumers may be far from satisfied (Blau, 1954). A Working

Party on Surplus Disposal was established by the CCP in pursuance of recommendations made by the seventh session of the FAO Conference to consider the most suitable means of disposing of agricultural surpluses, including the setting up of consultative machinery and the principles which should be observed by FAO member nations.[24] This led to the formulation of recommendations by FAO of *Principles of Surplus Disposal*, which were forwarded to FAO member governments in June 1954 and endorsed by the FAO Council at its twentieth session in September/October 1954.

The *Principles* are not legally binding but provided guidelines, a code of conduct, or what were called 'consultative obligations', for FAO member nations, and represent a commitment by 46 signatory countries. They embodied three general principles. First, solution to problems of agricultural surplus disposal should be sought, wherever possible, through efforts to increase consumption rather than through measures to restrict supplies. Second, disposal of excess stocks should be done in an orderly manner to avoid sharp falls in world market prices, particularly when prices were generally low. And third, where surpluses were disposed of under special terms, there should be an undertaking by both importing and exporting countries that such arrangements would be made without harmful interference with the normal patterns of production and international trade, by assurance against re-sales or trans-shipments of commodities supplied on concessional terms, and by the introduction of the concept of 'additional consumption', defined as 'consumption that would not have taken place in the absence of the transaction on special or concessional terms'. The normal mechanism of assuring such 'additionality' is the usual marketing requirement (UMR) provision of the food aid agreement, negotiated between the supplying and recipient country, which is included in the contractual arrangements. Following its use in the US assistance programmes, the UMR technique was adopted by FAO in 1970. It is 'a commitment by the recipient country to maintain the normal level of commercial imports of the commodity concerned, in addition to the imports provided under the concessional transactions'.

To monitor the implementation of the *Principles* and provide a forum for consultation, a special Consultative Subcommittee on Surplus Disposal (CSD), a subcommittee of FAO's Committee on Commodity Problems, was set up in Washington, DC in 1954 consisting of representatives of 45 member nations (27 developing and 18 developed), the European Union and 21 observer countries. The membership includes the major exporting countries of basic food commodities as well as others with significant export trade. The CSD meets monthly and is able to monitor the trade effects of the flow of food aid (as defined under the *Principles*) from supplying to recipient countries on a continuing basis. Member nations are generally represented by their agricultural or commercial counsellors or attaches. About 10 food aid supplying countries and the EU notify, consult and report on their food aid transactions.

When the *Principles* were first adopted in 1954, distinction was made between 'sales on concessional terms' and 'commercial sales'. It was 'assumed' that distinction between these two types of transactions would be 'self-evident'.

However, with experience gained from applying them, it became apparent that views on the meaning of 'normal commercial practices' differed among governments. Furthermore, as the objectives of economic assistance gradually took precedence over those of surplus disposal, related issues arose as to whether certain kinds of transactions should be regarded as 'concessional' or 'commercial' sales. Subsequently, various attempts have been made to find a generally acceptable distinction.[25] None has provided a definitive answer and the issue remains unresolved. Faced with this dilemma, a list of transactions was drawn up that were regarded as constituting 'food aid' that fall within the area of responsibility of the CSD. These transactions include: gifts or donations of food commodities by governments, intergovernmental organizations (principally WFP), and private, voluntary or non-governmental organizations (NGOs); monetary grants tied to food purchases; and sales and loans of food commodities on credit terms with a repayment period of three years or more (FAO, 1992, pp. 7–9 and Annex F). The list is not exclusive and other transactions may be included. Lack of clarity and agreement has led to an expanding 'grey area' between food aid, thus defined, and outright commercial transactions with no concessional element. A large part of agricultural exports of the major food exporting developed countries now take the form of credit and guarantee, and export enhancement, programmes (Shaw and Singer, 1995).

The vexed question of the disposal of agricultural surpluses was discussed at the eighth session of the FAO Conference in November 1955 (FAO, 1955b). The Conference reaffirmed the view, expressed two years previously, that measures to dispose of surpluses already in existence could not solve the surplus problem unless parallel measures were taken to avoid new surpluses. Consultations and action therefore had to be concerned with both the disposal of existing surpluses and the prevention of new surpluses. The latter implied the selective expansion of production and increased consumption, more efficient distribution, and higher nutritional levels, the co-ordinated development of agriculture, and the lessening of obstacles to trade.

Concerning the disposal of existing surpluses, the Conference took note of action taken on the three main aspects of the problem: the formulation of principles to be observed in the disposal of agricultural surpluses; the development of suitable methods of disposal; and the strengthening of intergovernmental machinery for consultation on these matters. It commended the guidelines and principles of surpluses disposal for all FAO member states that had been drawn up by the CCP and endorsed by the FAO Council. Regarding methods of surplus disposal, the Conference identified the use of surpluses for raising nutritional levels of vulnerable and under-privileged groups and for meeting famine conditions as 'one of the most desirable ways' of disposing of surplus products. It also commended the use of surpluses for aiding economic development in developing countries. It noted that the pilot study in India referred to above had shown that this could be done without harm to domestic or foreign producers when then unemployed or under-employed workers could be put to work on additional development projects and when the surpluses were fed into domestic markets at approximately the same rate as consumption of the products was increased by the additional buying power thus created. The Conference also endorsed the used of surpluses for establishing food reserve stocks. It also laid stress on the importance of ascertaining trends in production, consumption and trade of agricultural commodities on a commodity-by-commodity basis, and the international effects of national policies in food and agricultural matters.

The FAO report on the *Functions of a World Food Reserve* was presented to ECOSOC in the summer of 1956 and 'met with much response'. While recognizing the advantages in principle of multilateral action, ECOSOC reached the conclusion that 'it is not practicable to achieve under a single organization all the objectives set forth in General Assembly Resolution 827 (IX)', the resolution that had initiated the FAO report.[26] ECOSOC called for a further special study to be undertaken on 'the feasibility and, if feasible, the manner of using food reserves for meeting unforeseen food shortages'.

The UN General Assembly devoted 'a good deal of attention' to the issue of food reserves and to the FAO report that had been transmitted to ECOSOC at its eleventh session in January/February 1957. The FAO director-general participated in the General Assembly's debate which culminated in a request for the UN secretary-general, in co-operation with FAO, to carry out a study of national food reserves to present to ECOSOC.[27] The study should analyze

the possibilities and desirability of promoting by way of consultations between importing and exporting member countries, the use of surplus food stuffs in building up national reserve to be used in accordance with internationally agreed principles:

(a) to meet emergency situations;
(b) to prevent excessive price increases arising as a result of a failure in local food supplies;
(c) to prevent excessive price increases resulting from increased demand due to economic development programs, thus facilitating the economic development of less developed countries. (UN General Assembly resolution 1025 (XI))

Another UN General Assembly resolution (1026 (XI)) asked the UN secretary-general 'in consultation with FAO and other agencies, to explore the desirability of setting up a working party to examine the practical possibilities of implementing the various proposals made in the FAO report'. After consultations between the UN secretary-general and the FAO director-general, it was agreed not to establish a formal working group. Instead, FAO was asked to assume responsibility for arranging informal consultations with interested organizations and prepare the material for the report to ECOSOC. An informal meeting was convened by FAO in Geneva in the summer of 1957 attended by representatives of the secretariats of the UN, IBRD and the IMF. The point was made that the further FAO studies might usefully be centred on the subject of national food reserves which 'represented the most promising field for further inquiry and practical follow-up action'.

6
National Food Reserves in Developing Countries

Thus, the focus moved from the perspective of the potential scope and limitations of a world food reserve to the roles that national food reserves might play in developing countries. A working party had already been set up by the CSD to study the possible use of surplus agricultural commodities in building up national reserves and submitted its report in June 1957.[28] The FAO report on national food reserves began with a definition of such reserves for the purpose of the report as 'stocks held or controlled by governments on a continuous basis and subject to replenishment within reasonable periods' (FAO, 1958b). Three main roles were identifies for such stocks: as a contingency against local food shortages, transport problems and other difficulties in internal distribution; as a reserve against emergencies and other major unforeseen shortages; and as a means to thwart hoarding and prevent excessive price increases. It excluded stocks in private hands, or those held by governments for export or for strategic purposes. National food reserves were thus only part of the stocks held by a national community. Every community should hold some stocks but not every government decided to hold food reserves.

But why were stocks needed? After all, stocks meant capital locked up in uses that were not directly productive. They also needed to be looked after and involved continuing costs and administrative problems. These were serious consideration, particularly in developing countries where capital was scarce, returns from productive investment attractive, and administrative problems difficult to solve. Despite these drawbacks, the FAO report advocated that 'every country must hold stocks of its staple foodstuffs', from one harvest to the next in countries that produced enough of its own food requirements, and, in the case of importing countries, for the time until adequate replenishments can arrive and be distributed. It was good economic policy generally to spread supplies over time as evenly as possible because sharp peaks and troughs meant extra expense and waste of resources. The real cost of stock accumulations to a community could not, therefore, be judged merely on an accounting basis. If, for example, stocks could be built up during periods of glut when purchases would help to prevent prices from falling, and released during times of relative scarcity when prices were high, this would be a positive benefit to the community. Therefore, it would generally be necessary for importing or precariously self-sufficient countries to carry over some stocks, 'at least from one crop year to another'.

The amount of stocks needed varied with the circumstances and location of each country. Developing countries required a sizable cushion of stocks of staple foodstuffs for a number of reasons. Many of them were more liable than most developed countries to severe crop shortages owing to natural disasters, such as drought, floods, violent storms and earthquakes. Many relied very largely on their own crops rather than imports for their food. Local crop failure could cause severe shortage until emergency imports arrived. In many developing countries, a considerable proportion of agricultural output was retained by cultivators for their own consumption or use. Shortages were therefore likely to be accentuated in urban and other deficit areas. Markets were imperfect owing to poor transport and communications, and local shortages aggravated by hoarding and speculation. The effects of a crop shortage were much more serious in developing countries because consumption levels were so low. A reduction of 20–30 per cent might result in severe undernourishment, even starvation, in countries consuming little more than was needed for subsistence. And as population and incomes grew, demand for food could outpace the growth in domestic food production. The report acknowledged that no reserve, whatever its size, could meet a continuing drain on resources. At the same time, however, in periods of strain, it was a great advantage to have adequate stocks that enabled the increased demand to be met without a sharp rise in prices, which might slow down the pace of development.

But who held the food stocks in developing countries? Subsistence farming predominated in many developing countries. Farming families lived largely on what they produced, storing what was left after paying their dues and debts for their own needs until the next harvest. This was in marked contrast to farming in developed countries where most of the crop was sold to the market. Stocks held by subsistence farmers were of little use for stabilizing commercial supplies. Instead, subsistence farming tended to accentuate fluctuations in the volume reaching the market. Moreover, the reactions of subsistence farmers to price changes were difficult to predict. In times of poor crops, farmers, anticipating higher prices and wishing to make sure of sufficient food for their own needs, might offer less for sale than usual, thus accentuating the shortage. Instability was also heightened when the main crop was one for which there were cheaper substitutes. When prices were low, they might have to sell more of their crop of, say rice, and consume more cassava or millet and other cheaper foods. Other stocks may be held anywhere in the supply line from grower to final consumer, by traders, millers, shopkeepers, importers and exporters, or, especially if shortages are feared, by the final consumer. But it was not likely to be sufficient incentive for stocks to be held on a scale required for cushioning unforeseen major shortages. Storage costs were high and alternative returns to capital attractive, particularly where capital was scarce. Therefore, traders tended to aim at reducing their end-of-season stockholdings to a minimum required for tiding over until the new crop came in, unless there was good reason to anticipate rising prices. If a poor crop was expected, private traders might carry stocks into the next crop year. Otherwise, they had no incentive to carry stocks over.

A more or less self-sufficient country could have recourse to imports to supplement a poor crop thereby keep prices down and reducing private traders' profits. The conclusion was that in the absence of expectations of considerable price rises, traders were not likely to carry stocks adequate to meet a shortage due to a poor crop. Similarly, it was unlikely that commercial interests in normally importing countries would hold much more than enough stocks to fill the distribution pipelines until the next shipment arrived. The extent to which carrying costs could be passed on to the importing country in the form of higher prices depended on conditions of world supply and demand in international trade. In a buyer's market, they tended to be borne mainly by the exporting country. In food-exporting developing countries, carrying costs may be a heavy burden, usually borne by the growers. Future markets in commodities could serve a useful purpose in enabling manufacturers and others to avoid risks due to price changes but futures markets played little part in developing countries. Farmers, traders and others provided for the only hedging in those economies by hoarding or buying food grains when they thought their prices were likely to rise. Even when traders judged correctly that prices were likely to rise, their purchases could do harm by bringing about excessive increases in areas of temporary shortage to which supplies could not be easily transported. This illustrated the advantage of government-held stocks adequate to counteract such destabilizing speculation.

The paradox was that although the need for stockholding was greatest in a number of developing countries, they were the least able to afford to provide them. Such savings that could be made from their low incomes was required for directly productive investment to raise output and living standards. Therefore, before deciding to strengthen their stockholding through the establishment of national food reserves, they should carefully review their overall food policies and the various possible alternatives they might follow. Low productivity and instability should be attacked simultaneously on a number of fronts. The most appropriate and urgent measures would vary with the special circumstances of each country. These measures required capital in one form or another.

But developing countries had relatively little capital, which was also needed for other non-agricultural projects in the development programme. The pace of development was therefore inevitably slow, unless a country had some valuable resource, such as oil, to exploit, and the amount of external economic aid available to them was limited. A fundamental remedy for food shortages was to raise the level of output per worker, which was far below that of the more technically advanced developed countries. But this task was even more difficult in some developing countries where a substantial part of the limited resources for new investment was needed to expand consumption of a rapidly increasing population. In addition to the time lag between the expansion in total demand and supply, fluctuations occurred in the size of the crops and the level of demand. These fluctuations could not be forecast with sufficient accuracy in time for adequate measures to be taken to offset their effects because crop reporting and statistical services in many developing countries were inadequate. Therefore, the general conclusion was that 'the need for adequate stockholding to meet temporary and local food shortages is likely to recur, in underdeveloped countries, for quite a considerable number of years'.

The role of national food reserves

The FAO report identified three main arguments for national reserves in developing countries: the high degree of vulnerability to instability of food supplies; commercial interests could not be expected to hold large enough stocks or to sell them readily when local shortages developed; and imports took time and could not be relied upon to solve all the problems that called for immediate availability of supplies. (A fourth argument, the need for national food reserves to prevent sudden large calls on a country's foreign exchange reserves for imports, was dismissed as 'rather academic' as developing countries usually did not succeed in setting aside sufficient savings from their own resources for building up an adequate buffer of any kind, whether financial or physical.) The main uses of national food reserves, as set out in UN General Assembly resolution 1025 (XI) calling for the study, were examined.

Emergency relief

Emergency situations, often unforeseen, called for prompt and vigorous action by government in the afflicted country. Effective relief required an early 'first-line' defence with the help of physical stocks in hand. Three types of emergencies could occur: sudden, natural calamities such as earthquakes, floods and hurricanes; slower-maturing emergencies arising from food shortages caused by drought, crop failure, pests and diseases; and man-made emergencies arising from war and civil strife resulting in refugees and displaced persons. In a number of countries there was a perennial and serious danger of emergencies caused by nature. In others, there could be the lethal combination of more than one type of emergency, resulting in a sudden demand for emergency relief. Safeguards in the form of local food reserves were therefore very desirable and perhaps essential. Some districts in a country, especially in a large country with considerably different climatic conditions, were more liable to crop failures than others. A government should take into consideration, on the basis of past experience, which areas were most vulnerable to shortages, and to what extent, in deciding on the magnitude and location of food reserves.

Counteracting fluctuations and hoarding

A national food reserve could be used to lessen price fluctuations within a country. Excessive price fluctuation was harmful to the economy as a whole as well as to agricultural producers and consumers, and could distort the pattern of economic activity and investment. But stability of food prices was not the same thing as stabilization of farmers' incomes. Some rise in prices may be desirable when there is a short crop both to economize in consumption and to give farmers some

62 1945–70. Early Attempts: FAO's Pioneering Work

compensation for their reduced volume of sales. Releases from a national food reserve could keep price fluctuations within desirable limits and prevent excessive price fluctuations caused by hoarding, speculation and panic that would otherwise take place. A national food reserve might also take advantage of a heavy crop by adding to stocks relatively cheaply, preventing prices from falling to excessively low levels.

Even if it were possible, it was doubtful if absolute price stability should be the aim. The price system performed useful functions in providing producers incentive to use land and other resources in ways that the market required. But there could be no question that a number of developing countries suffered from excessive and harmful local price fluctuations. That caused hardship and damaged the country's economy. Such price fluctuations could be kept within reasonable limits by establishing a national food reserve. It could counteract hoarding and maintain supplies to the market whether crops fell or not, thereby preventing panic and sustaining confidence. The same effect could not be obtained from imports, which could not be speeded up at short notice.

A national food reserve operated in conjunction with a policy of price incentives for agriculture could also help a government procurement programme. The quantities offered by farmers for sale under such a programme depended, to some extent, on public confidence in the government's ability to deal with emergencies. With a food reserve large enough to enable government to deal effectively with temporary or local food shortages, the required degree of confidence might be created, and farmers induced to sell more than in the absence of the reserve. Similarly, food reserves should be large enough to discourage hoarding and convince speculators that they could not win in playing against the reserve. At the same time, confidence worked both ways. The stronger the reserve, the greater the confidence. But the stronger the confidence created by other means, the less the need for reserves. National food reserves should therefore be developed alongside such other measures that helped to maintain confidence in stable prices. Otherwise, the size of reserves required for anti-hoarding devices would be more than a government could afford.

Elbowroom for development

In developing countries, economic development can gradually raise real incomes but produces problems in transition. Development project may eventually increase agricultural output but only after a fairly long gestation period. Meanwhile, demand for staple foods may rise sharply through the multiplier effect. Increases in real incomes lead to considerable increases in the consumption of staples. Increased development expenditure also increases non-agricultural employment, which also increases the monetary demand for food. In the absence of increased market food supplies, this could lead to inflationary pressures. The existence of food reserves may cushion the effects of sudden inflationary pressures and allow time for adjustments to the scale of expenditures by meeting temporary needs until other measures are implemented to restore the balance between supply and demand. A national food reserve should be designed to deal with fluctuations of all types, both up and down, including fits and starts in the process of economic development.

Other subsidiary uses

The existence of a national food reserve could also be of help in the operation of crop insurance schemes aimed at compensating farmers for loss of income due to crop failures. A national food reserve and a crop insurance scheme might be under a co-ordinated management so that indemnities could be paid partly in cash and partly in food stocks. If the reserves could be built up on special terms, this could help where governments were deterred from establishing crop insurance schemes by the risk of heavy financial liability in the early years before adequate funds were built from insurance premiums. But the practicability of crop insurance schemes in developing countries was limited by various factors including: inadequate crop reporting methods, complex land tenure systems, lack of trained personnel, and the ignorance and poverty of farmers. Nevertheless, while such use of a national food reserve would be secondary, the possibility of initiating such schemes on a pilot scale should be considered. In addition, a reserve could enable a country to play the part of a 'good neighbour' by assisting a nearby country suffering from a severe temporary food shortage by sales or loans of food. Some assurance of reciprocity of such arrangements in case of need would add to security all round.

Multipurpose reserves

As has been shown, a national food reserve could be used for several different purposes. It would be too expensive to hold a reserve for release only in case of famine. It should also be available to prevent excessive price fluctuations. And multipurpose uses would spread the cost of maintaining a reserve and assist economic development by improving market structure and institutions, including transportation and storage facilities and the organization of wholesale and retail trading.

Commodity composition, storage, rotation and costs

It was difficult for governments in developing countries to maintain, administer and rotate food reserves of varied composition, particularly because of the need for decentralized storage and multipurpose uses.[29] In general, therefore, the bulk of national food reserves were likely to be held in wheat and rice, the composition determined by consumption habits of the area concerned and their relative availabilities and prices. Other considerations were that grains went further in terms of calories per unit cost, and that wheat and rice stored better over longer periods than other grains. However, food commodities other than grains could prove extremely useful in emergencies and in reducing the effects of inflationary tendencies on local prices.

The volume and kinds of food storage capacity available in developing countries were often inadequate and losses due to deterioration in stores very high. The important task in a national food storage programme was to hit on the optimum degree of storage protection and utilization per unit of cost. Labour-intensive storage construction could reduce costs and facilitate maintenance. The size of a national food reserve would be determined, among other things, by facilities available for rotation on terms that would not unduly disturb domestic markets. There was no evidence to suggest that the cost of government stockholding in developing countries was higher than in developed countries. Experience showed that once reasonably good storage capacity had been constructed and arrangements made for adequate maintenance and control, losses due to deterioration could be held down to a small proportion.

A range of factors affected storage costs. The cost of setting up and maintaining a national reserve depended mainly on its size, which depended on the circumstances of each country. The greater the geographical dispersion of stocks, the higher the storage costs. The composition of stocks would also affect storage costs. Costs would also depend on the availability of existing storage capacity and the need to construct new storage facilities. Costs varied widely by types of storage plants and of auxiliary equipment in different countries and by the design and material used.

The annual costs of a reserve programme included the charges for the services of the capital investment and those for current expenses for implementing the programme. The fixed costs were mainly those derived from the investment in storage space and administration. Variable costs related mainly to the investment in commodity stocks and their holding and handling. Storage space for a reserve programme could not be utilized continuously at full capacity as the reserve was drawn on to meet fluctuations. Therefore, costs could not be reckoned as merely proportional to the size of the stock carried. Since some costs were fixed independent of the actual size of stocks, the cost per ton was higher than when full capacity of storage was utilized. However, most storage facilities were 'versatile'. They could be used for other purposes and not necessarily left empty. The cost of replacement of bags was an important item when storage was not in bulk. Current expenditure on upkeep and repairs had to be added. Where reserve stocks were carried in stores rented from privately owned facilities, the rent paid included depreciation, interest charges on capital invested in the stores and a quota for current repairs. Physical losses in storage might be covered in many ways. In private stores losses might be covered by insurance premiums.

Governments carry their own risk since they could be self-insured at less than the cost of commercial insurance. In well-supervised warehouse, storage losses from rodents, insects, and moisture damage could be kept down by fairly simple preventive measures. More frequent rotation of stocks was necessary in developing countries, particularly in the tropics, to reduce losses. Rotation was largely a relatively inexpensive, labour-intensive, operation since wage rates were low. Turnover might be tied in with other government programmes, in which case its costs would not be entirely additional. Finally, the carrying costs included the cost of administration. A national reserve might be operated by an existing administration and the extra outlay might involve only direct supervisory and warehouse staff. Where a separate administrative unit was set up, the costs would be somewhat higher. A direct comparison of total carrying costs in different countries under different conditions was difficult to make because of the lack of data.

7
International Commodity Agreements

The 1930s and the post-war years saw intensive activity in negotiations for international commodity agreements in food and other commodities – wheat, sugar, coffee, cocoa, tea, olive oil, tin, copper, rubber (Goodwin and Mayall, 1979; Gordon-Ashworth, 1984). The US government played an active, often leading, part in these negotiations, which showed the scope and limitations of international commodity agreements as instruments for promoting economic stability and growth as well as world food security, particularly from the viewpoint of the developing countries (Blau, 1963).

In the closing years of the Second World War and the immediate post-war years, hopes were high for the creation of a widespread network of individual commodity agreements as part of a new international economic order. A number of resolutions of the UN, its specialized agencies, and other intergovernmental bodies urged the negotiation of commodity agreements, leading to preparatory work and discussion. Yet, almost twenty years later, by the beginning of the 1960s, only five international agreements had been concluded for wheat, sugar, coffee, tin and olive oil. Only those for wheat and tin qualified as producer–consumer agreements and contained some operative provisions designed to influence world trade in those commodities. The International Sugar Agreement continued formally in force until the end of 1963 but its operative provisions ceased to function from the beginning of 1962 owing the failure of governments to reach agreement on the reformulation of quotas. There had been a succession of one-year producer agreements for coffee by which the governments concerned agreed to limit exports. An agreement on olive oil provided only for a series of co-ordinated national measures without attempting to regulate international trade. The total value of world trade in these five commodities accounted for only about ten per cent of world trade in primary products at the beginning of the 1960s.

Frustration, and a growing sense of disappointment, was evident with the limited results attained, particularly on the part of the primary producing countries. Increasing attention was therefore paid to other mechanisms, which could either serve as a substitute for, or as a complement to, international commodity agreements. At the same time, governments explored the possibilities of new types of agreements of a more comprehensive kind.

Objective of commodity agreements

International commodity agreements were seen to have one of five objectives, or a combination of them, that could, *inter alia*, contribute directly or indirectly to food security:

- They could attempt to raise, or uphold, export earnings by means of arrangements among producers restricting production or exports or both.
- They could attempt to promote economic stability, both in producing and consuming countries, by preventing undue fluctuations of prices and quantities traded but without interfering with long-term trends.
- They could endeavour to mitigate the problems and hardships of such long-term adjustments as may be required in cases of persistent disequilibrium between production and consumption, particularly under conditions of inelastic supply and demand.
- They could try to counteract the shrinkage of markets to primary producers which resulted from protectionist measures or preferential arrangements in importing countries.
- And they could be used as instruments for intergovernmental commodity programming on more comprehensive lines, taking into account trade on both commercial and concessional terms, national policies relating to production, prices, and stocks, and the close links between problems of commodity trade, aid and development programmes.

One of the chief difficulties in the actual negotiation of international commodity agreements was that participating governments were not always fully conscious of which of these five objectives they were mainly aiming at, and the extent to which any one of these objectives, or combination of them, could be successfully attained by one or the other of the standard type of agreement techniques (Blau, 1963). The primary exporting countries were interested not just in price stability but in securing reasonable returns in terms of the manufactured goods that they bought. In 1950, work at the United Nations in New York by Hans Singer and then by Raul Prebisch at the UN Economic Commission for Latin America in Santiago, Chile, had shown that the net barter terms of trade between primary products and manufactures were subject to a long-run downward trend, which implied that without changes in the structure of the world economy, the gains from trade would continue to be distributed unequally and unfavourably between those nations exporting primary products (the developing countries) and those exporting manufactures (the developed countries).[30] The importing countries, on the other hand, were mainly interested in securing more stable conditions of trade and were prepared to consider any measure influencing the levels of exporters' returns only insofar as such measures formed part of a process or orderly adjustment of production to the changing conditions of the world markets.

The draft Havana Charter agreed at the UN conference in Havana, Cuba in 1948, when the International Trade Organization was successfully negotiated, but never ratified, and which was also intended to serve as a code of guiding principles governing international commodity negotiations, stated:

> The conditions under which primary commodities are produced, exchanged and consumed are such that international trade in those commodities may be affected by special difficulties such as a tendency towards persistent disequilibrium between production and consumption, the accumulation of burdensome stocks, and pronounced fluctuations in prices.

It was this problem of market instability that international commodity agreements were designed to cope, a problem of particular concern to developing countries and to others whose economies were largely dependent on the earnings of primary products in international trade (Hudson, 1960). The nature of the problem varied among commodities. In the case of tin, rubber, cocoa and coffee, for example, production tended to be concentrated in a relatively few countries and, at the beginning of the 1960s, more than 70 per cent of production entered world trade. The production of butter, sugar and wheat, on the other hand, occurred in a number of countries with the result that less than 30 per cent of aggregate world production was exported.

Chapter VI of the draft Havana Charter emphasized that no interested government should be excluded from negotiations and that 'participating countries which are mainly interested in imports of the commodity concerned shall, in decisions on substantive matters, have together a number of votes equal to that of those mainly interested in obtaining export markets for the commodity'. This provision made negotiation of individual commodity agreements more difficult. It implied that an agreement was negotiable only as regards matters on which there was an identity of interest of both parties or on points on which a 'bargaining balance' could be reached, that is, where the advantages and disadvantages of an agreement were in balance for each participant.

The two main objectives of international commodity agreements, according to Chapter VI of the Havana Charter, were: to prevent or moderate pronounced fluctuations in prices, without interfering with long-term trends; and to provide a framework for facilitating adjustments between production and consumption in order to securing long-term equilibrium between the forces of supply and demand. Eliminating or moderating price fluctuations were clearly in the interests of both exporting and importing countries but the interests of the former (the bulk of whose foreign exchange income was derived from the sale of one or a few primary commodities) was much greater than the latter (whose economies were not greatly affected by changes in the price of any one primary product).

The postulate of non-interference with long-term trends implied that prices resulting from an agreement should not differ, on average over a number of years, from what they would be in the absence of an agreement. The dilemma was that since the future was unknown, this 'neutral price' could be ascertained only *ex post*, whereas the technical solution of the problem presupposes that it was known *ex ante*. In the absence of such pre-knowledge, a commodity agreement

68   1945–70. Early Attempts: FAO's Pioneering Work

necessarily took on the character of a 'speculative deal', justified as a form of insurance against the risk of undue losses resulting from large and unexpected price variations. The fact that the conclusion of price-stabilizing commodity agreements proved so difficult in practice appeared to indicate that neither the exporters nor importers were prepared to pay a substantial premium for this kind of insurance. Moreover, for a number of commodities, it was difficult, or impossible, to speak of a representative world price. And the main concern of exporters was their total export proceeds (depending on volume as well as price) and the average level of such proceeds over a number of years, measured in terms of import purchasing power, not merely short-term fluctuations in money terms. Added to this was the finding of Singer and Prebisch of the long-term deterioration of the terms of trade against primary products. Therefore, commodity agreements discussed and negotiated in the 1950s were not, in themselves, a sufficient instrument, nor did they take sufficient account of the need for improved co-ordination of national policies in developed countries.

Types of agreements

By the 1960s, three types of agreements had been negotiated. Their subsequent histories illustrated the same fundamental difficulties.

Multilateral contract agreements: The main feature of this type of agreement was that it contained an obligation on importers or exporters to buy and sell certain guaranteed quantities at stipulated maximum or minimum prices whenever the free-market price reached or exceeded those limits. Such agreements had to cover a high proportion of the total trade of the participants and the spread of prices between floor and ceiling should not be too wide for them to be reasonably effective. They would then protect the real national income of both importing and exporting participants from fluctuations in the world price while preserving the free-market price as a mechanism of adjustment for securing a balance between world production and consumption.

International buffer stock: This second type of agreement, on which particularly high hopes had been set in the early post-war years, aimed to stabilize prices by an obligation to buy whenever the world price fell below a certain minimum level and to sell when the price rose above a certain maximum, combined perhaps with a discretionary right to buy or sell between these limits. The well-known problem of a buffer stock scheme was to provide adequate finance to enable the scheme's authority to carry out its functions. This was closely related to the difficulty of successfully forecasting the future relationship between supply and demand. In addition, was the problem of securing international agreement on a range of prices at levels consistent with the prospective movement of the long-term world price securing a balance between supply and demand. Unless the trend of this long-term world price was stable or rising, a buffer stock was unlikely to be successful in ironing out the fluctuations from the trend for more than a limited period of time. With a falling trend, the necessary downward adjustment of the operating range of prices could not be secured promptly, even if the difference between what was a fluctuation and what was a trend could be distinguished. With a rising trend, the same difficulty arose. But since this did not impair the finances of the buffer stock authority, but rather strengthened them, it did not prevent the authority from resuming operations subsequently, once agreement was secured on the revision of the operating range of prices.

Export restriction agreements: This third type of agreement made provision for the limitation of exports insofar as this was necessary in order to secure some degree of stability of prices. The Havana Charter laid down specific conditions for such agreements, which were designed to protect consumer interests and prevent the imposition of too rigid a pattern of production. Their effectiveness depended to a large degree on the comprehensiveness of the agreement, including: the extent to which it brought under control all important sources of export; the availability of substitutes; and the importance of international trade of the commodity in relation to world production and consumption. Moreover, to be effective, such agreements required the regulation of output by individual producers and not only of exports by the countries as a whole. Failure to secure worldwide participation in a quota arrangement on the part of exporting countries was less serious insofar as importing countries were brought in as participants and undertook to discriminate against non-participating exporters. At the same time, however, the very features likely to strengthen the effectiveness of such agreements as an instrument for raising or upholding export earnings in the short run were also those likely to endanger long-term prospects by sheltering high-cost producers and generating centrifugal forces that might eventually lead to the collapse of the whole agreement. Great care had therefore to be taken to set quotas realistically so as to allow for sufficient flexibility and to encourage efficiency and desirable structural adjustments in the primary exporting countries as well as expanding markets in importing countries.

Different categories of commodities and compensatory financing

One of the reasons for the comparative lack of success in many of the intergovernmental discussions of commodity questions was considered to be the generalized way in which they were approached without sufficient regard to the basic differences between different groups of commodities. Different categories of products had different types of problems.

By the 1960s, half of the total value of world commercial exports of primary products (excluding petroleum and the exports of the centrally planned economies) both originated in, and were absorbed by, the developed countries of North America, Western Europe, Oceania and Japan. The bulk of this trade consisted of temperate-zone agricultural products, mainly foodstuffs. The pattern of trade of this group of commodities was largely influenced by the domestic agricultural stabilization and support policies of virtually all the importing countries and of the United States, the largest exporter. The funds required for agricultural support were drawn from the non-agricultural sectors of the countries concerned.

70   *1945–70. Early Attempts: FAO's Pioneering Work*

This was very different from the situation prevailing in developing countries where virtually all incomes were low and where agriculture accounted for the dominant part of the national income. In these countries, there were no resources available for the price support of agricultural exports. And the export-producing sectors of their economies were often called upon to provide economic assistance for programmes to raise productivity in the even poorer agricultural subsistence sector, and for development and diversification generally.

The existence of an extended network of domestic agricultural policies in the developed countries had important consequences, providing as it did an effective barrier against any sudden large-scale contraction in agricultural incomes such as occurred in the great depression of the early 1930s. The existence of independent national policies of price and output regulation created a situation in which the patterns of production for some of the most important commodities, such as wheat, were completely divorced from world supply and demand relationships, resulting in large and growing surplus stocks. These policies led to the introduction of export subsidies or a two-price system on behalf of exporters, and of varying forms of import regulations for importers.

As we have seen, structural surpluses emerged as a consequence of remarkable technological progress, fuelled by national policies. These surpluses resulted in new forms of trade flows, on concessional terms, from the developed to developing countries. It was difficult to bring this concessional trade within the operative provisions of international commodity agreements. However, a beginning was made in evolving a new 'code of international ethics' through the acceptance of a flexible set of principles recommended by FAO in 1954 (FAO, 1954b).These principles encouraged the constructive use of surplus supplies, mainly in low-income, food-deficit, countries, while providing some safeguards for the interests of commercial exporters.

It was also possible to secure the acceptance by a large number of governments of a set of principles concerning national price stabilization and support policies (FAO, 1961a). These principles reflected 'the highest common denominator of international understanding' attainable by the 1960s from governments with differing, and partly conflicting, policies. This set of agreed principles did not imply any contractual obligations, and carried no sanctions. But they nevertheless marked an important step forward particularly as governments had been generally reluctant to accept contractual obligations that interfered with their sovereign rights in shaping domestic policies. Thus, while domestic agricultural policies of the developed countries had lessened their incentive, as compared with the early 1930s, to insure against violent price changes through international agreements, their incentives to secure access to markets increased, which required commodity agreements of a different character.

The nature of the problem was quite different for the other half of world commodity trade that originated from the developing countries. This trade consisted primarily of tropical agricultural products and, to a lesser extent, minerals. About three quarters of that trade was absorbed by the developed countries, mainly of North America and Western Europe, which in the early 1960s took about 85 per cent of the world imports on commercial terms of all primary products. (The only commodity mainly traded among developing countries was rice: only about four per cent of world rice production entered international trade.) In contrast to temperate-zone foodstuffs, tropical export products were subject to the problem of the narrowing of markets due to the protectionist measures of importing countries only in relatively few cases. For this reason, the primary exporting countries had relatively little to gain from the usual kind of multilateral negotiations for the reciprocal reduction of tariffs and quantitative restrictions. Indeed, they might tend to lose since their own exports were not predominantly hampered by trade restrictions while the concessions made in return might handicap them in developing new industries.

Analogous problems arose, however, on account of preferential arrangements. On the other hand, the markets for exports of raw materials from the developing countries (with some exceptions, such as petroleum) were affected by other causes. These included the growing use of synthetic materials, reduction in the amount of raw materials required per unit of finished product, and a shift in the pattern of industrial production which caused a decline in the relative importance of industries heavily dependent on imported materials. In addition, there was growing evidence of a structural over-production for a large number of tropical products through yield increases resulting from technological improvements and increases in the area planted. The spread of 'development consciousness' in the newly independent developing countries also stimulated increased production in order to increase the export earnings needed for economic growth. But FAO projections of the main tropical products up to 1970 indicated a growing excess of world production over consumption, even on the most optimistic assumptions concerning the growth of demand in high-income countries (FAO, 1962a).

The only long-term remedy, therefore, lay in the economic development of the developing countries themselves. This would allow a diversification of their domestic production. They would then become less dependent on a few basic commodities for their export earnings and less dependent on imports to cover their essential needs. But the prospects for their economic development were greatly dependent on their ability to maintain and increase their foreign receipts both through trade and aid. Singer and Prebisch had shown that history had been unkind to the developing countries. The long-run terms of trade were stacked against them and unless there were a more level playing field in international trade and development, developing countries would find it difficult to embark on a programme of industrialization of the import-substituting or export-substituting kind, or a combination of both, and divergence not convergence would have taken place between them and the developed countries, threatening world prosperity and peace (Singer, 1950; Prebisch, 1950).

The pressing need of developing countries was for more resources, particularly of foreign exchange, to sustain their development programmes. Economic aid had increased fairly rapidly in the early 1960s thanks in large part to the inspiration brought by President John F. Kennedy and his proposition, accepted by the UN General Assembly, that the 1960s should be declared the UN Decade of Development (UN, 1961b). This ushered in a newly accepted principle of international solidarity and burden-sharing in development co-operation and a greater willingness to give assistance to developing countries. But economic aid still constituted only a small fraction of the total foreign receipts of developing countries, and failed to compensate for the deterioration in their terms of trade. The first objective was therefore seen to be a reversal of the adverse trend of export earnings aided where necessary by policies of structural adjustment in both exporting and importing countries. Developing countries also urgently required assistance in replenishing their liquid reserves and for moderating the impact of fluctuations in the export earnings.

Another objective could be assisted by more liberal lending policies of the IMF, supported by the adoption of proposals on compensatory financing by a committee of UN experts (UN, 1961c).[31] The UN experts called for the creation of a central fund, known as the 'Development Insurance Fund', into which all member countries would pay contributions and against which members would make financial claims which would be paid automatically in stated circumstances. Such claims would be based on the decline of export proceeds in a particular year as against the average for the three preceding years, and would cover a proportion of the shortfall thus defined in excess of a minimum shortfall of five per cent for which no compensation was payable. The proposal was not implemented. However, in the 1960s, the IMF established two facilities designed to address the payments problems associated with export instability, particularly for countries highly dependent on primary commodities. A Compensatory Financing Facility (CFF), established in 1963, was designed to alleviate the balance of payments effects of export instability by providing assistance to countries experiencing temporary shortfalls in their exports due to factors largely outside their control. A Buffer Stock Financing Facility (BSFF), established in 1969, enabled the IMF to provide financial support to members involved in efforts to stabilize commodity prices through buffer stock operations under formal international commodity agreements in which the interests of both importing and exporting members were represented (Kaibni, 1988).

The adoption of a compensatory finance scheme did not obviate the need for individual commodity agreements. The UN experts emphasized that compensatory finance was complementary to commodity agreements, not an alternative to them. But what should such agreements serve? Commodity agreements could not be successful in stabilizing prices and in securing reasonable terms of trade unless they also succeeded in bringing world production and consumption of the commodity concerned into line. This was not a matter of international agreements alone. It required close co-ordination between international arrangements and national policies.

The main objective of commodity agreements was therefore seen as 'an orderly method through which patterns of production and trade could best be adjusted to the requirements of world demand over a longer period' (Blau, 1963). From this point of view, quota arrangements or multilateral contracts offered some of the elements required, for a limited range of commodities, provided they included provision for the co-ordination of the national policies of all the countries concerned, and for joint programming and adjustment of production patterns in both exporting and importing countries. They should also provide for co-ordinated measures influencing consumption, internal price levels and related commercial and fiscal policies, in addition to measures relating directly to the regulation of exports and imports. Such co-ordination called for a commodity-by-commodity approach of a broader kind. In this connection, international commodity consultations were useful even when they did not result in any formalized commodity agreement. With increasing emphasis on the importance of commodity export earning for the viability of developing countries, such consultations had an important role to play.

What conclusions could be down from this analysis of international commodity agreements? One was that there was no single panacea, no magic wand, to solve the world commodity problem in all its complexity. An attack on a single front could only reach limited objectives. Instead, there were a number of ways in which a genuine effort could produce useful results. What was needed was 'a concerted attack on a number of fronts', including: long-term lending and aid as part of a comprehensive development programme; compensatory finance; international agreements for the regulation of production, co-ordinated planning of the creation of new capacity, and guaranteed access to markets; long-term conditional and non-conditional individual commodity purchasing agreements, linked to discussions on trade, aid and development planning, all of which should be pursued 'simultaneously and with vigour'. Such was the challenge as seen at the beginning of the 1960s.

International Wheat Agreement

Negotiations concerning some form of international agreement for wheat were instructive, and the most directly related to the achievement of world food security. A series of international wheat conferences was held in the 1930s and 1940s (IJAA, 1949). The first international meeting to deal exclusively with the economic problems of wheat was held in London in 1930. This meeting, at which only representatives of exporting countries were present, considered a system of export quotas as a means of relieving the depressed wheat price situation but no agreement was reached. In 1933, when wheat prices had dropped to an all-time low point, the first International Wheat Agreement was signed by representatives of 9 exporting and 13 importing countries. This agreement was of the export quota type. A global quota of 550 million bushels was allocated among the exporters, and various arrangements were established with the aim of assuring supplies of wheat, later expanded to cover all grains, to importing countries and markets for exporting countries at equitable and stable prices (IWC, 1974). The agreement collapsed during its first year of operation when one exporter exceeded its quota. At the fourth wheat conference, which met in Washington, DC from July 1941 to April 1942, agreement was reached to establish an International Wheat Council, later changed to the International Grains Council, to facilitate continuous dialogue, which was temporarily based in Washington, DC before being moved to its permanent location in London, UK, where it remains.

74 *1945–70. Early Attempts: FAO's Pioneering Work*

This series of intense international negotiations revealed clearly the position not only of the United States, the biggest grains producer and exporter, but also of the other major grains producing and importing countries on three controversial issues: production policies, sales at special prices, and stocks. It was evident throughout the protracted negotiations that while consumers were far from forgotten, the primary initiative was with the producers. Even importing countries did not necessarily represent an exclusive consumers' interest. Many of them produced more grain than they imported, and they were generally committed to protecting their producers against low prices. This led to another overriding concern, the recurrence of large grain surplus stocks. As a counter-weight, two views had emerged strongly from the Second World War, which tended to play down the fear of mounting surpluses. The first was the belief that a policy of full employment would automatically obviate the prospect of burdensome surpluses. The second was that large numbers of people in the developing countries lived at below what was regarded as an acceptable nutritional standard. Increasing employment and raising nutrition levels were two objectives that would take care of any concern about being overwhelmed by mounting surpluses. This led to a third view, the need for providing more assistance to developing countries through greater burden-sharing in international co-operation expressed in the declaration of the first United Decade of Development of the 1960s (see above).

A major limitation to the reduction in market instability was the conflict between national policies in many countries and the basic aims of international wheat agreements. The dominant feature at the beginning of the 1960s continued to be the persistence of production in excess of effective demand as reflected in the large and increasing wheat stocks. The FAO Group on Grains concluded in its third report in 1960:

> The heart of the problem lies in the level of price or income guarantees to producers of wheat and other grains in many exporting as well as in importing countries. These guarantees, combined with other aspects of national agricultural policies, if maintained substantially unchanged, together with technological advance, to stimulate, year after year, an output larger than can be absorbed by normal effective demand. (FAO, 1960b)

This problem involved national adjustments in production, which could be achieved only by voluntarily subordinating national interest for the broader international good.

In this context, from the beginning of the 1960s, as their large stockpiles of grain were drawn down, the United States and Canada sought to share the burden of providing food aid to poor food-deficit countries with other major industrialized grain importing and exporting countries, especially in western Europe and Japan, which had, up until then, provided little or no food aid. Those countries were, it was argued, not strong enough economically to shoulder part of the burden. At the same time, the European Economic Community (now the European Union) and its member countries had accumulated large surpluses as a result of the agricultural protectionist measures under their Common Agricultural Policy that was also affecting United States and Canadian agricultural trade. The opportunity to address this issue came with the Kennedy Round of tariff negotiations under the General Agreement of Tariffs and Trade (GATT), which began in April 1963 (Wallerstein, 1980; Parotte, 1983; IWC, 1988). The primary focus of the Kennedy Round, as in previous GATT negotiations, was to reduce tariff barriers on industrial goods. The main participants, prompted by the United States and Canada, decided on this occasion that agricultural commodities, and more particularly wheat and coarse grains, should also be covered. Previously, agriculture had been excluded from such negotiations as a 'special case'. There was increasing concern in the early 1960s, however, about the degree and extent of agricultural protectionism, the widespread resort to non-tariff devices, and the serious effect of these measures on international trade in agricultural products.

Discussion centred on the formulation of an agreement covering world trade in grains, which would replace the existing International Wheat Agreement of 1962. In view of the concerns of the United States and Canada, the coverage of the proposed new agreement was extended to include aid in grain commodities on concessional terms and as grants (food aid). As the new aid commitments on a regular basis would be costly for the non-traditional food aid donors to undertake, concessions in their industrial trade sector were offered as part of the bargaining process. As a result, an International Grains Arrangement was negotiated at a conference convened by the International Wheat Council and UNCTAD in Rome in July/August 1967 with two inseparable parts, an International Wheat Agreement and, for the first time, a Food Aid Convention (IWC, 1988).

Food Aid Conventions

The object of the 1967 Food Aid Convention (FAC) was 'to carry out a food aid programme with the help of contributions for the benefit of developing countries'. Aid could be provided in the form of wheat, coarse grains or grain products (rice was included in subsequent FACs) suitable for human consumption and of a type and quality acceptable to recipients, or cash to purchase grains from signatories of the FAC for shipment as aid. A unique feature of the FAC was that each member agreed to provide a guaranteed minimum quantity of food in physical terms, irrespective of fluctuations in production, stocks and prices. Minimum commitments were based on complex calculations involving donor countries' grain production and consumption and GDP per capita. The United States proposed an annual minimum of ten million tons of cereal food aid in the aggregate. The 12 original members of the FAO finally agreed to provide a minimum of 4.5 million tons.[32]

Each FAC member was responsible for the allocation and shipment of its commitments. There was no stipulation about the destination of shipments other than that they should be made to developing countries, or about whether they should be provided on grant or non-commercial credit terms. (In fact, the food aid provided under the 1967 FAC was provided entirely on a grant basis). Multilateral channelling was, however, encouraged, with special reference made to the advantages of using WFP. This raised expectations of a large increase in WFP resources, which proved to be unfounded. While the Scandinavian countries, Finland, Norway and Sweden, channelled all their relatively small FAC contributions through WFP, the major donors provided either small amounts or none at all. And the EEC preferred to set up its own food aid administration and programme rather than rely on the services of WFP (Cathie, 1997). The result was that only about 5 or 6 per cent of the aggregate shipments of FAC grains were channelled annually through WFP during the three years of the 1967 FAC, which mirrored the proportion of food aid handled globally by WFP.

Further FACs were signed in 1971, 1980, 1986, 1995, 1999 and 2001, with changes in membership, commodity coverage, eligible recipient countries and principles. Minimum annual commitments also changed, reaching a peak in the 1980 FAC of 7.6 million tons and declining to 4.9 million tons in the 1999 FAC, although many of the signatories surpassed their minimum obligations in most years. The conventions gradually became more flexible in terms of the commodities covered and the way in which they could be acquired. Rice was included in the 1980 FAC, and pulses in the 1995 FAC. Substantive changes were made in the 1999 FAC, which was signed by 23 members. The list of eligible products was widened to include limited quantities of edible oil, root crops, skimmed milk powder, sugar, seeds for eligible products and products that were part of the traditional diet of vulnerable groups in developing countries.

How efficient has the FAC been in providing an effective safety net for food security in developing countries? One analysis has concluded that the quantities of food aid provided have been too small, and reduced at crucial periods, with the result that the FAC has 'contributed little to international food security' (Benson, 2000). A shift in emphasis away from a minimum quantitative commitment towards some form of obligation linked to need was suggested and a mechanism needed to be introduced to ensure continual assessment of the impact of FAC assistance in terms of international food security and other factors.

8
Freedom from Hunger Campaign

The 1960s began with an entirely new approach in the quest for world food security on the initiative of a new FAO director-general, the first, and so far the only one, from the Asia region. Binay Ranjan Sen, popularly known as B. R. Sen, had been India's Director-General of Food during wartime (1943–46), his primary task being to ensure equitable distribution of scarce food supplies for one-sixth of the world's population. He wrote: 'All my life I had been in the midst of hunger and poverty in all its stark reality' (Sen, 1982, p. 137). He had followed closely the discussions at the Hot Springs, Quebec and Copenhagen conferences and had seen that while they had opened a new chapter in international solidarity, they had also shown that the major powers were not prepared to establish some form of world food security arrangement under the control of a multilateral organization. A different strategy was therefore required that would be more acceptable to them but would also keep the goal of eliminating hunger alive.

The idea of mounting a world campaign against hunger was on Sen's mind when he became FAO's director-general in 1956. At the summer session of ECOSOC in 1957, he sketched out the main objectives of a 'Freedom from Hunger Campaign' (FFHC), which were: to attract worldwide attention to the problem; to secure the participation and co-operation of all concerned; to achieve a degree of enthusiasm and anticipation, which would result in more effective national and international action; and, in the process, establish a higher level of mutually profitable world trade to help raise the prosperity of both developed and developing countries. He reasoned that the problems of poverty, hunger and malnutrition were so vast in scale, and so serious in character, that a sustained campaign conducted over a number of years was necessary. He told ECOSOC that the main aim was to heighten awareness in the world and thus improve the foundations for effective and accelerated action, which would hopefully continue for the future. Three months later, he spoke at the FAO Council, when his ideas had clarified further. The campaign would be of an informational and promotional character. The expectation was that a climate of public opinion would be created that would force governments to intensify action programmes both at the national and international levels. The campaign would culminate in a 'World Food Congress' that would sum up its main lessons and conclusions. He suggested 1963 as the date for the meeting, which coincided with the twentieth anniversary of the Hot Springs conference that had given birth to FAO.

78   *1945–70. Early Attempts: FAO's Pioneering Work*

Sen's ideas were approved by the FAO Conference in its resolution 13/59 on 27 October 1960, which authorized an international campaign extending from 1960 through 1965 (later extended to 1970) under the leadership and general co-ordination of FAO (FAO, 1960a). The resolution noted that 'under its Constitution FAO was the principal agency within the United Nations family of international agencies responsible for the encouragement of aid to countries in raising levels of food production, consumption, and nutrition'. Invitations to participate in the FFHC would be made, 'as appropriate and approved by FAO', to member countries of FAO and the UN, the UN specialized agencies, international NGOs, religious groups, and individuals and private organizations. The resolution emphasized that the objectives of the FFHC could only be reached if the less developed countries formulated effective and useful projects, which would increase support for the campaign in the more highly developed countries. The resolution also authorized the director-general to make preparations for a World Food Congress in 1963, as Sen had proposed. A FFHC Trust Fund was created to finance activities carried out under the campaign.

The FFHC was officially launched on 1 July 1960. Sen clarified further the aims and objectives of the campaign in a letter to ministers of agriculture of FAO member countries (Sen, 1982, pp. 147–8). In his view, the problems of hunger and malnutrition had 'always been with man and has made man's history'. But they had been invested with a new dimension and new urgency by the explosive rate of population growth following the advance of science and social hygiene. The FFHC was intended to be 'primarily educational in character – to make the Governments and peoples all over the world aware of the nature of the problem so that integrated efforts can be made both nationally and internationally to overcome it'. Sen placed great store on people's participation in the FFHC. National FFHC committees were established in many developing and developed countries, including the United States, to help make people aware of the magnitude and dimensions of hunger, and of the measures needed to overcome it. Fund-raising was not the primary objective, although action projects had an important part to play by providing a means through which developed countries could express their solidarity with developing countries, assisting their efforts to implement their national development plans, and making available an additional source of skills, technical know-how and foreign exchange, which in developing counties could 'make all the difference'.

It was recognized that no lasting solution to the problem of hunger could be found without balanced economic and social development. The emphasis of the campaign was therefore on transforming subsistence agriculture into a market economy, on increasing productivity, and on quantitative and qualitative increases in food production. Hidden hunger, or malnutrition, the parent of many diseases prevalent in large segments of the world's population, could be cured only with provision of more plentiful supplies of food. Agricultural development had to be the 'spearhead' of economic and social development in developing countries, where the bulk of the population lived on the land. The essential savings required for investment in development programmes could accrue only if the income levels of rural communities were enhanced through increased productivity. There were many problems to be solved before 'the vicious circle of rural poverty' could be broken. But a start had to be made on two major objectives in developing countries: greater production of food, and higher purchasing power of the rural masses.

Sen explained that he made FFHC the central theme of all FAO activities during his time as director-general (1956–67). When he opened the campaign, he felt that he could best give expression to mounting international concern by quoting from one of his favourite poets, John Donne:

One man's hunger is every man's hunger – one man's freedom from hunger is neither a free nor a secure freedom until all men are free from hunger.

These words were taken as a key to the entire campaign. The FAO resolution approving the FFHC stated that it was intended 'to promote a spirit of re-dedication of the Organization [FAO] and its members to the achievement of the objectives of the Organization'. Sen felt that it needed the involvement of the whole organization with the director-general at the centre personally controlling and directing all of its activities bearing of the campaign. In expressing the idea of a continuing campaign, he explained:

one, of course, realizes that a radical transformation of economic conditions cannot be achieved in a few years. What we can hope for is the generation of a tempo of development which may break the cycle of stagnation and lead to self-sustaining growth. This campaign is not intended to be a special new programme in itself, but only to aid and intensify our work in FAO and at the same time the work of member governments as well as the vast masses of the people who depend on agriculture for their livelihood. (Sen, 1982, p. 139)

Sen realized that one of the first questions to be asked would be the extent of current world hunger and malnutrition that the FFHC would have to address. He therefore set in motion a world food survey in 1962 as one of his first campaign initiatives. The survey took nearly two years to complete. The first FAO world food survey, undertaken in 1946, was more or less an extension of the work of Boyd Orr, which had been carried out for the British people (Boyd Orr, 1936). Because there were serious gaps in statistical information, much of the material used was in the nature of intelligent guesswork. The second FAO world food survey in 1952 was somewhat more reliable as more realistic standards for calorie requirements could be established, which took account of such factors as age, sex, body weight and physical activity in different environments and temperatures. Ten years had passed since the 1952 survey during which not only had the impact of population growth revived Malthusian fears about adequate food supplies but also new and significant data on food consumption patterns had become available.

The 1962 survey was based on food balance sheets data for over 80 countries covering some 95 per cent of the world population (FAO, 1963a). It drew on food consumption and dietary surveys in various parts of the world and introduced new statistical techniques in the study of food supplies and needs. It provided a concrete basis for information and data and was quoted by world leaders in support of the FFHC. The survey showed that calorie supplies in Europe, North America and Oceania exceeded requirements by 20 per cent. In Africa, the Near East and Latin America they were about equal to requirements. In Asia and the Far East, supplies fell short by 11 per cent. The broad conclusion was that between one-third and one-half of the world's population suffered from malnutrition. While improvement had occurred in the developed countries since the 1952 world food survey, progress in the less developed countries was hardly enough to regain the unsatisfactory pre-war level.[33]

A prominent part of the FFHC was the publication of a series of 'basic studies' by FAO and other United Nations organizations covering a wide range of issues related to the problem of hunger. No less than 23 studies were produced covering such subjects as *Weather and Food* (WHO, 1962), *Nutrition and Working Efficiency* (FAO, 1962b), *Education and Training in Nutrition* (FAO, 1962c), *Population and Food Supplies* (UN, 1962b), *Aspects of Economic Development – The Background to Freedom from Hunger* (UN, 1962b), *Possibilities of Increasing World Food Production* (FAO, 1963b), *Malnutrition and Disease* (WHO, 1963), *Hunger and Social Policy* (ILO, 1963), *Education and Agricultural Development* (UNESCO, 1963) and *Towards a Strategy for Agricultural Development* (FAO, 1969). All these studies were essentially interconnected and dealt with different aspects of the same central theme, the problems of economic development in the developing countries. They provided background information and material for the briefs of delegates at sessions of ECOSOC, the UN General Assembly, the FAO Council and Conference, the other UN specialized agencies, and international NGOs. In particular, they served to increase awareness of the various dimensions of hunger and the importance of food and nutrition. The studies showed that although raising the levels of productivity and income in agriculture should provide the basic orientation of FFHC activities, such an aim could not be pursued in isolation. It was intimately bound up with the dynamics of general economic growth and with the social *milieu* in which various institutional factors operated to enhance or retard that growth. The problem had acquired a new dimension as a result of an unprecedented rate of population increase. And the farmer, upon whom prosperity and a sense of security the well-being of the community as a whole largely rested, had emerged as the central figure in any scheme for economic and social advancement.

FAO's *State of Food and Agriculture* in 1962 (FAO, 1962d) showed that farm income per head and per family was lower in almost all developing countries than in other occupations and that productivity depended not only on differences in technical knowledge and equipment but also on marketing facilities, price stability and the land tenure system. It brought out that agricultural development should keep pace with progress in other sectors, which benefited from a parallel development in agriculture. In the early stages of development, agriculture was the main source of manpower and investment resources. As a result,

Freedom from Hunger Campaign 81

FAO's programme of activities was reviewed and revised. Greater emphasis was placed on agricultural infrastructure, and on distributional, institutional and administrative aspects. It was also recognized that because of the operation of market forces and other economic factors, the economic and social welfare of the rural population depended largely on the buying power of others. On all these matters, thinking in FAO was influenced by the FFHC as the content and direction of FFHC itself were influenced by what emerged from these independent studies.

World Food Congress 1963

Sen took two initiatives in support of, and in preparation for, the World Food Congress, the high point in the FFHC, which was held in Washington, DC in June 1963 (Sen, 1982, pp. 150–4). He invited 28 world-renowned personalities, including several Nobel Prize winners, whose concern for the problem of hunger was well known, to Rome on 14 March 1963 with the objective of 'bringing their moral authority to bear on the aims and purposes' of the FFHC. This 'Special Assembly on Man's Right to Freedom from Hunger' as it was called was also intended to provide a dramatic opening for the 'World Freedom for Hunger Week', which followed immediately after. As Sen put it, not since the FFHC had been launched had such a range of interest been displayed in the problem of world hunger, nor had such a forceful analysis of the problem been presented from a single platform. The pronouncements of this group of eminent men and women showed a penetrating awareness of the social and political implications of many hundreds of millions of people being condemned to a life of hunger and poverty.

The Assembly's 'manifesto' highlighted some basic questions of fact and policy, which the forthcoming World Food Congress might address. Could food production keep pace with population growth within a framework of rational planning? Enough scientific knowledge and technological experience were available to bring about an agricultural revolution in the developing countries, but could this knowledge be applied within a social and institutional framework that had held up progress through its own inertia? Could external aid by itself be effective in stimulating economic growth in the absence of world commodity agreements that guaranteed fair and stable prices for the primary products of developing countries? Could the current inadequate levels of investment in development be significantly increased without drastically cutting down through international agreements the astronomical scale of expenditure on armaments? The manifesto stated:

> Freedom from hunger is man's first fundamental right. In order to achieve this, we suggest urgent and adequate national and international effort in which the Governments and the people are associated. More particularly, we desire to draw attention to the colossal waste of resources in the piling up of more and new forms of armaments and the immense assistance to the Campaign against Hunger that even a partial diversion of these funds could achieve. We feel that

82 1945–70. Early Attempts: FAO's Pioneering Work

international action for abolishing hunger will reduce tension and improve human relationships by bringing out the best instead of the worst in man. (Sen, 1982, pp. 314–15)

Sen explained that the main objective in observing the 'Freedom from Hunger Week' (March 17–23, 1963) was to 'heighten the feeling of world solidarity in winning man's first freedom – freedom from hunger'. As this event fell at the mid-point of the FFHC, it was an invitation to individuals and groups to participate in a tangible way in furthering the objectives of the campaign. Sen addressed letters to some 120 member governments of the UN system suggesting what actions might be taken for the observance of the event. These suggestions included the issuing of proclamations by governments and messages from heads of states, strengthening of the national FFHC committees, organization of agricultural and nutrition development programmes, adoption of relevant laws and administrative measures, religious observances, introduction of teaching programmes on FFHC into national education systems, and special media coverage.

President Kennedy issued a proclamation urging:

the American Freedom from Hunger Foundation to take national leadership in planning appropriate observance of this Week, and American citizens in all walks of life to participate in the observance of the National Freedom from Hunger Week'. (Sen, 1982, p. 152)

The high point in the FFHC was reached with the holding of a World Food Congress in Washington, DC in June 1963. The meeting was attended by 1,300 people from over 100 countries. Opening the congress, President Kennedy recalled that 20 years previously President Franklin D. Roosevelt had launched the conference at Hot Springs, that had led to the foundation of FAO, by declaring that 'freedom from want and freedom from fear go hand in hand'. Kennedy added:

so long as freedom from hunger is only half achieved, so long as two thirds of the nations have food deficits, no citizen, no nation, can afford to be satisfied. We have the ability, as members of the human race. We have the means, we have the capacity to eliminate hunger from the face of the earth in our lifetime. We need only the will. (FAO, 1965b, p. 63)

Among its proposals, the Congress stated that 'the formulation of a world plan, in quantitative terms, on the basis of nutritional needs, indicating the type and magnitude of external assistance needed in relation to local resources, and internationally coordinated should be undertaken in order to ensure that the world might be freed from hunger within the foreseeable future'. The Congress also proposed that both the FFHC and the national FFHC committees should be placed on a continuing basis and FAO's coordination of FFHC work should be widened and strengthened. The *Declaration of the Congress* echoed a number of the points contained in *Man's Right to Freedom from Hunger Manifesto* of the previous month (FAO, 1965a). Among other things, it declared that

> the persistence of hunger and malnutrition is unacceptable morally and socially, is incompatible with the dignity of human beings and the equality of opportunity to which they are entitled, and is a threat to social and international peace.

It urged that 'there be more equitable and rational sharing of world abundance, including an expanded and improved utilization of food surpluses for the purpose of economic and social development'. And it called for consideration to be given 'to the formulation of a world plan in quantitative terms on nutritional and economic development needs which would indicate the type and magnitude of external assistance needed. The aim would be to eliminate hunger within a specific period'.

The Congress laid responsibility for freeing the world of the scourge of hunger jointly with: the developing countries; developed nations ('realizing that freedom from hunger cannot long be secure in any part of this interdependent world unless it is secure in all the world'); the United Nations and its specialized agencies ('who must intensify and coordinate their efforts'); and with other international organizations and non-governmental organizations. The Congress urged that the task of eliminating hunger should be conceived within a framework of worldwide development dedicated to the fullest and most effective use of all human and natural resources, to ensure a faster rate of economic and social growth. The participants pledged themselves 'to take up the challenge of eliminating hunger and malnutrition as a primary task of this generation, thus creating basic conditions for peace and progress for all mankind'.

The resolution of the Congress recommended that a World Food Congress should be held periodically to review a world survey, presented by the director-general of FAO, of the world food situation together with a proposed programme for future action. Sen followed up the Congress meeting with a Young World Assembly in October 1965. From the beginning, he considered ways of engaging young people in the FFHC. He called together youth leaders from all parts of the world for a dialogue as to do this in meaningful ways. Sen also committed FAO to preparing an Indicative World Plan for Agricultural Development, which was completed by his successor, Addeke Boerma, in 1969 in response to the call by the Congress for the formulation of a world plan to reach a world free from hunger 'within the foreseeable future'. (see below).

In the meantime, an attempt was made to, what Sen described as, 'jump on the FFHC bandwagon' (Sen, 1982, pp. 170–2). Shortly after the World Food Congress, the UK delegation tabled a resolution (1943, XVIII) at the UN General Assembly, which was adopted by its Second Committee, proposing a 'World Campaign against Hunger, Disease and Ignorance' for the second half of the UN Development Decade of the 1960s. One of the objectives of the resolution was to enable the UN secretary-general to consider, in consultation with the heads of the UN specialized

84   *1945–70. Early Attempts: FAO's Pioneering Work*

agencies, how the resources of the UN system might best be mobilized to stimulate and channel the efforts and goodwill of private individuals and organizations in such a campaign. An appeal was made to all NGOs working for the FFHC to take up this wider campaign. The directors-general of ILO, UNESCO and WHO and others favoured the wider campaign.

Sen had serious reservations, which he put to the UN secretary-general, U Thant. Sen pointed out that the FFHC was not confined solely to food, and had already embraced health, education and other conditions essential for general economic development, as shown in the publications in the FFHC basic studies series. The FFHC had already received wide support from world leaders and, most significantly, had enlisted the effective participation of people and NGOs. He was, no doubt, also concerned that FAO's leadership role would be ceded to the UN secretary-general. Sen put his case to ECOSOC at its meeting in Geneva in these terms. The strength of the FFHC, he said, lay largely in its sharp focus on the concrete issues of hunger. The proposed new campaign seemed too wide and undefined in scope. There appeared to be two ways of implementing the UN General Assembly resolution: by enlarging the scope of the FFHC or by launching simultaneously campaigns of health and education independently by WHO and UNESCO with coordination provided by the UN coordinating machinery. ECOSOC came to the conclusion that the existing circumstances were not favourable for launching a wider campaign and the FFHC continued under Sen's leadership.

Two other FAO initiatives were to reflect on the world food security situation. In 1962, FAO conducted medium-term projections for agricultural commodities to the year 1970 (FAO, 1962a). The projections showed that demand for food would increase more rapidly in developing than in industrialized countries because of their greater population growth and increasing incomes as they strove to accelerate economic growth. Income elasticity of demand for food was also considerably higher than in the industrialized countries. According to FAO projections, growth in demand for food in the industrialized countries was 2 per cent, lower than the rate of growth of food production despite measures taken to reduce the area under production. Food surpluses would therefore accumulate. This led to second initiative on the realization that food surpluses might become a long-term phenomenon. Concessional food aid from food surpluses was therefore likely to continue through supply management programmes.

9
The Development of Food Aid

At the same time, a change in attitude toward agricultural surpluses was taking place, from 'surpluses disposal' to using surpluses to meet nutritional needs and assist economic development in the developing countries. In a landmark study, a CSD *ad hoc* group noted that 'the most significant change is that instead of contending with unintentional surpluses, the thinking is now directed more toward the planned use of existing and future surpluses for meeting new demands arising in many developing countries' (FAO, 1963c, p. 17). As a corollary, thinking in some quarters was also directed toward the deliberate over-production (as related to current effective demand) of agricultural commodities either as a consequence of internal agricultural policies or to make supplies available for non-commercial uses. At the same time, there were indications that some countries were making a conscious effort to avoid production of excessive surpluses.

A close interrelation existed between changes in the methods of surplus disposal and changes of attitude toward the accumulation of stocks in excess of normal commercial demand. The pressure and cost of mounting supplies resulted in the advocacy of stricter production controls and in the hastening of the search for larger market outlets, both commercial and concessional. On the other hand, increasing realization of the possibility of using surpluses as an adjunct to bilateral or multilateral aid programmes modified thought in some countries about the need for rigid reduction in output.

The CSD group analysed four aspects of the changing attitude towards agricultural surpluses. First, the production of surpluses, their causes and motives, and the change from unintentional over-production to supply management involving some over-production in excess of commercial demand and, by some governments, acceptance of over-supply. To meet the problem, emphasis was placed on the desirability of increasing world distribution and consumption which, together with adjusted national policies, would gradually result in the elimination of surpluses. With the emergence of substantial stocks in North America, despite the imposition of control on the area planted under several major crops, attention was turned to the utilization of surplus foods to the best advantage for producing and receiving countries. This tended to take some of the pressure off efforts to deal with the causes of surpluses, which would involve difficult political choices. However, the high cost of acquiring, storing and handling growing surpluses led to further considerations of the means of adjusting production to world needs. Hence, emphasis was placed on the concept of supply management. This included the idea of direct control of production by restricting quotas for specific commodities to those quantities required to meet commercial demands and food aid needs. Views were expressed in some international bodies concerning the possibility of accepting and justifying surplus production on the assumption that surpluses could be disposed of in non-commercial markets, primarily through international operations. Surplus accumulations could therefore be the result of: either unintentional or unplanned over-production; production efforts justified by domestic economic and social considerations; production to include commitments for bilateral or multilateral aid to developing countries; or a combination of these possibilities, in which case it was recognized that it would not be easy to distinguish the role played by each factor.

The possibility of European surpluses arising from the EEC Common Agricultural Policy (CAP) adding to an already over-burdened supply situation in North America, coupled with food deficiencies on many developing countries, led the French Ministers of Agriculture and Finance (M. Pisani and M. Baumgartner) to propose a fundamental change in the structure of world agricultural trade. Their central idea consisted of substituting a 'free' world market price by a 'managed minimum price', which would reflect the production price in the main importing countries. The countries participating in the scheme would see that all international commercial trade took place at or above the agreed price and would eliminate export subsidies. In the case of wheat, for example, the arrangement would be carried out through a progressive increase in the prices fixed by the International Wheat Agreement. An understanding would be reached among exporting countries on the amount of products to be sold on commercial markets with a view to reaching an agreed balance between commercial demand and sales. This, in turn, would determine the amount of a given commodity available for concessional transactions and grants. The more remunerative commercial markets would help the exporting countries to increase their participation in special sales and donations. Their share of the concessional markets would also be agreed upon to avoid any conflict. Under this concept, the twin reorganization of commercial and concessional markets would be closely linked.

Second, attention turned to the question of the use of surpluses. It was clear that there had been a shift from spasmodic programmes to relieve distress to highly organized and sophisticated long-term programmes for nutritional improvement and economic development. As the 1950s drew to a close, a number of forces came together to produce results. US food surpluses continued to accumulate. US food aid increased rapidly with the passage of PL 480. By the 1960s, it reached over 18 million tons a year at a cost of $1.6 billion (US, 1964b). At the same time, the US food aid programme became the subject of increasing criticism by politicians and academics alike. Senator Hubert Humphrey of Minnesota, who later became vice president in the administration of President Lyndon B. Johnson, wrote a scathing report that called for major reform measures and the establishment of what he called a 'food for peace' programme (Humphrey, 1958). 'Food will win the war

The Development of Food Aid   87

and write the peace' had become the wartime slogan of the US Department of Agriculture. Humphrey also recommended the creation of a new post of 'Peace Food Administrator' in the White House with the status of special assistant to the US president to provide a 'central guiding hand' for the inter-agency groups who were operating the PL480 programme.

President Eisenhower adopted Humphrey's recommendations in his farm message to Congress in January 1959 when he said:

> I am setting steps in motion to explore anew with other surplus-producing nations all practical means of utilizing the various agricultural surpluses of each in the interest of reinforcing peace and the well-being of friendly peoples throughout the world – in short, using food for peace. (*The New York Times*, 30 January 1959)

And he appointed a 'Food for Peace Coordinator', Don Paarlberg, who had been special assistant to the US Secretary of Agriculture, Ezra Taft Benson, in April 1960. But Eisenhower's food policy changes were regarded as representing 'more of an effort to repackage an old concept in a new format than the kind of fundamental reconceptualization of the program urged so energetically by Hubert Humphrey' in the short time remaining of the Eisenhower administration (Peterson, 1975; Wallerstein, 1980, p. 40).

Congressman George McGovern of South Dakota, who was later to become the first director of the US Food for Peace programme in the Kennedy administration, issued a press release in 1959 on a 'Food for Peace Resolution: American Farm Production a Force for Freedom and Peace', which he mailed to all members of the US Congress.[34] The resolution stated:

> many Americans and a considerable portion of the Congress are troubled by the paradox of mounting American farm surpluses and costly storage programs in a world where most of the people are crying for food . . . a broader and more imaginative use of surplus farm commodities can play a major part in advancing the economic development and political stability of underdeveloped nations.

B. R. Sen, FAO's director-general, recalled that the main preoccupation of the surplus-producing countries during a period of intense discussion at the end of the 1950s was that international agencies should do nothing to interfere with the normal channels of trade (Sen, 1982, pp. 198–9). In April 1959, stung by the criticisms of the Democratic Party, particularly those of Humphrey and McGovern, President Eisenhower urged the US Congress to adopt a 'food for peace' plan as a bold attack on the problem of surpluses. US Agricultural Secretary Ezra Benson was given charge of the plan. In his letter to Benson, President Eisenhower referred to FAO's efforts to launch a worldwide campaign against hunger. Benson called a conference in Washington, DC of the five major food-exporting countries, Argentina, Australia, Canada, France and the United States, to which Sen was invited to take part on behalf of FAO. The conference set up a Wheat Utilization

88   1945–70. Early Attempts: FAO's Pioneering Work

Committee (WUC), which served as a consultative body to the five governments and maintained a close working relationship with FAO. The activities of the WUC included making more effective use of wheat surpluses for the promotion of economic development, co-ordination of disposal programmes for economic development with other development activities, providing wheat to individual countries on concessional terms and safeguarding commercial markets.

As pressures mounted, and the FFHC had its educational and public relations effects, the idea of a multilateral food aid programme was born. During the presidential election campaign of 1960, Senator John F. Kennedy, the Democratic Party's nominee for president, said in a speech in South Dakota on 22 September during the presidential election campaign:

> I don't regard... agricultural surplus as a problem. I regard it as an opportunity... not only for our own people, but for people all around the world... I think the farmers can bring more credit, more lasting good will, more chance for freedom, more chance for peace, than almost any other group of Americans in the next ten years, if we recognize that food is strength, and food is peace, and food is freedom, and food is a helping hand to people around the world whose good will and friendship we want. (McGovern, 1977, pp. 82–3)

Kennedy proposed holding an international conference on food and agriculture, similar to the one convened by President Roosevelt at Hot Springs, Virginia in 1943:

> to deal on a constructive multilateral basis with the food needs of the world. This conference should, of course, be held under the sponsorship, and in cooperation with the United Nations Organization. This conference should have as its specific goal the organization of an agency to undertake the transfer of surplus food and fiber stocks from nations with surpluses to those nations in desperate need of such supplies to combat hunger and to promote economic development.[35]

In a press release in October 1960, he added 'pending such a conference and the creation of a "world food agency", negotiate long-term agreements for donor countries to supply food commodities for food-for-work schemes', clearly the embryo of what turned out to be the UN World Food Programme.[36] The president of the US National Farmers Union, James G. Patton, recommended that such a conference be held for the specific purpose of setting up a new agency, under but not in FAO, to administer a multilateral food aid operational programme for the dual purpose of spurring faster economic growth in the developing countries and at the same time building up the power of the United Nations in the attack on world poverty.[37]

The first public document containing a proposal for a multilateral food aid facility appears, however, to have come not from Senator Kennedy but from the then vice president, Richard M. Nixon, the Republican Party's nominee for

The Development of Food Aid 89

president (Wallerstein, 1980, pp. 167–9). During the 1960 presidential election campaign, Nixon suggested that the US should support the creation of a multilateral surplus food distribution system. His motives were mixed. It would not be harmful to US friends and allies since they were expected to participate in it. It would not be subjected to criticism directed against US bilateral aid, as it would be administered through the United Nations. And it would 'outinnovate' his presidential opponent, Senator Kennedy, who was also calling for new food aid initiatives, including a multilateral food aid mechanism. Ultimately, a proposal was presented to the UN General Assembly by President Dwight D. Eisenhower on 22 September 1960 when the US presidential election campaign for his successor was in full swing. In making the proposal for a multilateral food aid facility, he said:

> The United States is already carrying out substantial programs to make its surpluses available to countries in greatest need. My country is also ready to join other Members of the United Nations in devising a workable scheme to provide to Member States through the United Nations system relying on the advice and assistance of the Food and Agriculture Organization. I hope the Assembly, at this session, will seriously consider a specific program for carrying forward the promising food for peace program. (UN, 1960a)

The proposal was not without its critics. The delegation from the Soviet Union objected on grounds that the proposal had been promoted by domestic political considerations linked to the presidential election. The Ukrainian delegation felt that if the US considered the proposal to be so important, the FAO and other relevant UN organizations should have a special session to deal with it. The Argentine delegation considered the proposal might have dangerous results for other, particularly developing, countries. Furthermore, FAO had already established the FFHC and the US government had its own substantial food aid programme. It was difficulty to see why the UN General Assembly should assume responsibility for a problem that was already being dealt with by a specialized agency [FAO], which had competence in the matter, and possessed the technical ability for resolving it. Any UN General Assembly resolution on the subject would be mere duplication. The release of surpluses might have disastrous effects on the trade of developing agricultural-exporting countries [like Argentina] and reduce the foreign currency earnings needed to speed up their rate of development. In other words, the proposed aid would be at their expense. A vote was called for and the proposal was adopted with 36 countries for, 12 against, and 27 abstentions (UN, 1960b).

An Expanded Programme of Surplus Food Utilization

The bipartisan support for some form of multilateral food aid programme, the activities of the FFHC and the persistence of the FAO director-general finally paid off when the UN General Assembly passed a resolution on 27 October 1960 on the

'Provision of Food Surpluses to Food-Deficit people through the United Nations System' (UN, 1961c). FAO was invited, in consultation with others, to establish 'without delay' procedures by which, with the assistance of the UN system, 'the largest practicable quantities of surplus food may be made available on mutually agreeable terms as a transitional measure against hunger'. FAO was invited to submit a study of the subject for its approval. With Sen's prodding, the resolution endorsed the FFHC, urging all members of the UN and the UN-specialized agencies to support it in every way, and acknowledged the dominant part that FAO could play in dealing with the problem. It also recognized a central theme that FAO was developing, that the ultimate solution to the problem of hunger lay in an effective acceleration of economic development of the developing countries, using the large agricultural surpluses that could not be disposed of on commercial terms.

B. R. Sen appointed a small group of five 'high-level, independent experts' to assist him in preparing his report.[38] The group met at the height of the Keynesian consensus with its emphasis on full employment, active government demand management and the welfare state. Of the five members of the group, three were direct students of Keynes, the fourth was an economic development thinker in his own right, but fully in the Keynesian vein, and the fifth was an agricultural expert in the American 'New Deal' tradition of President Roosevelt. It was no surprise, therefore, that the group's report had a strong Keynesian flavour. The whole emphasis was to deal with the surplus problem not by curtailing production but by expanding demand. The expert group was very much aware of earlier FAO pioneering work and the proposals to set up a World Food Board and an International Commodity Clearing House, and the US Marshall Plan after Second World War. And it ensured that all its recommendations were in accordance with the FAO *Principles of Surplus Disposal*. Given such a like-minded group, and the wealth of documentation and experience available in FAO, the group's report was handed to the FAO director-general only 19 days after it commenced its work in Rome.

Certain basic considerations influenced the group's report (FAO, 1961a). Information available at the time indicated that over half the world's population was either undernourished or malnourished. The world's food problem was therefore seen as basically one of deficiencies, not surplus. Underdevelopment was recognized as the basic cause. Poverty for many beside plenty for a few was previously a general phenomenon, nationally and internationally. However, for about one-third of the world's population in the developed countries, it was a memory, fading rapidly or gradually as development took place. For the other two-thirds of the world's population, mainly in the developing countries, it was still a grim reality. Developing countries within the world economy were akin to under-privileged, low-income people within the national economies of developed countries. The expert group observed that with the growth of wealth in developed countries, inequalities of income had diminished. Equality of opportunity, full employment and a minimum of subsistence were accepted parts of the social philosophy of their welfare states. Nothing similar obtained, however, within the international community as a whole. The basic aim should be to apply the principles of social progress accepted within the rich countries to the world as a whole. In the group's view, only if this were done could we talk about a truly 'international community'.

In a spirit of optimism that matched the time, the group considered that the resources to implement a far-reaching programme of assistance were already available. In its opinion, a transfer of two-thirds to three quarters of 1 per cent of the Gross National Product (GNP) of the developed countries over a period of five years, and probably less for another decade, would provide sufficient means for helping people in developing countries to help themselves. (Under the Marshall Plan, the United States had transferred about 3 per cent of its annual GNP for four consecutive years from 1948.) The group noted that this would represent a much smaller international redistribution of income than the national redistribution on income achieved by progressive taxation within most developed countries, when they were less rich than they were in 1961. It pointedly added:

> To think that the developed world cannot spare three quarters of one cent from each dollar of its income for an international program of economic aid is to show failure of imagination and failure of will. (FAO, 1961c)

Food aid from the food surpluses that existed was seen to be an important part of the resources needed for economic development in the developing countries. Far from being a waste, it could be a blessing, if matched by other resources, and used as an essential part of a coherent aid programme (as it had been in the Marshall Plan), and, to borrow from the Keynesian concept, would 'turn the stone of surpluses into bread for development'. A central part of the expert group's case was that surplus food could form an important part of capital in its original sense of a 'subsistence fund'. If sufficient foodstuffs could not be supplied to meet the increased demand from the additionally employed workers on construction or other investments, then either more resources (circulating capital) would have to be spent on food imports or the amount of additional investment would have to be reduced. Additionally employed workers would have to be fed during the period of construction, before the fruits of their work and of investment could supply their needs, or enable them to buy their own subsistence. Without such a fund, additional investment would not be possible, and inflation would become rampant. Food surpluses used for economic development would enable hungry people to produce either their own food or other products to buy food. Freedom from hunger could ultimately be achieved only through freedom from poverty.

The group estimated that about $12,500 million of agricultural commodities would become available as 'surpluses' over a five-year period for use outside normal commercial market channels, either bilaterally or through the UN system. It recommended that about two-thirds of these resources should be used in economic development programmes and one-third for social development. Between $1,550 and $1,650 million of surplus food a year might be used for economic development programmes over a five-year period. The aim would be to provide developing

92   1945–70. Early Attempts: FAO's Pioneering Work

countries with a positive incentive for maximum national effort to increase their rate of growth. The primary criterion, therefore, was to maximize national effort, not to maximize income per dollar of aid. International aid should strengthen the national effort and shorten the time to reach the desired goal to the point where a satisfactory growth rate could be achieved on a self-sustaining basis.

A small part (about 8 per cent, or $200 million a year) of the total surplus food should be allocated for the establishment of national food reserves in developing countries to the extent that they could equip themselves with appropriate storage facilities and institutional and logistical arrangements to manage and handle the reserves. Surplus foods could be made available for the initial reserve stocks as one-time contributions, although this would not preclude that later contributions might be made to offset prolonged periods of sub-normal production caused by such factors as drought. Developed countries not supplying surplus food could provide other inputs, such as storage facilities.

In addition, an international emergency food reserve should be established to provide relief food grants to the victims of famine and other natural disasters. (No reference was made to man-made disasters.) The food grants would be provided from national food reserves held in contributing countries. The group estimated that about $150 million a year would be required for this purpose.

Resources should also be made available to promote social development. Two criteria were suggested for planning such programmes. The focus should be on moving gradually toward a situation in which the developing countries themselves would be able to take over these programmes. And action should be avoided that would depress prices to domestic producers or lessen incentive for maximum food production in the developing countries themselves. The channelling of food surpluses into social development programmes was not regarded as detrimental to local agricultural production since it represented additional consumption, and the beneficial effects of improved nutrition could be striking. Four types of social development programmes were identified. In land reform programmes, surplus food could be provided while land was redistributed and there might be a decrease in agricultural production. In school feeding programmes, meals could be provided to encourage school attendance and improve nutrition and food habits. Assistance might also be provided to poor students at the secondary and higher levels of education and in training programmes. And relief and welfare programmes for the old, handicapped and destitute might be supported.

While the major part of international aid would continue to be provided bilaterally, the expert group recommended that it should be supplied within a consultative, multilateral framework. This would ensure that all aid would be provided within coherent and consistent country assistance programmes. For incorporating the use of surplus food into development programmes, and advising on the general economic requirements of developing countries, the group recommended that FAO should work closely with the United Nations and in particular with the UN Regional Commissions. To ensure that surplus food was combined with additional financial and technical aid in packages of assistance, FAO and the UN should work closely with the World Bank. Much of the technical and training

The Development of Food Aid 93

work involved, as well as pilot projects and surveys, could lead to action by the UN Special Fund and the UN Expanded Programme for Technical Assistance (EPTA), later to be merged to become the UN Development Programme (UNDP).

The group favoured a country programming approach to the planning and use of international aid, including food aid, which incorporated three basic principles. First, the interests of the recipient, developing country should be paramount and should be determined by the needs of developing countries, not the availability of surplus food. Second, all potential recipients of additional food surpluses should be treated on a basis of equality so that each country had the same opportunity to benefit. And lastly, high and uniform standards should be applied in assuring that additional surplus food was only used for constructive objectives, which the involvement of international organizations could ensure.

The individual country programme, drawn up within a multilateral framework, would normally include an assessment of the additional financial and technical assistance required to accompany the surplus food, which would enhance the value of the total aid programme. An approximate idea of the amounts of aid available should be provided. Surplus-giving countries should, therefore, indicate their willingness to earmark surplus food as aid. Since it would not be known what proportion of the total aid requirements would be handled multilaterally, which would be determined by the recipient countries individually, part of the total earmarkings would be made available on a flexible basis for multilateral transactions.

The views of the expert group were reproduced in full in the FAO director-general's report, which was fittingly published in the FFHC basic studies series (FAO, 1961c). Although a number of their recommendations were well in advance of their time, their value was subsequently recognized. Crucially, they were well received by officials in key positions in the United States. For example, in a memorandum to President Kennedy, the US ambassador to the United Nations, Adlai Stevenson, described the report as 'one of the most remarkable documents on the subject'.[39] Willard Cochrane, director of the US Department of Agriculture's Agricultural Economics Service, found it 'an excellent report. The analysis of the role of food aid in economic development is, in my opinion, highly competent and informative. I know of no better analysis in the literature on economic development'.[40] In submitting his report, B. R. Sen made four 'basic principles'. First, surpluses in aid must be granted for the promotion of economic and social development. Second, the main decisions as to what course development should take place in the food-aided countries themselves. Third, aid would be more effective if it was integrated in national development programmes, and became part of a national effort, in which the use of every resource should be related to every other resource for achieving nationally agreed objectives and aspirations. He put it this way:

An operational plan for economic development is a charter of policy, which has to outline what the people may expect in time, and also the duties they have to undertake. It must receive support from all sections of the community.

94   1945–70. Early Attempts: FAO's Pioneering Work

However, while the architecture of the plan must be national, the techniques of its elaboration may profitably depend on assistance from abroad if that is needed. It is here that both donor countries and international organizations should concentrate their attention.

Fourth, plans for surplus utilization must not endanger the balance of the national economy in such ways as to allow short-term advantages, but result in long-term failure. Sen particularly underlined the need to avoid interference with the normal channels of trade and the importance of absorptive capacity in food aid recipient countries in order to make effective use of the aid provided.

In the meantime, a significant event had occurred, which resulted in a sea change in attitude toward the United Nations and the multilateral approach to international cooperation. Senator John F. Kennedy won the presidential election beating the two-term vice president Richard M. Nixon. During the presidential campaign, in October 1960, Kennedy announced that, should he win the election, he would appoint a 'committee of distinguished citizens' to make recommendations for his new administration 'to transfer the "food for peace" slogan into a truly effective long-range use of our food abundance'. Subsequently, after Kennedy had won the election, the committee was transformed into the American Food for Peace Council as a non-partisan advisory group to advise the president and the new director of the Food for Peace programme on the most effective use of US food surpluses.

In his inspiring inaugural address as president on 20 January 1961, Kennedy stated:

> The world is very different now. For man holds in his mortal hands the power to abolish all forms of human poverty and all forms of human life... To those people in the huts and villages of half the globe struggling to break the bonds of mass poverty, we pledge our best efforts to help them help themselves...
> If a free society cannot help the many who are poor, it cannot save the few who are rich. (US, 1963, pp. 1012–13)

So seized was the new president with the importance of US food surpluses to combat hunger at home and abroad, and as a tool for American foreign policy, that his first two executive orders on assuming the presidency related to these matters.[41] The first executive order, issued on the day after his inauguration, provided for an expanded programme of food distribution to needy families in the United States. The second executive order, issued three days later, outlined the responsibilities of the newly appointed director of the Food for Peace programme. In a memorandum to federal agencies of 24 February 1961, the president described further the director's role, adding that he would be 'located in the Executive Office of the President'.

In his State of the Union address on 30 January 1961, ten days after his inauguration, President Kennedy said

The Development of Food Aid   95

This Administration is expanding its Food for Peace Program in every possible way. The product of our abundance must be used more effectively to relieve hunger and help economic growth in all corners of the globe. And I have asked the Director of this Program to recommend additional ways in which these surpluses can advance the interest of world peace – including the establishment of world food reserves.[42]

In a 'Special Message to the Congress on Agriculture' on 16 March 1961, Kennedy outlined the policy framework that was to move the focus of the US food aid programme from disposal of surpluses to the constructive use of abundance both at home and abroad (US, 1963, pp. 192–200). In a 'Special Message to Congress on Foreign Aid' on 22 March 1961, Kennedy called for a comprehensive overhaul of US foreign aid, noting that its aid programmes and concepts were 'largely unsatisfactory and unsuited for our needs and for the needs of the underdeveloped world as it enters the Sixties' (US, 1963, pp. 192–200). He called for a new organizational structure for US aid but added that that was not enough. 'We need a new working concept. At the center of the new effort must be national development programs', which would include all types of US assistance, including the food for peace programme, 'while recognizing its essential role in our farm economy'.

Why was President Kennedy so interested in the Food for Peace programme? In an illuminating address to the American Food for Peace Council in San Francisco on 29 January 1962, Theodore Sorensen, special counsel to the president, identified three reasons.[43] It was a means of helping the president's agricultural policy of 'supply management', a programme of production controls combined with higher price support. It helped to fulfil the aims of Kennedy's foreign aid programme. And it could create the contentment and order on which freedom and peace could thrive by 'building the bodies, which in turn help to build the institutions of peace'.

Kennedy appointed George McGovern as the first director of the newly created Office of Food for Peace in the Executive Office of the President, and special assistant to him.[44] 'Food, farmers and his fellow men' were described as the three foundation stones on which McGovern's philosophy of life and his distinguished public service were built, underpinned by a strong and enduring belief that 'one person, despite weaknesses and mistakes, can make a difference' (*The New York Times*, 1961; McGovern, 1977, p. 297). McGovern was born and raised in a small rural community in South Dakota, one of the most agricultural states of America. Although not of farming stock, he witnessed at first hand the poverty of the farming community through the economic depression of the 1930s and the decline of farm incomes. He also saw the growing paradox of accumulating agricultural surpluses at a time when hunger existed at home and abroad. His concern for his fellow men stemmed from a deeply religious background. Son of a Wesleyan Methodist minister, he studied for the Methodist clergy until he changed to an academic career, with a strong interest in the history of American intellectual thought, before finally entering politics.

His commitment to the United Nations and to solving the problems of the world through the combined action of the 'brotherhood of man' was instilled in

96 1945–70. Early Attempts: FAO's Pioneering Work

him at an early age through the state's public school system and his post-graduate academic studies. These forces came together to create 'an old-fashioned free-enterprise capitalist and practical internationalist'. As a bomber pilot stationed in Italy during Second World War, he saw at first hand hunger and poverty in war-torn Europe that was reminiscent of scenes he had witnessed on the American prairies, and later to see on his first visits to Latin America as Food for Peace director.

Throughout his political career as congressman (1957–60) and later as senator (1963–68), McGovern consistently pursued his aims of giving fairness to the US farmer, sharing America's agricultural bounty at home and abroad, and supporting the United Nations and international action. As a member of the agricultural committees of both houses of Congress, he became a leading spokesman for the American farmer and an authority on American agriculture (McGovern, 1967a,b). Even before that, when he was building up the Democratic Party in South Dakota, a largely Republican state, he vigorously opposed the agricultural policies of the Eisenhower administration that from 1953 had led to a decline in farm prices and incomes and a rise in government-held grain stocks as farmers opted to leave their output in government hands rather than pay off their agricultural-support loans.

At the same time, he had a 'thoroughly realistic appreciation of the potentials and pitfalls of the [Food for Pace] program' (*The Washington Post*, 1961). He understood that food could not be a substitute for financial and technical assistance. There was a good case, therefore, for co-ordinating the Food for Peace programme with other aspects of US aid, without downgrading the programme in the process. Appropriations for the Food for Peace programme were largely a bookkeeping transaction in already sunk capital. Storage, transportation and administrative costs were real, but the food itself had been purchased by the government, and the use of food surpluses represented a saving in storage costs. Famine and emergency relief were important but they were only one aspect of a programme that had many possibilities for using food aid productively. But this required changes in attitude. At home, it was necessary to convince Americans that abundance was an asset rather than a curse. Abroad, it was necessary to persuade governments that food aid could contribute constructively to economic development and was not merely America dumping unwanted food or disrupting others' markets.

Shortly after taking office in January 1961, President Kennedy requested McGovern to undertake an evaluation of the past operations of the Food for Peace programme and propose ways of improving it. In his report to the president on 28 March 1961, McGovern wrote, among other things:

> we should support an expanded role for the FAO – a role where it will have responsibility for developing and executing a multi-lateral food distribution program. There should not be fear that a multi-lateral approach will conflict with the Food for Peace Program. On the contrary, world food needs are so great that there is need for both approached.[45]

B. R. Sen, the FAO director-general, had decided to call a meeting of an FAO Intergovernmental Advisory Committee in Rome between 5 and 12 April 1961

The Development of Food Aid   97

to discuss his report in response to the UN General Assembly resolution before submitting it for approval. Kennedy requested McGovern to represent the United States at the meeting.[46] Sen's study contained no specific proposals and the committee was called only to provide advice, not to present government positions. Furthermore, there had been no discussion, and hence no agreement, on any proposal in Washington prior to McGovern's departure for Rome. It therefore came as a complete surprise when McGovern suggested to the other members of the US delegation that a concrete proposal be made at the meeting in order to stimulate progress.[47] They felt that there was insufficient time to get any proposal approved in Washington. However, McGovern persisted. He requested the other members of the US delegation to draft a proposal in line with his thinking while he undertook to get clearance from the White House.

This unconventional procedure was even more unusual in that permission to proceed was sought over a weekend. McGovern contacted his deputy in the Office of Food for Peace, James Symington, by telephone and requested him to speak to Theodore Sorensen, special counsel to President Kennedy, about the draft proposal. Sorensen, a friend of McGovern who had the ear of the president, later spoke with McGovern by telephone, and 'within 24 hours' permission to go ahead was obtained. This demonstrated how in the early days of the Kennedy administration quick action could be taken through direct contact with the White House. It also showed the close relationship, and high regard, McGovern enjoyed with President Kennedy.

Although McGovern had not discussed the proposal, even in broad outline, with President Kennedy before he left for Rome, he felt that it reflected the president's views regarding a broader and more constructive use of food aid and his strong support for the United Nations, which the president had revealed both during the presidential election campaign and immediately after his inauguration. It also reflected the views expressed by McGovern in his report to the president on ways of improving the Food for Peace programme shortly before he left for Rome. The multilateral food aid programme that McGovern proposed was circumscribed in a number of ways. It was to be limited to $100 million in commodities and cash when, in 1961, the value of farm products shipped under the US food aid programme alone was $1.3 billion and US food surplus stocks had reached 112 million tons. It was restricted to three years, and to be conducted on an experimental basis, with a decision on its continuation dependent on an evaluation of experience. The activities of the experimental programme were to be restricted mainly to meeting emergencies, although pilot development projects were added, such as school lunches and labour-intensive works programmes, which the United States had recently introduced into its Food for Peace programme, in order 'to develop diversified experience'. Large-scale, bulk-supply, programme food aid that the United States and other donor countries were providing bilaterally was specifically excluded.

The proposal reflected perfectly the three dominant forces that fashioned McGovern's overriding philosophy throughout his public life: support for the American farmer; the constructive use of food surpluses; and resolving international problems through the medium of the United Nations. The elements of

98   1945–70. Early Attempts: FAO's Pioneering Work

McGovern's proposal were carefully crafted and based on a political judgement that they would be acceptable to all concerned in Washington, DC, bearing in mind past hostility to the United Nations and multilateral assistance in the Departments of Agriculture and State, and in the White House itself.

The proposal did not involve much additional funding. The resources pledged by the United States would, in the main, come out of sunken capital in the form of the large food surpluses that had accumulated in government-held stocks. No formal commitment was made of supplementary cash resources: that possibility would be 'explored' in Washington. The size of the total proposed resources ($100 million over three years) was calculated to be large enough to be meaningful to other delegations, but not too large to create opposition in Washington. And they were to be 'a supplement to bilateral arrangements', not a substitute for them. The project, not programme, approach proposed was to avoid the criticism that had already been made of the effects of US bulk programme food aid on international trade and domestic food production in recipient countries that had led the FAO to recommend its *Principles of Surplus Disposal*. It also facilitated evaluation of the impact of food aid on individual development projects and specific groups of poor and hungry people.

The proposal stressed the multilateral nature of the proposed new programme. (The word 'multilateral' occurred four times in McGovern's brief and concise statement.) It was to be 'a truly multilateral program with the widest possible contributions by member countries'. This served notice that the United States was not prepared to address the food problem of developing countries alone. International burden-sharing was needed to tackle their dimensions, politically and financially. This would help both to meet the costs involved and give an opportunity to all donors to contribute according to their comparative advantage in terms of food commodities (and the kinds of food needed), money for transportation and administration, and services, such as shipping.

FAO, and its director-general in particular, were given a major role in the proposed new multilateral programme. This was in recognition of FAO's mandate and its early work on world food security and food surplus concerns and issues. It also reflected confidence in the ability of FAO's director-general, B. R. Sen, to run the proposed programme effectively. McGovern had met with Sen in Washington, DC in February 1961. Both respected each other. McGovern wrote to President Kennedy, 'I think it is very important that assurance be given to Dr. Sen that the US Food for Peace Program will explore various possibilities of multilateral distribution of agricultural abundance', the first hint that he was already contemplating the ideas that were later to emerge in the personal initiative he took at the FAO Intergovernmental Advisory Committee meeting in Rome in April 1961.[48] For his part, Sen recognized the strategic role that McGovern played in advancing progress on his study concerning a multilateral food aid facility. In his autobiography he wrote

> This bold initiative by Senator McGovern, who was then Director of the Food
> for Peace Programme in the White House, finally got my proposal off the

The Development of Food Aid   99

ground. . . . Senator McGovern is one of the finest, most liberal political leaders I have come across. . . . I cherish him as a very close friend. (Sen, 1982, p. 202)

McGovern's proposal, and the concise, yet detailed, way in which it was presented, caught the delegates from other countries by surprise when he made it at the Intergovernmental Advisory Committee meeting on 10 April 1961. They called for an adjournment to consider how to respond. Eventually, however, the proposal was accepted. McGovern reported to President Kennedy on his proposal when he returned from Rome. Kennedy gave the proposal his personal endorsement at a press conference on 21 April 1961 (US, 1963, p. 307). Looking back at his initiative, McGovern still regards the proposal with satisfaction. It represented the best possible pragmatic political action at the time – an unambiguous proposal leading to concrete action.[49] The United States reiterated the proposal at the FAO Council meeting in Rome in June 1961. But discussion on McGovern's proposal was not quite over. Officials in the US delegation at the United Nations in New York were working on another, much larger, multilateral food aid proposal. McGovern had been briefed on this proposal. He was not opposed to it but was sceptical that it would clear the various US departments in Washington and the US Congress. That was why he went ahead with his proposal in Rome after obtaining clearance from the White House.[50]

In his first address to the UN General Assembly on 25 September 1961, President Kennedy had proposed that the decade of the 1960s should be designated as the 'United Nations Decade for Development'. He said

Political sovereignty is but a mockery without the means of meeting poverty and illiteracy and disease. Self-determination is but a slogan if the future holds no hope. That is why my Nation, which has freely shared its capital and technology to help others help themselves, now proposes officially designating the decade of the 1960s as the United Nations Decade for Development. Under the framework of that Resolution, the United Nations' existing efforts in promoting economic growth can be expanded and coordinated. New research, technical assistance and pilot projects can unlock the wealth of less developed lands and untapped water. And development can become a cooperative and not a competitive enterprise – to enable all nations, however diverse in their systems and beliefs, to become in fact as well as law free and equal nations. (US, 1963, p. 623)

The UN General Assembly approved Kennedy's proposal. It ushered in a new era and created an atmosphere for positive international action and burden sharing. Hopes were raised in many quarters, and especially among the developing countries, that the United States and other developed countries would be prepared to increase substantially their aid programmes, including food aid, as part of the UN development decade. An additional $400 million of food aid for economic and social development (as opposed to meeting emergencies, which was the

100   1945–70. Early Attempts: FAO's Pioneering Work

main purpose given in the McGovern proposal) was mentioned, although never officially, by the US government.[51] If approved, the larger food aid proposal was to be administered through the United Nations Special Fund in New York. The Special Fund had been set up as a new UN agency in 1958, following a US proposal in the UN General Assembly, to finance technical assistance provided largely by the UN specialized agencies. Paul Hoffman, a highly respected American, who had been administrator of the Marshall Plan which provided massive aid to war-torn Europe after the Second World War, had been appointed managing director of the Special Fund, an added reason for proposing the channelling of the larger food aid proposal through the fund. The rationale was that the prestige of the Special Fund would be enhanced, and optimal use of food surpluses assured through the fusion of financial, technical and food aid in one assistance programme.

The two food aid proposals had to be reconciled so that a common position could be presented by the US delegations at the FAO Conference and the UN General Assembly at the end of 1961.[52] McGovern initiated a meeting in New York with US representatives to the United Nations on 10 November 1961. A second meeting was held at the State Department in Washington, DC four days later. A limited experimental plan along the lines proposed by McGovern was generally favoured and the larger food aid proposal was not pursued. It was recognized, however, that if the three-year experimental multilateral food aid programme was successful, it could encourage, rather than foreclose, a larger UN food aid programme (McGovern, 1964, pp. 109–10). McGovern's proposal was preferred to other schemes. The Prime Minister of Canada, Lester Pearson, laid a proposal for a 'world food bank' before the UN General Assembly in 1959. A comprehensive commodity plan was also proposed (Haas, 1969, p. 155). These alternative proposals did not receive serious consideration, particularly after US opposition was known and McGovern's proposal was approved (Wallerstein, 1980, p. 170).

McGovern's proposal was incorporated into parallel resolutions, passed by the FAO Conference and UN General Assembly on 24 November and 19 December 1961 respectively, that resulted in the establishment of the UN World Food Programme (WFP), initially on a three-year, experimental basis (FAO, 1961b; UN, 1961a), which was later extended on a continuing basis 'for as long as multilateral food aid is found necessary' (WFP, 1965, p. 2).

A number of reasons were put forward for restricting WFP to the project approach in providing food aid in contrast to the programme approach adopted by the US food aid programme, which provided food aid in bulk for balance of payments and budgetary support, and for supporting US political and commercial objectives. The WFP experiment had specifically been proposed to test out the use of food aid in support of different types of development projects. The project approach was considered to be the best way to adhere to the FAO *Principles of Surplus Disposal* and to avoid disincentive to agricultural production in recipient countries and disruption of international trade that the US food aid programme had caused. The project approach facilitated evaluation of the effects of WFP aid on economic and social development. Furthermore, WFP food aid was to be supplementary to, and not in competition with, bilateral food aid and should

The Development of Food Aid   101

therefore be kept to a moderate size (Singer *et al.*, 1987, p. 29). It was much more difficult, and time-consuming, to disburse large amounts of aid – any aid – on a project-by-project basis than for macro-economic purposes using the bulk food aid programme approach. Other reasons were mentioned. It was hoped that WFP would attract more donors and hence forestall the creation of other large-scale bilateral food aid programmes, which would compete with those already established. This particularly applied to Western Europe where, through the Common Agricultural Policy of the European Economic Union, large-scale food surpluses had began to appear. Finally, the establishment of a small and circumscribed WFP also provided a token to the United Nations multilateral system at a modest cost and posed no threat to the large bilateral food aid programmes or to commercial trade.[53]

By the end of McGovern's short period as director of the Food for Peace programme in 1962, over a third of all US overseas economic aid was in the form of agricultural products. The Food for Peace programme had become 'the single most extensive foreign aid program in American history, with the exception of the Marshall Plan' (Knock, 1992, p. 3). Food aid commitments were 75 per cent higher than for any previous 18-month period, made possible in part by a $2 billion supplemental appropriation in the spring of 1961. The largest share was in the form of sales for foreign currencies, most of which was earmarked for development loans and grants. These funds had been used more effectively by coordinating them with other forms of US aid and by planning them on a multi-year basis. The number of countries using food aid grants for economic and social development had increased eightfold through food-for-work programmes and livestock development projects for which feed, not food, aid was provided. Nearly 70 million people had received food through American private voluntary organizations. And the number of children benefiting from a school lunch programme had increased to 35 million.

In his letter of resignation to President Kennedy of 18 July 1962 to seek election to the US Senate, McGovern summed up the multiple achievements of his 18-month period in office. Food for Peace had brought many mutual benefits to the United States and the developing countries by being: an outlet for costly farm storage; a device to support farm income; a commercial market development tool; a resource for economic development; an 'invaluable aid' to world health; a 'powerful corrective to the misery on which tyranny thrives'; an 'indispensable foundation stone' for a free and peaceful world by which 'the American farmer [was given] a vital role in US foreign policy'. McGovern singled out one 'priority recommendation'. He strongly urged that the 'United States take an even more active lead in providing a daily school lunch for every needy child in the world. No form of overseas assistance could return greater dividends for so little cost. We should undertake this task with renewed energy 'because it is right'. McGovern's work has been described as 'probably the single greatest humanitarian achievement of the Kennedy-Johnson era' (Knock, 1992, p. 10). He had showed that with vision and determination 'one person . . . can make a difference'.

McGovern continued to pursue his vision at home and abroad after he was elected to the US Senate for the state of South Dakota in 1963. In June 1965, he

102 1945–70. Early Attempts: FAO's Pioneering Work

introduced a bill, 'The International Food and Nutrition Act' (S2157), which called for a worldwide effort to eliminate hunger. The purpose of the act was:

> to provide for the use of the excess production and capacity of American agriculture and food industries and, so far as possible, in co-operation with other nations, to eliminate human hunger and malnutrition throughout the world, to assist underdeveloped nations in increasing their own production of food and other human requirements, and to encourage other developed nations to participate in a united effort to eliminate want as a potential cause for international disputes, aggression, or war.

The act, had it been passed, would have authorized the US president to allocate to appropriate agencies, including an agency of the United Nations, in addition to current programmes, $500 million for the fiscal year 1966, and for each fiscal year thereafter to 1970, to reach $3.5 billion in the seventh year, and for three years thereafter at that level, which was estimated to be seven per cent of the US military budget. The bill also made provision for the US president to negotiate with other nations, through the US ambassador to the United Nations, for an expansion of the UN World Food Programme or other multilateral agency of the UN to assume as much responsibility for world freedom from hunger as possible with the participation and support of the United States. The bill was read twice and referred to the Senate Committee on Foreign Relations. By then, the Vietnam war had come to divert and dominate attention and discussion in the US, and no further consideration was given to this bold initiative. McGovern vigorously opposed Nixon's food aid policy in the US Senate when Nixon became president. He was appalled to see the instrument of 'Food for Peace' transformed into an instrument of war (Wallerstein, 1980, pp. 193–7).

Had Kennedy not been assassinated, and perhaps served a second term, the evidence suggests that he would have pursued his aims of a strengthened United Nations and enlarged the UN programme of assistance with US support while, at the same time, continuing the use of an expanded US food aid programme in the causes of peace and development. In his State of the Union address on 11 January 1962, for example, he stated

> I see little merit in the impatience of those who would abandon this imperfect world instrument [the United Nations] because they dislike our imperfect world. For the troubles of a world organization merely reflect the troubles of the world itself. And if the organization is weakened, the troubles can only increase.... A newly expanded Food for Peace Program is feeding the hungry in many lands with the abundance of our productive farms – providing lunches for children in schools, wages for economic development, relief for the victims of flood and famine, and a better diet for millions whose daily bread is their chief concern. These programs help people; and by helping people, they help freedom. (US, 1963)

In this last address to the United Nations General Assembly on 20 September 1963, he said

> A United Nations Decade of Development is under way.... But more can be done...and...a worldwide program of farm productivity and food distribution, similar to our country's Food for Peace program, could now give every child the food he needs. (UN, 1963)

Kennedy's special counsel, Theodore Sorensen, called the Food for Peace programme 'a marked success' (Sorensen, 1965, p. 531). He noted how Kennedy had secured legislation authorizing its expansion and that within 18 months had shipped more food abroad than Hubert Hoover and his associates had shipped in ten years to the victims of the First World War. Preferring to pay for transporting food stored at the taxpayers' expense, Kennedy nearly doubled the programme's previous volume with such new uses as school lunch and food-for-work programmes in more than 80 developing countries.

Multilateral food aid study

During discussion on the future of WFP at the end of its three-year experimental period (1963–65), specific proposals were made for its transformation. The government of Israel called for the promotion of the multilateral food aid programme through the gradual and systematic increase of food production for food aid transfers at concessional prices or as grants rather than relying on unpredictable surpluses.[54] The government of Argentina proposed that WFP be converted into a multilateral 'World Food Fund'.[55] Uruguay suggested converting WFP into a 'World Food Bank'.[56] The Lebanon called for the establishment of a 'world commodity organization'.[57] And the Netherlands proposed the creation of an 'Emergency Food Supply Scheme'.[58] There was much support for the Argentine proposal. This related to a recommendation made at the UN Conference on Trade and Development in 1964 that in reviewing WFP's future, it 'may hereafter benefit both food-deficit developing countries and food-exporting developing countries' and that therefore 'due account be taken of the relationship and effects of a modified programme on the expansion and development of commodity trade of the developing countries' (UNCTAD, 1964). The Argentine proposal suggested that contributions to the proposed fund should be half in kind and half in cash, the cash being used to buy commodities in food exporting developing countries. The greater proportion of the fund's resources would be used as non-project aid in support of general development and mass feeding programmes. The fund would support rather than disrupt international commercial trade and its activities would be co-ordinated with international commodity agreements.

WFP's governing body agreed that the Argentine and UNCTAD proposals should be studied by an independent and authoritative specialist. S. R. Sen of India's Planning Commission was appointed to undertake the study (Sen, 1965). Sen concluded that the UNCTAD recommendation did not call for any basic modification of WFP's constitution. Regarding the Argentine proposal, Sen considered

104 1945–70. Early Attempts: FAO's Pioneering Work

that it contained a number of questions, such as the expansion and development of commodity trade, compensatory financing and improving the liquidity of developing countries, that required concerted action by a number of specialized agencies, such as UNCTAD, IMF and IBRD, and that 'it would not be desirable for WFP to combine the role of several of such organizations as the supporters of the World Food Fund idea would like to do'.

In reviewing his study, WFP's governing body felt that it went beyond its terms of reference. It therefore decided to refer the proposal to WFP's parent bodies, the UN and FAO, which led to a further study on multilateral food aid. A UN General Assembly resolution was passed in December 1965 that called on the UN secretary-general, in co-operation with the FAO director-general, to undertake a comprehensive, inter-agency study 'to examine, with a view to suggesting various alternative types of action, the means and policies which would be required for large-scale international action of a multilateral character for combating hunger effectively' (UN, 1965a). The resolution was passed immediately after the UN General Assembly had adopted another resolution approving the continuation of WFP after its three-year experimental period 'for as long as multilateral food aid is found feasible and desirable' (UN, 1965b). The resolution calling for the multilateral food aid study noted that 'the problem of hunger will continue to be one of the most serious problems facing the international community in the years to come' and that 'experience gained by the World Food Programme and the increase in its resources should enable it to enlarge its potential in this field'. It also noted that the various proposals intended to make WFP a larger and more effective instrument of international co-operation gave rise to fundamental issues that went beyond the terms of reference of WFP's governing body.[59]

The study, prepared at a time of critical food shortages in several developing regions, broke new grounds (UN, 1968b). It called for future food aid transfers to developing countries to be planned in response to forecasts of their needs and not by the food surpluses of developed countries, as in the past. Four main purposes were identified for food aid, each of which required different ways of estimating needs and different institutional arrangements for its supply: 'economically determined needs', defined as that part of the gap between domestic production and total effective demand that a food-deficit developing country could not import commercially without harming excessively its economic development; multipurpose food reserves; emergency food aid; and nutrition improvement programmes. The separation of emergency aid from other needs was particularly instructive and was to lead to future problems for WFP.

The study reasoned that the basic principle of future food aid operations, whether bilateral or multilateral, should be the planned provision of supplies, based as far as practicable, on a systematic analysis of the needs of each recipient developing country. It noted that FAO already projected long-term trends but the time period covered by these projections was too long to be useful for operational purposes. FAO therefore proposed the preparation of regular annual reviews of the medium-term food outlook.

The study also recommended that the international community should determine the minimum level of stockholding of the main food commodities that would provide satisfactory global food security in the event of unforeseen natural disasters. It also suggested that the national food reserves of developed countries might be extended to cover the emergency needs of developing countries. If such a principle were accepted internationally, it would be for the co-operating governments to decide whether to negotiate a maximum commitment for each country or whether it would be sufficient for them to act as an *ad hoc* consortium, called together when necessary by the FAO director-general.[60]

Regarding nutrition-improvement programmes for vulnerable groups, including young children and pregnant and nursing mothers, the study suggested that FAO's medium-term food outlook reviews could provide a continuous measure of progress by developing countries towards the attainment of established nutritional goals. But additional information would be required for building up special nutrition-raising programmes. UN agencies, including UNICEF and WFP, could assist national governments in developing countries in reaching these groups. Far more accurate data were required, however, if food aid programmes of this nature were to be systematically extended.

The study also suggested that the IBRD might assist in assessing requests for food aid in support of the national development plans of developing countries, as well as the need for associated financial and technical assistance. In addition, FAO might assess the impact of such aid on domestic food production and international trade in accordance with FAO's *Principles of Surplus Disposal*. And the IMF might consider the balance of payments aspects and the internal monetary impact in recipient countries of large-scale food aid transactions. To co-ordinate all food aid at the country level, it was suggested that WFP might join the aid consortia or consultative groups that had been set up under the auspices of the World Bank and UNDP for the major food-deficit developing countries.

The study concluded that the UN system's 'main contribution must come from its information and consultation activities'. These included: estimation of prospective food deficits of the four types identified above; early warning of food shortages; and an intergovernmental appraisal of the prospective food situation. By providing a clearer picture of requirements for food aid supplies, the commodities required, the supplies likely to be available, and the food aid operations currently being undertaken and planned, these 'informational activities', the study suggested, would assist governments in directing their food aid operations to where the need was most urgent, and would avoid any waste of resources.

Both ECOSOC and the FAO Conference endorsed the aim of using existing institutions, particularly WFP, in considering arrangements for expanded multilateral food aid. At the end of its discussion of the multilateral food aid study, the UN General Assembly requested the executive heads of the UN and FAO to give particular attention to the problems of co-ordinating all food aid programmes and to assessing the adequacy of existing multilateral institutional arrangements for handling a substantially increased volume of food aid.

Food aid during the Second UN Development Decade of the 1970s

During preparations for the implementation of the First UN Development Decade of the 1960s, WFP was seen as representing an experimental extension of the idea of multilateral aid in terms of physical commodities (UN, 1968a). Developed countries were urged to think more about the possibilities of bringing their surplus resources and capacities to bear on the promotion of development in developing countries. It was suggested that the whole area of supplementary aid in the form of surplus commodities and the utilization of surplus capacity deserved further exploration in the UN, where equal weight would be given to the legitimate protection of commercial trade and the interests of producers in developing countries as well as the inherent potential of such aid for speeding up development.

These considerations resurfaced during preparations for the Second UN Development Decade of the 1970s as a promising avenue for a significant increase in overall aid resources. An additional motive was to provide another opportunity to consider the various proposals for transforming WFP so that it might become a major force in world food aid. Six months after the UN secretary-general's multilateral food aid study was completed, the UN General assembly passed another resolution on 'Multilateral Food Aid' (UN, 1968a). On this occasion, the resolution was specifically directed to WFP's governing body, the Intergovernmental Committee (IGC). It called on the IGC to give its views on four specific issues: the UN secretary-general's and other studies on multilateral food aid; recommendations on food aid and related issues to assist in preparations for the Second UN Development Decade; ways and means of improving WFP, including resource allocations to WFP from the Food Aid Convention (FAC) of 1967; and, finally, examination of the possible inclusion of forms of aid in kind other than food in WFP's resources.

The IGC requested WFP's executive director to prepare the ground for its response to the UN General Assembly resolution. It agreed that he should be assisted by a group of qualified people,[61] with the support of the UN, FAO and WFP secretariats. The group was asked 'to consider and submit alternative policy choices for decision by the IGC'. Their report should be 'concrete and practical'. A comprehensive draft report prepared by the group was discussed by the IGC in April 1970. It was amended in the light of the comments of IGC delegations and was intended to establish a set of guidelines for WFP operations over the next ten years (WFP, 1970)

The IGC report stressed that the world food problem was an inseparable part of the broader problems of development. It was reasoned that, among other things, economic progress would raise food supplies through increased local production or commercial imports and increase effective demand, thereby improving nutrition. But despite considerable progress projected by the end of the Second Development Decade, many people in developing countries were expected to be unable to obtain sufficient food. At the same time, FAO and OECD projections indicated that during the 1970s developed countries would produce more

The Development of Food Aid   107

cereals and dairy products than could be absorbed in commercial markets. Food aid could help in transferring surpluses to needy people, subject to appropriate safeguards.

It was predicted that food stocks in developing as well as developed countries would increase during the 1970s. This could lead to enlarging the number of food aid donors, widening the commodity composition of food aid, and increasing the amount of reprocessing in recipient countries of the food aid commodities provided. But the volume and composition of food aid supplies might continue to reflect largely the stocks available in donor countries and, therefore, might be liable to considerable fluctuations. However, the annual average level around which these fluctuations might occur could be higher than the level of about $1.3 billion during the 1960s owing to the impact of technological improvements in agricultural production and an anticipated increase in aid. Various techniques had been proposed for increasing the involvement of food-exporting countries in food aid. The principal alternatives were the establishment of a multilateral fund to purchase food from developing countries, and the negotiation of international trade agreements, which might include special provisions for food aid.

No recommendation was given concerning the total volume of food aid that might be provided during the 1970s because of difficulties of forecasting likely availabilities and of assessing the capacity of receiving countries to use food aid effectively. However, one specific proposal was made. It was recommended that supplementary food should be provided to 60 million of the most vulnerable people in developing countries with about $600 million of food aid, which represented about half the total flow of food aid in 1970. While recognizing that food aid might continue to be provided mainly on a bilateral basis, the report recommended that the UN General Assembly should draw the attention of member states to the advantages of channelling a greater proportion of food aid through multilateral channels, particularly WFP. Those advantages included: focusing on agreed priorities with co-ordinated programmes of assistance; extending the number of food aid donors by allowing countries with small and intermittent surpluses to take part; obtaining a wider range of food commodities, more in keeping with the eating habits and customs of recipient countries; reducing transfer costs through more efficient, common shipping and transport arrangements; sharing the burden of providing aid; and taking the politics out of food aid programmes.

Concerning WFP itself, the report considered that while it should continue to pursue the project approach in the provision of food aid, to which it had been restricted by its constitution, WFP should also experiment with other approaches to help development. While WFP experience had shown that the project approach was effective, the number of sound projects that recipient countries could formulate and implement, and their administrative and budgetary capacities to handle, was limited. WFP and other aid programmes should help developing countries reduce those constraints. But there were a number of developmental needs that could be met in other ways. A solution might be found in what was called a 'multiproject approach' by which a number of projects could be considered jointly in the context of a country's development plan.[62] This would facilitate WFP's support

108 *1945–70. Early Attempts: FAO's Pioneering Work*

for integrated regional and area development programmes. It also had a number of other advantages. WFP commitments could be switched from activities within a multi-project that were performing badly to those progressing well. Small-scale activities could be incorporated or they could be brought together within the framework of what was called 'multi-purpose projects'. A number of small activities could then be supported in one approved projects without creating excessive overhead costs.

The report recognized that food aid could also support the national development plans of developing countries. Preference could be given to assisting countries whose development plans involved a considerable expansion of employment and thus the demand for food. Within this approach, food aid could be tied to an approved body of projects to be executed as part of a development plan. In addition, if there was a major expansion of WFP resources, contributions might be made on a significant scale for the establishment of national food reserves.

WFP collaboration with the UN and its specialized agencies 'should be deepened and become more sustained'. Close attention should be given to the association of WFP assistance with the technical services provided by the UN and its specialized agencies; the formulation by them of projects within their own mandates that could benefit from WFP assistance; provision of technical advice and support during the implementation of WFP-supported projects; and, specifically, closer collaboration with UNICEF.

The report also called for closer collaboration between WFP and international organizations outside the UN system and with bilateral food aid programmes. WFP aid had not been provided in association with food aid from other sources during its three-year experimental period because of the need to evaluate its performance before a decision was taken to continue its operations. This was no longer necessary. WFP could take part in consultative groups and aid consortia, and in jointly-financed projects, in which its aid could be combined with bilateral assistance. Collaboration with non-governmental organizations could also be 'substantially increased'.

The proposal that WFP should provide non-food items in kind, in addition to food commodities, proved to be a controversial issue. The non-food items that might be channelled through WFP were identified as fertilizers, pesticides, specific types of farm machinery, and storage equipment and materials. It was recognized that the impact of WFP-assisted projects could be considerably enhanced if food aid was accompanied by these non-food inputs. More aid could be provided by supplying non-food items at concessional prices than by providing food aid alone. And the surplus capacity of developed countries would be utilized, thereby creating greater employment.

However, certain negative factors were noted. In view of the lack of interest shown by potential donors in making non-food items available as aid through WFP, the danger of such aid displacing pledges of food, and the desirability of WFP concentrating its efforts on food aid, it was decided that it was inadvisable to embark on changes in WFP's operations. WFP did set up a small non-food items unit in 1974 to obtain such items directly related to WFP-assisted development

The Development of Food Aid 109

projects and emergency operations. These items included trucks to transport food from ports and border stations to project sites and distribution centres, storage and packaging materials, insecticides and fumigation liquids, and kitchen and canteen equipment. Tools, equipment and materials needed to implement WFP-assisted development projects were also supplied. Donors mainly provided these items in kind although some also made cash grants available to WFP on an annual basis for the purchase of the items required.

Further consideration of these multilateral food aid studies was interrupted by a world food crisis at the beginning of the 1970s, leading to a new agenda for action. In the meantime, food aid remained a controversial subject. Some, like Hans Singer, who played a major role in the international debate on food aid and the creation of WFP, have seen the opportunities that it can provide as well as the challenges its presents as an effective aid resource not only in times of emergency but also for addressing food insecurity and assisting the developmental aspirations of the hungry poor (Shaw, 2002b). Others have criticized food aid for creating disincentives for small farmers in recipient countries by depressing food prices, distorting markets, discouraging agricultural policy reform and fostering dependency, and the high transfer costs associated with the typing of food aid to donor countries and types of commodities (Clay and Stokke, 1991; Clay et al., 1998; Clay, 2005). They also point to it decline in absolute value and relative importance from over 20 per cent of total Official Development Assistance (ODA) in the mid-1960s to below five per cent since the mid-1990s, and the large increase in the relative share of food aid deliveries as humanitarian relief for increasing numbers of people caught up in crisis-related emergencies at the expense of development programme and project aid.[63] Controversy surrounding food aid has been heightened as it has become a key unresolved issue in the Doha Development Round, leading to a statement on food aid for sustainable food security (von Braun, 2003), and the call for a 'global food aid compact' (Barret and Maxwell, 2006), to reduce disputes and increase the effectiveness of food aid. Against this background, WFP has emerged as 'not only the world's largest humanitarian agency, but one of its most respected and effective' (Evans, 2006). And there is general agreement that, in many situations, food aid is often a necessary, if insufficient, resource for achieving sustainable food security, and that like all aid, much depends on the ways in which its is provided and used in concert with other types of aid resources.

Annex 9.1. Guidelines and Criteria for Food Aid

The Committee on Food Aid Policies and Programme recommends the following guidelines and criteria for bilateral and multilateral food aid programmes so that food aid can make a more effective contribution to the solution of the food problems of developing countries. As agreed by the [1974] World Food Conference and subsequently endorsed by the United Nations General Assembly, the long-term solution to the problem of food shortages in the developing countries lay in increased production in those countries. In the interim, food aid would continue to be needed for providing emergency relief, combating hunger and malnutrition, promoting economic and social development, and food security.

(a) Food aid should be provided in forms consistent with the development objectives of recipient countries, with the aim of promoting their long-term development efforts and ensuring that it neither acted as a disincentive to local food production nor had adverse effects on the domestic market and international trade, in particular of developing countries. For maximum effectiveness, project food aid should be coordinated, to the fullest extent possible, with financial and other forms of development assistance.

(b) In order to facilitate the effective planning and implementation of development and nutrition programmes, governments of recipient countries needed to have assurance of adequate food supplies over a sufficiently long period. To that end, all donor countries should make every effort to accept and implement forward planning, preferably on multi-annual basis, in physical terms as appropriate, so as to ensure continuity of food aid. Periodic assessments of food aid needs should be undertaken with a view to assisting planning and programming of its provision and use in donor and recipient countries respectively.

(c) Food aid in support of economic and social development projects should be programmed on a multi-annual basis, taking full account of the special needs and priorities of recipient countries and the nature of the projects themselves. Such multi-annual commitments could be subject to periodic revisions by mutual agreement as regards commodities to be supplied and the use of counterpart funds for various development activities in recipient countries.

(d) In the allocation of food aid resources, donor countries should give priority to low-income, food-deficit countries.* Due attention should also be given to the food aid needs of other developing countries in support of projects specifically designed to benefit the poorest segments of their populations. An important consideration in allocating food aid to the eligible countries should be a strong commitment on the part of their governments to development policies for achieving self-reliance, reducing poverty and improving nutritional status particularly in rural areas.

(e) For the poorest countries, donors should undertake to finance, to the maximum extent possible, transport and storage costs, as appropriate, of donated food commodities, for emergencies and for use in developmental projects, including special feeding projects, in food-for-work schemes and for other specified target groups in those countries.

(f) Food aid should be provided essentially on a grant basis to developing countries, in particular to the least-developed and most seriously affected among them.

(g) Donor countries should channel a more significant proportion of food aid through the World Food Programme and other multilateral institutions.

(h) Donor countries should make efforts to provide wherever possible cash resources with a view to financing food aid through triangular transactions between themselves, developing food exporting countries and recipient countries, including coverage of shipping costs wherever applicable, and further diversifying the varieties of food provided as aid. Such arrangements would increase the participation of developing exporting countries in providing food aid.

(i) In allocating and utilizing food aid, donor and recipient countries should give priority to

- Meeting emergency requirements. To that end, countries in a position to do so should earmark part of their national grain stocks or funds for emergency purposes as envisaged in the International Undertaking on World Food Security. Wherever possible, arrangements should be made to increase food aid levels to meet the needs of large-scale emergencies. Among other steps, countries which have not yet contributed to the International Emergency Food Reserve should do so, and other donors should make additional contributions so as to meet the minimum target, as established from time to time,[**] on a continuing basis with yearly replenishments.
- Activities designed to increase agricultural, and especially food, production, to raise incomes, to meet basic needs and stimulate self-reliance and to create opportunities for employment for the populations of developing countries, particularly in rural areas, including education and training geared to the achievement of these objectives.
- Nutrition intervention programmes, with special emphasis on projects for improving the nutritional status of the vulnerable groups of pre-school children and expectant and nursing mothers.

(j) Donor and recipient countries should also, wherever appropriate, use food, financial and technical assistance for the creation and maintenance of food reserves, including storage and transport facilities in developing countries.

[*] The Committee considered that the term 'low-income' covered countries eligible for concessional assistance by the International Development Association (of the World Bank). The poorest countries within this group should receive special attention.
[**] Currently 500,000 metric tons.
Source: WFP (1979) *Report of the Seventh Session of the United Nations/FAO Committee on Food Aid Policies and Programmes*. Document WFP/CFA: 7/21. Annex IV (Rome: World Food Programme.)

Part II

1970–90. The World Food Crisis of the 1970s and its Aftermath

All governments should accept the removal of the scourge of hunger and malnutrition, which at present afflicts many millions of human beings, as the objective of the international community as a whole, and should accept that *within a decade* [emphasis added] no child will go to bed hungry, that no family will fear for its next day's bread, and that no human being's future and capacities will be stunted by malnutrition.

(Henry Kissinger's opening statement, World Food Conference, Rome, Italy: 5 November 1974; incorporated into *Objectives and strategies of food production*. Resolution 1 adopted by the World Food Conference, UN, 1975)

Every man, woman and child has the inalienable right to be free from hunger and malnutrition in order to develop fully and maintain their physical and mental faculties. Society today already possesses sufficient resources, organizational ability, and technology and hence the competence to achieve this objective.

(*Universal Declaration on the Eradication of Hunger and Malnutrition*. World Food Conference, November 1974, UN, 1975)

10
World Food Crisis

Hunger, and humankind's concern about it, goes back to biblical times, to the story of Joseph and the seven fat and lean years. In more recent times, since the eighteenth century, a number of 'waves' of food-population pessimism have been detected.[1] One was stimulated by Thomas Malthus and his dire predictions in *An Essay on Population* in 1789, another by the writings of Sir William Crookes and others in the later 1890s. A third wave followed the devastation of the First World War, and a fourth with the Second World War. Then, beginning in 1965, southern Asia experienced two successive years of monsoon failure, requiring massive aid shipments and triggering new fears of impending world famine. By the end of the 1960s, the Green Revolution and its promise of improved wheat and rice yields, began to level off. At the same time, expectations were rising in the developing countries as they became independent. And booming economies and rising incomes in the more developed countries were bringing a demand for more and better food. Populations continued to expand, along with concern about the carrying capacity of planet earth. The stage was set for a sixth wave of world pessimism at the beginning of the 1970s. There was a certain irony in the fact that this new wave of crisis thinking came at a time when the world food situation had actually been improving over the previous two decades: world food production increased by more than half and production per capita had gone up by 22 per cent.

Events leading up to the world food crisis of the early 1970s demonstrated how unpredictable and fragile the world food security situation was, and how quickly it could change.[2] The crisis originated from a combination of longer-term problems and temporary set-backs and suddenly emerged in a pronounced form in 1972. In that year, world food output declined for the first time in more than 20 years. World grain markets had continued to suffer from heavy surpluses at the outset of the 1970s. Concessional sales and food aid in grains exceeded 12.5 million tons. There was an abrupt change in 1972, however, when a combination of factors came together in a chain reaction that created the immediate world food crisis. For the first time in recent decades, adverse weather conditions affected agricultural production in several parts of the world simultaneously. In that year, world cereal production in wheat, coarse grains and rice fell by 33 million tons

115

116   *1970–90. The World Food Crisis of the 1970s and its Aftermath*

(approximately 3 per cent), instead of increasing by 2 per cent (25 million tons) as the growth of world demand required. The lack of some 55 million tons was felt and resulted in short supplies and increased prices. The sudden drop in food production occurred at a time when Canada and the United States were grappling with supply-management measures designed to bring down their large food surpluses by taking land out of production in the so-called 'set-aside' programme.

The supply problem was aggravated when the Soviet Union, after a disastrous food harvest in 1972, became a major grains importer (Table 10.1). Concealing the size of their domestic grains shortfall, the Soviets quietly arranged contracts to import about 28 million tons of grain at concessional prices, mostly from the United States, in the largest commercial transaction in history (Brown, 1975; Morgan, 1979). This led to a record level of world trade in cereals. US farm exports hit a record $21.3 billion in fiscal year 1974, two-thirds larger than a year earlier (Rahe, 1974). This could only be done by drawing on stocks. Thus, carry-over stocks were sharply reduced in the main exporting countries to their lowest point for 21 years. FAO estimated that carryover cereal stocks fell from 201 million

Table 10.1   World cereal supplies, 1971/72 to 1973/74

Cereal supplies	1971/72	1972/73	1973/74
	Million metric tons		
Wheat			
Production[a]	353.6	346.2	377.9
Imports[b]	52.1	67.6	64.7
Developed countries[c]	22.8	33.7	22.7
Developing countries	29.3	33.9	42.0
Closing stocks of main exporting countries[d]	48.8	29.0	20.7
Coarse grains[e]			
Production[a]	651.4	633.5	674.9
Imports	47.4	55.4	62.7
Developed countries[c]	40.9	45.4	48.4
Developing countries	6.5	10.0	14.3
Closing stocks of main exporting countries[f]	55.6	39.6	31.8
Rice (milled equivalent)			
Production[a]	205.9	195.7	214.3
Imports[a]	7.7	7.6	7.4
Developed countries	1.6	1.4	1.3
Developing countries	6.1	6.2	6.1
Closing stocks of the main exporting countries[g]	9.1	6.3	3.7

[a] Calendar years, 1971, 1972, 1973.
[b] Including wheat flour in wheat equivalent.
[c] Excluding trade between EEC member countries.
[d] Argentina, Australia, Canada, European Economic Community (EEC), United States.
[e] Rye, barley, oats, maize, sorghum and millets, mixed grains.
[f] Argentina, Australia, Canada, United States.
[g] Japan, Pakistan, Thailand, United States.
Source: FAO Commodity Review and Outlook, 1973–1974, Rome 1974.

tons in 1970 to 105–110 million tons in 1974, representing 26 per cent and 12–13 per cent of world consumption respectively (FAO, 1974). Critically, cereal stocks held in the major exporting countries dropped from 97 to 41 million tons over the same period, representing respectively 11 per cent and 4 per cent of total world consumption. Stocks in many importing countries were also sharply reduced. World cereal prices, which had been historically very stable, increased fourfold. Prices, instead of repeating their stability in the rather similar events of the mid-1960s, were triggered off by the Soviet purchases. At the same time, the oil producing export countries (OPEC) raised petroleum prices to unprecedented levels, which had the immediate effect of increasing the cost of fertilizer production and transportation. The combination of these events created a grave financing situation for the food-deficit developing countries, worsened even further by a simultaneous cutback in food aid supplies. The result was a real threat of worldwide food shortages, and even famine (Table 10.2).

Contrary to popular belief, in spite of their difficulties, developing countries had actually expanded their agricultural output in the 1950s and 1960s just as

Table 10.2 Changes in export prices of selected agricultural commodities, 1971–74

Year/month	Wheat (US no. 2, hard winter, ordinary f.o.b Gulf)	Rice (Thai, white 5 per cent, f.o.b. Bangkok)	Maize (Yellow no. 2 f.o.b Gulf)	Soybeans (U.S., c.i.f. Rotterdam)
	U.S. dollars per metric ton			
1971	62	129	58	126
1972	70	151	56	140
1973	139	368[a]	98	290
1972 January	60	131	51	125
June	60	136	53	138
December	104	186	69	174
1973 January	108	179	79	214
June	106	205[b]	102	470
December	199	521	113	254
1974 January	214	538	122	261
February	220	575	131	271
March	191	603	126	265
April	162	630	114	235
May	142	625	114	227[c]
June	156[d]	596	117[d]	–
July	169[d]	517[d]	135[d]	–

[a]Since Thai rice was not quoted regularly on the world market from the second week of March to November 1973, the annual average is an approximation based on the few quotations available.
[b]First week of March.
[c]First three weeks.
[d]Last three weeks of the month.
Source: United Nations (1974) *United Nations World Food Conference. Assessment of the World Food Situation present and future.* New York: United Nation.

fast as the developed countries, a truly remarkable achievement. The difference lay in their rates of growth in demand for food (3.5 per cent per annum in the developing countries compared to 2.5 per cent in the developed world) due mainly to faster population growth. But agricultural performance was by no means uniform throughout the developing world. While food production in the sub-continent of India rose impressively under the impact of the Green Revolution, it stagnated in sub-Saharan Africa. As a consequence, the need for food imports rose markedly in developing countries at a time when their ability to purchase them on commercial terms did not increase commensurately.

In addition to the accumulating problems of food production and availability, there was the equally vital issue of the nutritional adequacy of available supplies within developing countries and the extent of under- and malnutrition. It was estimated that two-thirds of the developing world's population lived in countries where food output had risen more slowly than the effective demand for food. And in most of those countries, growth in effective demand had not been rapid enough to reduce the number of people living in extreme poverty. As a result, progress in food production in the developing countries, together with progress in economic development, although significant, had not been sufficient over the past 20 years to reduce appreciably the incidence of hunger and malnutrition. In many countries, the *proportion* of the population suffering from under-nourishment had declined but, taking the Third World as a whole, the *actual number* of hungry persons had increased. This was what was called 'the grim centre of the world's food problem' (UN, 1974a, p. 55).

Assessing prospects for the next ten years, aggregate world food demand in the 1970s and 1980s was conservatively calculated to grow at an annual rate of 2.4 per cent (2 per cent due to population increase and 0.4 per cent due to increased purchasing power). This aggregate projection masked differences between developed countries, where the demand growth rate was estimated at 1.5 per cent per annum, and the developing market economies, where it was projected to be 3.6 per cent in terms of farm value. It also masked differences among developing countries. In some countries, a combination of rapid population growth and rapid growth in incomes would double the demand for food between 1970 and 1985. On the other hand, there would remain 34 countries in 1985, with a total population of 800 million, where effective demand would still fall short of food energy requirements.

The emergency of 1972–74 was not an isolated accident. It was the first intimation of what might become a recurring manifestation of an underlying basic imbalance. The prospect of mass starvation was averted, at least temporarily, by good crops in 1973 and 1974, but half a million people were estimated to have died due to food shortages, high prices and inadequate arrangements for emergency food distribution. Many more were to suffer hunger and malnutrition, which reduced their health and productivity, and increased their exposure to ill-health in later years. Against this background, it was concluded that food aid on grant and concessional terms would continue to be needed 'at least for the next decade' (UN, 1974b, p. 187). Three basic considerations led to this conclusion. Many developing countries remained prone to chronic or emergency food shortages. Several continued to face balance of payments difficulties, which severely limited their capacity to import food on commercial terms and to alleviate inflationary pressures on their economies. And there was persistent need to accelerate development by raising consumption, nutritional and energy levels of vulnerable groups of their populations and increase employment and income through labour-intensive development projects.

A major problem, however, was instability resulting from lack of reasonable continuity in food aid supplies. From a maximum of 16.8 million of cereals in 1964/1965, statistically recorded food aid fell to 7 million tons in 1973/74.[3] Between 1954, when the United States PL 480 food aid programme started, and 1969, food aid shipments accounted for between 30 and 45 per cent of total annual food imports of developing countries. A part of the food aid provided consisted of outright grants but a growing proportion took the form of loans in kind or was transferred under long-term credit arrangements, which had to be repaid at some time in the future. The main reasons behind the decline in food aid were seen to be low stocks, high prices, and a relative scarcity of supply of grains in relation to commercial demand. As a result, with food aid availabilities sharply reduced, food supplies as well as development programmes and projects were adversely affected in many low-income, food-deficit developing countries. In effect, food aid flows shrank at the very time when they were most needed.

The fact that trends in food supply and demand extended to 1985 (on the assumption of no major policy changes) could lead to a serious imbalance in the international situation, highlighted the urgency for an in-depth discussion of modifications in governments' food and agricultural policies, as well as in other sectors. One set of problems related to periodic food crises resulting from circumstance beyond human control, such as the weather, earthquakes and other natural disasters, which called for some form of world food security stock arrangement that had been proposed in the past. Equally important was the need for action to deal with the long-term problem of persistent malnutrition. The 'central problem' needing attention was seen as how to expand food production more rapidly in the developing countries. Farmers, especially the hundreds of millions of small producers in the developing countries, could make their contributions only if they were enabled to communicate more effectively with extension workers, scientists and government authorities. An urgent problem related to the supply of fertilizers. However vigorously these objectives of production expansion were pursued, they could be expected to show results only after a lapse of time. The contribution that food aid could make during the interim period in meeting at least a part of the urgent food needs of deficit developing countries therefore also deserved careful consideration.

Many independent observers believed that the situation was more serious than that depicted in official documents. An articulate proponent of this view was Lester Brown who completed two seminal studies for the US Overseas Development Council (Brown, 1970; Brown and Eckholm, 1974). He was of the view, increasingly widely shared, that:

The complexities of the food problem is such that we must ask ourselves whether it may not now exceed our analytical capabilities. Very few can embrace the disciplines which are central to an understanding of what is happening in the world food situation. As an agricultural analyst looking back over half of this decade, I find we have not done a very good job in anticipating the major new trends and development. (Aziz, 1975b, p. 10)

Brown identified four major factors that contributed to the instability in the world food economy in the 1970s: the decline of grain reserves; the disappearance of idled cropland in the United States; the dangerous dependence of the world on the food surpluses of one geographic-climatic region, North America; and the decision by the Soviet government to offset shortfalls through massive imports rather than through belt-tightening (Brown and Eckholm, 1974; Brown, 1975). He went on to found The Worldwatch Institute in 1974 and later the Earth Policy Institute in 2001, both interdisciplinary bodies from which he has continued to present an alternative, controversial, and often less optimistic, view of the world food security situation than the UN and international institutions concerned with achieving world food security. Brown was not without his critics who accused him of using selected facts about the world food problem to repeatedly advocate 'a few essentially technological fixes for what is after all a deep social malaise', and for misconstruing the world food crisis in which there was 'a severe shortage of food in the hands of the poor, though not in general terms world-wide'; and so 'the Holy Grail of redistribution is probably the only real solution to malnutrition – if it is ever reached' (Taylor, 1975).

11
World Food Conference 1974

The first warning of the gathering world food crisis was disseminated to the world press by FAO director-general Addeke Boerma on 1 February 1973. In the face of a mounting world food crisis, the heads of state or governments of the Non-Aligned Countries, at their fourth conference held in Algiers, Algeria from 5 to 9 September 1973, urged that an emergency joint conference of FAO and UNCTAD should be convened at ministerial level in order to formulate a programme of international co-operation to overcome the increasing shortage of food and other commodities and maintain stable prices (UN, 1974c). Another important impetus for a high-level international discussion on food problems came from Henry Kissinger, the US Secretary of State in the Nixon and Ford administrations. In a statement to the UN General Assembly on 24 September 1973 he said:

> The growing threat to the world's food supply deserves the urgent attention of this Assembly ... No one country can cope with this problem. The United States therefore proposes: That a World Food Conference be organized under United Nations auspices in 1974 to discuss ways to maintain adequate food supplies, and to harness the efforts of all nations to meet the hunger and malnutrition resulting from natural disasters. (Kissinger, 1973)

Why did Kissinger take this initiative at a time when President Nixon's attention was taken up with the Watergate scandal that eventually led to his resignation? There was a mixture of motives. First were his foreign policy interests. In Southeast Asia and in the Middle East, he had 'skillfully utilized the food aid resources as a means of pursuing larger diplomatic and strategic interests' in the context of Nixon's 'food for war' and the 'power of food' policies (Wallerstein, 1980, p. 198). As the world food situation deteriorated after 1972, in his capacity as National Security Advisor to President Nixon, it fell to him to develop a US response. Kissinger ordered the preparation of a 'National Security Study Memorandum on Food', which was completed late in 1972. Another competing interest grew out of the serious and worsening international economic situation, and the prevailing idea in the Nixon and Ford administrations, supported by the Office of Management and Budget, the Council of Economic Advisors, the Council for International

Economic Policy and the Treasury Department, of controlling inflation in the US by fiscal constraint. Food aid was a billion-dollar programme. If various agencies were called upon to show restraint, why not cut back on food aid as well? (Gelb and Lake, 1974–75). Food aid was caught in a budgetary squeeze. Kissinger therefore sought to share the burden of meeting developing countries' food needs not only with other major food exporting countries but also with OPEC nations that might be encouraged to help meet the costs of distributing US food aid shipments.

Additionally, Kissinger wished to keep the initiative in the White House, and later the State Department, away from the US Department of Agriculture and Agriculture Secretary Butz, whose views on free enterprise agriculture were against expanding food aid. Hence the proposal to have the World Food Conference meet under UN auspices, which was State Department territory, rather than the FAO, which was USDA's bailiwick. Moreover, the USSR while a member of the UN was not a member of FAO, and it was important to ensure the Soviet's involvement to obtain a global view and solution to the world food security problem. There was another, more personal, reason. As usual in issues of US food policy, the influence of Senator Hubert Humphrey was involved. James Grant, then president of the US Overseas Development Council, invited Sartaj Aziz, then director of FAO's Commodities and Trade Division, to Washington, DC for a briefing on the impending world food crisis. Afterwards, he persuaded Senator Hubert Humphrey and others to send a memo to Henry Kissinger to propose that the UN convene an international food conference to find sustainable solutions to the world food crisis. There was considerable opposition in the US Senate to Kissinger's appointment as secretary of state. It was reported that Humphrey dropped his opposition to Kissinger's appointment on condition that Kissinger endorse the World Food Conference, which he did in his first address to the UN General Assembly as US Secretary of State (US, 1975a, p. 86; Ruttan, 1996, p. 572 ff. 54; Dil, 2000, p. 25).

The US government followed Kissinger's proposal by suggesting that an item on this matter be included on the agenda of the twenty-eighth session of the UN General Assembly. The proposal was supported by well-known international figures such as Algerian President Houari Boumedienne and West German Chancellor Willy Brandt. A similar item was included on the agenda of the fifty-fifth session of ECOSOC, which decided, on 18 October 1973, to recommend to the UN General Assembly that such a conference be held in 1974, and requested that the governing bodies of all UN agencies discuss their own contributions to such a meeting as an item of top priority. As the UN specialized agency with the mandate for food and agriculture, FAO's reaction was particularly important. After all, the proposal could be interpreted as an indirect criticism of the past performance of international organizations, particularly FAO, and might detract from its image and mandate. At its biennial conference in November 1973, recognizing that the UN could best generate the political momentum to sustain the nature of such a conference, the FAO Conference welcomed (in its resolution 1831(LV)) such an effort under UN auspices and recommended that the proposed conference should focus on the resolution of the food problem within the larger context of overall economic development. It noted that FAO's role in such an effort would be essential and authorized the FAO director-general to commit up to $500,000 from FAO's working capital. It was also suggested that the logical location for the conference secretariat, preparatory sessions and the conference itself would be at FAO headquarters.

At the same time, ECOSOC took special note of the remarks of the FAO Conference and recommended to the UN General Assembly on 1 December 1973 that the conference be convened under general UN auspices. UN General Assembly resolution 3180 (XXVIII) of 17 December 1973 accepted the offer from the Italian government to convene the meeting in Rome in November 1974. It also established that the conference should take place at the ministerial level, gave ECOSOC overall co-ordinating authority, and authorized the UN secretary-general, in consultation with the FAO director-general and UNCTAD secretary-general, to appoint a secretary-general for the conference and a small secretariat.

In spite of US reservations, Sayed Ahmed Marei, who came from an agricultural background and a land-owning family, held senior positions in the Egyptian government, was special assistant to the Egyptian president, Anwar Sadat, and Minister for Agriculture and Deputy Prime Minister, was appointed as secretary-general.[4] FAO supported his appointment because it was thought that he would be more amenable to that organization. As it turned out, that was not necessarily so (see below). He appointed three deputy secretaries-general, keeping in mind the need for geographical and ideological balance among developing, developed and socialist countries: Sartaj Aziz from Pakistan, director of FAO's Commodities and Trade Division, who was charged with the substantive concerns of the conference and the production of the conference documentation; John Hannah from the United States, former president of Michigan State University and head of USAID during the Nixon administration, was primarily responsible for administrative and public relations aspects; and Aleksei Roslov from the Soviet Union, a career diplomat with no previous experience in agricultural matters, whose responsibilities were described as 'elusive' but primarily intended to maintain a Soviet interest in the conference.

Preparations for the conference were carried out through a Preparatory Committee, which was open to all governments and recognized observers. The committee met in three sessions in New York, Geneva and Rome before the conference started. A meeting of 'Interested Delegations' met just before the third and crucial session of the Preparatory Committee in Rome to discuss specific proposals for consideration by the conference. And a working group, on the UNCTAD model, was set up to engage in behind-the-scene activities and informal meetings to finesse controversy and move head more easily and rapidly on agenda items. Important contributions were made by outside consultants who provided a balancing perspective to the views of the staff of the UN agencies. They worked with FAO staff under the direction of Sartaj Aziz, with funding provided by the Ford and Rockefeller Foundations and the Canadian Institute for International Cooperation. Don Paarlberg, a senior official in the US Department of Agriculture, was seconded to work with FAO officials in Rome to facilitate co-ordination of US and other views and material for the final draft of the document assessing the global food situation.

124   *1970–90. The World Food Crisis of the 1970s and its Aftermath*

Ironically, the conference was held in Rome, where FAO's headquarters is located, but in a different part of the city (at the Palazzo dei Congressi, in the EUR district of Rome) and under UN, not FAO, auspices. ECOSOC decided to convene the conference from 5 to 16 November 1974 and requested the UN secretary-general to invite all member states and interested organs and specialized agencies of the UN, the International Atomic Energy Agency, and the General Agreement on Tariffs and Trade to participate. Non-governmental organizations in consultative status with EOCSOC and FAO, and other NGOs that 'might have a specific contribution to make to the work of the conference', were invited to send observers. Representatives of the liberation movements recognized by the Organization of African Unity and the League of Arab States were also invited to participate without the right to vote.[5]

The Preparatory Committee submitted reports to ECOSOC. The FAO director-general submitted a report to ECOSOC entitled 'Appraisal of prospective food deficits and food needs'.[6] Numerous proposals for national and international action were drawn up by the Preparatory Committee on the basis of a detailed assessment of the world food situation before the conference was convened (UN, 1974a,b). ECOSOC 'expressed its belief' that the results of the conference would constitute an important contribution to the preparations for the special session of the UN General Assembly devoted to development and international economic cooperation. Sartaj Aziz was intimately involved in drafting the proposals for national and international action in the face of the world food crisis assisted by a task force that was set up in FAO on 15 January 1974 initially of 15 staff, which grew to include over 30 people.

In his personal diary, he described what motivated him to adopt a five-point strategy in preparing the draft documents for the Preparatory Committee (Dil, 2000, pp. 526–50). First, he did not want to present an over-pessimistic outlook and wished to convey the message that the world had the capacity to feed itself, if every effort was made. Second, the only viable long-term solution to the food problem was to increase food production in the developing countries, a different approach to that adopted in the mid-1960s when the effort was on 'food aid for the starving millions'. Third, the object of increasing production should, however, be pursued within a development framework that required investment, imports, technology but above all a more meaningful political and institutional environment. Fourth, to the extent possible, he thought that the conference should endorse concrete targets for each major aspect, investment, imports and research. Finally, while the longer term solution to the food problem was being sought, the conference should lay the foundation for a world food security system which should include: a coordinated stock policy; a new food aid policy with a commitment of 10 million tons a year for three years; and better arrangements for meeting emergencies, including an international emergency reserve of half a million tons. He noted that this package did not emerge all at once but developed gradually in discussions in Washington, Brussels, London and Geneva, and with 'scores of representatives' in Rome. Throughout preparations for the conference, which he described as a 'constant tug of war', he noted that a US team led by John Hannah and financed by the Ford and Rockefeller Foundations tried to take over the role of preparing the conference documentation on grounds that 'FAO cannot give you [Marei] objective advise'.

The broad outline was not very different from the ideas presented in four position papers that Aziz had prepared between February and May 1974 on: the scope and objectives of the World Food Conference, key proposals for the conference; the creation of an agricultural development fund; long-term policy proposals for food aid; and international food reserves for emergencies. But the precise recommendations went back and forth as a result of discussions, and the final decisions were made only in July 1974. The main problem was to get a package of proposals that was meaningful to developing countries and at least negotiable for the developed countries. Left to the G77, Aziz felt that they would ask for too much, as they had done at two UNCTAD conferences, and got nothing. He rewrote some of the chapters of the document containing the proposals for national and international action for the consideration of the conference but the most difficult task he found was to write a 35-page summary of the whole document as a 'strategy', which he did in a single day (Saturday, 20 July; 9 a.m.–9 p.m.). He considered that the most difficult of all topics was that pertaining to the follow-up of the conference. The 'most important element' was the proposed agricultural development fund. The second was an overall coordinating body. Marei had proposed the concept of a 'World Food Authority' on 25 June, which became 'the most controversial' element of the conference documentation. Aziz described how the threat of a new UN body on food set off almost panic reaction in FAO. Another issue that 'took a lot of spade work' was that of trade and stability. He found UNCTAD's contribution on the subject 'very inadequate' and had to 'work hard' on redrafting it only to find that 'developing countries were not interested in stability' and that it was 'a miracle that an agreed resolution on trade emerged from the conference'.

Proposals for national and international action

The Preparatory Committee's proposed national and international action in a structuralist and institutional strategy for resolving the world food problem that consisted of two parts. The first was the threat of famine, food shortages, or excessively high food prices following dislocations in supplies caused by some disaster or unexpected fluctuations in production. The second was the ever-present hunger of the world's poorest people. Action needed to be pursued on these two fronts simultaneously: a world food production policy and a world food security policy, which taken together could lay the foundation of a world food policy. Neither could be effective without the other. 'There can be no food security if there is not more food production'. Some delegations argued that the food problem was insoluble unless linked to broad economic and social changes. Others believed that a wide-ranging discussion could not lead to the formulation of specific steps. They preferred to focus on narrower questions of food production and consumption.

126 *1970–90. The World Food Crisis of the 1970s and its Aftermath*

Ultimately, the main lines of the strategy were grouped under five main headings. First, the 'highest priority' was accorded to measures for increasing food production in developing countries within the wider framework of development. It was estimated that the minimum requirement was to step up the average annual growth rate of food production from 2.6 per cent in the preceding twelve years to at least 3.6 per cent in the next twelve years. If not achieved, given the likely increase in demand, the developing countries as a whole might face annual deficits of approaching 85 million tons in normal years and over 100 million tons in years of bad crops. The four main elements for accelerating food production in the developing countries were identified as: agricultural inputs, including fertilizers and water; agricultural research and technology focused on the tropical and sub-tropical regions where most of the undernourished people lived; overall rural development; and investment.

The second element in the strategy were policies and programmes for improving consumption patterns in all countries, aimed at ensuring adequate food availability in developing countries, particularly to vulnerable groups. It was estimated that at least 40 per cent of the estimated 460 million undernourished people in the world were children. It was proposed that at least one quarter of these undernourished children should receive supplementary nutrition at a cost of $20 to provide 600 additional calories and 20 g of protein to each child every day. Another target might be to concentrate on the undernourished populations of those least developed countries that were prepared to attach high priority to special feeding programmes for these people at a cost of $50 million a year for a ten-year period.

The third element was strengthening world food security through measures including: a better early warning and food information system; more effective national and international stock-holding policies and improved arrangements for emergency relief; and food aid. The fundamental objectives of world food security were identified as ensuring that all countries can:

- meet emergencies that occur in an uncertain world without a substantial cutback in supplies of basic foodstuffs to their populations;
- rely on the availability of supplies on commercial or concessional terms when formulating their own development strategies; and
- make agricultural production decisions in the knowledge of reasonable market stability and the continuance of stable trading relationships.

This concept of food security embraced both the reduction of risks emanating from unstable production and the provision of mechanisms whereby individual countries could obtain assistance to meet specific food shortage problems. It was recognized that many developing countries would require concessional food aid on a continuing basis if they were to sustain even a minimum level of food security for their populations. It was therefore suggested that governments should accept a concept of forward planning for food aid programmes, say on a three-year basis, with the aim of providing a minimum quantity of 10 million tons of grain a year to take care of 'hard-core' food aid requirements, the cost to be shared equitably between food-exporting and other high-income countries. Food aid could then serve a triple purpose in circumstances likely to prevail over the next several years through: helping to build up national grain stocks and operating part of a proposed emergency reserve; easing balance of payments difficulties; and relieving hunger and malnutrition, thereby contributing to medium and long-term progress in developing countries.

The fourth element was specific objectives and measures in the area of international trade and adjustment that were relevant to the food problem, including measures toward stabilization and the expansion of markets for exports from developing countries. Trade was seen to have two important links with food security. The availability of imports of basic foodstuffs played a major part in offsetting problems of domestic production fluctuations. If backed up by adequate and appropriately managed stocks, trade could relieve developing countries of much of the uncertainty associated with rapid economic change. This required adequate foreign exchange resources to pay for such imports. Countries requiring food imports on a regular basis should have export opportunities for their products, agricultural and non-agricultural. Food-exporting developing countries needed to have assured outlets for their surplus food. This could be partly achieved by triangular deals in which cash resources available for food aid were utilized for purchases in developing countries.

The final elements were arrangements for implementing the recommendations of the conference. It was proposed that a new body should be created, perhaps called a World Food Authority, to implement or co-ordinate the implementation of the recommendations and decisions of the conference. Such an authority would have three functions. It would mobilize international financial assistance for agricultural development in the developing countries. It would provide support to a wider system of world food information and food security and facilitate observance of the International Undertaking on World Food Security that had been approved by the FAO Council and Conference (see below). And it would facilitate implementation of the longer-term food aid policy proposed for adoption by the conference. The proposed authority would consist of: a permanent intergovernmental council with half its members elected by the UN General Assembly and half by the FAO Conference; an agricultural development fund to provide assistance for increasing food production in developing countries with its own board of directors responsible to the permanent council, with weighted voting rights in proportion to contributions; a committee on food information and food stocks; and a committee on food aid. The proposed authority's main purpose would be to strengthen effective action by existing agencies and provide a mechanism whereby governments could better co-ordinate international action and policies in the three interrelated fields of food production, food security and food aid.

The World Food Conference was invited to do three things: endorse the main elements of the proposed world food strategy outlined above; recommend how the strategy as a whole and its various parts should be implemented; and indicate how additional resources required for its implementation should be mobilized.

Rome Forum

As part of the preparations for the World Food Conference, at the suggestion of Sartaj Aziz, the secretary-general of the conference, Sayed Marei, asked Barbara Ward (Lady Jackson), the eminent economist and president of the International Institute for Environment and Development, to convene a meeting of independent scholars, economists, scientists, politicians and business leaders from 15 countries 'to consider the issues that are likely to arise [at the conference], to examine the proposals that are put forward, and to give guidance and leadership in the search for solutions (Aziz, 1975b).[7] The meeting, called the *Rome Forum*, took place on the first two days of November 1974, and adopted a declaration, which was presented to the conference's secretary-general and circulated to delegates and other participants on the first working day of the conference on 5 November 1974.

The declaration began by recognizing that the world food crisis 'was more serious than any that has been faced since the end of World War II'. Immediate action to ensure access to basic supplies of food, fertilizer and petroleum was considered to be the conference's 'first order of business'. But action was also needed for the longer term, for which the group identified three priorities. First, it supported the strategy of restoring grain stocks, of financing them internationally, and placing them under international supervision with an agreed policy on floor and ceiling prices. It also supported the policy of setting aside a 10 million ton grain reserve for meeting emergencies and for directly attacking diseases and disabilities due to malnutrition, particularly among children. The group recognized that to establish grain stocks and a food reserve progressively over the next three years might mean, once again, some reduction in the high consumption standards of affluent communities. Since, however, those standards were often a cause of ill health, 'sane nutrition dictates more modest diets'.[8] Second, it supported the setting up of an early warning system of impending food crises. And third, it endorsed the proposal for establishing an agricultural fund of the order of $18–$20 billion a year, with a $5 billion input of external resources, four times higher than aid to the farm sector in 1974.

The group agreed that the 'chief hope' for a sustained and reliable food supply for people in the developing world lay in 'a maximum development of their own capacity to produce food'. Four priorities for agricultural investment were identified. First, to ensure that the benefits of modern agricultural technology were extended to the whole farming community. Second, to integrate a new environmental dimension into farm practices. Third, to accompany increased agricultural investment with a really large application of new resources to research. And fourth, to combine expanded agricultural and educational investment within a wider context of modernization – in transport and communications, new settlements, decentralized industry, and health services, including local centres for family welfare and planning.

The group emphasized that its proposals would have no hope of success unless mobilized behind the political will of governments and people, and a system of supervision and monitoring that kept up the momentum for reform long after the conference had ended. The various elements of an agreed programme should be administered in such a way as to enhance collective effect and give the weight and urgency they deserved as 'a central means of human survival'. Possibly, a 'Food Security Council' could provide this leadership, comparable in composition and responsibility to the UN Security Council. The issue was 'finally one of political will'. In the group's view, the conference 'will have failed unless this response is undertaken now'.

The Conference

The general public had been primed on the world food problem and the issues facing the World Food Conference in a blitz of newspaper and other media coverage before the conference was called to order in Rome. *The New York Times*, for example, after three months of investigation, which included hundreds of interviews around the world and the publication of ten major articles, concluded that the world food problem was 'a much more complicated matter than the economic interplay of supply, demand, and price' (*The New York Times*, 1974). The conference, which opened on 5 November and continued to 16 November 1974, was attended by delegates and observers from 131 countries, 26 UN bodies, 25 intergovernmental organizations, liberation movements and 161 NGOs, who arranged their own parallel meeting.

It is important to note that the conference was held after a number of important international meetings. The United Nations Conference on the Human Environment had taken place in Stockholm, Sweden in 1972. More immediately, a special session of the UN General Assembly was held in April 1974, which adopted on May 1 a declaration (3201 (S-VI)) on the establishment of a new international economic order based on more equitable relations between developing and developed countries. The resolution called for changes in trade and aid and for the international community to assist in increasing food production as well as speeding up industrial and technological development in developing countries. The conference was immediately preceded by the UN Population Conference in Bucharest, Romania in September/October 1974.[9] This was also a time when the Group of 77 non-aligned nations and the OPEC countries 'flexed their muscles'.

The leading article in the first issue of the conference newspaper, PAN, on 'Why you are here', caught the mood of the moment (Allen, 1974). For many years 'the plight of the hungry millions has provoked amongst the affluent few hardly a pang at all – and then less often of conscience than indigestion'. So what was different about this food crisis? 'First, it was preceded by a wave of optimism. Second, it was (and still is) the biggest ever. Third, it affected the rich developed countries'. The article explained why this was a 'very good time' to have the conference. The 'crude conjunction of biological, political and economic events has brought home the inescapable interdependence of all nations and the folly of governments' persistent refusal to behave accordingly. It is not a comfortable message. It has provoked in the massive industrial powers a kind of geopolitical

130 *1970–90. The World Food Crisis of the 1970s and its Aftermath*

change of life, for its logic is that a shared world must share resources, and the rich have most to give. . . . If a public relations opportunity like this won't get results, what will?'

The conference was opened by the UN secretary-general, Kurt Waldeim (UN, 1975). He noted that it was the last of the conferences and debates that had made 1974 a year of 'unprecedented United Nations activity in the economic field'. In his opinion, food was not only the major economic and social problem faced by the international community in the 'present difficult period of perplexity and change', it was 'without question the most immediately important'. He said that it was difficult to review the sequence of events that had led to the food crisis 'without being dismayed by the lack of foresight and common interest shown by individuals, governments and the international community'. One exception had been FAO, whose warnings had been clear. As a consequence, many developing countries had become heavy importers of food. The higher prices that they had to pay for their imports had placed a severe drain on their foreign exchange reserves. A UN Emergency Operation had been established to assist the countries most seriously affected but this did not provide the answer to the problem of global medium- and long-term food sufficiency. Food production would have to more than double by the end of the century to provide improved nutrition for those who needed it most. It was the task of the conference to determine how that could be achieved but already there were certain 'incontestable essentials'. Developing countries would have to reassess their planning priorities. And industrial nations would have to be prepared to assist in 'massive transfers of capital and technology'.

Waldheim then broadened his perspective. Taking his cue from the statements of President Ford and Secretary Kissinger at the UN General Assembly, he added:

> I am firmly convinced that we can no longer speak of the problem of food or energy in isolation from the other forces which are shaping our lives. Our global interdependence as people, and the constantly growing interrelationship between political, economic, social, economic, and population factors, will make it increasingly difficult for any of us to discuss major world issues except as against the background of commonly agreed goals established by the world community working in concert.

In the opening session, Sayed Marei, the secretary-general of the conference, reviewed the proposals for national and international action that were placed before the conference by the Preparatory Committee. In his judgement, the following points were dominant: the balance between the rate of a nation's population growth and its increased food production; national action in developing countries to increase their food production; maximum assistance by the international community, particularly for agricultural development; and the strengthening and expansion of research facilities. Efficient international machinery was needed, either through existing institutions or the establishment of new ones. He stressed that the world possessed the means to produce substantially more food and that although the nation–state remained the unit for putting the necessary policies into effect, those policies must form part of a 'coherent, efficient and equitable global strategy'. He concluded: 'We have arrived at a new watershed of history. The future of our species depends on which road we take from here. Let us not be prisoners of the past but servants of the future'.

As the leader of the free world and the dominant player in the world agricultural economy, much depended on the position the United States adopted at the conference. As the proposer of the conference, expectations were raised that the US would be prepared to allow scope for some major initiatives in contrast to the negative stance it had taken on the proposals put forward by FAO in the past. Henry Kissinger, who had originally proposed the holding of the conference, gave the keynote address to a packed and expectant audience. Setting the conference in a wider context that befitted his political and diplomatic concerns, he said:

> Our challenge goes far deeper than one area of human endeavour or one international conference. We are faced not just with the problem of food but with the accelerated momentum of our interdependence. The world is midway between the end of the Second World War and the beginning of the 21st Century. *We are stranded between the inadequacy of the nation-state and the emerging imperative of global community* (emphasis added). (UN, 1975)

He then threw down a challenge that:

> all governments should accept the removal of the scourge of hunger and malnutrition, which at present afflicts many millions of human beings, as the objective of the international community as a whole, and should accept the goal that *within a decade* [emphasis added] no child will go to bed hungry, that no family will fear for its next day's bread, and that no human being's future and capacities will be stunted by malnutrition.

He outlined a five-point, 25-year plan to 'free mankind from hunger':

- increased food production in the developed nations;
- accelerated food production in the developing world;
- improving distribution of food throughout the world;
- improving the quality and nutrition of food; and
- creating worldwide reserves against food crises.

He emphasized that 'Supplies alone do not guarantee man's nutritional requirements ... even with massive gains in food production, the world could still be haunted by the spectre of inadequate nutrition'. Linking the food crisis to the population explosion, he said that 'Our minimum objective of the next quarter century must be to more than double food production and to improve its quality'.

In a carefully worded proposal for an international grain reserves system, Kissinger said that the conference should 'organize a reserve coordination group to negotiate a detailed agreement on an international system of nationally-held

132 1970–90. The World Food Crisis of the 1970s and its Aftermath

grain reserves'. He added, 'a worldwide reserve of as much as 60 million tons of food [and feed grains] above present carryover levels may be needed to assure adequate food security'. He commended the FAO director-general, Addeke Boerma, for his initiative in proposing an international food reserve system. In Kissinger's opinion, such a system should include all major exporters as well as the largest importers, and should include the following main elements: exchange of information on levels of reserve and working stocks, on crop prospects, and on intentions regarding imports or exports; agreement on the size of global reserves required to protect against famine and price fluctuations; sharing of responsibility for holding reserves; guidelines on the management of national reserves, including conditions for adding to, or releases from, the reserves; preference for co-operating countries in the distribution of reserves; and procedures for adjustment of targets and settlement of disputes and measures for dealing with non-compliance. Kissinger emphasized the importance of increased research and more effective and widespread consultations. He proposed three new groups in the face of the inadequacy of the extant world-order based on autonomous nation states: exporters planning group, a food production and investment group, and a reserves co-ordinating group.

Contrary to expectations, he gave no indication as to whether the United States would increase its food aid resources. Rumour had it that Kissinger had personally appealed to President Ford to allow him to announce an increase in US food aid at the conference (US, 1974b, p. 10). He did say, however, that the United States would be prepared to raise output but that the oil-producing countries should play their part in financing the distribution of food aid. Kissinger then flew out of Rome to Cairo to continue his shuttle diplomacy aimed at ending the October 1973 war between Egypt and Israel, leaving Agriculture Secretary Earl L. Butz as leader of the US delegation.

Butz views differed sharply from those of Kissinger. He sought four outcomes from the conference:

- real dedication to increasing technical assistance so that eventually all countries could fend for themselves;
- an improved system of guidance for all countries on what food was needed and where;
- a better reporting system of areas and times of surplus and deficit; and
- attention to the immediate short-term problem of rescuing those countries most seriously affected by food and cash deficits.

He hoped that the conference would not spend a disproportionate time discussing the distribution of food. The essential problem as he saw it was food production. This should be the focus and not a wider world food strategy, including trade issues, that the Preparatory Committee and the Rome Forum had advocated. Butz made it clear that he had no intention of announcing a major increase in US food aid. And he was firmly against any international control of American food stockpiles. His attitude at the conference led to an atmosphere of tension not only with other delegations but also within the US delegation itself, leading to Sayed Marei's classic diplomatic understatement, 'I must say the Americans did their part to make the world aware of food problems' (Ruttan, 1996, p. 172).

By the time of the opening of the conference, the US was caught in an awkward conflict of four competing forces (Wallerstein, 1980, pp. 197–203). The absolute supply of grain available for export as trade or aid was limited by the reduced size of the US crop and depleted government-owned reserves. A World Hunger Action Coalition, composed of church groups, voluntary agencies and congressional leaders, had coalesced around the American Freedom from Hunger Foundation in demanding that the United States increase its food aid contributions. The poor world harvest had placed a huge demand on US food, causing growers and exporters to exert pressure on the Nixon, and later Ford, administrations to avoid any restrictions on free market trade. And inflation had continued in the United States causing consumers to demand that there should be no further food price increases.[10]

The embarrassment was accentuated when it was discovered that at the time of the world food crisis, and severe global food aid needs, 67 per cent of Title I PL 480 aid programmed in fiscal year 1973 was targeted for South Vietnam, Cambodia and South Korea, and for fiscal year 1974, South Vietnam's share had jumped to 40 per cent and Cambodia's to 29 per cent. Proceeds from the sale of Title I commodities could be used by the South Vietnamese and Cambodian governments to free foreign exchange in order to purchase desperately needed war materiel. The Nixon Administration 'had clearly chosen to place strategic, political considerations ahead of humanitarianism in its food aid policy' (Wallerstein, 1980, p. 196).

George McGovern, then chairman of the Select Committee on Nutrition and Human Needs in the US Senate, had made the same point in a report produced by the committee's staff, at his request, based on hearing before the National Nutrition Policy Study held in June 1974, shortly before the start of the World Food Conference (US, 1974a). He said that he thought the conference represented an opportunity for the United States, 'the world's pre-eminent agricultural producer', 'to set a tone and climate that would enable progress to be made not just on the food front but on the critical inflation front as well'. But, he noted, Secretary of Agriculture Butz, who had been named to head the US delegation to the conference, had said regarding the position the United States should take at the conference: 'If we go in with a bag of goodies we are going to come out in bad shape. Our ability to deliver is limited this year'.

He agreed that the United States should not promise more than it was able to deliver. But it was equally true that the United States was 'still the wealthiest and most powerful nation on earth with a strong heritage of doing good works, most especially in the area of sharing our agricultural abundance'. Yet the staff study found that US food aid had not only been shrinking but that 'in the struggle over short supplies political concerns have received a high priority'. In addition, a task force appointed by the US Council for Agricultural Science and Technology had reported in December 1973 that an international emergency food bank, if established, 'would have little effect on United States farm prices and incomes. That little effect, however, would be positive' (US, 1973). If the stocks for the bank were accumulated at the support price, this 'might prevent farmers from removing land from production' and 'there would be little or no effect upon returns to farmers', if stocks were released before target prices were reached.

The dilemma was accentuated when on the second day of plenary sessions of the conference, the Canadian Minister of External Affairs, Allan MacDachan, announced an additional pledge of $50 million for food aid, followed by Australia, West Germany and Sweden, who also announced increases. Kissinger wanted to include an announcement of increased US aid in his speech to the special session of the UN General Assembly on 15 April 1974. But Treasury Secretary George Schultz objected on fiscal and economic grounds. With Nixon 'immobilized' by Watergate, Kissinger decided to include a carefully worded statement promising 'a major effort to increase the quantity of food aid over the level we provided last year'. Butz, not only made no mention of Untied States increased food aid but, adding fuel to the fire, expressed strong belief in the value of the profit motive, saying: 'In my country, farmers respond to the motive of profit. The opportunity for farmers to own and operate their own farm is an incentive'. The Democratic senators attending the conference, including Dick Clark, Mark Hatfield, Hubert Humphrey and George McGovern, were outraged and demanded that a cable be sent on behalf of the World Hunger Action Coalition to President Ford, who had by now taken over from Nixon, requesting a minimum increase of food aid of 1 million tons for the 1975 fiscal year.

In an address to the UN General Assembly on 18 September 1974, President Ford said:

> The food and oil crises demonstrate the extent of our interdependence.... Energy is required to produce food and food to produce energy – and both to provide a decent life for every one.... A global strategy for food and energy is urgently required.... It has not been our policy to use food as a polit-ical weapon, despite the oil embargo and recent oil prices and production decisions.... however difficult our own economic situation, we recognize that the plight of others is worse.... to make certain that the more immediate needs for food are met this year, the United States will not only maintain the amount it spends for food shipments to nations in need but *it will increase this amount this year* (emphasis added).

Now, caught in the glare of wide media coverage devoted to the world conference, Ford decided to stand by his adopted policy of fiscal restraint and declined to increase US aid, apparently deciding that 'the inevitable international criticism of his decision would be outweighed in the long run by the domestic benefits of restraining federal spending' (Wallerstein, 1980, p. 202). In a press conference, Butz explained that the reasons for turning down the request were that: it would have pushed up grain prices; reduced the amount of grain available for other programmes; and would have a harmful effect on the US budget, and that the Democratic senators were 'making a lot of noise' in 'trying to make news for themselves'. Anne Armstrong, President Ford's adviser and a leading member of the US delegation to the conference said: 'If the aim of this conference was simply to meet short-term needs then I would have said – let's all stay home and just send money'. Adding insult to injury, Butz flew to the Middle East during the conference to sell grain to Egypt and Syria. Ironically, the US official stance at the conference proved ultimately to have been unnecessary. Grain prices declined in December 1974 and into January 1975, and the rate of domestic inflation also began to slow down. This made it possible for Butz to announce later a substantial increase in the final food aid budget for the 1975 fiscal year.

Taking other line, George McGovern, supported by the other Democratic senators at the conference, proposed that all nations should agree to a 10 per cent reduction in military expenditure, estimated to be running at $200 billion annually. At the same time, the oil producing countries should give up 10 per cent of their new annual oil revenue, equivalent to $7 billion. The $27 billion thus accumulated should be transferred to a new 'International Food and Rural Development Authority' to execute a seven-point food plan of price protection: and safeguards for farmers; research and development for better seeds, pesticides, planting, harvesting and storage; construction and distribution of: fertilizer plants; harnessing and conserving water for irrigation; establishment of food reserves; developing nutrition standards and education, and providing special feeding programmes for infants, mothers and old people; and dissemination of information and materials. In a highly charged statement that won applause, he told a press conference that it was not likely that foreign aid would be increased in the present difficult political climate. Money would have to be found by altering priorities within present budgets. 'The world had been fighting the wrong war, with the wrong weapons and the wrong sense of values'.

In his address to a packed auditorium on the afternoon of the opening day of the conference, Addeke Boerma, the director-general of FAO, began by referring to Boyd Orr's vision of a World Food Board thirty years previously, the idea of what he called 'a great world food scheme, which will bring freedom from want of food to all men'. Yet, a generation later, the world food problem was unsolved, and was worsening. He said: 'There are more people in want of food today than at any time since Boyd Orr spoke'. This was 'the greatest scandal of our time. For at the planetary level, there need be no crisis at all'. With less greed and more compassion the world would not today see death by hunger as a reality for some, and a threat for many, among its citizens. The conference had been called to deal with the immediate crisis but, in his opinion, its main objective must be a commitment to action on the longer-term world food problem. As FAO had pointed out as long ago as 1956, the main cause of under-nutrition and malnutrition was poverty, and the main remedy against poverty was economic development.

Boerma called for a world food policy, including nutrition, as an integral part of a world development policy, with a commitment to action. The main element of a world food policy was a massive drive for increased production in developing

136 *1970–90. The World Food Crisis of the 1970s and its Aftermath*

countries. This would involve many things. The structure of a modern state cannot be built on the ruins of famished human beings. There must be a just balance between investment in food and investment in other sectors. Capital must be combined with technology and managerial skill. And they must be complemented by vastly strengthened measures for world food security. Here he referred to FAO's submission to the conference of a proposal for an International Undertaking on World Food Security as a first and minimum step. Another element was food aid. He appealed to donors to adopt a long-term policy for food aid which included a firm commitment to provide at least 10 million tons of grain a year and to the conference to endorse the idea of an international reserve for emergency purposes at the very modest level of 500,000 tons of grain. He identified the final elements in a world food policy as trade and measures for international agricultural adjustment. He called for political will to achieve 'a final victory in the greatest and oldest battle of mankind'.

Other delegations expressed their views at what one US reporter called the 'Roman circus' (Egerstrom, 1983). The Soviet Deputy Minister of Agriculture, B. Runov, said that the Soviet Union supported the idea of an agricultural development fund first proposed by OPEC member nations. He noted that the Soviet Union was already helping countries most in need with technical assistance, and providing fertilizer plants and irrigation schemes. He felt that the best way to improve production quickly was through progressive reform of the economic and social system, citing progress in Uzbekhistan (*sic*). The Soviets did not offer anything substantive and refused to endorse the idea of an improved food information system. They were accused of only bringing cynicism to the conference, and their intervention on the grain market was seen as a material threat to the wellbeing of the developing countries.

China told Third World countries to aim for food self-sufficiency in order to keep their political independence. The reason why developing countries were in difficulties was due historically to 'the plunder and control by colonialism, imperialism and the super powers' who 'imposed on them a one-sided, single-product economy and extorted super-profits, and therefore these countries have been unable to develop their national economies'. Chinese Vice-Minister for Agriculture and Forestry, Hao Chung-Shih, identified the UN General Assembly's adoption of the resolution on the establishment of a new international economic order as a 'significant victory for the united struggle of Third World countries'. The tide of international affairs was now in their favour. He called on developed countries to transfer agricultural technology to developing countries, for food imports at fair and reasonable prices, and for the removal of rich nations' import tariffs.

Representatives of the EEC refused to talk about stabilizing grain prices. Instead, they invited the major grain consumers and traders to participate in negotiations to establish a system of grain reserves that they felt would impart a greater degree of stability in grain markets. A special audience for conference participants was held at Vatican City where Pope Paul VI reminded delegates that when he visited India in 1964 he had launched a special appeal for a truly substantial commitment to reduce world hunger, mainly through reduction in arms expenditure.

He said that freedom from hunger was attainable but stressed that simply reducing hunger was not enough. He talked of a crisis in civilization and method, 'when too much confidence is placed on the automatic nature of purely technical solution, while fundamental human values are forgotten'. He reiterated the Catholic Church's opposition to birth control. Much of his speech was taken up with the need for the modern world to stop underestimating the importance of agriculture. 'In a word', he said, 'it is necessary to give to the farming community responsibility for their own production and progress'. The president of the International Federation of Agricultural Producers (IFAP), Charles Monroe of Canada, said that pre-conference consultation with farmers had been 'woefully inadequate', and added, 'The farmers' main fear is that in producing more they will simply find themselves depressing market prices'.

Holding the conference in Rome under UN auspices was seen, implicitly, as a sign of lack of confidence in FAO to deal with the world food crisis. FAO's director-general, Addeke Boerma, thought that FAO could handle all the follow-up work of the conference. He proposed that a special meeting of the major grain exporters and a group of the hardest hit importing countries immediately after the conference ended to investigate in depth the amount of cereals available for export during the coming year and the import needs of grain-deficit countries. Sayed Marei had different ideas. He believed that a high-level political body was essential to get the decisions needed. At the important third and final session of the Preparatory Committee that met shortly before the conference commenced, he had said that an institutional framework was needed that 'would have to reflect the world community's political will to eliminate the scourge of hunger. It would have to be a credible organ for mobilizing the new resources needed and speak with greater authority to both developed and developing countries than any existing mechanisms'.

But there were signs by only the second day of the conference that the Preparatory Committee's proposal for a World Food Authority would not be passed. Governments seemed to be generally agreed that the world food question should be given a new priority status at the international level and that its various facets needed to be better coordinated. But, at the same time, there was resentment that the proposal for a new authority had come from the Preparatory Committee, specifically from Sayed Marei himself, rather than emerging from deliberations at the conference. Sayed Marei had been advised not to press for the proposal by including it in the Preparatory Committee's final documentation to the conference. His views was that a high-powered, co-ordinating political authority at the ministerial level was more likely to produce results than a new or modified UN bureaucratic body and that it was also more likely to yield resources particularly from the new potential donors from oil-producing states who were not comfortable working with existing international financial institutions that appeared to be structured in favour of the leading industrialized countries (Weiss and Jordan, 1976, p. 26). Two interventions, one at the conference and one at the UN General Assembly, seemed to support his case. The head delegate from the Sultanate of Oman stated that his delegation did not think that a new World Food Authority would flounder for lack of financial resources. President Gerald Ford in his address to the UN General Assembly linked food to what he called the oil-producing nations' responsibility to formulate a 'global strategy for food and energy'.

There was mounting consensus against creating another piece of bureaucratic UN machinery. It was predictable that the most energetic criticism of the proposed World Food Authority came from the FAO secretariat. This was seen as a threat to FAO's mandate and rival in its own realm of competence. They vigorously lobbied against the proposal and proposed instead that FAO itself should undertake the primary responsibility for follow-up procedures after the conference. They failed to appreciate that the mood in the conference was that there was need for a political committee of ministers when it came to making policy and to get things done rather than relying on the traditional UN bodies that had failed to produce results. Therefore, in place of the proposal before the conference, various alternatives were suggested, including a World Food Council (WFC) with the same membership as the UN Security Council. The objective behind this proposal was to obtain from governments the same degree of political commitment to solving the problems of food and hunger as they gave to the issue of war. Under this plan, the proposed council would be answerable to the UN General Assembly on political issues and to an upgraded FAO Council on technical matters. It would have two committees, one on aid and another on food security. It was appreciated that any new body would have to take account of feelings in the G77 (the group of non-aligned countries) that the UN specialized agencies, including FAO, had inclined to a western view of development due to the heavy weighting of staff in favour of the major contributing donors.

But there was disunity among G77 member delegations. A row broke out over the Algerian draft resolution that the proposed council should be appointed by the UN General Assembly to give it more teeth. Other G77 members wanted an upgraded version of the FAO Council. Eventually, the G77 united behind a formula making the proposed council directly responsible to the UN Security Council. The developed country group wanted the proposed council members to be elected by ECOSOC. The Soviet Union put forward a compromise calling on the UN General Assembly 'to consider setting up a world food policy coordinating body . . . under the guidance of ECOSOC'. The location of the proposed council was also seen to depend on which existing UN body it would be most closely linked.

The G77 also drew up plans for a radical alteration of the world trading system. Its draft resolution called for: a completely new deal for developing countries on world markets; food at reasonable prices; reduction of food consumption in the rich states; an end to restrictive practices in the from policies of developed countries; preference to Third World country exports, even if they competed with domestically produced products; and postponement of debt repayments.

At the end of the conference, Sayed Marei made an 'objective and dispassionate assessment' of the outcome of its work. In his view, its first accomplishment was the widespread interest and concern that the conference had generated regarding the problems of hunger and malnutrition. Participants had recognized that all lived in an interdependent world and that no country could live in isolation.

The conference had accepted the overall assessment and seriousness of the food situation and had agreed on a broad strategy and a minimum package of national and international action on three important fronts: increased food production, especially in the developing countries; improved consumption and distribution of food; and building a system of food security. He identified as a notable achievement of the conference its resolution concerning the setting up of an International Fund for Agricultural Development (IFAD). Although it was only a start and the full potential of such a fund had yet to be developed, the co-operation of many countries with potential resources, particularly the response of the oil-producing countries, had been most encouraging. The decision of the conference on food information and food security represented another landmark. For the first time, the international community had laid the foundations of a food security system that could ensure the availability of adequate food to all at reasonable prices. He also singled out the recommendation of the conference that all donors adopt the concept of forward-planning of food aid to provide at least 10 million tons of grain as food aid every year.

The main challenge now was the effective implementation of the conference's resolutions. One area where the action of the conference had fallen short of his expectations had been the short-term food problem. The most seriously affected countries needed at least seven to eight million tons of additional food grain in the next eight to nine months. Unless that amount was provided quickly, a large number of people would face starvation. The conference had resolved that 'within a decade no child will go to bed hungry, that no family will fear for its next day's bread, and that no human being's future and capacities will be stunted by malnutrition'. History would take that pledge as a yardstick for judging the adequacy of the policies framed and the action taken.

Conference resolutions

In the event, the conference did not reach agreement on the grand strategy and the overarching institutional arrangements proposed by the Preparatory Committee or the Rome Forum for achieving world food security. Instead, a resounding 'Universal Declaration on the Eradication of Hunger and Malnutrition' was adopted, in which the conference 'solemnly proclaimed' that:

> Every man, woman and child has the inalienable right to be free from hunger and malnutrition in order to develop fully and maintain their physical and mental faculties. Society today already possesses sufficient resources, organizational ability and technology and hence the competence to achieve this objective. Accordingly, the eradication is a common objective of all countries of the international community, especially of the developed countries and others in a position to help. (UN, 1975, p. 2)

The Declaration recognized that the 'grave food crisis that is afflicting the peoples of the developing countries' was 'not only fraught with grave economic and social

140 *1970–90. The World Food Crisis of the 1970s and its Aftermath*

implications but also jeopardizes the most fundamental principles and values associated with the right to life and human dignity enshrined in the *Universal Declaration of Human Rights*' adopted by the UN General Assembly in 1948 (UN General Assembly resolution 217 A (III)). It also recognized that the elimination of hunger and malnutrition, included as one of the objectives in the *United Nations Declaration on Social Progress and Development* (UN General Assembly resolution 2542 (XXIV)), was 'the common objective of all nations'. It was also consistent with the aims and objectives of the declaration on the establishment of a new international economic order adopted by the UN General Assembly at its sixth special session in 1974 (resolutions 3201 (S-VI) and 3202 (S-VI)). It recognized that it was 'a fundamental responsibility of Governments to work together for higher food production and a more equitable and efficient distribution of food between and within countries'. Developed countries and others able to do so were called upon to collaborate technically and financially with the developing countries in their efforts. The Declaration reiterated that 'All countries, big and small, rich or poor, are equal. All countries have the full right to participate in the decisions on the food problem'. It also contained a definition of a world food security system:

> The well-being of the peoples of the world largely depends on the adequate production and distribution of food as well as the establishment of a world food security system which would ensure adequate availability of, and reasonable prices for, food at all times, irrespective of period fluctuations and vagaries of weather and free of political and economic pressures, and should thus facilitate, amongst other things, the development process of developing countries.

Recognizing 'the common responsibility of the entire international community to ensure the availability at all times of adequate world supplies of basic food-stuffs by way of appropriate reserves, including emergency reserves', the Declaration called on countries to 'co-operate in the establishment of an effective system of world food security' by: participating in the operation of four objectives that had been approved at the conference: the Global Information and Early Warning System on Food and Agriculture; the International Undertaking on World Food Security; earmarking of stocks or funds, and developing international guidelines, for meeting international emergency food requirements; and implementing the concept of forward planning of food aid and making 'all efforts to provide commodities and/or financial assistance that will ensure adequate quantities of grains and other food commodities'.

In addition, 20 separate resolutions were adopted relating to the food production, food aid and food security aspects of the world food problem, a number of which reflected work already carried out by FAO, and arrangements to implement the conference resolutions. As with resolutions adopted at other UN conferences, these resolutions were not legally binding (UN, 1975) (see Annex 11.1). A separate declaration was issued by the NGOs participating in the conference (see below).

Food production: The first resolution adopted by the conference on *Objectives and Strategies of Food Production* incorporated the challenge that Kissinger had thrown down in his keynote address on the first day of the conference that 'within a decade' no one should suffer from food insecurity. Other resolutions covered a range of issues related to the need to increase food production including: priorities for agricultural and rural development; increasing the production and application of fertilizers; research, extension and training in food and agriculture; a world soil charter and assessment of land capability; scientific water management for irrigation, drainage and flood control; recognition of the role of women in food production; increased production and application of pesticides; a programme for the control of animal tryanosomiasis in Africa; the development of the seed industry; the establishment of an IFAD; and, following the proposal of George McGovern, reduction of military expenditures for the purpose of increasing food production.

Food aid: One of the resolutions adopted by the conference concerned *An Improved Policy for Food Aid*. The resolution recognized that

> while the ultimate solution to the problem of food shortages in developing countries lies in increased production in these countries, during the interim period food aid . . . will continue to be needed, primarily for meeting emergency and nutritional needs, as well as for stimulating rural employment through development projects.

The resolution affirmed the need for continuity of a minimum level of food aid in physical terms in order to insulate food aid programmes from the effects of excessive fluctuations in production and process. It recommended that all donor countries should accept the concept of forward planning of food aid and set a target of at least 10 million tons of grain a year, starting from 1975, plus adequate quantities of other food commodities. The need to increase the resources of WFP was recognized to enable it to play a greater and more effective role in providing development assistance to developing countries in promoting food security and in emergency operations (UN, 1975, p. 15). A proposal to provide a minimum share of the annual food aid target to WFP (20 per cent was indicated) on an assured basis was not approved (UN, 1974b, p. 193). Instead, donors were merely urged to channel 'a more significant proportion of food aid through WFP'. Another resolution referred specifically to the provision of *Food aid to the victims of colonial wars in Africa*.

Food security: The conference also adopted resolutions (details of which are given below) to improve world food security including: an *International Undertaking of World Food Security*; a *Global Information and Early Warning System on Food and Agriculture*, which many considered to be FAO's major contribution to the conference; *Policies and programmes to improve nutrition*; *Achievement of a desirable balance between population and food supply*; and *International trade, stabilization and agricultural adjustment*.

Follow-up measures: The proposed World Food Authority was not approved, nor was the proposal made during the conference to establish a World Food Security Council. Instead, in a resolution on follow-up arrangements, the conference

142 *1970–90. The World Food Crisis of the 1970s and its Aftermath*

agreed to establish a WFC (see below). In addition, the conference recommended that FAO establish a Committee on World Food Security (CFS) as a standing committee of the FAO Council. The functions of CFS would include: keeping current and prospective demand, supply and stock position for basic food-stuffs under continuous review; making periodic evaluations of the adequacy of current and prospective stock levels in exporting and importing countries; and reviewing steps taken by governments to implement the proposed International Undertaking on World Food Security. The CFS would submit periodic and special reports to the WFC.

The conference was concerned not only in increasing the level of food aid resources but also co-ordinating the policies and programmes of all countries involved in food aid. For this purpose, the conference recommended that the governing body of WFP should be reconstituted and called the Committee on Food Aid Policies and Programmes (CFA). In addition to its administration and supervision of WFP, the CFA would undertake the wider functions of providing a forum for intergovernmental consultations on national and international food aid programmes and policies, with particular reference to possibilities of securing improved co-ordination between bilateral and multilateral food aid; review periodically general trends in food aid requirements and availabilities; and recommend to governments, through the WFC, improvements in food aid policies and programmes on such matters as programme priorities, composition of food aid commodities, and other related subjects.

The conference resolved that the proposed IFAD should be administered by a Governing Board consisting of representatives of contributing developed countries, contributing developing countries, and potential recipient countries, taking into consideration the need for ensuring equitable distribution of representation among these three categories, and should submit periodically to the WFC information on the programmes of assistance approved by the Board.

NGO declaration

The non-governmental organizations participating in the conference issued their own declaration, which was delivered to the secretary-general of the conference. They identified a number of 'principles' to guide their combined action. These included: every human being has the right to a regular supply of food adequate for total development; basic nutritional needs in infancy must be met at whatever cost; people must not starve within a world where there is sufficient food for all, even if this means changes in the wasteful food habits of the affluent, wherever they live; hunger or food must not be used as a political weapon; food and other assistance must be made available as an expression of social justice and fundamental human right; food security and the maintenance of adequate, readily available reserves must have at least as high priority as military security; secracy on trade, crop, food and nutritional situations must cease to be used in a world which requires openness for early warning systems against hunger; human development in rural family life must come from the combined efforts of all; and the ultimate success of technological improvement and governmental and inter-governmental action depends on the development and mobilization of the human race potential, including training for appropriate skills, of every country and community.

The NGOs identified a number of 'crucial areas for early action'. Immediate follow-up action was needed to ascertain necessary levels of emergency food aid, food security stocks, fertilizer supply and capital funds for agricultural development. The implementation of the recommendations and decisions of the conference required the operation of an institutional framework to guide activities beyond the immediate future. The conference, following closely the World Population Conference and the establishment of a UN Environmental Programme, should be seen as a component of integrated development in the Second UN Development Decade. The problems of food, energy, water, pollution, depletion of resources, population, status of women and trade relations were all aspects of a profound change in world society. NGOs had a particular task in making people aware of this change and helping them to cope with it. Last, 'but not least', all these efforts would come to naught in times of major war or violence. NGOs would actively strive to eliminate, wherever possible, the underlying cause of international conflict and urge a drastic reduction in the world's armament budgets, the savings to be allocated toward integrated socio-economic development, including food production and purchases.

Impact of the conference

One month after the conference ended, the UN General Assembly adopted without a vote a resolution (3348 (XXIX)) on 17 December 1974, which endorsed the *Declaration on the Eradication of Hunger and Malnutrition* and the resolutions adopted at the conference (UN, 1975). It also called on governments and organizations of the UN system to take 'urgent' and 'speedy' action to implement the conference resolutions. The outcomes of the conference received a mixed reception internationally, leading some observers to suggest that in evaluating its achievements 'one must be careful not to exaggerate its importance' (Weiss and Jordan, 1976, p. 75). On the other hand, what might have happened without the conference? There can be little doubt that the conference served to generate widespread interest and concern about the problems of hunger and malnutrition and initiated action to alleviate them. The conference received 'high marks for its efforts to publicize the food issue and to institutionalize follow-up procedures' and 'focused the globe's attention on the lamentable human incapacity to satisfy the most basic of human needs' (Weiss and Jordan, 1976, p. 4). The conference 'was a success, too, because it did not, as such meetings often do, stop with adopting sound substantive Resolutions, but went on to assign responsibilities for effective follow-up' (Martin, 1974, p. 119). The main challenge after the conference was for the international community to effectively implement the 19 programmatic resolutions the conference had recommended. From the outset, there had been a clear realization of the need for more systematic approaches to agricultural development and food supplies. Since the Second World War, there had been many international conferences and other less formal meetings which had adopted laudable

144 *1970–90. The World Food Crisis of the 1970s and its Aftermath*

reports and resolutions but whose implementative machinery was totally inadequate to the task.

The most important factor in accounting for the success of the meeting was considered to be 'the almost total agreement that the time was right to discuss globally the problem of food' (Weiss and Jordan, 1976, p. 157). The urgency of the problem was perceived and acted upon by all concerned. Political pressure was brought to bear by individuals, private groups and organizations. National delegations were basically agreed upon the nature, dimensions and overall solutions to the problem. The fact that, 'The need to eat is shared by everyone', suggested that international discussion of global food supplies may be more advantageous than discussions on other global problems (Gardner, 1974, p. 46).

The leadership provided by the conference's secretary-general, Sayed Marei, who was not part of the career service of any international organization and an active political force, both during the preparations for and during the conference itself, was another important contributory factor. His deputy secretary-general, Sartaj Aziz, was the leading force in organizing the indispensable support and contributions of FAO, the formulation of proposals and policy ideas, preparation of the conference documentation, and in resolving differences and generating agreement before and during the conference. Before joining FAO, Aziz had been invited by Lester Pearson, the former Prime Minister of Canada, in 1969 to join the staff of the Commission on International Development that produced the famous report on *Partners in Development* at the request of the president of the IBRD, Robert McNamara (Pearson, 1969). Aziz attended a conference at Colombia University in New York in February 1970 to discuss the implications of the Pearson report organized by Barbara Ward who was a visiting professor at the university at the time. The conference adopted 'The Colombia Declaration' dethroning growth as the primary development objective and began the search for a more meaningful and broader concept of economic and social development.

Both the work on the commission and the conference had a profound effect on Aziz and his future work in the area of hunger and poverty (Dil, 2000, p. 24). One assessment was that 'the foresight and behind-the-scene efforts of Deputy Secretary-General Aziz ultimately influenced the content of all the important program resolutions of the Conference' (Weiss and Jordan, 1976, p. 103). Summing up his role in the conference, the *FAO House News* of December 1974 wrote: 'Mr Aziz was generally acknowledged as the backbone and the nerve and brain centre at the working level of the Conference'. One journalist wrote: 'On the word of almost every journalist who was in Rome that November, it was Mr Aziz who made the conference work and who shaped its two week's work so that at the end it voted unanimously for a comprehensive attack on world hunger' (Power, 1979). Barbara Ward said that 'without him there would have been no Rome Forum. I admire him for his wisdom, dedication, and hard work with which he organized the World Food Conference. He is a good man dedicated to improving the human condition and his work for the welfare of the hungry and poor deserves better recognition' (Dil, 2000, p. 24).

During the conference, Aziz gave, by his own count, between 20 and 25 press, radio and TV interviews and watched the major developments unfold from the 'control room'. He wrote Marei's closing speech, revised a number of the draft resolutions, and persuaded the drafting committee to include Kissinger's now famous goal ('within a decade no child will go to bed hungry ...') in the first resolution adopted at the conference. In many respects, the work of the Preparatory Committee and the meeting of interested delegations and working groups were as important as that of the conference itself in resolving differences and reaching agreement on basic issues before the conference began. And the arrangement of conference documentation into two comprehensive volumes, which separated the assessment of the food problem from proposals for action, rather than a plethora of separate papers, which had been the practice at previous international conferences, facilitated discussion and ultimate agreement. The conference could therefore begin with broad agreement on the nature and dimensions of the food problem and get down to business quickly to proposals for action.

The conference helped to reinstate the importance of agriculture in economic and social development and caused development economists to reconsider the emphasis they had placed on industrialization as the pathway to economic growth. It also re-emphasized the importance of the human factor in sustained and equitable economic advancement and rekindled the strong latent humanitarian forces that existed in the international community. While underlying the sovereignty of nations enshrined in the UN *Charter*, it also pointed to the responsibilities of governments in developing countries to take action to ensure the well-being of their own citizens, supported by increased and co-ordinated assistance from developed nations.

In accepting the dimensions and proportions of the world food problem, and recognizing the seriousness of the situation, in themselves important achievements (Wilson, 1974), governments implicitly reflected a sense of urgency in preparing for a conference at such short notice and explicitly agreed on a package of proposals for action based on three pillars: increased food production, especially in developing countries; the improvement of consumption and distribution of food; and an international system of world food security. Three categories of programmes emerged from the conference, which added to its positive achievements: financing agricultural development, food security and co-ordinated action (Gardner, 1974). Many believed the resolution to set up an IFAD as a key achievement of the conference. The institutional framework for co-operation among countries with potential resources, particularly the oil-producing (OPEC) countries as well as the developed OECD countries, was what many delegates and international officials believed to have been the essential *raison d'etre* of the conference. Progress was also made in terms of both an understanding of the concept of world food security and the foundations of a food security system was laid progress by bringing together the need for improved information and early warning, food aid and stock-holding arrangements, and fair and liberalized agricultural trade. And progress was also made in the essential need for co-ordinated action.

Rather than threatening the work and status of FAO, the conference had a rejuvenating effect. A number of the conference's resolutions were based on previous FAO work. In his post-mortem of the conference's results, FAO director-general Addeke Boerma said that FAO 'will consider a substantial change in its priorities for agricultural development as a result of the conference' (PAN, 1974). A special session of the FAO Council was held in March 1975 to discuss the future role of FAO in light of the decisions of the conference. Discussion centred around the fact that the overwhelming proportion of work for new programmes fell on FAO. A budget of approximately $185 million was proposed, an increase of $81 million over the previous biennium, about half of which was accounted for by new programmes and the other half by increased costs.

In this sense, the conference was a distinct advancement on previous international conferences. Shortly after the conference, Sartaj Aziz prophetically summed up the uncertainties surrounding the agreements reached on basic issues and the constraints of politics:

> These are very solid accomplishments, and if actions come near to matching words, it may in the course of time be regarded as the most successful UN conference ever held. Yet, will these decisions and recommendations taken together really solve the world food problem? Will they be implemented fully and effectively? (Aziz, 1974)

And he regretted that two main elements of food security, a global system of food reserves and a better deal for agricultural trade, had not been secured (Power, 1979).

His diary recorded that after the conference he was 'seriously worried and disillusioned' (Dil, 2000, p. 528). He found that the conference had brought out 'the selfish and sordid features of the world. Everyone was playing politics. The human or the moral angle was not important for everyone except in making speeches. No one paid any attention to the short-term problem while people are dying'. He thought that the United States had accepted the target for food aid because it gave a chance to put pressure on the Arabs and that 'even the Arabs accepted the proposal out of political pressure and not the love of humanity'. In the end, he thought whether the conference would solve the food problem 'very much an open question'. The ultimate solution lay with the developing countries themselves: 'the conference has at best given them a breathing space of a few years'.[11]

The establishment of a WFC as the designated institutional vehicle to ensure the implementation of the conference resolutions was seen as an effort to avoid the mistakes of the past when hunger and malnutrition were assigned low priority by governments and international organizations and to stimulate the mobilization of adequate financial and policy resources in order to achieve food security for all as the first of all human rights. On the other hand, although the conference recommended an impressive list of resolutions, it failed to agree on a grand design to achieve food security for all as proposed by the conference's Preparatory Committee and the Rome Forum of world authorities. The WFC was seen by some as a pale reflection of the originally proposed World Food Authority or World Food Security Council, which might have had the same prominence and authority of the UN Security Council. The conference failed to agree on proposals aimed at pegging international commodity prices, rationing food stuffs and indexing third world import costs to export prices. Particularly glaring, it did not come to terms with the all-pervasive effects of sharply rising oil prices on world food security. It was right to ask oil producers to help developing countries with their oil deficits, but oil producers also had the right to ask that developing countries should be helped through liberalizing trade and increasing their export revenues as well as through providing food aid.

The conference also exposed the serious divisions and contradictions among decision-makers and institutions in the United States, and between developing and developed countries, an ominous omen for future decisions and action on future world food security. The conference was considered to be a 'considerable success' from the US standpoint and the US objectives were considered to have been 'almost completely achieved' (US, 1974b, p. 39). The broad objective of the United States in entering the conference was described as 'the establishment of a substantive and organizational framework for concerted international efforts on several fronts to combat the food problem', which 'was wholly achieved'. The major accomplishment of the conference was regarded by the US as 'the creation of a series of follow-up activities and organizations to implement a wide range of specific, useful, and agreed upon recommendations for national and international action'. But the United States also recognized that whether the conference ultimately produced beneficial results depended on the 'degree of seriousness' with which follow-up action was pursued by international agencies and participating governments, 'particularly the major developed and developing nations'.

Ultimately, despite its achievements, the conference failed to agree that the world food problem was essentially a global political issue of the first magnitude that could neither be resolved by technicians or ministers of agriculture alone, nor by a single conference or by governments alone, nor in isolation from related world problems, including population, energy, environment and resources. And with its focus on 'the world food problem' and the need to increase production and stability of supplies, it failed to address adequately 'the world food security problem', including measures to ensure access of the poor to the food they needed. To the large and hungry portion of humanity, a conference to consider what can be done through common action might well have been seen as an event that was long overdue. But for others it was at best an important step in 'a crisis-ridden journey from here [1974] to the twenty-first century' (Wilson, 1974).

Barbara Ward captured the mood of the time in her Foreword to the book on the Rome Forum, *Hunger, Politics and Markets*, edited by Aziz and published after the conference (Aziz, 1975b). Referring to the numerous international conferences, special sessions of the UN General Assembly and the 'numberless' consultations that had taken place before the World Food Conference, and were planned to take place afterwards, she wrote: 'Our planet is in the middle of an unprecedented dialogue about itself. ... The whole world seems full of moving delegates, declarations, speeches, disclaimers, corridors of rumour, endless shifts behind

148   *1970–90. The World Food Crisis of the 1970s and its Aftermath*

the scenes ... Like an anthill that has received a sudden violent kick, the great termitery of Planet Earth is all movement and confusion. But the discoveries are real and the discussions of unprecedented urgency'.

She noted that in 1970, as in 1950, the wealthy 'developed' markets still had 80 per cent control of the world's wealth for not more than a fifth of the world's people. This relationship had to be grasped and understood for the world was undoubtedly a market but was not 'by any stretch of the imagination a community'. Demand for food would rise steadily as the world population doubled by the year 2010. But this would not all be 'effective demand' as three quarters of the increased demand would be among those with less than $200 a year and hence barely entered the market. And on the supply side, there would be a tendency to higher prices. Only North America had 'any hope' of providing immediate food surpluses on any scale as she put it: 'Leave grain to an uncontrolled market and only the rich will eat.' And, she noted, 'they are over-eating now. To have obesity a widespread disease in a starving world is itself a perversion of right order. "Grain shekhs" we can all become, using our appetites to rig the market'.

Then, she added provocatively

If the human race cannot agree on food, on what can they agree? If the self-proclaimed 'Christians' countries of the West who pray, 'Give us this day our daily bread', are not prepared to give it to anyone else, they deserve the mockery and collapse that follow upon too wide a breach between principle and practice. If those who worship Allah, the all-Merciful, the all-Compassionate, do not spontaneously help those whom their new wealth most depresses, they, too, weaken the ultimate moral cement of their own societies. 'The people of the Book' who have monopoly control of what the world most needs – bread and energy – are directly challenged to go beyond the idols of the market and to create instead a moral community for all mankind.

It was not as though the route forward were 'dark and unexplored'. In her view, the 'triple strategy' adopted by the World Food Conference – the creation of a 10 million ton grain reserve, a longer-term buffer stock plan, and, 'perhaps the most vital element', an agricultural development fund – 'meets the main weaknesses of the unmitigated market approach'. She regarded the chances of success 'better perhaps than one might fear', although the first meeting in 1975 of the WFC set up to monitor implementation of the conference's resolutions and coordinated the work of the concerned UN agencies 'was a setback since the developed countries committed themselves to little action and still seemed dedicated to the kind of preponderance in controls they inherited from a recent colonial past'. But, in her opinion, the seventh special session of the UN General Assembly held in September 1975 on development and international economic cooperation, which reaffirmed 'full support' for the resolutions of the World Food Conference (resolution 3362 (S-VII)), 'marked a genuine step forward towards a constructive dialogue on all points at issue', giving 'more elbow-room for the poor' and 'more dignity and equality in devising policy'.

Annex 11.1: Resolutions adopted by the World Food Conference

I. Objectives and strategies of food production.
II. Priorities for agricultural and rural development.
III. Fertilizers.
IV. Food and agricultural research, extension and training.
V. Policies and programmes to improve nutrition.
VI. World soil charter and land capability.
VII. Scientific water management: irrigation, drainage and flood control.
VIII. Women and food.
IX. Achievement of a desirable balance between population and food supply.
X. Pesticides.
XI. Programme for the control of African animal trypanosomiasis.
XII. Seed industry development.
XIII. International Fund for Agricultural Development.
XIV. Reduction of military expenditures for the purpose of increasing food production.
XV. Food aid to victims of colonial wars in Africa.
XVI. Global Information and Early Warning System on Food and Agriculture.
XVII. International Undertaking on World Food Security.
XVIII. An improved policy on food aid.
XIX. International trade, stabilization and agricultural adjustment.
XX. Payment of travel costs and other related expenses to representatives of national liberation movements.
XXI. Expression of thanks.
XXI. Arrangements for follow-up action, including appropriate operational machinery on the recommendations or resolutions of the Conference

Source: UN, 1975.

12
International Undertaking on World Food Security

The dramatic depletion of cereal stocks in the major exporting countries called public attention to the importance of maintaining an adequate year-round flow of food. In addition, the declared intention of the major exporting countries to prevent the accumulation of surpluses in the future caused all nations to re-examine their stock-holding policies. A resolution on an *International Undertaking on World Food Security* (IUWFS) had been endorsed in principle by the FAO Council at its sixty-third session in July 1974 (FAO, 1973, chapter 14, annex A). This resolution was submitted to, and endorsed by, the World Food Conference. In doing so, the participating governments accepted the following unprecedented responsibilities. They recognized that world food security was a common responsibility of all nations. They also agreed to cooperate to attain the objective of world food security, defined as

> ensuring, to the utmost, the availability at all times of adequate world supplies of basic food stuffs, primarily cereals, so as to avoid acute food shortages in the event of widespread crop failures or national disasters, sustain a steady expansion of production and consumption, and reduce fluctuations in production and prices.

Recognizing that food security had to be tackled from several sides, especially through strengthening the food production base of developing countries, appropriate national stock policies, food aid programmes, and other measures, including long-term trade agreements, governments undertook to adopt national and international measures to ensure an accelerated growth of food production, for which assistance was needed by the developing countries.

As regards stock-holding policies, all governments were required, in conformity with their institutional and constitutional constraints, to establish cereal stocks (at the end of the marketing year) that would maintain a minimum safe level of basic cereal stocks for the world as a whole. In periods of acute food shortages, nations holding stocks in excess of minimum safe levels for meeting domestic needs and emergencies undertook to make such supplies available for export on reasonable terms. Detailed guidelines for establishing and holding food stocks were incorporated into the IUWFS resolution and special assistance to developing countries was called for in financial, technical and food aid to increase food production, meet emergencies and establish food reserves. The resolution also recognized that the effective functioning of a world food security system depended on timely and adequate information. To keep governments informed, the FAO director-general was requested to prepare concise factual appraisals of the situation and outlook for the international cereals position during periods when world supplies were scarce. Intergovernmental consultations should also take place, with the assistance of FAO and other concerned intergovernmental organizations, on progress in implementing the IUWFS and on action required to resolve urgent food security problems. The IUWFS resolution was adopted by the FAO Council at its fifty-fourth session in November 1974 after the World Food Conference.

With the endorsement of the IUWFS, governments, for the first time in thirty years, accepted a proposal in favour of world food reserves (FAO, 1975). They had been fully aware, since the First World War, of the danger of food shortages and the need for greater stability in the world food economy. These anxieties had been standing items on the agendas of international meetings and had inspired a continuing stream of plans and proposals, which led to nothing or to calls for further studies. With the adoption of the IUWFS, a new attitude emerged due, in the main, to a sense of urgency generated by the severe food crisis of the early 1970s and the virtual disappearance of carryover stocks in the major food exporting countries. But it was also due to the fact that the proposal for an IUWFS, unlike previous attempts in the field of emergency planning, recognized the limits to which governments were willing to go in accepting commitments affecting their sovereignty.

The first lesson learnt from the failures of the past was that nations were not ready for internationally controlled supply schemes. The IUWFS was firmly grounded on national policies, national control of food production and stocks, and national financing, with some degree of international co-ordination. It followed the voluntary consultative approach developed for certain FAO commodity schemes. It also did not presuppose legally binding agreements on any specific formula for market stabilization or stockholding. Instead, it embodied a 'solemn pledge' by governments to achieve stated objectives without making this conditional upon the outcome of subsequent meetings. There were to be no more feasibility studies, which proved fatal to many past initiatives on world food security. Experts were now expected to say how, not whether, the necessary results could be attained.

Specialized bodies therefore set to work on the practical implementation of the IUWFS. They were confronted with the same difficulties that had dogged the attempts of their predecessors. But the ground had been cleared. They were now working in the context of an agreed global strategy defined by the World Food Conference. Streamlined machinery was set up in the field of information, co-ordinating procedures were established in FAO, WFP and the World Bank, and the need for a higher degree of world food security was a recognized element

152 *1970–90. The World Food Crisis of the 1970s and its Aftermath*

of the new international economic order expected to emerge from the Second UN Development Decade of the 1970s. A modicum of success was therefore anticipated. But it was also appreciated that success was bound to be severely limited and fall short of expectations if some major nations, particularly the United States and EEC countries, could not be persuaded to make the IUWFS a truly global scheme with global burden-sharing.

Minimum safe level of global food stocks

Agreement on the IUWFS inevitably raised the question as to what was the minimum 'safe' level of world cereal stocks. In 1974, the FAO secretariat prepared an estimate in the context of the objectives of world food security as defined in the IUWFS. At the same time, agreement was reached on the precise definitions of terms used in estimating the minimum 'safe' level of global cereal stocks, itself defined as 'the level of total carryover stocks required to ensure in the following season continuity of supplies on national and international markets, and to maintain consumption levels and safeguards against acute shortages in the event of crop failure or natural disaster'.

As the FAO secretariat acknowledged, there were many alternative ways of measuring the level of a minimum safe level of cereals to ensure the maintenance of desirable consumption levels in years of production shortfalls. By 1974, there was a sizeable literature on the subject and FAO's Intergovernmental Group on Grains had already addressed the subject (FAO, 1974). Each method had its own merits and shortcomings and looked at the same problems from different angles in an attempt to arrive at a figure for the world as a whole, or for individual countries, that would best reflect the concept of an adequate level of stocks. The inadequacy of basic data limited the significance of any single result achieved. Therefore, FAO used a variety of rather simple statistical methods in an effort to find a range of answers from which a final figure, based essentially on FAO's best 'judgement', could be derived.

The analysis aimed at measuring the disposable 'reserve' stocks (defined as 'all stocks in a country in excess of working stocks and stocks retained for strategic purposes') required to maintain consumption levels at the world level. This was not the summation of the stocks that each country alone would need to meet its own production shortfalls. And it did not measure the stocks required for complete price stability in world markets. It implied complete accessibility to the reserve stocks by all countries facing serious shortages irrespective of which country was holding the stocks. Working stocks were defined as 'the stocks required to assure a smooth and uninterrupted flow of supplies from the farmer or point of import to the processor and ultimately the consumer'. The estimated reserve stock was equal to the quantity that exporting countries would hold if they were keeping the total 'reserve' element for the world. To the extent that countries holding stocks were not prepared to put them at the disposal of other countries facing shortages, the total reserves to ensure maintenance of consumption levels for the world as a whole would be correspondingly higher. This would be offset partly, however, to the extent that large countries, notably the Soviet Union, that were responsible in the past for most of the production shortfalls, held national reserve stocks to meet their own major deficits in the future.

The *FAO* analysis was carried out for wheat, coarse grains and rice separately, and then aggregated to give a total for all cereals. The possibility of some substitution between the three cereals was taken into account, especially that of wheat for rice. Three basic methods were used to measure the level of emergency stocks. What was referred to as 'Method A' was an historical analysis of past trends in area, yields and domestic consumption in cereals exporting and importing countries to measure deviations from trends of these variables in the two trading groups. 'Method B' was a measurement of the maximum single-year shortfall in actual production below trend during the period 1955–72 for each grain at the world level as an indicator of the need for reserve stocks. It was argued that this method was imperfect to measure the need for reserve stocks because it implied that countries having production above trend would share their surpluses with deficit countries. 'Method C' was an historical analysis (for all countries for which stock data were available) of past ratios of carryover stocks ('supplies from crops harvested in the previous seasons (or from imports) that remain available in a country at the beginning of the new crop season') to total disappearance (domestic consumption plus exports) in exporting countries, and to total domestic consumption in importing countries, in order to identify those ratios that in the past related to normal or 'abnormal' situations in the grain economy.

The three methods gave similar results. They suggested that in order to maintain world consumption of cereals, the minimum 'safe' level of world stocks for all cereals would need to be within the range of 17–18 per cent of world cereals consumption. Of this total, the 'reserve' element would amount to 5–6 per cent of world consumption, the remainder representing the 'working stock' element. Based on the 1973/74 world cereal consumption level, the minimum 'safe' level of world stocks (including the Soviet Union and China) would be 225–230 million tons for all cereals (93–96 million tons wheat, 101 million tons coarse grains and 31–33 million tons rice), of which the reserve element would be 66–71 million tons (30–33 million tons wheat, 27 million tons coarse grains, and 9–11 million tons rice). At this level, the reserve would be sufficient to maintain world consumption levels for one year in around 95 per cent of the cases, thus leaving a 5 per cent risk of a production shortfall being larger than the reserve. The balance between the total safe level of stocks and the reserve element (159 million tons for all cereals) would be required for working stocks.

Sufficient has been said above to show that calculating a desirable level of world food stocks is a complicated business, and far from an exact science, for which assumptions and qualifications must be made. The FAO secretariat recognized that the desirable level of stocks could vary depending on the various objectives sought, for example, stabilization of prices within agreed limits, meeting emergency needs, and stabilizing supply. The specific purpose of the FAO secretariat's estimation was to assist in the evaluation of the adequacy of current and prospective stocks in line with the objectives of world food security as defined in the IUWFS, to assure a regular flow of basic foodstuffs to meet requirements in domestic and world markets in times of short crops and serious crop failure. This estimate was primarily based on an examination of past fluctuations in production so as to measure the possible magnitude of shortfalls in cereal supplies in any one year of crop failure. The purpose was to derive the smallest size of reserve stocks that would provide a designated level of world food security under a given set of assumption. It was considered more important to express the 'safe' level of stocks as a percentage of total consumption rather than in absolute terms to allow for automatic adjustment in line with the growth in food consumption.

The FAO secretariat acknowledged that the methods used to estimate the desirable cereal stock levels 'had several limitations'. Basic statistics of world stocks and consumption were incomplete and when available often included a large margin of error. A suitable and meaningful statistical methodology that would reflect all possible combinations was difficult to construct. The methods used may be inconsistent with each other and therefore the results may not be entirely compatible. And the statistical facts should be supplemented with well-informed judgements about the needs for these commodities. The estimates adopted were therefore a judgment that was regarded as reasonable in the light of actual experience and future expectations in the world grain economy. The estimates finally proposed and adopted were regarded as reasonable but it was recognized that as data improved, and greater experience was obtained through consultations, more accurate estimates may be developed in the future.

13
An International Grain Reserves System

After considerable internal deliberations in advance of the World Food Conference, the US government adopted a position favouring the negotiation of an international grain reserves system provided each country could chose its own method for holding and controlling the reserves. President Ford set forth the US position regarding food reserves in a speech at the United Nations on 18 September 1974 when he said

> to ensure that the survival of millions of our fellow men does not depend upon the vagaries of weather, the United States is prepared to join in a worldwide effort to negotiate, establish, and maintain an international system of food reserves. This system will work best if each nation is made responsible for managing the reserves that it will have available.

Secretary of State Kissinger amplified the US position in his keynote address to the conference (see above). While not endorsing any specific plan, US congressional support for negotiations looking toward an international food reserve system was expressed in legislation passed in 1974 and 1975. The US House of Representative resolution 1399 of 3 December 1974, stated that

> International agreement should be sought for a system of food reserves to meet food shortage emergencies and to provide insurance against unexpected shortfalls in food production, with costs to be equitably shared and farmers given firm safeguards against market price disruption from such a system.

In early 1975, when international price and supply pressures started to ease, the United States began considering various means by which an international structure could be created in order to prevent the recurrence of the extreme fluctuations in commodity prices experienced between 1972 and 1974. In this context, in both the US Senate and House of Representatives, H.R. 9005 of 1975 authorized and encouraged the US President to seek international agreement for a food reserve system to meet food shortage emergencies and to provide insurance against unexpected shortfalls in food production with the costs of such a system equitably

156   *1970–90. The World Food Crisis of the 1970s and its Aftermath*

shared among nations and with farmers and consumers given some safeguards against market price disruption from such a system.

After the World Food Conference, the principal forum for international discussion of a food reserve system was the International Wheat Council (IWC) (later changed to the International Grains Council) in London, UK. Wheat accounted for the largest share of food grains in international trade and IWC members were experienced in implementing the International Wheat Agreement with its conventions on wheat trade and food aid. In February 1975, at the US initiative, an *ad hoc* meeting of the major grain-producing, consuming and trading countries was convened at IWC headquarters in London to discuss the food security problem. At the council session that followed, a Preparatory Group was established to consider the possible bases for an agreement to replace the International Wheat Agreement. The group received various papers and met periodically throughout the year. At its third meeting on 29–30 September 1975, a paper was presented by the US delegation entitled *US Proposal for an International Grain Reserves System* (US, 1975b).[12] The plan had been awaited with great interest by the other participants because of the pre-eminent position of the United States in agricultural grain exports, which included about half of all world wheat trade, and the significance of US views for any agreement.

The US proposal was set forth in terms of concepts for an international grains reserves system rather than in the textual form of a treaty. The precise language for any such agreement would have to be negotiated. The principal features of the proposal were:

- the establishment of reserves totalling 30 million metric tons (25 million tons of wheat and 5 million tons of rice) in excess of working stocks;
- each participating nation would be responsible for holding an equitable share of the reserves, its share to be determined by such criteria as its volume of food grain trade, its financial capacity according to gross domestic product, and its variances in food production;
- each participating nation would pay for the cost of managing its reserves and would determine how its reserves are held;
- reserves should be built up, or released, according to guidelines for co-ordinated action triggered by quantitative indicators of amounts of grain available. The indicators would be based on stock levels and on deviations in production from long-term production trends;
- shortage situations could be met by a one- and, if necessary, a two-stage response: first, a warning stage, at which time a potential shortage would be identified and participants would consult on what action was warranted, and would co-ordinate on agreed conservation measures; second, should action under the warning stage be insufficient and a shortage stage reached, participants would be obliged to make their reserve stocks available up to the holding commitment of each;
- participants in the system would receive assured access to supplies from the system at market prices;

- to allow for the successful operation of the system, participants would have to supply timely information on crop prospects, supply availabilities and stocks, anticipated demand and international trade in grain; and
- developing countries would receive financial or food aid from developed countries to help them meet their reserve obligations.

The primary objective of the US proposal was to insure availability of grain in the event of serious production shortfalls. It was considered that a reserve system so large as to cover all possible contingencies would be too large and too costly to be practical. However, a less than completely comprehensive reserve could offset a substantial portion of likely shortfalls. Hence the proposal for a 30 million ton reserve, which was estimated to cover about 92.5 per cent of projected food grain shortfalls. (The 60 million ton reserve put forward by Kissinger at the World Food Conference included feed as well as food grains.) The US proposal at the International Wheat Council left open for later consideration whether the system should be extended to include coarse grains, used for livestock feed in some parts of the world and for human consumption in others. The US proposal recommended 'special assistance' to developing countries to help them carry their reserve shares under the system.

Proponents of the US proposal saw several significant advantages for the United States. The cost of holding reserve stocks would be spread among members of the system. In the past, as the largest producer of grains in international trade, the US had carried the major burden of holding stocks and customers had come to count on the US granary to make supplies available. The reserve would draw in supplies when production exceeded demand, thus helping to deter a depression of prices received by US producers. Stocks from the reserve would not depress prices to uneconomical levels because their release would be prevented except in times when demand exceeded normal supplies. The holding of reserves globally and the information and consultation procedures would work against sudden large and disruptive purchases, such as that by the Soviet Union in 1972. And the creation of a reserve system with its guarantees concerning supplies would provide an important assurance to customers of the reliability of the US as a supplier.

Differences of opinion concerning food reserves, particularly between the US Department of State under Secretary Kissinger and the US Department of Agriculture under Secretary Butz, had been expressed in inter-departmental discussions on the subject. The State Department tended to view a reserve system as a desirable means of moderating domestically and internationally disruptive effects of the wide fluctuations of grain prices. It saw a reserve system as a help in promoting world food security in general as well as an aid to poor countries suffering from unexpected food disasters. The US Agriculture Department tended to stress increasing production as the prime foundation for promoting world food security and that of developing countries. With a strong emphasis on free enterprise as the best system for increasing food production, it disliked proposals for governmental intervention in the market and particularly any scheme that might involve allocation of available supplies.

These differences were known to delegates during discussions on the US proposal for an international grains reserves system at the IWC and were not helpful to the US negotiating position. The representatives of the US agencies concerned appeared to be united in their opposition to a high-price support function for the proposed reserve, which would amount to an international subsidy for protective high-cost agricultural markets, such as that of the EEC. The Australian and Canadian delegates made some supportive comments. Delegates from the developing countries showed interest in what assistance might be available to them in maintaining reserves. The Japanese evinced interest in assistance in supply. The Soviet delegation was non-committal but 'unfriendly'. The Chinese, not members of the IWC, did not attend the discussions, adding to the presumption that they would not be interested in joining the proposed system. The sharpest questioning came from the EEC representative. While the proposal evoked much interest, the many reservations raised by the country representatives at the IWC resulted in that it failed to gain approval.

14
International Emergency Food Reserve

In the meantime, the UN General Assembly urged all countries to subscribe to the proposed *International Undertaking on World Food Security* and build up and maintain world food grain reserves to be held nationally and regionally, and located strategically, large enough to cover foreseeable major food production shortfalls. It was proposed that the wheat and rice components of the reserve should be 30 million tons. Pending the establishment of the reserve, developed countries, and developing countries in a position to do so, were urged to earmark stocks and/or funds to be placed at the disposal of WFP as an *International Emergency Food Reserve* (IEFR) to strengthen its capacity to deal with food crisis situations in developing countries. The aim was a target of not less than 500,000 tons, plus small quantities of other appropriate foodstuffs (UN, 1976).

When WFP was established in 1961, a small part of its resources were earmarked by its governing body for emergency food relief on the approval of the FAO director-general. Between the beginning of its operations to the time of the World Food Conference in 1974, 178 WFP emergency operations had been approved in 76 countries at a total cost of $136 million. In responding to emergency situations, WFP was handicapped not only by the size of the resources available for emergency food relief but also by its inability to respond quickly. Food commodities pledged were not held by WFP but kept in storage in donor countries around the world, which took time to release and deliver. WFP did not have its own transport and logistics facilities but had to purchase them with its limited cash resources. Attempts to convert WFP into a world food bank or a world food fund in the decade after it began operations might have increased its resources but they came to nothing.

At the Second World Food Congress in The Hague in 1970, the government of the Netherlands (FAO, 1970, p. 135), supported by the UN secretary-general (UN, 1971a, pp. 22–4), made a proposal to establish an 'Emergency Food Supply Scheme', which was presented to WFP's governing body for approval (WFP, 1971). The purpose of the scheme was to increase the effectiveness and operational speed of WFP emergency operations and thus increase its capacity to cope with disaster situations. The proposed scheme would be on a voluntary basis using resources already pledged to WFP. There was no obligation for donors to incur additional costs in food and storage. Participants would inform WFP of the type

160 *1970–90. The World Food Crisis of the 1970s and its Aftermath*

and quantities of commodities that could be made immediately available for emergencies. But even this 'minimalist' proposal did not receive approval.

The establishment of the IEFR offered the prospect of additional resources for WFP's emergency operations. Modalities of IEFR operations were approved by WFP's governing body in 1976 and revised and enlarged in 1978 after protracted deliberations (WFP, 1978) (see Annex 14.1).[13] The IEFR was seen as a continuing reserve with yearly replenishments determined by WFP's governing body. The reserve was originally regarded as a multilateral standby arrangement to provide WFP with an initial, quick-response capability. It did not involve WFP holding food stocks in specific locations. Instead, donors were required to announce their contributions to the reserve one year in advance, and in addition to their pledges to WFP's regular resources. Contributors were expected to ensure that their food donations would be shipped in the most expeditious manner. They were also required to assume responsibility for meeting transport and other related costs. Developing countries not in a position to make contributions to the reserve could make interest-free loans of commodities to be used by WFP in the initial stages of emergencies, especially where such arrangements could speed up food deliveries. Part of the contributions to the reserve were to be made in commodities such as rice and white sorghum to take account of the food habits of afflicted people.

Intensive discussion took place in WFP's governing body between 1980 and 1982 on the proposals of FAO's director-general, Edouard Saouma, to convert the IEFR into a 'legally binding convention' and to strengthen its operations by increasing its target to 2 million tons of food commodities (WFP, 1981, 1982). The proposals were not approved. The procedures for approval by the FAO director-general of WFP emergency food aid were applied to operations under the IEFR. The modalities made provision for changes in the existing procedures 'at a later stage in the light of experience'. No changes were subsequently proposed. The result was that donors were reluctant to give the FAO director-general unrestricted authority over the potentially much larger emergency resources that were expected to become available under the IEFR. Their contributions were therefore much lower than anticipated. They were also tied to emergency operations that they, not the FAO director-general, chose to support.

Later, the IEFR was modified in two important respects. A sub-set of WFP's regular resources devoted to assisting development projects was established in 1989 for assistance to refugees and displaced persons in protracted emergency situations lasting more than one year, which relieved pressure on the IEFR and WFP's emergency food aid resources. Up to $30 million a year was set aside for this purpose. In addition, to speed up IEFR operations, an 'Immediate Response Account' (IRA) was approved by WFP's governing body in 1991 with an annual target of $30 million in cash as an integral part of the reserve, to enable rapid purchase of food commodities close to where emergencies occurred.

While the IEFR has improved and strengthened WFP's ability to respond to emergencies, it has not lived up to its original expectations. The reserve is not like a banks account readily available for WFP to use. Nor is it a stock of food kept by WFP to be quickly drawn from in times of emergency. It is a voluntary facility to provide emergency relief from food stocks and budgeted funds kept in donor countries. Furthermore, donors were not expected to place *all* their contributions to the reserve at WFP's disposal, which would have made it a fully multilateral facility. Where contributions to the reserve are not placed at WFP's disposal, participating countries are required to keep WFP informed about their use in order to co-ordinate all food assistance provided from the reserve.

Donors have not fully respected the IEFR modalities that they approved. Contributions have not been fully announced in advance. A high proportion of contributions have been tied and designated to specific commodities and emergencies *after* they have occurred, eroding the multilateral nature of the reserve, and making it difficult to respond rapidly and flexibly to emergencies whenever and wherever they occur. Contributions to the reserve have fluctuated considerably. And cash contributions have fallen short of requirements. Consequently, a timely and adequate response to all, and especially to less publicized, emergencies has proved to be difficult. Therefore, the world still does not have an adequate international emergency food reserve. A truly multilateral and fully subscribed emergency reserve would help to take the politics out of emergency aid, avoid the hardship and suffering that afflicted populations might needlessly endure, and limit the costs and diversion of funds for development that result from a late and inadequate response to emergencies.

Annex 14.1. Modalities for the Operation of the International Emergency Food Reserve[*]

(a) The CFA (Committee on Food Aid Policies and Programmes) agreed to consider ways and means of implementing resolution 3362 (S-VII) of the United Nations General Assembly, which urged all countries to build up and maintain food grain reserves in accordance with the International Undertaking on World Food Security, and that, pending their establishment developed and developing countries in a position to do so should earmark stocks and/or funds to be placed at the disposal of the World Food Programme as an emergency reserve to strengthen the capacity of the programme to deal with crisis situations in developing countries. The aim should be a target of not less than 500,000 tons.

(b) The International Emergency Food Reserve (IEFR) of 500,000 tons should be a continuing reserve with yearly replenishments determined by the Committee on Food Aid Policies and Programmes and placed at the disposal of the World Food Programme. The Reserve should be in the nature of a standby arrangement; it would not necessarily entail the holding by WFP of physically separate stocks in specific localities.

[*]In addition, at its Thirty-second Session in December 1991, the CFA agreed to Establish an Immediate Response Account of at least $30 million annually, as an integral part of the IEFR, for the purpose of purchasing and delivering emergency food aid in food shortage situations.

(c) Participating countries should, over and above their regular pledged to WFP, indicate to WFP at the beginning of each calendar year or other appropriate 12-month period, availabilities of primarily food grains from stocks held in these countries. For that purpose the definition of emergencies adopted by the Intergovernmental Committee of the World Food Programme remained a valid guide.**

(d) WFP should direct requests to draw upon such availabilities or funds to the participating governments. Reserves not called upon on any one year will be carried over into the next year.

(e) Insofar as possible, all availabilities or funds should be placed at the disposal of WFP and contributing countries should preferably indicate their allocations to the Reserve for more than one year in advance. In cases where the availabilities or fund were not placed directly at the disposal of WFP, the participating countries should keep WFP informed about their use in order to achieve co-ordination of the food assistance under the emergency reserve.

(f) The present procedures of WFP for the approval of emergency food aid should also be applied to operations under the Reserve. The CFA might consider changes in the existing procedures at a later stage in the light of experience.

(g) Developing countries not in a position to make contributions in cash or in kind to the Reserve should, where possible, make interest-free loans of commodities to be used by WFP in the initial stages of emergencies especially where such arrangements would speed up delivery of commodities.

(h) The governments contributing food to the IEFR should also assume responsibility for meeting the expenses of its transport and other related costs. When food contributions come from developing countries unable to finance such expenses, the Programme will explore the possibility of meeting such costs with other donors.

(i) When resources allocated by contributing governments to the IEFR are placed at the disposal of WFP, such governments shall take all possible measures to see that food is shipped in the most expeditious manner.

(j) Part of the contributions to the IEFR should be made in commodities such as rice and white sorghum to take account of the food habits of afflicted peoples.

Source: CFA (1978) *Report of the Sixth Session of the Committee on Food Aid Policies and Programmes*, October 1978, Rome: World Food Programme, Annex IV.

**For purposes of WFP emergency operations, emergencies were defined as 'urgent situations in which there is clear evidence that an event has occurred which causes human suffering or loss of livestock and which the government concerned has not the means to remedy; and it is a demonstrably abnormal event which produced dislocation in the life of a community on an exceptional scale'.

15
Global Information and Early Warning System

Experience has repeatedly showed that accurate, timely and commonly available information of an impending disaster, coupled with a sound and speedy response, are key factors in mitigating the effects of emergencies. The returns from national and donor investment in early warning and response systems could therefore be considerable. Human and economic suffering and damage could be saved or mitigated, and enormous costs and diversion of resources in protracted relief programmes could be avoided. An international aid programme combining financial aid and technology with skills transfer deserves the highest priority. It is recognized that the first step is to improve national reporting services in collecting and analysing a range of factors affecting national food security. Only to the extent of the availability of reliable data at the national level can an international system function effectively.

The threat of unpredictable widespread famine was highly dramatized by the British scientist and author C. P. Snow in an address at Westminster College, Fulton, Missouri, in the United States (the place where earlier Winston Churchill had made his famous Iron Curtain speech) on 12 November 1968. Snow made the dire prophesy that 'many millions of people in poor countries are going to starve to death before our eyes – or, to complete the domestic picture, we shall see them doing so upon our television sets' (Snow, 1968). Snow continued:

> the rapidity and completeness of human communications are constantly presenting us with the sight of famine, suffering, violent death. We turn away, inside our safe drawing-rooms. It may be that these communications themselves help to make us callous. And yet, perhaps also there is the unadmitted thought that human lives are plentiful beyond belief?

Snow predicted that local hunger would spread into 'a sea of famine' by the mid-1970. He called for 'three tremendous social tasks': a concerted effort by the rich countries to produce food, money and technical assistance for the poor; an effort by the poor countries themselves, on the lines of India and Pakistan, to revolutionize their food production; and an effort by the poor countries, with assistance from the rich, to reduce or stop their population increase.

163

Six successive years of drought in the Sahelian countries of West Africa called for a major international relief effort in the three years 1973–75. Seven countries with a total population of 25 million people were most affected. As the situation worsened into widespread starvation, the immediate priority was to provide relief food quickly. During the three-year emergency operation, over 2.5 million tons of cereals were delivered to the region. Notwithstanding the unprecedented relief effort, it was estimated that 100,000 people died and one million head of cattle perished.

These dire warnings highlighted the need for an effective early warning system of impending disasters. FAO had for many years operated a system of regular reporting by member governments as part of its commodity market intelligence services and for its various statistical publications. Since the establishment in 1968 of an early warning system for food shortages, FAO and WFP field staff had sent in monthly data for over 70 countries. The experience of the Sahelian countries underlined the need to improve this service. The first step was for each country to review its data-collecting system. The second was to develop adequate arrangements at the international level. Following a decision of the FAO Conference in 1973, FAO began work on strengthening its Food Information System by incorporating an expanded Early Warning System, its food aid information service, and various commodity market intelligence services, linking it with the work of the specialized intergovernmental bodies. A third step was to extend and accelerate the communication of information by governments to the international system. Another step was to adapt the World Weather Watch System to better serve agricultural purposes.

The World Food Conference resolution welcomed the action taken by FAO and agreed that FAO was the most appropriate organization to operate and supervise the system. All governments were requested to take steps to amplify and improve their data collection and dissemination services and to participate in the system 'on a voluntary and regular basis'; in return they were to receive periodically the information this collected fully analyzed. The World Meteorological Organization (WMO) was requested, in co-operation with FAO, to provide regular assessments of current and recent weather on the basis of information assembled through the World Weather Watch, to expand joint research projects, particularly in arid and semi-arid areas, to strengthen weather monitoring systems at the national and regional levels, and to assess the probability of adverse weather conditions occurring in various agricultural areas, and on a better understanding of the causes of climatic variations.

16
International Trade, Stability and Agricultural Adjustment

ECOSOC and the Preparatory Committee for the World Food Conference recognized that proposals concerning international trade, stability and agricultural adjustment had a different character to those directly related to increasing agricultural production (UN, 1974b, pp. 199–222). They dealt with a more harmonized approach to integrating national food economies with world markets. Export trade was an important outlet for many foods. About a tenth of the value of the world's food, feed and beverages was traded internationally. For all cereals taken together, about one-eighth of the world's consumption came from imports. Trade in food, feed and some fisheries products in 1973, the year before the World Food Conference, amounted to some $70,000 million or about 15 per cent of total merchandise trade. Thus, food issues could not be considered in isolation from trade. The interdependence was too important, directly and indirectly.

While solution of the world food problem required increased production in the developing countries, it could not be expected that they should all become self-sufficient in food. It was only through a substantial trade in food and production requisites that a rational use could be made of the resource endowments of countries. In sum, the contribution of an expanding trade in food was an essential and increasingly strategic element in improving the world food security situation. But instability in world agricultural markets, reflected in excessive fluctuations in prices and uncertainty in the availability of agricultural products in world markets, was a recurrent problem. Yet for many developing countries, there would continue to be no practical alternative to expanding their agricultural exports as part of their drive for foreign exchange earnings.

Developing countries also faced structural food problems. In one group of developing countries, the economy, with poor resource endowments, generated neither enough basic foods nor enough foreign earnings. A second group consisted of developing countries, which were largely self-sufficient in basic foods physically or economically. A third group was made up of those countries with an export surplus of basic foods. International agricultural adjustments were required to address the problems of all three groups.

The conference resolution on international trade, stabilization and agricultural adjustment (resolution XIX) recognized the interrelationship between the world food problem and international trade and the role that international trade could play in solving the world food security problem. Governments were called upon to co-operate in promoting a steady and increasing expansion and liberalization of world food trade and remove discriminatory practices. They were also urged to take measures aimed at securing additional benefits for the international trade of developing countries and to take steps to deal with the problem of stabilizing world markets. Developed countries were called upon to review their farm support programmes for domestic food production to avoid detrimental effects on the food exports of developing countries. Governments were also encouraged to work together in a programme of international agricultural adjustment and to give the highest priority and most favourable terms to the least-developed, land-locked and island developing countries and to developing countries most seriously affected by economic crises.

17
World Food Council

The UN General Assembly approved the World Food Conference resolution establishing:

> a World Food Council, at the ministerial or plenipotentiary level, to function as an organ of the United Nations reporting to the General Assembly through the Economic and Social Council, and to serve as a co-ordinating mechanism to provide over-all, integrated and continuing attention for the successful co-ordination and follow-up of policies concerning food production, nutrition, food security, food trade and food aid, as well as other related matters, by all the agencies of the United Nations system. (UN, 1975, p. 18)[14]

At the World Food Conference in November 1974, the proposal for a World Food Council (WFC) was agreed to by more than a hundred sovereign countries in a two-week period, showing a sense of urgency any national legislature would find it hard to match (Cleveland, 1975, p. 28). Crucially, the United States supported adoption of the conference recommendation concerning the WFC, while noting significantly that it 'would have no authority beyond moral suasion to force action on the part of governments or UN bodies' (US, 1974b, p. 40). In taking this step, the conference appreciated 'the complex nature of the world food problem, which can only be solved through an integrated multi-disciplinary approach within the framework of economic and social development as a whole'.

The conference agreed that 'collective world food security should be promoted within a world food policy and its concept further defined and elaborated both to accelerate rural development and to improve international co-operation'. It also recognized that the work of the concerned international agencies needed to be co-ordinated and strengthened 'in an effective and integrated world food policy' (UN, 1975). WFC should consist of 36 members,[15] nominated by ECOSOC and elected by the UN General Assembly, 'taking into consideration balanced geographical representation'. Heads of the UN agencies concerned should be invited to attend its sessions. A WFC president would be elected 'on the basis of geographical rotation'. Critically, the conference agreed that WFC should be serviced 'within the framework of FAO' and have its headquarters in Rome. (The phrase 'within the framework of FAO' was removed by the UN General Assembly's

168   *1970–90. The World Food Crisis of the 1970s and its Aftermath*

Second Committee and WFC was to be directly funded from the budget of the UN secretariat and not from FAO.)

The Council would review periodically major problems and policy issues affecting the world food situation and all aspects of world food problems 'in order to adopt an integrated approach towards their solution'. Special attention would be given to the problems of the poorest and most seriously affected countries. In conducting its work, WFC would 'maintain contact with, receive reports from, give advice and make recommendations to, United Nations bodies and agencies, regarding the formulation and follow-up of world food policies'. This would include receiving periodic reports from the UN agencies concerned with food security issues, including: FAO's Committee on World Food Security, the FAO Commission on Fertilizers, FAO on progress in implementing it Global Information and Early warning System, WFP, IFAD, the CGIAR, and from the United Nations Conference on Trade and Development (UNCTAD) on the world food trade situation and on progress to increase trade liberalization and access to international markets for food products exported by developing countries. WFC would also work 'in full co-operation' with regional bodies to formulate and follow-up policies approved by the Council.

The establishment of WFC promised a new beginning in the quest for world food security. From the outset, however, the Council represented a compromise between those who did not want any new UN machinery to address the problems of world food security and the proposals for a World Food Authority or a World Food Security Council. It was the only UN body to be specifically set up at the ministerial or plenipotentiary level, reporting directly to the UN General Assembly through ECOSOC, with members serving for three years. This was carefully calibrated to give geographical and political balance between developing and developed countries and reflected the concern of the G77 that the Council should not become a tool of the powerful developed nations.[16]

Modus operandi

WFC ministerial sessions were to be held annually, which lasted for four or five days, preceded by a preparatory meeting of a similar period, usually at the location of the Council's headquarters in Rome. The Council's first session was held in Rome in June 1975 at which its 'Rules of Procedure', drafted by the secretariat of ECOSOC after consultation with the UN Office of Legal Affairs, were considered. A working group was set up to review and revise the draft, which was approved at its second session in 1976 (UN, 1977). A bureau, consisting of a president and three (later four) vice-presidents and a rapporteur, was elected by Council members for a biennium. In electing the WFC bureau, 'due respect should be paid to the principle of rotation and equitable geographical representation'. An executive director would be appointed by the UN secretary-general, in consultation with WFC members and with the FAO director-general, for a period of four years 'with due regard to the principle of geographical rotation'.[17] The UN secretary-general, in consultation with the executive director, would appoint 'an adequate number of staff' to the WFC secretariat 'taking into account the need for equitable geographical distribution in addition to professional competence and avoiding the appointment of persons who simultaneously perform functions in other agencies or institutions'.

In preparing the documentation and providing administrative, operational and other services for the Council, the secretariat would 'to the maximum extent' co-operate with, and rely on, existing international bodies in the field of food and agriculture, especially FAO. Funding of WFC activities was to be met out of the UN administrative budget and was to be closely controlled. Before any proposal involving expenditure from UN funds was approved by the Council, in accordance with UN financial regulations, the executive director, in consultation with the WFC president and the UN secretary-general, was required to prepare and circulate to Council members an estimate of the financial and administrative implications. While sessions of the Council would normally be held at WFC's headquarters in Rome, preceded by preparatory meetings, provision was made to hold sessions elsewhere at the invitation of governments that agreed to defray the costs involved, after consultation with the UN secretary-general.[18]

Sayed A. Marei, Assistant President of Egypt, who was secretary-general of the World Food Conference and a strong proponent of the proposal for some form of world food authority, was elected as the first president of WFC. John A. Hannah from the United States, former president of Michigan State University, head of the US Administration for International Development during the Nixon administration, president of the American Freedom from Hunger Foundation set up at the beginning of the Kennedy administration, and chairman of the World Hunger Action Coalition, who was chosen by Sayed Marei to be one of his three deputy secretaries-general for the World Food Conference, was appointed as WFC's first executive director, with Sartaj Aziz, one of the deputy secretaries-general of the World Food Conference who had played a major role in preparations for, and at, the conference (see above) as his deputy.

Significantly, Hannah had said at the end of the World Food Conference that 'the situation in the UN family will never be the same after this conference. This has been the value of calling a UN meeting rather than an FAO technical conference' (PAN, 1974). In his view, the conference 'had shown the global aspect and varied nature of the food problem that required the expertise of UN agencies such as WHO, UNICEF and ILO as well as FAO'. Although he would have preferred greater immediate response to short-term shortages, he felt that the conference had reached a turning point where world attention was focused on rural people and the plight of the hungry. Lessons had been given to both developed and developing countries. The former had been brought face to face with their moral and humanitarian responsibilities. Developing countries were beginning to realize that higher priority should be given to the human needs of their own people. As far as the United States was concerned, he considered that 'a better foreign aid bill was needed, written along the lines emphasized at the conference'. Much would depend on the ability of American NGOs to influence grass root and political opinion in the United States. The American people wanted to do something good after the trauma of recent scandals in the government (that had led to the resignation of President Nixon). In his view, the US delegation to the conference had not reflected the views of the American people. Many Americans had signed petitions proclaiming their willingness to share 'even if it meant sacrifice'. He intended as a follow-up to the conference 'to take the issues back to the people'.

At the outset, WFC faced a formidably array of issues and problems relating to the world food situation and world food security. Where should it begin, what should be its priorities, and what should be its programme of work? The main functions of the Council had been clearly spelled out in the World Food Conference resolution recommending its establishment (see below). The prompt action by the UN General Assembly to set up the WFC reflected the urgent need felt by governments for a high-level body with necessary political authority to take an integrated view of the world food problem and to take or initiate effective action on various aspects of the problem.

The main functions of the Council, which were laid out in the conference resolution (XXII.4), included (Table 17.1)

- periodic review of major problems and policy issues affecting the world food situation;
- periodic review of steps being proposed or taken to implement the World Food Conference resolutions and to resolve the problems by governments, the UN system and its regional organizations;
- recommendation of remedial action to resolve these problems;
- co-ordination of relevant UN bodies and agencies dealing with food production, nutrition, food security and food aid, giving special attention to the problems of the least-developed and most seriously affected countries; and
- maintaining contact with, receiving reports from, and giving advice and making recommendations to UN bodies and agencies for the formulation and follow-up of world food policies, and co-operation with regional bodies to formulate and follow-up policies approved by the council.

In essence, WFC was to be 'a political overview body' and 'to serve as the eyes, ears and conscience of the UN system regarding world food security issues'. It was to act as advocate, catalyst and co-ordinator, stimulating governments and the international community as a whole to adopt mutually beneficial policies and programmes to alleviate hunger and malnutrition in the world.

In a note to the Council at its first session in 1975, the executive director observed that the functions assigned to WFC were 'wide ranging, important and complex' and that 'it may not be practicable to deal with the whole range of subjects and issues simultaneously' (WFC, 1975a). He expected that the relative priority of various issues would change over time and some programmes or policy issues may be ready for decision earlier than others. The Council might therefore wish to consider the best manner in which it could fulfil its mandate by selecting specific issues or programmes for special attention at each session, while maintaining an overall view of the world food problem and of progress made in implementing the World Food Conference resolution.

Table 17.1 World Food Council and the World Food Security situation

Years	Cereals				Export Prices[a] (US dollars per ton)		
	Production (million tons)[b]	Trade (million tons)[c]	Stocks (million tons)	Stocks (as % of consumption)	Wheat	Maize	Rice
1971–72	1311	108	217	18	60	52	134
A. Crisis in the food economy							
1972–73	1273	133	172	14	91	72	171
1973–74	1376	135	186	15	177	116	584
1974–75	1339	134	179	14	163	132	439
B. Recovery in the food economy							
1975–76	1373	150	187	14	151	116	295
1976–77	1480	148	256	19	112	108	257
1977–78	1471	162	251	17	116	96	337
1978–79	1602	170	287	20	141	103	330
C. Setback in the food economy							
1979–80	1552	197	273	19	175	115	387
1980–81	1565	207	254	17	183	142	409
D. Recovery again							
1981–82	1648	212	301	20	170	118	440
1982–83	1707	195	346	22	160	115	300
1983–84	1643	204	286	18	154	146	241
1984–85	1800	216	339	21	148	123	217
1985–86	1839	181	427	26	129	105	188
1986–87	1852	184	457	27	110	73	186
E. Setback again							
1987–88	1791	198	401	24	123	86	220
1988–89	1733	205	310	18	167	118	284
F. Better balancing between supply and demand							
1989–90	1870	208	304	18	161	110	305
1990–91	1953	185	343	20	118	106	278
1991–92 (preliminary)	1878	208	319	19	150	110	302

[a]Price quotations refer to US No. 2 Hard winter Wheat, US No. 2 Yellow Maize and Thai 100 per cent, 2nd Grade Rice.
[b]Data refer to the calendar year of the first year shown.
[c]Data refer to world imports.
Sources: Different issues of *FAO Food Outlook and Statistical Supplements and FAO World Crop and Livestock Statistics*.

At its first session in 1975, WFC gave its revealing 'first views' of the conduct of its work. It agreed that 'as the world's highest political body dealing exclusively with food',[19] its main functions would be 'to monitor the world food situation in all its aspects, including what international agencies and governments were doing to develop short and long-term solutions to food problems', to determine, in its co-ordinating role, whether 'the world food strategy as a whole makes sense', to identify 'malfunctions, gaps and problem areas', and to exert its influence, *'through moral persuasion'* (emphasis added), to get any necessary improvements made. Ominously, in the face of this formidable array of tasks, it was agreed that the WFC secretariat should be 'small and of high professional competence' and should 'draw fully on the expertise of other agencies, especially FAO' (WFC, 1975b). While its reports should be of a 'high evaluative and analytical nature', the secretariat should not undertake major research efforts of its own but should rely on the agencies responsible for the subject, 'while exercising its own objectivity with respect to the conclusions it drew from them'. To accomplish this, the secretariat 'should feel free to call on all agencies for the information it required in a spirit of cooperation and shared concern'. The secretariat should maintain a 'close watch' over the efforts of international agencies and governments to increase food production and to improve world food security. And it should 'scrutinize, review and comment, frankly and impartially' on situations as it found them and should suggest improvements as and when necessary.

The Council was required to report annually to the UN General Assembly through ECOSOC. Members agreed that WFC reports 'should be different from the usual official style': they should 'convey the pulse of happenings on the world food scene and should command international attention'. The executive director should bring the Council's reports 'to the attention of all relevant international and national authorities'. It was agreed that: only a few problems should be put on the agenda of any session; ample time for preparation should be allowed; the dates of each sessions should be fixed with due regard to other relevant meetings; and that the secretariat should not duplicate documents which were readily available from other expert sources. At each session, the Council would need a report that concisely identified the major problems and evaluated the progress or impediments to their solutions at a world-wide level as well as the progress or needed improvement in programmes of agencies or nations.

The executive director's proposal that increasing food production in developing countries was 'the first priority' was accepted. The secretariat was requested to follow closely the various efforts underway to quantify the food problem in specific developing nations and regions and the amount and types of resources required to accelerate food production. It was also asked to report particularly on the establishment of the International Fund for Agricultural Development (IFAD), and begin work on 'a realistic and practical assessment' to determine the feasibility and implications of abolishing hunger and malnutrition 'within a decade' that had been agreed at the World Food Conference. The secretariat should also follow closely developments in world food security, including efforts to develop grain stock agreements, progress in attaining the 10 million ton food aid target established at the World Food Conference, and in meeting urgent food requirements of the most seriously affected countries.

It was recognized that it would be difficult to achieve WFC's main aims. The major factors affecting the world food problem should be the focus of attention, and action to deal with them stimulated, without duplicating the functions carried out by other bodies. It was therefore essential to follow 'a selective approach'. The Group of 77 (G77) submitted its own 'declaration', which was included in the report of the Council's first session (WFC, 1975b, pp. 24–5). It declared that it was 'essential' to maintain the WFC bureau that had been elected during the course of its first session (of Sayed Marei as president, vice-presidents from the USSR, Mexico and Bangladesh, and a rapporteur from the United Kingdom), to nominate 'an adequate secretariat with a balanced regional distribution, answerable to the Council', to maintain the composition and terms of reference of the working group on the drafting of WFC's rules of procedure, and to charge the WFC president, 'in whom the group reaffirms its confidence', with the task of convening the next session of the Council 'within a reasonable period of time'. In doing so, the G77 reiterated the concern it expressed at the World Food Conference of creating a body independent from other UN agencies and with a geographical balance that ensured that the views of the developing countries were not overwhelmed by those of developed nations.[20]

Views on WFC's priority concerns were reviewed and refined at subsequent Council sessions. At its second session in Rome in June 1976, on the recommendation of the UN Administrative Committee on Coordination (ACC)[21] to ECOSOC, the Council was called upon to keep under review the overall response to the World Food Conference resolution on policies and programmes to improve nutrition and suggest ways of expediting progress. The importance of international trade in food to the solution of the overall food problem was accepted, and it was agreed to follow closely progress on food trade issues in the light of discussions and negotiations in forums such as UNCTAD, IWC and GATT.

At its sixth session in Arusha, Tanzania, in June 1980, WFC recognized that it was a 'political instrument' (not an operational body) for realizing the objectives of eradicating hunger and malnutrition (WFC, 1980). At its seventh session in Novi Sad, Yugoslavia, in May 1981, members agreed that the Council 'should continue to assert its primary role, as the only expressly ministerial body of the United Nations, to focus on the political process of mobilizing support to resolve world food problems' (Williams, 1986). At the same session, Sayed Marei, WFC's first president, said that WFC 'was not created to function as a mere talk-shop where business ends with the delivery of statements; it was the standing follow-up mechanism of the World Food Conference'. He urged governments to endow it with their committed support (WFC, 1982b, p. 35). High priority was assigned to the food problems of Africa at the eighth session of the Council in Acapulco, Mexico, in June 1982 (WFC, 1982c, p. 30), which was intensified when, in 1984, ten years after the World Food Conference, it was decided that: 'All work conducted by the Council will provide a priority focus on African food problems, as directed by the United Nations Secretary-general for all elements of the United Nations system' (WFC, 1984f, p. 37).

In summary, within the three-pronged approach emerging from the World Food Conference of: recognizing the primary responsibility of governments; developing and implementing an effective and integrated world food policy; and achieving

174   *1970–90. The World Food Crisis of the 1970s and its Aftermath*

better co-ordination among international agencies; the main tasks of the WFC were perceived as

- reviewing major food and hunger issues with a view to advancing international understanding of them and the resolutions adopted by the conference and to monitor steps taken by governments and the UN system;
- recommending remedial action through WFC initiatives, thereby providing global policy direction; and
- monitoring and co-ordinating the relevant UN bodies and agencies (WFC, 1992).

It is against these three tasks that the performance of the WFC may be measured.

Major food and hunger issues

As standing items on its agenda, the Council reviewed the world food situation and progress in the implementation of the World Food Conference resolutions.

The world food situation

At its first session in June 1975, it was agreed that WFC's review of the world food situation should be 'deep, objective and penetrating. The review should convey the pulse of what was happening to the world food problems and show whether the longer term prospects were improving' (WFC, 1975b, p. 13). Its reviews were based on reports submitted by FAO, which gave implicit political support to FAO's work. In its 1975 review, the Council called for special attention to be given to the food needs of countries most seriously affected by the world food crisis by ensuring physical availability of 6–7 million tons of cereals by the end of the year.

By 1984, ten years after the World Food Conference, the Council noted that the global food situation had become 'more complex, interrelated and in some ways more precarious' (WFC, 1984f, p. 2). The growing imbalances and distortions that characterized the world food economy over the past decade were noted. It was regretted that despite an overall improvement in the aggregate world food supply situation, the risks of food insecurity were greater for many low-income developing countries, particularly because of natural and man-made calamities. The world was feeding nearly 1 billion more people in 1984 than ten years previously and there was 'ample food produced globally for all the world's people'. Yet there remained 'hundreds of millions of hungry and malnourished people'. The World Food Conference's goal of eliminating hunger and malnutrition within a decade 'had proved unattainable'.

The Council reaffirmed that hunger and malnutrition 'can be eradicated in our time' and agreed that the world food economy was characterized by large imbalances in the world agricultural economy between the performance of the major food-exporting countries and that of the food-deficit, largely, low-income countries. In the opinion of many, but not all, WFC members, the solution of the world food problem could be found only within the general process of restructuring international economic relations on a just and democratic basis and establishing a New International Economic Order. The Council agreed that sub-Saharan Africa was 'at the centre of the food problem', although most of the world's chronically undernourished still lived in Asia.

At its last session in 1992, the Council noted that most developing regions had made some headway during the decade of the 1980s in reducing the proportion (not number) of hungry and malnourished people. But sub-Saharan Africa remained a special concern. WFC appealed to the international community to help reverse Africa's deteriorating food and hunger situation and reiterated the need for a new Green Revolution. With the end of the Cold War and the break-up of the former Soviet Union, millions of people in the Eastern European region, including the Commonwealth of Independent States (CIS), were finding it increasingly difficult to gain access to adequate food as a result of the transitional effects of economic reform. The Council stressed that support to the region 'must remain additional' to, and not diverted from, official development assistance to developing countries.

World Food Conference resolutions

WFC was required to report to the UN General Assembly through ECOSOC on the implementation of the World Food Conference. In this role, it became what might be regarded as the guardian of the conference's resolution. Many, including this writer, feared that without the Council, the resolutions would be quickly forgotten, like those of many international conference before it. In carrying out this function, WFC had an impact particularly on the resolutions relating to food aid, the IFAD, and international agricultural trade.

The Council's influence on food aid was seen in a number of dimensions. Not only did it press for an increase in food aid toward the target set by the World Food Conference of 10 million tons of cereals annually but also for the establishment of an international emergency food reserve (IEFR). In particular, it called on the governing body of WFP to set guidelines and criteria for all food aid as a framework for implementing the resolution of the conference on an improved policy for food aid and to draw up modalities for the operation of the IEFR. After protracted discussion, especially concerning the relative priority to be given to food aid in support of food security schemes in developing countries and the concept of forward planning of food aid on a multi-annual basis, WFP's governing body agreed to a set of guidelines and criteria (see Annex 9.1). Although not legally binding, the guidelines recommended that two priorities should be given in the use of food aid: first, to low-income, food-deficit countries; and secondly, to meeting emergencies, to projects designed to increase agricultural, especially food, production, and to nutrition improvement programmes. Although not closely followed by bilateral food aid programmes, they provided the framework for WFP assistance for the next twenty years. As described above, WFP's governing body also drew up the modalities for the IEFR (see Annex 14.1).

The Council also kept up pressure on the developed and OPEC countries to reach agreement on their contributions to the IFAD. The director-general of the OPEC

Special Fund addressed WFC's second session in Rome in 1976 and announced that $400 million, half the resources of the OPEC fund, would be committed toward the IFAD target of $1,000 million, subject to developed countries contributing the balance of convertible initial resources. After protracted discussion, an agreement was reached in 1977 and IFAD began operations, directed by a governing council in which all member states were represented, and a president from Saudi Arabia and a vice-president from the United States. IFAD continues in operation today although with reduced resources.

International agricultural trade was a standing item on the Council's agenda from inception as an integral part of its programme to eradicate hunger and malnutrition. Developed countries were constantly encouraged to adjust their domestic agricultural and trade policies to facilitate increased food production in developing countries and stimulate their agricultural exports. It was noted that expansion and liberalization of trade had been slow and the initiatives of UNCTAD in multilateral trade negotiations were encouraged. At the fifth session of the Council, which was held in Ottawa, Canada, WFC's executive director pointed to the compounded effects of trade protectionism. If exports from developing countries were restricted, they were less able to import the food they need and to develop their economies, with a consequent adverse effect on the prospects of reducing poverty and hunger (WFC, 1979a, p. 30). Consumers and taxpayers in developed countries paid a heavy price for trade protection. Their export potential was reduced, inflation was more difficult to bring under control, and their economies were retarded from adjustment and restructuring towards new and more productive patterns. Inflation and recession in the developed countries not only affected the well-being of their own people but spilled over on other countries as well. Public opinion needed to be better informed of the costs of protectionist measures to their own and the broader international interest.

This message was carried forward to the next WFC ministerial session in Arusha, Tanzania in 1980. In a separate report emphasizing issues relating to developing countries' food imports, the executive director pointed out that the concept of a food import gap could be usefully disaggregated on a country basis (WFC, 1980). Overall figures for developing countries did not provide an adequate indication of the variety of problems involved. His report was a first attempt in that direction. It showed that while developing countries as a whole seemed to be spending a smaller proportion of their foreign earnings on food than they did two decades earlier, many countries had maintained that proportion, and some had even increased it. The 'relative import gap' (the relation between food availability and total imports) was also analysed in the context of each country's per capita average calorie intake. This showed that some countries, predominantly those in the lowest income category, had increased the proportion of their total imports accounted for by food but suffered a reduction in their per capita calorie intake. The executive director proposed that countries in that category should be identified and their problems studied in detail for priority assistance, which received wide support among WFC members. The executive director's report also called attention to the growing concentration of international grain supplies in North America and the need to diversify the sources of supply. Such diversification did not mean a reduction of grain exports. Many other, and particularly developing, countries had the potential to develop significant grain exports. The report suggested that measures designed to promote increased, and regionally more balanced, food production and trade, particularly from and to developing countries, should be explored.

Throughout the 1980s, WFC expressed 'deep concern' that the world-wide recession and financial crisis had set back prospects of increased food security for developing countries as it was closely related to overall economic and trade conditions. Ministers stressed the important impact of the international agricultural environment on the development and export earnings of many developing countries. Proliferation of import restrictions and increasing export subsidization by developed countries were seen to have contributed to international market instability and growing distortions in the allocation of resources in both developed and developing countries. The Council called on all countries to demonstrate 'the requisite political will' by refraining from creating tariff obstacles to agricultural imports, especially those from developing countries. An appeal was made to exporting countries to limit export subsidies and analogous practices that might hinder trade, especially that of developing countries.

The value of more open trade was affirmed and much more attention to building support for more orderly adjustments in trade policies and related structural adjustments of the major trading countries encouraged. Renewed trade negotiations were regarded as essential to reduce protectionism and expand export earnings of developing countries. Ministers emphasized that the WFC should continue its efforts to mobilize the necessary 'political determination' in pursuit of such negotiations in the GATT and other forums. The Council also reaffirmed its position against the use of food as an instrument of political pressure and agreed that efforts should also be stepped up to achieve a better balance between the domestic economic policies of developed countries and improved market opportunities and food security of the developing regions.

Remedial action and global policy direction: WFC initiatives

The Council also recommended remedial action and pointed to the direction global policy should take in the fight against hunger and malnutrition. It considered a wide range of initiatives on the basis of documents and reports submitted to it by the WFC secretariat. Some of the main initiatives are described below.

Food priority countries

One of the Council's first initiatives was to establish what were called 'food priority countries' (FPCs) that required special attention because of the seriousness of their food problems, their economic and other resource limitations, and their potential for increasing food production (WFC, 1976b, pp. 11–12). The FPCs were described as 'the heart of the food problem' (WFC, 1977b). The objective in selecting FPCs

178   *1970–90. The World Food Crisis of the 1970s and its Aftermath*

was, in the words of the Council, to lend a 'sharper sense of direction to the overall efforts to increase food production in the developing countries'. The following were criteria and guidelines established for determining FPCs:

- Per capita income of under $500 a year (in 1975 prices) with special emphasis on even lower income countries.
- A projected cereals deficit by 1985 of 500,000 tons or more and/or a cereals deficit of 20 per cent or more as a proportion of estimated cereal consumption.
- Degree of protein-calorie malnutrition in terms of the proportion of the population that was malnourished or in terms of the average availability of protein calories in relation to minimum requirements.
- Insufficient average increase in food production, total and per capita, during the last decade.
- Potential for rapid, efficient and socio-economically well-distributed increases in food production, including the availability of under-utilized resources to produce food.
- Serious balance of payments constraints which precluded necessary food imports.

On the basis of these criteria, 43 FPCs were identified, the situation of eight of which was regarded as 'extremely severe', 23 'very severe' and 12 'severe'. These FPCs accounted for more than half the population of developing countries (excluding China) and for over half their projected food deficits by 1985. In applying the above criteria, it was agreed that special consideration should be given to the need to support the intent of countries to implement policies and programmes specifically designed to ensure that productive efforts fully utilized the human and other resources of rural areas. They also contained practical measures to implement social and other reforms consistent with these objectives and with an equitable distribution of the food and income benefits of production programmes. It was also agreed that care should be taken not to interfere with the sovereign rights of each country to decide its own priorities and policies. The list of FPCs would be reviewed and further work carried out to refine and complement the criteria.

International agencies, including the regional banks, might be asked to co-operate with FPCs in determining specific measures and programmes to accelerate food production by at least 4 per cent per annum. They might also help in indicating other measures (such as food aid and nutrition programmes) that would be required to improve food supply while production was increased. It was noted that the FPCs overlapped with other groups of countries classified by the United Nations as deserving special attention. This underscored the commonality of problems among poor countries but the other classifications did not focus on the specific need to increase food production that was characteristic of the FPCs. The Council called on the international community 'effectively and substantially' to increase its official development assistance to food and agricultural production in order to achieve, 'as soon as possible', at least a 4 per cent sustained rate of growth of food production in developing countries. Their aid should take into account the estimate, provided by the WFC secretariat, of $8.3 billion in external resources on an annual basis, of which about $6.5 billion would be on concessional terms (WFC, 1977b).[22]

An international system of food security

At its second session in Rome in June 1976, the WFC secretariat submitted a document on 'an international system of food security' (WFC, 1976a). It was suggested that in view of the slow progress in implementing the International Undertaking on World Food Security, the continued threat of food insecurity, and the fragmentation of international efforts with different approaches to questions of food aid, food stocks, and food reserve management by different groups of countries, the WFC 'might wish to reaffirm its responsibility' to facilitate and expedite the creation of a suitable system of world food security and lend 'political impetus' to negotiations and discussions in the appropriate forums. It suggested that 'a more practical approach' to implementing a world food security system would be 'to take a disaggregated view of stocks in the light of the diverse concerns that have surfaced in various international fora, to break down the elements of a global stock policy into more manageable components, and to seek support for each element from different groups of countries, in relation to their own interest in that element'.

The main components of the proposed global stock policy were:

(a) An international reserve for emergencies with an initial target of 500,000 tons, as proposed by the UN General Assembly at it seventh special session in September 1975. Potential donors would be invited to indicate their contributions to the reserve and the WFP governing body would be asked to formulate appropriate criteria and procedures for the operation of the reserve.
(b) National reserves for providing emergency relief and, in special cases, the uncovered commercial import requirements of most seriously affected developing countries, which could be covered by countries earmarking a part of their national stocks. The normal size of such reserves at the beginning of each year would preferably be 25 per cent above the annual food aid programme of the country concerned. The FAO Committee on World Food Security would be requested to formulate special guidelines for these reserves.
(c) A food security reserve of 15–20 million tons to protect against well-defined commercial exigencies and to prevent abnormal fluctuations in grain prices. Governments would be urged to intensify their efforts in the appropriate forums to work out operational and other arrangements for such a reserve *taking into account the interests of both exporting and importing countries* (emphasis added). Such a reserve would neither be expected to stabilize prices within a narrow band, nor depress prices, nor provide grain on concessional terms to developing importers, but instead would be used to avert serious fluctuations in prices in the commercial markets.

180   *1970–90. The World Food Crisis of the 1970s and its Aftermath*

This initiative was seen by one observer as the brainchild of deputy executive director Aziz, who described it as a 'remarkably well thought out plan for breaking the impasse on how to create a global food reserve' (Power, 1976). It had the 'touch of a master of the craft of food diplomacy...Here in the guise of WFC is a new Joseph. It is up to the pharaohs of the world to make this conceptual breakthrough a political reality', which was not achieved.

Africa's food problems

The Council gave early attention to the acute food problems of Africa and discussed ways of overcoming them at seven of its annual sessions. At its second session in 1976, a report was received from the African Inter-Ministerial Committee for Food and its recommendations submitted to ECOSOC. The Council sponsored a regional consultation of African ministers for food and agricultural in Nairobi, Kenya in March 1982 and recommended 'urgently accelerated efforts' by African countries and international agencies taking into account the conclusions and recommendations of the consultation, which were included in the report of its eighth session (WFC, 1982b, annex III).[23] African ministers acknowledged that the causes of the deterioration of agriculture in the region were complex, exacerbated by natural and man-made disasters. They also recognized that to resolve their food problems effectively, African governments 'must disengage from the colonial legacies of urban-biased development, deeply embedded trade dependence, and unrealistic terms of trade'.

African ministers also observed the shortcomings of international agencies, which, in their view, tended to follow 'excessively narrow and strict criteria of project development without adequate attention to the broader social and economic aspects of national policies'. They also found that the 'multiplicity' of agencies, 'fragmentation' of projects and the 'complexity and diversity' of donor procedural requirements went beyond the administrative and co-ordinating capabilities of African nations. There was need for more integrated and simplified approaches, and better co-ordination of agency and donor efforts. While food provided a necessary and viable focus for improved development, development assistance agencies had been slow to recognize 'the focal concept of food'. Ministers supported the WFC emphasis on the development of staple food crops as a basis of attaining increased food self-sufficiency, and noted that in Africa, research, extension and supportive infrastructure had been weak in this area.

In 1986, the Council met in Rome for its twelfth session, immediately after a special session of the UN General Assembly was held on the critical economic situation in Africa, the first on a single region of the world, which adopted the United Nations Programme of Action for African Economic Recovery and Development 1986–90 (UN General Assembly resolution S-13/2, 1986). In the framework of the UN African action programme, the WFC executive director outlined what he called the 'imperative of food-centred development' for Africa's economic recovery (WFC, 1986a). The Council emphasized the importance of a 'quick start' if the UN programme was to be implemented within a five-year period. It would, 'as a political body', promote appropriate measures to translate the UN programme into specific action. It would also assist the UN secretary-general and the UN General Assembly in keeping progress under review and urged both recipient and donor countries to take effective steps towards the programme's implementation (WFC, 1986c).

In support of the UN Africa programme, WFC continued its food policy dialogue with donor countries, international aid agencies and African countries and institutions. A ministers' round table on food security in Africa, organized by the Development Policy Forum of the German Foundation for International Development in co-operation with the WFC president, was held in Berlin, Germany, in 1987 (DSE, 1987). The meeting was attended by African ministers and representatives of UN agencies. The principal message that emerged was that African countries faced difficult policy choices in trying to balance economic stabilization and the immediate protection of the already low welfare levels of their people. The international community, on the other hand, did not appear to be living up to its commitment, made at the UN General Assembly special session, to make 'every effort to provide sufficient resources to support and supplement the African development effort'. Africa could feed itself, and may even have the potential to become a major food exporter. But a number of African countries would remain food-import dependent. Given their ecological and related resource-endowment conditions, food self-sufficiency 'at all costs' should not be pursued. Population growth and rapid urbanization placed unprecedented demands on the food systems, urging the transformation of Africa's subsistence agriculture into a market-oriented economic sector. Development of human resources and institutions were key priorities, with special emphasis on the role of women. Co-operation with other developing countries and regions was recognized as important for achieving food security in Africa, and the practical steps taken by WFC to promote South–South co-operation were welcomed. In the context of the UN African programme, WFC ministers called for action on four fronts: more adequate support for African countries' adjustment and policy reform efforts; a major effort to reach a solution to Africa's debt crisis; significant improvement in the international trade and economic environment, in favour of African exports and terms of trade; and a revival of genuine North–South dialogue.

The Council continued to promote the proposal for the establishment of food policy management training programmes in Africa in support of national and regional food strategies (see below). This was done through visits to 20 African government and training institutions. A high-level workshop was held in the Netherlands, in 1988, by WFC and the European Centre for Development Policy Management with senior experts from African and international institutions. And a consultation on food policy management training programmes in Africa was held in Abidjan, Côte d'Ivoire in 1989, organized jointly by WFC and the African Development Bank with representatives of African governments, regional and training institutions, and interested bilateral and multilateral agencies. The consultation reaffirmed the need for strengthening African expertise in food policy management and proposed several types of training programmes that could be carried out in existing African institutions.

National food strategies

WFC invested more time and effort in promoting what were called 'national food strategies' as a planning tool for countries to deal with their particular food problems than perhaps any other single subject it promoted. This was done largely on the initiative of its executive director, Maurice J. Williams, previously chairman of OECD's Development Assistance Committee, who took over from John Hannah in 1978 and served as executive head of the WFC secretariat for eight years until 1986. Salahuddin Ahmed, previously permanent representative of Bangladesh to FAO, was appointed as his deputy. The Council began discussing the concept of national food strategies after its endorsement at its fifth session in Ottawa, Canada in 1979. What motivated the WFC executive director to take this initiative? (Williams, 1984). Many developing countries continued to have increasing food deficits in the years immediately following the 1974 World Food Conference. This suggested that government approaches to resolving their food problems were proving inadequate. Production shortfalls and high import bills indicated that special attention should be given to the food sector. But it should not simply 'tag along' with the rest of a country's economy and development objectives. Specific and concerted attention was required. Apart from expanding food production, *equal attention* (emphasis added) would be required for the demand side concerns of ensuring acceptable consumption levels and undernourished for the poor and promoting their income generating potential.[24]

The resolution of national food and hunger problems was therefore seen to require constant and long-range attention to a host of factors that directly and indirectly affected both food production and consumption. The concept of national food strategies emerged from seven consultations organized by WFC during 1979 among representatives of developing and developed countries and assistance agencies (WFC, 1982a). Concerned by the lack of progress towards the eradication of hunger, participants were asked to identify the major obstacles they encountered in their efforts to increase food production and consumption and to suggest specific ways to overcome them. This pointed to the need for greater focus on national food policies in a new structure of co-ordinated international support. It also called for policy adjustments in a framework of priorities that kept a country's perceptions of its food needs *at the centre of the development process* (emphasis added) and enabled development agencies to direct and project their assistance programmes.

Critically, a national food strategy[25] was country-specific in two senses. It was formulated, and adapted, to the particular circumstances of each country. And its thrust and content were entirely matters for each country's policy-makers to determine. It differed from other approaches in several important ways. It:

- linked more directly consumption needs to production objectives as a basis for meeting those needs;
- emphasized the integration of policies and project activities and avoided fragmentation of efforts;

- included provisions for strengthening the institutions necessary for its implementation as a continuing process designed to sustain adequate priority for the food sector;
- facilitated national decisions over time covering the whole range of activities affecting food; and equally
- facilitated the increased and co-ordinated international assistance needed for its implementation; and ultimately
- was directed toward a paramount aim of development – 'a world without hunger'.

At its core, a national food strategy was seen as an integrated policy approach to food production, distribution and consumption. It encompassed the broad economic and social policies and reforms that affected the wider distribution of incomes and people's access to food. It served as a mechanism to give institutional expression to the priority for food and the elimination of hunger, and transcended sectoral divisions in national decision-making. It therefore facilitated the co-ordination of national efforts and the mobilization and cohesion of international assistance.

Williams saw what was termed the 'food policy dilemma' as perhaps the most fundamental issue to be tackled. This involved the policy choices of how to raise prices as an incentive to increase domestic food production while simultaneously safeguarding the nutrition of the poor. Resolving this dilemma required a clear understanding of the short- and long-term trade-offs involved in the pursuit of both production and consumption objectives. This, in turn, widened the focus to include such concerns as employment and income generation and consumer food subsidy programmes.

The national food strategy concept caught the attention of both developing and developed countries. By 1982, some 50 developing countries were said to be engaged in food strategy reviews, 32 of them with WFC-arranged assistance. Other countries also initiated food strategy reviews without specific external assistance. A number of bilateral development agencies and UN bodies and development banks offered support. National food strategies were endorsed by the UN General Assembly and at the conferences of UN and other organizations. At a 1981 summit meeting in Cancun, Mexico, 22 heads of states of developing and developed countries agreed that 'developing countries should define and put into operation, with the aid of ample and effective international support, national food strategies' as a first step to overcoming world hunger. This strong and widespread support culminated in the 1982 meeting of representatives of 44 developing countries fully endorsing the integrated approach of national food strategies to resolve food problems as a priority for global negotiations.

Subsequently, the Council, in co-operation with other bodies, carried out seven reviews of the experience of countries, particularly in Africa, in implementing national food strategies. Over 30 papers and reports were produced, between 1984 and 1992 (e.g., WFC, 1984a; RTI, 1984; Lipton and Heald, 1985; WFC, 1985a; George, 1987; Shapouri, Missiaen and Rosu, 1992). The Council also drew

184 *1970–90. The World Food Crisis of the 1970s and its Aftermath*

up detailed guidelines for the preparation and implementation of national food strategies, including institutional considerations, and addressed some important issues such as the co-ordination of international support. A number of lessons were learned (Williams, 1984). Because a number of sectors of a country's economy were involved in planning and implementing national food strategies, leadership from the highest political level, and inter-ministerial support and co-ordination, were of paramount importance. Adequate institutions and trained manpower were necessary, hence the need for training, public management and sustained institutional support. Policy change and programme innovation involved political and economic risks and required special efforts to overcome organizational inertia and resistance to change. Similarly, adjustments were required in the assistance policies and programmes of development agencies. There were no 'quick fixes' and a long-term and sustained effort was required by national governments and the international community to resolve the national and global food problems and end the scourge of hunger. And the replication of successful experience among developing countries and regions was not easy. One criticism was that national food strategies involved so many aspects of a country's development that it was difficult to distinguish the concept from that of general economic development. And with so many government and international agencies involved, co-ordination among them proved to be particularly difficult.

Eradicating hunger and malnutrition

Encouraged by its executive directors and supported by its secretariat, the Council never lost sight of its mission to seek ways and means to eradicating hunger and malnutrition. Various approaches were taken by the Council to address the issue. 'Improving nutrition' was the message at the WFC's third session in 1977. A broad approach to nutritional problems in their social and economic context was 'strongly supported'. It was also recognized that increased food production and economic development, although important elements in eradicating hunger and improving nutrition, were by themselves insufficient to achieve those objectives while people were unable to afford an adequate diet by reason of unemployment or poverty (WFC, 1977b). The importance of introducing nutrition improvement as a major objective in national development was emphasized. The WFC president proposed that the Council's bureau adopt 'a direct and high level involvement' in the actions related to nutrition and consult the agencies and governments involved to ensure rapid and effective implementation of the Council's recommendations.

'Mobilizing greater effort in the struggle to overcome hunger' was the theme at its eighth session in 1982 (WFC, 1982b). The executive director noted the commitment among all groups of countries that the eradication of hunger was 'a priority for development' but stress that 'the Council should further accelerate progress towards the achievement of that priority'. He emphasized that food and hunger issues 'must remain at the centre of the global development agenda', until hunger was completely eradicated.

A number of 'direct measures' to reduce hunger were proposed on the basis of a report prepared by its secretariat (WFC, 1982e). The WFC secretariat, with inputs from international consultants, developed the idea of an 'international food entitlement scheme', focused on international support for direct measures at the national level to eradicate hunger and malnutrition, including various types of consumer subsidy and related programmes. This idea was not pursued.[26] Instead, the WFC secretariat report identified a number of ways to improve access of the poor to food, including: the prospects for the hungry to grow more food; labour-intensive investment programmes; productive credits for low-income people; subsidizing supplementary food; and food aid to meet food import requirements.

In response to the rhetorical question raised in the report as to whether it was possible to eliminate hunger by the end of the century, it was observed that given present trends world hunger was 'likely to be more widespread'. But, as Maurice Williams, WFC's executive director, pointed out, the costs of an accelerated programme of direct measures to reduce hunger as part of a campaign to raise productivity and generate incomes and assets 'lie within the capacity of world economic resources' (Williams, 1982). He recognized that the political, social and administrative constraints were 'real and should not be underestimated'. But if such efforts were launched, 'there are prospects that the objective of food and jobs for all can still be achieved by the turn of the century'.

The Council recognized that 'changes were necessary in the national policies of many governments and in the programmes of many development agencies'. The trickle-down theory in which the 'normal' process of development was assumed to lead eventually to food self-sufficiency for the hungry had not worked in the past, and would not work in the future. The problem of extreme poverty and hunger occurred in most of the developing countries, in a context of overall food shortage, but it could not be resolved solely by measures to assure higher food availability, neither by faster agricultural growth nor larger levels of food aid. It was necessary to adopt a 'strategic package' of policies and measures that increased food production through appropriate incentive policies for producers as well as to establish schemes to generate employment, incomes and assets specifically for the poor, and supplement domestic food supplies by imports.

These were all essential elements of a national food strategy to achieve increased food self-sufficiency for people and nations. Eliminating hunger was 'the most urgent priority of the international community' and the 'mandated goal' of the Council. But unless decisive measures were taken urgently, hunger would continue to grow. The Council's discussions provided 'broadly support' for the basic thrust of the proposals contained in the executive director's report. It recommended that countries should adopt specific hunger-eradication plans to supplement their planned production programmes. And emphasis was laid on measures to improve job and income opportunities effecting more equitable food distribution. The food security concept should be reoriented to include not only global and national food security aspects but also, in particular, the food security of individuals. The main task of hunger eradication along with food self-sufficiency rested with developing countries strengthened by effective development-assistance co-operation (Williams and Stephens, 1984).

186 *1970–90. The World Food Crisis of the 1970s and its Aftermath*

The Council called for 'a renewal of the commitment to eradicate hunger' at its tenth session in 1982 (WFC, 1984f). The executive director emphasized that developing countries required sufficient resources to increase their food and agricultural production. External trade and increased export earnings were important but until such time as they were improved, more external assistance was required. ECOSOC had requested WFC to carry out an assessment of resources provided through the UN system for the food and agricultural system toward meeting the objectives of the World Food Conference (WFC, 1984f). On the basis of that assessment, he made a proposal to increase external assistance by $5 billion over the next five-year period to reverse the trend of declining assistance to the sector. He regarded this as a 'minimum amount', which would be additional to existing commitments in support of food policy adjustments in developing countries and channelled through existing aid mechanisms and institutions. Half could be in the form of food aid to support consumption and nutrition objectives, and half in capital and technical assistance directed to related food production efforts a as part of food policy support packages.

A number of Council delegates (but not all) supported the executive director's proposal. Most delegates (but not all) from developed countries indicated their willingness to assist developing countries in their efforts to restructure policies to promote new investment and growth but were unable to make positive commitment to the executive director's proposal. All delegates urged improved effectiveness in multilateral operations given the scarce resources available and the pressing agricultural investment needs. Most delegates reaffirmed that food should not be used as a measure or instrument of political pressure. And there was consensus that peace and disarmament were requisite to the elimination of poverty and eradication of hunger.

'Improving access to food by the undernourished' was the focus of the Council's discussions at its eleventh session in 1985 (WFC, 1985b). In its view, renewal by the UN General Assembly of the commitment to eradicate hunger and malnutrition was based on the recognition that these scourges were essentially man-made and could be eliminated through human resolve. The Council once again 'strongly urged' governments to take 'determined and more sharply-focused' action that made the elimination of hunger and malnutrition 'a truly central objective in national development'. Specifically, it recommended that political determination should be focused on four objectives:

- Prevention of loss of life and human suffering caused by famine through both immediate action to improve disaster preparedness and management and longer-term efforts to remove the root causes of famine. The Council recommended that FAO should be encouraged, with the support of all governments and private organization, to accelerate well co-ordinated assistance to drought-prone countries for the establishment and improvement of national early warning systems. In addition, all disaster-prone countries should prepare contingency plans to strengthen their preparedness and capacity to deal with crises and efforts should be made to improve the effectiveness of emergency food aid and relief.

- Drastic reduction of infant deaths from malnutrition and disease and protection of the gains achieved, especially in times of economic crisis. Council ministers were encouraged by progress with nutrition and health interventions to reduce infant mortality and ensure the healthy development of the next generation but recommended that this momentum 'must be maintained'.
- Efforts to alleviate the factors that led to growing world hunger in the immediate period ahead. As part of the efforts to halt growing hunger during the 1980s, Council ministers attached high priority to action which protect the already fragile food and nutrition levels of low-income families. They requested governments facing difficult economic adjustments and budgetary restrictions to take measures to prevent a deterioration in the food and nutrition levels of low-income people. International financial institutions, especially the IMF, were requested to take food security and poverty issues into account in the design of adjustment programmes to assist developing countries restore their financial and economic health. And development agencies were requested to assist governments identify economic policy alternatives and implement programmes to protect and improve the food security of the poor.
- Redirected programmes for a substantial reduction of chronic hunger in the 1990s. Council ministers 'strongly emphasized' that this would require some reorientation of development priorities and policies to meet the multiple objectives of growth, equity, self-reliance, improved efficiency and productivity, with a view to bringing about a more equitable participation of all people in development.

It was recognized that realization of these objectives required fundamental changes, which were 'the prerogative of sovereign nations'. WFC's role was to be that of an 'untiring advocate for the poor and hungry'. Elimination of hunger and malnutrition should not become 'empty rhetoric' if hunger was not to be perpetuated in the future. UN and other development agencies were invited to carry out a comprehensive assessment of the social, economic and administrative factors that reduced hunger and chronic under-nutrition and improved food security.

The paradox of growing hunger amidst record food surpluses caused the Council to address the potential for hunger reduction through 'food-surplus-based development assistance' at its fourteenth session in 1988 (WFC, 1988d). The WFC secretariat report on this subject contained a proposal for an 'International Hunger Initiative' (WFC, 1988b). The initiative, described as a kind of 'standstill and roll-back agreement', called for a firm commitment by all participating countries for joint action that would halt the growth of hunger and malnutrition and reduce the number of people affected. The primary beneficiaries of the initiative would be hungry people in low-income food-deficit countries where food consumption levels per capita had been declining. Under the initiative, developed food-surplus countries would commit a portion of their surpluses, plus some finance towards meeting shipping costs, developed non-food-surplus countries would provide complementary finance, and developing countries would commit themselves to using the assistance provided under the initiative in ways most suited to meeting the objective of limiting the growth of hunger and poverty and meet local currency costs. The WFC secretariat proposed that the initiative be established on a trial basis, of say three to five years, and continued if it proved effective. The Council was requested to endorse the initiative in principle and establish a consultative group of interested governments and international organizations to work out modalities.

The proposed initiative was supported 'in principle' but many WFC ministers felt that it did not go far enough. They felt that it dealt more with food aid and the utilization of food surpluses than with the eradication of hunger and did not take adequate account of the problems inherent in increased food aid. Instead, a much broader initiative, called 'The Cyprus Initiative Against Hunger in the World', was articulated and supported (see below). The initiative focused more directly on the possibility of hunger eradication in the foreseeable future and how to go about it, which, in the Council's view, could make a significant contribution to food security in the long run.

At its fifteenth session in 1989, the Council adopted 'The Cairo Declaration' (see below), which, among other things, significantly committed WFC ministers to set an example to the rest of the world by putting into place policies and programmes to reduce hunger and malnutrition *in their own countries* (emphasis added) as well as at the global level. They undertook to review the action taken to provide food security for all at its sixteenth session in 1990. To assist them, the executive director produced a review on a range of national policies and programmes to reduce hunger and poverty. The review drew on four regional consultations that the WFC secretariat had organized to identify additional and more effective measures and to draw attention to the constraints and problems that countries faced in their implementation (WFC, 1990a).

The review made a number of recommendations for WFC ministers' approval. Ministers from developing countries were requested to consult with their cabinet colleagues on practical ways to increase government efforts to reduce hunger including: setting specific national hunger-reduction targets for each year until the end of the decade of the 1990s; reviewing and strengthening national food strategies; upgrading inter-ministerial co-ordination; allocating additional resources to deliver effective programmes; and improving national capacity to collect data on hunger and monitor progress. Other recommendations included giving priority support to small farmers, food-subsidy schemes and nutrition interventions for the poor and most vulnerable groups, and employment-generation in rural and urban areas.

Ministers from developed countries were requested to give priority to ensuring that development assistance promoted equitable economic growth. The WFC's president was requested to convey to the governing bodies of the international financial institutions the wish of the Council that more effective measures were taken to ensure that the welfare of the hungry poor was given the greatest importance in the design and implementation of economic adjustment programmes. It was also recommended that the WFC secretariat prepare a report on the status and prospects for increasing food production in developing countries on a sustainable basis, which would include the potential for major technological advances through a new 'green revolution'.

In response to the executive director's review, the Council agreed unanimously that the development process must increasingly take into account the needs of the poor and called for 'multi-level, equitable, human-centred development policies' to be implemented in order to counter earlier neglect and distribute benefits more fairly. Many delegates stressed that agricultural policies and programmes that focused on the small farmer were doubly effective by simultaneously raising incomes of the poor and increasing agricultural output. Special attention to the creation of employment and income-earning opportunities in both rural and urban areas was emphasized. The important role that food subsidies and direct interventions could play in alleviating hunger and malnutrition was also recognized. Ministers from developing countries recognized that sound economic policies and measures to fight hunger and poverty were primarily a domestic responsibility. Developed-country ministers noted that hunger and poverty were already being given greater attention in development co-operation.

On the last occasion it address issues of hunger and poverty, at its seventeenth session in 1991, WFC stressed the need to focus development assistance specifically on the objective of their alleviation, encouraged by a report by the WFC secretariat on the subject (WFC, 1991a). Council ministers from developed countries recognized the need for a constant re-examination of the focus on hunger and poverty alleviation in the development co-operation programmes, which WFC ministers from developing countries supported (WFC, 1991b).

Food crisis contingency planning

It was predicted that the 1980s would be a 'food-crisis-prone decade'. The Council therefore agreed to consider specific contingency measures to counteract problems as they occurred. At its sixth session in 1980, the WFC executive director presented a proposal for strengthening food crisis contingency planning that had two parts. The first part was the constitution of a food security contingency reserve of 12 million tons of food grains to be held in advance or as part of a new International Wheat Agreement (WFC, 1980). Developing countries might hold up to five million tons, financed through OPEC and developed countries' assistance, and multilateral agencies and bilateral donors would provide additional technical and financial assistance and food aid to increase storage capacity and meet the costs of holding the reserves. The second part was a 'world food crisis pledge' to avoid the catastrophe of the world food crisis of the early 1970s. Its elements included an undertaking on the part of countries to act, in periods of tight international food grain markets, to minimize unilateral or destabilizing action, and to establish specific logistical stand-by procedures. The proposal also included special provisions for assistance to developing countries during an eventual world food crisis. It reiterated the need for the establishment of a food financing facility in IMF and an additional flow of food aid in case of global crisis. The executive director stressed that a 'true and reliable' contingency arrangement could not be left to voluntary or unilateral commitments. 'It must have the character of a binding international instrument'. The actions that the proposed pledge would put into motion would concern the international community as a whole because its impact would affect the actions of all nations and their ability to deal with a world food crisis. The negotiation of the pledge and the monitoring of its provisions should therefore be the responsibility of the United Nations.

The Council shared the executive director's concern for the coming decade of the 1980s. All but three WFC members agreed that if the International Wheat Agreement could not be brought to a successful conclusion by mid-1981, 'serious consideration' should be given to alternative ways of establishing a contingency reserve of 'an adequate size' in advance of, and for eventual incorporation into, a new International Wheat Agreement. Regarding the proposed 'World Food Crisis Contingency Pledge', the Council considered that it could be a 'major help' towards meeting a major world food crisis like that of the early 1970s. It requested the WFC secretariat to explore further the possible modalities of such an arrangement with the appropriate agencies.

A developing country-owned reserve

The possibility of establishing developing country-owned food reserves, within the overall objectives of achieving world food security and market stability, as part of a strategy to mobilize greater effort in the struggle to overcome hunger, was discussed by the Council at its eighth session in 1982 (WFC, 1982b). The executive director reported on consultations he had held on the possible establishment of such reserves. In the view of the experts he had met, grain markets were likely to be as volatile in the future as they had been in the past, with increasing food security risks for developing countries. There was therefore a strong case for building up reserves by developing countries as part of their national food policies as well as for protection against external uncertainty. Making available adequate financing to assist them when international prices were low therefore seemed 'very reasonable'. If enough countries, both exporters and importers, showed interest, a good case could be made for the use of the IMF buffer stock facility that had been relatively idle since its establishment in 1969. It was estimated that the sum of individual reserves needed to satisfy the commercial cereal annual requirements for the 72 low-income countries that at the time qualified for soft loans through the World Bank's International Development Association (IDA) facility would amount to 7 million tons of wheat, 3 million tons of coarse grains, and 1.3 million tons of rice. These estimates limited the reserves of any one country to a maximum of 500,000 tons of wheat, 500,000 tons of coarse grains, and 50,000 tons of rice but it was considered that only a few of the eligible countries would have annual commercial requirements above those limits.

The executive director recommended that while the acquisition of stocks with concessionary financing should be co-ordinated and undertaken according to agreed international criteria, the use of the stocks by individual countries would be decided principally by national needs and policies. This would have a market-stabilizing effect, nationally and internationally, and preserve maximum food security flexibility for governments. Each developing country would decide on the volume of reserve stocks it was prepared to acquire and hold on their location. A consultative group of donor agencies would help developing countries establish storage and management capability for which training of government personnel would also be provided. The proposal for developing country-owned reserves was considered to be both technically and financially feasible. It could be started with a few interested countries and enlarged progressively. While there was broad support in the Council for the concept of developing country-owned reserves, some member recognized the need for further work on a number of issues involved. There was agreement, however, that if effective the proposal would be beneficial for both importing and exporting countries. Markets would be supported at times of large supplies and falling prices, thereby introducing a degree of long-term supply continuity. Farmers would benefit from incentives. Importers would benefit from the continuity of supply and the measure of stability that the use of stocks would provide during periods of shortage.

Many Council members, particularly those from developing countries, considered that the proposal should move forward towards intergovernmental discussion. They stressed the need for speedy action so that the advantage could be taken of the favourable global grain supply situation to build reserves at minimum cost and to assist farmers in the process. Representatives of socialist countries also generally supported the proposal and suggested that although many problems remained they could be solved by an intergovernmental working group. While expressing interest, members from food-exporting developed countries called for more study of the technical, financial and modalities of the proposal. The Council requested the WFC president and executive director to continue the process of consultations on the proposal with the help of other interested agencies. It also stressed that if global negotiations were launched at the United Nations, the proposal could become part of a wider effort in food security and international co-operation.

Food security and environmental management

Stimulated by the UN General Assembly resolution on 'Environmental Perspective to the Year 2000 and Beyond' adopted in December 1987 (UN, 1987b), and by the report of the World Commission on Environment and Development (UNEP, 1987), the Council examined the links between food security and the environment at its fourteenth session in 1988 (WFC, 1988e). Two reports were prepared by the WFC secretariat in co-operation with UNEP (WFC, 1988c; WFC, 1988d). WFC and UNEP had also signed a memorandum of understanding in October 1987 by which they had agreed to strengthen their mutual collaboration. The executive director of UNEP introduced the subject at the Council's session.

The Council considered that environmental degradation jeopardized the food security of present and future generations. It called for the pursuit of sustainable global food security through productive systems that safeguarded the natural resources and protected the environment; and noted with concern that extreme poverty of rural people and population pressure were among the major causes of environmental degradation. The situation was made worse in a number of developing countries because of over-exploitation of resources resulting from the need

192 *1970–90. The World Food Crisis of the 1970s and its Aftermath*

for financial resources to comply with structural adjustment programmes and the servicing of external debt. Effective action to prevent further environmental damage and to achieve sustainable food security in the developing world could be facilitated by a concerted effort by the international community to improve global economic conditions. Environmentally sound agricultural management practices should form an integral part of national food strategies and that environmental concerns be integrated into economic development policies and programmes. Close co-operation between the secretariats of WFC and UNEP was requested and with other UN agencies concerned.

Developing countries food security and changes in eastern Europe and the CIS

Dramatic political changes that resulted from the break-up of political order in the USSR and eastern Europe, the creation of 15 sovereign states, and the transition to market economies of countries in eastern Europe, caused the Council to consider the effects of these changes on food security both within the region and on the food security of developing countries. The WFC executive director stated that by its mandate, WFC was called upon to contribute to advancing the understanding of, and the international dialogue on, the food security issues involved in changes in Eastern Europe and the former USSR as a basis for global policy making in support of the world's hungry poor. In a progress report to the Council, he identified two possible outcomes (WFC, 1992a). Changing patterns of financial flows at commercial terms and development and emergency assistance, with substantial amounts going to Eastern Europe, could have negative effects in developing countries.[27] On the other hand, a successful transformation of the economies in Eastern Europe was likely to contribute to greater food security globally and low-income developing countries particularly.

The Council discussed these implications at its eighteenth session in 1992 (WFC, 1992a). It stressed that all future support to the eastern European region 'must remain additional to official development assistance flows to the developing countries and must by no means divert needed assistance from the developing countries'. It was 'confident' that economic progress and a successful transformation of the economies of Eastern Europe would be stimulating for the world economy and of 'great benefit' for the developing world. A reduction of net food imports in the region could result in a net export situation in the long run by mobilizing its large food production potential. This could ease world food market prices with a positive effect for most food importing developing countries. Economic progress would also enable the region to assume and expand its development assistance to developing countries. Many developing countries would also gain from the changing patterns of trade and the expanded opportunities for food and non-food trade. However, changing patterns of financial flows on commercial terms, with substantial amounts going to Eastern Europe, could have a negative effect on developing countries. In general, a successful transformation of Eastern European economies would contribute to greater food security globally and in the low-income, food-deficit countries in particular.

National and international migration and food security

At its seventeenth session in Helsingor, Denmark in 1991, the Danish Minister for Agriculture presented a proposal to place the subject of national and international migration on WFC's agenda, which his government considered to be closely linked to food security (WFC, 1991b). He said that the magnitude of the problem was not fully known but the risk of large and accelerated migration of people within and from developing countries might constitute 'one of the greatest challenges of the generation'. Such migration had an influence on the food security situation of countries and on the development process. The proposal was accepted. The Danish Ministry of Agriculture commissioned a paper on the subject, which contained case studies on Bangladesh, Bolivia, the Sahelian countries of West Africa and the Sudan (WFC, 1991c).

The Council discussed the issue at its eighteenth session in 1992 (WFC, 1992c). Consultations undertaken by the executive director with member governments and international agencies highlighted the seriousness and complexities of the problem as one of the potentially major political and development challenges during the transition from the second to the third millennium. In addition to migration within and between developing countries, there was pressure from mass movements of people, from south to north and from east to west, of potentially unprecedented dimensions. It was noted that some migration flows could be more easily traced to food-insecurity causes than others, although true causal relationships were often difficult to determine. The problem of refugees and displaced people and the issue of migration and food security were important enough to be kept on the agenda of the United Nations until appropriate action in the relevant operational institutions was assured. The Council requested the WFC secretariat to encourage further study and policy development in this field and agreed to review progress in the future.

Strategic perspectives

Another way adopted by WFC to fulfil its mandate and keep the objective of eliminating hunger and poverty before the international community was to make projections of progress, or the lack of it, at appropriate times, and to recommend concrete actions to stimulate positive trends. On the threshold of the decade of the 1980s, at its fifth session in 1979, the prospects for world food security in the 1980s were reviewed in the light of three substantial reports (WFC, 1979a–c). The first contained a detailed assessment of the prospects for various dimensions of world food security during the decade and proposals for action by the WFC executive director. The second contained the FAO Plan of Action on World Food Security that the Committee on World Food Security made available to the Council. And the third concerned international trade issues following UNCTAD V and the Tokyo Round of Multilateral Trade Negotiations. The UN General Assembly recommended that the WFC 'consider the impact of trade including the protectionist measures harming the exports of developing countries on the

194   *1970–90. The World Food Crisis of the 1970s and its Aftermath*

solution of the food problems of developing countries and put forward specific recommendations thereon' (resolution 33/90).

In submitting his assessment, the executive director took the opportunity to clarify the concept of world food security, which, in his view, was 'not a uniformly understood concept', and was used 'with a variety of meanings'. To him, in a broad sense, it meant 'food security at the village or family level among the poorest people so that their food consumption can at least be maintained at current levels, and progressively improved over time'. In a narrower, more specialized, sense, it meant 'the stability of the international wheat market, the most widely traded food'. Proposed solutions varied according to the scope of its definition and there were many different conceptions and views. He considered that the broad concept should serve as the basis for assessing proposed policy measures. Given the complexity of the problems of food security, he felt that it was analytically useful to recognize three different, but related, aspects: the adequacy of food production and consumption systems within countries, including the distribution of income; the adequacy of infrastructure for food distribution and information concerning crop and market conditions; and international trade and adjustment, aid flows and the stability of international food markets.

On the basis of his assessment, the executive director made five recommendations for the Council's approval. First, country and regional assessments of the food security infrastructure needs of developing countries, with a request to the World Bank and FAO to expand their activities in this area. Second, agreement on a world food grain stabilization reserve of 20–30 million tons under internationally agreed and binding rules. Third, agreement on a 10-million ton Food Aid Convention to be reached in 1979. Fourth, immediate achievement of the 500,000 ton target for the IEFR, and endorsement of a 'relatively modest' enlargement to 750,000 tons by 1981. And finally, support for the establishment of a Financial Food Facility within the IMF.

The Council agreed that a world food security system was necessary to minimize the consequences of the shortfalls in production that would 'inevitably arise'. It reaffirmed the importance of concluding a new International Wheat Agreement with a new Food Aid Convention of at least 10 million tons as 'key elements' of world food security. It endorsed the guidelines and criteria for food aid developed by the WFP's governing body at the Council's request, recommended that arrangements should be made to ensure that additional food aid was provided to assist developing countries build national food reserves, and urged all countries to contribute to the immediate achievement of 500,000-ton target for the IEFR and consider its enlargement in response to growing emergency needs. And it endorsed the FAO Plan of Action on World Food Security,[28] and the FAO request that IMF establish a food financing facility. On international trade, the Council reaffirmed its support for changes in international trade to ensure access in favour of developing countries exports, and endorsed the initiatives taken by UNCTAD V in the field of food production and trade. It also recommended that developing countries expand trade among themselves and efforts to increase public awareness of the cost of protectionism to consumers and taxpayers as well as its negative effects on economic development (WFC, 1979d).

The adoption by the UN General Assembly of the International Development Strategy (IDS) for the Third United Nations Development Decade of the 1980s (UN, 1980) presented another occasion for the Council to carry out a strategic perspective of future prospects for the elimination of hunger and malnutrition (WFC, 1981). Some satisfaction could be gained from the fact that the IDS had taken note of WFC's work and recommendations and had included the target of eradicating hunger *by the end of the century* (emphasis added). However, it regretted the fact that its elimination 'within a decade', the goal set at the 1974 World Food Conference, 'was no longer feasible'. The situation of growing mass hunger and malnutrition was 'an affront to humanity'. The Council called on all governments and agencies to redouble their efforts to eliminate hunger and lead the world to co-operative development for all people. The Council was convinced that progress towards peace and disarmament, including the reduction in military expenditure called for in the IDS, were crucial for the international community to be able to develop its full capacity to feed a growing population. 'Food for all may be difficult to achieve without peace, as much as peace will not be possible in the long run without food and development for all' (WFC, 1981).

Ten years after the World Food Conference, WFC asked for a special assessment on progress in meeting food objectives and the priority tasks that remained to be achieved. The WFC president decided that at least part of the assessment should be carried out by an independent panel of highly qualified individuals with wide-ranging development experience who were not associated formally with either governments or international organizations and who would be capable of 'rigorously independent judgement'. The intention was to avoid the pitfalls often associated with self-serving institutional evaluations. The WFC president selected the panel of individuals from different regions of the world in order to ensure a broad perspective.[29]

The panel's report was presented to the Council at its tenth session in 1984 (WFC, 1984c). The assessment concluded that many of the dire forecasts made in 1974 'have not been borne out'. Aggregate food and agricultural production had reached record levels, with corresponding low real prices for most internationally traded cereals and agricultural commodities. The threat of global food scarcity 'now seems remote', although the possibility of major production shortfalls 'is still in evidence'. Identifying the hungry and formulating effective programmes for them had undergone 'major shifts in thinking and emphasis', as chronic undernutrition had proved to be 'a much more intractable and deep-seated problem'. Between 400 and 600 million people, especially in the low-income countries of Asia, Africa and Latin America still went without adequate food. The paradox of growing output and starving millions was the dilemma of the world food situation dealt with in the panel's assessment.

The assessment implicitly sought to distinguish between the world *hunger* problem and the world *food* problem, although it was acknowledged that the two were 'closely intertwined'. In the panel's opinion, 'hunger will not be ultimately overcome until the undernourished have access to meaningful employment and income-generating opportunities'. In the meantime, direct measures would be needed to provide the poor and undernourished with access to the food they required. The panel stressed that the problem of hunger must be tackled primarily at the national level where short-term and long-run policy decisions were required to provide immediate needs without hindering long-term solutions. At the global level, the panel identified the food problem as the inability to reconcile the increasing commercialization of domestic and international agricultural trade with divergent national agricultural policies and expanding food surpluses. In its view, without some measure of adjustment, the low-income countries would continue to face the greatest burden. Changes in agricultural and trade policies were necessary in the industrially advanced countries although, given past distortions, the process of change could only be gradual. Developed countries should shape national agricultural policies by understanding their implications on international prices and their impact on low-income countries. This was the nexus where the global food and hunger problems came together.

A report prepared by North American NGOs was also presented to the Council at its tenth session in 1984 (WFC, 1984d) and a statement was also made by NGOs attending that session (WFC, 1984e). The NGO report called for more collaborative and effective partnership among multilateral agencies, governments and NGOs. The WFC secretariat had analysed 'in cogent and challenging ways' the continuing reality of world hunger and had proposed strategies for dealing with it more effectively than in the past. It was now up to WFC ministers, on behalf of their governments and the international community, to respond to take steps to make the agreed-upon goal of food security a reality for all the people of the world.

The WFC ministers concluded that to meet the objectives of the World Food Conference, the major tasks ahead included:

- Sustained efforts by the developing countries at the national or regional level to increase food production and improve access to increased food supplies, the integrated food strategy approach (see below) playing an increasingly important role in the years ahead.
- A renewed commitment to an accelerated reduction of chronic hunger and malnutrition, integrating more effective direct hunger-reducing measures (see below) into the process of economic and social development.
- A major concentrated effort by African countries and the international community to resolve the African food and development crisis (see below), and the concomitant need for increased resources and for further improvements in the utilization of resources.
- Further identification and negotiation of measures for strengthening the access of developing countries to food supplies in the event of global food shortages.
- Real efforts by developed countries to reduce trade protectionism and international market instability, in support of food security and development objectives of all countries.

World Food Council 197

- Efforts to resolve the serious financial problems in general and liquidity problems in particular, confronting developing countries, which are caused to a large degree by the impact of increases in interest rates
- A commitment to sustained and increase development assistance, with a strengthened role for multilateral agencies, and improved coordination of international assistance (WFC, 1984f, p. 4).

WFC declarations

The Council issued resounding declarations at Manila, the Philippines (in 1977), Mexico City, Mexico (1978), Beijing, China (1987), Nicosia, Cyprus (1988) and Cairo, Egypt (1989) as acts of solidarity and in order to get its messages across to ECOSOC, the UN General Assembly, and the international community.[30]

Manila Communiqué of the World Food Council: A Programme of Action to Eradicate Hunger and Malnutrition (WFC, 1977b).[31]

The communiqué was adopted at the third session of the Council in Manila in 1977. In it, the Council stated that it was encouraged by some recent improvements in the world food supply situation. Increases in production had permitted the rebuilding of grain stocks in some countries. And it expressed satisfaction that, 'with the help of the Council', pledges for the $1 billion IFAD had been achieved and the fund was expected soon to be in operation. However, it expressed concerned that there was no assurance that improvement in the world food situation would continue. It called for urgent action to accelerate food production, especially in food-deficit countries, create an adequate food reserve, expand and improve food aid, improve human nutrition, and liberalize and improve food trade, in line with the resolutions of the 1974 World Food Conference. Its 'greatest concern' was the absence of 'systematic and concerted action' to implement the *Universal Declaration on the Eradication of Hunger and Malnutrition*, with its proclamation that 'Every man, woman and child has the inalienable right to be free from hunger and malnutrition' (endorsed by the UN General Assembly after approval at the 1974 World Food Conference). Achievement of that goal was 'critical to the welfare and human development of over 500 million of the world's population'.

A series of measures were recommended as basic components of an integrated programme of action to eradicate hunger and malnutrition. Governments and international agencies were called upon to act 'as matters of the highest priority' on six key areas:

- To increase food production, special treatment should be given to countries designated as 'food priority'. Official development assistance to food and agricultural production should be increased to achieve at least a 4 per cent sustained rate of growth in food production in developing countries, and a package of specific inputs should be provided to reach that goal.
- To improve and ensure world food security, countries with grain stocks were requested to convert a portion of their stocks into national reserves in 1977,

198   *1970–90. The World Food Crisis of the 1970s and its Aftermath*

while intensified efforts were underway to develop an adequate food reserve programme in appropriate international negotiations, and to ensure continuity of supplies to countries relying on imports to feed their people, especially poor, food-deficit countries. Other measures included: the establishment of an international system of nationally held reserves, and adequate food aid supplies as part of a new International Grains Arrangement with a new Food Aid Convention by June 1978; adoption of the objectives and main elements of the International Undertaking on World Food Security; and support to the IEFR of 500,000 tons of cereals by the end of 1977.

- To increase and improve the use of food aid by reaching the minimum annual level of food aid in cereals of 10 tons in 1977/78, adopting the forward planning of food aid supplies, and developing and implementing an improved policy framework for food aid.
- To improve human nutrition, all governments were called upon to give high priority to reducing hunger and improve nutrition in accordance with the appropriate resolution of the World Food Conference. Bilateral and multilateral agencies were requested to assist developing countries develop and implement nutrition plans, policies and programmes, and measures to monitor and evaluate their results.
- To improve the contribution of trade to the solution of food problems, all countries, and particularly developed nations, were encouraged to make 'serious efforts' to stabilize, liberalize and expand world trade, and for negotiation of the UNCTAD Integrated Programme for Commodities to be 'speedily concluded'.
- To ensure that these recommendations were integrated with other development policies and programmes to advance development and reduce poverty, and to assure overall development consistent with the Council's food and nutrition objectives, donors were requested to increase their ODA to reach the target of 7 per cent of GDP envisaged at the seventh special session by the UN General Assembly by the end of the decade. Governments and international agencies were recommended to give 'major support' towards the implementation of the 'basic needs approach' endorsed by the 1976 ILO World Employment Conference (ILO, 1976).

The communique was unanimously endorsed by ECOSOC in its resolution 2114 (LXII) of 4 August 1977, and adopted in full by the UN General Assembly in its resolution 32/52 of 8 December 1977.

Mexico Declaration of the World Food Council (WFC, 1978)[32]

Shortly after he had become WFC executive director, in his statement to the Second Committee of the UN General Assembly on 20 October 1978, in which he reported on WFC's session in Mexico City, Maurice Williams stressed that the eradication of hunger and malnutrition 'must be the key elements in the [UN] Third Development Strategy [of the 1980s] – indeed, it may well be our central preoccupation until the year 2000' (Williams, 1978). He noted that there was 'a general understanding' of the measures that had to be taken to achieve that objective. What was needed was agreement on the precise measures that were required to translate 'willingness in principle into action in practice'. In his message delivered at the WFC session, the UN secretary-general had reminded the Council that 'the search for a meaningful and positive consensus among governments is at the heart of the Council's work'. The Council had progressively refined its approach to the difficult problems of establishing a real priority for food and getting agreement on it. The Mexico Declaration laid out a practical programme to achieve that result. Williams sought 'with confidence' the strong endorsement of the UN General Assembly 'in order to provide a firm basis for its [WFC's] continuing work'.

The Mexico Declaration was in the form of an international wakeup call. The declaration listed the positive achievements of the Council in the direction of fulfilling the goals it had set, including: promoting the establishment of IFAD, which had approved its first project in April 1978; stimulating contributions to the IEFR; promoting machinery to accelerate action in the field of nutrition within the UN system; encouraging the initiation of food and nutrition strategies for specific developing countries; and stimulating actions to eradicate hunger and malnutrition through adoption of the Manila Communiqué. However, on closer examination of the world food situation, the Council had found that the rate of progress in solving fundamental food problems was 'far too slow'. Employment and income opportunities of the rural poor 'lagged seriously behind' population growth. Food production had increased by only 1 per cent in developing countries and food prices had risen significantly, creating difficulties for consumers, especially in FPCs. Progress in formulating a new international wheat agreement had been slow. In sum, although government and international organizations did respond to the world food crisis of the early 1970s, progress had been 'limited and uneven'.

A number of facts were listed that led to the Council's 'fears for the future', including: world food production had grown more slowly in the 1970s than in the previous decade; per capita food production had declined in the FPCs; the number of undernourished people continued to increase; external assistance for increasing food production was little improved in real terms and was substantially below the Council's target of $8.3 billion; many developing countries had not been able to increase their priority for food production and improved nutrition owing to limited resources; a new international wheat agreement, with provision for a cereal reserve, and at least 10 million tons of food aid on a secure basis, had not been formulated; and trade barriers, instability and, in some cases, mounting protectionism handicapped food trade, production and the development efforts of many developing countries. The Council called for this 'dangerous situation' to be corrected 'or else the pace and direction of progress will continue to fall short of the objectives of the World Food Conference and the Manila Communiqué'.

The Council recognized its responsibility 'as a guiding force within the United Nations on all food matters'. It also sought the 'full co-operation' of governments, international organizations and forums whose operational decisions it recognized. And it recalled that the World Food Conference had recognized that the important food problems could not be solved without assigning greater political priority to

200   *1970–90. The World Food Crisis of the 1970s and its Aftermath*

food and without agreements between governments and agencies to undertake joint obligations to solve those problems. In the Council's opinion, such priority and joint commitments 'have not become a reality' and 'there continued to be weaknesses in the world food system'. The Council's mandate required it 'to take further steps to correct these weaknesses'. It noted that more was required of the Council 'to overcome the obstacles to efficient and rapid progress in food production'. Widespread hunger and malnutrition and their negative consequences on development were 'such grave concerns' that action must be initiated to eradicate these conditions. The response of the UN system to the nutrition recommendations of the Manila Communiqué was 'positive, but, as yet, too limited'. The world community needed a better framework for action to which countries and agencies could respond to. Two 'urgent concerns' were identified:

- The necessity of allocating a share of resources that would be freed as a result of the reduction of military expenditure to finance measures directed to advancing the development of developing countries, especially their food situation, was reiterated.[33]
- Bearing in mind the serious situation that again confronted countries in the Sahelian zone of West Africa owing to climatic conditions, governments and multilateral agencies were 'expressly requested' to supply or increase the necessary emergency food aid and to support the efforts of the governments of the region to ensure long-term development of their food production.

The Mexico Declaration then listed in detail the Council's recommendations concerning the implementation of the Manila Communiqué. It was to take almost a decade before the Council issued another 'declaration'.

Beijing Declaration of the World Food Council (WFC, 1987a)[34]

The Beijing Declaration was another clarion call for concerted international action to eliminate hunger and malnutrition. Coming towards the end of a decade of world recession and non-development, it stated that thirteen years after the World Food Conference, although total food production had increased, the number of undernourished people had risen. This 'untenable situation' had 'deep historical root causes and complex social and economic factors'. In the face of this disorder, 'which was affecting innocent human beings', the Council:

- once again proclaimed that access to food constituted a human right that must be defended by governments, peoples and the international community;
- affirmed, in the light of the experience of a number of developing countries, that humanity can feed itself if it adopted the proper means;
- proclaimed that those means depended on the political will of governments and the international community to win the common battle against hunger; and
- acknowledged that the development of agricultural production required a favourable international climate, and was contingent upon the convergence of financial, economic and social policies implemented by each country within the framework of the concept of national food strategies.

Moreover, the Council was convinced that agriculture was a vital sector for establishing a social, economic and financial equilibrium in developing countries and that the debts incurred by many developing countries, especially the least-developed, should not result in increased poverty for rural populations. Therefore, the Council:

- called upon those responsible for national economic adjustment programmes to give priority to the requirements of integrated rural development as they affected the living conditions of both rural and urban populations;
- urged developed countries and major financing bodies to take into consideration the great difficulties of developing countries to repay their debts and to set up the necessary financial instruments for national economic recovery;
- urged those responsible for trade negotiations to re-establish a healthy and equitable exchange of agricultural products and to allow the fair participation of developing countries;
- believed that governments and international organizations must further encourage regional and South–South co-operation, particularly in support of food production, agro-industries, trade, and management and institution-building;
- affirmed that the support of the countries of the North for the peoples of the developing South remained essential;
- recognized that peace and stability were essential for the development of agricultural production; and
- proclaimed the Council members' intention to join together and, in their united strength and interest, 'eliminate the scourge of hunger forever'.

The declaration address four major issues. First was the global state of hunger and malnutrition and the impact of economic adjustment on food and hunger problems. The Council proclaimed that the conclusion emerging from its review was clear. The world was 'moving away from the central objective of the World Food Conference to eliminate hunger and malnutrition'. That objective required fundamental policy change, which placed improvement of the human condition at the 'front and centre of economic development', and comprehensive economic and social measures. The Council urged 'all governments and international assistance agencies to make the well-being of all people the central objective of development and to focus all development policies to pursue this end'. It recommended the governments 'redouble their food-strategy efforts', requested the WFC secretariat to intensify its efforts to facilitate North–South and South–South co-operation in support of national and regional food strategies, and resolved to sharpen the focus on hunger-related poverty reduction in its future work. And it 'noted with interest' the recommendations of the consultation on 'The Impact of Economic Adjustment on People's Food Security and Nutritional Levels in Developing Countries' organized by the WFC secretariat in collaboration with UNICEF and ILO in May 1987 (WFC, 1987b).[35]

The second issue was the impact of international agricultural trade and related national policies on food and development. The UN General Assembly (resolution 41/191) requested the Council to assess, within its mandate, 'the impact of the present agricultural trade situation in all its aspects and to maintain an active interest in the progress and outcome of multilateral negotiations on agricultural trade issues'. The Beijing declaration noted that growing protectionism, the decline of commodity prices, deterioration in the terms of trade, and limited access to markets had had a negative impact on the situation of international agricultural trade, and impeded efforts of the developing countries to overcome hunger and malnutrition. The WFC president and executive director were invited to consider the possibility of using the large food surpluses and technical and financial assistance to accelerate economic development of developing countries. The declaration recommended that in order to solve the problems of world agricultural trade, national policy reforms should go hand-in-hand with efforts to improve the international trade and economic environment and that 'special and differential treatment' should be given in agricultural trade to developing countries, particularly the least-developed, in the Uruguay Round of multilateral trade negotiations.

Regional and South–South co-operation in food and agriculture was the third issue to be addressed in the Beijing declaration. The regional development banks and economic commissions and donor countries were urged, in liaison with the Council, to facilitate practical arrangements to increase the financing of technical and economic co-operation among developing countries. The Council also recommended in particular that greater attention be given to the expansion of tripartite arrangement through which developed countries helped finance South–South co-operation.

Finally, attention was turned to the activities of multilateral assistance agencies in the reduction of hunger. The declaration expressed the Council's 'general appreciation and encouragement' for the work of the multilateral agencies and highlighted in particular: the continuing development of FAO Global Information and Early Warning System, FAO's feasibility study to assess the net benefits of increased aid-in-kind of farm inputs, IFAD's special programme for sub-Saharan African countries affected by drought and desertification, and WFP's programme to improve food aid delivery in the African food emergency.

The Cyprus Initiative against Hunger in the World (WFC, 1988e)[36]

At its fourteenth session in Nicosia, Cyprus in 1988, the Council discussed the potential for reducing hunger through food-surplus based development assistance. It was noted that increasing world hunger amid growing food surpluses was 'a cruel fact of our time'. Against this background, the WFC secretariat proposed an 'International Hunger Initiative' (1988b) based on a combination of concessional food transfers from food-surplus countries, financial assistance from non-food-surplus developed countries, and the efforts of developing countries themselves, to alleviate hunger and poverty. While the proposal met with widespread interest and support, it was observed that food 'surpluses' and hunger were separate problems. The Council's primary concern was 'the solution of the problem of hunger'. The secretariat's proposal was therefore considered to represent a limited contribution to the much broader efforts required to address hunger problems. The Council's discussions brought to the fore that past policies and programmes had not succeeded in reducing hunger and malnutrition. Future progress critically hinged on a better understanding of why efforts of the international community had proved insufficient. At the same time, the Council emphasized that more studies would not feed hungry people. Immediate and more effective action was required, drawing upon the lessons of the past. In this spirit, the Council decided to launch *The Cyprus Initiative against Hunger in the World*.

The initiative called for 'an urgent review and assessment of the efforts made to date in reducing hunger and for the identification of ways for improving current policies and programmes and pragmatic, feasible and potentially effective new initiatives towards meeting the Council's fundamental objective: the elimination of hunger and malnutrition'. The WFC president was requested to present a full, action-oriented report to the Council at its next session in 1989. In order to assist the president, a 'small and informal *ad hoc* consultative group' was established composed of representatives of states members of the United Nations convened by the Council's regional vice-presidents, relevant international organizations, and the WFC president'.[37] The group's mandate was:

> to review and assess the policies and instruments available to combat chronic hunger and malnutrition in developing countries, particularly in low-income, food-deficit countries, and identify the reasons and obstacles that may have hindered their greater impact; consider concrete and realistic measures that could make existing policies and instruments more effective; identify workable initiatives; and recommend a course of action to combat hunger more effectively.

The proposals of the group were to be first examined at a meeting of the WFC bureau by the end of 1988 before being presented to the Council at its session in 1989.

The Cairo Declaration (WFC, 1989f)[38]

The WFC president's comprehensive report in response to the *Cyprus Initiative* was discussed by the Council at its fifteenth session in Cairo, Egypt in 1989. The four-part report comprised a review of global hunger fifteen years after the World Food Conference, an assessment of the effectiveness of current policies and programmes in reducing hunger, and a proposed programme of co-operative action (WFC, 1989a-e). Deliberations focused on urgently needed action, out of which emerged the *Cairo Declaration*. The Council admitted that its discussions 'were not free of some frustration and impatience' with an international community that '[had] not yet succeeded in turning its energies sufficiently toward a problem that morally must be solved and practically can be solved'. Hunger continued to grow because 'we have not tried hard enough to eradicate it, even thought we have the resources to do so'.

204 *1970–90. The World Food Crisis of the 1970s and its Aftermath*

The declaration stated that the 'tragedy of hunger has many faces': starvation caused by famine, often associated with violent conflict or war, and natural disasters; the silent suffering of the growing number of undernourished; the millions of malnourished children, women and elderly who are unable to meet their special food and health needs; and the many lives lost to or ruined by disorders caused by deficiencies of micro-nutrients, such as vitamin A and iodine. While different forms of hunger had specific causes requiring appropriate responses, they were generally rooted in poverty and a failure to share food and wealth adequately within and between countries, as demonstrated with the growth in the number of hungry people, despite record-level global food stocks. The problem of access to food by those who needed it had been made worse by the economic difficulties of the 1980s.

The Council reiterated that the elimination of hunger and poverty 'must be made a central objective of national policies'. To increase food production, food strategies should emphasize domestic research and extension, the timely provision of inputs at prices farmers can afford, and appropriate production incentives for ecologically sustainable agricultural practices. An improved international economic environment was necessary for the growth of the economies of developing countries, and would contribute to the elimination of hunger through generating economic activity, provided that domestic policies were in place to direct part of its benefits to the poor. It was necessary to increase resource flows to developing countries and solve the problem of foreign debt. And it was important to achieve a positive outcome of the multilateral trade negotiations undertaken within the framework of the GATT Uruguay Round and to expand trade among the developing countries themselves.

The *Cairo Declaration* contained a specific 'call to action' (WFC, 1989f). Council members agreed that they could serve 'as an example to the rest of the world' if they strengthened their own political determination to eradicate hunger, commensurate with the magnitude and urgency of the problem. They recognized that each country must take its own initiatives in the fight against hunger and poverty but achievements would be greater when WFC member and non-members worked together and co-ordinated their efforts. In this spirit, the Council accepted the steps articulated in the 'Programme of Co-operative Action' that the WFC president proposed (which was annexed to the *Cairo Declaration*), as a framework for its individual and collective action to combat hunger. Specifically, WFC members undertook to:

- review their policies and programmes to provide food security for all people, and devise a package of corrective measures to address inadequacies, and report to the next session of the Council;
- make all efforts to achieve, *during the next decade* (emphasis added), the elimination of starvation and death caused by famine, a 'substantial reduction' of malnutrition and mortality among young children, a 'tangible reduction' in chronic hunger, and 'the elimination' of major nutritional deficiency diseases;

- adopt, evaluate and improve food strategies as an important instrument to fight hunger within broader developmental efforts focused on the improvement of the human condition; and
- co-operate among each other, and with other countries, in the fight against hunger and malnutrition.

Other specific measures mentioned in the declaration included: acceptance, in principle, by the Council of the proposal for an international agreement on the safe passage of emergency food aid in times of civil strife, war and natural disasters; a call to donor countries to streamline their administrative procedures to ensure more timely and flexible response to emergency requests; training programmes in food policy management and support of food strategies in Africa at the national and regional levels; and increased South-South co-operation on food and agriculture at the regional and interregional levels with the support of the concerned UN agencies.

To raise the level of political support nationally and internationally, the declaration proposed that the eradication of hunger and malnutrition should be a 'major theme' on the agenda of the special session of the UN General Assembly on international economic co-operation in 1990, and a 'central objective' for the international development strategy for the 1990s. The Council's president was requested to convey the conclusions and recommendations of the *Cairo Declaration* to the G7 countries prior to its summit in Paris in July 1989. And the Council decided that its future programme of work would be as determined in the *Cairo Declaration*.

Beijing Proposal emerging from the symposium on Sustainable Agriculture and Rural Development

The final act of the Council was to co-sponsor an international symposium on sustainable agriculture and rural development in Beijing, China in May 1993. The symposium was organized by the Chinese government and attended by over 160 participants, including representatives from 24 countries and international organizations. Some 100 papers were prepared for the meeting, including one by the WFC secretariat (WFC, 1993). The WFC paper argued that in many developing countries a new Green Revolution was needed to meet the growing demand for food but that it should be significantly different from the first Green Revolution. It should be 'green' in an ecologically sustainable sense, but also socially sustainable. The paper called for new strategic directions in technology development and application for sustainable food security, guided by the three basic objectives of productivity, sustainability and equity. Five major new directions were identified: a focus on agro-ecological zones to achieve sustainable food security; the development of a farming systems approach and livelihood research; the integration of conventional research with modern biotechnology; participatory research and extension by farmers; and improving the links between research and policy. The paper also addressed the trade-offs between sustainability, food production growth and hunger and poverty alleviation, many of which should be understood as long-term 'inter-generational' trade-offs.

The *Beijing Proposal* emerging from the symposium contained four major recommendations:

- the establishment of a regional association for world sustainable agriculture and rural development;
- the foundation of an Institute of International Sustainable Agriculture and Rural Development in China;
- the setting up of a key research and development project on international sustainable agriculture and rural development; and
- the holding of annual international workshops in different regions of China or countries in the Asia and Pacific region on sustainable agriculture and rural development.

A co-ordinating mechanism

An important function of the WFC, established by the World Food Conference and approved by the UN General Assembly, was to serve as a 'co-ordinating mechanism' to provide 'over-all, integrated and continuing attention for the successful co-ordination and follow-up of policies concerning food production, nutrition, food security, food trade and food aid, and related matters by all the agencies of the UN system' (UN, 1975). A number of ways were approved for carrying out that role. At its first session in 1975, the Council decided to allow its president, or his representative, to attend sessions of the governing bodies of the relevant UN bodies. The WFC president and the executive director also met with the executive heads of UN bodies individually or collectively and organized consultations with relevant UN organizations on specific subjects within the Council's mandate.

The scale and complexity of the Council's co-ordinating function was revealed when it requested the WFC secretariat to review co-ordination among the UN agencies towards meeting the common objective of eliminating hunger and malnutrition (WFC, 1990b). The review found that well over 30 multilateral institutions were 'in a significant way' related to hunger and malnutrition issues (see Figure 17.1). The mandates of most of these institutions were directed at fostering economic development and human welfare. Some were specifically called upon to assist in raising nutritional levels, such as FAO, IFAD, UNICEF, WFP and WHO. Other addressed aspects related to food security in terms of the supply of, or access to, food as well as relevant macro-economic policies. A substantial number of institutions provided technical, financial or research support. About two-thirds of the bodies listed were involved in one way or another in macro-economic policies and structural adjustment programmes that related to food security in general and for low-income groups in particular. There were some 15 institutions that provided operational, research or political support for country food strategies and food security policies. At least a dozen were involved in food production, processing and distribution activities. The activities of most of the agencies had a bearing on employment and income-generating opportunities and on nutrition and health activities.

207

Figure 17.1 United Nations bodies with an interest in food and nutrition security

UN Body	Special Interest*	UN Body	Special Interest*
FAO	Agricultural protection, rural development, employment, income generation, marketing, trade, food security, nutrition, food emergencies/early warning, agrarian reform, structural adjustment, environment	UN Centre for Human Rights	Food as a human right
		UN Centre for Human Settlements (Habitat)	Food security and viable and sustainable settlements
IAEA	Irradiation of food		
IBRD/IDA	Macro policy, structural adjustment, programme and project lending for food security and nutrition improvement, CGIAR secretariat	UN Centre for Social Development and Humanitarian Affairs	Food policy in context of social development
		UNCTAD	Food trade and agricultural subsidies
IFAD	Agricultural production, rural development, agrarian reform, structural adjustment, employment, income generation, environment	UNCTC	Food production and trade of transnationals
		UNDHA	Humanitarian operations
		UNDP	Technical cooperation and grant aid for programmes and projects for food security and nutrition, management of round-table process
ILO	Employment, income generation, training, social protection, entitlement programmes, structural adjustment, rural development		
		UNEP	Food production, food security, environment and sustainability
IMF	Macro policy, structural adjustment, financing of food imports		
INSTRAW	Women and food security	UNESCO	Formal and informal education on food and nutrition and related issues
UNFPA	Food security and population questions		
		UNRWA	Food security and nutrition for Palestinian refugees
UNHCR	Refugees and food security and nutrition issues		
UNICEF	Food security and nutrition programmes, mothers and children, structural adjustment	UN Secretariat and Departments (New York)	UN General Assembly and Security Council, general over-sight, political questions, macro policy, structural adjustment, population, environment, sustainability
UNIDO	Agro-industry, food processing		
UNITAR	Training programmes in food security, nutrition and related issues	UNU (including WIDER)	Research and teaching on food security issues
UN Regional Commissions (5)	Food security and nutrition in regional policy and context	WFP	Development and emergency food aid for food security and nutrition
UNRISD	Research on food security and related issues	WHO	Health and nutrition programmes, food standards (with FAO)

*The special interest indicated for each UN body is illustrative and not definitive. There are also 15 international centres of the Consultative Group on International Agricultural Research (CGIAR) including the International Food Policy Research (IFPRI), related to the United Nations system. In addition, there are three regional banks and the World Trade Organisation (WTO), whose special interests relate to food security that have cooperative arrangements with the United Nations system.

Source: WFC (1990); Maxwell and Shaw (1995); Shaw (1999).

208   *1970–90. The World Food Crisis of the 1970s and its Aftermath*

While most agencies were engaged in some food security related activity, only a few of them were found to 'focus sharply' on hunger and poverty alleviation, including IFAD, UNICEF and WFP, which concentrated their assistance on small farmers, the rural poor, and nutritionally vulnerable groups, and humanitarian assistance agencies such as UNDRO and UNHCR. Agency priorities were generally widely set, reflecting different interests within their governing bodies. The review found that hunger-alleviation and food security objectives were not well integrated into agencies' overall activities. There was need for more effective internal co-ordination within agencies, particularly the larger ones. And given the dispersion of priorities, many institutions spread their limited resources over a wide range of activities, generating large numbers of small-scale projects, endangering the quality of the agencies' work and their impact on hunger and poverty reduction.

Given the multi-institutional structure and 'sectorization' of the UN system, efforts had been made to ensure co-ordination among the system's institutions. At the intergovernmental level, ECOSOC was charged with co-ordinating the economic and social work of the UN system. At the inter-secretariat level, ACC was created as a mechanism through which, under the chairmanship of the UN secretary-general, the activities of the UN bodies could be co-ordinated. To foster co-operation at the technical level, the ACC established a number of sub-committees and task forces in such areas as rural development, long-term development objectives, and information systems. An ACC Subcommittee on Nutrition (SCN) was established in 1977. WFC worked closely with, and through, the SCN in its attempts to harmonize the UN agencies' perceptions of the nature and causes of hunger problems and feasible policy responses. With the encouragement of the Council, the SCN had increased its efforts to improve the information base of the magnitude of malnutrition and stimulated the development of strategies to eliminate nutritional-deficiency diseases. Over the years, a number of co-ordination-related organs had been added to the UN system's machinery including: an Advisory Committee on Administrative and Budgetary Questions (established in 1962); a Committee on Programme and Co-ordination (1964); a Joint Inspection Unit (1968); an Office for Programme Planning and Co-ordination (1977); a Consultative Committee on Substantive Questions (1977); and a Director-General for Development and International Economic Co-operation (1977). At the developing country level, UNDP was expected to play a co-ordinating role for UN operational activities. It was to serve as a central funding and programming agency, under the leadership of a UN resident co-ordinator, to ensure system-wide co-ordination in the country context. To facilitate policy dialogue and co-ordinate aid programmes among donors at the country level, the World Bank instituted the practice of chairing 'consultative groups' in the early 1960s and the UNDP initiated a process of 'round table' discussions in the 1970s.

Despite the various co-ordination arrangements, extensive reviews had found co-ordination within the UN system to be deficient. The UN agencies were perceived to compete excessively, and joint programming of their operational activities remained 'mostly inadequate' (UN, 1987c). The general conclusion of these assessments was that ECOSOC had failed to bring the economic and social activities of the UN system closer together and that the ACC should make its role more effective and establish clearer priorities. At the country level, UNDP had generally not fulfilled expectations, and the UN resident co-ordinator, although formally representing the UN secretary-general in the country, could only occasionally exercise the leadership expected. These deficiencies were addressed by the UN General Assembly at its forty-fourth session in 1989, which made a number of recommendations directed at their possible solution (UN, 1989).

The WFC review noted that while much remained to be done to make the UN co-ordination machinery effective, there had been many additional efforts to facilitate collaboration, including inter-agency arrangements. An inventory prepared by the ACC listed close to 100 such arrangements within and outside formal UN system co-ordination machinery. Most of these were consultative headquarters arrangements but some provided technical and financial assistance at the country-level. Among the principal problems impeding co-ordination were the different cycles of financing and programming operated by each agency and the different decision-making structures and degree of devolved responsibility between their headquarters and field staffs. Other difficulties included major differences in project management procedures, agreement on leadership among the agencies concerned, and differences in administrative structures. The World Bank consultative groups and UNDP round tables were created to provide a broad framework for co-operation without going into sectoral or sub-sectoral details. They had therefore not been expected to serve as forums for dialogue with a major focus on hunger reduction. But sectoral committees or groups had been set up following consultative group and round table meetings and could therefore be used to introduce and pursue hunger-alleviation objectives. The review gave examples of collaborative efforts among UN agencies with food security and other social objectives in structural adjustment programmes, the development of food strategy and food security policy, in agricultural research, particularly through the CGIAR, and in the elimination of nutritional deficiency diseases.

From its overview, the WFC secretariat drew two general conclusions. First, with over 30 multilateral institutions involved in hunger and malnutrition issues, the need for a central focus on hunger in the UN system remained as important as it was when WFC was established sixteen years previously. To meet the challenges ahead, the secretariat concluded that the Council would need to further strengthen its monitoring, assessment and promotional roles. Second, improved co-ordination was most critically needed at the country level. Multilateral and bilateral assistance agencies could support developing countries' efforts by adjusting their own aid management and co-ordination procedures to developing countries' needs, including improvements in the internal co-ordination of hunger-focused action within the agencies themselves: and by providing management support to improve developing countries' capacity to plan and manage their national policies and programmes and external aid.

From these two conclusions, the WFC secretariat made three groups of recommendations: first, to improve the capacity of developing countries to plan, manage

210 *1970–90. The World Food Crisis of the 1970s and its Aftermath*

and co-ordinate national hunger-focused action and external aid; second, to strengthen existing co-ordination mechanisms in the UN system; and, third, to explore opportunities for informal co-ordination arrangements. The Council noted that in its regional consultations on improving co-ordination, developing countries emphasized that co-ordination of external assistance was primarily the responsibility of the developing countries themselves, which would be facilitated by better co-ordination of their domestic activities (WFC, 1990b). In the light of the growing complexity of hunger and poverty problems, the Council felt that its role in providing 'a central, undivided focus on hunger within the UN system' was now more important than at the time of its establishment. It agreed to encourage an enhanced hunger focus and improved co-ordination among all relevant international agencies and governing bodies. Council members welcomed the proposal, endorsed by the UN secretary-general, for the creation of an inter-secretariat consultative mechanism among the four Rome-based food organizations, FAO, IFAD, WFC and WFP.

Assessment

The above account shows the considerable work and initiatives of the Council as the political overview body in the UN system in the fight against hunger and malnutrition. As a ministerial body, it had: lent its weight, *inter alia*, to: the establishment of IFAD; the increase in food aid through an enlarged Food Aid Convention; the establishment of an IEFR with agreed modalities; the elaboration of international food aid guidelines and criteria; and the creation of an IMF cereal financing facility. Among its major initiatives, the Council had established criteria for the identification of FPCs as a focus of attention; urged particular concern be given to the special food problems of Africa; developed the concept of national food strategies; attempted to keep international attention focused on the various dimensions of the goal of eradicating hunger and malnutrition; advocated food crisis contingency planning; recommended developing country-owned food reserves; drew attention to the importance of environmental management in the quest for food security; warned of the possible diversion of assistance from developing countries to the countries of Eastern Europe with the break-up of the former Soviet Unions; and address the problem of international migration and its threat to food security. It carried out strategic perspectives on future prospects for achieving the elimination of hunger and malnutrition. And it issued four resounding declarations as clarion calls to ECOSOC, the UN General Assembly, and the international community on the elimination of hunger and malnutrition.

The Council's contributions toward helping to shape and promote an effective hunger-focused world food policy were therefore significant. As a report of the UN Joint Inspection Unit, the 'watchdog' of the UN system's performance, stated, 'the World Food Council is the only body which each year brings together ministers and whose deliberations have a real effect on the shape of operations' (Bertrand, 1985, p. 21). It was the ministerial character, and the political weight it carried, that made the Council a unique policy forum. The WFC president, and especially its executive director, backed by a small, dedicated secretariat, played important roles in formulating and advocating WFC policy proposals and consensus building.[39] Despite their Herculean efforts, they were given neither the authority nor the means to carry out the co-ordinating role expected of the WFC for all relevant bodies of the UN system.[40]

Although much was achieved, there was disquiet both within and outside the Council about the way in which it functioned. By its fifth session in 1979, frustration with the way the Council conducted its business broke to the surface when the WFC president, Arturo R. Tanco, Jr., Minister of Agriculture of the Philippines, called a meeting of heads of delegations of member and non-member states to discuss the Council's future programme of work. They 'strongly recommended' that more ministers of government should attend future Council sessions and reached agreement on 10 points for the future organization of the Council's work (WFC, 1979d, p. 32). Preparatory meetings were 'necessary and important' in assisting WFC ministerial sessions, but the work of those meetings 'must be properly structured'. The nature of the Council's reports to ECOSOC and the UN General Assembly would depend on the subjects to be taken up, but time should not be taken at plenary meetings in drafting the reports. Representatives of member states should not spend time describing their countries' progress in food and agriculture. Long statements of this nature could be filed to be read by those interested. And a voluntary restraint on the length of speeches should be exercised by all. Representatives should address themselves to the agenda items and discuss issues thoroughly rather than make speeches or engage in a general debate. To function properly as a monitoring and co-ordinating body, the Council should receive reports from governments and international agencies on what they were doing. A change of format was needed to allow for more informal meetings and for smaller groups to get together to work informally. Informal meetings of ministers and other heads of delegations should be held at the beginning of Council sessions. The WFC bureau and executive director should warn members in advance of any new commitments to be made or sought so that they could be prepared to respond. The agenda for each session should consist of 'only a few carefully selected items' and should 'possibly' include case studies of countries with successful food and agricultural programmes. And the WFC president and bureau should 'continue to be very active'. The Council unanimously adopted the ten points and agreed to follow them in conducting its future work.

But there was no discernable change in the way in which the Council conducted its business or reported to the UN General Assembly on its work. As a result, another WFC president, Eugene Whelan, Minister of Agriculture of Canada, had a private meeting with Council ministers at their eleventh session in 1985 to discuss the future work and organization of the Council and consider what changes might be necessary to 'revitalize' its work and 'facilitate the resolution of persistent world food problems' (WFC, 1985b, p. 30). The meeting concluded that the Council 'should clearly return to its original mandate, as specified in the World Food Conference resolution'. It considered that it was timely to conduct a review of

212 1970–90. The World Food Crisis of the 1970s and its Aftermath

the Council's *modus operandi*, 'ideally by the [UN] Secretary-General's Office with a small committee of member states'. The review 'would aim to ensure that the Council has adequate authority and independence to discharge its responsibility'. The UN secretary-general, Perez de Cuellar, appointed a small advisory group to evaluate the effectiveness of the WFC and recommend ways in which the Council might more effectively accomplish its objectives.[41] The group held meetings in Rome, Washington, DC, Paris and New York, and consultations with governments and other institutions.

The advisory group presented its report to the UN secretary-general in February 1986. Its recommendations and suggestions were distributed to Council members in March 1986 (WFC, 1986b). The group considered three options:

- strengthening the Council through improvements in its organization, *modus operandi*, and programmes and methods of work, but with very modest additions to its resources and staff;
- a major upgrading of the Council's work, with significant structural and budgetary changes; and
- a basic redesign of the Council's role, by integrating its work more closely with the broad development functions of UN headquarters in New York.

The group focused on the first option as it could be implemented largely within existing resources. The second option would, in effect, mean developing a structure and level of resources commensurate with the Council's mandate as conceived by the 1974 World Food Conference. By way of example, the group noted that the Council's enhanced functions might include: a major expansion of its role in co-ordination of support for food-related emergencies, such as the crisis in Africa; the direct mobilization of resources for the implementation of food strategies and other food-related programmes; a central monitoring role of the activities of the relevant UN agencies; and a considerable increase in its capacity to address directly the broader dimensions of the food problem, such as investment, trade and development policy in general.

A number of replies to the group's written request favoured strengthening action along these and similar lines. In part, therefore, the question was one of degree. The group observed that the Council would need a much larger staff to undertake such an expanded role. In order to make any fundamental change, some respondents stressed that it would be essential to endow the Council, and its executive director, with substantially increased authority, at least as great as that of the UN agencies that the Council was required to co-ordinate and monitor. The third option would entail relocating the Council's headquarters in New York and integrating its role, as the food advisory arm of the UN secretary-general and the UN Director-General for Development and International Co-operation, into the broader development function of the UN. Under this option, food-related issues would be left to FAO and the co-ordinating role of the UN would be strengthened. In due course, the group felt that the Council could probably evolve into the first ministerial 'World Development Council'.

The group stressed that the first, 'favoured', option was evolutionary rather than revolutionary in nature. But it was important to appreciate that it did involve real change and required 'energetic support' of governments if it was to be successfully implemented. The group made nine recommendations to bring this about, each one of which was accompanied by detailed suggestions for their implementation:

- In order to reinforce the Council's political authority to the maximum, as a unique policy forum for food-related issues, its ministerial character should be conserved and enhanced.
- The role and authority of the WFC president, and the Council itself, should be strengthened.
- The Council's programme should be increasingly concentrated on key priority issues.
- Discussion on the issues selected for WFC annual ministerial session should be intensively prepared with the involvement of the maximum number of informed sources.
- The Council should place continuously greater emphasis on the inter-sectoral issues that place food at the heart of the development process.
- Continuous action should be taken to ensure that the Council's recommendations were followed up and acted upon.
- Within the UN system, the role of the Council should be more clearly defined through greater interaction with the other agencies concerned with food.
- The Council's role vis-à-vis UN headquarters should be clarified and the linkages strengthened.
- The WFC secretariat's staffing resources should be strengthened.

Conscious of the tight financial situation of the UN and that substantial additional resources could not be expected, the group pointed out that the majority of its recommendation had no financial implications. Where they did, they were not large and could be possibly offset by curtailment of some activities and redistribution of resultant savings (e.g., the elimination of the Council's preparatory meetings prior to ministerial session would yield some $75,000 a year, and by reorganization of staff). Governments wishing the Council to continue and increase its effectiveness would need to demonstrate that commitment by supporting the small additional outlay that may be entailed in implementing the group's recommendations. The group pointedly added that the Council's budget of less than $2 million a year was 'hardly excessive in relation to the exceptional responsibilities with which it has been entrusted' (*sic*).

The Council discussed measures to strengthen its role in the light of the advisory group's report at its twelfth session in 1986 (WFC, 1986c, pp. 4-5). There was consensus that WFC was playing a unique political role at the ministerial level and should continue to do so within its existing mandate. It was agreed that the Council should continue to be a 'political catalyst, a forum for discussion of policy ideas and proposals' through its role of monitoring world food problems. It was recognized that the Council should not have an operational role but should continue to play its part in 'stimulating action'. The Council's mandate and terms approved by the UN General Assembly 'should not be amended', but every effort should be made to strengthen it through 'improvements in its organization, programme and method of work, within the framework of its terms of reference, keeping in view the current budgetary constraints'. The necessity of ensuring the Council's individual identity was endorsed as were the proposals of the advisory group to improve co-operation with other UN bodies. Greater visibility of the Council in the UN should be acquired by having the WFC president report directly on its work in plenary sessions of the UN General Assembly. The Council's president and bureau were called upon to assure the 'continuity and thrust' of WFC activities between annual ministerial sessions and to promote initiatives and meetings which concerned their region's food security.

The thirteenth session of the Council in 1987, which was held in Beijing, China, marked an important juncture in its attempts to strengthen its role for three reasons. First, the Council reverted to the approach adopted at its meeting in Manila in the Philippines in 1977, and in Mexico City, Mexico a year later, of issuing a declaration to galvanize attention to its work and cause, which was extended to its next two annual sessions in 1988 and 1989. Second, ECOSOC had established a special commission to conduct an in-depth study of the UN intergovernmental structure and functions in the economic and social fields on which the views of the Council were requested. The terms of reference of the commission included simplifying the intergovernmental structure, avoiding duplication, defining precisely the areas of responsibility of the UN bodies, and strengthening co-ordination of activities. Third, a new executive director, Gerald I. Trant, previously Canadian Deputy Minister of Agriculture, (but no deputy executive director) had been appointed and the Council was required to submit to the UN General Assembly its draft medium-term work plan for the period 1990–95.

Ministers recommended to ECOSOC's special commission that account should be taken of the fact that the Council was 'the highest political body in the United Nations system dealing with food' and that it 'reviews and recommends remedial action on major problems or policy issues affecting all aspects of the world food situation'. The Council was 'an overall ministerial level policy body, not an operational one'. The other UN bodies concerned with food were all operational in character. Consequently, their activities did not duplicate those of the Council. Ministers were unanimous in their support of the Council retaining its own independent identify as a political body for addressing food and hunger issues. They emphasized that its mandate could not be fulfilled if the Council were merged with, or its functions taken over by, another UN body.

The draft outline of the Council's medium-term work plan (1990–95) prepared by the executive director was approved by ministers (WFC, 1987c). The intergovernmental objectives of the plan were described as 'acting as a catalyst for concerted action by all to eliminate hunger and malnutrition and their poverty-related causes'. The objectives of the WFC secretariat were defined as 'providing analytical synthesis and policy documentation for ministerial consideration, identifying major problems and policy issues affecting the world food situation in a timely fashion, consulting regularly with governments and UN bodies, and working with NGOs and the general public to raise awareness of food, hunger and poverty problems'. During the period 1990–95, the regular Council activities of advocacy, policy review and problem prediction and broad-based policy consultation would be 'continued, expanded and improved'. Areas of emphasis would include: monitoring and promotion of progress towards the elimination of hunger and malnutrition; international agricultural trade and national agricultural policies, including sustained support to national food strategies and greater efforts to monitor and assess food strategy experience; follow-up on regional and South–South co-operation in food and agriculture; and international economic policy issues, including debt problems and aid flows, as they related to food and hunger problems. Ministers observed that the continuing increase in the number of the world's hungry and malnourished was testimony to the fact that past efforts to eliminate hunger and malnutrition had failed. One of the Council's responsibilities was to probe the causes of that failure and propose remedies. And the Council should review the hunger-related activities of the UN agencies and assess their impact.

At the beginning of the 1990s, disquiet concerning the need to strengthen and improve the Council's effectiveness resurfaced against the background of attempts to 'revitalize' the UN system in the economic and social sectors, initiated by the UN secretary-general, Boutros Boutros-Ghali. A number of suggestions were made at the Council's seventeenth session in 1991 including: shortening the agenda for ministerial sessions and providing secretariat background information in such a way as to better facilitate an exchange of views and discussion among ministers; providing assessment and follow-up of ministerial decisions and recommendations with special attention to practical ways and means of removing obstacles to eradicating hunger and malnutrition; requesting and making greater use of reports from other intergovernmental bodies that pursued similar objectives; using expert groups to report to WFC on special issues, within available resources; and holding biennial ministerial sessions. The WFC president was requested to convene a consultation between regional representatives of member states on these issues and to report to the Council at its next session.

At its eighteenth session in 1992, which turned out to be the last time that the Council met, the need for greater leadership and co-ordination in the fight against hunger was discussed. A discussion framework paper (WFC, 1992b) identified priority areas for a strengthened WFC including: more active participation by Council members; being in the forefront in vetting sensitive political issues relevant to the solution of hunger problems; and placing greater emphasis on the follow-up of its recommendations, initiatives and commitments. It was observed that strengthening the work of the Council would greatly benefit from increased resources. The WFC president, Issa Kalantari, Minister of Agriculture of Iran, said that he had received an indication from the UN secretary-general, Perez de Cuellar, of possible increased resources to strengthen the work of the Council. He wrote to his successor, Boutros Boutros-Ghali, expressing the view that it was now time to greatly strengthen the Council's role. The discussion paper recognized that

216   *1970–90. The World Food Crisis of the 1970s and its Aftermath*

new ways of approaching the preparation, conduct and follow-up of ministerial sessions were required, with implications for the functioning of the WFC bureau and secretariat. The ministerial composition of the Council might also be reconsidered. As the perception of world hunger had shifted over the years from a food production problem, within the responsibility of ministers of agriculture, to a multifaceted development problem, participation in the Council might be broadened to include economic and development co-operation ministers, leading to a 'world development council', as had been suggested in the report of the advisory group on the WFC (see above). But it could not be 'over-emphasized' that as long as a broader UN development council did not exist, a strengthened WFC as the UN system's highest policy-making and co-ordinating body on food, hunger and poverty issues 'will be essential'.

Minister agreed that 'the Council has fallen short of achieving the political leadership and co-ordination role expected from its founders at the 1974 World Food Conference' (WFC, 1992c, p. 7). There was consensus that the objectives of the conference were as important in 1992 as they were in 1974 and that 'food and hunger issues must remain at the centre of national and international development efforts'. There was also 'broadly based agreement' that in a rapidly changing world 'there can be no continuation of the *status quo* for the World Food Council or for the United Nations as a whole'. Therefore, there was 'general agreement' on the need for review of the role and functioning of the Council in the wider context of global food security management and the overall restructuring of the social and economic activities of the UN system. For this purpose, the Council agreed to establish an *ad hoc* committee to develop further specific proposals, which would be open to all WFC member states at the level of minister or his delegate.

The report of the *ad hoc* committee was to be submitted by the WFC president to the president of the UN General Assembly by mid-October 1992 in accordance with a detailed timetable that was approved by the Council. The Council also recommended that in view of the global food situation, and the close linkage between the environment and food production, and considering the importance of the UN Conference on Environment and Development that was held in 1992, the *ad hoc* committee should consider recommending to the UN General Assembly the possibility of holding a second World Food Conference in 1994. The Council proposed that the UN General Assembly, in its restructuring of the UN economic and social system, review the mandate, operations and future role of the Council after taking into account the report of the *ad hoc* committee.

Council members had a two-day meeting in New York in September 1992 at which they gave their views on WFC's future (WFC, 1992d). The meeting took place at a time when reform and revitalization of the UN system was under active consideration. ECOSOC had established an open-ended *ad hoc* working group on the role of the UN system in enhancing international development co-operation. And restructuring of the UN system was on the agenda of the forty-seventh session of the UN General Assembly that started on 15 September. There was therefore considerable pressure on the *ad hoc* committee to complete its work and submit its report. The meeting was opened by the WFC president, Issa Kalantari. He added to the tension by drawing attention to the fact that the document before the meeting had been prepared by the UN, and not the WFC, secretariat, and that it fell short of what Council members had requested the WFC secretariat to do. He distinguished between two sets of options. The first, which implied the dissolution of WFC as a separate entity, contained three proposals. One suggested transferring the Council's policy leadership and co-ordination functions to ECOSOC. Another suggested that the task of co-ordinating UN agency operational activities be transferred to the ACC, while WFC's analytical functions should be integrated into the FAO. A third proposal saw the full integration of the Council's mandate and functions into FAO. In the second set of options, while emphasizing the need for the Council to co-operate closer with the UN system on hunger-alleviation activities, the separate identity of the Council would be retained.

The WFC president considered that a majority of Council members believed that, with adequate reform, the Council could fulfil its mandate more effectively. They had made a number of proposals for reform, which he grouped into three categories. First, focusing WFC's future work more on policy guidance at the international level so that a harmonized and effective world food policy within the UN system could be implemented. Second, centring discussion at each ministerial session on one major theme and eliminating formal speeches to make room for more dialogue and possibly more private meetings of heads of delegations. The general view was to keep the ministerial composition of the Council unchanged, since ministers of agriculture were well placed to deal with the multi-sectoral agenda of the Council in consultation with their colleagues from other ministries. The implication was, however, that more than in the past, the preparatory process for ministerial sessions would have to create room for such consultations. Third, holding biennial ministerial sessions, which would facilitate more thorough preparation and follow-up, although some members cautioned that this risked losing continuity in the political priority for food and hunger issues. There was also a preference among WFC members for having Rome as a fixed venue for ministerial sessions, close to the operational UN food agencies, rather than rotating them among the capitals of member countries.

The WFC president gave his own personal observations on these options. He expressed doubt that ECOSOC could provide a central policy-leadership role in food and hunger issues as it already had the considerable task of addressing the full range of economic and social development issues. It was hard to conceive that it could engage in in-depth and high-level discussions of food and hunger problems and it was uncertain whether it could attract ministers of agriculture to attend sessions on a regular basis since it had already proved difficult to attract them to ECOSOC's high-level segments. He also took issue with the proposal to integrate the Council's mandate and functions into FAO. In his opinion, FAO did not stand above the sectoral lines along which the UN system was organized. It was therefore not well placed to provide policy guidance to, and monitor the policies of, other multilateral agencies. Instead, he supported the proposal for a reformed Council with a *substantially new approach to the Council's functioning* (original emphasis). In his view, the work of the Council should be understood 'as

218   *1970–90. The World Food Crisis of the 1970s and its Aftermath*

a continuum in which ministerial sessions constitute the high point in an ongoing process rather than an end in themselves'. It was his 'strong personal belief' that a WFC, reformed in accordance with the proposals of Council members, and the additional considerations he had to offer, could 'more than adequately fulfil its mandate'.

The statement by the UN secretary-general, Boutros Boutros-Ghali, which was delivered by UN Under-Secretary-General Chaolzhi Ji, put the future of the Council in a different perspective. The die was cast. Ominously, no successor had been appointed in place of Gerald Trant whose term of office as WFC executive director expired on 30 June 1992. The UN secretary-general recognized that the functions entrusted to the WFC when it was established 'were indeed far reaching'. It seemed evident that the Council 'has not been able to accomplish this ambitious mandate', even though members had explored the possibilities for improving it's functioning on several occasions. Meanwhile, the UN system had established or strengthened structures and made advances in directing the world's attention to the problem of hunger and enhancing understanding of issues relating to food security. The functions of the Council were being reviewed within the overall framework of the restructuring of the economic and social sectors of the United Nations. This 'revitalization process' aimed to enhance the role of ECOSOC as a 'central forum' for major economic, social and related issues and to strengthen its coordinating functions relating the UN system as well as promoting an integrated approach to the policy and programme aspects of the economic and social issues. It also aimed at making the 'most cost-effective use' of the resources available to the UN.

The UN secretary-general said that it was his intention to strengthen the capacity of the United Nations to deal with development issues 'in an integrated way'. He was also seeking ways to strengthen the role and contributions of the UN agencies and to enable the United Nations to draw more systematically on them. The role of the United Nations in relation to food issues should be viewed in that light. The best course would be to centre the co-ordination of food issues more closely around the newly-restructured ECOSOC, which would include procedures for regular reporting from FAO, WFP and IFAD. Drawing on the demonstrated capabilities of those agencies would ensure coherent management of the policy and operational aspects of the world food problem. This would advance the original objectives of the 1974 World Food Conference and enhance the effectiveness of the restructuring process. 'A primary objective will be more effective [UN] organization-wide distribution of responsibilities, based on a clear understanding of our priorities'. The UN secretary-general was also seeking to enhance interagency coordination through the ACC.

Eighteen Council members made interventions at the meeting. Fourteen were in favour of retaining the WFC but with various proposals for its reform. Four members (Canada, Denmark, Japan and the United States) supported the dissolution of the Council and a distribution of its functions and responsibilities along the lines indicated by the UN secretary-general. In the ensuing debate in the ECOSOC and the UN General Assembly, with no fanfare or ceremony, after almost two decade, the Council was disbanded, one of the few UN bodies to be closed after their creation. For some, the Council was seen as the victim of a restructuring process in the UN system that had to demonstrate to the major developed countries that the UN secretary-general meant business in cost-cutting and streamlining the UN decision-making apparatus. For others, the Council had served its time, had demonstrated its ineffectiveness, and interest had moved on to other priorities.

In many ways, the Council and its work had served as a microcosm of the complexities and difficulties of achieving world food security. A number of reasons have been put forward for its demise (Talbot, 1990; Maxwell and Shaw, 1995; Shaw and Clay, 1998, Shaw, 1999). Some pointed to the compromise that led to the establishment of the Council at the 1994 World Food Conference when agreement was not reached on the original proposal of the preparatory committee to set up a World Food Authority or on the proposal made during the conference for a World Food Security Council. In setting up the compromise Council, delegates were as much influenced by what they did not want to create as what they intended to do. As a result, the Council was given many of the far reaching roles and responsibilities of the originally conceived World Food Authority without the authority and resources required to carry them out. The Council was therefore never able to command the leadership and co-ordination roles expected of it, and the respect and attention that was required for it to fulfil its functions.

Born out of a world food crisis, which quickly passed, its utility for developing and developed countries also waned. Crucially, the Council was never really able to distinguish between the world food problem and the world food security problem. Members consisted mainly of ministers of agriculture who had neither the mandate nor experience to cover the range of food security issues outside the agricultural sector nor legally binding control over the activities of the large number of UN agencies whose work related to food security. WFC's role became a confused mixture of general advocacy and action plans. Its four to five day sessions, which took place once a year, preceded by a brief preparatory meeting, covered too many agenda items, were often too broad in scope, and insufficiently focused on monitoring key action programmes. Insufficient attention was given to inter-sessional activities to keep the focus and maintain the momentum. Its secretariat and resources were far too small to perform its wide-ranging functions effectively.

Co-operation from key UN agencies was essential for the secretariat to carry out its work. Yet there was resentment to the Council's establishment, which was seen by some agencies as unnecessary, adding to the institutional inconsistency that already existed among the numerous bodies concerned with world food security. And its location, as a UN agency, at FAO headquarters in Rome, Italy, away from UN headquarters in New York, was a major impediment, particularly as FAO saw itself as playing a major and co-ordinating role in the UN system for policies and activities related to food security and nutrition.

FAO director-general Boerma had offered to place premises at FAO headquarters at the disposal of WFC free of charge and even entered a $240,000 subsidy in favour of the Council in his draft budget for 1976–77. His successor, Eduoard Saouma, withdrew the subsidy and asked WFC to pay rent, just as FAO was required to pay rent for the offices it occupied at UN headquarters in New York. Saouma considered that the WFC had both negative and positive effects (Saouma, 1993, p. 9). In his view, born out of a crisis of confidence in FAO, and apparently conceived as a 'war machine' against FAO, the Council did not succeed in destroying FAO but 'seriously undermined its credibility'. On the other hand, Saouma considered that the WFC had the merit of placing the debate on world food security 'in its proper context', by 'going beyond the technical and scientific vision of development, and stressing the importance of the social aspects' and the need to focus on the poor. In this sense, he considered that 'the WFC represented an opportunity for FAO's own renewal'.

Yet, as the Council agreed at its last session in 1992, the need for a central, undivided focus within the UN system on the achievement of food security for all remained as important as when the Council was established in 1974. The experience of the WFC has shown that the solution does not lie in the establishment of a separate body without executing authority and with a mandate that cuts across that of other agencies. Nor does it lie in giving co-ordinating responsibility to a single agency with restricted sectoral membership and a limited sectoral mandate. No single agency or institution has the resources, capacity or competence to overcome food insecurity alone. And it should not be left to NGOs and the private sector, important as their contributions can be. Proposals have been made to overcome these problems. Many commentators have detailed the problems of bureaucratic fragmentation in the UN system and the need for centralized co-ordination on all economic and social affairs (e.g., UN, 1969; Bertrand, 1985). As one observer has put it:

> The need to introduce a certain amount of order and clarity into the extraordinary diversity of activities - too often marginal – of international organizations, and the desire to condense these activities, through a concentration of effort, into a number of programmes whose effectiveness is beyond question are as old as the United Nations system itself. (Bertrand, 1985, p. 1)

A structure already exists to bring about improved and strengthened co-ordination in the UN system in the form of the ACC, which provides a point of contact for UN bodies at the top executive level with the UN secretary-general as chairman. In 1997, under the reform measures proposed by UN secretary-general, Kofi Annan, a UN development group was established, composed of the concerned UN funds and programmes, but not the UN specialized agencies, to coordinate their development activities. With a strengthened service staff, drawing heavily on the UN Department for Economic and Social Affairs, these co-ordinating bodies might become a kind of policy planning forum at the global level. But changes in structure, procedures and attitudes will be needed to create a central and permanent co-ordinating mechanism for all UN bodies, including the UN specialized agencies.

A 'UN Economic Security Council' has been advocated as a decision-making forum at the highest level to review threats to global human security and agree

World Food Council 221

on required action (UNDP, 1994; ul Haq, 1995). The creation of a 'UN Economic and Social Security Council' has been proposed to provide a structure to deal with issues of world governance and world action toward poverty and social needs in a systematic and politically realistic way (Stewart and Daws, 1998). In either case, achieving world food security would be one of the primary tasks. The Group of Seven (G7) leading industrialized countries and the Group of Fifteen (G15) developing countries have been called upon to establish a joint high-level steering committee for sustainable food security. And because of the difficulties of establishing a new UN body, a proposal has been made to add responsibility for world food security to the extended tasks of the UN Security Council (Singer, 1995). Whatever decisions are taken on UN reform, it is necessary to have a focal point at the highest political level, which would ensure that food security is advocated and managed as a central issue embedded in world and national action for achieving economic and social development and peace, with cohesive and coordinated programmes of international development assistance.

Annex 17.1: World Food Council Presidents and Executive Directors

Presidents

1975–77 Sayed A. Marei (Egypt). Assistant President.
1977–81 Arturo R. Tanco, Jr. (Philippines). Secretary of Agriculture
1981–83 Francisco Merino Rabago (Mexico). Secretary of Agriculture and Water Resources
1983–85 Eugene Whelan (Canada). Minister of Agriculture
1985–87 Henri Nallet (France). Minister of Agriculture
1987–89 Eduardo Pesqueira Olea (Mexico) Minister of Agriculture and Water Resources
1989–91 Youssef Amin Wally (Egypt). Deputy Prime Minister and Minister for Agriculture
and land
reclamation*
1991–93 Issa Kalantari (Iran). Minister of Agriculture

Executive Director

1975–78 John A. Hannah (United States)
1978–86 Maurice J. Williams (United States)
1986–92 Gerald I. Trant (Canada)

*Andreas Gavrielides, Minister of Agriculture and Natural Resources of Cyprus served as Acting President at the Council's seventeenth session in Helsingor, Denmark in 1991 owing to the illness of WFC President Youssif Wally.

18
ILO World Employment Conference, 1976

In 1976, the impetus that had been generated at the 1974 World Food Conference was continued and given a new and broadened, and for some, unexpected focus at the ILO World Employment Conference or, to give it its full name, the 'Tripartite World Conference on Employment, Income Distribution and Social Progress and the International Division of Labour' (ILO, 1976).[42] As befitted the mandate of ILO, the conference was concerned with the problems of employment in the world but it also saw those problems in the context of the concept of satisfying 'basic needs' (which included ensuring food security but also other essential requirements, see below) and the changing international economic order. The focus on 'base needs' arose out of the work being conducted simultaneously at the Bariloche and Dag Hammarskjold Foundations and the ILO.[43] The decision to hold the conference was in no small measure due to the pressure exercised by the debate in the UN General Assembly over a new international economic order. There was also a link to the results of the employment missions of ILO's World Employment Programme, particularly that of the mission to Kenya in 1972, out of which came the concept of 'distribution from growth'.[44]

As noted above, the sixth special session of the UN General Assembly in 1974 had adopted a 'Programme of Action on the Establishment of a New International Economic Order and the Charter of Economic Rights and Duties of States' (resolution 3202 (S-VI)). In a sense, this paved the way for the Lima Declaration and Plan of Action on Industrial Development and Co-operation, adopted in 1975 by the Second General Conference of UNIDO, which established as a target an increase in the developing countries' share of world industrial production from 7 per cent in 1973 to at least 25 per cent by the end of the century. The adoption by the seventh special session of the UN General Assembly in 1975 of a resolution on 'Development and International Economic Co-operation' (resolution 3362 (S-VII)) called for more assistance to be provided to increase food production and facilitate socio-economic reforms in developing countries with a view to achieving integrated rural development. The thrust of these measures was to bring about major reforms in international economic relations and changes in the structure of world trade and production. Increasing food production was viewed as an urgent need in both UN General Assembly special session resolutions.

These preoccupations were obviously in the minds of the conference planners at ILO, but there was another concern, which made the approach adopted at the conference unique. Although developing countries had achieved significant economic and social progress since the Second World War, there still remained a high incidence of poverty, as evidenced by the large proportion of the world's population whose basic needs remained unmet. Poverty and employment problems were seen as closely linked, though the relationship was complex. Not all the unemployed were poor. And many poor people worked hard, often for long hours, but obtained a meagre reward for their efforts. The ILO conference therefore adopted a 'Declaration of Principles' and a 'Programme of Action', which explicitly linked the promotion of employment with the satisfaction of basic needs. Basic needs were defined as including two elements: first, certain minimum requirements of a family for private consumption, including adequate food, shelter and clothing as well as certain household equipment and furniture; and second, essential services provided by and for the community, such as safe drinking water, sanitation, public transport and health, education and cultural facilities. The conference also stressed the importance, in a basic-needs policy, of both the participation of people in making decisions which affected them through organizations of their own choice, and employment, which yielded an output and income and imparted a feeling of self-respect and dignity.

The Declaration of Principles approved by the conference noted that past development strategies based on rapid economic growth had not led, in most developing countries, to the eradication of poverty and unemployment. The development processes in those countries had produced an employment structure characterized by a large proportion of the rural labour force with high levels of under- and unemployment. Major shifts in the development strategies at both national and international levels were needed in order to ensure full employment and an adequate income 'to every inhabitant of the One World in the shortest possible time'. The declaration also recognized that one of the primary objectives of national development efforts and international economic relations 'must be to achieve full employment and to satisfy the basic needs of all people'. The conference was therefore seen as a major initiative on the part of ILO to establish a more equitable international economic order through appropriate strategies to eradicate poverty and promote full, productive employment to satisfy basic needs, which included food security.

The Programme of Action approved by the conference stated that 'Strategies and national development plans and policies should include explicitly *as a priority objective* (emphasis added) the promotion of employment and the satisfaction of the basic needs of each country's population'. It clarified that the concept of basic needs was a 'country-specific and dynamic concept' that should not be interpreted to mean the minimum necessary for subsistence but should be 'placed within a context of national independence, the dignity of individuals and peoples and their freedom to chart their destiny without hindrance'. But it also crucially emphasized that the satisfaction of basic needs in developing countries 'could not be achieved without both acceleration of economic growth and measures aimed at changing the pattern of growth and access to the use of productive resources by the lowest income groups'.

The essential elements of a national employment-centred development strategy aimed at satisfying basic needs for all were spelled out:

- increasing the volume and productivity of work in order to increase the incomes of the lowest income groups;
- strengthening the production and distribution system of essential goods and services to correspond with the new pattern of demand;
- increasing resource mobilization for investment; the introduction of progressive income and wealth taxation policies; the adoption of credit policies to ensure employment creation and increased production of basic goods and services;
- the control of the utilization and processing of natural resources as well as the establishment of basic industries that would generate self-reliant and harmonious economic development;
- developing inter-regional trade, especially among the developing countries, in order to promote collective self-reliance and to ensure the satisfaction of basic import needs without depending permanently on external aid;
- a planned increase in investment in order to achieve diversification of employment and technological progress and to overcome other regional and social inequalities;
- reform of the price mechanism in order to achieve greater equity and efficiency in resource allocation and to ensure sufficient income to small producers;
- reform of the fiscal system to provide employment-linked incentives and more socially just patterns of income distribution;
- safeguarding ecological and environmental balances;
- provision by the government of the policy framework to guide the private and public sectors towards meeting basic needs, and making its own industrial enterprises model employers; in many cases this can only be done in a national planning framework; and
- the development of human resources through education and vocational training.

A target was set for achieving full employment by the year 2000. Social policies should be designed to increase the welfare of working people, especially women, the young and the aged. The action programme contained specific sections on international manpower movements and the effects on employment and technology for productive employment creation in developing countries. And although the conference was unable to reach consensus on the role of multinational enterprises in developing countries (a 'Tripartite Declaration of Principles concerning Multinational Enterprises and Social Policy was, however, adopted by the ILO in 1977) the action programme did set out in detail the roles and responsibilities of governments, employers and workers in a common tripartite effort.

The conference formulated a number of recommendations for action by the ILO, in co-operation with other international organizations and its member states.

In particular, it asked member states to supply the ILO with a quantitative evaluation of basic needs for the lowest income groups of their population, and with a description of their policies to implement a basic-needs strategy. On the basis of their replies, ILO was asked to prepare a report for a future ILO annual conference defining the basic needs concept more precisely and a survey of the replies received from member states.

A report was prepared for the sixty-fifth session of the ILO annual conference, which was held in Geneva in 1979 (ILO, 1979). The survey showed the continuing and growing 'poverty gap' between poor and rich nations. It also showed the gap that existed among developing countries, between those rapidly industrializing and other medium-income countries which, on average, had made good progress towards meeting the basic needs of their population, and those countries that registered slow or retrogressive change. Several hundred million people in sub-Saharan Africa and South Asia were estimated to be affected and, even on extremely optimistic assumptions, 'the prospect is that by the year 2000 a few hundred million would still be in absolute poverty' (World Bank, 1978). The 'islands of poverty' in many other developing countries also called for a reappraisal of the national and international policies that resulted in such an unequal pattern of growth.

The ILO report further concluded that while accelerated growth was the first prerequisite of progress, un- and under-employment, including low-productivity employment yielding inadequate incomes, was 'at the heart of the problem of poverty'. It projected that these factors would reach 'increasingly intolerable proportions' as a result of the rapid growth of the labour force unless 'present patterns of growth are changed and much more determined efforts are made to ensure that all members of the active population are able to contribute to sustained growth and development through their productive efforts and thereby receive a share of its fruits'. It was therefore imperative to pursue resolutely the implementation of the Programme of Action adopted at the 1976 World Employment Conference, which defined the main lines of an approach designed to promote employment and achieve the satisfaction of basic needs in a context of growth and international co-operation.

Concerning elaboration of the employment and basic-needs approach to development, the ILO report showed that while the approach placed stress on the employment and higher productivity of millions of small producers at work in rural and urban informal activities, it also recognized the importance of industrialization and a better balance in development and the creation of linkages between industry and agriculture. The fear that concentration on employment generation might slow growth might also have be based on the notion that rapid growth was a function of the assimilation of new technology and that this required primary emphasis on the modern sector embodying the latest techniques. Raising productivity was in effect the continuous application of improved technology in all branches of economic activity. Emphasis on rural development would result in increased food production. And with a greater and more stable access to overseas markets, the scope for productive employment in export production would grow.

226   1970–90. The World Food Crisis of the 1970s and its Aftermath

But the proposed approach to development also stressed the need for participation at all levels of the economy. Clearly, designing and implementing the development strategies and policies that would promote simultaneously economic growth, employment of poverty alleviation, leading to the satisfaction of basic needs, was no simple task and the difficulties should not be underestimated. But experience had established certain basic facts. First, the formulation of basic-needs targets and strategies was essentially a matter for each country. Second, a multi-pronged attack was required in which many policy elements must be reconciled. And third, provided there is political will, basic-needs policies could be successfully carried out in countries with widely differing social and political systems.

There seemed to be certain national ingredients that were common to successful basic-needs strategies, including:

- efforts to raise the level and productivity of employment through an appropriate mix of products and technology, widespread education and training, and land reform where necessary;
- a fairer and more widespread provision of essential services and the appropriate orientation and design of delivery systems;
- effective participation of the mass of the people in the development process through various economic and political mechanisms;
- successful integration of the agricultural sector and the rural population with the over-all development strategy; and
- a balance and mutually re-enforcing relationship between capital-intensive and labour intensive technology, between the modern and informal sectors and between rural and urban areas.

But the magnitude of the effort needed was such, particularly in the poorest developing countries, that without a favourable international framework, elimination of poverty and the satisfaction of basic needs 'may have to be postponed to an intolerably late date'. Substantial assistance and fairer and more equitable international trade would be required.

However, there was a twist in the tail. Despite encouraging developments and overwhelming support for the basic-needs approach at the World Employment Conference, there was increasing criticism from developing countries, particularly from the G77. What explained this distrust of a basic-needs approach to development? Some of the objections appeared to result from a misreading of the basic-needs approach. In an attempt to set forth a coherent strategy, the ILO planners had to allow for some diversity of approach among the well over 100 very different developing countries represented at the conference. The United States representative's 'fundamental differences' with the conference report was that 'it places too little emphasis on the importance of growth in the context of an employment-oriented development strategy [and] overstates the possible contribution to development of redistribution of assets' (US, 1976, p. 18).

The report might have included a more extended and detailed discussion of how redistribution of assets and income could generate employment, and how employment could generate increased output and faster growth. But it is difficult to understand how the strategy outlined in the conference report could be fairly accused of indifference to growth. The report contained numerous references to the need for growth as an essential and integral part of the basic needs strategy. Redistribution *with growth* (emphasis added) was the aim. Some feared that the basic needs strategy emphasized consumption and redistribution at the expense of production and investment, that it rejected the use of efficient modern technologies, and that it would therefore sacrifice tomorrow's development for a small increase in welfare today. Others questioned the feasibility of the policies advocated. Still others felt that there might be a conflict between a basic-needs approach and the achievement of the objectives of a new international economic order.

But significant changes in development strategies and in development assistance to match them were already in the wind (US, 1980). A new kind of US foreign economic aid bill that sought to change the whole approach to development by concentrating directly on the problems of the poor was passed in 1973 (Howe, 1974). The president of the World Bank, Robert McNamara, pointed to 'the need to reorient development policies in order to provide a more equitable distribution of the benefits of economic growth'. He outlined changes in Bank policy designed to help the small farmer and the rural poor and urged eradication of 'absolute poverty' by the end of the century in his address to the Bank's Board of Governors in Nairobi, Kenya in September 1973 (McNamara, 1973). And the annual report of the chairman of the Development Assistance Committee (DAC) of the OECD concluded that 'there has been a growing loss of confidence... in the development strategy which was widely accepted in the 1960s [which] gave priority to GNP growth and... the modern sector..., leaving too many people in deep poverty' and supported a strategy of higher priority to food production and rural development (OECD, 1973). And so it came to pass that many (but not all) development economists and practitioners came to accept that improving the lot of the poor was best done by attacking their basic problems directly rather than assuming that they would benefit eventually from a 'trickle down' of the benefits of overall economic growth and, most significantly, that enhancing social equity need not deter, and may even accelerate, overall economic growth (Grant, 1973).

After the arrival of President Carter in the White House in January 1977, the United States actively pursued a 'basic human needs' policy. Robert MacNamara was also converted to the 'basic needs' approach and the World Bank adopted 'redistribution of growth' as the 'signature concept' of its approach to poverty alleviation (Kapur *et al.*, 1997, vol. 1, p. 263). But this support by the leading country and leading development institution and economists paradoxically made many developing countries suspicious. They wanted *international* redistribution while basic needs involved a lot of *national* redistribution. The basic-needs approach was interpreted as a tactic by the developed nations to divert the developing world from achieving a fundamental structural change in the world economic order without which divergence, not convergence, between them would continue and increase.

The director-general of ILO, addressing ECOSOC in July 1978, attempted to dispel these misunderstandings and misgivings. Pleading earnestly for action to create growth and employment as necessary conditions for meeting the basic needs of the very poor, he explained that the basic-needs approach was not an alternative to the strategy for economic growth but represented the introduction of a new variable into the general equation of development. It was not a collection of non-productive social assistance measures, which some had called 'charity', but an instrument of growth, an instrument to create economic infrastructures and, accordingly, and an instrument to stimulate employment. He recalled 'three convictions' that underpinned the approach. The first was that insufficient attention had been given to the relationship between capital and labour in the production process. The second was that more vigorous national action against poverty, based on the expansion of productive employment, could help the self-sustained development of the less developed countries by permitting a more rational and productive use of their human resources and 'natural genius'. The third proposition was that vigorous implementation of those measures or policies was meaningful only in a new international economic framework. This last point was fundamental. In the eyes of developing countries, progress in establishing this new international economic framework had been slow, even halting.

In the face of strong, and sometimes over-zealous, advocacy, the basic-needs approach risked eliciting scepticism, and even suspicion. As the DAC chairman of the OECD countries expressed it, there was a 'fear that Northern development agencies will seek to apply it [the basic-needs approach] according to their own values and experience use it to condition economic assistance, in an interventionist way – perhaps as an excuse for not tackling international issues of structural change and economic development' (OECD, 1978, p. 29). It was recognized that it would be difficult to overcome such fears unless industrialized countries improved their performance in development assistance and made it clearly responsive to needs as perceived by the developing countries themselves, and faced realistically the need to encourage appropriate structural adjustments in the world economy.

Perhaps the most significant development that occurred since the World Employment Conference was the increasing stress laid on the need for parallel changes, in favour of poorer people but also poorer countries, and the relation between the two in the world economic order. This was apparent in the conclusions adopted by the conference of ministers of labour of non-aligned and other developing countries in Tunis, Tunisia in April 1978. The conference, while stating as a first objective in a programme of co-operation among developing countries the need 'to accelerate the formulation and implementation of policies for full, productive and remunerative employment . . . in the interest of better satisfaction of national basic needs', emphasized that employment and basic-needs policies, among various objectives of development, would be facilitated by the fundamental changes that were urgently needed in the international economic order to create favourable conditions for rapid economic growth of developing nations.

In 1977, the secretary-general of UNCTAD stressed the link between international and domestic reforms when he said:

> A new international economic order can have little meaning if it is not matched by, and does not promote, a new order within the societies of developing countries... [through] new strategies, new styles of development... that pay attention to social problems and equitable distribution of the benefits of growth, and which make a frontal attack on mass poverty and unemployment. (UNCTAD, 1977)

A similar preoccupation was reflected in the development charter adopted by the International Confederation of Free Trade Unions (ICFTU) in May 1978. The charter endorsed the need for a new economic order in the interests of the people of both developing and developed countries in order, in particular, to check those trends that had led to a continuing impoverishment of developing countries. It also stressed that the creation of 'fair shares between nations' was 'the achievement of fair shares within nations, so that the mass of the people benefited from economic and social development' (ICFTU, 1978).

Nevertheless, the growing opposition to the basic-needs approach was testimony to the fact that even with sound economic arguments, and the best of intentions, the views and aspirations of developing countries needed to be fully taking into consideration when launching any new initiative. The basic needs concept continues today under a number of names and guises, including 'participation strategies', 'employment-oriented strategies' and a 'people-oriented strategy for development'. Its legacy can be found in the 'human development' concept postulated in the UNDP annual *Human Development Reports* that began in 1990 and have continued to this day. Its legacy can also be seen in the resurgence of the fight against poverty, without the economic framework, however, that the basic needs concept provided, and in the continuing work on income distribution and the quest for food security. And it was not until the 1990s that it was fully recognized that:

> Today, understanding the labour market is as important for addressing the food security problems of the rural and urban poor in developing countries as understanding the food market. It is now widely accepted that food security is at least as much a matter of poverty – limited access to food – as it is a matter of supply – limited availability of food. (Dreze and Sen, 1989; von Braun, 1995)

19
Food Entitlement

Yet another concept entered the general debate on the quest for food security from Amartya Sen's clinical examination of famines, first in India in 1976 and 1977 (Sen, 1976, 1977), and then in a seminal publication in 1981 (Sen, 1981).[45] Sen's thesis was that in major famines in the past, the problem was not so much lack of food but of poor people's access to it. The cause, in his view, was a breakdown in what he called their 'entitlement'. This related to his concept of economic development as a process of expanding people's 'capabilities', or what they are able to do (Sen, 1982). Sen's view is that the goal not only of economics but of society as a whole should be the enlargement of what he calls 'positive human freedom' and the capability to enjoy it (Sen, 1999). He believes that the issue of 'social choice' should be of concern not only to economists but also to the public (Dreze and Sen, 1989). His insistence on making larger moral and cultural concerns preconditions for answering economic questions echoes Socrates' challenge, 'man, know thyself', and Plato's comparison of the human soul to a chariot pulled by the two horses of 'reason' and 'emotion'.

Sen explained that his concept differed from both judging economic progress by the amounts of goods and services produced, or from focusing just on utilities. It also provided a broader vision than that of fulfilling basic needs. He described it as a process 'of enhancing the freedom that people can positively enjoy'. One of the most elementary freedoms, in his opinion, is that from starvation, hunger, malnutrition and related morbidities. He states that the capability to lead a well-nourished existence has 'a pre-eminent position' in the list of capabilities that are valued. Sen explained that the capabilities of a person depends, among other things, on the 'bundles of goods and services over which the person can establish command'. In each society, there are rules that govern who can have the use of what. In a private ownership market economy, use depends essentially on 'ownership and exchange'.

Sen applied these notions to food security. What we can eat depends on what food we are able to acquire. The mere presence of food in the economy or market place does not entitle a person to consume it. In each social structure, given the prevailing legal, political and economic arrangements, people can establish command over some alternative bundle of commodities which they can choose to consume. He referred to the set of alternative bundles of commodities over which a person can establish command as that person's 'entitlement', defined in terms of ownership rights. Sen identified different types of entitlement. For example, people who grow their own food are entitled to what is grown (adjusted for any obligations there may be, e.g., to money-lenders). They can sell or exchange what is grown within their entitlement. A wage labourer's entitlement is equated by what can be bought with the wages earned. People's entitlements can also depend on what they are endowed with, what is owned initially, and what can be acquired through exchange. And entitlement can be attained through social or legal rights in a society, and from the state in the form of social security programmes, including the right of work or other benefits.

The entitlement approach to food problems contrasted with other approaches in that it took account of the distributional patterns that held in a particular society or in a specific situation. It focused on the command people could exercise over commodities and on what determined the distribution of those commodities. Extending this concept of entitlement to a study of the great Bengal famine in India in 1943, the Wollo famine in Ethiopia of 1973, and the famine in Bangladesh in 1974, Sen found that acute food shortage occurred among poor people because of the breakdown in their entitlements and not because, as was commonly misunderstood food, was not available, which led to a broadening of the definition of food security (see below). Thus, in famine situations, the availability of food had often not been the critical factor, but people's access to it. Famines did not affect all groups of people equally. They were typically very selective in their effects, even when they occurred on a large scale. In order to understand famines and their effects, therefore, it was necessary to examine the entitlements of particular occupational groups.

The proportion of the population affected by regular or sporadic entitlement failures varied among countries and regions. In many African countries, endemic failure of entitlement covered a relatively large proportion of the population. The decline in entitlement to food in that region was related to a decline in the value of the output produced. The fact that the bulk of output was food made the problem look spuriously like one of a Malthusian decline of average food output per head. But the same crisis of command over food would have taken place had there been a decline in non-food crops or in industrial output. The value of output of farmers was their means of economic command. It was not a matter of primary importance whether the decline was in food or non-food output, the former affecting direct entitlement to food and the latter indirect access through trade and exchange.

This led to Sen's concept of entitlement protection (Dreze and Sen, 1989, pp. 104–21). Entitlement failures could arise either from a decline in initial ownership or endowment or from a worsening of exchange possibilities through, for example, a decline in employment opportunities, a fall in wages, or a rise in food prices. Increasing landlessness in many developing countries had therefore contributed to the possibilities of entitlement failure. There was also the further issue of uncertainty of command over food when the survival of a person depended on trading non-food goods for foodstuffs. Sen therefore reasoned that effective famine prevention called for much more than simply rushing food to the victims. It involved a network of decisions relating to diverse policy areas, such as the generation of employment and incomes, the delivery of health care, the stabilization of food prices, the provision of drinking water, and the rehabilitation of the rural economy. People's entitlement to food depended not only on the operation of economic forces, including market mechanisms, but also on political ones. Standards of legitimacy, operations of rights, and availability of actual opportunities were all relevant to the entitlement approach to food and hunger, which went beyond the narrow domain of traditional economics.

Entitlement protection therefore has many different facets. As Sen explained, the occupational characteristics of the affected population, the pattern of intra-family divisions, the structure of markets, the nature of co-operative village institutions, and the mobility of vulnerable groups are some of the numerous considerations that are relevant to the choice of a strategy of entitlement protection when a famine threatens. There are significant differences among and within countries in these and other respects and interventions to prevent famine must come to grips with those differences. Sen concluded that entitlement protection almost always call for 'mixed systems', involving the use of different instruments to provide direct or indirect support to all vulnerable groups. He identified the provision of employment, perhaps with cash wages, combined with unconditional relief for the unemployable, as one of the more effective options in many circumstances. But detailed examination of public works programmes in Ethiopia during the peak of the famine of 1985–86, when there was a general shortage of food, showed the advantages of using food rather than cash as wages (von Braun *et al.*, 1991; Webb and von Braun, 1994; Holt, 1995). Sen also recognized that other factors were at work. He famously observed that famines do not occur in democratic countries with a free press, comparing the experiences of China and India, and wrote at length on the role of public action (Dreze and Sen, 1989).

The value of Sen's entitlement approach is that it analyses famines as disasters caused by many factors, not just as food crises. His empirical studies brought out several distinct ways in which famines can develop, defying the stereotyped uniformity of what was referred to as 'food availability decline' (FAD). He noted that while famine victims share a common predicament, the economic forces leading to that predicament can be very different. That famines can take place without a substantial FAD was of interest mainly because of the hold that the food availability approach had on the usual famine analysis, which had led to disastrous policy failures in the past. (He pointed out, e.g., that the failure to anticipate the Bengal famine in India in 1943 which killed about three million people and the inability to recognize it when it came was due to the government's overriding concern with aggregate food availability statistics, which showed no FAD, instead of changes in food price and employment, the real causes of the famine.) The entitlement approach concentrated on the ability of different sections of the population to establish command over food using the entitlement relations operating in a society depending on its legal, economic, social and political characteristics.

From this, Sen drew five general observations (Sen, 1984):

- The entitlement approach provides a general framework for analysing famines, rather than one particular hypothesis about their causation. It characterizes the nature and causes of entitlement failures, where they occur. The contrast between different types of entitlement failures is important in understanding the precise causation of famines, and in devising famine policies: anticipation, relief and prevention.
- Famines can arise in overall boom conditions (as in Benegal in 1943) as well as in slump condition (as in Ethiopia in 1973). In the fight for market command over food, one group can suffer precisely from another group's prosperity, 'with the Devil taking the hindmost'.
- It is important to distinguish between decline of food availability and that of direct entitlement to food. The former is concerned with how much total food there is in the economy, while the latter deals with each food grower's output of food that he/she is entitled to consume directly. Moving food into an area may not help the affected population. What may be needed is the generation of food entitlement.
- Entitlement shifts also explain why there have been cases of food moving out of famine areas rather than into them. A famine-affected region may lose out in market competition with people from other areas, and may thus lose a part of even the food supply it has. The classic case of this 'food counter-movement' was the Irish famine of the 1840s (Woodham-Smith, 1962).
- The focus on entitlement had the effect of emphasizing legal rights. Other relevant factors, such as market forces, can be seen as operating through such a system of legal relations (ownership rights, contractual obligations, legal exchanges and so on). The law stands between food availability and food entitlement, and 'famine deaths can reflect legality with a vengeance'.

Like many pioneers, Sen has not been without his detractors (Clay, 1991). His work on the Bengal famine in India that led to his theory of famines came under a barrage of criticism in the journal *Food Policy* as being 'untenable, both because of analytical errors and because it was factually inaccurate', claims which Sen refuted (Bowbrick, 1986). Another reservation concerns what is regarded as the oversimplified contrast between famine and the problems of endemic hunger or under-nutrition, questioning whether the contrast of the aggregate food availability and entitlement approach to famines has created a straw man (Stewart, 1982). Other contributors to the debate on the causes of famine have emphasized that famine is an extreme situation that results from a concatenation process, not a single cause (Currey, 1978). Famine in this sense will occur when there is a problem of the breakdown of governance caused by civil war, lack of social control, or government insensitivity to the conditions if its people.

It has already been noted above that another alternative for policy analysis has been made in a World Bank study which distinguishes between transitory and chronic food insecurity (World Bank, 1986). Other analysts have also distinguished between food insecurity, structural poverty and under-nutrition (Maxwell, 1990; AJAE, 1990). Still others have found Sen's use of the term 'entitlement' unfortunate, even confusing, and in an extreme case as nothing more than 'a fancy name for elementary ideas fairly well understood by economists, though not necessarily by policy makers' (Srinivasan, 1983). Social scientists other than economists have not found the entitlement concept useful for their understanding of the causes of famine and people's reaction to it (de Waal, 1990). Thus, there are those who feel that Sen has complicated what might have been simple by imposing his own special framework on entitlement theory. And those who see Sen's remarkable ability to 'discover the obvious' by simultaneously consume and transform a wide array of existing knowledge into an enabling framework of convincing theory as a powerful tool for positive action for which he was awarded the Nobel Prize in Economics in 1998. This controversy has resulted in less application of the entitlement concept than might otherwise have been expected.

20
Pragmatism and Politics

The year 1976 marked a major juncture in FAO's history with the election of a new director-general, Edouard Saouma, a Maronite Christian from the Lebanon with a distinctly different personality, and sharply different views, from his predecessor. An agricultural engineer, who had been director-general of Lebanon's National Agricultural Research Institute and Minister of Agriculture, Saouma joined FAO in 1962, fourteen years before becoming executive head of the organization, first as regional representative for Southwest Asia in New Delhi, India (1962–65), and then for ten years as director of FAO's Land and Water Development Division in Rome (1965–75). He was to be elected three consecutive times (in 1975, 1981 and 1987) and to serve for eighteen years as FAO's director-general. Saouma immediately displayed a very different personality and character from that of his amiable and co-operative predecessor (Murray, 1989). His style of leadership was 'perceived by many as self-perpetuating by whatever means, preoccupied with personal prestige, and egocentric toward authority' (Abbott, 1992, p. ix). He established an unrivalled position, creating enemies in donor countries and support in the developing world, that ensured his election as director-general on three occasions (Pilon, 1988).

Saouma witnessed what he, and others in FAO, regarded as misguided leadership by his predecessor, and humiliation for his organization, at the 1974 World Food Conference (Saouma, 1993). Boerma completed the Indicative World Plan for Agricultural Developed that had been begun by B. R. Sen in 1969. It estimated that to meet the world's food requirements, production in the developing countries would need to increase by 4 per cent a year. Boerma shared the optimistic view of many analysts that hunger was liable to threaten only a fairly limited number of people in the future. Technical progress and the 'green revolution' would make it possible to cover all needs and avoid any negative effects on the environment and social fabric. Emphasis was therefore placed on research and the dissemination of new technologies, and on consolidating FAO's work in technical studies and surveys.

In Saouma's view, priority was accorded to work, such as master plans and econometric studies, which, however sound and well-documented, 'were liable to be of more use to university researchers than to practitioners'. In the meantime, FAO's regional offices gradually lost their role as an effective FAO presence in the developing world. They tended to conduct their own autonomous policy, with the result that, in Saouma's view: 'Instead of decentralization we now have feudalism'. At the World Food Conference, Saouma watched as, from a position of weakness, 'the FAO Secretariat was unable to oppose the establishment of bodies whose mandate impinged on its own. In the face of this, my predecessor preferred compromise to confrontation'. He noted that Boerma had even offered to place premises at FAO headquarters at the disposal of the World Food Council free of charge, and entered a $240,000 subsidy in favour of the WFC in his draft budget for 1976–77.

Saouma soon revealed his hand. The FAO Conference had adopted the programme of work and budget prepared by Boerma for the 1976–77 biennium shortly before Saouma took office. As Saouma described it, 'anxious to restore to FAO the importance it was in danger of losing, following the World Food Conference', Boerma had requested a 'massive increase' in FAO's budget, which he planned to allocate to strengthen FAO's regional offices, creating over 500 posts (some 300 at FAO headquarters), and assigning additional resources to studies, publications, meetings and travel. Saouma describes how 'a careful reading of the Constitution gave me inspiration'. His view was that the text 'clearly expresses the primacy of the Member Nations'. FAO 'before anything else' was a place where they could meet, enter into dialogue, and agree on joint action, 'with the assistance of the body of specialists they have established to help them'. It also called for FAO to be aware of the needs of each country, for which 'FAO should be by their side, in their homeland, and not only exercising vigilance from far away in Rome'.

With this vision of what his organization stood for, Saouma called for an extraordinary session on FAO's Council in July 1976 to amend Boerma's FAO budget for 1976–77 and begin to repair the damage that he considered his predecessor had done. He reduced the number of proposed new posts by 330, dispensed with 155 proposed meetings, and reduced the number of FAO publications and documents. These amendments resulted in savings of over $20 million out of a total budget of $167 million. Saouma allocated these newly released resources mainly in three areas. First, he strengthened FAO's Investment Centre, which worked in conjunction with the World Bank, regional banks and other financial sources to identify, design and appraise agricultural investment project, which some saw as a counterweight to the newly established International Fund for Agricultural Development. Second, he set up a Technical Cooperation Programme (TCP) to respond quickly to the requests of countries in case of need in addition to funds provided by UNDP and other donors. This innovation was the one to which Saouma attached the greatest value. But, as he recognized, it was also the most controversial. Opponents accused him of creating a 'slush fund' for his own personal use to curry favour in developing countries. The third innovation was hardly less controversial. He established 78 FAO country offices with FAO country representatives serving some 106 developing countries. With these three components, Saouma planned 'to give FAO new impetus and a new dimension', and, some would add, to give him political control. They were also to put him on a collision course with the major developed countries that paid the bulk of FAO's assessed contributions, which led to financial crisis as they reduced or delayed their payments.

Saouma saw the value in his scheme of things of retaining FAO's interest and involvement in activities to achieve world food security through a mixture of pragmatic and political action. For him, food security constituted one of FAO's major objectives in the context of the New International Economic Order defined by the United Nations. At the fortieth anniversary of FAO in 1985 he proclaimed 'we must strive to attain food security for the whole earth' (Saouma, 1993, p. 128). He actively used the newly created FAO Committee on World Food Security (CFS), established following a resolution of the World Food Conference in 1976, as a foil to the World Food Council. And he organized a World Conference on Agrarian Reform and Rural Development, held at FAO headquarters in Rome in July 1979, which established FAO as the UN lead agency for the coordination of UN agencies action in this field.

Preparedness for large-scale and acute food shortages

Pragmatically, not wishing to play the iconoclast, he continued the work started under his predecessor on FAO's Global Information and Early Warning System (see above). This work was continued further when an *ad hoc* Working Party on Preparedness for Acute and Large-scale Food Shortages was set up by the CFS in 1980 with the objective of avoiding the experience of the food crisis of the early 1970s. Several documents were prepared for the working party, including one on objective indicators to signal acute and large-scale food shortages (FAO, 1980a). Such shortages were defined as 'a large decline in supplies for current consumption of basic foods below the level needed to maintain normal consumption'. The main purpose of the indicators was to provide a clear signal in advance of an impending large-scale food shortage so that there was sufficient time to prevent its occurrence, or at least to minimize its effects. The indicators would have four characteristics. First, to provide significant lead-time, with a trade-off between timeliness and accuracy. Second, to be simple and understandable. Third, to be economical in the resources necessary to monitor them. And finally, preferably quantitative rather than qualitative. At the national level, the indicators should indicate severe production, marketing and import problems, serious deterioration in the nutritional situation, and large numbers of refugees and displaced persons. At the global level, the indicators would show unduly low level of exporters' supplies, substantial production shortfalls, prospective import requirements substantially exceeding export availabilities, substantial and sudden price increases, falling stock levels, falling food aid supplies, and exceptionally large rises in prospective import bills.

At the same time, ways of improving national preparedness to meet acute and large-scale food shortages, including improvements in internal distribution networks, were developed, drawing on earlier work done in FAO and the UN (Masefield, 1967; UN, 1952b; FAO, 1980b). As each emergency had its own peculiarities, uniform procedures and guidelines were not prescribed. Instead,

238 *1970–90. The World Food Crisis of the 1970s and its Aftermath*

common features were identified, which made it possible to draw up certain broad types of relief activities and related tasks and administrative procedures, which could be brought into action in the event of a food disaster. A codification of relief activities, tasks and procedures would facilitate quick action and ensure efficient relief work. Reserve stocks, if held by governments, could be drawn down to meet urgent requirements until arrangements could be made to procure supplies. The establishment of disaster units, on a stand-by basis, in countries at risk and in donor countries, could monitor impending emergency conditions and prepare and modify contingency plans. And the establishment of early warning systems could provide lead-time for remedial action.

Food Security Assistance Scheme

A Food Security Assistance Scheme (FSAS) was established in 1976 to assist developing countries in pursuing the goal of food security (FAO, 1984a). The FSAS attempted to deal not only with short-term food supply problems but also with improvements in food production and distribution on a continuous basis. It exemplified a merger of efforts under FAO's regular programme of work with projects funded from extra-budgetary resources entrusted to FAO by donors, and identified projects and helped to mobilize funds under other multilateral and bilateral aid programmes. The FSAS mobilized over $50 million in its first eight years of operation. Initially concentrating on food reserves, storage and emergency needs, the scheme was gradually broadened to deal with other elements of a food security system, including marketing, information systems, and economic and social incentives to food production.

To assist the CFS in its review of food security assistance requirements, a detailed survey of the cereals storage needs in developing countries was carried out in 1981(FAO, 1981). The survey noted that one of the most striking phenomena of the 1970s had been the growth and changing pattern of trade and consumption of cereals in developing countries. Increasing population, growing urbanization, and changing income levels and diets had generated demand for imported food and feed grains. Total cereal imports by developing countries (excluding China) doubled from 35 million to 70 million tons during the 1970s, creating strains on port, storage and transportation facilities. During the same period, annual production in developing countries grew by some 77 million tons. The annual flow of domestic and imported supplies through storage and marketing systems in developing countries (excluding China) increase by 113 million tons during the 1980s. About 40 per cent, or 45 million tons, of this increase was accounted for by low-income developing countries. According to the World Bank, storage and related processing capacity in those countries had increased by about 3–4 per cent a year since 1960, while cereals and other foods entering commercial markets had grown at about double that rate. This resulted in shortages and bottlenecks throughout the storage and transportation systems of those countries.

The implications were of great consequence to storage and infrastructure, both in terms of volume and in kind. The FAO survey focused on what was regarded as 'the prime areas of concern' of farm, village and commercial storage, national and regional storage and infrastructure for national and regional food reserves, and port facilities. It was estimated that $2.6 billion would be needed for additional storage capacity and $45 billion would be required in additional new investment needed for cereals transport by 1990, or an average annual capital investment of $4.5 billion, to maintain pace with the projected increase in cereal production in developing countries. All food security projects funded by FAO's FSAS were from pledges from donors in addition to their contributions to FAO's regular programme. The level of funding via this channel (targeted at $10 million a year but actually reaching $8 million in 1980) was considerably below requirements for identified projects. Additional funding was sought from other donors and from the UNDP, WFP, the World Bank and regional development banks.

To reinforce the impact of the FSAS, Saouma launched a Special Action Programme for the Prevention of Food Losses (PFL) after harvest in developing countries in 1977. Its essential aim was to help small farmers reduce the considerable post-harvest food losses, which were estimated at more than 20 per cent in many countries, thereby contributing directly to increasing food availability. The programme, which was financed by voluntary contributions from FAO member countries, initially benefited from a capital of nearly $10 million accruing from the FAO budget surpluses for the years 1976–77. Saouma also proposed a Food Security Action Programme, which was adopted by the FAO Conference in 1979. This programme called for more aid to low-income, food-deficit countries to enable them to cope with their import needs and to compensate for insufficient food production, lack of storage facilities, and construction of national food reserves. With the objective of reducing dependence on food imports and food aid, the programme called on developing countries to increase mutual co-operation to boost food production, foster trade among them, and establish regional and sub-regional reserves.

As an example, FAO undertook a feasibility study on fostering food security among eight countries in the Sahelian region of West Africa, including a project to expand national and regional storage capacity. The study led to a proposal to construct storage facilities at the national level for an additional 120,000 tons in order to bring national security stocks to 312,500 tons. At the regional level, the study proposed the establishment of five security stock storage centres with a total capacity of 152,000 tons. The costs involved $104 million for buildings and equipment and $107 million to establish grain reserve stocks. Donor countries and international financial institutions turned the project down. They felt that priority should be given to increasing agricultural production. They did not accept the FAO argument that increased food production depended on the institution of appropriate grain pricing policies supported by reserve stocks.

Another element that developing countries needed for their food security, which FAO recognized, was balance of payments support in the event of exceptional variations in their food import bills (FAO, 1979a). The attempt to conclude a new International Wheat Agreement with legally binding provisions for wheat prices, reserves and special assistance to developing countries, was suspended in February

240   *1970–90. The World Food Crisis of the 1970s and its Aftermath*

1979. With this setback, the need became more urgent to improve international arrangements for food, financial and other assistance to developing countries facing acute food security problems due to periodic crop failures. One such measure was identified as special balance of payments support to help at least the poorest countries to finance the exceptional upward variations in their food import bills. FAO joined with the WFC to press for such assistance. At the annual meetings of the Board of Governors of the IMF and World Bank in Belgrade, Yugoslavia in October 1979, several delegations also urged the liberalization of access to IMF financing facilities or the setting up of a special food import facility to deal with recurrent emergencies created by natural calamities and abrupt variations in food grain prices.

A food financing facility

In June 1979, the FAO Council recommended that the IMF be invited to consider providing balance of payments support during food emergencies, which was later endorsed by the WFC at its fifth ministerial session in Ottawa, Canada in September 1979 (see above). This recommendation was transmitted by the director-general of FAO to the Managing Director of the IMF, who agreed to present it to the IMF Board. A paper was prepared jointly by FAO and the WFC in support of the recommendation. The paper argued that no country should be expected to adjust food consumption below survival levels for whatever reason. If a country was to avoid a fall in consumption levels during a food crisis, it should either draw on existing reserves, increase its commercial food imports, or obtain additional aid. For many poor developing countries, the first two options were very limited. Hence, the need for additional support.

Food insecurity in those countries was a cyclical problem. The need for balance of payments support to meet the cost of increased food imports periodical seemed to fall within IMF's mandate. A food financing facility operated by IMF would only be concerned with short-term balance of payments needs arising mainly from crop failures or world price movements. The objective would be to help minimize the worst consequences as measured in starvation, hunger and malnutrition and by the undue disruption in poor countries' development efforts. The need for such a facility was acutely felt in 1979. World cereal production had fallen for the first time since 1974 and export prices as well as ocean freight rates for gains had risen substantially. At the same time, a large number of developing countries suffered production shortfalls.

The FAO/WFC paper attempted to quantify the magnitude of the problem facing poor countries in the period 1965–77 from a sample of 50 low-income, food-deficit countries. In this period, in all but four years, consumption exceeded trend. But in those four years it fell by amounts ranging from 6 to 11 million tons, or roughly three to four per cent below the trend figure. These shortfalls from trend were matched by a decline in the index of actual per capita consumption. There was little growth in per capita consumption during this period, with the index value increasing from 100 in 1965 to 103.3 in 1977. A disaggregated picture of the 50 countries included in the sample showed that in 24 of those countries, the trend in per capita consumption over the period 1965–77 was negative. When broken down on a regional basis, the shortfalls in cereals consumption average 6.4 per cent below the norm in Africa, 5.8 below in Latin America and 4.6 per cent below in Asia. Another FAO study of cereal production data in 55 low-income, food-deficit countries had shown that a shortfall in production larger than 5 per cent could be expected to give rise to emergency needs. Cereal imports for the same 50 sample countries over the same period showed a stead upward trend, showing the major difficulties that low-income, food-deficit countries faced in offsetting fluctuations in food production and/or import price increases by means of increased expenditure on food imports.

The FAO/WFC paper also addressed the question of 'criteria for eligibility' to draw on the proposed IMF facility. One underlying principle could be a 'consumption criteria' of some kind. Another might be that without special foreign exchange credit to finance food imports, a country would experience severe balance of payments strains. The paper stressed that whatever facility was established, it should provide for quick action on requests by countries for drawings to cover exceptional food import needs. It was recognized that quick quantification of the degree and extent to which an existing situation constituted a food-related balance of payments emergency 'may sometimes entail difficulties', but FAO stood ready to offer whatever assistance was required, drawing on its considerable experience and extensive database.

The relationship of the facility to food aid would also have to be taken into account. Food aid had not always been timely and well-directed. It would continue to be 'an important factor in the food security of many developing countries for the foreseeable future'. But financial help through an IMF facility would provide additional flexibility to countries in making import procurement decisions in times of crisis. One final issue of principle was that of the repayment terms for drawings from a food financing facility, which might be related to broader considerations of their overall debt burden and financial prospects. In May 1981, the IMF Executive Board decided, for an initial period of four years, to extend its Compensatory Financing Facility so that financial assistance could be provided to countries which encountered a balance of payments difficulty as a result of an excess in the cost of their cereal imports. Drawings from the facility were less than anticipated because, some argued, the terms for access to the facility were set too high to make it attractive or acceptable.

A revised concept of world food security

An evaluation of the FSAS found that the scheme did not have the conclusive answer to the problem of world food security not only because of limited resources but because of the broader elements of food security that lay outside its command (FAO, 1987b). Therefore, in 1983, FAO's concept of food security was broadened on the basis of a proposal from its director-general (FAO, 1982b). The concept of world food security was redefined as: 'The ultimate objective of world food security

242   *1970–90. The World Food Crisis of the 1970s and its Aftermath*

should be to ensure that all people at all times have both physical and economic access to the basic food they need'. To the two original elements of ensuring production of adequate food supplies (with particular attention to the problems of accelerating food production in the low-income, food-deficit countries) and maximizing stability in the flow of food supplies was added the third element of 'securing access to available supplies on the part of those who need them'. This third element no doubt took into account the work of Amartya Sen described above. It also gave prominence to forces that lay outside the mandate of FAO to address, calling for co-ordinated action with other agencies and programmes.

Explaining the changing perceptions of world food security, the director-general noted that, as originally embodied in the *International Undertaking on World Food Security*, world food security was sought through specific action on a relatively narrow front, although pursued within a much broader general framework. Special emphasis was placed on measures designed to ensure the physical availability of food supplies in the event of widespread crop failure, particularly to sustain levels of consumption in the most vulnerable countries. This concept of world food security became, in the director-general's opinion, too closely linked to negotiations on an International Grains Agreement, which created an impression that food security for individual countries could be assured if larger grain stocks were available globally and fluctuations in international grain prices contained within reasonable limits. Yet many poorer developing countries would still be helpless when faced with inadequate production levels, a widening import gap, low consumption levels and a deteriorating balance of payments position, which 'constitute the hard core of their food insecurity'.

Experience had shown that while a satisfactory rate of growth in food production was, in most cases, 'a necessary condition for achieving food security', it would not by itself suffice to ensure that food was available in sufficient quantities to those who needed it. The elimination of chronic malnutrition and hunger had thus been accepted as 'the ultimate goal of a strategy for food security'. There was growing evidence (as Amartya Sen had shown) that many emergencies and famines had been caused by not so much by a catastrophic fall in food production but by a sudden drop in the purchasing power of specific social groups, such as rural labourers or nomadic pastoralists. It was also recognized that degrees of food security could vary widely between different areas in a single country. Temporary or chronic malnutrition could exist on a considerable scale even if total food supplies at the national level appeared to be satisfactory. While the problem of mobilizing sufficient emergency assistance to meet natural or man-made disasters had acquired greater prominence, increasing attention was also being paid to the financing and food aid problems of poor and vulnerable countries facing surges in their cereal imports, even when aggregate world supplies were sufficient. The question of expanding their foreign exchange earnings and real purchasing power from exports was also been increasingly seen as an issue with major food security implications for developing countries.

The conceptual framework of world food security thus included very broad policy issues relating to agricultural and rural development, food production, improved access to food and international trade. Action to enhance world food security accordingly had to be taken on a broad front but had 'still to remain within a manageable focus so as to make a maximum impact on the most pressing problems'. Thus, for the 1980s, the director-general recommended that the components of world food security should be linked to three specific goals: 'adequacy of food supplies; stability in food supplies and markets; and security of access to supplies'. The director-general concluded by observing that 'the paradox of world food security was that an apparently simple problem, which has existed in one form or another since the draw of history, was in fact extraordinarily complex, being affected by a vast range of economic, social and even political issues'. He therefore suggested 'a more systematic approach to these wider issues, coupled with specific measures having a narrower focus'. He called for consensus as: 'Food security is too fundamental an issue to be treated as just one subject among others to be banded about in negotiations between and within groups of countries'.

The FAO Conference adopted a resolution on 'World Food Security' in 1983. It endorsed the director-general's revised and broadened concept of world food security. It also called on regional and sub-regional bodies to review their policy objectives with a view to promoting regional and sub-regional food security and requested the director-general to continue to assist them.

Regional and sub-regional food security schemes

The FSAS focused on the food security needs of individual developing countries. This focus was extended in 1982 to foster the collective self-reliance of developing countries through regional and sub-regional food security schemes (FAO, 1982a). The FAO Plan of Action on World Food Security adopted by the FAO Council in June 1979 contained a separate section on the collective self-reliance of developing countries, including the setting up of regional reserves. In the same year, the FAO Conference (in resolution 3/79) requested the director-general to assist countries interested in participating in regional or sub-regional reserves with a view to facilitating co-operation among them. The FAO secretariat responded by giving technical advice to the Arab Organization for Agricultural Development on the food security scheme it was preparing. As described above, it also organized with the Sahelian countries of West Africa a detailed study and projects for the Sahelian zone. It collaborated with the UN Economic Commission for West Asia (ECWA) in examining the opportunities for sub-regional co-operation in West Asia. It assisted the Southern Africa Development Conference (SADCC) and the Latin America Economic System (SELA) in preparing regional food security projects. And it prepared a special study on regional food security for the FAO Regional Conference for Asia and the Pacific.

The response of governments and regional organizations was cautious but a number of actions were taken. An ASEAN Food Security Reserve Agreement was signed in 1979 by countries of the Association of South-East Asian Nations for the establishment of an emergency rice reserve, co-ordination of national food stock policies, and exchange of information and consultations. An Arab food reserve stock was agreed in April 1980 to be located either on a sub-regional or national basis, with central management. A food security system among non-aligned countries was proposed in January 1981. A grain reserve system for the Sahel was promoted in July 1981 (see above). And regional co-operation to promote food security was proposed by SELA in August 1981.

The case for regional and sub-regional food security rested on a number of premises. Food security had dimensions that transgressed national boundaries. Solutions to some of the problems of national food security could be provided within a regional framework. A regional food security scheme could assist in the movement of food supplies in several ways. At times of severe shortage, a regional organization could raise a more authoritative voice to draw attention to impending famine or drought and help mobilize external help. Insufficient domestic production was a long-run food security problem faced by a number of developing countries that could be better addressed through regional co-operation and exchange of experience, joint production and marketing arrangements, and regional agreements on agricultural experimentation and research. Regional schemes could be more economical in their management and demand for funds than an unrelated series of national schemes. On the other hand, experience was to show that regional and sub-regional food security scheme shared a number of the problems faced by their national counterpart. Problems of location, ownership, storage, stock rotation, conditions for release and replenishment, and above all costs, generally made practical regional working arrangements difficult and deterred donor support.

Indicative world plan for agricultural development

While this detailed, pragmatic work on food security continued, Saouma did not lose sight of FAO's obligation to provide member nations with a global perspective on world agriculture. Neither did he disguise his criticism of his predecessor's Indicative World Plan for Agriculture (IWP), which was initiated by B. R. Sen after the First World Food Congress in 1983 and completed and published in 1969, for 'lacking realism'. Sen described the IWP as 'FAO's most important pioneering exercise in global planning', which led to various perspective studies of a comprehensive nature in the UN system (Sen, 1982, pp. 182–5). It was the only detailed study of the long-term future perspectives available when the international development strategy for the second UN development decade of the 1970s was prepared. With hindsight, Sen considered that one central lesson was that global plans of this nature should be 'firmly based on the political realities of the individual member countries and their programmes and aspirations. Otherwise such Plans become mere intellectual exercises, collecting dust of shelves' (Sen, 1982, p. 185).

As he pointed out, the IWP did not constitute a 'plan' in the usual sense of the word. The emphasis was more on the word 'indicative', since it set out primarily to present an analysis of the main problems that world agriculture would probably face during the coming fifteen years. The aim was to offer governments an international framework for drafting their national plans and policies, and to orient the work of FAO. Controversy and criticism surrounding the preparation of the IWP surfaced when it was presented to the FAO Conference in 1969. But even Saouma recognized that the IWP broke new ground in drawing attention to the major problems faced in a study of its kind and by proposing a scheme, concepts and indicators which continued to be valid. It also provided the information for the preparatory documentation for the 1974 World Food Conference and the agricultural growth target adopted in the international strategy for the Second UN Development Decade of the 1970s of 4 per cent.

The IWP was essentially a blueprint of a strategy for development to 1985. It defined five major strategic objectives: increasing agricultural productivity, especially by extending the use of high yielding cereals through the Green Revolution; closing the protein gap; eliminating waste; mobilizing human resources more effectively; and promoting foreign exchange earnings and savings in developing countries, all contributing toward establishing the right relationship between population growth and food production. In many respects, the IWP was a unique and pioneering experience in international perspective planning. On the basis of collating and synthesizing global material, it attempted to look into the future and influence it by proposing specific objectives together with recommendations for their attainment. As its first task, the IWP tried to establish the magnitude of the food and population problem. It forecast that by 1985, demand for food in the developing countries would be almost two and a half times what it was in 1962. Two-thirds of the increase would be due to population growth and one-third to rising incomes. The conclusion reached was that merely to maintain the existing inadequate patterns of consumption in developing countries, an increase of 80 per cent in food supplies would be required by 1985. If the income and population effects were multiplied, total demand would increase by 140 per cent. An annual rate of increase in food production would be required of 3.9 per cent, while only 2.7 per cent was reached in the previous ten years.

The IWP recommended raising productivity through more intensive use of resources rather than extending the net area cultivated as in the past. It recommended expanding the area under high-yielding varieties of cereals by 1985 from one-twentieth to one-third of the cereals area planted, and increasing investment in research, irrigation and inputs, such as farm equipment, chemical fertilizers and pesticides, as well as in the provision of adequate storage, marketing and processing facilities. The IWP also addressed the problem of rural unemployment and recommended labour intensive public works programmes with the aim of creating additional productive capacity and not merely of providing work, training of the manpower needed to provide essential agricultural services, and a rapid expansion of credit to farmers.

The IWP was heavily criticized on a number of points. Questions were raised concerning its assumptions, scope and methodology. The scope and problems of international co-operation were considered to be insufficiently developed. The question of rural institutions required for the distribution of inputs and the storage and marketing of the perceived additional food production were regarded as being treated too academically. The importance of inter-disciplinary research was found

246   *1970–90. The World Food Crisis of the 1970s and its Aftermath*

to be insufficiently emphasized. And the IWP was considered to have failed to go beyond generalities in its conclusions and recommendations concerning the pattern of international trade. Following these criticisms, the FAO Conference at its session in November 1969 (resolution 1/69), called on FAO to continue its planning work within the framework of a 'Perspective Study for World Agricultural Development', with more extensive coverage, updated statistics, and closer consultations with governments and regional bodies within the context of the strategy for the Second UN Development Decade of the 1970s. The study should also give more attention to changes in income structure and other social and economic factors as well as the problems of international trade policies and the need for international agricultural adjustment.

World food surveys

Saouma continued the tradition started by Boyd Orr in 1946 of FAO carrying out periodic world food surveys. The second survey, conducted in 1952, was followed by a third survey implemented by B. R. Sen at the start of the Freedom from Hunger Campaign in 1963. Two surveys were conducted by Saouma, one in 1977 (FAO, 1977) and the second in 1987 (FAO, 1987a). Although the results of these five world food surveys could not be directly compared in view of the different methodologies and techniques used, they gave a general idea of where progress had taken place, and what problems remained, over the past forty years since the end of the Second World War.

What stood out was the extraordinary progress in food and agriculture. A better-fed world had been achieved, but there were serious exceptions. Most notably was the successful response to the challenge of feeding the rapidly growing world population, at levels of average per caput food consumption that had been constantly improving in both quantity and quality. Fears in the 1960s and 1970s of chronic food shortages over the larger part of the world had proved to be unfounded. However, at the regional level, sub-Saharan Africa in particular still faced a critical problem of producing more adequate food supplies.

In the early 1960s, only five developing countries, with a combined population of 100 million, had average food supplies of more than 2,500 calories per head that was regarded as adequate for a healthy and productive life. Progress was modest up to the early 1970s and the time of the world food crisis. Thereafter, there was a real surge in food consumption levels. By 1979/81, 32 countries, with a combined population of nearly 600 million, had exceeded the 2500-calorie mark. By 1983/85, this group comprised, with the notable addition of China, 35 countries with a total population of 1.86 million people.

The Fifth World Food Survey of 1987 showed a mixed picture. With the entry of China into the group of countries with a high level of food availability per person, over half the total population of developing countries had food supplies exceeding 2,500 calories. At the same time, however, the overall economic crisis of the 1980s virtually arrested the rising trend of average calorie consumption in Latin America. The situation in sub-Saharan Africa was even worse, where there were the additional adverse effects of drought and deteriorating agricultural conditions. Per caput food availabilities were lower in 1983/85 than in 1979/81 in 30 of the 94 developing countries, 24 of them in sub-Saharan Africa.

Two significant developments largely accounted for whatever improvements took place. First, was the rapid growth of incomes and foreign-exchange availability of the oil-exporting and some other middle income countries in the 1970s. Secondly, favourable developments took place in food production in a number of other countries, including low-income ones. The most spectacular gains in this group came in China from the late 1970s, but in many non-African low-income countries gains in food availability, though modest, were solidly based on improved performances in domestic agriculture. Improvements took place in the other low-income countries but only slowly and the 1970s witnessed a reversal of the trend towards improvement, resulting in a tripling of the population living in countries with average per caput availabilities less than 1900 calories.

Food availabilities were only one measure. Access to available supplies was another. In most of the low-income countries, the very poor simply did not have access to enough food to lead a normal life. Consequently, the numbers of under-nourished people in developing countries (outside the Asian centrally planned economies) were conservatively estimated by FAO to have risen slightly over the 1970s. By the mid-1980s, most of the over half a billion undernourished lived in Asia, followed by Africa, although the trend was for the numbers to remain stationary in Asia and to rise in Africa. The general picture to emerge was that while there was a rise in consumption levels, a large undernourished population was left behind. The composition of food consumption continued to change in both developing and developed countries. The share of cereals directly consumed for food declined, together with pulses, roots and tubers, while the share of vegetable products rose. Animal products, consumed in much larger quantities in developed countries, supplied a rising share of calorie intake, and still more of consumer expenditure on food. Two additional and significant changes were the doubling of consumption of wheat in developing countries in the two decades between to early 1960s and early 1980s, and the rising indirect use of cereals as livestock feed in both developing and developed countries.

Among many questions that remained to be answered, three problems were identified as of 'very great concern' to food and agriculture in the 1980s and beyond: trade and related production adjustments, access to food, and the environment. Disarray in agricultural trade, and its underlying protectionism, and the impact on world food security of the agricultural policies of industrialized countries, created 'tremendous real costs' for both developing and developed countries, and 'cried out' for a more effective framework and rules (FAO, 1987a). Retardation, not cessation, required in the growth of production of developed market economies would cause severe adjustment difficulties in the medium term. At the same time, the poor of the world needed improved access to food. The paradox of hunger affecting hundreds of millions of people and excess supplies still remained to be solved, worsened by the stabilization and structural adjustment programmes that developing countries were required to undertake, with

248   *1970–90. The World Food Crisis of the 1970s and its Aftermath*

their negative effects on the food security of the poor (FAO, 1989). Likewise, the world had left unanswered the question of how best to be prepared for any widespread occurrence of crop failures. The third problem, which was becoming more serious, was the protection of agricultural resources and the environment from pollution and degradation, for which there was more publicity than action. Agriculture was also very much involved in the external debt problem of many developing countries, and efforts to slow the rate of urbanization, and with the location of industries outside urban centres. Finally, there remained 'the complex and acute problem' of rehabilitating agriculture in sub-Saharan Africa and avoiding the recurrence of famines or minimizing their impacts.

World agriculture: towards 2000

Saouma decided to continue FAO's work of exploring the future of world agriculture 'in as realistic way as possible', while avoiding the trap into which the IWP had fallen in what he called 'diffuse planning'. He therefore conceived the idea of publishing a major study on world agriculture that would have the dual purpose of constituting FAO's contribution towards the preparation by the UN of a new international development strategy for the Third UN Development Decade of the 1980s, and of helping FAO formulate its own policies and work programme. The study relied on the usable components of the IWP, documents prepared for a Perspective Study of World Agricultural Development, and the first reports of the Club of Rome, which appeared in 1972, and which shed new light on the problem of the limits to growth (Meadows, 1972).

The study, entitled *World Agriculture: Toward 2000,* took almost a decade to complete, from the submission of a provisional version of the work to the FAO Conference in 1979 to the presentation of the final version to the FAO Conference in 1987, and its publication for wider readership in 1988 (Alexandratos, 1988). Its purpose was to provide a perspective analysis of likely trends in food and agriculture up to the end of the century. Saouma presented the provisional version of the study to FAO Conference delegates in 1979 in the following terms:

> It is not, of course, a set of prophecies or predictions. We must at all times remember that it is simply an analysis of the implications of a path of growth derived from certain assumptions about demographic and economic growth rates. The resultant data and situations represent what could happen if the assumptions were in fact justified by experience. (Saouma, 1993, p. 54)

In other words, the results of the study were only as valid as the assumptions on which it was based.

Three scenarios were drawn up. One was called a 'trend scenario' because it was based on a simple extrapolation of past trends in production and consumption. As might be expected, it showed that the rift between rich and poor countries would continue to widen and the number of malnourished and underfed would increase further. A second, 'intermediate scenario' was based on medium growth in developing countries, with agricultural production rising by roughly 3.1 per cent a year. In this case, the number of undernourished would diminish only slightly, the divergence between urban and rural incomes would become more pronounced, and overall improvement would remain limited. According to the third and 'most optimistic scenario', developing countries would reach the growth targets established for the international development strategy of the 1980s of 7 per cent growth in GDP a year, and yearly increases in agricultural production of 3.7 per cent (compared with 2.9 per cent during the previous decade). With profound changes in agriculture in developing countries, including doubling investment and tripling inputs, it was projected that agricultural production would double between 1980 and the year 2000, and the number of undernourished would fall to 250 million. Even with such spectacular progress, the scourge of hunger would not be eliminated. And it was recognized that tremendous efforts would be needed on other fronts in order to make food more accessible to the poor including: improving access to education, training and employment; bringing about dynamic and balanced rural development; developing the non-agricultural sectors of the economy; and, above all, raising incomes.

To answer the question to what extent, and at what rate, world agriculture could increase, FAO moved from macro-economic speculation to detailed technical analysis. A *Soil Map of the World*, which took seventeen years to complete, had been produced as a result of co-operation with UNESCO that had started in 1961. To this was added work on the capacity of the world's agro-ecological zones based on low, medium and high levels of inputs (FAO, 1978–81). A special study of African agriculture projected over a quarter of a century showed that over 60 per cent of the population would be deficient in food if the level of inputs remained low (FAO, 1986). These factors were taken into account in the revised and updated version of *World Agriculture: Towards 2000*, which was submitted to the FAO Conference in 1987. The new edition broadened the scope of the study to cover virtually the entire world, including China. It took account of the deteriorating world economic situation that had developed since the beginning of the 1980s. And it introduced new considerations, such as the need for environmental protection, and developments in technology and research.

The final study showed that nutrition had improved but not everywhere (Alexandratos, 1988, pp. 3–10). Average per caput food availability for direct human consumption was projected to rise from 2,420 calories in 1983/85 to 2620 calories in the year 2000. But in its *Fifth World Food Survey*, published in 1987, FAO estimated that between 335 million and 500 million people in developing countries were undernourished in 1979/81 (FAO, 1987a). Total agricultural production was projected to rise by 3 per cent a year between 1983/85 and the year 2000, lower than the 3.3 per cent growth rate achieved in the preceding fifteen years, with significant differences among the developing regions. The net cereals deficits of the developing countries, which had risen by three and a half times in the past fifteen years to nearly 70 million tons in 1983/85, were projected to grow, but at a much slower rate, to about 110

250 *1970–90. The World Food Crisis of the 1970s and its Aftermath*

million tons by 2000. And the agricultural trade surpluses of developing countries were expected to continue to decline.

In conclusion, the picture for the developing countries emerging from the study was one of continuing development of their agricultural sector overall but with some significant black spots. The unfavourable overall economic environment of the 1980s constrained growth of demand. Export opportunities were limited by protectionism. There was only minimal improvement in the food situation in sub-Saharan Africa. And there was no decrease in the total number of undernourished people. Regarding food security, the study noted that this had become a leading issue following the world food crisis of the early 1970s. The 1974 World Food Conference had sought to abolish hunger by a combination of national and international measures, including a commitment on food aid. But some major developed countries 'did not find the goal of a formal stock policy at the global level acceptable'. Increasing experience with various institutional arrangements (including the World Food Council and FAO's CFS) had led to a better understanding of food security but 'meeting any food crisis still depended essentially on effective *ad hoc* action by individual countries'. And the recent African famines pointed again to the urgent need for effective national and international arrangements for a quicker response action.

As a sequel to *World Agriculture: Towards 2000*, a study of the prospects for agriculture in FAO's European region to the year 2000 was initiated, which was extended to include the countries of North America and the UN Economic Commission for Europe, including the USSR (Alexandratos, 1990). The study discussed policy issues and options in the context of national and international efforts towards agricultural policy reform, including progressive and concerted reduction of agricultural support measures and social and other concerns, including food security. Regarding issues of trade and relations with the developing countries, the study noted that much of the impetus for policy reform, particularly in the market economies, had come from 'undesirable trade-distorting effects', which resulted from the pursuit of predominantly domestic goals in agricultural policy. The key question for the future was the extent to which countries would accept that national agricultural policy should be subjected to the discipline imposed by the need for the orderly development of international economic relations. In practical terms, this translated into a quest for policies to meet domestic farm income and related goals by means that minimized distortions of markets. It also implied a greater role for market forces in determining production and consumption patterns and trade flows. Developing countries as a group stood to gain from improved market access.

Successful policy reform in the industrial countries would greatly reduce or eliminate their structural food surpluses. This could adversely affect concessional exports to developing countries. Given the extreme scarcity of foreign exchange faced by many developing countries, they might not be able to maintain their levels of food imports. In particular, food security of low-income, food-deficit countries, which depended substantially on concessional import, could suffer. The study concluded that the net effect on the welfare of developing countries of trade

Pragmatism and Politics 251

liberalization in cereals was much less clear than for other commodities. More generally, benefits to developing countries from trade liberalization would also depend on complementary changes in their own policies, which often discriminated directly and indirectly against agriculture.

Food aid and food security

Saouma also saw the potential advantage for him in the role that food aid could play in food security. We have already seen in Part I that FAO played a major role in the evolution of food aid from a surplus disposal mechanism to a resource for development, and in the establishment of a multilateral food aid facility through the creation of the UN World Food Programme (WFP). A unique and unprecedented feature of WFP's constitution in the UN system was that it was to operate as a joint undertaking between two parent bodies, the United Nations in New York and FAO in Rome.[46] From his election, Saouma considered that he had *de facto* control of WFP. He was jointly responsible with the UN secretary-general for the appointment of WFP's executive director and WFP senior staff, after consultation with WFP's governing body. In reality, it was the director-general who took the initiative in these appointments.

The unequal partnership was carried further when it was decided to locate WFP at FAO headquarters in Rome where its governing body also met. Saouma insisted in seeing all policy papers and draft reports of WFP's governing body before they were submitted for discussion and adoption. In addition, the WFP secretariat was not created as a self-contained entity but had to rely on the technical, financial and administrative services of other UN organizations, particularly FAO, on a reimbursable basis. FAO's director-general was entrusted with the financial management of WFP's resources and with the approval of WFP's emergency assistance. There were many reasons for this complex arrangement. But basically it was to assist, not control, the fledgling organization, which was originally set up as a three-year experimental programme (1963–65) with an uncertain future, to undertake its work through cost-saving measures. With limited funds, Saouma saw the possibility of extending the resources over which he could gain control through food aid. Moreover, the FAO CFS gave him a mechanism for pursuing his political goals. It was to take a ten-year struggle (1982–92) to liberate WFP from Saouma's domination (Ingram, 2006).

Against this background, FAO produced a document that was presented to the CFS setting out the potential roles that food aid could play in the pursuit of food security (FAO, 1985b). The paper recognized that food aid alone could not achieve food security, and was only one component in the complex process of reaching that goal. A crucial problem was therefore how to ensure that it was used in a favourable policy environment and in proper balance with complementary technical and financial resources in appropriate packages of assistance. It also noted that food aid could be used in many ways to help strengthen all three of the components of FAO's broadened definition of food security: increasing food production; stabilizing food supply and ensuring access to food availabilities.

252 1970–90. The World Food Crisis of the 1970s and its Aftermath

The direct and indirect links between food aid and food production were numerous. Food aid provided balance of payments support, which could be used to finance agricultural development. But this could pose a policy risk. A recipient government could give lower priority to domestic food production as a result of receiving food aid and thus accentuate long-term food insecurity because it could bridge its food deficit without structural change or expenditure of its own foreign exchange resources. To ensure a positive impact, therefore, the food aid provided and the foreign exchange saved from not having to purchase food imports should be used to support an overall food security programme, which included specific measures to promote food production. The released foreign exchange could be used to import agricultural production inputs, machinery and equipment, or essential consumption goods for distribution in rural areas where, for lack of goods to buy, farmers had no incentive to increase food production or sell their output. Relaxation of foreign exchanges constraints could also have a broader developmental effect, making it possible to increase or maintain rates of investment, employment and incomes, thereby increasing effective demand for food, which, in turn, would encourage production.

Food aid could also provide budgetary support in recipient countries. Where food aid commodities were sold, the counterpart funds generated could be used to promote food production by helping to finance agricultural development projects or various incentive measures for farmers. The importance of such budgetary support depended on the volume of food aid in relation to government expenditure, the terms on which the food aid commodities are sold and the readiness of recipient governments and donors to agree on their use. Disincentive risks, such as the danger that the commodity composition of the food aid provided would distort domestic consumption patterns in the recipient countries or disrupt internal food system underlined the need for using counterpart funds to strengthen the position of local food producers and maintain their market share.

Food aid could also be used as a development resource directly to increase food production in developing countries in a number of ways. It could support labour-intensive food-for-work projects to construct or improve the infrastructure needed to increase food production as in land development and improvement projects involving irrigation, drainage, food control and other works, or in land settlement or resettlement schemes or agricultural adjustment programmes in which small farmers are assisted in transforming their traditional, low-yielding farming practices into modern farming systems. Other ways included supporting agricultural training programmes, assisting women's role in agricultural production, and protecting the environment, and livestock, dairy, forestry and fisheries development projects, leading to the phasing out of the need for food aid. Set against these advantages, potential disadvantages should be guarded against including: depressing food prices and creating a disincentive for local agricultural production, distorting recipient government policies and disrupting trade, creating a dependency syndrome, the political and commercial forces that motivated food aid donors, and the inferiority of food aid as a doubly tied aid resources.

Food aid also had the potential of having a significant stabilizing effect on food supplies (see below). It could help to limit the damaging impact of production fluctuations on consumption and price levels in recipient countries and enable them to establish and replenish national food stocks and reserves. Food aid could also help improve access to food by the poor in recipient countries both through income-generation in labour-intensive work projects and through subsidized food distribution nutrition-improvement and education and training programmes. But like all forms of aid, attaining the many potential benefits of food aid depended both on the ways in which it was provided by donors and the precise ways in which it was used by the recipients.

The FAO paper identified a number of ways of improving the contribution of food aid to food security. For recipient countries, these included a better integration of food aid within national food security programmes, developing national preparedness plans, including early warning systems, to contend with major food shortages, the development of storage and distribution systems, giving high priority to food security objectives in the use of counterpart funds generated from food aid sales, and committing local resources to food-aided projects when food aid is finally phased out, thereby ensuring the maintenance and follow-up.

For donor countries, multi-year country programming of food aid was identified as a 'crucial factor' in effective utilization of food aid as part of a package of development resources. In addition, timely and co-ordinated response, including the pre-positioning of food stocks, the provision of complementary resources, including cash and technical assistance, and the promotion of triangular transactions (whereby a donor provided a food commodity which could be exchanged for another food commodity in a developing countries for use as food aid) were mentioned as other ways of strengthening the contribution of food aid for food security. As far as multilateral food aid was concerned, improvement could be made by increasing the dependability of food aid, particularly through an enlarged and revised FAC, and improving the responsiveness to large-scale food shortages through, *inter alia*, increasing the stand-by resources of the International Emergency Food Reserve (IEFR) to 2 million tons (FAO, 1983b), strengthening the emergency provisions of the Food Aid Convention, establishing a system of interim food reserves, and creating a food aid insurance schemes (first suggested in 1973 and reiterated at a Food Security Symposium organized by FAO in 1985) under which donor countries would guarantee to provide food aid to developing countries experiencing supply deficits in excess of a specified percentage below trend.

FAO studied the responsiveness of food aid in cereals to fluctuations in supply in donor and recipient countries over the fifteen year period 1970–1985 (FAO, 1985b). Taking the three cereal commodity groups (wheat, coarse grains and rice) and the five major donors (Australia, Canada, the European Economic Community (EEC), Japan and the United States), the study noted that cereal food aid disbursements as a percentage of total development assistance declined over time, and were much more volatile than other forms of assistance. This indicated that, by and large, the food aid programmes of the major donor countries had been influenced 'first and foremost by conditions in their agricultural sectors and only secondarily by development objectives'. Overall expenditure on food aid by donors was determined by budgetary allocations, which were made in monetary terms well ahead of food aid shipments. The quantity shipped depended largely on food commodity prices at the time of shipment. The level of carryover stocks and export prices explained a 'considerable part' of the year-to-year variability of food aid provided by the Canada, Japan and the United States, while for Australia and the EEC, the level of their food aid shipments was 'very closely linked' to their minimum commitments under the FAC. Concerning the price effect on food aid shipments, while the current year world price was a significant factor for wheat, the previous year's world price was significant for coarse grains and, to some extent, rice. The effect of carryover stocks was 'substantial' on food aid in rice, 'moderate' for wheat, and 'relatively small' for coarse grains.

The FAO analysis of the factors influencing donors' food aid shipments also showed that the level of production in the rest of the world was in general negatively correlated with food aid shipments. Donors did, in general, respond to the increased needs of recipient countries arising from short-term production shortfalls. However, this response was partial, estimated to cover only about 13 per cent of cereal production shortfalls for low-income, food-deficit countries as a whole (excluding China and India). For the most seriously affected, least-developed countries, the response was somewhat better, covering about 20 per cent of production shortfalls. Donors gave higher priority to low-income, food-deficit countries, which received between 85 and 90 per cent of total food aid in cereals, but the volume of food aid provided was inadequate to meet the needs of some of those countries. Total food aid shipments accounted for only 18 per cent of their food imports during the 1980s compared to 30 per cent in the 1970s. Food aid availabilities had stagnated at around 9 million tons a year while requirements were estimated at over 20 million tons of cereals a year (FAO, 1983b).

In conclusion, the FAO study observed that since the beginning of the food aid system as a permanent mechanism of transferring resources from rich to poor countries, the motives for providing food aid had shifted considerably from a surplus disposal regime toward developmental objectives and consideration of specific short-term needs of recipient countries. The availability of a large part of food aid had been institutionalized through successive FACs. However, the extent to which food aid varied from year to year depended 'to a considerable degree' on the availability of surpluses in donor countries. This implied that in the short-term, prospects for increasing the volume of food aid would depend 'to a considerable extent' on the size of cereal surpluses in donor countries. However, domestic considerations in donor countries dictated that their farm policies increasingly aimed at keeping the level of cereal production under control. The volume of future food aid could therefore be significantly influences by the degree of success that these domestic farm policies brought about a balance between production and demand.

There were, of course, other factors that had an increasing influence of donors' decisions concerning the level of the food aid they provided. These related particularly to the role of food aid as an effect development resource and its more specific roles as one component in the complex process of strengthening food security in developing countries. It was recognized that food aid had a vital and irreplaceable role in increasing access of the poor to food, improving the diet of vulnerable groups, and in relieving food emergencies and famine. As the FAO paper on *Food Aid and Food Security* had shown, food aid could play many roles as a development resource to promote development in low-income, food-deficit countries, leading toward the promotion of food security. Much depended on how successful food aid was in playing those roles.

Plan of Action on World Food Security

It was not long before Saouma, the self-appointed guardian of the rights of the developing countries, pursued the moral as well as the material aspects of food security, and crossed over from a pragmatic approach into the realms of politics. Like his predecessors, he soon found that going beyond the pragmatic would meet with the resistance that major developed countries had shown from the days of the first FAO director-general, Boyd Orr. Nevertheless, he considered that FAO had a dual role: alerting the world's moral conscience; and undertaking concrete, pragmatic action in concert with others. We saw above that Saouma had tried and failed to convert the IEFR into a legally binding convention and to increase its target to 2 million tons. In 1979, Saouma proposed a five-point *Plan of Action on World Food Security*. He considered that the plan was necessary to implement the *International Undertaking on World Food Security* that had been recommended by the FAO Conference and the World Food Conference and endorsed by the UN General Assembly (FAO, 1979b). At the same time, he urged governments to reach agreement on a new international grains arrangement with adequate stock, price and food aid provisions, and with special provisions for developing countries, which he regarded were essential for an effective world food security system.

The five points of his proposed plan were:

- adoption by all countries of national reserve stock policies and targets in accordance with the provisions of the International Undertaking in World Food Security;
- establishment by the CFS of criteria for releases from such reserves;
- adoption of special measures to assist low-income food-deficit countries to meet current food import requirements and emergency needs;
- new arrangements to intensify and coordinate assistance to developing countries in strengthening their food security, including the establishment of food reserves; and
- measures to promote the collective self-reliance of developing countries through regional and other mutual aid schemes.

The Committee of the Whole of the United Nations established under UN General Assembly resolution 32/714 at its session in March 1979, welcomed Saouma's initiative in proposing the plan. The FAO Council approved the plan at its session in June 1979. In doing so, the Council reaffirmed 'the common responsibility of the entire international community to assure the availability at all times of adequate supplies of basic food stuffs in accordance with the objectives of the International Undertaking on World Food Security'. It also recognized that 'in the absence of a coordinated system of national and regional food stocks, the world is still not adequately protected against acute food shortages in the event of widespread crop failures or other disasters' and that 'additional assistance is needed to meet the growing import needs and emergency requirements of developing countries as well as to strengthen their food security programmes'. The Council stressed, however, that the Plan of Action was not a substitute for a new international grains arrangement, and urged that such an arrangement be concluded as quickly as possible.

World Food Security Compact

Not content that the plan was sufficient to raise the world's moral conscience, Saouma launched the idea of a *World Food Security Compact* in the CFS at its session in April 1983 (FAO, 1983a). An outline of the compact was also contained in a document on 'World Food Security: Selected Issues and Approaches' that was presented to the CFS at its session in April 1984 (FAO, 1984b). This led to heated discussions and deep disputes. The CFS came back to the proposal twice at it sessions in 1984 and 1985. The compact set out some fundamental principles. It identified food and nutrition security as a human rights question, specifically the 'fundamental right of everyone to be free from hunger'. It recognized that it was poverty that prevented 'the human right to food' from being exercised, and proclaimed that 'no one can remain indifferent to the distress of others'. Relieving misery in the immediate future, and working for economic and social development in the long run, remained essential elements to achieve food security, equal to growth in food production, stability of supplies, and access by all to available food. At the same time, 'food should not be used as a mean of exerting political pressure'.

The compact called on governments in the developing countries to stimulate food production by motivating farmers, adopting mechanisms involving early warning systems, establishing food reserves and relief distribution plans, giving priority to the needs of the poor, especially small farmers, and developing regional co-operation. Developed countries were invited to take into account the interests of the international community, and primarily the weakest countries, in their production, storage and import policies, and provide aid in the form of agricultural inputs and food. Concerning international trade, the compact appealed for recognition of 'the moral dimensions of commercial relations' and for concern for the 'common good' to counterbalance that of national interest. The compact also called on NGOs to redouble their efforts to make the public more aware of the need for world food security, and invited individuals to recognize their 'sacred obligation' to help others and to make a personal commitment, along with NGOs, to arouse the moral conscience. Dedicated to affirming humanity's common responsibility on food security, the compact ended with the words: 'The enemy is indifference'.

What motivated Saouma to propose the compact? He explained that experience gained in implementing the food security programme described above led him to think that FAO should apply a wider and more precise definition to the concept of food security (Saouma, 1993, pp. 82–3). In this spirit, food security was defined in accordance with its main aim: 'to achieve the ultimate objective of ensuring that all people at all times are in a position to product or procure the basic food they need'. Three components were identified in pursuing this objective: raising food production to an adequate level; ensuring stability of supplies; and guaranteeing the poorest access to food. While the first two components entailed a whole set of political and technical measures, the third brought out the ethical dimension of the problem. This broadened concept of food security contained what Saouma called 'the germ of a standard of behaviour'. It meant 'rejecting the scandalous paradox of hunger in a world of plenty', both at the individual level (the poor lacked food while the rich spent fortunes on slimming) and at the national level (some countries fought against scarcity and famine while others were glutted with surpluses). From this situation, Saouma explained that 'the idea of a codification, or statement of moral rules for observance by countries, organizations, and plain citizens quite naturally came to mind'. Hence, the World Food Security Compact.

But why did it cause so much heated debate and dissention? On first reading, it could be regarded as a harmless document. It contained no legally or financially binding provisions and repeated existing agreements and commitments in outlining the broad lines of a long-term strategy concerning the establishment of a 'world food security system'. What, then, were the points of contention? In the view of some delegates, the initial draft compact seemed 'superfluous'. By simply repeating existing agreements and commitments, its usefulness and effectiveness were questioned. They contested the idea that by grouping together in one text a collection of principles scattered among several international instruments, the proposed compact could have any positive impact on public opinion. A more radical objection harked back to the founding of FAO and the days of Boyd Orr. Should FAO, a UN technical agency, state an opinion on questions concerning moral commitment and political will? Surely, these were matters more correctly discussed at the United Nations and elsewhere. FAO should stick to providing technical assistance, analysis, and to monitoring. Closely linked to this objection were the reservations, prompted by inclusion in the draft compact of the concept of food security in terms of human rights, the injunction that food should not be used as a political weapon, the reference to a basic set of principles, the duties and responsibilities of governments in developing and developed nations, and the roles and involvement of NGOs and the common man. While some delegations felt that the draft compact went too far, others found it 'too anodyne, too timorous and nor incisive enough'. The CFS decided by a majority, but not by consensus, to accept the draft and send it to the FAO Council for approval and to the FAO Conference for adoption.

At this point, Saouma admitted that to reach unanimous agreement with no reservations on all points 'would have been rather unrealistic'. At the same time, while famine was ravaging a large part of Africa and many developing countries were suffering from privation and malnutrition, 'any word, any sign, that could bring us nearer to the ideal of food security was extremely important'. He, therefore, redrafted the compact before sending the revised text to the FAO Council 'in order to make it more easily acceptable to all'. Nevertheless, a small number of major developed countries maintained their reservations, and dissociated themselves from the compact that was adopted by the FAO Conference in November 1985. Their objections were illuminating. Apart for calling for more consultation in preparing the compact, and that the text should have been more explicit as to its voluntary and non-binding nature, they considered that the compact was unnecessary to stimulate further action this field. They also considered that the compact was unbalanced and unclear regarding the obligations of developing and developed countries, and the roles of food trade and NGOs, in strengthening food security. The majority of FAO member states, in supporting the compact, considered that it set out 'the moral values and lines of action' that all should follow in attaining 'the commonly shared objective of improved world food security and the elimination of hunger and malnutrition' and that it 'would strengthen the resolve of all people to pursue the objective of food security'.

21
World Bank Perspective

Inevitably, the World Bank joined the chorus in addressing the issues and options for ensuring food security in the developing countries in a seminal study that appeared first as an internal report in 1985 (World Bank, 1985) and then as a Bank publication in 1986 (World Bank, 1986).[47] The study noted that the world had 'ample food'. Food production had grown faster than the unprecedented growth of population. World cereal prices had been falling. And there was enough food available worldwide so that countries that did not produce all the food they needed could import it, *if* they could afford to do so. Yet famines still occurred as part of the problem of widespread hunger and malnutrition. A 'continuing tragedy' was that over one-third of the population of the developing world, about 730 million people, did not have enough food, and some 340 million of them were acutely undernourished. But what were the causes of hunger? No doubt inspired by the work of Amartya Sen, the study emphasized that inadequate food supply was no longer the source of the problem. Food security, defined as 'dependable access to enough food for an active, healthy life', was the 'most fundamental need'. But many countries did not have strategies for helping most of their people achieve food security. And of those which did, some had strategies that were ineffective or self-defeating in the long run.

The study's unique contribution to the general debate was that it distinguished between two kinds of food insecurity: chronic and transitory. Chronic food insecurity was defined as 'a *continuously* (original emphasis) inadequate diet caused by the inability to acquire food'. It affected households that persistently lacked the ability either to buy enough food or to produce their own. Transitory food insecurity was defined as 'a *temporary* (original emphasis) decline in a household's access to enough food'. It resulted from instability in food prices, food production, or household incomes, and in its worst form produced famine.

The central message of the Bank's policy study was that from the many forces that conspired to leave underfed almost one person in five, 'one stands out above all others: poverty'. Poverty, or lack of purchasing power, was 'likely to be relieved by economic growth, which would ultimately provide most households with enough income to acquire enough food'. Such growth should, therefore, continue to be 'a primary goal of economic policy'. But there were two difficulties.

259

First, economic growth takes time. And second, given the distribution of assets and opportunities, the purchasing power of large numbers of poor people would increase only slowly, and some would remain in poverty. The Bank's policy study analyzed how the second set of difficulties could be address at the national level, and how the international community could assist. It stressed that while there were no universally valid solutions, four principles were essential for understanding and formulating remedies for food insecurity:

- The objectives of poverty alleviation and food security converged because the lack of food security was usually caused by lack of purchasing power.
- Food self-sufficiency, or a rapid increase in food production, would not necessarily increase food security in a country, although these goals may be desirable for other reasons.
- In the long term, poverty alleviation linked with economic growth was the best way to reduce malnutrition. But in the shorter run, redistributing purchasing power and food itself towards the undernourished could help. Governments could, therefore, do much to improve the food security of their people if programmes for redistribution were carefully designed and selected on a cost-effectiveness basis.
- Transitory food insecurity could best be reduced through measures that facilitated trade and provided income relief.

The study pointed out that by looking at factors that typically affected food consumption, it could be seen that food security problems resulted more from a lack of purchasing power among the poor than from inadequate levels of food production at the country level for four basic reasons. First, the energy lacking in the diets of the food insecure was only a small faction (less than 10 per cent) of the energy in the food supply (net domestic production plus imports) of most nations. This gap could usually be eliminated when rising effective demand induced higher levels of food production or imports, sufficient to fill the energy deficit. Second, a study of 50 developing countries showed a strong association between the energy content of the national diet and per capita income. Increases in domestic food production did not necessarily improve food security unless food prices also fell relative to incomes, thus raising the purchasing power of the poor. The additional food produced may simply substitute for imports, or be exported. There was no necessary link between national food self-sufficiency and food security. Where a country could not produce food efficiently, attaining self-sufficiency could reduce a country's purchasing power, and therefore its food security. Third, it was striking how the annual variation in domestic food prices in developing countries was so much greater (by a factor of two and a half times) than in industrialized countries. This instability reflected not only foreign exchange constraints but also uneven demand for food because of unstable household incomes. Finally, perhaps the most telling evidence came from the study of famine victims, as Amartya Sen had shown. Supply problems arising from natural and man-made disasters could certainly aggravate food insecurity. But famine could be caused when there was no generalized food shortage and markets were full and the victims lacked the purchasing power to buy it. The causes of food insecurity therefore suggested that it could be relieved only by raising the real incomes of households so that they could afford to acquire enough food. This could be done in two ways: by giving people the opportunity to earn an adequate income; and by ensuring an abundant food supply through domestic production or imports.

The study next identified the different kinds of interventions that could be used to address chronic and transitory food insecurity. Regarding chronic food insecurity, beyond the array of measures to accelerate economic growth, create employment, and reduce poverty, three kinds of interventions could be used: increasing food supply (through production or imports), subsidized consumer prices, and targeted income transfers (as, e.g., through public works programmes). These interventions were likely to have different short-run effects on the three main groups of people facing chronic food insecurity: the urban poor, the rural landless, and small-scale farmers. Interventions that increased incomes, or reduced consumer prices without lowering producer prices, clearly improve food security. With such interventions, none of the people facing chronic food insecurity would suffer a decline in their real incomes. But some food supply policies might increase food security for some poverty groups but reduce it for others. And some initial benefits of interventions could be eroded over time. For example, lower food prices might eventually lead to lower nominal wages. The long-run gains to workers would then be largely limited to the growth in employment from the implicit wage subsidy. Since all interventions have costs, a comprehensive analysis of the size and incidence of benefits would have to consider the direct and indirect effects, other than changes in food prices and employment, of those costs. The choice of interventions would need to be based on a balanced concern for budgetary and economic costs, the administrative and political feasibility of different interventions, and their expected benefits.

Transitory food insecurity could best be reduced through measures that facilitate trade and provide income relief to afflicted people, such as food stamps or child-feeding programmes. In most countries, 'the surest and probably cheapest ways' to stabilize domestic food prices was through international trade. Imports or exports, combined with variable levies to insulate domestic food prices from changing international prices, could offset instability in domestic production almost automatically. But such policies could wreak havoc with the budget and balance of payments, unless governments held large foreign exchange reserves and could rely on more food aid or international schemes, such as the IMF's Compensatory Financing Facility for cereal imports.

Many governments often tried to stabilize food supplies and prices in costly and ineffective ways. As a result, interventions of this kind aggravate rather than reduce the instability of supply and prices. Some governments also kept excessive buffer stocks. Countries with access to foreign exchange usually found it cheaper to stabilize prices by varying their exports and imports, even when world market prices were unstable. Production could also be stabilized through investing in measures such as irrigation or pest control, or improving market efficiency. But stable food prices and efficient domestic marketing were not always enough to prevent transitory food insecurity. Also, they could not prevent famines brought on by bad weather or economic crisis. Then, the afflicted groups could be given temporary employment with wages paid in cash and/or food, and those who could not work, food subsidizes. But relief should be carefully targeted to those who suffer a fall in real income. As well as cost-effectiveness, the selection of a package of appropriate interventions in any country required attention to the size and makeup of the target population, the government's ability to administer and finance interventions, and political feasibility.

There was no one optimum solution to the problem of food security any more than there was one solution to the problem of poverty. The Bank study made it clear that to help developing countries improve their food security, the international community should:

- intensify efforts to accelerate growth through productive investment, policy reform and adjustment assistance;
- help design, for the short- and medium-term, cost-effective programmes to alleviate chronic hunger and prevent transitory food insecurity, including famines, paying special attention to the needs of the very young, among whom malnutrition could cause irreversible damage;
- help countries co-ordinate food aid with other forms of economic assistance.

Other cost-effective programmes to strengthen food security might include improving the nutrition of vulnerable groups through food and other forms of income transfer, nutrition education, better drinking water and preventive health and family planning services. Assistance might also be given to improve the capacity of developing countries to handle sharp, sporadic increases in food imports and intra-regional food transfers, and to manage small strategically located emergency food stocks. Promotion of crop diversification, public employment and transport facilities might be supported, particularly in climatically unstable regions where it may be difficult to sustain adequate food consumption in years of bad weather.

The study noted that aid-in-kind accounted for a significant portion of official development assistance. It advocated that this form of assistance should be planned and managed with as much care as financial aid. An increasing share of food aid was used to directly augment the incomes of the poor and their nutritional status. Better integration with overall country development programmes would greatly enhance the long-term benefits of such aid. The food aid provided should have a high value to the recipients relative to the delivery costs. And exchanging donated food for cash and buying local foods may often be more advantageous to recipients. The cost-effectiveness of famine relief could be improved by detecting emergencies earlier, reducing response time, and providing aid in cash as well as food. Multi-year commitments by food aid donor, with flexible drawings against those commitments in accordance with the needs of recipient countries, were required so that food aid could more effectively alleviate transitory food insecurity.

And food aid donors should co-ordinate their efforts with other development institutions to improve the effectiveness of all external assistance. Food security in developing countries could also be enhanced if action was taken to reduce trade restrictions on their exports. The terms of trade for internationally traded goods greatly affected the real incomes of vulnerable groups, who often worked in the labour-intensive production of export goods. Multilateral actions that stabilized food prices and major exchange rates, as well as technical assistance to help developing countries manage trade risks would also contribute to food security.

In conclusion, the World Bank study observed that much foreign assistance for food security has been sought to accelerate agricultural development and increase food production. These were important aspects of the problem when they affected the real incomes of vulnerable consumers and producers. But progress in reducing food insecurity had been 'disappointing, partly because of the widely held misperception that food shortages are the root of the problem'. Ironically, food insecurity had worsened in many countries, even when per capita food production increased. 'Increasing the food supply will not eliminate the problem unless it also improves the incomes and purchasing power of the poor'. The often predicted Malthusian nightmare of population outstripping food production had not materialized. Instead, the world faced a 'narrower problem': many people did not have enough to eat, despite there being enough food for all. This was not a failure of food production or of agricultural technology. It was a failure to provide all people with the opportunity to secure enough food, 'something that is very difficult to do in low-income countries'. The roots of the predicament ranged from improper macro-economic policies to the economic and political structures of local societies. 'The causes of food insecurity are complex and so are its remedies'. The problem had been tackled successfully in some countries. This should be repeated in many others.

22
Food Subsidies

Interest in consumer food subsidy programmes was accentuated during the 1980s not only because of concern with the increasing number of hungry people in developing countries as their access to food deteriorated but also because of the social dimensions of structural adjustment programmes that the World Bank and IMF were advocating and the need to find effective compensatory measures to protect the poor during the economic adjustment process. Research and experience showed that consumer food subsidies aimed at reducing consumer food prices below the free-market level could be a double-edged sword. They could be a powerful and cost-effective policy tool to reach certain social, economic and political goals, or they could be harmful to growth and equity. As with so many other policy tools, the question was not whether consumer food subsidies were good or bad but when and how they were applied. And subsidies were only one means of keeping consumer prices low: they were also open to abuse.

Research undertaken at IFPRI over a period of almost ten years (1978–86) provided the results of consumer-oriented food subsidy programmes in a number of diverse developing countries (Pinstrup-Andersen, 1988). These programmes had different objectives, which included improving the real purchasing power or nutritional status of the poor, maintaining low urban nominal wages, reducing energy and nutrient deficiencies in low-income population groups, or assuring social and political stability by protecting poor households from deteriorations in their already low standard of living while structural adjustment programmes were implemented. They also took many forms: directly government-financed or indirectly supported through fiscal or exchange rate policy, and generally applied or highly targeted at specific population groups.

While subsidy programmes were effective policy tools for reaching specific government objectives, including those aimed at enhancing the health, nutrition and general well-being of the most disadvantaged groups of the population, usually urban consumers, they often represented a large drain on government revenue, introduced price distortions into an economy, and large economic costs to farmers and to the economy as a whole. Therefore, their alleviation was expected to contribute to economic growth, which in turn would assist in effectively dealing with economic crises. They were thus often the target when governments sought ways of reducing expenditure and inflation during economic reform during the 1980s. Capping or reducing food subsidies was part of about one-third of 94 adjustment programmes supported by the IMF.

Used imaginatively, food subsidies could be effective in reaching specific and limited policy goals with little or no negative effect on economic growth and could result in healthier children, more productive adults and stronger economic growth in the longer run. Conversely, used indiscriminately, they were unlikely to be the most cost-effective means to improve the welfare of the poor in the short run and have disastrous effects on economic growth in the longer term. While consumer food subsidies had a positive role to play, in many cases that role was not properly specified. Failure to design or modify subsidy programmes to achieve objectives in the lost cost-effective manner, and failure to discontinue or replace inappropriate programmes, resulted in high fiscal and economic costs and misallocation of resources and transfers. In Egypt, the annual costs of subsidy programmes during the first half of the 1980s were $2 billion, or about 6 per cent of GNP.

Consumer food subsidies were rarely, if ever, the most efficient way to deal with long-term structural problems. Their proper role was to compensate for the effects of inappropriate development strategies, asset distribution, institutions and policy measures. They enhanced the purchasing power of the poor and lowered and stabilized food prices. They may not be needed in countries following a development strategy that emphasized employment generation and productivity growth among the poor, equitable asset distribution, cost-saving technological changes in food production, and improvements in food marketing. Institutional changes and policy measures that provided the poor with access to productive assets and skills could greatly reduce the need to enhance their incomes through food subsidies.

An important role could be played by consumer food subsidies in countries where the development strategy was biased toward capital-intensive urban development rather than employment-intensive rural development, where there was little emphasis on expanding food production at lower unit costs, and on reducing food-marketing costs, where market institutions were not effective in dealing with price fluctuations, or where the poor could not maintain a minimum living standard. Food subsidies might also be needed to compensate the poor for negative effects of regressive distortions in other sectors of the economy.

Food subsidies had resulted in large transfers from food producers or governments to consumers. In Sri Lanka, for example, a subsidized food ration scheme contributed 16 per cent of the incomes of the poorest decile of the population in 1978–79. In Egypt, food subsidies accounted for 13 per cent of the incomes of the urban poor and 17 per cent of the incomes of the rural poor in the early 1980s. And in Bangladesh, the value of food subsidies received by the urban poor was 15–25 per cent of total income. Benefits of similar magnitude were estimated for several other countries. However, IFPRI's research showed that most subsidy programmes were not targeted on the poor. Better-off consumers usually received larger absolute transfers, although they generally made up a smaller percentage of total incomes.

Food subsidy programmes had a positive effect on household food security and nutrition in several countries. The provision of fixed rations at pre-determined prices was particularly effective in ensuring access by household to staple foods, especially in urban areas. Food consumption among low-income consumers also increased. But long-run benefits were lower as wages tended to adjust to changing food prices, particularly where minimum wage laws or labour unions maintained at least a certain degree of indexing between prices and wages. The implication was that government savings from reduced food subsidies would be partly offset by increased public sector wages. Where the subsidy cost was borne by donors of foreign food aid, government savings from reducing or removing explicit food subsidies could be less than expected.

Food subsidy programmes based on foreign food aid resulted in net gains to governments, thus providing a source of government revenue that would disappear if both food aid and subsidies were discontinued. Benefits to recipients may also be less than the value of the transfer when explicit subsidies were financed in such a way as to result in higher rates of inflation and therefore higher prices for other commodities purchased by poor households. Costs to governments could also be high, particularly in the case of explicit untargeted subsidies. During the first half of the 1980s, 16–18 per cent of total government expenditure in Egypt was spent on food subsidies. Similarly, during the mid-1970s, 15 per cent of government expenditures in Sri Lanka went to food subsidies. However, government expenditures fell as the real prices of food procured on international markets declined.

IFPRI research showed that in the short run, food subsidies were but one of many ways in which governments could increase the purchasing power of the poor and compensate for losses in real incomes caused by economic recession or adjustment, or by inappropriate development strategies. Cash as well as food transfers were among the alternatives. But cash transfers not linked to food tended to be less palatable politically than transfers linked to food, such as food stamps, targeted food-price subsidies and food-supplementation schemes. There were other arguments in favour of food transfers. Political resistance to programmes directly aimed at reducing starvation and malnutrition was likely to be much less than political resistance to cash transfers. Cash transfers were also difficult to implement: the cost of necessary control measures to avoid fraud and excessive leakage to non-target groups was usually high. Self-targeting, which could be possible if food subsidies were aimed at foods consumed by the poor, was not possible with cash transfers. Also, food may be available from foreign aid at a cost to governments in recipient countries considerably below its market value, thus making food-related transfers less expensive. Food aid could also be monetized (sold) and the proceeds used to buy locally produced food, or it could be exchanged for local food that could be made available to the poor.

Food-aided subsidies could also provide compensation for those adversely affected by economic adjustment programmes, such as those who lost their jobs, or those who could not afford price increases in basic food commodities (WFP, 1987). The most appropriate compensatory measure would be to provide productive, income-earning employment in food-for-work schemes that created the infrastructure needed to increase agricultural and food production and general economic development. However, in the short run, it might also be necessary to provide compensatory nutrition programmes. But compensatory measures also entitled dangers. Unless attention was given to targeting, they would not reach those most in need. And they could be subjected to political pressures and manipulations that could divert them from their original purposes, and significantly increase their costs. The most serious concern was that food-aided compensatory measures could be used to try to make socially and politically palatable adjustment programmes that involved disproportionate costs for the poor.

Food supplements or direct feeding of individuals deficient in calories and proteins, usually children and pregnant and lactating women, were adopted in some countries in an attempt to focus more sharply on improved nutrition and, at the same time, reduce leakage to non-target households. However, leakages among the members of poor households occurred through reductions in the allocation of food to target individuals, and households may reduce food acquisitions from other sources. If nutritional improvement was the sole objective of a food subsidy programme, it was likely to be most cost-effective if combined with a primary health-care programme, which included growth monitoring, nutrition education, vaccinations, and preventative and curative health measures. But adequate, trained staff was necessary, otherwise food subsidies could become merely a handout and stimulate a curative rather than preventive approach to removing the effects of nutritional deficiencies, and scarce medical and health personnel may be diverted from carrying out their professional duties to supervise the distribution of food. One solution might be to charge private retailers with the distribution of subsidized foods, accompanied by the distribution of food stamps to targeted households at health centres. In addition, malnutrition was likely to be caused by a set of factors, only some of which could be offset by a food subsidy. Thus, a combined programme was likely to be more cost-effective than a food subsidy alone.

The effectiveness and efficiency of a subsidy programme depended crucially on its design and how it was implemented. There was no ideal type of subsidy programme because the same system that was effective and efficient may be unsuitable in a different place. A food stamp programme, for example, was best suited to more developed economies with effective administrations and infrastructure. Modifications of existing programmes may improve their performance. Pursuing rationing or price stabilization goals efficiently may require programmes that were different from those needed to ensure efficient income transfers. Many existing programmes and policies had changed over time from public distribution schemes aimed at assuring poor households access to certain rations of basic staples at fixed prices to food-linked income-transfer programmes. Some changes were caused by default rather than design as when inability to increase the prices of food rations at the same rate as price increases in the open market, rendering the subsidy programmes cost-ineffective.

Targeting poor household was found to be a key element in achieving income-transfer or nutritional goals at reduced costs. But this was often logistically difficult, and could result in economic losses for non-targeted households, and therefore incur political opposition. The political costs of reducing subsidies, especially if done without appropriate political preparation, may be higher than the economic gains. The benefits of food subsidies to political leaders could be important and perhaps sufficient to sustain then when other redistribution programmes are ended. But it could also result in their abuse. And there was a point beyond which increases in administrative staff and costs involved in reaching poor households could be supported. Often, a balance has to be struck between criteria that focus on the poorest households and less exacting criteria that address affliction on a community or area basis, without dissipating scarce resources and impact, or biasing benefits in favour of any one particular group. Many of the difficulties involved may be overcome if the target population itself was involved in the design, implementation and evaluation of subsidy programmes. Risk assessment and vulnerability mapping could provide useful operational tools for focusing attention on those most in need and for determining the types and amounts of assistance required. In the absence of reliable data, appropriate rapid appraisal and beneficiary participation techniques could be used to establish the parameters for targeting, which could be more finely defined through the operation of intervention programmes.

The IFPRI research findings concluded that 'consumer food subsidy programmes should be seen as a temporary but important means to ensure that the poor can acquire sufficient food for nutritional requirements while such capacity is being created'. To be cost-effective, 'it is essential that the programmes be targeted'. But opportunities for using food subsidies to create self-sustaining income-generating capacity among the poor 'have not been fully exploited and should be pursued'. The most important lesson learned was that consumer food subsidies could be 'a powerful and cost-effective policy tool to reach certain social, economic, and political goals, or they can be harmful to growth and equity'. This depended on when and how they were applied.

Part III

The 1990s and Beyond: International Conferences

Member States must give effect to agreements already reached to make all efforts to meet four goals during the decade:
– eliminate starvations and death caused by famine;
– reduce malnutrition and mortality among children substantially;
– reduce chronic hunger tangibly; and
– eliminate major nutritional diseases.

> (*International Development Strategy for the Fourth United Nations Development Decade*, UN General Assembly resolution 45/199, 21 December 1990)

We ... declare our determination to eliminate hunger and to reduce all forms of malnutrition. Hunger and malnutrition are unacceptable in a world that has both the knowledge and the resources to end this human catastrophe. We recognize that access to nutritionally adequate and safe food is a right of each individual. We recognize that globally there is enough food for all and that inequitable access is the main problem.

> (*World Declaration on Nutrition*, International Conference on Nutrition, Rome, Italy, 11 December 1992)

The world now produces enough food to feed its population. The problem is not simply technical. It is a political and social problem. It is a problem of access to food supplies, of distribution, and of entitlement. Above all, it is a problem of political will.

> (Boutros Boutros-Ghali, *Conference on Overcoming Global Hunger*, Washington, DC, 30 November 1993)

Eradicate extreme poverty and hunger: halve, between 1990 and 2015, the proportion of the world's population whose income is less thanUS$1 a day and who suffer from hunger.

> (UN Millennium Development Goals and Targets, *UN Millennium Declaration*, 2000)

23
International Development Strategy for the 1990s

The 1980s came to be characterized as 'the lost decade of development'. The goals and objectives on the International Development Strategy (IDS) for the Third United Nations Development Decade of the 1980s were for the most part unattained. Adverse and unanticipated developments in the world economy wiped out the premises on which growth had been expected. For the developing countries, the external economic environment over the decade of the 1980s generally resulted in shrinking resource flows, declining commodity prices, rising interest rates, and increasing barriers to market access. During the 1980s, overall growth in the developing countries averaged 3 per cent annually and a per capita growth of 1 per cent. (Over the preceding two decades, overall growth of these countries averaged 5.5 per cent and a per capita growth of 3 per cent.)

The 1980s saw a widening of the gap between rich and poor countries. It also witnessed political tensions and conflicts as well as natural and man-made disasters that were costly and disruptive. In many developing countries, where economic conditions stagnated or declined during the decade, absolute poverty became more widespread and conditions deteriorated with regard to nutrition and food security, job creation and education, health care and infant mortality, and housing and sanitation as economic recession took hold, worsened by ill-conceived and misdirected economic adjustment policies and programmes foisted on poor developing countries by the international financial institutions. The erosion of living standards and social services also brought mounting political unrest.

This was the background to preparations for a new IDS for the Fourth United Nations Development Decade of the 1990s, which was adopted by the UN General Assembly in December 1990 (UN, 1990). The principal aim of the strategy was to ensure that the 1990s were 'a decade of accelerated development in the developing countries and strengthened international co-operation'. Six inter-related goals were established:

- A surge in the pace of economic growth in the developing countries.
- A development process that was responsive to social needs, sought a significant reduction in extreme poverty, promoted the development and

272 The 1990s and Beyond: International Conferences

utilization of human resources and skills, and was environmentally sound and sustainable.

- An improvement of the international system of money, finance and trade so as to support the development process.
- A setting of strength and stability in the world economy and sound macroeconomic management, nationally and internationally.
- A decisive strengthening in international development co-operation. Official development assistance had on average remained at only half of the internationally agreed target of 0.7 per cent of the gross national product of donor countries.
- A special effort to deal with the problems of the least developed countries, the weakest among the developing countries.

It was realized that these goals and objectives posed 'a big challenge'.

The IDS for the 1990s stated that the international community agreed that the objective of eradicating poverty 'is of the highest priority', which called for policies and measures on two broad fronts. First, 'a style of development' in which economic progress was distributed as widely as possible and not concentrated excessively on a few localities and sectors or limited groups of the population. Second, it required, to the extent that poor and vulnerable sections of the population were not reached by that process, special supplementary programmes and actions that were directly targeted to bring benefits to those groups.

The IDS recognized that the call for an acceleration of development placed special focus on policies and measures aimed at raising agricultural output and at strengthening food security. It also emphasized that the struggle against poverty was 'the shared responsibility of all countries'. Poverty eradication, as well as broad humanitarian and social goals, such as the advancement in the quality of development, broad participation, larger choice and better opportunities for all, needed the full support of the international community. With a positive and optimistic tone, it announced that: 'A substantial reduction in hunger and malnutrition is within reach'. There was 'considerable scope for international food aid going beyond emergency situations'. Echoing the *Cairo Declaration* of the World Food Council (see Part II), it called on UN member states to give effect to agreements already reached to make all efforts to meet four goals during the decade of the 1990s:

- 'elimination' of starvation and death caused by famine;
- reduction of malnutrition and mortality among children 'substantially';
- 'tangible' reduction of chronic hunger; and
- 'elimination' of major nutritional diseases.

Apart from the eradication of poverty, the IDS identified three other 'priority aspects of development': the development of human resources, for which education and health 'must receive special attention'; the integration of population programmes with economic and social strategies, it being noted that 'the 1990s will see the largest increase in the population of developing countries of any decade in history, an increase of well over 20 per cent; and protection and enhancement of the environment, 'the common concern of all'.

24
International Conferences

The organizations of the UN system were seen to have a 'special responsibility' for the pursuit of the goals and objectives of the IDS for the 1990s. The IDS called for 'greater coherence by closer inter-agency co-operation and co-ordination and by organizational measures that strengthened the contribution of the [UN] system to development'. It was noted that major conferences of the UN system had already been scheduled for the initial years of the IDS, and that others would follow (UN, 1991). These would be 'important occasions' for reaching agreements that would give more specific content to the actions and commitments needed to realize the goals of the IDS and to develop priorities for the twenty-first century (UN, 1997). They would also serve to establish or restate the leadership positions of various UN agencies within their respective fields. These international conferences were to give a special context in which the quest for food security was considered along with other major issues during the 1990s and beyond. They also became the target of heated controversy and disputed perspectives in the vast literature that was to emerge on the subject of the value of these UN-sponsored world conference.[1]

It is important to see these conferences in the context in which they emerged. From one perspective, they can be seen to occur after a decade of non-development brought on by world recession and the patent failure to devise a development strategy that was both equitable and sustainable. From another perspective, the conferences were seen to represent a release from the restrictions imposed with the ending of the Cold War and a determination to address key issues in development in a multilateral context that would give new life to the United Nations, the one world organization. They formed the context for an extended debate about the relationship between global governance and diplomacy and the role of the state and societal forces in the post-Cold War era (Cooper, 2004).

The series of UN conferences of the 1990s was therefore seen to shift the focus of UN attention away from attempts to accommodate globalization through integrated economic interaction towards the promotion of universal social values and demand for transparency and greater inclusion by the developing country in international power structures and decision-making processes.

In this sense, they also could be seen as a sign of frustration with the established structure of UN debate fundamentally to address issues of world importance and reach agreement for decisive action. Seen in this perspective, the UN-sponsored conferences represented 'test sites' of change in international relations, which could not be separated from the overall fortunes of the United Nations itself.

As has been pointed out, the world conferences 'rose to the top of the intellectual and policy agenda at a time of transition' (Berridge, 1991; Weiss, Forsythe and Coate, 1994). Once released from the older constraints of bipolarity and East/West rivalry, the UN gained recognition as an essential ingredient in the building of an authentic new world order based on collective action with a commitment both to inspire and to solve problems on a global level (Clark, 2001; Hall, 1996; Williams, 1998). The UN conferences provided an opportunity for at least some actors in the international system to think beyond the narrow parameters imposed by the structure of the Cold War. At the same time, the limitations on such an ambitious range of goals must also be acknowledged, and the UN's 'moment of opportunity' did not last long. Any hope of a widely shared agreement concerning the legitimacy or capacity of the UN to champion an ambitious cluster of reform-oriented initiatives eroded with attempts to move forward either on a basis of a cluster of principled ideas or with a changed architecture.

Many of the traditional flaws of the UN system, instead of being corrected, persisted and were even exacerbated under the definition of new responsibilities. And the paradox was that the additional responsibilities that emerged from the UN conferences were not matched by increased resources or concomitant reform of the UN system, leading to increased and often unfair criticism. In addition, leadership at the world conferences was of uneven quality. Sometimes it was innovative, even inspiring, at other times, muted or proffered in an extremely cautious manner. But the truth was that the UN could only be as robust as its member states allowed it to be, leading to the conclusion that the 'management of the world conferences remained an unwieldy and highly differentiated enterprise' (Cooper, 2004).

Given these impediments, the UN conferences were seen to fall far short of the claims, negative or positive, often attributed to them. On the negative side, the UN conferences were often condemned for their excessive reach and as part of a plan, even conspiracy, by one group to impose a radically altered way of doing things in the international arena, imperceptibly leading towards the objective of a global welfare state governed by a world government. More commonly, the conferences were stigmatized for being a waste of resources and providing another channel and excuse for regulation. For the critics, the UN conferences were seen as an irrelevant form of diplomatic activity, a diversion from the 'real business' of diplomacy through bilateral dialogue and bargaining. They were dismissed as 'a babel of voices, a confusion of tongues' that served no very useful purpose, or 'little more than contemporary froth' in world politics (Watson, 1982).[2]

For the proponents of global transformation, the world conferences were often damned with faint praise because, in their view, they did not go far enough. Indeed, they may have even delayed the goal of stimulating bottom-up multilateralism by trying to impose top-down global governance. One analyst put it this way: 'The UN conferences on global issues held during the first half of the 1990s illustrated [a] new political energy . . . But what was lacking was a cross-issue orientation that would be necessary to sustain coherent politics from below that could in some ways balance the coherence of neo-liberalism in its different, but mutually reinforcing, forms' (Falk, 2000). Despite the criticisms and reservations, the impact of the UN world conferences should not be minimized. Perhaps too much was realistically expected of them. In one, contested, view, all these conferences were a 'continuum. They are cumulative in their content and the results of one influenced the others' (Boutros-Ghali, 1995, p. 49). A good deal of learning and cross-fertilization also took place on both the procedural and substantive levels. And a large amount of thematic continuity may be traced throughout the entire series.

A more balanced assessment of the UN conferences would recognize their strengths as well as their weaknesses (Schechter, 2005). On the positive side, they were important agents in advocacy and setting standards and targets. They were instrumental in establishing coordination, or where it should be. They generated basic data and information that have helped to give a common conception of the magnitude of the problems address, and how best to tackle them. And they contributed to an increased flow of resources, national and international, in the particular field of concern. On the negative side of the balance sheet, they revealed that the record of coordination among organization of the UN system was at best chequered and that the quality of aid and operational performance of the UN bodies has been very uneven. They also showed that the UN system has not been very good at agreeing a consensus on how to tackle problems of common interest. The conferences were also better at issuing general statements of intent than at turning these into actionable statutes with legal force. It should be remembered that agreements reached at the conferences were not legally binding. They did not generally provide a forum for real international policy negotiation. The politico-bureaucratic problems of the UN system were also revealed, both within and among the agencies of the UN system, and the cross-cutting mandates of the various UN bodies has led to institutional incoherency and lack of central leadership on many global issues. Despite these shortcomings, the series of UN conferences did incrementally lead to the identification of key objectives in the Millennium Development Goals as an international reference for measuring and tracking improvements in the human condition globally. They offer a comprehensive and multi-dimensional development framework and set quantifiable targets.

While the focus will be on those conferences that were directly relevant to the quest for food security, it is also recognized that given the multidimensional character of food security, many of the other conferences were also important and served to broaden both the understanding of the array of factors that led to food insecurity and, concomitantly, the measures that need to be address to overcome it.

Annex 24.1 International Conferences: 1990–2005

1990 World Conference on Education for All, Jomtien, Thailand.
Second United Nations Conference on the Least Developed Countries, Paris, France.
World Summit for Children, United Nations, New York, USA.
1991 The UNIDO Conference on Ecologically Sustainable Industrial Development, Copenhagen, Denmark.
1992 International Conference on Water and the Environment, Dublin, Ireland.
UNCTAD VIII, Cartagena, Colombia.
World Assembly on Ageing, Vienna, Austria.
United Nations Conference on Environment and Development, Rio de Janeiro, Brazil.
International Conference on Nutrition, Rome, Italy.
1993 World Bank Conference on Overcoming Global Hunger, Washington, DC, USA.
UN World Conference on Human Rights, Vienna, Austria.
1994 International Conference on Population and Development, Cairo, Egypt.
Global Conference on the Sustainable Development of Small Island Developing States, Bridgetown, Barbados.
World Conference on Natural Disaster Reduction, Yokohama, Japan.
1995 UN World Summit on Social Development, Copenhagen, Denmark.
Fourth UN Conference on Women: Action for Equality, Development, and Peace, Beijing, China.
International Conference on A 2020 Vision for Food, Agriculture, and the Environment, Washington, DC, USA.
The Ninth United Nations Conference on the Prevention of Crime and the Treatment of Offenders, Cairo, Egypt.
1996 World Food Summit, Rome, Italy.
UNCTAD IX, Midrand, South Africa.
1997 United Nations Conference on Human Settlements (Habitat II), Istanbul, Turkey.
2000 United Nations Millennium Summit, United Nations, New York, USA.
World Education Forum, Dakar, Senegal.
2001 Third United Nations Conference on the Least Developed Countries, Brussels, Belgium.
World Conference against Racism, Durban, South Africa.
World Food Summit, five years after, Rome, Italy.

278 *The 1990s and Beyond: International Conferences*

2002   International Conference on Financing for Development, Monterrey, Mexico.
           Second World Assembly on Ageing, Madrid, Spain.
           World Assembly for Sustainable Development, Johannesburg, South Africa.

2005   World Summit, United Nations, New York.

Special sessions of the UN General Assembly reviewed progress made after the UN Conference on Environment and Development (in 1997), Small Island Developing States (1999), Population and Development (1999), Women (2000), Social Development (2000), Human Settlements (2001), Children (2001) and HIV/AIDS (2001).

25
World Summit for Children, 1990

On 29–30 September 1990, the largest gathering of world leaders in history assembled at the United Nations in New York to attend the *World Summit for Children* (WSC).[3] It was fitting that first among of the series of international conferences held in the 1990s was that concerned with the well-being of children. It was recognized that children were the most vulnerable segment of society, and had suffered particularly during the 1980s, as two seminal studies by UNICEF revealed. The first had shown the full and staggering effects of the world recession of the 1980s on children in many parts of the developing world (UNICEF, 1984). The study also helped to change the perspective on development. It concluded with the view that: 'the world needed to be confronted with the consequences of the current economic policies and the possibilities of clear alternatives. We were used to describing the flows of money and wealth, with their effects on human life seen as incidental consequences. If we instead started with the focus on people, the same international links could be traced in a wholly new light. The human consequences would be brought to the fore, with economic numbers becoming background. When this glimpse of another reality became an accepted and legitimate preoccupation of national and international policy, more hope could be taken for the welfare and future of the world's children, the next generation'.

The study set the scene for another seminal study by UNICEF on *Adjustment with a Human Face* (Cornia, Jolly and Stewart, 1987). The concept was first launched by Richard Jolly, then UNICEF deputy executive director (programmes), in the Barbara Ward Lecture at the 18th Society for International Development World Conference in Rome, Italy in July 1985, with the inspiration and support of the distinguished economist Barbara Ward and James P. Grant, UNICEF's executive director at the time. The study was seen as a frontal attack and criticism of the economic adjustment programmes advocated and supported by the World Bank and IMF. It showed that in many developing countries the position of the poor had worsened during these adjustment programmes, with deterioration in nutrition levels and educational achievements of children. Investment rates frequently slowed or fell. With reduced expenditure on both human and physical resources, the prospects for economic growth in the medium term worsened. And

280 *The 1990s and Beyond: International Conferences*

the poor and their children were made to meet the social costs of the adjustment programmes seen in worsening health, education, employment and incomes. To take a extreme example, if malnutrition among young children increased, leading to irreversible loss of physical and metal capacity, this could in no sense be described as 'laying the foundation for viable future economic growth', the purported reason for adjustment programmes (Shaw and Singer, 1988). It was clear that alternative adjustment packages were needed. The objective of the alternative approach proposed by UNICEF was to combine adjustment with protection of the vulnerable and the restoration of economic growth.[4]

The WSC was held less than a year after the adoption by the UN General Assembly of the *Convention on the Rights of the Child*, which provided a new opportunity to make respect for children's rights and welfare truly universal. The summit adopted a *World Declaration* and a *Plan of Action*, which included 27 goals for the survival, development and protection of children and youth that was endorsed by the UN General Assembly (UNICEF, 1991). The declaration proclaimed the overall objective: 'to give every child a better future'. It called for a 'universal effort to promote the well-being of children . . . not only for the present generation, but for all generations to come. There can be no task nobler than giving every child a better future'.

At the eighteenth special session of the UN General Assembly held in April 1990, the international community affirmed that a most important challenge for the 1990s was the need to revitalize economic growth and social development in the developing countries and to address together the problems of abject poverty and hunger that continued to afflict many people. As the most vulnerable segment of human society, children were seen to have a particular stake in sustainable economic growth and poverty alleviation, without which their well-being could not be secured. The challenge facing those who prepared for the WSC was indeed formidable. Hunger and malnutrition in their different forms contributed to about half the deaths of young children. More than 20 million children suffered from severe malnutrition and 150 million were underweight. About 350 million women suffered from nutritional anaemia. Improving nutrition was considered to require three things: adequate household security; a healthy environment and control of infection; and adequate maternal and child care.

The WSC set an example for the other UN and international conferences that were to come later in the 1990s by laying out specific goals, with verifiable targets, for children during the forthcoming decade that were formulated through extensive consultation in various international forums attended by virtually all governments, the relevant UN agencies and NGOs. And specific provision was made to closely monitor progress. Seven major goals to be achieved between 1990 and 2000 were adopted:

- Reduction of infant and under-five child mortality rate by one-third, or to 50 and 70 per 1,000 live births, respectively, whichever was less.
- Reduction of maternal mortality rate by half.
- Reduction of severe and moderate malnutrition among under-five children by half.

World Summit for Children, 1990 281

- Universal access to safe drinking water and to sanitary means of excreta disposal.
- Universal access to basic education and completion of primary education by at least 80 per cent of the primary school-age children.
- Reduction of the adult illiteracy rate (the appropriate age group to be determined by each country) to at least half its 1990 level, with emphasis on female literacy.
- Improved protection of children in especially difficult circumstances.

Supporting and sectoral goals were also approved. These covered the health and education of women, including special attention to the health and nutrition of the female child and to pregnant and lactating women. Eight nutrition-related goals were adopted:

- Reduction in severe as well as moderate malnutrition among under-five children by half of the 1990 level.
- Reduction of the rate of low birth weight (2.5 kg or less) to less than 10 per cent.
- Reduction of iron deficiency anaemia in women by one-third of the 1990 levels.
- Virtual elimination of iodine deficiency disorders.
- Virtual elimination of vitamin A deficiency and its consequences, including blindness.
- Empowerment of all women to breastfeed their children exclusively for four to six months and to continue breastfeeding, with complementary food, well into the second year.
- Growth promotion and its regular monitoring to be institutionalized in all countries by the end of the 1990s.
- Dissemination of knowledge and supporting services to increase food production to ensure household food security.

Six child health targets were established:

- Global eradication of poliomyelitis by 2000.
- Elimination of neonatal tetanus by 1995.
- Reduction by 95 per cent in measles deaths and reduction by 90 per cent of measles cases compared to pre-immunization levels by 1995, as well as a major step to the global eradication of measles in the longer term.
- Maintenance of the high level of immunization coverage (at least 90 per cent of children below one year of age by 2000) against major diseases.
- Reduction by 50 per cent in deaths due to diarrhoea in children under five and 25 per cent reduction in diarrhoea incidence rate.
- Reduction by one-third in deaths due to acute respiratory infections in children under five.

In addition, the goal of providing universal access to safe drinking water and sanitation was approved as well as universal access to basic education and the achievement of primary education by at least 80 per cent of primary

282 *The 1990s and Beyond: International Conferences*

school-age children, with emphasis on reducing disparities between boys and girls, and reduction in adult illiteracy rates to at least half the 1990 level, with emphasis on female literacy. A *Plan of Action* for the implementation of the *World Declaration* was drawn up as a guide for national governments, international organizations, bilateral aid agencies and NGOs on the understanding that: 'As today's children are the citizens of tomorrow's world, their survival, protection and development is the prerequisite for the future development of humanity'.

A mid-decade review of progress towards meeting the WSC goals was submitted by the UN secretary-general to the UN General Assembly in 1996. A *UN Special Session on Children* was held in May 2002, the first such session to be devoted exclusively to children and the first to include children as official delegates to review progress and re-energize the global commitment to children's rights. The special session was attended by more than 7000 students including 70 heads of states and governments and delegates from 190 countries, 187 of which took the floor during the plenary debates. Some 155 countries had submitted national action programmes aimed at implementing the WSC goals during the 1990s. Over 100 countries had conducted monitoring surveys. National progress reports were submitted by over 130 countries in 2000, which formed the basis of a report by the UN secretary-general in May 2001 entitled *We the Children: End-decade review of the follow-up to the World Summit on Children*. The report showed that on the most far-reaching summit goal – reduction of under-five mortality by one-third – there had been 'important but insufficient progress'. Globally, infant and child mortality had been reduced by 11 per cent, impressive given the population growth, and more than 60 countries had met the WSC goal. However, in 14 countries, mostly in sub-Saharan Africa, under-five mortality had actually increased. Significant progress had been made in reducing diseases, and routine immunization had been achieved for 75 per cent of the world's children. But still approximately 11 million children died each year before their fifth birthday. About 600 million children, or about 40 per cent of all children in developing countries, lived in abject poverty. And 30 million children were not routinely vaccinated, resulting in millions of deaths from preventable killer diseases.

During the decade of the 1990s, under-five malnutrition was reduced from 177 million to about 150 million children, despite population growth. Overall, malnutrition was reduced from 32 per cent to 28 per cent of all children in developing countries. One hundred developing countries had met the summit goal of less than 10 per cent low-birth weight levels. Almost 75 per cent of households in developing countries were using iodized salt and gains had been made in breast-feeding. Still, malnutrition had not been reduced by the 50 per cent, as stipulated in the WSC goals: two-thirds of all malnourished children were in Asia, while in sub-Saharan Africa, the number of malnourished children had increased during the decade since the WSC. Women's health had not significantly improved since the 1990 summit. More than half a million women died each year as a result of pregnancy and childbirth. Globally, four in 1,000 women died from pregnancy-related causes, and there had been little progress in reducing anaemia among pregnant women. Much of the children's health and nutrition challenge could be traced to inadequate sanitation and unsafe drinking water. During the 1990s, access to improved water supplies increased from 77 per cent to 82 per cent of the global population and access to improved sanitation increased from 51 per cent to 61 per cent. The UN secretary-general's report concluded that 'much work had been accomplished but much still remained to do'. Three main barriers to progress were identified: lack of investment as the resources promised in 1990 had yet to materialize; misplaced priorities and lack of commitment with developing countries spending on average more on military expenditure than on basic education or health care, while developed countries spent ten times more on defence than on international development assistance; and discrimination on the basis of ethnicity, gender, religion and on the basis of childhood itself, with children coming low on the list of priorities.

Opening the special session, the UN secretary-general, Kofi Annan, was brutally frank. He said:

We, the grown-ups, have failed you [the children] deplorably. One in three of you has suffered from malnutrition before you turned five years old. One in four of you have not been immunized against any disease. Almost one in five of you is not attending school. We, the grown-ups, must reverse this list of failures.

The UN special session adopted a new declaration and plan of action, entitled *A World Fit for Children*, which included 21 specific goals and targets for the next decade, a number of which were incorporated into the Millennium Development Goals (see below). The declaration emerging from the special session (resolution S-27/2) recognized that not only renewed political will was required but also additional resources at both the national and international levels. Ten 'guiding principles' were listed in a 'global movement' that would: put children first, eradicate poverty, invest in children, leave no child behind, care for every child, educate every child, protect children from harm and exploitation, protect children from war, combat HIV/AIDS, listen to children and ensure their participation and protect the earth for children. The declaration noted that since the WSC in 1990 many goals and targets relevant to children had been endorsed by major UN summits and conferences and their review processes, which were 'strongly reaffirmed'. As a step towards building a strong foundation for attaining the 2015 international development targets and the Millennium Development Goals (see below), it was resolved to achieve the unmet goals and objectives as well as a consistent set of intermediate targets and benchmarks during the course of the next decade (2000–10) in the following priority areas, each with its own targets and strategies: promoting healthy lives; providing quality education; protecting against abuse, exploitation and violence and combating HIV/AIDS.

The plan of action set out three 'necessary outcomes': the best possible start in life for children; access to a quality basic education, including free and compulsory

284 The 1990s and Beyond: International Conferences

primary education; and ample opportunity for children and adolescents to develop their individual capacities. It identified chronic poverty as the 'single biggest obstacle' to meeting the needs and protecting and promoting the rights of children. 'It must to be tackled on all fronts, from the provision of basic services to the creation of employment opportunities, from the availability of micro-credit to investment in infrastructure, from debt relief to fair trade practices'. Owing to poverty and lack of access to basic social services, more than 10 million children below the age of five, nearly half of them in their neonatal period, died every year of preventable diseases and malnutrition.

The plan of action set the following goals in conformity with other UN conferences, summits and special sessions of the UN General Assembly:

(a) reduction in infant and under-five mortality rates by at least one-third, in pursuit of the goal of reducing it by two-third by 2015;
(b) reduction in the maternal mortality ratio by at least one-third, in pursuit of the goal of reducing it by three-quarters by 2015;
(c) reduction of malnutrition among children under five years of age by at least one-third, with special attention to children under two years of age, and reduction in the rate of low birth weight by at least one-third of the current rate;
(d) reduction in the proportion of households without access to hygienic sanitation facilities and affordable and safe drinking water by at least one-third;
(e) development and implementation of national early childhood development policies and programmes to ensure the enhancement of children's physical, social, emotional, spiritual and cognitive development;
(f) development and implementation of national health policies and programmes for adolescents, including goals and indicators, to promote their physical and mental health; and
(g) access through the primary health care system to reproductive health for all individuals of appropriate age as soon as possible and no later than 2015.

Provision was made for the follow-up and assessment of these goals. The action plan ended with the commitment 'to spare no effort in continuing with the creation of a world fit for children... In giving high priority to the rights of children... we serve the best interests of all humanity and ensure the well-being of all children in all societies'.

What was learned in the decade after the WSC was held? Recognizing children's rights in the *Convention on the Rights of the Child* had led to establishing internationally recognized agreement on goals for their future. But it was also recognized that focus on adolescents (10- to 19-year-olds, who numbered over one billion) was also necessary as this was a critical period in shaping their future lives. More resources, both national and international, were required to achieve the goals set. The UN attempted to mobilize more support through a 20–20 initiative through which recipients and donor nations would agree to invest 20 per cent of their resources in basic social services. The clear, measurable goals established at the 1990 summit proved valuable, if not altogether successful, in

World Summit for Children, 1990 285

making progress in key areas. However, the international community urged attention to broader-based strategies in the 1990s aimed at strengthening the public health infrastructure more broadly. But the unforeseen HIV/AIDS pandemic that emerged during the 1990s not only presented an important and new challenge on the international agenda but a major obstacle to achieving many of the WSC goals.

26
UN Conference on Environment and Development, 1992

The *UN Conference on Environment and Development*, commonly known as the *Earth Summit*, held in Rio de Janeiro, Brazil between 3 and 14 June 1992, was regarded as an historic turning point for humanity in reaching agreement on the principles and actions necessary to achieve environmentally sustainable development, an essential requirement for reaching world food security (UN, 1993a).

The relationship between economic development and environmental protection brought together in the concept of 'sustainable development' was first placed on the international agenda at the *UN Conference on Human Environment* held in Stockholm in 1972 (UN, 1972). A number of writers and commissions had pointed out the increasing effects of unbridled economic growth on environmental degradation. Two contributors stood out. Barbara Ward, the eminent British economist, who dramatized the scale of the problem in her seminal work *Only One World* (1972) written for the Stockholm conference, and Lester Brown, who founded The Worldwatch Institute in 1974. The Stockholm conference led to the setting up of the United Nations Environmental Programme (UNEP), which today continues to act as a global analyst and UN watchdog for the protection of the environment. It also led to the creation of the International Institute for Environment and Development, with Barbara Ward as its first president.[5] In 1973, the United Nations Sudano-Sahelian Office (UNSO) was set up to spearhead efforts to reverse the spread of desertification in West Africa. But the impact of the Stockholm conference was disappointing and little was done to integrate environmental concerns into national economic planning and decision-making, although the UN adopted a *World Charter for Nature* in October 1982, and the FAO conference adopted a *Charter for the Soil* in November 1981, and invited all members and non-members of FAO to subscribe to an *International Undertaking on Plant Genetic Resources* in November 1983. Overall, the environment continued to deteriorate and problems, such as ozone depletion, global warming and water pollution, grew more serious, while destruction of natural resources accelerated at an alarming rate.

In 1983, the UN set up a World Commission on Environment and Development, under the leadership of Mrs. Gro Harlem Brundland of Norway, to develop concrete proposals for reversing the trend in environmental degradation.

The commission submitted its report and recommendations to the UN General Assembly in 1987 (UN, 1987a). In it, Mrs. Brundtland emphasized the 'new concepts of management that both preserve the essential sovereignty of the individual, his culture, community and nation, and permit the degree of management at the regional and global level needed to guide our common destiny on our Earth'. The integrating concept, central to the commission's report, was 'sustainable livelihood security'. Livelihood was defined as 'adequate stocks and flows of food and cash to meet basic needs'. Security referred to 'secure ownership of, or access to, resources and income-earning activities, including reserves and assets to offset risk, ease shocks and meet contingencies'. And sustainable referred to 'the maintenance or enhancement of resource productivity on a long-term basis'. Sustainable livelihood security was considered to be basic for three practical reasons. First, it was a precondition for a stable human population. Second, secure resources and adequate livelihoods were prerequisites for good husbandry and sustainable management. And third, sustainable livelihood security reversed destabilizing processes.

The commission set up a Panel on Food Security, Agriculture, Forestry and Environment to indicate how humankind could be insulated from hunger on an ecologically sustainable basis. The panel proposed a seven-point action plan for achieving sustainable food and nutrition security to be converted into appropriate local-level action plans, starting with the village as the primary unit of development, in promoting 'a symphonic agricultural system where appropriate attention is paid in every link in the chain beginning with production and ending with consumption', helping 'to produce more and more food from less and less land in the decades and centuries ahead'. The seven points were

- development of an international code for the sustainable and equitable use of life-support systems;
- inclusion of sustainable livelihood for all in the *UN Declaration on Human Rights*;
- initiation of a new agricultural system for nutrition security;
- ensuring equality of opportunity for access to technology;
- organizing skills for sustainable livelihood security in every country;
- reorientation of international action and assistance so that it is to be consistent with integrated national conservation and sustainable livelihood strategies; and
- promotion of political commitment and accountability.

In 1989, the UN General Assembly called for a global meeting to devise integrated strategies that would halt and reverse the negative impact of human behaviour on the physical environment and promote environmentally sustainable economic development. The resulting *Earth Summit* was described a being 'unprecedented' for a UN conference in terms of both its size and the scope of its concerns (UN, 1997). Two decades after the Stockholm conference, governments were being asked to rethink ways of bringing about economic development, and at the same time, find ways to halt the destruction of irreplaceable natural resources and pollution of the planet.

288 *The 1990s and Beyond: International Conferences*

At the conference, representatives of 178 governments, 108 of whom were heads of states of governments, adopted three major agreements aimed at changing the traditional approach to development that were negotiated over the two and a half years leading up to the conference and finalized at Rio de Janeiro.

The *Rio Declaration on Environment and Development*, a series of 27 'principles' defining the rights and responsibilities of states, reaffirmed the Declaration of the UN Conference on the Human Environment adopted at Stockholm in June 1972, and sought to build upon it. The declaration recognized 'the integral and interdependent nature of the Earth', and established the principles, *inter alia*, that

- 'Human beings are the centre of concerns for sustainable development. They are entitled a healthy and productive life in harmony with nature'.
- 'States have, in accordance with the *Charter of the United Nations* and the principles of international law, the sovereign right to exploit their own resources pursuant to own their environmental and developmental policies, and the responsibility to ensure that activities within their jurisdiction or control do not cause damage to the environment of other States or of areas beyond the limits of national jurisdiction'.
- 'The right to development must be fulfilled so as to equitably meet developmental and environmental needs of present and future generations'.
- 'In order to achieve sustainable development, environmental protection shall constitute an integral part of the development process and cannot be considered in isolation to it'.
- 'All States and all people shall cooperate in the essential task of eradicating poverty as an indispensable requirement for sustainable development'.
- 'The special situation and needs of developing countries, particularly the least developed and the most environmentally vulnerable, shall be given special priority'.
- 'The developed countries acknowledge the responsibility that they must bear in the international pursuit of sustainable development'.
- 'Where there are threats of serious or irreversible damage, lack of full scientific certainty shall not be used as a reason for postponing cost-effective measures to prevent environmental degradation'.
- 'Women have a vital role in environmental management and development. Their full participation is therefore essential to achieve sustainable development'.

Agenda 21: Programme of Action for Sustainable Development, a wide-ranging blueprint for global action into the twenty-first century to achieve sustainable development worldwide into the twenty-first century, consisted of four sections:

- Social and Economic Dimensions;
- Conservation and Management of Resources for Development;
- Strengthening the Roles of Major Groups;
- Means of Implementation.

The 40 'programme areas' that constituted *Agenda 21* were described in terms of the basis for action, objectives, activities and means of implementation, and covered 270 pages of the report of the conference (UN, 1993a). The secretariat of the conference estimated that the average annual costs of implementing all the activities listed in *Agenda 21* in developing countries to be $600 billion, with $125 billion contributed by the international community.[6] These were 'indicative' or 'order-of-magnitude' costs to be reviewed by governments. Actual costs would depend on, *inter alia*, the specific strategies and programmes governments decided upon for implementation. In the programme area on 'combating poverty' in the section on the 'Social and Economic Dimensions', it was recognized that 'poverty is a complex multidimensional problem with origins in both the national and international domain'. It was agreed that no uniform solution could be found for global application. Rather, country-specific programmes were 'crucial'. Eradicating poverty and hunger, greater equity in income distribution, and the development of human resources were identified as 'major challenges everywhere'. The struggle against poverty was 'the shared responsibility of all countries'. The major cause of the deterioration of the global environment was 'the unsustainable pattern of consumption and production, particularly in industrialized countries', which were 'a matter of grave concern, aggravating poverty and imbalances'.

The preamble of *Agenda 21* began:

Humanity stands at a defining moment in history. We are confronted with a perpetuation of disparities between and within nations, a worsening of poverty, hunger, ill health and illiteracy, and the continuing deterioration of the ecosystems on which we depend for our well-being. However, integration of environment and development concerns and greater attention to them will lead to the fulfilment of basic needs, improved living standards for all, better protected and managed ecosystems and safer, more prosperous future. No nation can achieve this on its own; but together we can – in a global partnership for sustainable development.

The preamble ended:

Agenda 21 is a dynamic programme. It will be carried out by the various actors according to the different situations, capacities and priorities of countries and regions in full respect of all the principles contained in the *Rio Declaration on Environment and Development*. It could evolve over time in the light of changing needs and circumstances. This process marks the beginning of a new global partnership for sustainable development.

The *Statement of Forest Principles* was described as a 'non-binding authoritative statement of principles for a global consensus on management, conservation and sustainable development of all types of forests'.

At the closing session of the Rio conference, Maurice Strong, the conference secretary-general, called the summit a 'historic moment for humanity'. He said that

290   *The 1990s and Beyond: International Conferences*

although *Agenda 21* had been weakened by compromise and negotiation, it was still the most comprehensive and, if implemented, effective programme of action ever sanctioned by the international community. While the agreements approved were not legally binding, they carried a strong moral obligation to ensure their full implementation, which continue to the present. The summit's messages were transmitted by almost 10,000 on-site journalists and heard by millions around the world. They were reviewed at a special session of the UN General Assembly in June 1997.

At the *Earth Summit*, two legally binding conventions, the *United Nations Framework Convention on Climate Change* and the *Convention on Biological Diversity*, which aimed at preventing global climate change and the eradication of the diversity of biological species, were opened for signature. A new legally binding agreement on high seas fishing was also opened for signature in December 1995. At the summit, governments also requested the UN to hold negotiations for an international legal agreement to prevent the degradation of dry lands. The resulting *International Convention to Combat Desertification in Those Countries Experiencing Serious Drought and/or Desertification, particularly in Africa* entered into force in December 1995. Subsequently, a *Protocol* was signed by 156 countries (including every industrialized country except Australia and the United States) in Kyoto, Japan in 1997 to cut greenhouse gas emissions. The protocol expires in 2012. A series of conferences of the parties to the *UN Framework Convention on Climate Change* has been held with a view to set new targets and to persuade all industrialized and developing countries, especially the largest of them, to join in a common worldwide effort. The summit also called for the UN to convene a *Global Conference on the Sustainable Development of Small Island Developing States*, which was held in Barbados in May 1994.

UNEP has been described as the 'environmental conscience' of the UN system and the lead agency for UN bodies involved in environmental protection. UNEP helped to negotiate and now administers the *Vienna Convention for the Protection of the Ozone Layer* (1985) and the *Montreal Protocol* (1987) and its amendments. Three new bodies were created within the UN to ensure the implementation of *Agenda 21*: the UN Commission on Sustainable Development (CSD), which first met in June 1993, whose secretariat is provided by the Division for Sustainable Development of the UN Department of Economic and Social Affairs; the Inter-agency Committee on Sustainable Development, set up by the UN secretary-general in 1992 to ensure co-operation and co-ordination by the relevant organizations of the UN system in the follow-up of the Earth Summit; and a High-level Advisory Board on Sustainable Development, established in 1993 to advise the UN secretary-general and the inter-agency commission on issues relating to the implementation of *Agenda 21*.

A *Global Environment Facility* (GEF) was launched in 1991 and restructured in 1994 to provide new and additional external funds to support developing countries' efforts to implement sustainable development practices and protect the global environment. GEF projects, principally carried out by UNDP, UNEP and the World Bank, conserve and make sustainable use of biological diversity, address global climate change, reverse the degradation of international waters, phase out substances that deplete the ozone layer, combat land degradation and drought, and reduce and eliminate the production and use of certain persistent organic pollutants. In 1991, a Multilateral Fund was set up to assist developing countries in complying with their obligations under the Montreal Protocol, the international treaty to phase out substances that damage the ozone layer.

The *Earth Summit* threw down a marker for environmentally sustainable development that has been difficult to ignore. In so doing, it enlarged the framework within which food security should be considered and programmes to achieve it designed and implemented. At the same time, the full complexity of the problem was revealed and another complication added. Sustainable development has come to mean 'all things to all people' and almost anything that is perceived as 'good' can fall under its umbrella, thus ignoring the inevitable trade-offs between productivity, equitability, stability and sustainability (Conway, 2003). With so many development agencies and programmes professing to be engaged in sustainable development, depending on how it is defined, one critic has found that they have seldom been able to be particularly innovating in 'conceptualizing' and 'operationalizing' sustainable development, and co-operation and co-ordination among them to be limited (Barraclough, 2002). And some prominent developed and developing countries have yet to join in the global effort to 'save the planet' for future generations.

A decade after the *Earth Summit*, it was hardly a secret, or even a point of dispute, that progress in implementing sustainable development was 'extremely disappointing', with poverty deepening and environmental degradation worsening. In 2001, the UN General Assembly called for a *World Summit on Sustainable Development* (WSSD) to be held in Johannesburg, South Africa, in 2002, not for another philosophical or political debate but as a 'summit of action and results'. The CSD, with the support of the UN Division on Sustainable Development, acted as the Preparatory Committee for the WSSD and held four sessions between April 2001 and June 2002 during which drafts of the summit's principal documents, a 'Political Declaration' entitled the *Johannesburg Declaration on Sustainable Development* and the *Plan of Implementation of the World Summit for Sustainable Development*, were drawn up. The president of South Africa, Thabo Mbeki, presided over the WSSD, with Nitin Desai, chief of the UN Department on Sustainable Development, as secretary-general of the summit.

The summit brought together a wide range of interests. Over 22,000 people, including 100 heads of state, and 8,000 representatives from NGOs, business and other major groups, and 4,000 members of the press and media, attended the official segment of the WSSD in Johannesburg for the ten-day conference between 26 August and 4 September 2002. At least as many people attended parallel events. The summit marked a major departure from previous UN conferences in its structure and outcomes that offered an example of the way in which the international community might approach problem solving in the future. There was a new level of dialogue between all the stakeholders, especially between representatives of governments, civil society and the private sector. Participants were forced to confront the arguments, and the needs, of other actors in an interactive dialogue. For the first time, the outcome documents were not the only products of the summit. The meeting also resulted in the launch of voluntary partnerships, each of which brought additional resources to support the implementation of sustainable development. These partnerships, tied to government commitments, provided a built-in mechanism to ensure implementation. The official summit events included a multi-stakeholder event, four high-level round tables and thematic plenary meetings. More than 220 partnerships were launched at the WSSD. In addition, more than 150 parallel events were held in conjunction with the summit.

The UN secretary-general, Kofi Annan, in opening the summit, referred to the six countries in southern Africa where 13 million people were being threatened by famine. He dramatically used this situation as a reminder of 'what happens when we fail to plan and protect the long-term future of our planet'. He said that if one word should guide the summit's deliberations, it was 'responsibility' for each other, 'but especially the poor, the vulnerable and the oppressed – as fellow members of a single human family and most of all, responsibility for the future – for our children and their children'. He reminded his audience that over the past decade, at conferences and summit meetings, 'the world has drawn up a far-reaching blueprint for a stable, prosperous twenty-first century'. A key component of the blueprint was the relationship between human beings and the natural environment. But, 'all is not well!' There should be no more disguising 'the perilous state of the earth', or 'pretend that conservation is too expensive', when the cost of failure to act would be far greater. He said, 'Let us stop being economically defensive, and start being politically courageous'. He called for facing up to the 'uncomfortable truth' that the model of development that the world was pursuing had been 'fruitful for the few, but flawed for the many'.

Tentative steps had been taken to improve the situation but at Johannesburg, Kofi Annan said, 'we must do more'. The focus from now on must be on implementing the many agreements that had been reached, including the Millennium Development Goals (MDGs). Sustainability was one of the goals. It was also a prerequisite for reaching all the others. Action must start with governments. The richest countries must lead the way. They had the wealth and technology, and they contributed disproportionately to global environmental problems. Civil society groups had a crucial role, as partners, advocates and watchdogs, as did commercial enterprises. Without the private sector, 'sustainable development will remain only a distant dream'. Action should no wait for 'tomorrow's technological breakthroughs'. Progress could be far quicker than is commonly believed. He called for a 'new chapter' to be opened, 'a chapter of responsibility, partnership and implementation'.

Speaking at the opening session, Thabo Meku said that the goal of shared prosperity was achievable because 'for the first time in human history, human society possesses the capacity, the knowledge and the resources to eradicate poverty and underdevelopment'. What was required was agreement on 'the concept of common but differentiated responsibility'. He regretted that not much progress had been made in realizing 'the grand vision' contained in *Agenda 21* and other international agreements. 'The global community has not yet demonstrated the will to implement the decisions it freely adopted'. He singled out the UN Millennium Summit (2000) because its outcome, the *Millennium Declaration* (see below) constituted a united pledge made by the world's political leaders to meet the MDGs, which 'must inform the outcome of this summit'. A global agenda for sustainable development already existed from which the WSSD should proceed.

The president called the theme of the summit, 'people, planet and prosperity', with a focus on the improvement of people's lives everywhere through sustainable development. What was required was agreement on practical measures. The *Johannesburg Plan of Implementation* 'must be a credible and meaningful global plan of action for the realization of the goals that humanity had already set itself'. The 'political declaration' should constitute 'an honest pledge' to implement the programme of action contained in the implementation plan. Necessary consultation would take place to ensure that it was truly owned by all and constituted a genuine commitment to act. Mbeki noted that the WSSD came after a long and intensive process of global interaction. The expectation was that the summit would live up to its promise of being a fitting culmination to a decade of international debate and discussion by adopting practical programmes for translating the dream of sustainable development into reality and bringing into being a new global society that was 'caring and humane'.

Nitin Desai, the secretary-general of the summit, set the meeting in context. The WSSD was 'the last in a great cycle of global conferences' that the UN had begun in the 1990s that addressed all the major dimensions of economic and social dimensions. Taken together, these conferences had defined not just a framework for development policy and co-operation but a 'comprehensive vision of what human progress is all about'. The Earth Summit of 1992 was perhaps the most ambitious of all the conferences. It had launched a number of major conventions which, together, put before the world a truly ambitious agenda, combing the social, economic and environmental dimensions of development and focusing on the challenges in three key areas: the eradication of poverty; adoption of a pattern of consumption and production that was ecologically more sustainable; and the management of critical ecosystems, such as forests and oceans, in a more holistic and integrated way. There had been some successes, heightened awareness and many concrete achievements. NGOs had done some very creative things, especially at the local level. But overall, the record was 'very poor'.

He reminded participants that the world had changed rapidly in the decade since the *Earth Summit*. Globalization was a word hardly used at Rio, and the AIDS pandemic hardly mentioned. Information technology had been developed, but there was no worldwide web at Rio. It had not been possible to connect these changes and adapt them to the implementation of the Rio agenda. But there were other equally fundamental reasons. The Rio agenda had presumed an improvement in the macroeconomic climate for development, which did not happen. There had been a decade of declining ODA. Market access and debt relief had come at the end of the decade since Rio, and were still quite modest. But there were still other reasons. It was not yet truly grasped what it meant to bring these

294 *The 1990s and Beyond: International Conferences*

things together. 'We have been working along sectoral lines' and that 'simply does not work'. Another factor was that Rio was a 'grand vision' that produced a 'road map'. But a 'route map' was also needed with a beginning and an end, and resources to get there, with a 'medium-term framework'.

There had been many examples of local successes. These needed to be brought together in order to scale them up. Desai felt that if the medium-term framework of the Millennium Summit of 2000 (see below) was connected with the larger vision of sustainable development, and if the successful implementation of the Doha and Monterrey meetings (see below) were used on the financial side, then 'we can show results'. Hence the design on a plan of implementation at Johannesburg that focused on targets, timetables, goals and activities that could lead to concrete results. Desai stressed the importance of partnerships 'to connect dynamism at the local level with commitments that governments need to make, with a capacity to implement'. Partnerships marked 'a new stage in the involvement of civil society in the UN'. However, he reminded his audience that this was a medium-term framework. Halving the number of people in poverty, and giving them access to safe water, by 2015 was only halfway to sustainability. There was still a long way to go. The focus was on the medium term because 'we want action. There must be a sense of urgency'.

The *Political Declaration* of the summit, a document of some five pages and 37 paragraphs, was adopted on 4 September 2002. It reaffirmed the commitment to sustainable development and committed participants to 'building a humane, equitable and caring global society, cognizant of the need for human dignity for all'. It pointedly referred to the appeal of children, made at the beginning of the summit, to recognize that 'the future belongs to them', and the challenge 'to ensure that through our actions they will inherit a world free of indignity and indecency occasioned by poverty, environmental degradation and patterns of unsustainable development'. In response, the declaration stated, 'we are united and moved by a deeply felt sense that we urgently need to create a new and better world of hope'. Thus, the summit assumed 'collective responsibility' to 'advance and strengthen the interdependent and mutually reinforcing pillars of sustainable development – economic development, social development and environmental protection – at the local, national, regional and global levels', through the WSSD's *Plan of Implementation*. Recognizing that 'humankind is at a crossroads', the declaration announced a 'common resolve' to produce 'a practical and visible plan to bring about poverty eradication and human development'.

The declaration recognized that poverty reduction, changing consumption and production patterns and protecting and managing the natural resource base for economic and social development were 'overarching objectives of, and essential requirements for, sustainable development'. It also acknowledged that a 'deep fault line' divided human society between the rich and the poor and the 'ever-increasing gap' between the developed and developing worlds that 'pose a major threat to global prosperity, security and stability'. The global environment continued to suffer. Globalization had added a new dimension to the challenge. There was a risk of 'entrenching' global disparities and unless action was taken that fundamentally changed their lives, the world's poor 'may lose confidence in their representatives and the democratic systems', seeing their representative as nothing more than, to use the biblical phrase, 'sounding brass or tinkling cymbals'. The declaration therefore called for 'constructive partnerships for change and for the achievement of the common goal of sustainable development'. The focus of the summit was on the 'indivisibility of human dignity'.

Decisions were reached on targets, timetables and partnerships to speedily increase access to such basic requirements as clean water, sanitation, adequate shelter, energy, health care, food security and the protection of biodiversity. At the same time, access was sought to financial resources, benefits from the opening of markets, ensuring capacity-building, using modern technology to bring about development and make sure that there is technology transfer, human resource development, education and training 'to banish underdevelopment forever'. The declaration pledged to place particular focus on, and give priority to, the fight against the worldwide conditions that posed severe threats to sustainable development, which it listed as including chronic hunger, malnutrition, foreign occupation, armed conflict, illicit drug problems, organized crime, corruption, natural disasters, illicit arms trafficking, trafficking in persons, terrorism, intolerance and incitement to racial, ethnic, religious and other hatreds, xenophobia, and endemic, communicable and chronic diseases, in particular HIV/AIDS, malaria and tuberculosis. And it announced commitment to ensuring women's empowerment, emancipation and gender equality.

It was recognized that global society had the means and was endowed with the resources to address the challenges of poverty eradication and sustainable development confronting all humanity. But it was also emphasized that sustainable development required a long-term perspective and broad-based participation, including the private sector, in policy formulation, decision-making and implementation at all levels. It was agreed to provide assistance to increase income-generating employment opportunities in accordance with the *Declaration on Fundamental Principles and Rights at Work* of the ILO (ILO, 1998), to strengthen and improve governance at all levels, and more effective, democratic international and multilateral institutions to achieve the goals of sustainable development. The leadership role of the United Nations was supported as 'the most universal and representative organization in the world, which is best placed to promote sustainable development'. A commitment was made to monitor progress at regular intervals towards the achievement of sustainable development goals and objectives. The declaration ended with a commitment to 'act together', 'united by a common determination to save our planet, promote human development and achieve universal prosperity and peace'.

The declaration was backed up by a 60 page *Plan of Implementation*, which reaffirmed the fundamental principles and action programme of the Earth Summit, and committed action to achieved the development goals of the major UN conferences of the 1990s. Eradicating poverty was identified as the 'greatest global challenge' and indispensable requirement' for sustainable development, particularly in the developing countries. Each country had 'primary responsibility' for its own sustainable development, for which concerted and concrete measures were required. The implementation plan set targets for halving, by 2015, the proportion of the world's population whose income was less than one dollar a day, and the proportion of the people suffering from hunger, and, by the same date, halving the proportion of people without access to safe drinking water, in accordance with the MDGs established by world leaders at the UN Millennium Summit in 2000 (see below). A voluntary 'world solidarity fund' was established to eradicate poverty and promote social, economic and human development in developing countries pursuant to modalities to be determined by the UN General Assembly, avoiding duplication with existing UN funds and encouraging the private sector and individual citizens to provide funding.

Fundamental changes in the way societies produced and consumed were called for within a ten-year framework of development programmes. The *United Nations Framework Convention on Climate Change* was regarded as the 'key instrument' for addressing climate change. The entry into force of the *Kyoto Protocol* of that Convention was stressed, preferably by the tenth anniversary of the Earth Summit in 2002, in order to embark on the required reduction of greenhouse gas emissions. Globalization offered opportunities and challenges for sustainable development, involving new opportunities for trade and advanced technology, including information technology, growth in world economic development and improvements in living standards. But globalization should be fully inclusive and equitable. Developing countries, especially in Africa, and countries with economies in transition faced special problems in responding to the challenges and opportunities of globalization. A substantially increased effort and an effective institutional framework were required by countries and the international community to achieve the goals of sustainable development in which the economic, social and environmental dimension would be integrated in a balanced manner. This required strengthening collaboration within and between the UN system and other institutions. The UN General Assembly was called upon to adopt sustainable development as a 'key element' of the overarching framework for UN activities and further promote UN system-wide inter-agency co-operation and co-ordination, with the support of ECOSOC, in sustainable development. The UN Commission for Sustainable Development should also be strengthened to review and monitor progress.

The Johannesburg summit resuscitated the agreements reached at the *Earth Summit* ten years earlier and paved the way for further action towards the goals of sustained development. Yet despite all the targets, timetables and commitments made, there was realization that there were no 'silver bullet' solutions to aid the fight against poverty and a continually deteriorating natural environment. Practical and sustained steps were needed to address many of the world's pressing problems. As an implementation-focused summit, there were no agreements that would lead to new treaties, and many of the agreed targets had already been set at previous conferences and summits, especially the MDGs. But some important new targets were established, such as the use and production of chemicals by 2020 in ways that did not lead to significant adverse effects on human health and the environment; the maintenance or restoration depleted fish stocks by 2015; and the achievement by 2010 of a significant reduction in the current rate of loss of biological diversity.

The question was raised whether the summit would make a genuine difference, the true test for what was billed as an implementation conference. For the first time, the outcome documents were not the sole products of the summit. The summit also resulted in the launch of more than 300 voluntary partnerships, each of which would bring additional efforts to support sustainable development. These partnerships, tied to government commitments, were expected to provide a built-in mechanism to ensure implementation. There was a new level of dialogue between all the stakeholders, especially between governments, civil society and the private sector. At the end of the summit, Desai said that 'Johannesburg gives us a solid basis for implementation and action to go forward'. Although the *Plan of Implementation* was much shorter than *Agenda 21* approved at the *Earth Summit*, he felt that in many ways it was more targeted and focused. He said, 'We have agreed on global priorities for action and we have agreed to take action'. He considered that the results of the summit were 'far more comprehensive than any previous outcome. We have put together not only a work plan but we have identified the actors who are expected to achieve results'. In his view, *Agenda 21* 'was only a very general statement'. At Johannesburg, 'we agreed on a ten-year programme on production and consumption, a concept that not only will affect the developing countries, but the development of the richer countries as well'. He considered that a 'high level of specificity' had been achieved, that would require 'new and additional resources'. The partnership agreements had moved away from the 'donor-driven frameworks' of the past and allowed representatives of developing and developed countries to sit down together and formulate plans. But, he warned, partnerships were not a substitute for government responsibilities and commitments.

Kofi Annan told the press on the last day of the summit, 'I think we have to be careful not to expect conferences like this to produce miracles. But we do expect conferences like this to generate political commitment, momentum and energy for the attainment of goals'. Commitments were made on expanding access to water and sanitation, energy, improving agricultural yields, managing toxic chemicals, protecting biodiversity and improving ecosystem management – not just by governments, but also by NGOs, intergovernmental organizations and businesses through voluntary partnership initiatives. Following through on these commitments would be, in the view of the UN secretary-general, the yardstick of success or failure, when he said, 'We invited the leaders of the world to come here and commit themselves to sustainable development, to protecting our planet, to maintaining the essential balance and to go back home and take action. It is on the ground that we will have to test how really successful we are. But we have started off well. Johannesburg is a beginning. I am not saying Johannesburg is the end of it'.

As usual, participants came to the summit with different agendas, and not all were pleased with its outcomes. NGOs felt that the summit did not go far enough

298 *The 1990s and Beyond: International Conferences*

in setting targets for increasing the use of renewable energies. The Danish prime minister, Anders Fosh Rasmussen, who was president of the European Union at the time, said, 'The conference has concluded a global deal reconnecting free trade and increased development assistance and has committed to good governance as well as a better environment'. The Venezuelan president, Hugo Chavez, speaking as chairman of the G77 – which represented 132 developing countries – said he would have liked the summit to achieve much more but that because of time constraints 'the generalities that had been set out could be seen as retrograde'. He would have preferred emphasis on human rights, such as 'the right to housing, health, drinking water and life'. The US secretary of state, Colin Powell, called the summit a 'successful effort. I think it shows that we have a shared vision of how to move forward. I think it shows that the world is committed to sustainable development'. He added, however, that 'the real challenge is not just what is aid in the statements, but the action that will be taken in the months and years ahead'.

A series of step were taken to strengthen co-ordination within the UN system to follow up agreements reached at the Johannesburg summit. The UN System Chief Executive Board (CEB), through its High-Level Committee on Programmes, took the lead in co-ordinating system-wide follow-up activities in the key areas of freshwater, water and sanitation, energy, oceans and coastal areas, and consumption and production patterns. Specific actions included setting up co-ordination bodies for water, oceans and energy, strengthening inter-agency support for the International Strategy for Disaster Reduction, and endorsing a ten-year framework of programmes on changing unsustainable patterns of consumption and production. The CSD was confirmed as the high-level forum for sustainable development in the UN system and was responsible for reviewing progress in the implementation of *Agenda 21* and for providing policy guidance to follow-up the Johannesburg *Plan of Implementation*. The UN Division for Sustainable Development, which provides the substantive secretariat to the CSD, was designated as an authoritative source of expertise within the UN system on sustainable development.

27
International Conference on Water and the Environment, 1992

Access to safe water and hygienic sanitation is an essential part of the quest for food security and a sustainable environment, as recognized by past international conferences. But, as the UN Conference on Water held at Mar del Plata, Argentina, in 1977 noted, relatively little attention had been attached to the systematic measurement of water resources and the compilation and processing of whatever data were available had been seriously neglected. To heighten international awareness, the UN declared the 1980s as the International Drinking Water and Sanitation Decade, and a Water Supply and Sanitation Collaborative Council (WSSCC) was established to stimulate and monitor progress. Despite failure to meet the quantitative goals established for the decade, much was learnt from the experience gained, including realization of the importance of comprehensive and balanced county-specific approaches to water and sanitation problems. It was also appreciated that the achievement of the goals set at the beginning of the decade would take more time and investment than originally thought. A Global Consultation on Safe Water and Sanitation for the 1990s was held in New Delhi, India, in 1990. The New Delhi Statement that was approved at the end of the consultation, and appropriately entitled 'Some for all rather than more for some', stated that: 'Safe water and proper means of waste disposal . . . must be at the centre of integrated water resource management'. And the World Declaration on the Survival, Protection and Development of Children' adopted at the World Summit for Children in 1990 stated: 'We will promote the provision of clean water in all communities for all their children, as well as universal access to sanitation'.

As the *Earth Summit* held in Rio de Janeiro earlier in June 1992 had recognized, scarcity and misuse of fresh water posed a serious and growing threat to sustainable development and protection of the environment. Not only food security but also human health and welfare, industrial development and the ecosystems on which they depended were all at risk, unless water and land resources were managed more effectively than they had been in the past. Inspired by the Earth Summit, an *International Conference on Water and the Environment* was held in Dublin, Ireland, between 26 and 31 June 1992, just 12 days after the Earth Summit ended. The conference was attended by about 500 participants, including government-designated experts from 100 countries and representatives

300 *The 1990s and Beyond: International Conferences*

of 80 international, intergovernmental and non-governmental organizations. The experts saw the emerging global water resources situation as critical.

At the closing session, the conference adopted the *Dublin Statement* and conference report. The statement emphasized that the problems highlighted during the conference were not speculative in nature nor were they likely to take affect in the distant future. They were already present. The future survival of many millions of people demanded immediate and effective action. The conference participants called for fundamental new approaches to the assessment, development and management of fresh water resources, which could only be brought about through political commitment and involvement from the highest levels of government to the smallest communities. That commitment would need to be backed up by substantial and immediate investment, public awareness campaigns, legislative and institutional changes, technology development and capacity building. Underlying all should be a greater recognition of the interdependence of all people and of their place in the natural world.

The *Dublin Statement* set out what were called for 'guiding principles'. First, fresh water was a finite and valuable resource, essential to sustain life, development and the environment. As such, a holistic approach was required for the effective management of water resources, which linked social and economic development with protection of natural ecosystems, and land and water uses across the whole of a catchment area or groundwater aquifer. Second, water development and management should be based on a participatory approach, involving users, planners and policy-makers at all levels. Decisions should be taken at the lowest appropriate level, with full public consultation and involvement of users in the planning and implementation of water projects. Third, was the recognition that women played a central part in the provision, management and safeguarding of water resources. But the 'pivotal role' of women had seldom been reflected in institutional arrangements for the development and management of water resources. Positive policies were required to address women's specific needs and to equip and empower them to participate at all levels in water resource programmes *in ways defined by them*. Finally, water had an economic value in all its competing uses and should be recognized as an economic good. The basic right of all human beings was to have access to clean water and sanitation at appropriate prices. Past failure to recognize the economic value of water had led to wasteful and environmentally damaging uses. Management of water as an economic good was an important way of achieving efficient and equitable use and of encouraging conservation and protection of water resources.

Recommendations were made in an *Action Agenda* to enable countries to tackle their water resource problems on a wide range of fronts resulting in a number of major benefits. One major benefit was seen to be the alleviation of poverty and disease. At the start of the 1990s, over a quarter of the world's population still lacked the basic human needs of enough food, a clean water supply and hygienic means of sanitation. It was recommended that priority be given to water resource development and management to accelerate the provision of these basic human needs to the unserved millions. Another major benefit was protection against natural disasters. Economic losses from drought, floods and other natural disasters had increased three-fold between the 1960s and the 1980s, setting development back for many years, because investments had not been made in basic data collection and disaster preparedness. Projected climate change and rising sea levels would intensify the risk for some, while also threatening the apparent security of existing water resources. Disaster preparedness was recommended that could drastically reduce damage and loss of life.

Yet another major benefit could come from water conservation and reuse. The current pattern of water use involved excessive waste. There was great scope for water savings in agriculture, industry and domestic water supplies. Irrigated agriculture accounted for about 80 per cent of the world's water use. In many irrigation schemes, up to 60 per cent of the water was lost. Recycling could reduce water consumption of many industrial users by a half or more. Water savings could significantly defer investment in costly new water resource development and have considerable impact on the sustainability of water use. And more savings could come from multiple water use. Sustainable urban development could also be achieved. The situation in the majority of the world's major cities was described as 'appalling and getting worse'. It was recommended that future guaranteed urban water supplies should be based on appropriate water charges and discharge costs. Residual contamination of land and water should no longer be seen as a reasonable trade-off for the jobs and prosperity brought by industrial growth.

Other major benefits were recognized. Achieving food security was a high priority in many countries, and agriculture had not only to provide additional food for rising populations but also save water for other uses. The challenge was to develop and apply water-saving technology and management methods and, through capacity building, enable communities to introduce institutions and incentives for the rural population to adopt new approaches for both rain fed and irrigated agriculture and to have better access to potable water supply and sanitation services. It was recognized that this was an 'immense' task, but it was not impossible, provided appropriate policies and programmes were adopted at all levels, local, national and international. Protecting aquatic ecosystems could also provide a major benefit. It was time that water was regarded as a vital part of the environment and a home for many forms of life on which the well-being of humans ultimately depended. Disruption of water flows had reduced productivity in many such ecosystems. Integrated management of river basins provided the opportunity to safeguard aquatic ecosystems and make their benefits available to society on a sustainable basis. The most appropriate geographic entity for planning and managing water resources was the river basin. It was predicted that in the coming decades, management of international watersheds would greatly increase in importance. High priority should be given to the preparation and implementation of integrated management plans endorsed by all affected governments and backed by international agreements. The essential function of existing international basin organizations was reconciling and harmonizing the interests of riparian countries, monitoring water quality, developing concrete action programmes, exchanging information, enforcing agreements and resolving water conflicts.

The implementation of action programmes for water and sustainable development would require substantial investment not only in the capital projects concerned but crucially in building the capacity of people and institutions to plan and implement those projects. Measurement of the components of the water cycle and other characteristics of the environment affecting water use was an essential basis for undertaking effective water management. Research and analysis techniques, applied on an inter-disciplinary basis, permitted an understanding of these data and their application to many uses. With the threat of global warming, the need for measurement and data exchange on the hydrological cycle was evident. All actions identified in the Dublin conference report required well-trained and qualified personnel. Regarding follow-up of the Dublin Statement, all governments were recommended to initiate periodic assessments of the progress made. At the international level, it was recommended that the UN bodies concerned with water should be strengthened to undertake assessment of follow-up action. A world water forum or council was proposed, and a full assessment of implementation was recommended by the year 2000.

The importance of water and sanitation was reflected in the agreements and reports of a number of the international conferences held during the remainder of 1990s and into the next millennium. Three world water forums were held in Marakesh, Morocco in 1997, The Hague, the Netherlands in 2000 and Tokyo, Japan in 2003. In 2001, WSSCC launched a water, sanitation and hygiene (WASH) campaign to mobilize political awareness and support towards ending the suffering of the 1.1 billion people without access to safe water and the 2.6 billion people without adequate sanitation. WASH was further endorsed by the UN Commission on Sustainable Development in April 2005 as a major programme to reach the water and sanitation Millennium Development Goals (MDGs). In 2006, the UNDP *Human Development* Report focused on water issues; *World Water Week*, in Stockholm, Sweden, examined in detail benefit sharing and transboundary water issues; and the *Mexico World Water Forum*, at which the second *UN World Water Assessment Report* on shared responsibility was launched, was attended by over 10,000 participants (and at least as many protestors).

The UN report emphasized the importance of governance over water development projects and that close attention should be given to empowerment and rights as well as the choice of technology. Research undertaken continues to highlight the importance of understanding how embedded and complex political economies work at different levels, and how greater understanding becomes increasingly important as water management challenges increase, especially as solutions are being sought in large-scale infrastructure projects, as shown in China and funded by the World Bank. Sector analysis that helps in analysing power relations and political economies, the new aid architecture, and the inter-linkages across economic sectors has now become particularly necessary.

The importance of water and sanitation is reflected in the MDGs approved by world leaders in 2000 (see below). The challenge is great but the potential gains considerable. It is estimated that 1.1 billion people are without safe water and 2.6 billion without improved sanitation, probably a significant under estimate owing to the omission of those living in slums and informal settlements. Those excluded are largely the world's poor, of whom women and girls suffer disproportionately. The economic case for action is illustrated by an estimated societal gain of $8 in costs saved or productivity gains from each $1 invested in improved water and sanitation facilities, which out-performs all other comparable development investments (UNDP, 2006).

28
International Conference on Nutrition, 1992

Between 5 and 11 December 1992, delegates from 159 countries and the European Economic Community (including 137 ministers) and representatives from 144 NGOs, 11 intergovernmental organizations and 16 UN bodies attended an *International Conference on Nutrition* (ICN), jointly organized by FAO and WHO, at FAO headquarters in Rome, Italy. The two organizations had co-operated in the past in efforts to overcome the scourge of malnutrition. As we saw earlier (in Part I), attempts had been made to marry health and agriculture during the League of Nations that had led to important advances in the new science of nutrition.

WHO had co-operated with FAO in the Freedom from Hunger Campaign that B. R. Sen had launched during the 1970s. The two organizations took up the issue of nutrition in their own special spheres but had a long history of working together, particularly to ensure food safety through the preparation and issuance of food standards. This collaboration was formalized in 1961 by the setting up of a joint Codex Alimentarius Commission with the aim of protecting consumers and promoting international trade in foodstuffs by: formulating standards on food safety, pesticides, veterinary drug residues and contaminants; setting labelling requirements and standards for analysis and sampling; recommending uniform codes of hygienic handling requirements, and promoting mutual recognition of systems for food inspection and certification.

Food and nutrition security had figured prominently among the issues discussed at FAO's founding conference, and if Boyd Orr had had his way, would have been the central objectives around which the work of FAO would have been based. But on his departure, in the view observers voiced over the years, the focus of the organization changed, *viz*:

> When he [Boyd.Orr] left the Food and Agricultural Organization, it lapsed into a pedestrian and narrowly functional concern from which he had tried to save it . . . [I]t was clearly more concerned with the commodities than with the people who needed these commodities (Richie Calder, 'Introduction' in Boyd Orr (1966)); and

The Food and Agricultural Organization of the United Nations (FAO), like most departments of agriculture around the world, is dominated by producers' organizations (Borgstrom (1969)).

FAO's human focus was revived during Sen's Freedom from Hunger Campaign but nutrition became the focus of only one division among the many administrative units at FAO headquarters in Rome. It therefore came as somewhat of a surprise that the proposal for an ICN was submitted to the UN Administrative Co-ordinating Committee (ACC) by its Subcommittee on Nutrition, especially as a number of other international conferences had already been planned. Despite opposition, the ACC and the governing bodies of both FAO and WHO approved the idea of a jointly sponsored international conference.

As with other UN international conferences, a Preparatory Committee was appointed, under the chairmanship of Ibrahim Adam of Ghana, to prepare for the ICN. The conference took two years to prepare, which included eight regional meetings. A final global preparatory meeting was held in Geneva, Switzerland in August 1991, which brought together representatives of over 150 countries as well as experts in various fields. In addition, 154 countries prepared reports assessing their individual nutritional status. Out of this intensive consultative process a *World Declaration and Plan of Action for Nutrition* was drafted, which was presented to the ICN for discussion and approval.

A background document was also prepared giving a global assessment of the status of nutrition based on the latest information and data available and the findings and conclusions of intensive consultation (FAO and WHO, 1992a). The document also analysed causal factors, under the three categories of food, health and care, and considered the broader policies and programmes that could have an impact on nutritional well-being. Concerning the scope and dimension of the nutrition problem, the assessment concluded that: 'Hunger and malnutrition remain as the most devastating problems facing the majority of the world's poor... No one can doubt the seriousness of the problem, which afflicts millions of human beings'. One in five people in the developing world was considered to be 'chronically undernourished'. About 192 million children suffered from protein-energy malnutrition. And over two billion experienced micro-nutrient deficiencies. In addition, diet-related non-communicable diseases existed, or were emerging, as public health problems in many countries.

The global assessment recognized that while these numbers and trends were 'alarming', progress had been made in reducing the prevalence of nutritional problems, and many countries had been 'remarkably successful' in addressing issues of hunger and malnutrition. For developing countries as a whole, there had been a consistent decline during the previous twenty years (1970–90) in both the proportion and absolute numbers of chronically undernourished people. In 1969–71, about 941 million were chronically undernourished compared to 786 million in 1988–90, a reduction from 36 to 20 per cent of the developing world's population. Dietary energy supplies in developing countries had continued to increase in the 1980s, although at a slower rate than in the previous decade. According to FAO estimates, 'in 1988–90 there was enough food to meet the energy needs of the world's population, if it were distributed according to individual requirements'.

By the end of the 1980s, roughly 60 per cent of the world's population was living in countries that had more than 2,600 kilocalories available per person per day. However, there were 11 countries, mostly in sub-Saharan Africa, with a total population of 123 million, where dietary energy supplies were grossly insufficient (less than 2,000 kilocalories per person per day). Protein-energy malnutrition was widespread throughout the world, primarily among children. About 192 million children under five suffered from acute or chronic protein-energy malnutrition, which increased during the annual periods of food shortage and in times of famine and social unrest. The percentage of underweight children under five had declined over the past fifteen years, but the absolute numbers had remained fairly stable due to population increases. The number of underweight children was highest in Asia (155 million), although the number was declining. In Africa, however, the number of underweight children had increased from 20 million in 1975 to 27 million in 1990. Mortality rates in children under five, which were correlated with underweight status, were much higher in developing countries (120 deaths per 1,000 live births), particularly in the least developed countries (200 deaths per 1,000 live births) than in developed countries (20 deaths per 1,000 live births). The percentage of low birth weight (LBW) infants (less than or equal to 2.5 kg), an indicator of foetal undernourishment due to maternal under-nutrition or infections, was also much higher in developing than in developed countries. The prevalence of LBW in 1991 was nearly 19 per cent in developing countries, with very high rates in Southeast Asia and Africa, compared to over 6 per cent in developed countries. Micro-nutrient deficiencies were widespread, the most prevalent being lack of iron (over 2 billion people affected), lack of iodine (over 1 billion people at risk) and insufficient vitamin A (40 million affected).

The background document assessed the factors influencing nutritional status. It concluded that nutritional status was affected by a wide range of factors but stressed that 'poverty is the root cause of malnutrition' in the trilogy of food, health and care issues. Nutritional well-being was influenced by the nutrient content of foods consumed in relation to requirements, which, in turn, was determined by a range of factors. Stability of food availability was a 'cornerstone' of nutritional well-being, and food safety and quality had an important influence on nutrition. Various infections had a major impact on nutritional status. The interaction of infection and inadequate food consumption led to what was called the 'malnutrition-infection complex'. Poorly nourished persons were more susceptible to many infections. It was necessary to improve environmental health conditions to break this complex. And improved health services could also contribute to improved nutritional well-being. Care and sound feeding practices were another essential element of good health and nutrition.

Specific strategies and actions to improve nutrition needed to be developed according to the particular needs and circumstances prevailing in each country and the resources that were available. Common areas of action were identified, including:

- improving household food security;
- protecting consumers through improved food quality and safety;
- preventing specific micro-nutrient deficiencies;
- promoting appropriate diets and health lifestyles;
- preventing and managing infectious diseases;
- caring for the socio-economically deprived and nutritionally vulnerable; and
- assessing, analysing and monitoring nutrition situations.

A clear perception of the nature and magnitude of nutritional problems, and the factors and policies that influenced them, was a first step in formulating the strategies for meeting the nutrition challenge. It was also necessary to keep in mind the basic principles that were essential for the success of the policies aimed at improving nutritional well-being as well as the contributions that governments, NGOs, local communities, the private sector and the international community, including international organizations, could make in this endeavour. The task of meeting the nutrition challenge was 'formidable', but it was 'attainable provided there is a global commitment and concerted actions'. A fundamental need was simply to focus the attention of planners and policy-makers on the need to make improvements in human welfare 'the primary objective of the development process'. Economic development was important but what was required was 'a common commitment to allowing people the opportunities to improve themselves, while ensuring that the benefits of economic development and social development are equitably distributed'.

The Conference[7]

His Holiness, Pope John Paul II gave the inaugural address at the opening of the ICN (FAO and WHO, 1992b). He noted that the conference sought a world in which 'each individual can enjoy a standard of living that benefits human dignity'. He observed that 'while the inalienable right to food has been asserted, we must ensure that this right is applied'. He declared that while 'it is not the Church's role to propose technical solutions, it will fully support the strengthening of international solidarity and the promotion of justice'. In this spirit, he called on the conference 'to work for a world in which no one is denied his or her daily bread or health care'.

Edouard Saouma, FAO's director-general, said that 'This is a great day in the history of FAO'. His organization was honoured to host the first world conference on nutrition. It represented the crowning achievement of past efforts. He recalled the proposal of Stanley Bruce to the League of Nations in 1935 to bring about 'the marriage of health and agriculture'. In his view, the mandate for the conference had come from the entire UN system and the texts of the *World Declaration on Nutrition* and the *Plan of Action for Nutrition* that were before the conference for approval represented the thinking of the entire United Nations family. For the first time, a world meeting was dealing with a topic that had 'implications for the survival of humanity'. He said:

> We have always known that people's health and their physical and mental development – and thus their capacity to learn, to work, and to play their full role in society – are wholly dependent on nutrition. Humans' most fundamental need and right is access to sufficient supplies of nutritionally adequate food. The major declarations on human rights mention this only in passing, so obvious and inalienable does it seem. But sometimes even the most obvious truths must be spelled out; and so we hail the *Declaration of Barcelona*, adopted in March 1992, which, in solemnly reaffirming the right of all humans to their fair share of food, defined the nature and scope of this right.

Saouma recalled the view of his predecessor, B. R. Sen, that 'one person's hunger is everyone's hunger', the inference being that if some are hungry, it is the duty of all to come to their aid. He referred to his *World Food Security Compact* that had been adopted by the FAO Conference in November 1985, which he considered was 'of continuing relevance'. FAO's role in nutrition was 'both varied and wide-ranging . . . the entire range of FAO's activities is directly and indirectly aimed at advancing nutrition'. He was not asking for the creation of a special fund or of new agencies. What he wanted was 'the world to feel the weight of the nutrition challenge inherent in every political, economic, and social decision in the fight against poverty, and the establishment of a new world economic order'.

The director-general of WHO, Dr. Hiroshi Nakajima, recalled that the conference was being held 18 years after the 1974 World Food Conference, which had focused on food-security issues. He said:

> We now know that food security alone is not enough to prevent problems of nutrition. This is why we address the nutritional security of all people. We are building a bridge that spans health and agriculture to achieve sustainable development.

He considered that the impact of nutrition could not be underestimated. It was central to health. Good nutrition prolonged a healthy life. And sound nutritional status was essential to good health, which was the key to socio-economic development. Therefore, he felt that, in a larger sense, the conference was also about the place of nutrition in development policy. Nutrition was an investment for human development and the aim of development was to improve the human condition. If this fundamental connection were kept in mind, 'difficult matters of direction, priority and resource allocation will be made clear'. The guiding principle was that 'nutrition is the key to health, long life and investment of human resources'. But programmes were needed to put this principle into practice.

In his view, reforms to improve health and nutrition throughout the world could not be carried out by any one international agency. The full participation of all multilateral, bilateral and non-governmental organizations must be obtained as equal partners in what he called a 'planetary pact' for nutritional well-being. But the real follow-up of the conference would take place in countries and communities, with a special focus on countries in greatest need and on populations that needed help most. Over 60 per cent of WHO's resources were devoted to technical co-operation for basic health development, including nutrition, that built on local experience and local initiatives using the primary health care approach. The ultimate goal was 'health and nutritional well-being for all, for a better, longer, and more productive life'. The conference provided the opportunity to start 'to build the political commitment for an inter-sectoral campaign for nutritional well-being'.

The draft declaration and action plan that had been presented to the conference was revised, following suggested modifications, by a drafting committee, and review by the conference commission of the whole. The revised text was adopted unanimously by the conference. Representatives of each of the regional groups endorsed the *Declaration* and *Plan of Action*. They called for full and effective implementation by all concerned, and stressed their willingness to work together.

World Declaration on Nutrition

The conference declaration proclaimed:

> our determination to eliminate hunger and to reduce all forms of malnutrition. Hunger and malnutrition are unacceptable in a world that has both the knowledge and the resources to end this human catastrophe. We recognize that access to nutritionally adequate and safe food is a right of each individual. We recognize that globally there is enough food for all and that inequitable access is the main problem.... we pledge to act in solidarity to ensure that freedom from hunger becomes a reality. We also declare our firm commitment to work together to ensure sustained nutritional well-being for all people in a peaceful, just and environmentally safe world.

The declaration went on to express 'the deepest concern [with] the unacceptable fact that about 780 million people in developing countries – 20 per cent of their combined population – still do not have access to enough food to meet their basic daily needs for nutritional well-being' and 'the high prevalence and increasing numbers of malnourished children under five years of age in parts of Africa, Asia and Latin American and the Caribbean'. Moreover, 'more than 2000 million people, mostly women and children, are deficient in one or more micronutrients' and '[h]undreds of millions of people also suffer from communicable and non-communicable diseases caused by contaminated food and water' and from 'excessive or unbalanced dietary intake' which 'often lead to premature deaths in both developed and developing countries'.

The declaration called on the United Nations 'to consider urgently the issue of declaring an International Decade of Food and Nutrition, within existing structures and available resources, in order to give additional emphasis to achieving

310   *The 1990s and Beyond: International Conferences*

the objectives of this World Declaration on Nutrition'. It recognized that 'poverty and the lack of education, which are often the effects of underdevelopment, are the primary causes of hunger and undernutrition'. The declaration committed conference participants 'to ensuring that development programmes and policies lead to a sustainable improvement in human welfare'. They recognized that 'the nutritional well-being of all people is a pre-condition for the development of societies and that it should be a key objective of progress in human development'. Policies and programmes 'must be directed towards those most in need' and the 'rights of women and adolescent girls to adequate nutrition is crucial'. 'Food aid may be used to assist in emergencies, to provide relief to refugees and displaced persons and to support household food security and community and economic development' but '[c]are must be taken to avoid creating dependency and to avoid negative impacts on food habits and on local food production and marketing'. Each government had 'prime responsibility to protect and promote food security and the nutritional well-being of its people, especially the vulnerable groups' but the efforts of low-income countries 'should be supported by actions of the international community as a whole', including 'an increase in official development assistance in order to reach the accepted United Nations target of 0.7 per cent of GNP of developed countries as reiterated at the 1992 *United Nations Conference on Environment and Development*, renegotiation or alleviation of external debt, and further liberalization and expansion of world trade'.

The objectives of a number of previous international conferences and documents[8] were reaffirmed, including the *Fourth United Nations Decade for Development* and the *World Summit for Children*, which were annexed to the report of the conference (FAO and WHO, 1992b, Annex I). As a basis for the *Plan of Action for Nutrition*, and a guide for the formulation of national action plans, including the development of measurable goals and objectives within time frames, conference participants pledged to make all efforts to eliminate *before the end of this decade* (emphasis added):

- famine and famine-related deaths;
- starvation and nutritional deficiency diseases in communities affected by natural and man-made disasters; and
- iodine and vitamin A deficiencies.

They also pledged to reduce substantially *within this decade* (emphasis added):

- starvation and widespread chronic hunger;
- under-nutrition, especially among children, women and the aged;
- other important micro-nutrient deficiencies, including iron;
- diet-related communicable and non-communicable diseases;
- social and other impediments to optimal breast-feeding; and
- inadequate sanitation and poor hygiene, including unsafe drinking water.

They resolved 'to eliminate progressively the causes that lead to the scandal of hunger and all forms of malnutrition in the midst of abundance'. And they adopted the *Plan of Action for Nutrition* and affirmed their 'determination to revise or prepare, *before the end of 1994* (emphasis added), our national plans of action, including attainable goals and measurable targets, based on the principles and relevant strategies in the attached *Plan of Action for Nutrition*. We pledge to implement it'.

Plan of Action for Nutrition

The *Plan of Action for Nutrition*, which was attached to the *World Declaration on Nutrition*, began by noting that 'Despite considerable progress in recent decades, the world still falls far short of the goal of adequate food and nutrition for all', and that 'Eradicating hunger and malnutrition is within the reach of humankind'. The action plan was designed 'to provide guidelines for governments', in partnership with others, 'to achieve the objectives of the *World Declaration on Nutrition*'. It built upon previous work and represented 'a major step in preparing and implementing national nutrition improvement plans in the coming years'.[9] Its four 'overall objectives' were described as:

- ensuring continued access by all people to sufficient supplies of safe foods for a nutritionally adequate diet;
- achieving and maintaining health and nutritional well-being of all people;
- achieving environmentally sound and socially sustainable development to contribute to improved nutrition and health; and
- eliminating famines and famine deaths.

Thirteen wide-ranging 'major policy guidelines' were included, which related to: a commitment to promoting nutritional well-being; strengthening agricultural policies; environmentally sound and sustainable development; growth with equity and the need for both economic growth and equitable sharing of the benefits by all segments of the population; priority given to the most nutritionally vulnerable groups; focus on Africa; people's participation; focus on women and gender equality; the development of human resources; population policies; health policies; promoting nutritional well-being through strengthening economic and technical co-operation among countries; and allocating adequate resources.

The action plan stressed that improved nutrition required the co-ordinated efforts of a number of actors and institutions. Therefore, 'national intersectoral coordination mechanisms are needed to ensure the concerted implementation, monitoring and evaluation of policies, plans and programmes' for which community involvement was 'imperative'. Many inter-sectoral issues had to be addressed with close co-operation and co-ordination by all. Six specific issues were highlighted. The action plan pointed out that the 'basic goal of protecting and promoting nutritional well-being for all will be achieved only through a combination of policies involving various sectors at various levels of responsibility'. Based on the worldwide consultations held in preparation for the ICN strategies, and actions to be considered by governments were laid out in detail, grouped under

312 *The 1990s and Beyond: International Conferences*

nine 'action-oriented themes', which allowed 'each sector and actor to determine how it can best address nutritional problems, taking into account the specific needs and conditions of each country':

- Incorporating nutritional objectives, considerations and components into development policies and programmes.
- Improving household food security.[10]
- Protecting consumers through improved food quality and safety.
- Preventing and managing infectious diseases.
- Promoting breast-feeding.
- Caring for the socio-economically deprived and nutritionally vulnerable.
- Preventing and controlling specific micro-nutrient deficiencies.
- Promoting appropriate diets and health styles.
- Assessing, analysing and monitoring nutrition situations.

The action plan recognized that the recommendations of the ICN 'need to be translated into priority actions in accordance with the realities found in each country and must be supported by action at the international level'. The strategies would vary from country to country, and the responsibilities rested with a variety of agents, from government institutions to individuals. Responsibility for action was spelled out at the national and international levels and recommendations were made for implementing the conference's decisions. The action plan concluded that 'the ICN should be viewed as a milestone in the continuing process to eliminate hunger and malnutrition . . . and to prevent an increase in the incidence of diet-related diseases'.

29
World Conference on Human Rights, 1993

At the founding conference of the United Nations in San Francisco in 1945, the determined lobbying of a group of about 40 NGOs resulted in the inclusion of some provisions on human rights in the UN *Charter*, which laid the foundations for human rights concerns in the world body and the post-war era of international law making (UN, 1945). The preamble of the *Charter* reaffirmed 'faith in fundamental human rights, in the dignity and worth of the human person, in equal rights of men and women and of nations large and small' and determination 'to establish conditions under which justice and respect for the obligations arising from treaties and other sources of international law can be maintained' as well as saving 'succeeding generations from the scourge of war' and promoting 'social progress and better standards of life in larger freedom'. Article 1 of the UN *Charter* established that one of the four principles of the UN was to promote and encourage 'respect for human rights and for fundamental freedoms for all without distinction as to race, sex, language, or religion'. Two others were to maintain international peace and security and to promote economic and social development. The fourth was to be 'a centre for harmonizing the actions of nations in the attainment of these common ends'.

Article 55 of the *Charter*, in chapter IX on 'International Economic and Social Cooperation', states:

> With a view to the creation of conditions of stability and well-being which are necessary for peaceful and friendly relations among nations based on respect for the principle of equal rights and self-determination of peoples, the United Nations shall promote:
>
> a. higher standards of living, full employment, and conditions of economic and social progress and development;
>
> b. solutions of international economic, social, health, and related problems; and international cultural and educational co-operation; and
>
> c. universal respect for, and observance of, human rights and fundamental freedoms for all without distinction as to race, sex, language, or religion.

314 *The 1990s and Beyond: International Conferences*

All UN members pledged themselves to take 'joint and separate action in co-operation with the Organization' for the achievement of these objectives. Other provision of the *Charter* committed states to take action in co-operation with the UN to achieve universal respect for human rights.

Three years after the UN was created, on 10 December 1948, the UN General Assembly adopted and proclaimed the *Universal Declaration of Human Rights* (UDHR) as 'a common standard of achievement for all people and all nations', laying the cornerstone and reference point of contemporary human rights law (UN, 1948a). Its 30 articles spelled out basic civil, cultural, economic, political and social rights that all human beings, in every country, should enjoy. Later, the broadest legally binding human rights agreements negotiated under UN auspices, adopted by the UN General Assembly in 1966, were the *International Covenant on Economic, Social and Cultural Rights*, and the *International Covenant on Civil and Political Rights*, which entered into force in 1976. These two instruments, together with the UDHR, comprised the *International Bill of Right* and took the evolution of human rights a step further by translating these rights into legally binding commitments, with committees to monitor the compliance of state parties. The UDHR served as the inspiration for some 80 conventions and declarations concluded by the UN on a wide range of issues.

An international conference on human rights was held in Tehran, Iran in 1968.But widespread abuse and lack of co-operation among the many bodies involved in human rights led the UN General Assembly to call for another world meeting in 1989 that would review and assess progress made in the field of human rights since the adoption of the UDHR and identify obstacle and ways in which they might be overcome. The conference agenda, approved by the UN General Assembly in 1992, also included examination of the links between development, democracy and economic, cultural, social and political right, and evaluation of the effectiveness of UN methods and mechanism with the aim of recommending ways to ensure adequate financial and other resources for UN human rights activities.

Starting in 1991, four preparatory meetings and three regional meetings, in Tunis, San Jose and Bangkok, were held to prepare for the conference. Not surprisingly, these meetings raised many difficulties on key issues, such as sovereignty, universality, the role of NGOs, and questions concerning feasibility, viability and the impartiality of human rights instruments. Intense exchanges took place between representatives of governments, UN bodies and NGOs in the search for common ground. At the final preparatory meeting in May 1993, the preparatory committee prepared a draft of the final document to be placed before the conference.

The conference took place in Vienna between 14 and 25 June 1993 hosted by the Austrian government. The conference organizers and secretariat was the UN Centre for Human Rights. The conference secretary-general was Ibrahim Fall, the UN Assistant Secretary-General for Human Rights. Some 7,000 participants, including representatives of 171 countries and 800 NGOs, attended the conference. On the last day of the conference, the *Vienna Declaration and Programme of Action* was adopted, which was subsequently endorsed by the UN General Assembly in its resolution 48/121, presenting to the international community a 'common plan' for strengthening human rights throughout the world (UN, 1993b).

In a message to the conference, the UN secretary-general, Boutros Boutros-Ghali, told delegates that by reaching agreement 'they had renewed the international community's commitment to the promotion and protection of human rights' and congratulated them for having forged 'a new vision of global action for human rights into the next century'. At the final plenary session, Ibrahim Fall, the conference's secretary-general, said that the *Vienna Declaration* provided the international community with a 'new framework of planning, dialogue and co-operation' that would enable 'a holistic approach' to the promotion of human rights and involve 'actors at all levels, national and international'. He concluded, 'the Member States of the United Nations have solemnly pledged to respect human rights and fundamental freedoms and to undertake individually and collectively actions and programmes to make the enjoyment of human rights a reality for every human being'.

In its preamble, the *Vienna Declaration* considered that 'the promotion of human rights is a matter of priority for the international community, and that the Conference affords a unique opportunity to carry out a comprehensive analysis of the international human rights system and of the machinery for the protection of human rights, in order to enhance and thus promote a fuller observance of those rights in a just and balance manner'. It reaffirmed commitment to the purposes and principles of the UN *Charter* and the *Universal Declaration of Human Rights*. And it acknowledged that 'the human person is the central subject of human rights and fundamental freedoms, and consequently should be the principal beneficiary and should participate actively in the realization of these rights and freedoms'. Among the 39 principles adopted in the *Vienna Declaration*, the conference reaffirmed 'the solemn commitment of all States to fulfil their obligations to promote universal respect for, and observance and protection of, all human rights and fundamental freedoms for all in accordance with the *Charter of the United Nations*, other instruments to human rights, and international law. The universal nature of these rights and freedoms is beyond question'. All people had the right of self-determination and by virtue of that right they freely determined their economic, social and cultural development. Democracy, development and respect for human rights and fundamental freedoms were considered to be 'interdependent and mutually reinforcing'.

The right to development, as established in the *Declaration on the Right to Development*, was reaffirmed as 'a universal and inalienable right and an integral part of fundamental human rights'. States were called upon to co-operate with each other in ensuring development and eliminating obstacles to development. Everyone had the right to enjoy the benefits of scientific progress and its applications. The international community was called upon to make all efforts to help alleviate the external debt burden of developing countries. The immediate alleviation and eventual elimination of widespread extreme poverty, which was seen to inhibited the full and effective enjoyment of human rights, 'must remain a high priority for the international community'. The human rights of women and of the girl child

316 *The 1990s and Beyond: International Conferences*

were 'an unalienable, integral and indivisible part of universal human rights'. The full and equal participation of women in political, civil, economic and cultural life, at the national, regional and international levels, and the eradication of all forms of discrimination on grounds of sex were declared to be 'priority objectives of the international community'. The early ratification of the *Convention on the Rights of the Child* was welcomed as was recognition of the human rights of children in the *World Declaration on the Survival, Protection and Development of Children* and *Plan of Action* adopted at the *World Summit for Children* in 1990.

The section of the *Vienna Declaration* entitled 'Increased coordination on human rights within the United Nations system' contained 18 recommendations covering a wide range of issues. These included providing adequate resources, strengthening the UN Centre for Human Rights, which 'should assume a larger role in the promotion of human rights', adapting and strengthening the UN machinery for human rights, and establishing the post of a UN High Commissioner for Human Rights. In a section on 'Equality, dignity and tolerance', the *Vienna Declaration* called for the elimination of racism and racial discrimination and established the human rights of national, ethnic, religious and linguistic minorities, indigenous peoples, migratory workers and disabled persons. It urged 'the full and equal enjoyment of all human rights and that this be a priority for Governments and the United Nations'. Education in human rights was called for, which resulted in the UN General Assembly proclaiming in 1994 the *UN Decade for Human Rights Education* (1995–2004). Regarding the follow-up of the Vienna conference, the *Declaration* requested the UN secretary-general to invite all UN agencies related to human rights to report on progress in the implementation of the *Vienna Declaration* on the occasion of the fiftieth anniversary of the proclamation of the *Universal Declaration of Human Rights* in 1998.

Thus, the *Vienna Declaration* marked the culmination of a long process of review and debate over the status of human rights machinery throughout the world. It also marked the beginning of a renewed effort to strengthen and further implement the body of human rights instruments that had been constructed since the adoption of the UN *Charter* in 1945 and the *Declaration of Human Rights* in 1948. It recognized the interdependence between democracy, development and human rights, and prepared the way for future co-operation by international organizations and national agencies in the promotion of all human rights, including the right to development. It also took historic new steps to promote and protect the rights of women, children, minority groups and indigenous peoples. It made concrete recommendations for strengthening and harmonizing the monitoring capacity of the UN system, including the establishment of a UN High Commissioner for Human Rights, which was created by the UN General Assembly by its resolution 48/141 of 20 December 1993.[11] The *Vienna Declaration* also emphasized the need for speedy ratification of other human rights instruments and for additional resources for the UN Centre for Human Rights. The High Commissioner and the Centre for Human rights became the focal point for human rights in the UN system.

Despite the far-reaching and historic proclamations of the Vienna conference, blatant violations of human rights continue in many parts of the world. Matters came to a head when the UN Commission on Human Rights, established in 1946 as the major UN body to promote and protect human rights, and once revered as the creator of the major universal human-rights rules and instruments, became thoroughly discredited when a number of countries regarded as serial abusers of human rights were elected on to the commission and sought to protect themselves from criticism. In 2005, the UN secretary-general called for the replacement of the commission, which met for just six months once a year, by a leaner, tougher, year-round Human Rights Council, which would be ready to act whenever serious abuse was discovered and whose country members would have a solid record on human rights.

Agreement was reached on the need for a new body on a par with the UN Security Council that would meet several times a year, including, when necessary, for emergencies. The new UN Human Rights Council met for the first time in Geneva in June 2006. Unlike the former Human Rights Commission, whose 53 members were nominated by the UN regional blocs, the 47 members of the new Council were elected by the UN General Assembly, which, proponents of the new body feel, will make it more difficult for human rights violators to win a seat. The United States did not seek election to the new body asserting that the changes to the defunct commission did not go far enough.

30
World Conference on Overcoming Global Hunger, 1993

To register its concern, and in keeping with the institution's motto, 'Our dream is a world without poverty', the World Bank organized and hosted a *World Conference on Overcoming Global Hunger* that was held at The American University in Washington, DC on 30 November and 1 December 1993. The conference was attended by over 1,200 participants, including former US President Jimmy Carter, the UN secretary-general, Boutros Boutros-Ghali, the president of the World Bank, Lewis T. Preston, and the administrator of USAID, Brian Atwood.[12] The World Bank had responded to the call of US Congressman Tony Hall's appeal[13] for a conference to be organized at which those most knowledgeable about hunger and malnutrition in the developing world could meet to formulate an agenda for action (Serageldin and Landell-Mills, 1994).

The objectives of the conference were to:

(a) identify the major elements of an effective strategy to reduce hunger and to generate the necessary political will;
(b) build consensus on a priority agenda to reduce global hunger;
(c) assist the World Bank in defining what it can do; and
(d) raise international awareness of the scope and magnitude of the problem.

Conference participants were organized into three groups that addressed: the impact of macroeconomic reform on poverty; the lessons from targeted interventions; and the political economy of hunger. The conference was preceded by a one-day preparatory workshop attended by representatives of NGOs, researcher and staff members of bilateral and multilateral agencies, including IFAD, UNDP, UNICEF, WFP and the World Bank.

The report of the conference noted that 'hunger is not a simple phenomenon that yields to simple solutions'. The means to overcoming hunger cut across the whole spectrum of development challenges, including raising agricultural production, developing human resources, creating jobs and improving governance. The UN secretary-general, Boutros Boutros-Ghali, said that no one seriously disputed that hunger was an evil that should be eradicated. Nevertheless, hunger existed despite the universal consensus that it should not, and despite all efforts to eradicate it. He recognized three basic causes of hunger: it arose during a sudden crisis, it came from poverty, and it was caused by an imbalance between the growth of population and food supply. He went on:

> The world now produces enough food to feed its population. The problem is not simply technical. It is a political and social problem. It is a problem of access to food supplies, of distribution, and of entitlement. Above all, it is a problem of political will ... Economic growth and prosperity, peace and stability, institution building, and targeted assistance would all help eradicate hunger. We have the understanding, we have the means, we have the tools to remove the shame of hunger from the world. With the political will we can, together, so do.
>
> (Serageldin and Landell-Mills, 1994, p. 81)

Jimmy Carter spoke of the need to develop collaboration between NGOs and international organizations to fight hunger from his perspective as head of his own non-governmental organization (Serageldin and Landell-Mills, 1994, pp. 103–6). He identified a number of the 'generic problems' that existed. Major agencies were reluctant to change basic policies, even in the face of failure. There were too many fragmented, uncoordinated, even competing, programmes within developing countries. Assistance programmes needed to be country-specific and comprehensive, for which a co-operative task-force approach was needed both among donors and within recipient countries. Top priority should be given to the development of the capacity of local people to meet their own needs. The relationship between research and practical needs in the developing world was inadequate. Assistance programme managers were moved around too frequently. NGOs were mostly excluded from participation in a comprehensive approach to alleviating hunger. Public interest in eradicating hunger had waned because there was enough food but inadequate attention was focused on the critical problem of unequal distribution both internationally and within developing countries. There was also a failure to acknowledge that disease was still 'the greatest cause of malnutrition'.

Protectionism in rich nations was 'a cruel and most often ignored affliction on starving people'. Deforestation was rapidly becoming the most critical issue in many poverty-stricken areas. And perhaps overriding all other issues in the long run was population growth. He recognized that a lot had been learned, 'sometimes the hard way'. Whenever possible, efforts had been combined in health, nutrition and agriculture. For food production alone, the efforts of his organization were based on the lessons learned during the green revolution in India and Pakistan. Top national leaders should share responsibility with donors. Self-reliance should always be emphasized. Poor people, and particularly women, should be directly involved, with minimal impact on people's culture. Advanced technology should be introduced, where appropriate. And regular meetings should be held involving top government officials, agricultural experts, farmers and others for a frank assessment of successes and failures.

320   *The 1990s and Beyond: International Conferences*

An NGO statement presented to the conference on 30 November called for 'true participation' with the World Bank in the fight against hunger, people-centred macroeconomic policies, improved project quality and development impact, and an increase in the Bank's targeted interventions to half of IDA lending and 45 per cent of all Bank assistance. In a concluding statement on behalf of NGOs, Carolyn Long, president of the NGO InterAction, called for a 'pro-poor task force' or 'campaign headquarters' in the World Bank to end poverty and hunger, a group that would 'seize on the urgency of this need and make it happen'. She announced that NGOs were ready to work with the Bank, USAID, UN agencies and others to move forward and win a new campaign to end poverty and hunger.

The conference chairman proclaimed it an 'abiding disgrace' that a sixth of humanity was hungry in a world where food was plentiful. That hunger persisted despite the many conferences and initiatives organized to overcome it was a 'profound challenge' to the development community. He said that the consensus that emerged from the conference focused on the need for a more collaborative effort on the part of the international community. The key to reaching the poorest of the poor was to assist them directly to raise their earning capacity through 'participatory community-based programmes'. Only by involving poor people directly in the design and management of programmes could sustainable improvements in their welfare be achieved. Agreement was needed on specific actions that benefited the poorest. Most often, the poorest groups were women. The empowerment of women was therefore at the core of any sustained action to deal with poverty and hunger. He found that there was widespread agreement that 'hunger must be tackled with a broad-based, poverty-reduction strategy because it was extreme poverty that was the main cause of hunger, not insufficient food production'. Eradicating hunger and malnutrition were attainable goals but it depended on a collaborative effort for this common purpose. Eradicating hunger was an objective to which all decent human beings must be devoted. He ended: 'I say that hunger is unconscionable and unacceptable. We must become the new abolitionists.[14] We must not fail'.

In his closing remark, Serageldin identified what he regarded as the basic points from an emerging consensus. The problem of hunger was closely identified with extreme poverty rather than with the production of food. The attack of hunger was therefore an integral part of an anti-poverty strategy. The promotion of broad-based development was recognized as the essential condition for reducing poverty on a large scale. In addition, there was recognition that complementary action at the grassroots level to reach the poorest of the poor was essential. The link between health and hunger was now better understood and so certain types of interventions (such as the provision of vitamin A, iodine and iron supplements) that cost little but had a profound effect should be promoted.[15] Policies that increased access of the poor to assets, and to credit and extensions services that increased returns to their assets, should be assisted.

31
International Conference on Population and Development, 1994

Ever since Thomas Malthus made his dire prediction in 1798 that the growth of population would outrun food production, leading to mass starvation (Malthus, 1817), intensive debate has taken place on what later came to be characterized as 'defusing the population time bomb' (Ehrlich, 1968). Reaching agreement on population issues was to prove to be particularly difficult, and often acrimonious, in the international conferences in Rome, Italy in 1954, Belgrade, Yugoslavia in 1965, Bucharest, Romania in 1974, and Mexico City, Mexico in 1984. When the call for another international conference on population was made at the beginning of the 1990s, to avoid the difficulties of past debates, the aim was not to consider population issues in isolation but to link them in a broader framework of developmental concerns.

In 1991, ECOSOC explicitly linked population and development when it decided on the name of the proposed conference. In the same year, as preparations for the 1992 *UN Conference on the Environment and Development* focused attention on how to achieve sustainable development, the first session of the preparatory committee on the proposed *International Conference on Population and Development* (ICPD) resolved that population and sustainable development would be the themes of the conference. Given the tensions surrounding population issues, rigorous arrangements were made in preparation for the conference. In addition to three meetings of the preparatory committee, five regional meetings were held and a number of sub-regional and expert groups and *ad hoc* round tables were held on issues identified by ECOSOC as requiring the greatest attention, and national reports were prepared by over 140 countries. The UN General Assembly, in its resolution 48/186, endorsed the ICPD by deciding to make its preparatory committee a subsidiary body of the Assembly, giving the conference a status comparable to that of the *UN Conference on the Environment and Development*. Debate in the Second Committee of the UN General Assembly on a proposed annotated outline of the main document to be approved at the ICPD further guided the conference secretariat in preparing the final draft for negotiation at the final session of the conference's preparatory committee in April 1994.

322 *The 1990s and Beyond: International Conferences*

The ICPD was held in Cairo, Egypt, between 5 and 13 September 1994. Over 10,700 registered participants from governments in 179 countries, and from inter-governmental organizations, UN bodies, NGOs and the new media, attended to conference (UN, 1994). In addition, some 4,200 representatives of 1,500 NGOs from 113 countries attended a parallel meeting called NGO Forum '94. The President of Egypt, Mohamed Hosni Mubarak, was declared the president of the conference and Safis Nadik, executive director of the UN Population Fund (UNFPA), its secretary-general. UNFPA and the UN Population Division organ-ized the conference and acted as its secretariat. The week-long plenary session was addressed by 249 speakers, including the UN secretary-general, seven prime ministers and the vice-president of the United States, Al Gore. Other parallel activities included the International Youth NGO Consultation on Population and Development, the International Conference on Parliamentarians on Population and Development and the 1994 Parliamentarians' Day Assembly organized by the Inter-Parliamentary Union. The UN Population Division's Population Inform-ation Network provided an electronic communications and reference centre at the conference site. Four independent daily newspapers were produced in Cairo for distribution at the conference. And the UN Department of Public Information and the UNFPA co-sponsored an 'Encounter for Journalists' on ICPD issues.

At the end of the conference, after a week of intense negotiations, a *Programme of Action* was adopted by acclimation as a guide for national and international action for the next twenty years.[16] In its 16 chapters, the 115-page document covered a wide range of issues. As its preamble explained, the conference was explicitly given a broader mandate on development issues than previous population conferences, 'reflecting the growing awareness that population, poverty, patterns of production and consumption and the environment are so closely interconnected that none of them can be considered in isolation'. The ICPD had followed and built upon other important recent conferences and was seen as making significant contribu-tions to other forthcoming major conferences in the 1990s. The objectives and recommendations of the *Programme of Action* 'collectively addressed the critical challenges and interrelationships between population and sustained economic growth in the context of sustained development'. It recognized that over the next twenty years, governments were not expected to meet the goals and objectives of the ICPD single-handedly. All members of, and groups in, society 'have the right, and indeed the responsibility, to play an active part in efforts to reach those goals'.

A set of 15 'principles' was included in the *Programme of Action*, which provided a 'careful balance' between the recognition of individual human rights and the right to development of nations. Each principle contained specific recommendations of action to achieve them. The wording of most principles was directly derived from agreed international language from relevant declarations, conventions and covenants. Implementation of the recommendations was 'the sovereign rights of each country'. International co-operation and universal solidarity were regarded as 'crucial in order to improve the quality of life for all people'. The principles touched upon the main issues in the field of population and development. The principles reaffirmed that human beings were at the centre of concerns for sustainable development 'since people are the most important and valuable resources of any country'. Consequently, the right to development 'must be fulfilled so as to meet equitably the population, development and environmental needs of present and future generations'.

In addition, states were called upon to reduce and eliminate unsustainable patterns of production and consumption and promote appropriate policies, including population-related policies, to achieve sustainable development and a higher quality of life for all people. Accordingly, advancing gender equality and the empowerment of women, the elimination of all kinds of violence against women and ensuring women's ability to control their own fertility were 'cornerstones' of population and development-related programmes. States should also take all appropriate measures to ensure, on the basis of equality, universal access to health care services, including reproductive health care, family planning and sexual health. All couples and individuals had the 'basic right' to decide freely and responsibly the number and spacing of their children and to have 'information, education and means to do so'. The family was identified as the 'basic unit of society' and as such 'should be strengthened'. But it was acknowledged that there were various forms of the family in different cultural, political and social systems.

Concerning the interrelationships between population, sustainable economic growth and sustainable development, there was general agreement that persistent widespread poverty and serious social and gender inequalities had significant impact on, and in turn were influenced by, demographic factors such as population growth, structure and distribution. It was also generally recognized that efforts to slow population growth, reduce poverty, achieve economic progress, improve environmental protection and reduce unsustainable development 'were essential to eradicating poverty'. Meeting the basic needs of a growing population was dependent on a healthy environment. The empowerment of women and improvement of their status were important ends in themselves and were essential to achieve sustainable development. Elimination of all forms of discrimination against girls was essential as was the enlistment of male responsibility and participation as men 'exercised preponderant power in nearly every sphere of life'. The family was the 'basic unit of society' but faced considerable changes and pressures. Development policies and laws were required to better support the family.

The objective was to facilitate 'demographic transition' as soon as possible in countries where there was imbalance between demographic rates and social, economic and environmental goals, which would also 'contribute to the stabilization of the world population'. Reproductive health was defined as 'a state of complete physical, mental and social well-being in all matters relating to the reproductive system and to its functions and processes'. All countries were called upon to strive to make reproductive health accessible through the primary health care system to all individuals of appropriate age 'as soon as possible and no later than 2015'. It was recommended that countries should assign sufficient resources so that 'primary health services covered the entire population'.

324 *The 1990s and Beyond: International Conferences*

All countries should reduce mortality and morbidity and seek to make primary health care, including reproductive health care, 'universally available by the end of the current decade [by the year 2000]'. Countries should aim to achieve 'by 2005 a life expectancy greater than 75 years. Countries with the highest levels of mortality should aim to achieve by 2005 a life expectancy at birth greater than 65 years and by 2015 greater than 70 years. Access to health care services should be made available for all people and 'especially the most underserved and vulnerable groups'. Governments should seek to make basic health care services more sustainable financially, while ensuring equitable access.

Specific targets were set. Countries should strive to reduce their infant and under-five mortality rates by one-third or to 50–70 per 1,000 live births, respectively, whichever was less, by the year 2000. By 2005, countries with intermediate levels should aim to achieve an infant mortality rate below 50 deaths per 1,000 births and an under-five mortality rate below 60 deaths per 100 births. By 2015, all countries should aim to achieve an infant mortality rate below 35 per 1,000 live births and an under-five mortality rate below 45 per 1,000 births. Countries with indigenous peoples should achieve infant and under-five mortality rates among indigenous people that are the same as those of the general population. Maternal mortality rates should be reduced by one-half of the 1990 levels by 2000 and a further half by 2015. All countries should reduce maternal morbidity and mortality rates to levels where they would no longer constitute a public health problem. In no cases should abortion be promoted as a method of family planning. Concerning HIV/AIDS, the main objective was to prevent and reduce the spread of the disease, to minimize the impact of HIV infection and to ensure that HIV-infected individuals had adequate medical care and were not discriminated against.

It was recognized that the process of urbanization was 'intrinsic' to economic and social development and that, as a consequence, both developing and developed countries were in the process of shifting from predominantly rural to urban societies. The objective was to foster a more balanced distribution of population by promoting sustained development in both sending and receiving areas. In many countries, a single city dominated the urban system, posing economic, social and environmental challenges. But large urban agglomerations were often the most dynamic centres of economic and cultural activity. Governments were called upon to respond to the needs of all citizens, including migrants and internally displaced persons.

International economic, political and cultural interrelations played an important role in determining the flow of people between countries. International migration was linked to such interrelations and both affected, and was affected by, the development process. Poverty and environmental degradation together with the absence of peace and security and the violation of human rights were all factors affecting international migration. Orderly international migration could have positive effects in both countries of origin and destination. Governments were urged to address the root causes of migration, to make remaining in one's country a viable option for all people.

Education was a 'key' in sustained development. The increase in education of women and girls contributed to women's empowerment, to postponement of marriage and to the reduction of family size. When mothers were better educated, their children's survival rate tended to increase. Four objectives were identified:

(a) achieving universal access to quality education, in particular to primary and technical education and job training;
(b) combating illiteracy and elimination of gender disparity in educational opportunities and support;
(c) promoting non-formal education for young people; and
(d) improving the content of the curriculum.

It was recommended that investment in education and job training should be given 'high priority in development budgets' and should take into account the range and level of future workforce skill requirements.

The importance of 'valid, reliable, timely, cultural relevant, and internationally comparable population data for policy and programme development was stressed. Research, particularly biomedical research, had been instrumental in giving more people access to a greater range of safe and effective modern methods for regulating fertility. Social and economic research was also needed to enable programmes to take into account the views of the intended beneficiaries, especially women, adolescents and other less-empowered groups.

Where leadership was strongly committed to economic growth, human resource development, gender equality and equity and meeting the health particularly the reproductive health, needs of the population, countries had been able to make population and development programmes successful. Population and development were intrinsically interrelated and progress in any area could catalyse improvements in others. The need to involve intended beneficiaries in the design and implementation of population-related policies, plans and programmes was stressed. The main objective was to foster active involvement of elected representatives of people and build up capacity and self-reliance to undertake concrete national action.

Estimates of the funding levels required to meet developing countries' needs, and the needs of countries with economies in transition, were made in the period 2000–15 for basic reproductive services, including family planning, prevention of sexually transmitted diseases, including HIV/AIDS, population data collection, analysis and dissemination, policy formulation and research. On the basis of past experience, it was estimated that implementation of programmes in these areas would cost $17.0 billion in 2000, $18.5 billion in 2005, $20.5 billion in 2010 and $21.7 billion in 2015. It was tentatively estimated that up to two-thirds of the costs would be met by the countries themselves, with one-third coming from external sources, with considerable variations between and within regions. Governments were urged to devote an increasing proportion of their public sector expenditures to the social sectors, with particular focus on the eradication of poverty in the context of sustainable development.

International co-operation should be provided, consistent with national population and development priorities. National capacity building and the transfer

326   The 1990s and Beyond: International Conferences

of technology and know-how were regarded as the 'core objective' of international co-operation. The need for complementary resource flows from donor countries were estimated to be (in 1993 dollars) in the order of \$5.7 billion in 2000, \$6.1 billion in 2005, \$6.8 billion in 2010 and \$7.2 billion in 2015. Government and international organizations should integrate NGOs and local community groups into their decision-making and facilitate the contributions that NGOs could make towards finding solutions to population and development concerns and, in particular, ensure implementation of the *Plan of Action* approved by the conference. Governments should also ensure the essential roles and participation of women's organizations in the design and implementation of population and development programmes and identify new areas of co-operation with the private sector.

Regarding the follow-up of the conference's decisions, at the national level action it should include policy guidance, building political support on populations and development issues, resource mobilization, co-ordination and accountability of implementation efforts, problem solving, sharing experience within and between countries, and monitoring and reporting on progress achieved. Implementation of the *Programme of Action* should be part of an integrated follow-up effort of the major international conferences held in the 1990s. At the international level, the UN General Assembly should organize a regular review of action taken to implement agreement reached at the conference, and ECOSOC should promote an integrated approach and provide UN system-wide co-ordination and guidance in monitoring implementation and should review the UN reporting system. The UN General Assembly should also review the roles, responsibilities, mandates and comparative advantages of the intergovernmental bodies and UN organizations addressing population and development issues, including consideration of establishing a separate executive board for the UNFPA, and ensure interrelationships between policy guidance, research, standard-setting and operations. Similarly, ECOSOC should consider the respective roles of the UN organs dealing with population and development issues, and the UN specialized agencies and related organizations should strengthen and adjust their activities as a follow-up of the conference.

Speaking at a joint meeting of the staffs of the World Bank and IMF on 4 November 1994, Nafis Sadik, the secretary-general of the conference and executive director of UNFPA, said that the conference had adopted a new and forward-looking *Programme of Action* for the next twenty years, which was viewed by many, especially by women's groups, as a major breakthrough in conventional thinking on population and development issues that went beyond human numbers and demographic targets and explicitly placed human beings at the centre of all population and development activities. The international community had acknowledged that investing in people, and in their health and education, was the key to sustained economic growth and sustained development. The *Programme of Action* adopted by the conference was an approach that attacked macro-problems by addressing micro-needs at the local level, without undermining the responsibilities and sovereignty of governments. Its central goal was the improvement of the quality of life of all people. The population dimension was no longer seen in isolation, and a framework of action was provided for the entire international community.

In her view, there were at least six aspects that stood out in setting the conference apart from earlier international conferences and documents on population issues: the integration of population concerns into sustained development; the empowerment of women; the integration of family planning into the wider context of reproductive health; the setting of quantitative goals; the establishment of partnerships with NGOs; and the mobilization of resources, including reaching agreement on new financial investments in the areas of reproductive health and family planning. Success would depend on the willingness of all concerned to turn the recommendations of the conference into tangible and effective action. She concluded: 'We know what is needed and we have a 20-year work plan. The international community has every reason to be optimistic; let us make sure our optimism is justified'.

A special session of the UN General Assembly (known as *ICPD + 5*) was held in 1999 to review progress towards meeting the ICPD goals at which agreement was reached on a new set of benchmarks in four areas:

Education and literacy: Governments and civil society, with the assistance of the international community, should as quickly as possible, and in any case before 2015, meet the ICPD goal of achieving universal access to primary education, eliminate the gender gap in primary and secondary education by 2005 and strive to ensure that by 2010 the net primary school enrolment ratio for children of both sexes would be at least 90 per cent compared with an estimated 85 per cent in 2000, reduce the rate of illiteracy of women and men and at least have it for women and girls by 2005 compared with the rate in 1990.

Reproductive health care and unmet need for contraception: By 2015, governments should strive to provide all primary health care and family planning facilities, directly or through referral, with the widest achievable range of safe and effective family planning and contraceptive methods and related services. By 2005, 60 per cent of such facilities should be able to offer this range of service, and by 2010, 80 per cent. The gap between contraceptive use and the proportion of individuals expressing a desire to space or limit their families should be closed by at least 50 per cent by 2005, 75 per cent by 2010 and 100 per cent by 2050. Demographic goals should not be imposed.

Maternal mortality reduction: By 2005, where the maternal mortality rate was very high, at least 40 per cent of all births should be assisted by skilled attendants, by 2010 at least 50 per cent and by 2015 at least 60 per cent. All countries should continue their efforts so that globally, by 2005, 80 per cent of all births should be assisted by skilled attendants, 85 per cent by 2010 and 90 per cent by 2015.

HIV/AIDS: By 2005, at least 90 per cent and by 2010 at least 95 per cent, of young men and women, aged 15–24 years, should have access to information, education and services necessary to develop the life skills required to reduce their vulnerability to HIV infection. HIV infection rates in persons 15–24 years of age should be reduced by 2005 by 25 per cent in the most affected countries and by 2010 reduced globally by 25 per cent.

32
World Summit for Social Development, 1995

As with the other major conferences held during the 1990s, the decision to hold the *World Summit for Social Development* (popularly known as the *Social Summit*) was triggered by growing concern among UN member states, and the UN secretariat, that widespread social problems had been seriously neglected and in some cases had become unmanageable (UN, 1995a). Among the reasons given for convening the summit was that while prosperity had expanded for some, it was accompanied by an expansion of 'unspeakable poverty' for others. This 'glaring contradiction' was unacceptable and needed to be corrected through urgent action. The process of globalization was seen as a double-edged sword. While offering the prospect of new opportunities for sustained economic growth and development of the world economy, the rapid process of change and adjustment had been accompanied by intensified poverty, unemployment and social disintegration. More than one billion people lived in 'abject poverty, most of whom go hungry every day'. A large proportion of them had 'very limited access to income, resources, education, health care or nutrition, particularly in Africa and the least developed countries'.

A major cause of the continued deterioration of the global environment was 'the unsustainable pattern of consumption and production, particularly in industrialized countries'. The continued growth of the world's population, its structure and distribution and its relationship with poverty and social and gender equality, challenged the 'adaptive capacities' of governments, individuals, social institutions and the natural environment. Over 120 million people worldwide were officially unemployed and many more were underemployed. More women than men lived in 'absolute poverty', with serious consequences for them and their children. Women carried a disproportionate share of the problems of coping with poverty, social disintegration, unemployment, environmental degradation and the effects of war. One of the world's largest minorities, more than one in 10, was people with disabilities. Millions of people worldwide were refugees or internally displaced persons. Communicable diseases constituted a serious health problem and were a major hindrance to social development and often the cause of poverty and social exclusion. The challenge was 'to establish a people-centred framework for social development ... to build a culture of cooperation and partnership, and

The *Social Summit* was mandated by the UN General Assembly (resolution 47/92) in December 1992 and was organized principally by the UN Department for Policy Coordination and Sustainable Development. It was held in Copenhagen, Denmark, between 6 and 12 March 1995 and attended by over 14,000 participants, including delegates from 186 countries (with 117 heads of state or governments, the largest gathering yet of world leaders), 2,300 representatives from 811 NGOs, and 2,800 journalists. In addition, some 12,000 NGO representatives and others met nearby in a parallel event called NGO Forum '95. The Danish Prime Minister, Poul Nyrup Rasmussen, was president of the summit and Ambassador Juan Somavia of Chile served as chairman of the summit's main committee and its pre-summit Preparatory Committee, which drafted and finalized the summit's main agreements during three two-week preparatory sessions that began in January 1994, a week of informal consultations in October 1994, and five days of negotiations in Copenhagen during the summit.

Although the *Summit* was the first major UN conference specifically on social development issue, it was closely linked to the other major conferences that had gone before it and drew extensively on their recommendations in an integrated framework. It focused on three core principles: the eradication of poverty, the expansion of productive employment and reduction of unemployment, and the promotion of social integration. A thirty-page *Copenhagen Declaration on Social Development* was adopted, which began:

> For the first time in history, at the invitation of the United Nations, we gather as heads of State and Government to recognize the significance of social development and human well-being for all and to give these goals the highest priority both now and into the twenty-first century. We acknowledge that the people of the world have shown in different ways an urgent need to address profound social problems, especially poverty, unemployment, and social exclusion, that affect every country. It is our task to address both their underlying and structural causes and their distressing consequences in order to reduce uncertainty and insecurity in the life of people.

The *Declaration* made 10 ground-breaking commitments, each one of which contained specific action to be taken at the national and international levels to achieve them:

- eradicate absolute poverty by a target date to be set by each country;
- support full employment as a basic policy goal;
- promote social integration based on the enhancement and protection of all human beings;
- achieve equality and equity between women and men;
- accelerate the development of Africa and the least developed countries;
- ensure that structural adjustment programmes include social development goals;

- increase resources allocated to social development;
- create an economic, political, social, cultural and legal environment that will enable people to achieve social development;
- attain universal and equitable access to education and primary health care; and
- strengthen co-operation for social development through the UN.

These commitments were couched within 'a political, economic, ethical, and spiritual vision for social development that is based on human dignity, human rights, equality, respect, peace, democracy, mutual responsibility and cooperation, and full respect for the various religious and ethical values and cultural backgrounds of people'. Accordingly, the 'highest priority' was given to 'the promotion of social progress, justice and the betterment of human condition, based on full participation by all'. To this end, a framework of action was defined, based on 21 principles and goals, beginning by placing 'people at the centre of development' and directing 'economies to meet human needs more effectively'. The declaration acknowledged that it was the primary responsibility of states to attain these goals but that the international community needed to contribute 'in order to reduce inequalities among people and narrow the gap between developed and developing countries in a global effort to reduce social tensions, and to create greater social and economic stability and security'.

The *Copenhagen Declaration* was backed up by a detailed 87-page *Programme of Action of the World Summit for Social Development*, which outlined policies, actions and measures to implement the principles and fulfil the commitments enunciated in the declaration under five chapter headings: An Enabling Environment for Social Development; Reduction of Poverty; Expansion of Productive Employment and Reduction of Unemployment; Social Integration; and Implementation and Follow-up. In creating an enabling environment for social development, the action programme declared that: 'Social development is inseparable from the cultural, ecological, economic, political and spiritual environment in which it takes place. It cannot be pursued as a sectoral initiative'. And the 'ultimate aim of social development is to improve and enhance the quality of life of all people'. It required a favourable national and international economic, political and legal environment. Concerning the eradication of poverty, it was recognized that: 'Over one billion people in the world today live under unacceptable conditions of poverty, mostly in developing countries, and particularly in rural areas of low-income Asia and the Pacific, Africa, Latin America and the Caribbean, and the least developed countries'.

Poverty had 'various manifestations' in which hunger and malnutrition were seen to be embedded along with lack of income and productive resources sufficient to ensure sustainable livelihoods, ill health, limited or lack of access to education and other basic services, increased morbidity and mortality from illness, homelessness and inadequate housing, unsafe environments, and social discrimination and exclusion. It was also characterized by a lack of participation in decision-making and in civil, social and cultural life. Absolute poverty was defined as 'a condition characterized by severe deprivation of basic human needs, including food, safe drinking water, sanitation facilities, health, shelter, education and information. It depends not only on income but also on access to social services'. Poverty was therefore seen as 'a complex multidimensional problem with origins in both the national and international domain. No uniform solutions can be found for global application'. Productive work and employment were regarded as 'central elements' in development as well as 'decisive elements' of human dignity. While globalization and rapid technological development 'give rise to increased labour mobility, bringing new employment opportunities', they were also seen as creating 'new uncertainties'. The aim of social integration was defined as 'to create "a society for all", in which every individual, each with rights and responsibilities, has an active role to play'.

Regarding implementation and follow-up of the *Social Summit* agreements: 'Nothing short of a renewed and massive political will at the national and international levels to invest in people and their well-being will achieve the objectives of social development'. Primary responsibility lay with governments, although international co-operation and assistance were 'essential'. The UN General Assembly, described as 'the highest intergovernmental mechanism', was identified as the 'principal policy-making and appraisal organ' on matters relating to the follow-up of the summit. It was called upon to review steps taken to eradicate poverty in 1996 as part of the activities relating to an International Year for the Eradication of Poverty. The General Assembly was also requested to hold a special session in the year 2000 to conduct an overall review and appraisal of the implementation of the outcome of the summit. As no single UN agency could meet the challenge alone, the UNDP was given a specific mandate to organize UN system efforts towards capacity-building at the local, national and regional levels and to support the coordinated implementation of social development programmes through its new work of country offices.

A UN Commission for Social Development, which reports to ECOSOC, was given primary responsibility for the follow-up and review of implementation of the social summit. As requested, the UN General Assembly proclaimed 1996 the *International Year for the Eradication of Poverty* and a decade on this theme (1997–2006). The UN General Assembly also held a special session in 2000, which drew on the results of the series of seminars, The Copenhagen Seminars for Social Progress, organized by the Government of Denmark. The social summit and the other world conferences of the 1990s highlighted the need for a unified, inter-UN agency approach to conference follow-up and implementation. For this purpose, the UN Administrative Committee on Coordination (ACC) established three UN inter-agency tasks forces, on Employment and Sustainable Livelihoods (chaired by ILO), Basic Social Services for All (chaired by UNFPA) and Enabling Environment for Economic and Social Development (chaired by the World Bank). A UN Commission on the Status of Women, under ECOSOC, examines progress towards women's equality throughout the world and makes recommendations for promoting women's rights.

In a *Foreword* to the UN publication on the *Social Summit* (UN, 1995a), the UN secretary-general, Boutros Boutros-Ghali, described the *Copenhagen Declaration and*

Programme of Action as 'a new social contract at the global level'. He regarded the presence of so many world leaders at Copenhagen gave 'immense political weight' to its agreements and reflected 'a sense of solidarity within nations and between nations'. He said: 'We cannot permit those who are privileged to ignore those who are poor, vulnerable and disadvantaged'. He considered that the potential for co-operation 'has never been greater'. The east–west divide had disappeared and the north–south confrontation was gradually giving way to a more global approach. The new economic and social challenge was 'not confrontation but divergence – the widening divide between those who can make it on their own and those who cannot and will need the cooperation of the international community'. But, he continued, 'not even the strongest economies today... can escape the problems of social development, of poverty, unemployment and social disintegration'. He ended: 'Together we must continue our collective efforts to help shape a better common future for all nations, communities and people'.

A special session of the UN General Assembly was held in Geneva, Switzerland, between 26 June and 1 July 2000 to assess the achievement made since the *Social Summit* was held and to discuss new initiatives. Based on a report by the UN secretary-general, the review and appraisal of developments since 1995 showed that further action was required for the full implementation of the agreements made at Copenhagen. It was also clear that 'there is no single universal path to achieving social development and that all have experience, knowledge and information worth sharing'. Globalization and continued rapid technological advances offered 'unprecedented opportunities' for social and economic development but, at the same time, they continued to present 'serious challenges, including financial crises, insecurity, poverty, exclusion and inequality within and among societies'. And considerable obstacles to further integration and full participation in the global economy remained to developing countries.

One of the 'most important development' since the *Social Summit* was 'the increased priority which social development has been given in the national and international policy objectives'. But globalization had presented 'new challenges'. Gender mainstreaming was now 'widely accepted' but in some parts of the world the implementation of this concept had 'often not started'. One the most significant outcomes of the *Social Summit* was 'to place the goal of eradicating poverty at the centre of national and international policy agendas'. But progress in eradicating poverty 'had been mixed', reducing unemployment 'had been slow and uneven' and, regarding social integration, 'social exclusion and marginalization continued... especially for women and girls'. For Africa and the least developed countries, many of the objectives undertaken at the Social Summit 'have yet to be fulfilled'. Resources at the national and international levels for social development were still inadequate, despite the 20/20 initiative to encourage governments and donors to increase resources earmarked for basic social services, and overall Official Development Assistance (ODA) continued to decline. Capacity-building to implement social policies and programmes was also 'inadequate'.

World Summit for Social Development, 1995 333

The special session adopted a resolution (S-24/2) on 'Further initiatives for social development', which listed 10 new 'commitments':

1. To create an economic, political, social, cultural and legal environment that will enable people to achieve social development.
2. To eradicate poverty in the world through decisive national actions and international co-operation, as an ethical, social, political and economic imperative of humankind.
3. To promote the goal of full employment as a basic priority of economic and social policies and to enable all men and women to attain secure and sustainable livelihoods through freely chosen productive employment and work.
4. To promote social integration by fostering societies that are stable, safe and just and that are based on the promotion and protection of all human rights as well as on non-discrimination, tolerance, respect for diversity, equality of opportunity, solidarity, security and participation of all people, including disadvantaged and vulnerable groups and persons.
5. To promote full respect for human dignity and to achieve equality and equity between women and men, and to recognize and enhance the participation and leadership roles of women in political, civil, economic, social and cultural life.
6. To promote and attain the goals of universal and equitable access to quality education, the highest attainable standards of physical and mental health and the access of all to primary health care, making particular efforts to rectify inequalities, relating to social conditions, without distinction as to race, national origin, gender, age or disability, respecting and promoting our common and particular cultures, striving to strengthen the role of culture in development and contributing to the full development of human resources and to social development, with the purpose of eradicating poverty, promoting full and productive employment and fostering social integration.
7. To accelerate the economic, social and human resource development of Africa and the least developed countries.
8. To ensure that when structural adjustment programmes are agreed to they include social development goals, in particular eradicating poverty, promoting full and productive employment and enhancing social integration.
9. To increase significantly and/or utilize more efficiently the resources allocated to social development in order to achieve the goals of the Summit through national action and regional and international co-operation.
10. To promote an improved and strengthened framework for international, regional and sub-regional co-operation for social development in a spirit of partnership, through the United Nations and other multilateral institutions.

33
A 2020 Vision for Food, Agriculture and the Environment, 1995

Since the beginning of the 1990s, the International Food Policy Research Institute (IFPRI) in Washington, DC (the policy arm of the Consultative Group on International Agricultural Research (CGIAR) of 15 international agricultural research centres, 13 of which are located in developing countries, 'to mobilize agricultural science to reduce poverty, foster human well being, promote agricultural growth and protect the environment'), became, in the words of its director-general, Per Pinstrup-Andersen, 'increasingly concerned at the apparent complacency of the international community about the future of the world's food situation' (IFPRI, 1995a). As a result, in late 1993, IFPRI began an initiative looking forward to the year 2020 'to identify the critical issues that must be confronted if the world's growing population is to be fed and the livelihoods of today's poor and hungry are to be improved'. This initiative, called *A 2020 Vision for Food, Agriculture and the Environment*, had as its goals: 'to seek consensus about the problems of ensuring adequate future food supplies while protecting the world's natural resources for future generations, to create a vision of what the future should look like, and to recommend steps that must be taken immediately to make that vision come true'.

IFPRI organized research, workshops and seminars, and a series of publications on specific topics and geographical regions of the developing world relating to the future world food situation. To reach and involve an increasing circle of participants, and disseminate its findings, IFPRI organized an international conference of representatives from NGOs, governments and aid agencies as well as researchers and other interested parties to discuss its research findings and to begin the process of identifying solutions to the urgent problems of hunger, poverty and environmental degradation. The conference, held in Washington, DC between 13 and 15 June 1995, was co-hosted with the National Geographic Society. More than 500 people from 50 countries participated in the conference. Some 30 speakers summarized state-of-the-art knowledge and thinking on particular issues, including a vision of the world at 2020, the impact of population growth, improving natural resources to feed the world, the contribution of technology, the march of malnutrition, and the dimensions of the world food problem, seen from the perspective of the different regions of the developing world, leading to a global vision and an identification of the required action.

A 2020 Vision for Food, Agriculture and the Environment, 1995   335

Addressing the challenge facing a 2020 vision, IFPRI's director-general said: 'The world has won important battles in the area of food security, but the war has not yet been won. Failure to take appropriate action now may result in a loss of future battles. And many more battles must be fought'. He defined IFPRI's 2020 vision as: 'a world where every person has economic and physical access to sufficient food to sustain a healthy and productive life; where malnutrition is absent; and where food originates from efficient, effective, and low-cost agricultural systems that are compatible with sustainable use and management of natural resources'. This vision was 'based on the principle affirmed by the United Nations and its members that freedom from hunger is a human right'. He emphasized seven points in achieving this vision:

- It would be a 'tremendous challenge' to achieve the 2020 Vision with the world's population increasing to 8 billion, diets changing towards more livestock products, and the need to eradicate already existing food insecurity and malnutrition.
- The world's natural resources can support the 2020 Vision.
- Although food production would need to rise 'a great deal' to meet food demands by 2020, IFPRI's projections indicated that these demands could be met at the global level without price increases.
- The world had missed opportunities for alleviating poverty and food insecurity through agricultural growth during the last ten to fifteen years.
- Broad-based economic growth and reduced food prices would not dramatically reduce the number of malnourished children unless accompanied by access to primary health care, clean water and good sanitation along with education, empowerment of women and good child care. While considerable progress had been made in providing these services, 'much more' must be done if the 2020Vision is to be achieved.
- Low-income developing countries needed to increase their rate of investment to achieve the 2020 Vision. Higher-income developing countries invested more than 35 per cent of their incomes while investments in sub-Saharan Africa were around 15 per cent and falling. Foreign financial assistance 'may be of some help' in increasing investments in low-income developing countries, but domestic savings rates must be increased as well. International capital was less likely to be available for low-income, food-deficit countries than for higher-income, rapidly growing developing countries. Re-allocation of international assistance and domestic government funds would be necessary to achieve the 2020 Vision.
- To help developing countries achieve the 2020 Vision may be 'good business' for donor countries. Developing countries with healthy populations and growing economies made good markets for industrialized countries.

He concluded by reiterating three main points:

(a) Although the global food situation looked good, as we moved towards 2020, 'tremendous human suffering due to food insecurity, hunger, and malnutrition' occurred in large parts of the world; and natural resources degradation was rampant'.

(b) The world's natural resources were 'sufficient' to remove this suffering by 2020. The 'most important question' was not whether we can feed the world but whether civil society and governments in both developing and developed countries had the 'political will' to feed the world and to commit to taking the actions that are needed today. 'Failure to take action will affect us all'.

(c) The agricultural sector played an essential role in leading broad-based economic growth and industrialization in higher-income developing countries of Asia. Many low-income developing countries were failing to take advantage of that lesson.

At the end of the conference, IFPRI's director-general highlighted a six-point programme of action for achieving the 2020 Vision beginning with a broad look at the direction the world should take. He said: 'The 2020 Vision will be achieved only if broad-based economic growth is accelerated, particularly in the poorest developing countries'. Such growth should involve agriculture, which in the least-developed countries employed three-quarters of the labour force, generated nearly half the national income, and produced more than half of all export earnings. Global food supplies were sufficient to meet current market demand but this was not a sign to reduce investment in agriculture. Many people still went hungry, and the agricultural sector offered 'tremendous opportunities' for accelerating economic growth and reducing poverty and hunger in both rural and urban areas. The 2020 Vision also required that research, technology, infrastructure and competitive markets should be put to work to reduce costs of producing and marketing each unit of food. Sound practices for managing natural resources should be adopted to assure that more intensive farming methods are sustainable, to prevent or minimize environmental degradation and to maintain biodiversity. The poor, especially women, should gain greater access to productive assets, markets, employment, education, clean water and sanitation, primary health care and reproductive health care services. Women should also be given a greater voice in decision-making at all levels. And the conditions that led to large-scale migration of people, such as civil strife, armed conflict, poverty and environmental degradation, should be addressed.

On the basis of this general assessment, the six areas of action required to achieve the 2020 Vision were:

- Developing country governments must be strengthened to undertake activities best done by governments. NGOs and the private sector cannot achieve the 2020 Vision alone.
- Developing countries must invest in poor people. Widespread poverty, food insecurity, malnutrition and poor health are not just morally unacceptable; they are a deplorable waste of resources. Eliminating these problems is essential to achieve the 2020 Vision and should take top priority in low-income developing countries. In addition, through legislation and other incentives, governments should help empower women to gain gender equality.

- Developing countries must increase agricultural growth. Doing so is the most efficient way of alleviating poverty, protecting the environment and generating broad-based economic growth. Raising agricultural growth will require strengthening agricultural research and extension systems.
- Agriculture must be made more productive in ways that are sustainable and adopt sound management practices of natural resources.
- Food marketing systems must be improved in low-income developing countries. It is too expensive to get food from the farmer to the consumer.
- Foreign assistance should be available to countries that have demonstrated a commitment to reducing poverty, hunger and malnutrition, and to protect the environment – goals embedded in the 2020 Vision. More and better-directed international development assistance is required focused on four areas:

    (a) activities with large international benefits, such as international agricultural research and alleviation of global environmental problems;
    (b) investments in items with high social payoffs and long-term benefits, such as primary health care, nutrition programmes, agricultural research, and physical and institutional infrastructure;
    (c) programmes to foster more efficient and effective use and allocation of resources shared by more than one country, such as water; and
    (d) efforts to assure that low-income developing countries realized their fair share of the benefits from international trade liberalization.

In his summing up at the end of the conference, Keith Bezanson, then president of the International Development Research Centre in Canada,[17] broke IFPRI's 2020 Vision down into what he considered were its four 'very basic elements': food security, food affordability, nutrition adequacy, and environmental sustainability. He found nothing new in the 2020 Vision. It was nothing more than a restatement of 'one of the most universal, most fundamental, and most widespread aspirations of the human species ... [that] goes back to the very dawn of prehistory'. So, he asked: 'Why, then, do we need a 2020 Vision?' He felt that there was a strong consensus shared by all at the conference, which was perhaps best set in the context of two recent global conferences: the 1992 *Conference on Environment and Development* in Rio de Janeiro and the 1994 *Conference on Population and Development* in Cairo.

In his view, both conferences were designed to serve as wake-up calls on human complacency about the state of the natural environment and the demographic 'time-bomb'. The 2020 Vision was a third wake-up call on the pressing need for 'vast improvements' in food productivity as the 'third pillar' of the problems faced by humankind, which, according to IFPRI's projections, required a doubling of cereal production within the next twenty-five years. He found that there was general acceptance that the 2020 Vision could be achieved. But the division of opinion between the pessimists and optimists – the Cassandras and the Pollyannas – remained, with an important difference. The division now seemed to be over not whether it could be done, but whether it will be done: between the optimists of the one-world school and the pessimists of the Malthusian persuasion.

338 *The 1990s and Beyond: International Conferences*

Another problem was that 'we have made our subject very complex'. IFPRI had taken the right course in trying to deal with 'the richness, complexity, and contradictory nature' of the subject without 'succumbing to the temptation of oversimplification'. But complexity had made it more difficult to reach consensus. The need to apply 'the very best of scientific knowledge' to the subject carried the risk of 'inconclusiveness' and therefore of 'inaction'.

IFPRI followed up the conference with an extended version of the 2020 Vision and initiated a series of policy briefs, discussion papers, new articles and books that have continued to the present (IFRPI, 1995b). Considerable disagreement prevailed on the magnitude and nature of the world's food and environment problems. A 'dangerous sense of complacency' about the future seemed to develop. It was for that reason that IFPRI had launched it 2020 Vision initiative both to better inform and to develop and pursue a course of action. The initiative built on food policy research by IFPRI and others and relied on data from many sources, most notably FAO. IFPRI's research and global food model (IMPACT) suggested that 'the world is far from approaching bio-physical limits to global food production. Warning signs, however, suggest that growth in food production has begun to lag. Increases in food production did not keep pace with population growth in more than 50 developing countries in the 1980s and early 1990s'. About 800 million people, 20 per cent of the developing world's population, were food-insecure in 1995. They lacked economic and physical access to the food required to lead healthy and productive lives. Their numbers had declined from 950 million in 1970 primarily because of a 50 per cent reduction in the number of food-insure people in East Asia. South Asia still had about 270 million hungry people, while sub-Saharan Africa had emerged as 'a major locus of hunger', where the number of hungry people had increased by 46 per cent since 1970 to 175 million in 1995. And the prospects for reducing malnutrition among the world's children was 'grim' with about 185 million children under the age of six years seriously underweight for their age.

Hidden hunger, in the form of micro-nutrient deficiencies, was pervasive, even where food consumption was adequate. Nearly 2 billion people worldwide were iron-deficient, resulting in anaemia in 1.2 billion. More than half the pregnant women in the developing world were anaemic. Some 1.25 million pre-school children suffered from vitamin A deficiency, resulting in eye damage to 1.4 million of them. And more than 600 million people had iodine-deficiency disorders. In IFPRI's view, 'Hunger is, and will remain, the primary challenge confronting developing countries'. But IFPRI research found a paradoxical nutrition-related trend of obesity emerging in some areas, particularly in urban locations. With the change in diet to more fatty foods, such as livestock products, and more sedentary occupations, obesity was becoming a serious public health problem in developing as well as developed countries resulting in increased chronic diseases such as heart condition. IFPRI posed the question, what if we do not take action? Existing resources were sufficient to achieve the 2020 Vision, if the global community took appropriate action, including the necessary re-allocation of resources. If appropriate action is not taken, a time would come when natural resource constraints would dictate our future. Failure to act now would result in more human misery and more degradation of natural resources, which in turn would impose misery on future generations and cause continued misallocation of scarce resources. A world of extreme poverty on the part of many and overt material excesses for some would create an unstable world, politically, economically and socially, and falling living standards for all.

34
Fourth World Conference on Women, 1995

The *Fourth World Conference on Women* held in Beijing, China, from 4 to 15 September 1995 marked the end of two decades of intense international debate on the empowerment of women and their role in the development process. The first world conference on women had been held in Mexico City in 1975, after which the following ten years (1976–85) had been declared the *United Nations Decade for Women*. A second world conference was held in Copenhagen, Denmark, in 1980 and a third in Nairobi, Kenya, in 1985. Increasing research and practical experience over this period had shown that women played pivotal roles in the social and economic development of their families, communities and nations. But this was often done in the face of formidable political, cultural, social and economic constraints.

Nowhere was this more evident than in maintaining what was described as the 'three pillars of food security': sustainable food production, economic access to available food, and nutritional security for all family members (Quisumbling *et al.*, 1995). Improvements in household welfare depended not only on the level of household income, but also on who earned and controlled that income. Women, relative to men, tended to have a higher propensity to spend more of their income on food for the family and on improvements in nutrition, health, education and general growth and development for their children. And ensuring household nutritional security through the combination of food and other factors, such as childcare and access to clean water and sanitation, were almost the exclusive domain of women. This raised questions of how to take these gender-sensitive factors into account in the design, implementation and evaluation of development policies and programmes. The *United Nations Decade for Women* and the four world conferences provided the impetus that helped to make a difference.

The Beijing conference built upon the consensus that had been achieved at the three previous world conferences and finally established gender at the centre of development policies. Since 1975, the discourse on women's advancement and its relation with the development process has evolved. Essentially, the focus shifted from an intellectual and political approach of 'women in development' to a new approach of 'gender in development', and later, to 'gender mainstreaming' as a strategy to promote gender equality (UN, 1999). A new understanding of development began to emerge in the 1970s as the underlying assumptions of modernization theory, the paradigm of economic development after the Second World War that postulated the newly emerging nations could best develop by following in the footsteps of the developed nations, came under critical scrutiny.

As we saw in Part II, increased attention was paid to questions of social justice, poverty and welfare under the rubric of 'basic needs' and 'distribution from/with growth', which broadened the earlier focus on the technical aspects of economic growth. In this context, integration of women into development efforts became an increasing area of concern in the 1970s. Thus, while the status of women was not a major topic of concern in the *United Nations First Development Decade* of the 1960s, it was included as an objective in the *United Nations Second Development Decade* of the 1970s. Researchers and practitioners made it a central topic of debate on development, especially after Ester Boserup's pioneering book *Women's Role in Economic Development* (Boserup, 1970)[18], and 'women in development' became a field of study in its own right. Besides energizing research, advocacy and policy efforts in promoting women's rights, the world conferences also gave 'women in development' official recognition at both the national and intergovernmental levels. Governments established national institutions to deal with the promotion of policy, research and programmes aimed at women's advancement and participation in development. And within the UN system, in addition to the Commission on the Status of Women, under ECOSOC, the Division for the Advancement of Women in the UN Department of Economic and Social Affairs, with a special adviser to the UN secretary-general on gender issues and the advancement of women who oversees the work of the division and co-ordinate and chairs the UN Inter-Agency Network on Women and Gender Equality, a UN Committee on the Elimination of Discrimination against Women, an International Research and Training Institute for the Advancement of Women and a UN Development Fund for Women were established in 1976 to provide an institutional framework for research, training and operational activities in the area of women and development.

The early discussions on women in development focused on two different concerns: women had either been excluded from the benefits of development or had been included in ways that had marginalized them. It did not address the basic structure of inequality in the relationship between men and women. This realization opened a new debate and resulted in the wider emphasis placed on the concept of 'gender' and a shift to a new approach of 'gender and development'. Gender was defined as 'the social meaning given to biological sex differences'. It was seen as an ideological and cultural constraint, which affected a whole range of factors, including the distribution of resources, wealth, work, decision-making and political power, and the enjoyment of rights and entitlements within the family as well as in public life. In short, gender relations entailed asymmetry of power between men and women as a pervasive trait. This led to the politics of gender relations and to restructuring institutions, rather than simply equality in access

342   *The 1990s and Beyond: International Conferences*

to resources, as the focal point of developmental progress and to what came to be known as 'gender mainstreaming'. Experience showed that there were no 'best' recommendations of general applicability.

The appropriate choice depended mainly on local and national characteristics, hence the importance of gender mainstreaming, which was defined by ECOSOC in 1997 as:

> the process of assuring the implications for men and women of any planned action, including legislation, policies and programmes, in all areas and at all levels. It is a strategy for making women's as well as men's concerns and experiences an integral dimension of the design, implementation, monitoring and evaluation of policies and programmes in all political, economic and social spheres so that women and men benefit equally and inequality is not perpetuated. The ultimate goal is to achieve gender equality (ECOSOC, agreed conclusion 1997/2).

Achieving gender equality required that gender roles and the basic institutions involved – government, the market and the family – were re-organized. Mainstreaming therefore aimed at 'transformative change', which, in turn, required that women take an active part in policies and decision-making at all levels of society. The UN conferences of the 1990s were especially effective in this transformation process.

The decision by the UN General Assembly in 1990 to convene the Beijing conference was spurred by the momentum that had been built up at the three previous world conferences on women and the *UN Decade for Women* and by growing concern, reflected in ECOSOC and other forums, at the uneven pace of implementation of agreements reached at the last conference in Nairobi, Kenya, in 1985. Despite progress in some areas, the objectives of ensuring equality for women, preventing violence against women and advancing their participation in efforts to promote peace and in economic and political decision-making were lagging. The fourth world conference on women was organized by the Commission on the Status of Women, with the UN Division for the Advancement of Women serving as the conference secretariat. The UN assistant secretary-general in the UN division, Mrs. Gertrude Mongella, was secretary-general of the conference, which was attended by participants from 189 countries and more than 5,000 representatives from 2,100 NGOs. Nearly 30,000 people attended the parallel and independent NGO Forum '95.

The conference adopted the *Beijing Declaration and Platform for Action*, which was subsequently endorsed by the UN General Assembly, with the objective of seeking fundamental change through immediate action and accountability in order to reach the targets set by the year 2000 (UN, 1995b). Governments were called upon to prepare national action plans by the end of 1996, with support from civil society. The *Beijing Declaration* embodied the commitment of the international community to the advancement of women by ensuring that a gender perspective was reflected in all policies and programmes at the national, regional and international levels. It proclaimed that the international community was 'determined to advance the goals of equality, development and peace for all women everywhere in the interest of all humanity'. Women's empowerment and their full participation on the basis of equality in all spheres of society were regarded as 'fundamental' for achieving these goals. Women's rights were 'human rights'. And the eradication of poverty based on sustained economic growth required 'involvement of women in economic and social development'.

The *Platform for Action* was seen as an agenda for women's empowerment. It identified 12, what were called, 'critical areas of concern' for priority action to achieve the advancement and empowerment of women: the persistent and increasing burden of poverty on women; inequalities and inadequacies in and unequal access to education and training, and to health care and related services; violence against women; the effects of armed or other kinds of conflict on women, including living under foreign occupation; inequality in economic structures and policies in all forms of productive activities and in access to resources; inequality between men and women in the sharing of power and decision-making at all levels; insufficient mechanisms at all levels to promote the advancement of women; stereotyping of women and inequality in women's access to and participation in all communication systems, especially in the media; gender inequalities in the management of natural resources and the safeguarding of the environment; and persistent discrimination against and violation of the rights of the girl child. In each of these critical areas of concern, the problem was diagnosed and strategic objectives proposed with concrete actions to be taken by the various parties involved.

Five years after the Beijing conference, a special session of the UN General Assembly was convened to review progress and make further recommendations. In preparation for the special session, governments were asked to report on their national actions to implement the Beijing *Platform for Action*. By the start of the special session, 153 member states and two observers had responded. The special session also had before it the latest *World Survey on the Role of Women in Development* as one of its basic documents.[19] Review of the national reports showed that some profound changes had taken place in the status and role of women in the years since the start of the *UN Decade for Women* in 1976, some more markedly since the Beijing conference. Women had entered the labour force in unprecedented numbers, increasing the potential for their ability to participate in economic decision-making at various levels starting with the household. Women were seen as major actors in the rise of civil society throughout the world, stimulating pressure for increased awareness of the gender equality dimensions of all issues and demanding a role in national and global decision-making processes. The role of NGOs, especially women's organizations, in putting the concerns of women and gender equality on the national and international agenda was acknowledged by many governments. But, despite much progress, the responses showed that much more needed to be done to implement the Beijing *Platform for Action*. Two major areas, violence and poverty, continued to be major obstacles to gender equality. Globalization had added new dimensions in both areas, creating new challenges. Overall, there had been no major breakthrough regarding equal sharing of decision-making in political structures at both the national and international levels. In most countries, representation of women remained low.

344 *The 1990s and Beyond: International Conferences*

Following the Beijing conference, ECOSOC, in its resolution E/1996/6, had requested the Commission on the Status of Women to identify emerging issues, trends and new approaches affecting the situation of women and equality between women and men that required urgent consideration and make recommendations thereon. The UN General Assembly, in its resolution A/Res/52/231, also requested a report on emerging issues to be submitted to the Commission on the Status of Women. In order to comply with these resolutions, an international workshop on *Beijing ± 5 – Future Actions and Initiatives* was convened by the UN Division for the Advancement of Women and held at UN House in Beirut, Lebanon, from 8 to 10 November 1999, the results of which were placed before the special session of the UN General Assembly in 2000 at which 148 member states and representatives of NGOs made interventions.

Addressing the opening session, the UN secretary-general, Kofi Annan, emphasized that progress had been made since the Beijing conference. Women's human rights had gained recognition; violence against women was now an illegal act in almost every country; and there had been worldwide mobilization against harmful traditional practices. But, he acknowledged, much remained to be done, including addressing new challenges, such as HIV/AIDS and increased armed conflict. While women entered the labour force in unprecedented numbers, the gender divide still persisted; women earned less and were involved in informal and unpaid work. There had been no major breakthrough in women's participation in decision-making processes and little progress in the legislation in favour of women's rights to own land and other property. The UN secretary-general focused on the importance of education for integration into the labour force, which would give women more choice and enable them to provide better nutrition, health care and education for their children.

On 16 November 2000, the UN General Assembly adopted by consensus resolution S-23/3 on the 'Further Actions and Initiatives to Implement the Beijing Platform for Action' (UN, 2000a). The special session reaffirmed the importance of gender mainstreaming in all areas and at all levels and complementarity between mainstreaming and special activities targeting women. Many actions were identified to be taken at the national and international levels. A number of these activities set new targets and reconfirmed earlier ones. The report of the *ad hoc* committee of the whole of the session was annexed to the UN General Assembly's resolution, which assessed the achievements in, and obstacles to, the implementation of the 12 critical areas of concerned identified at the Beijing conference (UN, 2000a). It noted that progress had been made in increasing recognition of the gender dimensions of poverty and in recognizing that gender equality 'is one of the factors of specific importance for eradicating poverty'. Progress had been made by pursuing a two-pronged approach of promoting employment and income-generating activities for women and providing access to basic social services, including education and health care. Microcredit and other financial instruments for women had emerged as a 'successful strategy' for economic empowerment and had widened economic opportunities for some women living in poverty, particularly in rural areas. Policy development had taken account of the

Fourth World Conference on Women, 1995   345

particular needs of female-headed households. Research had enhanced the understanding of the differing impacts of poverty on women and men and tools had
been developed to assist with this assessment. But many factors had contributed
to widening inequality between women and men, including income inequality,
unemployment and the 'deepening' of poverty levels of the most vulnerable and
marginalized groups.

There was increasing awareness that education was one of the most valuable
means of achieving gender equality and the empowerment of women. Similarly,
there was increasing realization among policy-makers and planners of the need
for programmes to cover all aspects of health throughout women's life cycle, high-
lighting especially the problems associated with the emergence of the HIV/AIDS
pandemic. Violence against women was now seen as a human rights issue as was
the effects of armed conflict on women, which had a different destructive impact
on them than on men. Increased participation of women in the labour market and
subsequent gains in their economic autonomy were recognized but the importance of a gender perspective in the development of macroeconomic policy was
still not widely recognized. Many women still worked in rural areas and in the
informal economy as subsistence producers and in the service sector with low
levels of income and little job and social security. There was growing acceptance
of the importance and full participation of women in decision-making but the
gap between *de jure* and *de facto* equality persisted. Gender mainstreaming was
widely acknowledged as a strategy to enhance the impact of policies to promote
gender equality but inadequate financial and human resources and a lack of political will and commitment were seen as the main obstacles confronting national
institutions.

Legal reforms had been undertaken to prohibit all forms of discrimination
and discriminatory provisions, including the *Convention on the Elimination of All
Forms of Discrimination against Women* (UN General Assembly resolution 34/80),
but gender discrimination continued to cause threat to women's enjoyment of
human rights and fundamental freedoms. Negative, violent and degrading images
of women had increased in different forms using new communication technologies in some instances and bias against women remained in the media. There was
recognition of the link between gender equality, poverty eradication, sustainable
development and environmental protection, but there remained lack of public
awareness about the environmental risks faced by women and the benefit of gender
equality for promoting environmental protection. Concerning the girl child, there
had been some progress at the primary level of education, less so at the secondary
and tertiary level, but the persistence of poverty and discriminatory and negative
cultural customs and practices acted against girls.

After the special session, the UN General Assembly invited ECOSOC to continue
to promote and coordinate follow-up of the outcomes of the major UN conferences and summits and to ensure gender mainstreaming as an integral part of
its work. The UN General Assembly also reaffirmed the need for the mobilization of resources at the national level, the promotion of an active and visible
policy of mainstreaming a gender perspective by the UN, including through the

346 *The 1990s and Beyond: International Conferences*

work of the UN special adviser on gender issues and the advancement of women and through the maintenance of gender units and focal points. The UN Security Council adopted a resolution (1325 (2000)) on 'Women, Peace and Security' on 31 October 2000. The UN Commission on the Status of Women adopted a new multiyear work programme for 2002–06 in March 2001. And a special session of the UN General Assembly was held in June 2001 to address and review the problem of HIV/AIDS.

35
World Food Summit, 1996

Two decades after the 1974 *World Food Conference*, the election of a new director-general of FAO resulted in a call for another world meeting on food security. In his first policy statement to the FAO Council in May 1994, following his election in November 1993, Jacques Diouf from Senegal, the first African director-general of FAO, proposed that a *World Food Summit* (WFS) be held in 1996 in the context of the changes relating to the programmes, structures and policies of FAO that the FAO Conference had empowered him to make (FAO, 1994a). In making his proposal, he said

> The challenges facing this Organization are the challenges of Member Nations. It is Member Nations and their people who cannot accept the human tragedy of 800 million people without adequate food, be they those condemned to abject poverty and misery, be they the 192 million children whose hunger today points to deprivation of opportunities tomorrow. It is Member Nations who face the challenge of feeding 9,000 million people by the year 2030. Accordingly, it is Member Nations who rightly insist that their Organization for food and agriculture effectively help them in dealing with these challenges.

Diouf referred to FAO's constitution in which member nations had 'made a solemn pledge to raise levels of nutrition and standards of living and thereby contribute toward ensuring humanity's freedom from hunger. There can be no higher purpose'. He noted that since FAO's establishment, 'impressive progress toward food security had been made' and that by the time of the International Conference on Nutrition in 1992, 'for the first time the absolute as well as the share of the world population that was in a state of undernutrition had declined'. Yet food was not distributed equitably. While some regions produced more food than they needed, others, particularly sub-Saharan Africa, did not. Therefore, 'unless appropriate and concerted actions were taken by all concerned, the incidence of undernutrition in the developing countries will continue to be unduly high'.

Although approved by the FAO Council and Conference, the call for another world food conference had a mixed reception internationally. In clear contrast to preparations for the 1994 World Food Conference, there was no widespread

348   *The 1990s and Beyond: International Conferences*

sense of a deepening food crisis that necessitated a major initiative on economic, humanitarian or political grounds.

FAO's own assessment of the world food security situation concluded that it showed only 'a modest deterioration in 1993/94 compared to the previous year' (FAO, 1994b). A tighter world cereals market situation and accompanying price hike in 1995 temporarily raised concern about problems of unstable supply and the possible effects of the GATT Uruguay Round, but these pressures eased during 1996.

The timing of the WFS was also far from ideal. Coming at the end of a series of international conference held during the first half of the 1990s, there was a distinct feeling of conference fatigue. There was also a widespread perception in official circles that there were too many institutional arrangements, too many bodies with overlapping mandates and duplication of responsibilities, not just in the areas of food security but in the whole international system for supporting human security and development. The effect of contracting aid funds resulted in resources being spread even more thinly, raising problems of aid effectiveness and efficiency. Holding the summit in November 1996 conflicted with other competing attractions. The newly established WTO was to hold its first meeting within weeks. Most significantly, the attention of the major force in world food supplies, trade and aid, the United States, was focused on its presidential election. Within the United Nation, the impending election of a new secretary-general was a further distraction. And the outbreak of a large-scale human-made disaster in central Africa also drew attention away from the summit.

Concern was also expressed as to what was the real purpose of the summit. Were there any hidden agendas? In its position paper prepared for the summit, the United States considered that the 'primary focus [of the WFS] is the unfinished job of enhancing food security for that 700–800 million people who are still food-insecure. In this sense, the crisis is perceived to be geographically concentrated – not the global crisis of the early 1970s' (US, 1996). It acknowledged, however, that there were global concerns about the longer term capacity of the world to meet ever-increasing food needs without destroying the environment and natural resource base, particularly as economic pressures and policy changes had reduced global public investment in agricultural research and financial support for agricultural development. Nevertheless, the United States pointedly recalled that FAO member states had agreed that the WFS was not a conference about pledging new resources, was not aimed at creating new financial mechanisms, institutions or bureaucracies, and would not reopen agreements reached in other forums. Rather, the WFS was 'designed to examine realistic approaches to food security'. In so doing, 'it was essential that current market conditions and strong grain prices not divert the Summit from its primary purpose of addressing the long-term challenge of global food security'. The United States was concerned that failure to keep the current situation in proper perspective could lead to calls for inappropriate market-distorting actions and policy changes, and that whatever short-term benefits such changes might provide would make the road to long-term global food security even harder.

Significantly, a major shift had taken place in the concept of food security since the 1994 World Food Conference. Then world food security was erroneously equated with the world food problem. In 1983, FAO revised and broadened its concept of food security. To the two dimensions of ensuring adequate food production and maximizing stability of food supplies was added the third dimension of securing access to available food, which required that balanced attention be given to both the demand as well as the supply side of the food security equation. The work of the World Food Council and the international conferences of the early part of the 1990s dealing with a wide range of issues and concerns related to achieving world food security, extended the concept further. In its position paper prepared for the WFS, the United States defined food security as having three dimensions:

- availability of sufficient quantities of food of appropriate quality, supplied through domestic production or imports;
- access by households and individuals to adequate resources to acquire appropriate foods for a nutritious diet; and
- utilization of food through adequate diet, water, sanitation and health care.

Achievement of these three dimensions had to be sustainable economically, socially, politically and environmentally, preserving the long-term productive capacity of the natural resource base. But all three dimensions could be seriously undermined by a number of 'root causes', which, apart from natural disasters, included: war and civil strife; inappropriate national policies; inadequate development, dissemination, adaptation, and adoption of agricultural and other research and technology; barriers to trade; environmental degradation; poverty, population growth, gender inequality; and poor health.

The complexity of food security as an all-embracing, multifaceted and multisectoral concept had two significant implications. The first was that many of the issue and their resolution lay outside the mandate of FAO. Thus, as the United Kingdom put it in its policy paper for the WFS, a wide range of organizations had important parts to play according to their remits and comparative advantages (UK, 1996). FAO could provide particularly valuable inputs by concentrating on strengthening the international knowledge base on food production issues and food trade. But because of the very wide range of factors influencing food security, the full participation of all the intergovernmental and United Nations system processes involved in co-ordinating the international follow-up to the other international conferences of the 1990s was also essential.

The second implication was related to the problem of institutional incoherence (Maxwell and Shaw, 1995; Shaw, 1999; Shaw and Clay, 1998). Influenced by a series of UN conferences held between the 1974 World Food Conference and the WFS on key issues related to food security, a number of UN agencies, many bilateral programmes, and most NGOs had made improving food security one of their main objectives. More than 30 UN bodies are directly or indirectly involved in food and nutrition security objectives (see Figure 17.1). In addition, the activities of the three regional development banks and the WTO as well as the 15 international centres of the Consultative Group on International Agricultural Research (CGIAR) also have a bearing on food security.

The SCN estimated that between 1987 and 1991, these UN bodies and bilateral sources for sectors related to food security (including nutrition, health, water, sanitation, child welfare, women, literacy, community development and food aid programmes) provided an average of over $58 billion a year, of which 60 per cent was supplied bilaterally and 40 per cent by the UN system, principally the World Bank (SCN, 1995). Total financial expenditure (excluding food aid) on projects designed to have a direct impact on improving nutrition in developing countries (a narrower and shorter-term concept than the more complex and longer-term concept of achieving food security) is estimated to have averaged $144 million a year during the same period (1987–91), representing 0.2 per cent of total Official Development Assistance (ODA). These funds averaged $0.04 per person per year for all developing countries and were unlikely to have had a major impact on the nutritional situation (*sic*). In contrast, world military expenditure rose to about $1,000 billion a year, four-fifths in industrial countries and one-fifth in developing countries (Sivard, 1991). With so many aid agencies involved in food security, there is a danger that as the issue becomes 'everybody's business', it will become 'nobody's business'. After the demise of the World Food Council, there is no single forum or body through which a major international or national crisis would automatically be considered or overall aid policy reviewed and negotiated. And with shrinking resources spread among a growing number of disparate and often conflicting projects, the effectiveness and efficiency of aid has been compromised.

Such was the background to preparations for the WFS. The WFS was unique among the international conferences of the early part of the 1990s in that the summit's main documents, the *Rome Declaration on World Food Security* and *World Food Summit Plan of Action*, were hammered out over a period of 18 months prior to the summit in a series of regional and co-ordination meetings and adopted unanimously at the beginning of the WFS. These documents were described as 'laying the foundations for diverse paths to a common objective – food security, at the individual, household, national, regional and global levels' (FAO, 1996). Completing these documents was complicated by disagreements over such issues as: the relationship of trade liberalization and food security; legal recognition of a right to food; the link between population stabilization and reproductive health of women and food security; and responsibility within the UN system for implementation and monitoring the action plan adopted by the summit. FAO's Committee on World Food Security drafted the final summit documents. Some 6,600 delegates and observers from 190 countries, including heads of state and ministers of agriculture and aid, assembled at FAO headquarters in Rome on 13 November 1996 for the five-day meeting. A parallel *Forum on Food Security* was held at the same time by representatives of over 1,200 NGOs from 80 countries.

Among the pointed interventions made in a series of 'scoldings and self-flagellation' during the five-day summit, delegates heard a harsh assessment from Pope John Paul II, who called disparities in nutrition among and within countries 'intolerable for humanity'. The pontiff criticized what he saw as the global causes of hunger: the diversion of food money to weaponry; crippling levels of

World Food Summit, 1996 351

international debt; refugees forced from their agricultural lands; trade embargoes 'imposed without due consideration for the hungry'; and 'arbitrary stabilization of the world population, or even its reduction', which, he said could not solve the problem. The Vatican's country paper prepared for the summit stated that 'the right to food is a universal human right'.

The UN secretary-general, Boutros Boutros-Ghali, arrived at the summit from cobbling together a military relief mission to ease the humanitarian crisis in eastern Zaire (now the Democratic Republic of Congo) where hunger and starvation affected more than a million people. He decried the destruction and waste of food around the world as hundreds of millions starved. He called the extent of the world's hunger, with 200 million children under five undernourished, and one dying every eight seconds, 'a rude shock to our conception of equity and social justice'. He urged the international community to launch 'a new and generalized mobilization against hunger'.

President Castro of Cuba, who also had a meeting with the Pope, blasted the gathering for failing to address the causes of world hunger, which, he said, were 'capitalism, neo-liberalism, the laws of a wild market, the external debt, under-development and conditions of inequity' (Bohlen, 1996). Castro also attacked 'absurd' economic blockades (a reference to the United States blockade of Cuba), which he said only compounded hunger and misery. 'Where are the ethics, the justification, the respect for human rights', he asked, 'what is the sense of these policies?' The US Agricultural Secretary, Dan Glickman, head of the US delegation to the summit, declared 'I don't think this conference is going to eliminate hunger overnight, But I think the world is a better place because of it' (Trueheart, 1996).

The FAO director-general said that the summit's basic documents had been adopted by consensus 'in a spirit of give and take'. At a news conference disrupted by protesters shouting 'farce', he stated: 'If it depended on me, I certainly would not have set an objective whereby 400 million people continue not to have access to adequate food' (Holmes, 1996). He criticized the size of his organization's budget as 'less than what nine developed countries spend on dog and cat food in six days and, listen to me, less than five per cent of what the inhabitants of one developed country spend each year on slimming products to counter the effects of over-eating'.

The *Declaration* adopted by the WFS reaffirmed 'the right of everyone to have access to safe and nutritious food, consistent with the right to adequate food and the fundamental right of everyone to be free from hunger'. It was considered both 'intolerable' and 'unacceptable' that 'more than 800 million people throughout the world, and particularly in developing countries, do not have enough food to meet their basic nutritional needs'. A target was set to 'reduce the number of undernourished people to half their present level no later than 2015'. The *Declaration* also reaffirmed that

> a peaceful, stable and enabling political, social and economic environment is the essential foundation which will enable States to give adequate priority to food security and poverty reduction. Democracy, promotion and protection of

352 *The 1990s and Beyond: International Conferences*

all human rights and fundamental freedoms, including the right to development, and the full and equal participation of men and women are essential for achieving sustainable food security for all.

Poverty was identified as 'a major cause' of food insecurity and 'poverty eradication' as 'critical to improve access to food'. Conflict, terrorism, corruption and environmental degradation were also listed as contributing 'significantly' to food insecurity. Increased food production was required within the framework of sustainable management of natural resources, elimination of unsustainable patterns of consumption and production, particularly in industrialized countries, and stabilization of the world population. The 'multifaceted character' of food security required concerted national action and effective international assistance.

The *World Food Summit Plan of Action* stated that in order to achieve food security for all:

> Each nation must adopt a strategy consistent with its resources and capacities to achieve its individual goals and, and the same time, cooperate regionally and internationally in order to organize collective solutions to global issues of food security. In a world of increasing interlinked institutions, societies and economies, coordinated and shared responsibilities are essential.

It reiterated that availability of enough food for all could be attained and referred to the remarkable achievement that the 5.8 billion people in the world at the time had, on average, 15 per cent more food per person than the global population of 4 billion had two decades previously. Harmful seasonal and inter-annual instability of food supplies could be reduced. But a warning was issued that further large increases in world food production, through the sustainable management of natural resources, was required to feed a growing population, and achieve improved diets. Unless national governments and the international community addressed the multifaceted causes underlying food insecurity, the number of hungry and malnourished people would remain very high in developing countries, particularly in sub-Saharan Africa; and sustainable food security would not be achieved.

The *Plan of Action* 'envisaged an ongoing effort to eradicate hunger in all countries', with an immediate view to reducing the number of undernourished people by half, no later than by 2015. A mid-term review would be conducted by 2010 to ascertain whether it was possible to achieve this target. The action plan contained seven 'commitment areas', with a total of 27 'objectives and targets', relating to:

- ensuring an enabling political, social and economic environment most conducive to achieving sustainable food security for all;
- implementing policies aimed at eradicating poverty and inequality and improving physical and economic access by all, at all times, to sufficient, nutritionally adequate and safe food and its effective utilization;
- pursuing participatory agricultural and rural development policies and practices in high and low potential areas;

World Food Summit, 1996 353

- striving to ensure that trade policies are conducive to fostering food security for all through a fair and market-oriented world trade system;
- endeavouring to prevent and be prepared for natural disasters and man-made emergencies and to meet transitory and emergency food requirements in ways that encouraged recovery, rehabilitation, development and a capacity to satisfy future needs;
- promoting optimal allocation and use of public and private investments to foster human resources, sustainable agricultural systems and rural development in high and low potential areas; and
- implementing, monitoring and following-up the *Plan of Action* at all levels in co-operation with the international community. Implementation was 'the sovereign right and responsibility of each State'. Monitoring would be conducted by the FAO Committee on World Food Security.

So, was this *déjà vu*, or something new (ODI, 1997)? It was easy to be cynical about the outcome of the WFS. Seen in a historical context, would it prove to be yet another failure in the many attempts to achieve world food security over the past half century? Coming at the end of a long series of international conferences held over the previous five years, there was a feeling of resignation, even resentment, that yet another expensive talk-shop, resulting in an unrealistic action plan, and inadequate commitment of additional resources, would once again raise false hopes and lead nowhere. Much of this was reflected in the press coverage that focused on the contrast between the subject matter, the elimination of hunger and malnutrition, and the 6,000 delegates enjoying the gastronomical delights of Rome. Questions were asked about what had happened to the 23 resolutions adopted by the 1974 World Food Conference, all the work of the World Food Council, and agreements reached at all the other international conferences. Critics argued that what the summit achieved was only a restatement of commitments acceptable to every government rephrased in the sustainable, participatory, gender-sensitive, anti-poverty, environmentally friendly terms of the moment.

On closer examination, some significant progress was made and previous gains were secured. As one commentator aptly put it, the WFS ensured that food and food security was back on the international menu (Maxwell, 1996a). From the relatively straightforward concept of food self-sufficiency as a way of ensuring food security, a counter-intuitive view of global development emerged based on the premise that those who are short of food would only be able to obtain it in the longer run if they could pay for it, leading to the concept of food self-reliance. This view highlighted the importance of employment and markets, as well as increased food production and stability of supplies. It also led to market protection and the concept of the welfare state and the need for safety nets for the unemployed and disadvantaged. These factors, in turn, disrupted the functioning of markets, and undermined comparative advantage, leading to the call for market liberalization. The chain of causality went on, leading back to food insecurity.

354   *The 1990s and Beyond: International Conferences*

The WFS action plan attempted to break this cycle. A multifaceted concept of food security was adopted, which recognized the multidimensional and interrelated causes of food insecurity, although the consequences of this in terms of leadership and concerted global action were not pursued. Throughout the action plan, reference was made to the agreements reached at the earlier international conferences of the 1990s. Substantively, the negotiators saw off the extreme Malthusians who considered the answer to world food security problems to be a combination of rigorous population control and massive efforts to produce more food in high potential areas. The needs of the poor and vulnerable living in low potential areas were also addressed.

One of the new and specific proposals committed governments to monitoring progress in reducing chronic hunger. Its implementation involved the use of vulnerability and risk mapping to target vulnerable, food insecure people and monitor hunger reduction strategies. More broadly, the process leading to the summit gave greater coherence to the ways in which governments and aid agencies discussed food security; the presentation of their policy and reviews of recent performance was also made in more similar terms. The summit also gave further impetus to discussions on international trade and food security. The recommendation for the creation of a WTO Working Group for Trade and Food Security was adopted at the 1996 WTO Ministerial Conference in Singapore.

As in the case of the other international conferences, the agreements reached at the WFS were non-legally binding. No new aid commitments were made, and no new institutional arrangements were proposed. Implementation of the recommendations contained in the action plan was the sovereign right and responsibility of each state. Co-ordination of international co-operation, especially among agencies of the UN system, was to be carried out 'using existing mechanisms and forums'. At the developing country level, representatives of the UN agencies were required to work with the UN resident co-ordinator to support implementation of the WFS action plan.

There was one issue that cast a shadow over agreements reached at the WFS. The position of the US government throughout the negotiations leading to the adoption of the WFS *Declaration* was negative on any legal right or rights to food. Its position was summed up in an 'interpretative statement' issued at the close of the summit:

> In joining consensus on this or other similar paragraphs in the Rome Declaration on World Food Security and the World Food Summit Plan of Action, the United States does not recognize any change in the current state of conventional or customary law regarding rights to food. The United States believes that the attainment of any 'right to food' or 'fundamental right to be free from hunger' is a goal or aspiration to be realized progressively that does not give rise to any international obligations nor diminish the responsibilities of national governments towards their citizens. The United States understands and accepts the provisions of the 'right of everyone to have access to safe and nutritious food' as an integral component of the right to a standard of living

adequate for health and well-being, as set forth in the Universal Declaration of Human Rights, which includes the opportunity to secure food, clothing, housing, medical care and necessary social services.

(FAO, 1997, p. 50)

Why was the United States the only country attending the summit to voice such strong opposition to the definition and implementation of the rights relating to food? One view was that declaring food a 'right' could lead to legal actions requiring the provision of food aid or to special provisions for food in international trade agreements, which linked this issue with provisions taken by various countries or NGOs on the trade liberalization issue (Hanrahan, 1996). A similar view was that the United States, which led rich nations to calls at the summit to make free trade the key to ending the poverty that was at the root of hunger, feared that recognition of a 'right to food' could lead to law suits from poor nations seeking aid and special trade provisions (Holmes, 1996).

Whatever the reason, a significant legal obstacle to the early implementation of the right to food was the US position that this right not be regarded with the same respect as other human rights, such as civil and political rights (Buckingham, 1998). This stance had not always been consistently maintained. In fact, the US position, at least from the perspective of the White House, had at times been very positive towards the realization of economic rights, as in President Roosevelt's four 'freedoms' State of the Union address in 1941, which included the 'freedom from want' (McGovern, 2001). And the US delegation to the 1974 World Food Conference had endorsed the conference's declaration, which proclaimed that 'every man, woman and child has the inalienable right to be free from hunger and malnutrition' (UN, 1975).

Reference was made to actors and institutions in civil society in the implementation and monitoring of the summit's *Plan of Action*. In affirming this role, the NGO Forum on Food Security, held at the same time as the summit, set out its own alternative model for achieving food security based on decentralization and a break-up of the concentration of wealth and power. The NGOs collective statement, *Profit for the Few or Food for All. Food Sovereignty and Security to Eliminate Globalisation of Hunger*, highlighted six key elements in its alternative strategy:

- strengthening the capacity of family farmers, including indigenous peoples, women, and youths, along with local and regional food systems;
- reversing the concentration of wealth and power and prevention of further concentration;
- changing farming systems toward a model based on agro-ecological principles;
- recognizing that prime responsibility for ensuring food security must rest with national and local governments and states, whose capacity must be strengthened and mechanisms for ensuring accountability enhanced;
- ensuring participation of people's organizations and NGOs at all levels, which must be strengthened and deepened; and

356 *The 1990s and Beyond: International Conferences*

- guaranteeing the right to food through international law and ensuring that food sovereignty takes precedence over macro-economic policies and trade liberalization: food cannot be considered as a commodity because of its social and cultural dimensions.

The most obvious differences in emphasis between the summit's and the NGOs' statements concerned the role of trade and markets and the right to food. Following ratification of the Final Act of the Uruguay Round, governments of the major food exporting developed countries saw market globalization and liberalization as largely positive in effect. For them, trade reduced fluctuations in food consumption, relieved part of the burden of stockholding and promoted economic growth. However, developing countries and NGOs were largely critical of the effects of both trade liberalization (particularly because of the lack of accountability or transnational corporations operating with the global economy) and of structural adjustment programmes on the poor and food insecure. The NGO Forum regarded hunger and malnutrition as fundamentally questions of justice, hence the right to the sustenance of life should come before the quest for profit. Without this, the scourge of hunger and malnutrition would continue. The NGO Forum's message was simple: '*Queremos una tierra para vivir*'. The WFS *Plan of Action* committed the UN only to exploring the legal ramifications of a universal right to food which, in a dissenting vote, the United States representative interpreted as an objective or aspiration, not a binding commitment or obligation.

What, then, was the overall balance sheet of the WFS? One view might be that it was a costly process in terms of limited financial and human resources, with limited outcomes. An alternative view might be that in a global economy, where policy agendas are defined by international media events, the issues of hunger and food security were put back on the international menu along with the major issues discussed at the other international conferences of the first half of the 1990s (Maxwell, 1996a). Whether it would make a real difference remained to be seen.

World Food Summit: Five Years Later, 2002

At the request of the FAO Council, another summit (WFS+5) was held at FAO headquarters in Rome between 10 and 13 June 2002, hosted by the Government of Italy, and chaired by the President of the Italian Council of Ministers, Silvio Berlusconi (FAO, 2002a). Delegates from 179 countries and the European Community attended the meeting. Parallel meetings were held at the same time in Rome, including a Multistakeholder Dialogue, a Meeting of Parliamentarians, an NGO forum, a Private Sector Forum and a Meeting on Rural Women.

At the inaugural ceremony, the UN secretary-general, Kofi Annan, reminded participants that at the WFC of 1996, the international community set a goal of cutting by half the number of hungry children, women and men by 2015. He noted that the target (of halving the proposition, not number, of hungry people by 2015) had been subsequently incorporated into the Millennium Development

Goals agreed by world leaders at the United Nations Millennium Summit in New York in September 2000. But with already one third of the time passed, 'progress has been far too slow'. He called for the meeting to give 'renewed life' to the 800 million hungry people 'by agreeing on concrete action'.

He continued:

> There is no shortage of food on the planet. But while some countries produce more than they need to feed their people, others do not, and many of them cannot afford to import enough to make up the gap. Even more shamefully, the same happens within countries. There are countries which have enough food for their people and yet many of them go hungry.

He recognized that hunger and poverty were 'closely linked'. 'The devastating cycle of generational hunger and poverty must be broken'. About 70 per cent of the hungry poor of the developing world lived in rural areas. He called for improving agricultural production and living standards in the countryside but stressed that 'success will also depend on developments beyond the farm gate' and on a 'secure a central place for women, who play a critical role in agriculture in developing countries'.

The UN secretary-general pointed out that if the WTS goal of halving the number of hungry by 2015 was to be achieved:

> we need a comprehensive and coherent approach that addresses the multiple dimensions of hunger by pursuing *simultaneously* (emphasis added) wider access to food and agriculture and rural development. We need an anti-hunger programme that could become a common framework around which global and national capacities to fight hunger can be mobilized. We know that fighting hunger makes economic and social sense.

He regarded it as a key step towards achieving all the development goals that were agreed at the Millennium Summit in 2000. It was fitting that WFS+5 came in the middle of a crucial cycle of conferences aimed at helping to improve the lives of people everywhere, from the free trade talks in Doha, via the financing for development meeting in Monterrey, to the sustainable development conference in Johannesburg. He concluded

> Hunger is one of the worst violations of human dignity. In a world of plenty, ending hunger is within our grasp. Failure to reach this goal should fill every one of us with shame. . . . It is time to do what we have long promised to do – eliminate hunger from the face of the earth

Jacques Diouf, FAO's director-general, gave vent to his sense of frustration when he spoke at the *WFS+5* opening ceremony. He noted that while there had been major international meetings in recent years, it was only in the last year (2001), in Genoa, Italy, that, for the first time, the G8 summit had paid any attention

358 *The 1990s and Beyond: International Conferences*

to food security. He observed that while famines 'stirred emotions and triggered waves of solidarity among public opinion', chronic hunger was 'only met with indifference, penalized for existing in silence and for not providing shock images on our television screens'. Yet, 'it also degrades biologically and intellectually, excluding the undernourished from the opportunities of life'. Hunger weighed heavily on the economies of countries it affected, causing an estimated 1 per cent a year loss in the rate of economic growth through reduced productivity and nutritional effects.

Diouf informed the meeting that since the 1996 summit, 150 developing and transition countries had prepared national food security strategies, and agricultural trade strategies had been drawn up for regional economic organizations. A special programme for food security for small farmers had been put into effect in 69 countries. A programme of prevention against transboundary animal and plant pests and diseases was also underway. And a programme to mobilize public opinion had also been in operation since 1997. Progress had been made in the realization of the right to food. Despite these positive developments, concessional assistance for agriculture had fallen by 50 per cent between 1990 and 2000, even though it was the source of employment and income of 70 per cent of the world's population.

Critically, the number of undernourished had fallen by 6 million a year instead of the 22 million required to reach the WFS target. At this rate, he estimated that the target would be met 45 years behind schedule. He stated that 'we know how to fight hunger'. An anti-hunger programme launched shortly before the meeting started would 'serve as a basis for work and dialogue among partners to mobilize the resources still needed'. In his opinion, the resources and technology existed to eliminate 'the insufferable spectre of cyclical famine and the inexorable deprivation of chronic hunger'. In the broader perspective of eliminating poverty, progress needed to rest on the three pillars of food, health and education. The mobilization of an international alliance against hunger would revive the essential political will required if the destiny of the world's hungry was to regain centre stage.

WFS+5 adopted an *International Alliance Against Hunger* (IAAH), which contained three substantive sections concerning political will, the challenges ahead, and the resources needed (FAO, 2002a). The IAAH, *inter alia*, reaffirmed 'the right of everyone to have access to safe and nutritious food' and that trade was a 'key element' in achieving world food security. Concerning political will, the FAO Council was invited to establish an Intergovernmental Working Group 'to elaborate, in a period of two years, a set of voluntary guidelines' to support FAO member states' efforts to achieve 'the progressive realization of the right to adequate food' in the context of national food security. FAO and other relevant UN bodies were requested to assist the working group, which would report on its work to the FAO Committee on World Food Security.

The United States repeated the reservation that it had voiced at the 1996 WFS concerning the right to food. In addition, it understood 'the right of access to food to mean the opportunity to secure food, and not guaranteed entitlement'. The United States stated that it was 'committed to concrete action to meet the objectives of the World Food Summit' but was concerned that the 'sterile debate' over 'voluntary guidelines' would 'distract attention from the real work of reducing poverty and hunger'. In an explanatory note, Norway stated that it would have preferred the expression 'code of conduct' instead of 'voluntary guidelines' because it was 'clearer and more definite'. However, it hoped that the action requested would lead to a useful instrument that would have the same function as a code of conduct on the right to adequate food, and would lead to such a code in the future.

In the 'challenges' section of the IAAH, the need to assure gender equality and to support empowerment of women was reaffirmed and the 'continuing and vital role of women in agriculture, nutrition and food security and the need to integrate a gender perspective in all aspects of food security' was recognized. The need for nutritionally adequate and safe food was emphasized, and the need for attention to nutritional issues as an integral part of addressing food security was highlighted.

Concerning resources, voluntary contributions to FAO's *Trust Fund for Food Security and Food Safety* were called for. Countries were urged to sign and ratify the *International Treaty on Plant Genetic Resources for Food and Agriculture*. During the meeting, 53 nations and the European Community signed the treaty.

The statement by the NGO Forum that took place during *WFS+5* expressed 'disappointment in, and rejection of, the official Declaration of the World Food Summit: five years later'. Far from analyzing and correcting the problems that had made it impossible to make progress over the past five years since the 1996 WFS toward eliminating hunger, the new action plan 'continues the error of more of the same failed medicine with destructive prescriptions that will make the situation even worse'. There would be no progress without a reversal of current policies and trends. Food sovereignty meant the primacy of peoples' and communities' right to food and to food production over trade concerns. The liberal economic policies imposed by the World Bank, the WTO and the IMF and northern countries and multilateral and regional free trade agreements should be ended and agriculture removed from the WTO. A Convention on Food Sovereignty was called for in order to 'enshrine the principles of food sovereignty in international law' and institute it 'as the principal policy framework for addressing food and agriculture'.

To reach the WFS goal of halving the number of hungry people in the world by 2015, FAO launched a Special Programme for Food Security (SPFS) as its 'flagship initiative'. Through projects in over 100 countries, the SPFS promotes what are described as 'effective, tangible solutions' to the elimination of hunger, undernourishment and poverty. Since 1995, $770 million from donors and national governments have been invested in FAO-designed food security programmes. The SPFS initiative helps to achieve food security in two ways: through assisting national governments run focused, well-planned national food security programmes, and through working closely with regional economic organizations to develop regional programmes for food security that optimize regional conditions for attaining food security in areas like trade policy. The SPFS is not a stand-alone initiative. Its goals and vision have been integrated into major international efforts including the

Comprehensive Africa Agriculture Development Programme and the *New Partnership for Africa's Development*, and the *UN Millennium Project for* achieving the *UN Millennium Development Goals*.

The final declaration of *WFS+5, The International Alliance Against Hunger* (IAAH), set in motion the initial steps for establishing a global partnership reminiscent of B. R. Sen's Freedom from Hunger Campaign. The initial working group formed in late 2002 consisted of representatives of the four Rome-based food agencies (FAO, IFAD, WFP and the International Plant Genetic Resources Institute (IPGRI), which acted on behalf of the CGIAR). This group was expanded to include representatives of NGOs and civil society organizations (CSOs). The IAAH is a voluntary association of local, national and international institutions and organizations that share a common mission to eradicate hunger through a combination of political will and practical action. At the end of 2005, governments and CSOs in 93 countries had expressed interest in establishing a national alliance against hunger. The IAAH has four focus areas: advocacy, accountability, resource mobilization and co-ordination. The aims of the IAAH are; to strengthen national and global commitment and action to end hunger; to facilitate dialogue on the most effective measures to reduce hunger; to amplify and add value to the contributions and capacities of members; and to promote the emergence of mutually supportive action in involving governments and other stakeholders in the fight against hunger. A principal function is to nurture the emergence and growth of strong national alliances against hunger.

36
World Agricultural Trade: WTO and the Doha Ministerial Declaration, 2001

The importance of world agricultural trade for achieving world food security was recognized at a number of international conferences throughout the 1990s. The conclusion of the GATT Uruguay Round of multilateral trade negotiations and the setting up of the World Trade Organization (WTO) in 1995 provided a major opportunity for reaching agreement on fair and free world trade within a liberalizing global economy. However, progress towards this aim proved elusive at the first three WTO ministerial meetings at Singapore in 1996, Geneva, Switzerland, in 1998 and Seattle, USA, in 1999. Promise of a break-through came at the fourth WTO ministerial meeting that was held in Doha, Qatar, in 2001. Negotiations on agricultural trade began in early 2000. By November 2001, at the time of the Doha ministerial meeting, 121 governments had submitted a large number of negotiating proposals.

The *Ministerial Declaration* that emerged from the meeting provided the framework for significant progress (WTO, 2001). In it, ministers declared their determination 'to maintain the process of reform and liberalization of trade policies' and pledged 'to reject the use of protectionism'. They recognized that international trade 'can play a major role in the promotion of economic development and the alleviation of poverty'. The special problems of the least-developed countries were recognized and a commitment was made to address their marginalization in international trade and to improve their effective participation in the multilateral trading system. To implement the ministerial declaration, a 'broad and balanced' work programme was agreed upon which sought to place the interests of developing countries at its heart. Concerning agricultural trade, the work programme recalled the long-term objective of the WTO *Agreement on Agriculture* to establish a fair and market-oriented trading system and prevent restrictions and distortions in world agricultural markets. A commitment was made to comprehensive negotiations aimed at: substantial improvements in market access; reduction and eventual phasing out of all forms of export subsidies; and substantial reductions in trade-distorting domestic support, with special and differential treatment for developing countries to enable them to take account of the development needs, including food security and rural development. Non-trade concerns would also be taken into account in negotiations. Modalities for further commitments would be established by no later than 31 March 2003.

Doha set a development agenda of considerable promise. Agreement to substantially reduce trade barriers in agriculture was the key to the ministerial meeting's success. But progress on the commitments made at Doha has proved to be difficult and tardy. Agriculture in many developed countries remains a highly sensitive and protected sector. Changes in agricultural policies in the European Union (EU) and the United States – two major players in world agricultural trade – have, since Doha, been moving in the wrong direction and have tended to exacerbate rather than reduce agricultural protection.

Many developing countries also have considerable agricultural protection and are reluctant to make reciprocal concessions to further Doha agreed negotiations. The G77 and China have also noted with great concern that the benefits of the existing multilateral trading system continue to elude the developing countries and have expressed disappointment at the lack of any meaningful progress on implementation of the Doha agreements. The WTO ministerial meeting in Hong Kong in 2005 renewed resolve to complete the Doha work programme in 2006. At that meeting, the EU, US and Japan pledged to phase out all their direct subsidies to food exports. At the same time, developing countries such as Brazil and India called for easier access to developed markets for prepared foods and cuts in overall farm subsidies. They claimed that developed countries spent six times as much on farm subsidies as the total world aid budget. An emergency meeting in Geneva, Switzerland, in July 2006 of the six 'core negotiators' of the Doha round of multilateral trade negotiations – Australia, Brazil, EU, India, Japan and the US – collapsed over irreconcilable differences about the liberalization of world agricultural trade. The US continued to argue for big cuts in farm import tariffs to open up markets for its farmers, which was rejected by the EU, India and Japan. They said that the US should first go further in offering to cut its agricultural subsidies. The Doha round will now enter indefinite suspension, unless a consensus in the WTO's 149 member countries can be found to revive it, throwing into doubt the future of WTO itself as an effect forum for reaching agreement in multilateral trade negotiations.

How much will trade liberalization help the poor and what is the likely impact of failure to reach agreement in the WTO? Trade liberalization is expected to act positively on development and poverty reduction (Bouet, 2006). Recent empirical studies have identified several key linkages through which trade liberalization helps development: the price and availability of goods, factor prices, government transfers, incentives for investment and innovation, terms of trade and short-run risks. Regarding the positive effect on poverty reduction, traditional argument focuses on two linkages: the fact that a large proportion of poor people work in the agricultural sector, where trade distortions are particularly high; and that liberalization could lead to higher world agricultural prices and raise activity and remuneration in the agricultural sector in developing countries. But it is also recognized that greater openness in agricultural trade can have negative effects. Government transfers can shrink as liberalization cuts receipts of trade-related taxes. Terms of trade can deteriorate as liberalization affects world prices. And liberalization can impose adjustment costs and raise short-run risk owing to competition from imports and re-allocation of productive factors. As a result, it is uncertain how much trade liberalization would reduce poverty and, by implication, food insecurity.

Many studies have attempted to assess the benefits of trade liberalization, using the multicountry computable general equilibrium (CGE) model, with mixed results. A survey of 16 assessments using CGE models of the global consequences of full trade liberalization from 1999 to 2005 highlighted a major divergence (Bouet, 2006). The implied increase in world welfare ranged from 0.3 to 3.1 per cent. Estimates of the number of people lifted out of poverty also ranged widely, from 72 million to 440 million. A simulation of full trade liberalization run at IFPRI using its MIRAGE model concluded that it would increase world real income by 0.33 per cent after ten years of implementation. It would lead to a higher rate of growth in middle-income countries (0.4 per cent) and in the least-developed countries (0.8 per cent), than in the rich countries (0.3 per cent). It would also contribute to poverty alleviation, as gains would go to unskilled labour in many developing regions, especially in Latin America and part of sub-Saharan Africa. And it would also reduce world income inequality. But some developing countries might also be hurt by trade liberalization. Some countries' terms of trade may be reduced as rising world prices for agricultural commodities would adversely affect net food importers or because preferential access to certain markets could be eroded. The main conclusion was a general trend toward greater trade pessimism for two main reasons: the world is already more globalized than previously expected or acknowledged; and some economic linkages, especially the dynamic ones, remain uncertain.

Nevertheless, international trade reform is still regarded as highly desirable, the benefits of which could be increased if domestic reforms were put in place simultaneously, leading to more efficient markets and more stable and predictable domestic institutions. Studies concluded confirm that trade reform must be very ambitious to improve welfare and have a positive impact on development. They also point to several policy recommendations related to the now suspended *Doha Development Agenda*:

- Tariff cuts should be large and progressive. A sensitive products clause could have very negative consequences on the extent of liberalization even if it concerned a limited number of products.
- Agriculture is the main area where distortions should be cut.
- Developing countries should liberalize their own economies.

These reforms could drastically change agricultural policies in the developed countries and their levels of output but it is a price worth paying to promote development and reduce poverty, and hence, food insecurity.

37
UN Millennium Summit, 2000

With the approach of a new millennium, the UN secretary-general, Kofi Annan, proposed that a 'Millennium Assembly of the United Nations' be held in the year 2000 with the overall theme of 'The United Nations in the Twenty-First Century' and four sub-themes: peace and security, including disarmament; development, including poverty eradication; human rights; and strengthening the United Nations. The UN General Assembly adopted the proposal and agreed that a three-day *UN Millennium Summit* be held at the start of it fifty-fifth session in September 2000.

The UN secretary-general prepared a report to assist the UN General Assembly in its deliberations during the *Millennium Summit* (Annan, 2000). He identified four priorities in applying the values set out in the UN *Charter* to the problems of the new century. First, freeing people from the 'abject and dehumanizing' poverty in which over one billion citizens of the world were confined. Second, freeing people from the scourge of war. Third, freeing people from the danger of living on a planet 'irredeemably spoilt' by human activities, and whose resources could no longer provide for their needs. And finally, making the United Nations a more effective instrument in pursing these three priorities by: reforming the UN Security Council; giving the UN the necessary resources to carry out its mandate; ensuring that the UN secretariat could make the best use of those resources; and by providing an opportunity for NGOs and other non-state actors to make their 'indisputable contribution' to the work of the United Nations. In his opinion, these priorities were 'clear and achievable', if there was the will to reach them. No state or organization could solve all the world's problems alone. Building a safer and more equitable world in the new century required the determined efforts of every state and citizen.

The UN secretary-general acknowledged that while there was much to be grateful for, there were still many things to deplore and correct. He considered that the 'central challenge' was to ensure that globalization became a positive force for all, instead of leaving many people behind. People had to be put at the centre of everything: more must be done, and it must be done better. He endeavoured to convey a series of 'clear and simple messages'. Extreme poverty was an affront to common humanity and made many other problems worse. Despite significant achievements, nearly half of the world's population lived on less than two dollars a day: 1.2 billion lived on less the one dollar a day. Nowhere was a global commitment to poverty reduction more needed than in sub-Saharan Africa. Income inequality persisted. While 1 billion people living in developed countries earned 60 per cent of the world's income, 3.5 billion people in low-income countries earned less than 20 per cent. The world's population had reached 6 billion, the last 1 billion taking only twelve years, the shortest in history. By 2025, another 2 billion would be added. During the next generation, the global urban population would double to 5 billion people. The message conveyed in the secretary-general's report was that: 'We are all impoverished if the poor are denied opportunities to make a living'. Debt relief, additional aid and domestic and foreign investment opportunities were needed.

The report of the UN secretary-general called on the international community to adopt a target of halving the proportion of people living in extreme poverty by the year 2015. The only hope of significantly reducing poverty was through 'sustained and broad based income growth'. New employment opportunities enabled women to expand the range of critical choices open to them. The surest route to growth was through 'successfully engaging in the global economy, combined with effective social policies'. Education was the 'key' to the new global economy. It was regarded as 'central' to development, social progress and human freedom. Universal access to primary and secondary education was 'vital' and could only be achieved by closing the education gender gap. Basic health care and enabling social policies had brought dramatic increases in life expectancy and sharp declines in infant mortality. But young people and children needed to be protected from HIV and provided with effective and affordable vaccines. The digital revolution had created a brand new economic sector that did not exist before. The power of information technology could transform economic and social activity.

Addressing the *Millennium Summit*, the UN secretary-general said that the meeting was the largest gathering of political leaders the world had ever seen. His report to the summit attempted to identify the main challenges facing the world at the beginning of the new millennium and to sketch out an action plan for addressing them. One word encapsulated the changes the world was living through, 'globalization', with its benefits and dangers. One problem was that the opportunities it brought were far from being equally distributed. The overarching challenge was to make globalization mean more than bigger markets. 'We must learn to govern better and – above all – how to govern better together'. Drawing from President Franklin D. Roosevelt's 1941 State of the Union address, he identified the global issues that needed to be addressed under three headings: freedom from want, freedom from fear, and freedom of future generations to sustain their lives on this planet.

At the end of the *Millennium Summit*, a *United Nations Millennium Declaration* was adopted, which drew substantially from the UN secretary-general's report. In many ways, the *Declaration* was a fitting climax to the series of UN conferences and meetings that had taken place over the decade of the 1990s (UN, 2000b).

It re-affirmed the faith of world leaders in the UN and its charter 'as indispensable foundations of a more peaceful, prosperous and just world'. It recognized the 'collective responsibility' to uphold the principles of human dignity, equality and equity at the global level and the duty of world leaders to all people, especially the most vulnerable and particularly to children to whom the future belonged. And it listed certain fundamental values considered to be essential to international relations in the twenty-first century including: freedom, equality, solidarity, tolerance, respect of nature, and shared responsibility.

In order to translate these shared values into action, the *Declaration* identified 'key objectives', to which special significance was assigned, under the headings of: peace, security and disarmament; development and poverty eradication; protecting our common environment; human rights, democracy and good governance; protecting the vulnerable; meeting the special needs of Africa; and strengthening the United Nations. No effort was to be spared to free people from the scourge of war, both within and between countries, which had claimed more than 5 million lives in the 1990s. People were to be freed from the 'abject and dehumanizing conditions of extreme poverty', to which more than a billion were subjected. Humanity was to be spared from the threat of living on a planet irredeemably spoilt by human activities. Democracy was to be promoted, the rule of law strengthened, and human rights and fundamental freedoms, including the right to development, respected. The vulnerable were to be given every assistance and protection to lead normal lives. Africa was to be brought into the mainstream of the world economy. And the United Nations was to be made a more effective instrument for pursuing the priorities recognized in the declaration.

A series of specific target was set in what became known as the *Millennium Development Goals* (MDGs), drawing from the goals and targets that had been established at previous UN conferences (Annex 37.1). Among the steps to strengthen the United Nations, the *Declaration* re-affirmed the central position of the UN General Assembly as 'the chief deliberative, policy-making and representative organ of the United Nations', and 'the indispensable common house of the entire human family', resolved to intensify efforts to achieve a 'comprehensive reform' of the UN Security Council 'in all its aspects', strengthen further ECOSOC and the International Court of Justice, and ensure 'greater policy coherence and better cooperation' between the United Nation, its agencies, the Bretton Woods institutions and the WTO and other multilateral bodies to achieve 'a fully coordinated approach to the problems of peace and development'.

Annex 37.1 Millennium development goals and targets

1. *Eradicating extreme poverty and hunger*

- Halve, between 1990 and 2015, the proportion of the world's population whose income is less that one dollar a day.
- Halve, between 1990 and 2015, the proportion of people who suffer from hunger.

2. *Achieve universal primary education*

- Ensure that, by 2015, children everywhere, boys and girls alike, will be able to complete a full course of primary education.

3. *Promote gender equality and empower women*

- Eliminate gender disparity in primary and secondary education, preferably by 2005, and in all levels of education no later than 2015.

4. *Reduce child mortality*

- Reduce by two-thirds, between 1990 and 2015, under-five child mortality.

5. *Improve maternal health*

- Reduce by three-quarters, between 1990 and 2015, the maternal mortality ratio.

6. *Combat HIV/AIDS, malaria and other diseases*

- Halt by 2015 and begin to reverse the spread of HIV/AIDS.
- Halt by 2015 and begin to reverse the incidence of malaria and other major diseases.

7. *Ensure environmental sustainability*

- Integrate the principles of sustainable development into country policies and programmes and reverse the loss of environmental resources.
- Halve, by 2015, the proportion of people without sustainable access to safe drinking water and basic sanitation.
- Achieve, by 2020, a significant improvement in the lives of at least 100 million slum-dwellers.

8. *Develop a global partnership for development*

- Develop further an open, rules-based, predictable, non-discriminatory trading and financial system (including a commitment to good governance, development, and poverty reduction, nationally and internationally).
- Address the special needs of the least developed countries (includes tariff- and quota-free access for least developed countries exports; enhanced programme of debt relief for heavily indebted poor countries and cancellation of official bilateral debts; and more generous ODA for countries committed to poverty reduction).
- Address the special needs of landlocked countries and small island developing (through the Programme of Action for the Sustainable Development of Small Island Developing States and the outcome of the twenty-second special session of the General Assembly).
- Deal comprehensively with the debt problems of developing countries through national and international measures in order to make debt sustainable in the long term.

- In cooperation with developing countries, develop and implement strategies for decent and productive work for youth.
- In co-operation with pharmaceutical companies, provide access to afford-able, essential drugs in developing countries.
- In cooperation with the private sector, make available the benefits of new technologies, especially information and communications.

(Annan, 2000; UN, 2000b)

38
International Conference on Financing for Development, 2002

From its earliest days, the UN General Assembly and UN secretariat paid special attention to the financing of development in the developing countries, including a protracted attempt to establish a Special United Nations Fund for Economic Development (SUNFED) between 1949 and 1959, which did not succeed but which led to the creation of the International Development Association (IDA), the soft lending facility of the World Bank (Shaw, 2005a). The series of international conferences of the 1990s, culminating in the *Millennium Summit* and the MDGs in 2000, intensified the need to address again ways of financing development in the developing countries and the need for developed countries to increase their official development assistance. Responding to increasing pressure, an *International Conference on Financing for Development* was held in Monterrey, Mexico, between 18 and 22 March 2002. The meeting was attended by 50 heads of state or government, over 200 ministers, and leaders from the private sector and civil society, and senior officials from the major intergovernmental financial, trade, economic and monetary organizations (UN, 2002).

It was the first quadripartite exchange of views between governments, civil society, the business community, and the institutional stakeholders on global economic issues. Discussions took place not only in plenary sessions but also in 12 separate roundtables. The conference was widely regarded as a turning point in the approach to development co-operation by the international community and a new point of reference for policy-making on the interconnections of domestic and international finance, trade and other development issues. It was the first UN-sponsored summit-level meeting to address, in an integrated way, key financial and related issues pertaining to global development. The committee preparing for the conference adopted a broad agenda covering six major inter-related themes, each integral to financing for development: the mobilization of domestic financial resources for development; mobilizing international resources; foreign direct investment and other private flows; international trade as an engine for development; increasing international and technical co-operation for development through, *inter alia*, ODA, external debt servicing and addressing systemic issues; and enhancing the coherence and consistency of the international monetary, financial and trading systems in support of development. An integrated approach to these themes was taken as a key distinguishing element in the financing for development process.

Speaking at the opening session, the Mexican president, Vicente Fox Quesada, said that for decades the nations of the world had endeavoured to come to grips with the problems of development and poverty through international co-operation. But the results, in his opinion, had been 'meagre, belated and discouraging'. He went on: 'It is our responsibility to pave the way today for a century of bridges, not barriers; a century of encounters, not wars; of shared responsibilities and achievements, not isolated efforts'. It was a time 'to change, but to change in order to build'. He found that the conference marked the beginning of a new concept of development and provided the 'spark' for a new movement designed to combat marginalization and underdevelopment. If the twenty-first century was to be a 'century of development for all, we must be prepared to undertake bold action – challenging former attitudes and looking for new ideas and actions'. He found that the conference was not an isolated event but part of a global movement in pursuit of development. The *Millennium Summit* had marked the beginning of a new effort to eradicate marginalization. At Doha, emphasis had been placed on promoting fairer participation by developing countries in world trade. And at Johannesburg, the importance of sustainable environmental development had been recognized. All must contribute to the new world development agenda, in a 'century of bridges and encounters, not walls and barriers'.

The UN secretary-general, Kofi Annan, called for people to be given a chance to improve their lives, denied by multiple hardships, each of which made it harder to escape from the others: poverty, hunger, disease, oppression, conflict, pollution and depletion of natural resources. In his opinion: 'Development means enabling people to escape from that vicious cycle'. Development required resources, human, natural and, critically, financial. He said: 'We live in one world, where no one can feel comfortable or safe while so many are suffering and deprived'. Developing countries had asked for a chance to make their own voices heard and ensure that their interests are taken into account when the management of the global economy is discussed, and a chance to trade their way out of poverty. The promise of Doha 'must be fulfilled' as well as relief from an unsustainable burden of debt, and a helping hand up in the form of a significant increase in ODA. He reminded his audience that at the *Millennium Summit* in 2000, world political leaders had agreed to use the first fifteen years of the new century to begin a major onslaught on poverty, illiteracy and disease through reaching the MDGs. But serious studies had concurred that those goals could not be achieved without at least an additional $50 billion a year in official development aid, roughly double the current level.

The clearest and most immediate test of the Monterrey conference was whether donors would be prepared to provide that aid. Some donors were still sceptical that aid worked; there was abundant evidence that it did. But as vital as aid was, it did not provide the complete answer. Development was a complex process involving many actors working together, not against each other. In preparing for the Monterrey conference, the UN, WTO and the Bretton Woods institutions had worked together as never before with the result that 'we are all tackling the issues together, in a coherent fashion'. The *Monterrey Consensus* (MC), which the conference was to approve, was not in his view a weak document, as some had claimed. It could mark a 'turning point' in the lives of poor people throughout the world. 'Let's make sure that it does'.

The president of the World Bank, James D. Wolfensohn, regarded the conference as a good opportunity 'to reinforce our collective commitment to expand the opportunities and resources necessary to halve world poverty by 2015' and to meet the other MDGs. But, he reminded participants, development was 'a long road' and the challenges ahead should not be underestimated. He felt that perhaps for the first time in an international meeting there was greater consensus than ever before about what needed to be done and that the opportunity should not be squandered. All people had a right to human dignity and to control their own lives, and a right to opportunity, in education, trade and building a better future for their children. 'We must not fail them'. We had come to view as normal a world where less than 20 per cent of the population, in the rich countries, dominated the world's wealth and resources and consumed 80 per cent of its income. But there was only one world. Something new was begun at Monterrey, a new global partnership based on an understanding that leaders of the developing and developed world were united by a global responsibility based on ethics, experience and self-interest. Opportunity and empowerment, not charity, could benefit all. Long-term peace and stability would not be created until it was acknowledged that we were a common humanity with a common destiny in which our futures were indivisible.

The managing director of the IMF, Horst Koehler, said: 'We need to work for a better globalization – one that provides opportunities for all and one in which risks are contained'. Integration into the global economy was good for growth, which was essential for fighting poverty. He saw four priorities for the international community in producing faster, stronger and more comprehensive support for developing countries:

- trade, which was the most important avenue for self-help;
- reaching the target of 0.7 per cent of GNP for ODA;
- debt relief; and
- creating institutional capacity, which more than political will was responsible for slow progress in the reforms needed to fight poverty.

The director-general of WTO, Mike Moore, delivered a 'clear and simple message' to the conference. In his opinion, poverty in all its forms was the greatest single threat to peace, democracy, human rights and the environment. It was a 'time-bomb against the heart of liberty'. It could be conquered. We had the tools but we needed the courage and focus to make use of them. One of the tools was trade liberalization. It could make a 'huge contribution' to the generation of resources for the financing of development. The basic priority of the international trading community should be, as the Doha development agenda had recognized, the creation of conditions in which developing countries could maximize the gains they were able to reap from trade. He identified four key areas that required action:

- agriculture, the backbone of most developing countries;
- textiles and clothing, the greatest export earners of many developing countries;
- tariff peaks reduction; and
- tariff escalation, which tilted the tables against the development of indigenous processing transformation to enable developing countries to diversify out of dependence on a few primary products for their foreign exchange.

The *Monterrey Consensus* (MC) adopted by the conference provided a vision of a new global approach to financing development. It reflected the comprehensive agenda and holistic approach that was taken by the conference and established a platform for the future. It also embraced as part of the agreed policy package important concerns about social protection, income distribution, employment and gender equality and the concept of partnership in the financing of development. In confronting the challenges of financing for development, the MC stated: 'Our goal is to eradicate poverty, achieve sustained economic growth and promote sustainable development as we advance to a fully inclusive and equitable global economic system'. It noted, with concern, the estimates of a 'dramatic shortfall' in the resources required to achieve the internationally agreed development goals, including the MDGs and to ensure that the twenty-first century became 'the century of development for all'. It called for a 'new partnership' between developing and developed countries, declaring that 'our resolve to act together is stronger than ever'. Each country had 'primary responsibility' for its own economic and social development but national development efforts needed to be supported by 'an enabling international economic environment'. It was recognized that globalization offered both opportunities and challenges. In an increasingly globalizing, interdependent, world economy, a holistic approach to the interconnected national, international and systemic challenges of financing for development, and involving sustainable, gender-sensitive, people-centred approaches in all parts of the world, was essential. Peace and development were 'mutually reinforcing'. The *UN Charter* was upheld and, building on the values expressed in the *Millennium Declaration* of 2000, a commitment was made to promoting national and global economic systems based on the principles of justice, equity, democracy, participation, transparency, accountability and inclusion.

In mobilizing domestic financial resources for development, it was noted that good governance was essential for sustainable development and that fighting corruption at all levels was a priority. In mobilizing international resources, private capital flows, particularly foreign direct investment, along with international financial stability were regarded as 'vital components'. International trade was described as 'an engine for development'. It was recognized that a universal, rule-based, open, non-discriminatory and equitable multilateral trading system, as well as meaningful trade liberalization, could substantially stimulate development worldwide and benefit countries at all stages of development. ODA played an 'essential role' as a complement to other sources of financing for development, especially in those countries with the least capacity to attract private direct investment. A major priority was to build development partnerships, particularly in support of the neediest, and to maximize the poverty reduction impact of ODA. Developed countries that had not done so were urged to make concrete efforts towards the target of 0.7 per cent of GNP as ODA to developing countries: 0.15–0.20 per cent of GNP of developed countries should be provided to the least developed countries.

Developing countries were encouraged to use ODA effectively in helping to achieve internationally agreed development goals and target, including the MDGs. All involved should strive to make ODA more effective (eight ways to do this were mentioned) and innovative sources of financing should be explored provided they did not unduly burden developing countries. It was recognized that external debt relief could play a 'key role' in liberating resources for development. The MC also addressed systemic issues, and it was openly recognized at last the need to enhance the coherence and consistency of the international monetary, financial and trading systems in support of development. A commitment was made to ensure follow-up of the MC. Building a global alliance for development would require 'unremitting effort'. Fuller use should be made of the UN General Assembly and ECOSOC. A call was made for a follow-up international conference to review the implementation of the MC and for the UN secretary-general to submit annual reports on progress made.

The UN secretary-general prepared a report for the UN General Assembly's High Level Dialogue on *Financing for Development* in June 2005 (UN, 2006). The *UN Economic and Social Survey 2005* also contained a special section of 'Financing for Development'. Against the background of a continuous decline in ODA, the UN General Assembly requested further exploration of ways to generate new public and private resources that would complement national development efforts. Motivated by the complex, multidimensional process of development for which governments had both individual and shared responsibilities, the UN General Assembly requested a systematic, comprehensive and integrated high-level international and intergovernmental consideration of financing for development that would lead to a broader-based partnership for development.

The MC had brought the importance of ODA back to the centre of discussion on financing internationally agreed development goals, including the MDGs. At the time of the Monterrey conference in 2002, ODA had fallen to the historically low level of 0.2 per cent of donor countries' GNP. After the conference, a number of important measures were taken to improve both the quantity and quality of aid. ODA increased to $78.6 billion in 2004 (in current $US). If the commitments made at Monterrey were fulfilled, the ratio would rise to 0.30 per cent in 2006. ODA to the least-developed countries recovered even more strongly to over $23 billion in 2003, a 60 per cent increase over 2001 but still well below the agreed target of 0.15 to 0.2 per cent. The European Union agreed to increase ODA from € 34.5 billion in 2004 to € 67 billion in 2010.

At the G8 summit meeting at Gleneagles, Scotland, in July 2005, additional commitments were made to increase ODA. According to the Development Assistance Committee (DAC) of the OECD, the new commitments will increase ODA by around $50 billion a year by 2010. A doubling of aid to Africa by 2010 was announced, valued at 425 billion a year. The United States announced that it would double its aid to sub-Saharan Africa by 2010 and Canada by 2008–09. Japan committed to doubling its ODA by $10 billion over the next five years and doubling its aid to Africa in the next three years. Significant steps were also taken to improve aid effectiveness, with a commitment to improve coherence and consistency and to stay engaged in the dialogue on the agreements reached at Monterrey.

39
World Summit, 2005

In May 2004, at the request of the UN secretary-general, the UN General Assembly decided to convene at the commencement of its sixtieth session in 2005 in New York a high-level plenary meeting of the General Assembly to comprehensively review the implementation of the *Millennium Declaration* and the integrated follow-up of the major UN conferences of the 1990s in the economic, social and related fields. The General Assembly requested the UN secretary-general to submit a comprehensive report on the *Millennium Declaration*, including progress in meeting the MDGs and their financing. The report would also draw on the findings of the *High-level Panel on Threats, Challenges and Change* that the UN secretary-general had established in 2003. The meeting was held between 14 and 16 September 2005 at the level of heads of state and government. A civil society *Millennium Forum* was also held and a *High-level Dialogue on Financing for Development* at the ministerial level.

The UN secretary-general said in his report to the UN General Assembly that the second millennium summit, called the *Millennium + 5 Summit*, was an event of 'decisive importance' (Annan, 2005). The The secretary-general wrote that the decisions taken 'may determine the whole future of the United Nations' and offer the best chance, 'perhaps our only chance to ensure a safer, more just and more prosperous world – for us and our children and grandchildren'. Putting it more graphically, he said that 'we have come to a fork in the road'. The report set out what the UN secretary-general called 'an agenda of highest priorities' for consideration at the 2005 *World Summit*, which drew from the work of the *High-level Panel on Threats, Challenges and Change* and the *Millennium Project* that he had commissioned (see below).

He recalled that the *Millennium Declaration* of 2000 had called for a 'global partnership' to achieve the MDGs by 2015. But much had happened in the five years since the *Millennium Summit*, including international terrorism and the horrendous attack of 11 September 2001 in New York and Washington, DC; violent conflict in over 40 countries resulting in 25 million displaced persons and 11–12 million refugees; the spread of HIV/AIDS, with over 20 million deaths and over 40 million affected; and the continuation of abject and dehumanizing poverty with more than 1 billion people living on less than a dollar a day and 20,000 dying each day from poverty. Global wealth had grown but was less evenly distributed both between and within countries. Insufficient action had been taken to achieve the MDGs. The scale of long-term challenges, as diverse as international migration and climate change, was far greater than the collective action taken to meet them. And there had been a decline in public confidence in the UN, for opposite reasons, as shown in the debate over the war in Iraq. But, the UN secretary-general stressed, 'our problems are not beyond our power to meet them . . . However, we must come together to bring about far-reaching change'.

The report pointed out that the multifaceted challenge of development cut across a wide array of interlinked issues. The UN conferences and summits of the 1990s had helped build a comprehensive normative framework around these linkages for the first time by mapping out a broad vision of shared development priorities. This had laid the groundwork for the *Millennium Summit* to set out a series of time-bound targets by 2015 that were later crystallized into the MDGs. The *Millennium Project* would propose an action plan to achieve the MDGs. But, the UN secretary-general pointed out, the MDGs were part of an even larger development agenda and did not encompass some of the broader issues covered in the UN conferences and summits of the 1990s. Nevertheless, he called on developing countries with extreme poverty by 2006 to adopt and begin to implement a national development strategy bold enough to meet the MDG targets by 2015. This required a specific framework of action. Investment strategies to achieve the MDGs would not work unless they were supported by states with transparent, accountable systems of governance, grounded in the rule of law, which encompassed civil and political as well as economic and social rights and underpinned by accountable and efficient public administrations. Many of the poorest countries required capacity-building investment to put in place and maintain the necessary infrastructure and to train and employ qualified personnel. Good governance, strong institutions and a commitment to root out corruption and mismanagement were necessary. It was crucial to provide decent jobs that both provided income and empowered the poor, especially women and young people. Civil society organizations also had a 'critical role' to play in 'making poverty history'.

The report identified seven broad 'clusters' of public investment and policies to address the MDGs, and set the foundations for private sector-led growth, as elaborated in the *Millennium Project*:

- gender equality; overcoming pervasive gender bias;
- the environment: investing in better resource management;
- rural development: increasing food output and incomes;
- urban development: promoting jobs, upgrading slums and developing alternatives to new slum formation;
- health system: ensuring universal access to essential services;
- education: ensuring universal primary education and expanding secondary and higher education; and
- science, technology and innovation: building national capacities.

Quoting from the work of the *Millennium Project* (see below), the UN secretary-general stated that the investment costs for the MDGs alone in a typical low-income country would be roughly \$75 per capita in 2006, rising to approximately \$140 in 2015 (in constant dollar terms), equivalent to one-third to one half of their annual per capita incomes, and far beyond the resources of most low-income countries. A big push in development assistance was needed to create conditions for greater private investment and an exit strategy from aid. He therefore urged developed countries that had not already done so to establish timetables to achieve the 0.7 per cent target of gross national income for ODA by no later than 2015, starting with significant increases no later than 2006 and reaching 0.5 per cent by 2009.

Starting in 2005, he suggested that developing countries that put forward sound, transparent and accountable national strategies and required increased development assistance should receive a significant increase in aid of sufficient quality and arriving with sufficient speed to enable them to achieve the MDGs. For this purpose, he recommended that the international community should launch in 2005 an *International Finance Facility* (IFF) 'to support an immediate front-loading of ODA', underpinned by scaled-up commitments to achieve the 0.7 per cent ODA target no later than 2015. In addition, in the longer term, other innovative sources of finance for development should also be considered to supplement the IFF. These steps should be supplemented by immediate action to support a series of what he called 'quick wins' – relatively inexpensive, high-impact initiatives with the potential to generate short-term gains and save millions of lives.

In the follow-up to the March 2005 Paris *High-level Forum on Aid Effectiveness*, he proposed that donor countries should set, by September 2005, timetables and monitorable targets for aligning their aid delivery mechanisms with partner countries' MDG-based national strategies. Regarding debt and debt servicing, he proposed that debt sustainability should be redefined as 'the level of debt that allows a country to achieve the MDGs by 2015 without an increase in debt ratios'. Concerning trade, he identified as an 'urgent priority' the establishment of a timetable for developed countries to dismantle market access barriers and begin phasing out trade-distorting domestic subsidies, especially in agriculture. To address this priority, he suggested that the Doha round of multilateral trade negotiations should fulfil its development promise and be completed no later than 2006. As a first step, member states should provide duty-free and quote-free market access for all exports from the least developed countries. But he warned that efforts to defeat poverty and pursue sustainable development would be in vain if environmental degradation and natural resource depletion continued unabated. He listed three major challenges that required urgent attention by the international community – desertification, biodiversity and climate change – that should be addressed by developing a more inclusive international framework with broader participation by all major countries, developing and developed. Other priorities he identified for global action included infectious diseases surveillance and monitoring, natural disasters, science and technology for development, regional infrastructure and institutions, global institutions, and migration. The 'urgent task' in 2005 was to implement in full the commitments already made and to render genuinely operational the framework already in place.

378 *The 1990s and Beyond: International Conferences*

The report called for a set of proposals to provide 'freedom from fear' and 'freedom to live in dignity' to match those to provide 'freedom from want'. Drawing from the report of the *High-level Panel on Threats, Challenges and Change* (UN, 2004), the UN secretary-general proposed that these should include the panel's vision of collective security and the case for a more comprehensive concept of collective security, and a strategy against terrorism, organized crime, control of weapons of mass destruction, peacekeeping and peace-building, and strengthening the role of the UN Security Council. At the same time, democracy should be promoted, the rule of law strengthened, and respect for all internationally recognized human rights and fundamental freedoms should be observed. To achieve these aims, the UN secretary-general proposed that the UN Office of High Commissioner for Human Rights should be strengthened and the UN Commission for Human Rights replaced by a Human Rights Council. The UN secretary-general also called for a strengthening of the major components of the UN, including the UN General Assembly, the UN Security Council, ECOSOC and the UN secretariat, and for improving coherence and co-operation among the UN bodies.

Speaking at the beginning on the 2005 *World Summit*, the UN secretary-general referred to the 'deep divisions' among member states and the 'under performance of our collective institutions', which had led to a 'proliferation of ad hoc responses' that were 'destabilizing and dangerous'. He recalled that he had appointed a *High-level Panel on Threats, Challenges and Change* and had commissioned a *Millennium Project* to meet the MDGs. Their reports would set the agenda for reform. He had put forward what he regarded as a 'balanced set of ambitious proposals' that had been negotiated to produce the outcome document for the 2005 summit. In the meantime, there were some encouraging signs. A 'democracy fund' had been created and a convention against nuclear terrorism had been finalized. An addition $50 billion a year had been provided in the fight against poverty by 2015. The 0.7 target for ODA had gained new support, innovative sources of financing were coming to fruition, and progress had been made in debt relief. By agreement on the outcome document, these achievements would be locked in and progress in development would be matched by commitments to good governance and national plans to achieve the MDGs by 2015. He ended with reference to what President Franklin D. Roosevelt once called 'the courage to fulfil our responsibilities in an admittedly imperfect world' and that 'precisely because our world is imperfect, we need the United Nations'.

The *World Summit* approved an outcome document that brought together in one place agreements reached at the major UN conferences and summits of the 1990s (UN, 2005a). It reaffirmed the *Millennium Declaration* of 2000 and recognized the 'valuable role' of the major UN conferences and summits in mobilizing the international community and guiding the work of the United Nations. It recognized peace, collective security, development and human rights as the 'pillars' of the United Nations system and foundations of collective security. There was a general commitment to adopt national development strategies by 2006 to achieve internationally agreed development goals, with the support of increased development assistance. The DAC/OECD estimate that ODA to all developing countries would increase by around $50 billion a year by 2010 due to recent substantial increases in aid was highlighted. At the same time, concrete, effective and timely action would be taken to implement all agreed commitments on aid effectiveness. A commitment was also made to put in place policies to ensure adequate investment in health, clean water and sanitation, housing and education, and the provision of public goods and social safety nets to protect vulnerable and disadvantaged sections of society. The 'critical role' of education in poverty eradication was recognized and support to ensure free and compulsory access to primary education, the elimination of gender inequality and renewed efforts to improve girls' education. It was also resolved to make the goals of full and productive employment and decent work for all, including women and young people, a 'central objective' of national and international policies, while eliminating the worst forms of child labour.

A commitment was made to take further action through international co-operation on promoting clean energy, energy efficiency and conservation, and in enhancing private investment, technology transfer and capacity building in developing countries and in assisting them in integrating their sustainable development strategies. Increased investment in health systems in developing countries was also recommended in order to achieve universal access to treatment for HIV/AIDS, malaria and tuberculosis by 2010 and to reproductive health by 2015.

Concerning peace and collective security, it was agreed that the UN Security Council should consider ways to strengthen its monitoring and enforcement roles in counter-terrorism but this fell short of adopting a comprehensive counter-terrorism strategy proposed by the UN secretary-general. Regarding peacekeeping, support was given for the development of a ten-year capacity building plan with the African Union but the proposed establishment of a Peace-building Commission and a Peace-building Fund was not approved. Strengthening the Office of the High Commissioner for Human Rights by doubling its regular budget resources was approved, as was mainstreaming human rights throughout the UN system, but more work was called for on the responsibilities of individual states to protect their populations from genocide, war crimes, ethnic cleansing and comes against humanity. It was recognized that individuals were entitled to freedom from fear and from want, with equal opportunity to enjoy their rights and develop their human potential, but further discussion was called for in the UN General Assembly and on the definition of the notion of human security.

Support was given to strengthening the effectiveness of the UN humanitarian response, in part by improving the *Central Emergency Revolving Fund*. It was also agreed to explore the feasibility of a more coherent institutional framework to address environmental issues. But further discussion was needed on the reform of the UN Security Council to make it more broadly representative, efficient and transparent, to strengthen ECOSOC's co-ordination role, policy review and dialogue on economic and social issues, the creation of a Human Rights Council to replace the Commission on Human Rights, the establishment of an independent ethics office to the UN General Assembly, an independent external evaluation of the UN, and the creation of an independent oversight advisory committee.

380   *The 1990s and Beyond: International Conferences*

Following weeks of intense negotiation and numerous draft text, the final outcome document approved by the UN General Assembly showed all the hallmarks of compromise. At the *Millennium Summit* in 2000, world leaders had resolved to meet a number of MDGs. But in the five years since the summit, many governments had not acted on their promises, and the gap between rich and poor countries continued to widen. Many calculated that the world would not meet the MDGs by 2015. For this reason, many states, rich and poor alike, were not keen to raise any further hopes, or to make further promises. Even the relatively cautious reform package of the secretary-general had failed to rally strong government support. 'Massive' last-minute changes by the United States further 'unravelled' the process. The final summit outcome document disappointed those who had hoped for strong and creative solutions to the world's problems. Delegates expressed mixed feelings about the document. A few were pleased while others felt that priority issues had become diluted to the point of meaninglessness.

In April 2006, a special high-level meeting was held between the UN and the Bretton Woods institutions, WTO and UNCTAD to discuss coherence, co-ordination and co-operation in the context of the *Monterrey Consensus* and the outcome document of the 2005 *World Summit* (UN, 2006). It was noted that the outcome document had reaffirmed the *Monterrey Consensus* and recognized that mobilizing financial resources for development and their effective use in developing countries was 'central' to a global partnership for development in support of the achievement of internationally agreed development goals. Subsequently, in its resolution 60/188 of 22 December 2005, the UN General Assembly resolved 'to continue to make full use of the existing institutional arrangements for reviewing the implementation of the Monterrey Consensus' and stressed the importance of the full involvement of all relevant stakeholders. ECOSOC also held its ninth special high-level meeting with the international financial and trade institutions in April 2006.

Attention was focused on four sub-themes. First, implementation of, and support for, national development strategies towards the achievement of internationally agreed development goals, including the MDGs. The role of employment policy for achieving the goal of full and productive employment and the removal of corruption as a serious barrier to development were considered to be particularly important for achieving the MDGs. Second, the development dimension of the *Doha Work Programme* should be completed. The *Doha Round* had reached a critical stage among the 149 WTO members to reach conclusion by the end of 2006. Third, additional measures were needed to implement and build on initiatives taken to enhance debt sustainability. In 2005, agreement was reached on the Multilateral Debt Relief Initiative to cancel an estimated $55 billion in debt owed by Highly Indebted Poor Countries (HIPCs) to multilateral institutions. It was proposed that additional countries should receive debt reliefs for which additional resources would be required. Finally, the development efforts of middle-income developing countries should be supported. Ways and means should be found to mitigate the effects of international financial volatility, increasing investment in infrastructure, enhancing the transfer of technology and skills, and strengthening South–South co-operation.

Part IV

Assessment. The Graveyard of Aspirations

A country [civilization] should not be judged by its wealth but by the way it treats its poor and hungry.

(Adapted from Franklin D. Roosevelt, *Inaugural Address*, 1941)

The UN was not created to take humanity to heaven, but to save it from hell.

(Dag Hammerskjold, UN Secretary-General, 1953–61)

The record of addressing global hunger, malnutrition and food insecurity in their various manifestations over the past two decades [1980s and 1990s] is one of both qualified success and unjustifiable failure.

(Uwe Kracht and Manfred Schulz (eds), *Food Security and Nutrition. The Global Challenge*, 1999)

40
Redefining the Concept of Food Security

As one observer has put it, in the years since the 1974 World Food Conference, the concept of food security has 'evolved, developed, multiplied and diversified' (Maxwell, 1996b). One count put the number of definitions of 'food security' at close to two hundred (Smith *et al.*, 1993). With the failure to achieve Boyd Orr's grand vision of a World Food Board, and the adamant objection of the world's most powerful countries to proposals for a multilateral world food security arrangement, the early conceptual work of FAO focused on increasing food production, particularly in the developing countries, stabilizing food supplies, using the food surpluses of developed countries constructively and creatively, creating world and national food reserves, stimulating world agricultural trade, negotiating international commodity agreements, and increasing concern and understanding through B. R. Sen's Freedom from Hunger Campaign.

After the world food crisis of the early 1970s and the 1974 World Food Conference, the continued tendency was to equate the world food security problem with the world food problem by concentrating attention of increasing food production, stabilizing food supplies and using food surpluses, despite the efforts of the World Food Council to broaden the focus of attention. The ILO World Employment Conference of 1976, with its concept of 'basic needs', and the work of Amartya Sen and his concept of food 'entitlement', led to an understanding and acceptance of the importance of assuring access to food by the hungry poor, thereby moving the concept of food security out from a purely agricultural sector concern into the broader arena of poverty and development problems (see Figure 40.1). This process was carried further by the series of international conferences of the 1990s described in Part III. In essence, food insecurity is now being seen as the eye of the storm of interlocking national and global concerns to which it contributes and whose solution lies in tackling those concerns holistically.

This broader concept of world food security may be depicted graphically in many ways. Here, it is represented as three concentric circles. The innermost circle – the eye of the storm – includes a series of interlocking food and nutrition security concerns the relative importance of which varies from location to location. Those local concerns are surrounded by a number of wider regional and national concerns, such as basic services, technology, assets and human rights, that impact on how the local concerns are played out. They in turn, are affected by overarching

Figure 40.1 The broad concept of food and nutrition security: the eye of the storm

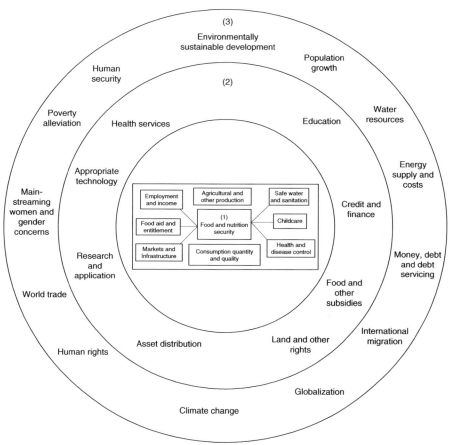

1. Interlocking local food and nutrition security concerns
2. Basic services, technology, assets and rights
3. Overarching major concerns

major global concerns, such as environmentally sustainable development, water resources, world trade, human security and rights, climate change and the current pattern of globalization, which penetrate and affect the concerns in the two inner circles. This enlarging, refining and redefining process carries with it two important implications. First, it highlights the problem of institutional incoherence. With so many multilateral, bilateral and non-governmental organizations and international institutions involved, food security has tended to become everybody's concern and so, in reality, no one's concern. And it has made the problem of developing common and coherent policies, priorities and programmes to attain world food security especially difficult. These problems will be addressed in Part IV of this history.

Another view is that the evolution of thinking about food security reflects three shifts in the definitions of the term from: the global and the national to the household and the individual; a 'food first' to a livelihood perspective; and objective indicators to subjective perceptions (Maxwell, 2001). Five phases of food security policy and practice have been detected: the 1970s, following the world food crisis and the 1974 World Food Conference when the objective was to establish a global food security system; the first half of the 1980s, with Amartya Sen's food entitlement concept and the counterproductive effects of IMF and World Bank structural adjustment programmes; the second half of the 1980s when the Africa famine of 1984–85, UNICEF's work on *Adjustment with a Human Face*, and the publication of Jean Dreze and Amartya Sen's *Hunger and Public Action* renewed impetus to action on hunger and its causes; and the 1990s with its series of international conferences which emphasized poverty as the major cause of hunger and malnutrition and broadened the concept of food security.

This broadening of the concept of world food security, with its multifaceted and multidimensional aspects, in many ways mirrors the evolving views on development theory and practice. The 1960s saw the recognition of the importance of the human factor in development, which gave a whole new perspective. The starting point should be people, not money and wealth. Sustained and equitable development depended not on the creation of wealth but on the capacity of people to create wealth. This led in the 1970s to the emphasis on equity in development and debunking of the concept of the trickle down effect of the benefits of development to the poorest. In its place came the basic needs strategy, the importance of employment and markets, the implementation of direct measures to reach and benefit the poorest, and the concept of re-distributing the benefits of growth to them. The 1980s witnessed world economic recession and what was described as 'the lost decade of development' during which the poor were marginalized and forced to bear the social costs of economic adjustment programmes imposed on developing countries by the international financial institutions. The 1990s saw the re-discovery of the importance of human development, epitomized in the annual *Human Development Reports* of the UNDP, and the mainstreaming women and gender issues into development (Emmerij *et al.*, 2001; Jolly *et al.*, 2004).

Another important development, which is described below, is the large and dramatic ways in which the world food system has evolved since 1945 (Maxwell and Slater, 2004). From a situation of food shortages in the developing countries and the use of the so-called food 'surpluses' of the developed countries, the focus switched to the importance of ensuring access by poor people to the food they needed through increasing employment and purchasing power. At the same time, powerful forces entered the world food system, including the emergence of large multinational food corporations, which led to the increasing commercialization and control of the food chain, and population growth and urbanization, which resulted in a considerable expansion of world food trade.

Another significant development has been the changing patterns of food consumption, the emergence of the fast food industry and supermarket chains, and the emergence of obesity, not malnutrition, as a major killer in the developed world and in parts of the developing world as well. The industrialization of food is systematically destroying traditional food cultures. The sheer novelty and glamour of what is called the 'Western diet', with its large number of new food products introduced every year, and the marketing power used to sell these products, has overwhelmed the force of tradition and left the general public relying on science, journalism and marketing when deciding what to eat. What has come to be called 'nutritionism', which arose to help better deal with the problems of the Western diet, has largely been used by the food industry to sell more food and undermine the authority of traditional ways of eating. And fast food has become good business for the health care industry which, in the United States, is estimated at more than $200 billion a year in unsustainable diet-related health care costs (Pollan, 2007).

Food habits are not immutable and can be changed by many factors, such as government import and pricing policies, changes in the relative prices of food commodities, increasing income, transport and logistical improvements and changes in fuel costs. As migration has taken place from rural to urban areas, a significant factor that has changed eating habits has been women's participation in income-earning activities outside the home, particularly in the informal sector. And it is now recognized that the prospects of reducing poverty and hence malnutrition and hunger around the world are being shaped by changes in the international economy caused by such factors as modifications in the international rules and institutions governing trade and finance, the flow of private capital as well as ODA, and the global impact of growth in the major developing countries, particularly China and India. It has also led to the accusation of an 'international organization of hunger' through the interdependence and hegemony of countries and regimes and the powerful domination of a small number of developed nations (Uvin, 1994).

41
Dimensions of Poverty and Food Insecurity

'Make poverty history' was the clarion call of Nelson Mandela at a mass rally in Trafalgar Square in London on 3 February 2005. The former South African president, world statesman with the greatest moral authority who was awarded the Nobel Peace Prize in 1993, called on world leaders 'to act with courage and vision'. For him: 'Overcoming poverty is not a gesture of charity. It is an act of justice. It is a fundamental human right, the right to dignity and a decent life. While poverty persists, there is no true freedom'. He repeated his message at a meeting of the finance ministers of the G7 leading group of industrialized countries the following day.

Hunger, malnutrition and poverty are intricately interlinked. Poverty is now generally regarded as the root cause of hunger and malnutrition. What is not always understood, however, is that hunger and malnutrition can, in turn, be major causes of poverty. They can affect the capabilities and capacities of individuals attempting to escape from poverty in several ways, including:

- reducing the capacity for physical activity and hence the productive potential of the labour, usually their only asset, of those who suffer from hunger;
- impairing people's ability to develop physically and mentally, retarding child growth, reducing cognitive ability and seriously inhibiting school attendance and performance, thus compromising the effectiveness of investment in education;
- causing serious long-term damage to health, linked to higher rates of disease and premature death;
- causing inter-generational disadvantages, for example, hungry mothers give birth to underweight children who start life with a handicap; and
- contributing to social and political instability that further undermines government capacity to reduce poverty (FAO/IFAD/WFP, 2002).

Poverty also has various dimensions. UN organizations and other international institutions have recently published a number of annual and special reports on various aspects and dimensions of poverty that are read in isolation, often only by specialized groups of readers. If read simultaneously by the general public, they give a compounded picture of the various dimensions of poverty and food insecurity, and their interrelationships, and what might be done to reduce and eventually eradicate them in meeting the Millennium Development Goals (MDGs) approved at the UN in 2000. The MDGs have become an international reference for measuring and tracking improvements in the human condition in developing countries. They offer a comprehensive and multidimensional development framework and set clear quantifiable targets to be achieved by 2015.

Food and nutrition insecurity

At a number of international conferences, the international community has recognized food security as one of the most fundamental of human rights. It has also been agreed that the world possesses enough resources and know-how to eradicate hunger and malnutrition. Achieving food security has been the subject of countless international conventions, declarations, compacts and resolutions. According to one calculation, more than 120 have been addressed on various issues relating to the right to food since the League of Nations was founded (Pinstrup-Andersen *et al.*, 1995). Yet despite some progress, it is estimated that 852 million people worldwide were undernourished in the period 2000–02, most of them women and children (FAO, 2004). This figure includes 815 million in the developing countries, 28 million in countries in transition and 9 million in the industrialized countries (see Table 41.1). Hunger and malnutrition kill more people every year than AIDS, malaria and tuberculosis combined. More people die silently from hunger than in wars. And malnutrition often leads to disease, devastating the lives of hungry poor people. Some 150 million children under the age of five in the developing countries are affected by chronic protein-energy malnutrition (Table 41.2). One child dies every five second from hunger-related causes.

The causes of hunger are many, often rooted in poverty. Millions of people have experienced famine and death caused by natural and man-made disasters, as the large-scale humanitarian disasters that occurred in the genocide in Rwanda, the Asian *tsunami*, the Pakistan earthquake, and the on-going humanitarian catastrophe in Darfur, Sudan, have shown. After each event, the international community has said 'never again', but C. P. Snow's dire prophesy made in 1968 continues to unfold. Four steps should be taken to handle future humanitarian catastrophes (Shaw, 2004a). First, agreement should be reached at the United Nations to give the UN secretary-general the power to take whatever speedy action is necessary in accordance with Article VII of the UN *Charter* on 'Action with respect to threats to the peace, breaches of the peace, and acts of aggression'. Article 99 of the *Charter* authorizes the UN secretary-general to bring to the attention of the UN Security Council any matter which, in his opinion, may threaten the maintenance of peace and security (which could involve voicing the wishes of the people against its government). He already has authority to request the UN World Food Programme to provide emergency humanitarian assistance to people caught up in war and civil conflict if the government concerned does not make a request to do so.

Table 41.1 Undernutrition in the developing world, 1979–81 to 2000–02

Developing regions and countries	Number of undernourished people (millions)				Proportion of undernourished people in total population (%)			
	1979–1981	1990–1992	1995–1997[a]	2000–2002	1979–1981	1990–1992	1995–1997[a]	2000–2002
Developing world	920.0	823.8	796.7	814.6	28	20	18	17
Asia and the Pacific	727.3	569.2	509.5	519.0	32	20	17	16
East Asia	307.3	198.8	155.1	151.7	29	16	12	11
China	303.8	193.5	145.6	135.3	30	16	12	11
South Asia	330.6	291.3	287.3	301.1	37	26	23	22
India	261.5	214.5	194.7	213.7	38	25	21	21
Latin America and the Caribbean	45.9	59.5	54.8	52.9	13	13	11	10
Near East and North Africa	21.5	24.8	34.9	39.2	9	8	10	10
Sub-Saharan Africa	125.4	170.4	197.4	203.5	36	36	36	33
Countries in transition	na	na	23.3	28.3	na	na	6	7

[a]For countries in transition 1993–95.
na – data not available
Source: FAO (2002c and 2004).

Table 41.2 The effects of protein-energy malnutrition on preschool children, 1980–2005

Region	Prevalence(%)						Numbers (million)					
	980	1985	1990	1995	2000	2005	1980	1985	1990	1995	2000	2005
Stunted (height for age)												
Africa	39.0	37.8	36.9	36.1	35.2	34.5	32.8	36.4	39.6	41.9	45.1	48.5
Asia	55.1	48.2	41.1	35.4	30.1	25.7	176.8	166.4	154.6	130.8	109.4	92.4
Latin America and Caribbean	24.3	21.1	18.3	15.9	13.7	11.8	12.7	11.3	10.0	8.8	7.6	6.5
All developing countries	48.6	43.2	37.9	33.5	29.6	26.5	222.6	214.4	204.3	181.5	162.1	147.5
Underweight (weight for age)												
Africa	23.5	23.5	23.6	23.9	24.2	24.5	19.8	22.6	25.3	27.8	30.9	34.5
Asia	45.4	40.5	35.1	31.5	27.9	24.8	145.6	139.6	131.9	116.3	101.2	89.2
Latin America and Caribbean	12.5	10.5	8.7	7.3	6.1	5.0	6.5	5.6	4.8	4.0	3.4	2.8
All developing countries	37.6	33.9	30.1	27.3	24.8	22.7	172.1	168.1	162.2	148.2	135.5	126.5
Wasted (weight for height)[a]												
Africa				7.3	8.3	9.5				8.5	8.5	13.3
Asia				9.7	9.2	8.9				35.7	33.5	32.0
Latin America and Caribbean				1.6	1.6	1.5				0.9	0.9	0.8
All developing countries				8.3	8.2	8.3				45.2	45.1	46.2

[a]No data for 1980, 1985, 1990.
Source: WHO data.

Second, a multilateral humanitarian fund should be established to provide food and other basic needs quickly to victims of disasters. Some action has been taken to create such a fund but the shortcomings of the International Emergency Food Reserve established in 1975 (see Part II) should be avoided. Third, the UN World Food Programme, the largest and most respected humanitarian organization, should be given responsibility for co-ordinating the international response to future humanitarian disasters, thereby removing the institutional incoherence and incompetence resulting from many aid agencies acting independently. Finally, the artificial separation between relief and development assistance should be removed, thereby ensuring that humanitarian aid is followed up with assistance for reconstruction, rehabilitation and development that would help prevent the recurrence of future disasters.

More than 2,000 million people are affected by various forms of micro-nutrient malnutrition, such as vitamin A, iodine and iron deficiency (Table 41.3). And a growing number of children and adults in both developed and developing countries are becoming obese. Hunger and malnutrition are killing nearly 6 million children each year (a figure roughly equal to the entire pre-school population of a large country, such as Japan) (FAO, 2005b). Hunger and malnutrition are among the root causes of poverty, illiteracy, disease and mortality of millions of people in the developing world. Progress towards reducing the number of hungry people has been 'very slow', and the international community is far from reaching its hunger reduction targets and commitments set at the *World Food Summit* (WFS) in 1996 and the UN *Millennium Summit* in 2000. At the current pace, only South America and the Caribbean region will reach the MDG target of cutting the *proportion* of hungry people by half by 2015. None will reach the more ambitious WFS goal of halving the *number* of hungry people by that date.[1]

But, who are the hungry poor, where are they concentrated, and why are they hungry and malnourished?[2] Understanding what has been called the 'anatomy'

Table 41.3 Population affected by micro-nutrient malnutrition (millions), 2001/2004

Region (WHO definition)	Vitamin A deficiency and xerophthalmia[a]	Iron-deficient or anaemic
Africa	35	240
Americas	8	140
South/Southeast Asia	58	780
Western Pacific and China	17	600
Europe	*na*	80
Eastern Mediterranean	13	180
Total	131	2020

[a] Pre-school children only.
na – data not available.
Source: WHO data for iron. SCN (2004) for vitamin A.

of hunger and food insecurity and its determinants in terms of who are the undernourished in its various manifestations as they affect different groups of people and their underlying causes is crucial for effective local, national and global strategies for their eradication (Kracht, 2005). The causes of food shortages are varied and complex (FAO, 2003). Many countries have been plagued by severe food shortages for a decade or longer. Conflict and economic problems have been cited as the main causes of more than 35 per cent of food emergencies during the period 1992 to 2003. Thirty-three countries, particularly in sub-Saharan Africa, have been described as 'food emergency hotspots'. They have experienced food emergencies during more than half of the seventeen-year period between 1986 and 2003. Many conflict-induced complex emergencies that may also coincide with drought are persistent and turn into long-term crises. Eight countries suffered emergencies in fifteen or more years between 1986 and 2003, with war or civil strife as a major cause.

Ethiopia is an example of an extreme case. In 1973, 1.5 million people were affected by famine. In 1984, the number was 6 million; in 2003, 14 million. Almost half of Ethiopia's children are said to be malnourished but do not die. They suffer a different fate. Robbed of vital nutrients, they grow up stunted and sickly, weaklings in a land that runs on manual labour. Some become intellectually stunted and drop out of school. According to the Ethiopian Economic Association, the underlying trend is for the number of people requiring food assistance to rise by 3.5 per cent a year, to reach 50 million in 20 years' time, unless significant steps are taken to halt and reverse that trend. Ethiopia has received more relief aid than any other country. But it has had less development aid than any needy nation. In sub-Saharan Africa, 5 million children under the age of five died in 2005, 40 per cent of such deaths worldwide. Malnutrition was a major contributor to half of these deaths. In this region, children under five not only died at 22 times the rate of children in wealthy countries but also twice the rate for the entire developing world. In this region, too, 33 million more children under five are living with malnutrition. In UN surveys from 1995 to 2003, nearly half of under-five children were stunted or wasted, markers of malnutrition and harbingers of physical and mental problems. While dead children are mourned, intellectual and physical stunting are less obvious until it is too late, when it is time to go to school.

As the only region in the world currently facing widespread chronic food insecurity as well as persistent threats of famine, sub-Saharan Africa should be given special consideration by the international community, as has been expressed at a number of international conferences. It has been correctly argued that Africa's persistent vulnerability 'is due as much to a failure of understanding as a to a failure of interventions' (Devereux and Maxwell, 2001). It has been suggested that a starting point for improved understanding would be acceptance of five propositions, namely:

- Hunger and poverty in Africa must now be seen as the most urgent and intractable problems.
- A precondition for tackling poverty in Africa lies in improving the production, marketing and consumption of food: national and household food security must be at the heart of poverty reduction.

Dimensions of Poverty and Food Insecurity 393

- Food security policy faces unprecedented challenges associated with a range of internal and external influences: for example, the impact of new technology, conflicts, HIV/AIDS and the effects of globalization.
- Food security management requires better collaboration across sectors, disciplines and institutions: it is too complex to be left to one specialist ministry such as agriculture.
- The problems and failures of the past should not lead to pessimism and cynicism about the future: the challenge is to put the right institutions and policies in place, nationally and internationally (Devereux and Maxwell, 2001).

As food aid will be required for a number of years to come in many countries in sub-Saharan Africa in order to achieve food security, it has been proposed that an international conference should be held to arrive at common policies and co-ordinated programmes for future food aid to the region (Shaw, 2002a).

Hunger and poverty are still predominantly rural phenomena and are likely to remain so for the next decade at least. Some 75 per cent of the hungry poor live and work in rural areas. Projections suggest that over 60 per cent will continue to do so in 2025. Some people and places are more vulnerable to poverty and food insecurity than others. The International Fund for Agricultural Development (IFAD) has identified seven groups of people and their relative importance in different regions of the world who are particularly prone to food insecurity (IFAD, 2001). *Smallholders* living in dry land areas in West and Central Africa, Asia and the Pacific and Latin America face a much higher risk than those living and working in irrigated rural areas. In Africa, smallholders are the largest poverty group. *Pastoralists* who depend on livestock for some or all of their subsistence are another high-risk group. These estimated 675 million rural people are highly vulnerable to drought and flood, resource degradation, outbreaks of disease and increasing pressure as human population increases and grazing areas shrink. Another high-risk group are *artisan fishermen* who have to supplement and diversify their incomes in a number of ways.

Wage labourers, especially landless or casually employed farm-workers are almost everywhere among those most likely to be poor and hungry. So too are *indigenous people and scheduled castes and tribes* in the regions of Latin America and the Caribbean, the Near East and North Africa, and Asia and the Pacific. *Female single-headed households* are also among the most vulnerable to poverty and hunger, as are *HIV/AIDS affected communities*. The interaction between food insecurity and HIV/AIDS is particularly pronounced (FAO, 2003). Since the HIV/AIDS epidemic began, 25 million people have died of the disease, another 42 million are infected and, during the present decade, 'AIDS is expected to claim more lives than all the wars and disasters of the past 50 years'. The disease causes and exacerbates food insecurity in many ways, particularly by drastically debilitating and reducing the most productive part of the agricultural labour force. While it has become a major cause of hunger, the reverse is also true. Incorporating HIV prevention, nutrition care for people living with HIV/AIDS and AIDS mitigation measures into food security and nutrition programmes can help reduce the spread and

394 Assessment. The Graveyard of Aspirations

impact of the disease. When short-term food emergencies intersect the long-wave HIV/AIDS crisis, household food security is likely to be the single most important HIV prevention strategy and AIDS mitigation response.

FAO has developed a generic classification of people particularly vulnerable to food insecurity that identified six broad groups (FAO, 1999). These include: a substantial array of marginal populations in urban areas; people in at-risk social groups, including indigenous people and ethnic minorities; members of low-income households within vulnerable livelihoods, such as those included in IFAD's classification; migrant workers and their families; dependent people living alone or in low-income households with large families and the victims of conflict.

A different approach classified hungry people into four broad groups based on the household's principal means of obtaining food: low-income farm households, rural landless and low-income non-farm households, low-income urban households and poor herders, fishermen and forest people dependent on community or public resources (Task Force Hunger, 2005). These four food-insecure groups were complemented by six 'cross-cutting' groups: pregnant and lactating women, newborn infants, children under five, micro-nutrient deficient individuals, victims of extreme natural or man-made disasters and HIV/AIDS and other adult disabilities (Figure 41.1).

For each of these groups, the principal causes of under- and malnutrition, the approximate size of each group and its geographical concentration were estimated. This suggested that about half of the hungry are in low-income farm households, mainly in high-risk production environments; about 22 per cent are rural landless and low-income non-farm households, mainly in higher-potential agricultural regions; about 20 per cent are urban households and some 8 per cent are herders, fishermen and forest-dependent households relying on community or public resources. This suggested that on a global basis, according to these estimates, 80 per cent of the undernourished population of developing countries live in rural areas.

While these classifications provide a broad indication of who, and where, the hungry poor are on a global scale, they are of limited value in operational terms. At the 1996 *World Food Summit*, it was agreed to establish *Food Insecurity and Vulnerability Information and Mapping Systems* (FIVIMS) in order to identify groups and households particularly vulnerable to food insecurity along with the reasons for their food insecurity (FAO, 1996). FAO was requested to provide the technical secretariat for FIVIMS on behalf of an inter-agency working group comprising over 25 members from bilateral and multilateral organizations, international NGOs and regional organizations (FAO, 2000a). WFP is a close collaborator in FIVIMS with its *Vulnerability Analysis and Mapping* (VAM) created in 1994 (WFP, 2004). While FIVIMS provides guidance on norms and standards for use by national information and mapping systems, VAM supports the application of these common approaches at the country level. The common objective is to identify who are food insecure or vulnerable to food insecurity, why are they so, and where they live.

Hunger and malnutrition inflict heavy costs on individuals, households, communities and nations (FAO, 2004). Undernourishment and deficiencies in

Figure 41.1 A classification of hungry people

Food-insecure classes	Principal causes of hunger/malnutrition	Percentage of undernourished	Geographic 'hotspots' of hunger
Low-income farm households	Increased production pressure on low-productivity, high-risk or degraded lands; remoteness from markets; poor market institutions	50% of total (400 million)	Dry lands: Sahel, southern Africa, South Asia, NE Brazil; mountains: Mesoamerica, Andes, E Africa, Himalayas, SE Asia
Rural landless and low income non-farm households	Inadequate income; weak social networks; lack of access to productive resources; lack of employment	22% of total (176 million)	Asia, Central America
Low-income urban households	Inadequate income to purchase food; weak social networks, low productivity, wages	20% of total (160 million)	China, India, Zambia
Poor herders, fishers, forest people dependent on community or public resources	Pressure on natural resources; pollution; disruption of resource flows; loss of local rights	8% of total (64 million)	Dry lands: Africa, lowland Asia; forest regions or Amazonia, Himalayas, SE Asia
Cross-cutting above groups			
Pregnant and lactating women	Added dietary needs for pregnancy and breastfeeding, inadequate food and micro-nutrient intake	Several hundred million	South Central Asia, SE Asia
Newborn infants	Inadequate foetal nutrition due to maternal malnutrition	30 million	South Central Asia, SE Asia
Children under five years	Inadequate child care, poor feeding practices, infectious disease, poor water, low status of women	150 million	South Central Asia, SE Asia, East Africa, West Africa
Micro-nutrient-deficient individuals	Teenage girls and women (iron); nutrient-deficient diets/soils; lack of sunlight; lack of protein, fruit, vegetables	2 billion	Widely distributed
Victims of extreme events (natural disasters, war and civil conflict)	Disruption of food systems, loss of assets; aid not delivered, low farm investment	60 million	Recent victims in Sahel, Horn of Africa, Southern Africa
HIV/AIDS and other adult disabilities	Inability to produce or access food; increased dependency ratio; depleted social networks	36 million infected	Sub-Saharan Africa, but moving to Asia

Source: Adapted from Task Force Hunger (2005): Kracht (2005).

essential minerals and vitamins are said to cost the lives of more than 5 million children every year. Households in the developing world lose more than 200 million years of productive life of family members whose lives are cut short or impaired by disabilities related to malnutrition. Developing countries lose billions of income in lost productivity and consumption. Every year, more than 20 million low birth-weight (LBW) babies are born in the developing world. From the moment of birth, the scales are tipped against them in a 'vicious cycle of deprivation'. The risk of neonatal death is four times higher in infants weighing less than 2.5 kg and 18 times higher for those who weigh less than 2.0 kg. Almost one-third of all children in developing countries are stunted. The damage to physical and cognitive development is usually irreversible. The costs in blighted health and opportunities extend not only throughout the victim's life but also on to the next generation, as mothers give birth to LBW babies. WHO estimates that more than 3.7 million deaths in 2000 could be attributed to underweight. And deficiencies in the three micro-nutrients, iron, vitamin A and zinc, each caused an additional 750,000–850,000 deaths.

Childhood poverty and malnutrition has been found to portend high costs in adult life. Children who grow up poor and malnourished can cost the country in which they live because as adults they are less productive, earn less, have more health-related expenses and may resort to crime as members of a marginalized underclass. This indicates that investing resources in poverty reduction is more cost effective than generally thought. One measure used to quantify the impact of malnutrition on both poor health and increased mortality is called 'disability-adjusted life years' (DALYs), the sum of years lost as a result of both premature death and disabilities, adjusted for severity. A *Global Burden of Disease Study*, sponsored by WHO and the World Bank, ranks being underweight as the single most significant risk factor for DALYs worldwide and for both death and DALYs in the group of high-mortality developing countries. This group includes almost 70 countries with a combined population of more than 2.3 billion people. Overall, childhood and maternal undernutrition are estimated to cost more than 220 million DALYs in developing countries. When other nutrition-related risk factors are taken into account, the toll rises to almost 340 million DALYs, representing a loss of productivity equivalent to having a disaster kill or disable the entire population of a country larger than the United States.

While the human cost of hunger is morally unacceptable, the economic costs of hunger are unaffordable, not only for the individuals concerned but also for the economic development and prosperity of the nations in which they live. The costs of hunger come in several distinct forms. The direct medical expenditure of treatment throughout the developing world is estimated at around $30 billion a year. These direct costs are dwarfed by indirect costs of low productivity and income caused by premature death, disability, absenteeism and lower educational and occupational opportunities. Provisional estimates suggest that these indirect costs range in the hundreds of billions of dollars.

Coming at the costs of hunger from another direction, FAO conducted a macro economic study to estimate the benefits of reducing undernourishment by an amount sufficient to meet the WFS and MDG targets of reducing the number and proportion of hungry people by half by 2015. The study estimated the value of increased production that would be unleashed if the target were met. Based only on increased life expectancy, the total discounted value over the years up to 2015 was estimated at about $3 trillion, which translates into an annuity benefit of $120 billion a year. The FAO study recognizes that the calculation underestimates the true costs of hunger. However, it also estimated that an increase of $24 billion a year in public investment, associated with additional private investment, would make it possible to attain the WFS and MDG targets. This would boost GDP by $120 billion a year as a result of longer and healthier lives. The FAO director-general found the costs of not taking action to reduce hunger worldwide as 'staggering' and the costs of interventions that could sharply reduce hunger as 'trivial' by comparison. As he put it: 'the question is not whether we can afford to take urgent and immediate action needed to reach and surpass the WFS goal. The question is whether was can afford not to. And the answer is an emphatic, resounding no' (FAO, 2004).

The *Fifth Report on the World Nutrition Situation* by the UN Standing Committee on Nutrition (SCN) underlines that *food and nutrition security* are not the same (SCN, 2004).[3] Nutrition is both the outcome and the process of providing the nutrients needed for health, growth, development and survival. Although food as a source of these nutrients is an important part of this process, it is not by itself sufficient. Other necessary inputs include good caring practices and health services. The report also outlines how reducing malnutrition is central to achieving the MDGs. It also makes the case for recognizing nutritional status as a key MDG indicator of poverty and hunger as an important first step in recognizing that measures to improve nutrition have a role to play in global development. Improving nutrition can accelerate improvements in other development objectives. For example, the MDG of universal primary education (UPE) is set back as malnourished children are less likely to enrol in school, or more likely to enrol later, and hunger and malnutrition reduced mental capacity and school performance. In achieving the MDG of promoting gender equality and the empowerment of women, better-nourished girls are more likely to stay in school and to have more control over future choices.

The MDG of reducing child mortality is confronted by the fact that malnutrition is directly or indirectly associated with more than half of all child mortality and that malnutrition is the main contributor to the burden of disease in the developing world. An anti-female bias in the allocation of food, health and care compromises the MDG of improving maternal health: malnutrition is associated with most risk factors in maternal mortality. And malnutrition hastens the onset of AIDS among the HIV-positive and weakens resistance to infection and reduces survival rates, thereby confronting the MDG of halting and reversing the spread of HIV/AIDS, malaria and other major diseases.

In these and many other ways, improving nutrition can help the attainment of other development objectives. But this will require greater awareness of the substantive links involved, which will call for a readiness and capacity of nutrition professionals to engage with broader development processes.

398 *Assessment. The Graveyard of Aspirations*

The perspective of world food insecurity as it affects children, the most vulnerable group, has been portrayed through the annual publication of UNICEF's *State of the World's Children*. The publication for 2005 gives a relentless account of how nearly half of the two billion children throughout the world are robbed of their childhood through the triple, and often interrelated, realities of poverty, armed conflict and HIV/AIDS (UNICEF, 2005). Drawing on an empirical study commissioned by UNICEF, the report looks at how poverty affects children in the developing world through what is called 'severe deprivation' on seven areas. Over 16 per cent of children under five suffer from 'nutrition deprivation' and are severely malnourished. Most of them already had low weight at birth, many are anaemic, weak and vulnerable to disease, and some have learning problems, if they ever go to school, resulting in the chilling prospect that they will probably remain among the poorest of the poor throughout their lives. About 400 million children, on average one in five children, have 'water deprivation', with no access to safe water. One in three children, a total of over 500 million children, has no access to sanitation facilities and suffers from 'sanitation deprivation'. Around 270 million children, about 14 per cent, have 'health deprivation', with no access to health care services. Over 640 million children experience 'shelter deprivation', with inadequate housing. Over 140 million children, 13 per cent of those between seven and eighteen years of age, have 'education deprivation' in that they have never attended school. And over 300 million children have 'information deprivation', lacking access to television, radio, telephone or newspapers. Over one billion children, more than half the child population in the developing countries, suffer from at least one of these forms of severe deprivation. About 700 million children suffer from two or more forms of deprivation. The fact that every second child is deprived of even the minimum opportunities of life is correctly described as 'alarming'.

Deprivation in one aspect often accentuates deprivations in other areas, with compounding effect. Children in rural areas are more exposed to extreme forms of deprivation. Severe deprivation among children is not confined to low-income countries. Many children in extreme poverty live in countries with fairly high levels of national income. Gender discrimination is an underlying factor of severe deprivation. Poverty denies children safety, dignity and protection. Material deprivation exposes children to exploitation and abuse. Child protection abuses reinforce the generational cycle of poverty. Families form the first line of defence for children. The further they are from their families, the more vulnerable they are. Strategies for tackling child deprivation include: harnessing globalization and economic growth for children's benefits; promoting local solutions and participatory planning for development; strengthening the protective environment for children and involving children themselves in helping to understand what child poverty means. Reaching the MDGs would go a long way to reducing the material poverty that children experience in developing countries. Protecting childhood from poverty is a global as well as a national responsibility. Interventions that address child deprivation need to be designed and owned locally, with families and children part of the solution. And strengthening the protective environment is essential for children at every level.

But as if poverty were not enough, the UNICEF 2005 report shows how poverty is accentuated by two other threats to childhood in the developing world. Armed conflict and violence rob children of a secure family life. The nature and complexity of warfare have changed in recent years. Between 1990 and 2003, there were 59 major armed conflicts in 48 locations: four involved war between states, 55 occurred within nations. An estimated 90 per cent of global conflict-related deaths since 1990 have been of civilians, and 80 per cent of these have been of women and children. Many of the victims suffer from the catastrophic impact of conflict on the health of the entire society. Many developing countries are locked in a vicious cycle in which poverty generates the desperation, fear and struggle for resources that can lead to conflict, which in turn aggravates poverty that can continue from one generation to the next. Of the world's 20 poorest countries, 16 have suffered a major civil war in the past fifteen years.

Conflict impacts childhood in many direct and indirect ways. During the 1990s, some 20 million children were forced by conflict or human rights violations to leave their homes and join the growing numbers of refugees and internally displaced persons. Many children were conscripted, kidnapped or pressured into joining armed groups or gangs. Many were orphaned, abducted, raped or left with emotional scars and psychological trauma from exposure to violence, poverty or loss of family members, relatives and other loved ones. But as if poverty and armed conflict were not enough to destroy childhood, a third major threat has been the spread of HIV/AIDS.

Children do not have to have HIV/AIDS to be devastated by it, although many have contracted the disease, or been born with it. When HIV/AIDS enters a household by infecting one or both parents, the UNICEF report describes how 'the very fabric of a child's life falls apart'. The statistics are numbing. By 2003, 15 million children under the age of 18 had been orphaned by HIV/AIDS, eight out of 10 of them in sub-Saharan Africa. It is estimated that by 2010 over 18 million African children will have lost one or both parents. Millions more live in households with sick and dying family members and also suffer the pernicious effects of HIV/AIDS. The compounded effects are awesome. Families and communities feel the strain. Women take on the greater burden of care. Children are increasingly forced to head households, which deprive them of their education and rights and deepens child poverty. And children orphaned or made more vulnerable to HIV/AIDS are more exposed to exploitation, abuse and violence.

The UNICEF report advocates a human rights-based approach to development in combating the threats that children face. In a contribution to the report, Joseph Stiglitz, winner of the Nobel Prize in Economics and former Chief Economist and Senior Vice-President of the World Bank, now a professor at Columbia University in New York, states: 'What makes the poverty children experience so appalling is that it would cost very little to do something about it'. He quotes the average cost of educating a child in developing countries at about $40 and of achieving UPE by 2015, one of the MDGs, at about £9.1 billion annually or less than $100 billion over the next ten years. To put this in perspective, he quotes global defence spending in 2003 at over $956 billion ($879 billion at constant 2000 prices and

400 *Assessment. The Graveyard of Aspirations*

exchange rates) (SIPRI, 2004). And he estimates that a one per cent reduction in annual global military spending could provide primary education for all children around the world. He finds the disparity in health no less glaring and expresses the view that the world could easily meet the expenses of basic health care for the least-developed countries 'if it is willing'. He calculates the average yearly cost of servicing sub-Saharan Africa's external debt at roughly $80 per household, almost half the average amount ($173) each family spends on health and education combined. He therefore argues that faster and deeper debt-service relief for the poorest countries could free up additional resources for social expenditure, which would go a long way towards ameliorating poverty. Similarly, he notes that UNICEF's projected cost of immunizing children for the whole of 2004 is about $187 million, about 0.2 per cent of global military expenditure. He concludes: 'Lack of resources is not, and cannot be, an excuse'. And the eradication of poverty among children is not simply a matter of self-interest. It is a question of what is 'morally right'.

UNICEF and the World Bank joined forces to provide a perspective on global efforts to address malnutrition and to evaluate how the two organizations could contribute to overcoming it (Gillespie *et al.*, 2003).[4] According to the joint study, global nutrition has improved in the past decade, but 'slowly and unevenly'. It was estimated that worldwide more than 180 million children under the age of five (nearly one in three) were stunted. Malnutrition, implicated in half of all child deaths, also caused considerable illness and cognitive under-development. UNICEF had identified 23 developing countries where more than 30 per cent of children under five were moderately or severely underweight (UNICEF, 2004). About one billion adults in developing countries were under-weight; an estimated 1.6 billion were anaemic. They suffered from lower resist-ance to infection, impaired work capacity and reduced economic productivity. As growing evidence demonstrated, foetal malnutrition threatened survival, growth and development in childhood, and increased the risk of chronic diseases in later life. That was why, the joint study concluded, that the MDGs could not be reached without 'significant progress in eliminating malnutrition'. And yet, the joint assessment found, the prospects for eliminating malnutrition were 'grim'.

Seven key findings emerged from the joint assessment. First, nutrition was improving only slowly in some regions but stagnant in others. Second, nutrition was 'sidelined' in poverty agendas despite its potential to improve health, mental development and productivity. Third, while nutrition professionals broadly agreed on key interventions, and on success factors for implementation, this was not reflected in action. Fourth, few large-scale programmes were rigorously monitored and evaluated. Fifth, inadequate capacity to tackle malnutrition was a major factor limiting progress towards poverty reduction. Sixth, per capita spending on nutrition was generally low and poorly targeted. And finally, better collaboration between the two organizations, and with numerous other agencies involved in combating malnutrition, could strengthen nutrition action.

A five-point action programme was recommended to apply known solutions with the intensity needed to eliminate nutrition deprivation: position nutrition

Dimensions of Poverty and Food Insecurity 401

squarely on the poverty and human development policy agenda, ensure that large-scale actions incorporate best practices, use information systematically for decision-making at all levels, develop the capacity to address malnutrition and increase financing for effective nutrition-relevant actions. Each dimension of the programme was described as an entry point. Local conditions and existing capacity may favour one entry point over another, but for maximum impact all five dimensions needed action.

The joint assessment concluded that UNICEF and the World Bank have complementary approaches. In partnership with countries and other agencies, it was recommended that both organizations should together 'jump start' a global effort to eliminate nutritional deprivation 'one and for all'. It was frankly admitted that while UNICEF had shown an ability to mobilize resources around nutritional issues, particularly in breastfeeding and micro-nutrient programmes, it had been less successful in mobilizing resources for a broad-based effort to tackle overarching nutritional concerns. Similarly, while the World Bank investments had focused on integrated community-based programmes, emphasizing micro-nutrient interventions and better feeding and care of infants, they had been limited to too few countries, and the volume of resources and number of staff assigned to work on nutrition issues were small. (Only about 10 per cent of the Bank's lending in the health, nutrition and population sector was said to be allocated to nutrition operations.)

In many ways, the UNICEF–World Bank relationship represented a microcosm of the problems inherent in trying to establish coherent and complementary actions among the numerous organizations and agencies involved in addressing malnutrition and nutritional concerns. While both organizations shared a common vision for nutrition, they differed significantly on processes and institutional means. It was suggested that potential complementarities could be realized by allying UNICEF's country-level grassroots presence, technical expertise and operational knowledge with the Bank's greater convening power and rigour of evaluation. UNICEF supported country programmes and directly advocated policy change. The World Bank used analytical work and the project approach to influence policy at the macro-level. Both approaches were needed that strongly supported each other. In order to tackle malnutrition seriously, it was recommended that both organizations should consider a special joint initiative to reach the goals and targets established at the *World Summit for Children* in 1990 and the *UN Millennium Summit* in 2000. Both organizations recognized that: 'Nutrition has been sidelines for too long. The time to act is now'.

There is another factor, rarely mentioned in official publications of international organizations, that was highlighted in Peter Griffiths' *The Economist's Tale* (Griffiths, 2003).[5] His book is a diary of four months working in Sierra Leone as an interface between the government and the World Bank. He witnessed at first hand the pressures put on civil servants, politicians, aid workers, consultants and World Bank officials in a food crisis that could have developed into a full-blown famine. He described how the World Bank, obsessed with the free market and the prescriptions of the Washington Consensus, imposed a secret agreement banning

402 *Assessment. The Graveyard of Aspirations*

all government food imports and subsidies as part of an economic structural adjustment programme. The collapsing economy meant that the private sector would not import. Famine loomed. No ministry or state marketing organization official could change the agreement. It had to be a top-level government decision whether Sierra Leone would stand against the World Bank's judgement.

Those who have worked in developing countries will be very familiar with Griffiths' account of the interaction between government officials and aid workers, discussions within the expatriate community and corruption in high places. They will have observed the power of the World Bank not only as a major source of external assistance but also as the co-ordinator of much of the aid provided by donor countries, and its prescribed solutions to developing country problems made in Washington, DC rather than on the basis of careful investigation in the field. This often led to what has been called 'asymmetric information', where one side (the World Bank) in a transaction has different perceptions from the other (a developing country), which distorts market signals and produces market failures. In Griffiths' view, it is individuals who cause poverty, underdevelopment and famine by their actions, or their failure to act, and by their failure to speak up. From his experience, he found some individuals incompetent, or dishonest, while others were 'downright evil'. Some are pressed to be so by their employers, families or society. Others tolerate this because they are afraid of losing their jobs or worse. He concludes that workers in the aid industry have to bow to pressure from clients, consultancy forms, donor organizations and the whole aid system if they are to continue to work in aid. In his view, unless the aid industry tackles this problem, 'it will achieve as little in the future as it did in the past'. Griffiths account will no doubt be controversial and dismissed as unrepresentative of the general situation, but there is more than a little reality in what his experience reveals.

Another book is welcome for providing a new scientific and comprehensive study of disease-related malnutrition in which the causes, consequences and prevalence of disease-related malnutrition and the results of numerous studies that demonstrate the benefits of nutritional support (Stratton, Green and Elia, 2003). The consequences of disease-related malnutrition are numerous, including shorter survival rates, lower functional capacity, longer treatment, greater complications and higher costs. Nutritional support in the form of nutritional supplements lead to an improvement in patient outcomes. It would be particularly useful if a practical field manual could be produced, based on the book's findings, for government and aid officials working in the forefront of the attack on hunger and malnutrition.

IFPRI has continued its major contributions to both an understanding of the causes of world food insecurity and their solution through its *2020 Vision* programme under a new director-general, Joachim von Braun, on the retirement of Per Pinstrup-Andersen in 2003.[6] The institute has identified nine 'driving forces' that it regards as 'critical' in efforts to achieve its *2020 Vision*: accelerating globalization and further trade liberalization, sweeping technological changes, degradation of natural resources and increasing water scarcity, health and nutrition crises, rapid urbanization, the changing nature of farming in developing countries with small-scale family farms under threat, continued conflict, climate change and changing roles and responsibilities of key actors, especially local governments, business and industry and NGOs, as national governments played new and diminished roles (IFPRI, 2002). IFPRI has also emphasized that rapid economic growth is essential to achieve sustainable food security for all by 2020 but the challenge is to achieve that growth in a way that benefited the poor through what was called 'pro-poor economic growth'. This kind of growth, together with empowerment of the poor and effective provision of public goods and services, would be the 'foundation' of any successful attempt to achieve IFPRI's *2020 Vision*. The specific and most appropriate policies and priorities would vary according to local and national circumstances. In IFPRI's view, these would be: investing in human resources; improving access to productive resources and remunerative employment; improving market, infrastructure and institutions; expanding appropriate research, knowledge and technology; improving natural resource management; good governance and pro-poor national and international trade and macroeconomic policies.

The themes from IFPRI's *2020 Vision* were 'extended and deepened' in a book on *Ending Hunger in our Lifetime* that the institute published in 2003 (Ringe *et al.*, 2003). In their foreword to the book, IFPRI's director-general, Joachim Von Braun, and the president of the non-denominational NGO, Bread for the World, David Beckmann, wrote:

> Hunger, and the misery that accompanies it, have been scourges for millennia. But in a global society, increasing interconnected communities can no longer conjure [up] excuses for failing to banish the chronic, recurring, hunger-related crises affecting their neighbors. In fact, the global community stands indicted for knowing much about how to reduce hunger, but not doing so. In this context, 'business as usual' takes on a distinctly unethical meaning, describing as it does a global effort falling far short of ending hunger anytime soon, even by 2050. . . . No one can pretend that ending hunger will be easy, but it *must* and can be done (original emphasis).

As they point out, the book presents a wide-ranging array of ideas, arguments, facts and figures on ending hunger and complements the work of IFPRI's *2020 Vision* initiative. One of its main themes is that global peace and stability can only be achieved by ending the deprivation of the world's poor. The authors' predict that the WFS goal of halving the world's hungry by 2015 'will almost certainly not be reached'. However, their analysis shows that global hunger could be substantially reduced by 2025 and chronic mass hunger ended by 2050. They point out that this is no more ambitious than the near-elimination of the many infectious diseases that stalked the world a century ago. But they recognize that unlike vaccination against diseases, food insecurity will need a larger set of changes if it is to be eradicated, including: institutional reforms in trade policies; the rehabilitation and renewal of commitments to multilateral aid; significant reforms in natural resource management and major new investment in agricultural science

404 *Assessment. The Graveyard of Aspirations*

and technology. They believe that while national governments will play a central role in facilitating these changes, part of the burden will fall on the private sector, NGOs and civil society, and that broad international co-operation among rich and poor countries will be essential if the fight against hunger, misery and discontent is to succeed.

The authors acknowledge that some improvements have taken place. Some developing countries have substantially improved the education, health and nutrition of their people. Investments in agriculture have shifted to focus on small peasant farmers, improved irrigation, rural roads, electricity and agricultural research and education. Yields of staple crops have increased. But without major changes in more countries, progress against poverty and hunger will be 'too slow to win the fight'. The authors observe that the ways of improving poverty, health and food security are closely interconnected, and so co-operation should be strengthened among the various international agencies involved. (Seventeen bilateral agencies, multilateral organizations and NGOs said to be 'striving to end hunger' are listed in an appendix in the book, which might have been doubled in number.) They call for: reform of the World Bank to support pro-poor growth and to shift its resources towards grants for the poorest countries and poorest segments of the populations of middle-income countries; expanded roles for FAO and WHO; an effective organization to address international environmental issues; the same standards of accountability, transparency and legitimacy for NGOs that they seek to impose on international organizations; and increase in the efficiency of the global food distribution system; a fair and just involvement of developing countries in the international market economy and much greater foreign assistance.

The book ends with a quotation from Amartya Sen, winner of 1998 Nobel Prize in Economics:

> The contemporary age is not short of terrible and nasty happenings, but the persistence of extensive hunger in a world of unprecedented prosperity is surely one of the worst.... [M]assive endemic hunger causes misery in many parts of the world – debilitating hundreds of millions and killing a sizable proportion of them with statistical regularity. What makes this widespread hunger even more of a tragedy is the way we have come to accept and tolerate it as an integral part of the modern world, as if it is a tragedy that is essentially unpreventable.
> (Sen, 1999, p. 204)

echoing the thoughts of C. P. Snow (1968).

IFPRI's annual report for 2003–04 begins with an essay on 'Agriculture, Food Security, Nutrition and the Millennium Development Goals', which makes a strong case for the central importance of food and nutrition security in attaining the MDGs (IFPRI, 2004b).[7] The most effective strategy for making steady, sustainable progress to the attainment of the MDGs is said to serve all the goals in an integrated way and that each goal should have a well-defined package of technologies at the field level. Environmentally friendly agriculture and rural development are regarded as key to achieve faster, sustainable human and economic development, which is needed to achieve all the MDGs. Concerning the MDG of eradicating extreme hunger and poverty, it is pointed out that it is necessary to have an understanding of the ways in which these two 'injustices' interconnect. The essay shows the strong direct relationships between agricultural productivity, hunger and poverty. By increasing food availability and incomes, and contributing to asset diversity and economic growth, higher agricultural productivity and supportive pro-poor policies allow people to break out of the poverty–hunger–malnutrition trap. IFPRI's global food model is used, which assumes that investment in five areas (rural road construction, education, clean water provision, agricultural research and irrigation) is the most effective way to reduce malnutrition, hunger and poverty. In this way, it is estimated that reaching the MDG of halving child malnutrition would cost $161 billion, about $16 billion a year more than current expenditures.

A three-pronged strategy is advocated to achieve the MDG of UPE: food for children in school, incentives (food or cash) for parents, and support services (such as crèches) for working mothers and improvements in agricultural productivity and market functioning to assure adequate food supply and access. Regarding the MDG of promoting gender equality and empowering women, it is observed that many women are farmers who depend on agriculture to secure food and income for their families. Improvements in agriculture and access to services, such as labour-saving technology, finance and credit, and legal and economic rights, could contribute both to increasing incomes and to empowering women economically and boost agricultural productivity further.

The links between agricultural improvement and the MDG of reducing child mortality and improving maternal health are also shown. Improving food and nutrition security for poor households with the help of agriculture and ensuring that households allocate food equitably are crucial steps. To attain the MDG of disease control, the resources of the agricultural sector need to be co-ordinated with those of the health sector to meet the joint challenges of poverty reduction and disease eradication. A productive agricultural sector can reduce pressures on the environment and assist in meeting the MDGs relating to sustainable development but this outcome is not automatic. Food and nutrition insecure people generally tried to safeguard their environments but often fail because of lack of resources and the capacity to organize the needed collective action at the local level. It is acknowledged that wrestling with the problems of development will require countries to work together at the regional and global levels. Creation of what is called a 'global partnership for development' will require increased commitments in the pursuit of pro-poor growth. Policy actions that improve agricultural productivity and food and nutrition security are regarded as essential components of a successful MDG strategy.

IFPRI's director-general notes 'with dismay that there is slow progress against hunger in 2003/2004' (IFPRI, 2004b). At the same time, he is encouraged by political leaders' broader recognition of the hunger problem and by some action initiatives around the world based on a new understanding of the importance of agricultural and rural growth and good nutrition and health for development. He notes that demand for IFPRI's work is changing and growing. IFPRI's annual report outlines a number of changes in the institution, including: the integration of the International Service for Agricultural Research (ISNAR) into IFPRI; major new funding for the expansion of its HarvestPlus programme, which aims to combat the scourge of 'hidden hunger', the inadequate level of micro-nutrients that afflicts over 2 billion people, and greater decentralization of its operations through the establishment of offices in Addis Ababa, New Delhi and Costa Rica to bring its work closer to the people whom IFPRI researchers study and serve and with whom they collaborate.

A major undertaking in 2004 was an all-Africa conference organized by IFPRI as part of its *2020 Vision* programme on 'Assuring Food and Nutrition Security in Africa by 2020: Prioritizing Actions, Strengthening Actors, and Financing Partnerships'. To assure its relevance, impact and follow-up, the conference, which was held in Kampala, Uganda, was designed in close consultation with key partners and actor in Africa (IFPRI, 2004a). In June 2000, the G8 summit of leading industrialized countries pledged support for IFPRI's 'Strategic Analysis and Knowledge Support Systems' for agricultural and market analysis in Africa as part of an overall strategy to end the cycle of famine, raise agricultural productivity and promote rural development.

The report of the Task Force Hunger, an independent group of experts who formed one of the 13 task forces that carried out the analytical work for the *UN Millennium Project* commissioned by the UN secretary-general (see below), concluded that 'hunger can be halved by 2015 and eventually eradicated from our planet' (Task Force Hunger, 2005). In its opinion, that goal is well within the reach of human capabilities but, the task force stress, will require focused and unprecedented levels of effort by all involved. While progress in reducing hunger is acknowledged, this has not been done quickly or broadly enough. The task force does not propose a stand-alone strategy for fighting hunger. Instead, a plan is set forth that forms part of a larger effort to address all the MDGs simultaneously. At the global level, the task force recommends moving from the political commitment to end hunger, which has repeatedly been made, to effective action.

The key message for political leaders is that halving world hunger is 'well within our means'. But if that goal is to be met, governments in developed countries must increase and improve their Official Development Assistance (ODA), especially for agriculture and nutrition, and increase attention given to capacity-building in the developing countries. At the national level, government policies can make or break efforts to end hunger, and good governance (including the rule of law, removing corruption and respect for human rights) was essential for promoting food security. Five recommendations are made for community-level interventions: increasing agricultural productivity among food-insecure farmers; improving nutrition for the chronically hungry and vulnerable; reducing the vulnerability of the acutely hungry through productive safety nets; increasing incomes and making markets work for the poor; and restoring and conserving the natural resources essential for food security. Within these five broad recommendations, the task force identifies

40 proposed interventions. It is recognized that not every intervention will be appropriate to every country and locality. An important step would be to identify the priority interventions for the local conditions that prevail.

An alternative, controversial and less-optimistic view of the state of world food and nutrition security is given by Lester Brown, president of the Earth Policy Institute, an independent environmental research organization he founded in 2001. He presents the case for redefining world food security by pointing out that for 40 years international trade negotiations were dominated by the main grain-exporting countries but now the world may be moving into a period dominated not by food surpluses but by shortages (Brown, 2004). If this were to happen, as Brown puts it, the issue becomes not exporters' access to markets but importers' access to supplies, in what he calls 'the politics of food scarcity'. He considers that the big test of the international community's capacity to manage scarcity may come when China turns to the world market for massive imports of grain every year, demand on a scale that could quickly overwhelm world grain markets.

In a previous publication, Brown predicted rapid industrialization, urbanization, loss of cropland, increasing population and incomes, and diminishing water supplies will override the rise in land productivity, leading to a decline in grain production, increasing demand for a variety of foods, particularly meat, dairy produce and other grain-dependent goods and a sharp rise in import demand. The result has been to turn China abruptly from an exporter to a net importer of grain and other foodstuffs. So, he raised the question, 'who will feed China?' (Brown, 1997). Given the size of China's population, he projects that grain imports could have a major impact on world grain trade and prices, which could seriously affect poor, food-deficit countries, and world food security. When this happens, China will have to look to the United States, which controls nearly half the world's grain exports. He paints what he calls 'fascinating geopolitical situation': 1.3 billion Chinese consumers, who have a $120 billion trade surplus with the US, will compete with Americans for US grains, driving up food prices. In such a situation thirty years ago, the United States would have simply restricted exports; today, however, it has a stake in a politically stable China. The Chinese economy is not only the engine powering the Asian economy, but also the only large economy worldwide that has 'maintained a full head of steam in recent years'. Furthermore, the risk is that China's entry into the world market on a massive scale will drive grain prices so high that many low-income developing countries will not be able to import the grain they need. Opposite views have been expressed (Rosegrant *et al.*, 1997) and an optimistic view presented that China's foresight in dealing with the up-coming challenge will likely determine whether the production–demand gap turns into a major crisis or becomes an opportunity to more effectively develop the nation's food economy, including producing food abroad in countries with land capacity, such as Brazil and Sudan (Riches, 1997). However, the merit of Brown's work is that it has drawn attention to one of the major threats to future world food security and has provoked a respond (Shaw, 1997a).

408 *Assessment. The Graveyard of Aspirations*

Brown takes his argument further. He notes that because the last half-century has been dominated by excessive production and market surpluses, the world has little experience in dealing with 'the politics of scarcity', apart from a brief period in the early 1970s, which resulted in the 1974 World Food Conference. He argues that as surpluses are replaced by scarcity, more attention will need to be paid to carryover grain stocks. In his view, one reason why food shortages do not get the attention they once did is because famine, in effect, has been redefined. Given the growing integration of the world grain economy, and today's capacity to move grain around the world, he notes that famine is concentrated less in specific geographical regions and much more among low-income groups. In his opinion, this is likely to increase as scarcity drives up prices. Thus, in his opinion, future food security will depend on stabilizing four agricultural resources: cropland, water, rangeland and the earth's climate system. This poses a more complex challenge, as the world today faces a situation far different from that of half a century ago. Brown notes that diminishing returns are setting in on several fronts, including the quality of new land that can be brought into production, the production response to additional fertilizer applications, the opportunity for drilling new irrigation wells, and the potential of research investments to produce technologies that will boost production dramatically.

Ensuring future food security can, in Brown's view, no longer be left to ministries of agriculture alone, if it ever could, but will depend on an integrated effort of several government departments, echoing the news he expressed during the 1974 World Food Conference. And strong national political leadership will be essential, without which 'deterioration in the food situation may be unavoidable'. Similarly, he calls for better integration among the international agencies concerned with global food security. He concludes that in a world that is increasingly integrated economically, food security is now a global issue that gets little attention in the UN Security Council or at the G8 summit meetings. He reasons that everyone has a stake in securing future food supplies but the complexity of the challenge is matched by the enormity of the effort required to reverse trends that are undermining future food security. In addition, he observes, we have inherited 'the mindset, policies, and fiscal priorities from an era of food security that no longer exists'. Moreover, unless we recognize the nature of the era we are entering and adopt new policies and priorities, world food security could begin to deteriorate and 'quickly eclipse terrorism as the overriding concern of governments'. Many will take issue with Brown's views and perspectives but they amount to a wakeup call that should not be ignored (Shaw, 2005b).

The focus of this book is on food insecurity in the developing world where most of the hungry and malnourished live. But hunger and absolute poverty re-emerged as a significant social issue in many rich industrialized countries during the 1980s and 1990s (Riches, 1997). In Canada, 2.5 million people a year were said to receive food from chartable food banks in the 1990s. In the United States, it was estimated that 35 million people could not afford to buy enough food to maintain good health, including 13 million children. And in Australia and New Zealand, food banks have proliferated in recent years. These are small numbers when compared with the millions of hungry poor throughout the developing world. But they stand in stark contract to increasing economic prosperity and common standards of human decency, and violate national and international human rights obligations.

But another phenomenon has emerged that shows the paradox of hunger in a world of plenty in a new and stark light. Obesity, not hunger, has emerged as the killer in the rich industrialized countries and is threatening to invade the Third World as well. No where is this more prevalent than in the United States, although it is quickly taking hold in European countries and elsewhere in the developed world. America has thus become a microcosm of the disparities in the global food and nutrition security situation and other nations in the rich and poor world would do well to take careful note of the consequences (Shaw, 2004b).

The full extent of the obesity crisis in the United States was revealed by Eric Schlosser, an award-winning journalist, in his book *Fast Food Nation* (Schlosser, 2002). He describes in vivid detail the incredible rise of the fast food industry during the last three decades to the point where it has infiltrated every 'nook and cranny' of American society. According to Schlosser, in 1970, Americans spent about $6 billion on fast food; in 2001, they spent more than $110 billion – more than on movies, books, magazines, newspapers, videos and recorded music combined. Schlosser maintains that what people eat is determined by a complex interplay of social, economic and technological forces. He attributes the extraordinary growth in the fast food industry to fundamental changes in American society brought about, among other things, by women entering the workforce in record number (about two-thirds of mothers with young children work outside the home). The result is that more than half of the American adults and about a quarter of all American children are said to be obese or overweight.[8]

Although the rise in obesity has numerous complex causes, Schlosser argues that genetics is not one of them, as the pool of American genetics has not changed radically in the past few decades. What has changed is the nation's way of eating and living. Put simply, when people eat more and move less, they become obese. Americans have become increasingly sedentary and as they eat more meals outside the home, they consume more calories, less fibre and more fat. Another theory is that of the 'thrifty gene' (*The Economist*, 2003). Humans were designed to cope with deprivation, not plenty. They were perfectly tuned to store energy in good years to see them through lean periods. But when the bad times no longer come, they are stuck with that energy, stored around their expanding bellies.

Whatever the cause, Schlosser points out the cost of America's obesity epidemic. Obesity is now second only to smoking as a cause of mortality in the United States. The United States Centers for Disease Control and Prevention (CDC) estimates that about 280,000 Americans die every year as a direct result of being overweight. The annual health care cost in the United States stemming from obesity now approaches $240 billion. In addition, as they are made to become increasingly aware of their increasing bulk through various forms of advertising, Americans spend more than $33 billion on weight-loss schemes and diet products.

410 *Assessment. The Graveyard of Aspirations*

Schlosser proposes a number of ways of attacking the obesity crisis including: legislation banning advertising that preys on children; stopping subsidizing dead-end jobs; tougher food safety laws and intensifying the fight against a dangerous concentration of economic power. But he maintains that the first step towards meaningful change is, in his opinion, by far the easiest: 'stop buying fast food'. This may be easier said than done, as the book by Marion Nestle on *Food Politics* shows (see below) (Nestle, 2003). Nonetheless, as he points out, nobody in the United States is forced to buy fast food. The executives who run the fast food industry will offer whatever sells at a profit. A boycott, refusal to buy, can speak much louder than word.

Marion Nestle, professor and chair of the Department of Nutrition, Food Studies and Public Health at New York University, takes Schlosser's analysis even further by showing the power of politics in an oversupply situation. Her book is an almost clinical examination of how the food industry influences nutrition and health in the United States. She explains that US food supply contains enough to feed everyone in the country nearly twice over, even taking account of exports. Over-abundant supply, combined with an affluent society that can afford to buy more food than is needed, sets the stage for aggressive competition. The food industry must compete fiercely for every dollar spent on food. Food companies therefore expend extraordinary resources to develop and market products that will sell, regardless of their effects on nutrition, weight and health. To satisfy stockholders, they must convince people to eat more of their products instead of those of their competitors. This they do through a labyrinth of means including advertising and public relations and by working tirelessly to convince government officials, nutrition professionals and the media that their products promote health, much of which she describes as a 'virtually invisible part of contemporary culture that attracts only occasional notice'. Nestle exposes the ways the food companies use political processes ('entirely conventional and nearly always legal') to obtain government and professional support for the sale of their products. Her purpose is both to illuminate the extent to which the food industry determines what people eat, and to generate much wider discussion of its marketing methods and use of the political system.

In her 25 years as a nutrition educator, Nestle found that food industry practices were rarely discussed and embedded in a closed political syndrome. Most food company officials maintain that any food product can be included in a balanced, varied and moderate diet, and that their companies are helping to promote good health, when they fund the activities of nutritional professionals. Most agricultural and health officials understand that their federal agencies are headed by political appointees whose concerns reflect those of the political party in power and whose actions must be acceptable to the US Congress. Members of Congress must, in turn, be sensitive to the concerns of corporations that help fund their political campaigns. In this political system, the actions of food companies, through their well-rewarded lobbyists, are regarded as normal, legal and thoroughly analogous to the workings of any other major industry, like tobacco, in influencing health experts, federal agencies and Congress.

Nestle first became aware of the food industry as an influence on government nutrition policies and on the opinions of nutrition experts when she worked for the US Public Health Service and managed the editorial production of the first (and as yet only) *Surgeon General's Report on Nutrition and Health*, which appeared in 1988. This was an ambitious government effort to summarize the entire body of research linking dietary factors to leading chronic diseases. But the ground rules established for writing the report was that there should be no restrictions recommended on any category of food, which in the industry-friendly climate of the time would have prohibited its publication. Political expediency explains why no subsequent report has appeared despite Congress passing a law in 1990 that required such a report to be issued biannually.

Nestle's book examines in detail the process of undermining dietary advice with an historical account of the period 1900 to 1990 during which the message has been transformed from 'eat more' to 'eat less'. She shows how the food industry used lobbyists, lawsuits, financial contributions, public relations, threats and biased information to convince Congress, federal agencies, nutrition and health professionals and the general public that the science relating diet to health was so confusing that they need not worry about diets. She concludes that while nutritionists try to educate the general public that some foods are better than others and to eat less, the actions of food companies add to the confusion and in some ways create it. As she points out, food choices have economic, polit-ical, social and environmental consequences that place health improvements in conflict with other considerations.

Therefore, she asks what should health and nutrition professionals and concerned citizens do to improve the social and political environment in which people make food choices? And how can we make sure that the actions taken are responsible and effective? She draws an analogy from the anti-smoking campaign strategy with its four principle elements – research, message, target and tactics. And she makes proposals in the fields of education, food labelling and advertising, health care and training, transportation and urban development, and taxation to promote better food choices and more active lifestyles. Ultimately, like Schlosser, she believes that 'voting with forks' will be the most effective strategy every time a meal is eaten. But this must be extended beyond the food choices of individuals into the larger political arena. She points out that there are countless community, state and national organizations that could join together when issues of mutual interest emerge and concludes that this ability to exercise democratic power holds hope for achieving a more equitable balance in matters pertaining to food and health.

In many ways, Nestle's sentiments are echoed in other book. Written by the director and consultant at the Yale Center for Eating and Weight Disorders, *Food Fights* described what is called the 'inside story' of the American food industry and the nation's obesity crisis and makes recommendations to overcome it (Brownell and Horgen, 2004). The authors point out that obesity and its associated diseases came 'quickly, with little fanfare'. Most alarming, in their opinion, has been in the national inaction in the face of the crisis, the near total surrender to powerful

412 *Assessment. The Graveyard of Aspirations*

food industry, and the lack of innovation in preventing further deterioration. As they aptly put it: 'big food and big money have led to big people'. They note that the CDC has labelled the obesity problem as an epidemic, with almost two-thirds of people in the United States either overweight or obese, and the increase in overweight children trice that seen in adults. They note that other nations in the developing as well as the developed worlds are following 'in hot pursuit'. The authors feel that it is wrong to blame the global epidemic solely on the spread of the American fast food industry but recognize that revered and hated, American food represents affluence and innovation.

The authors describe in vivid detail what they call the 'toxic environment' in which obesity has flourished – a sedentary lifestyle, lack of physical activity, junk food, soft drinks and oversized meals – all leading to the 'inexorable economic march to obesity'. They call for fundamental changes, including: 'thinking differently' in appreciating that a changing environment has caused the world's obesity epidemic and that that environment is the logical lace to intervene; getting global priorities right in recognizing that over-nutrition now rivals hunger as the world's leading nutrition issue, and learning from the successes of some countries; increasing physical activity; objecting to the 'commercialization of childhood', which treats children as market objects; improving school lunch programmes and showing that healthy eating and activity are connected with academic performance; reducing the size of meals; making the public aware of the powerful economic forces that contribute to obesity; interacting with the food industry; and encouraging political leaders to be bold and innovative in addressing the obesity crisis and removing the political barriers to taking effective action.

The WHO International Task Force on Obesity estimates that 1.3 billion people globally are overweight or obese. A WHO/FAO expert consultation on diet, nutrition and the prevention of chronic diseases has suggested a strategy for dietary changes, including limits on sugar consumption as well as policies that might make it easier for people to eat more healthily. Stricter labelling requirements have been proposed as part of the UN *Cartagena Protocol*, which is meant to prevent biotechnology hazards by giving countries enough information about gene-altered products to help them decide whether to reject imports. Governments, both national and regional, have a role to play. The unbridled activities of the food industry must be curbed in the interest of consumer, with a distinct separation of government responsibility for the promotion of food production from that of its protection of food consumers. Government should insist on clearer food labelling so that consumers can make informed choices. And they have a duty to protect children. Equally, individuals and parent must assume personal responsibility in eating wisely.

It is increasingly being realized that like hunger, obesity must be addressed holistically and not bit by bit like pieces of a jigsaw puzzle that lie scattered and unconnected. Both have personal, national and global consequences that go well beyond their nutritional significance. It would be grotesquely perverse if attention to world hunger and food insecurity were to be diverted by a focus on the obesity epidemic. Both crises must be overcome.

The population dimension

No discussion of world food security is complete without consideration of the population dimension of poverty (Leisinger *et al.*, 2002). It is now generally accepted that the problem of food insecurity can be overcome. As was pointed out earlier, the division of opinion between the optimists and pessimists remains but with an important difference. The division now seems to be over not whether it can be done but whether it will be done: between the optimists of the one-world school and the pessimists of the Malthusian persuasion. The race between the relentless rise of the world's population and the growth of food production can be traced back to biblical times.

The UN Population Division has shown the astonishing growth in the world's population, from the first billion people reached in 1804, to 2 billion in 1927, 3 billion in 1960, 4 billion in 1974, 5 billion in 1987 and 6 billion in 1999 (UN, 2001). The UN projections of future world population growth give three possible trajectories. Under what is called a 'low-fertility' scenario, world population is expected to peak at 7.5 billion by 2040 and then fall to 7.4 billion in 2050. A 'medium-growth' scenario would result in world population reaching 8.9 billion by 2050 and 9.2 billion in 2075. Under the 'high-growth' variant, world population would rise to 10.6 billion by 2050 and to 14 billion by 2099. The latest UN population projections show somewhat lower population growth than previously expected, reflecting lower fertility and higher mortality related to AIDS.

The year 2004 marked the tenth anniversary of the landmark *International Conference on Population and Development* (ICPD), held in Cairo, Egypt in 1994 (see Part III). The conference adopted a wide-ranging twenty-year action plan and agreed to work towards universal access to family planning and reproductive health by 2015 and targets that were incorporated into the MDGs at the *UN Millennium Summit* in 2000. The central premise of the ICPD was that population size, growth, age structure and rural–urban distribution had a critical impact on development prospects and, specifically, on prospects for raising the living standards of the poor, which included improving their food security. Reflecting this understanding, the ICPD called on countries to 'fully integrate population concerns into development strategies, planning, and decision making and resource allocation at all levels'.

A report to mark the tenth anniversary of the ICPD gave the latest population projections of the UN Population Division and prospects for meeting the ICPD goals (UNFPA, 2004). The world's population grew by 76 million people in 2004, 73 million of them in developing countries, to reach 6.5 billion (UN, 2005b). Some 5.2 billion live in the least-developed countries where the population grew 16 times as fast as in the industrialized countries. Six countries accounted for about half the world's population increase: India, with 21 per cent of world population growth; China, 12 per cent; Pakistan, 5 per cent; and Bangladesh, Nigeria and the United States 4 per cent each. According to these latest UN population projections, the population of India will overtake that of China before 2030, earlier than previously expected. The combined populations of developed countries is expected

414 *Assessment. The Graveyard of Aspirations*

to remain virtually unchanged between 2005 and 2050, at about 1.2 billion, less than the populations of either China or India. In contrast, the total population of the least-developed countries is projected to more than double.

The UNFPA report recalled that at the ICPD in 1994, participants pledged to invest a combined $17 billion a year by the turn of the century, rising to $22 billion by 2015 in basic reproductive health services and related activities in developing countries. Developing countries undertook to provide two-thirds of total investment with the remaining one-third coming from external sources. Halfway to 2015, developing countries were said to have met at least 80 per cent of their promised contributions while the wealthier donor countries had only provided half their pledges. Nevertheless, the ICPD has invoked some successes in advancing a human rights agenda to address critical health and development challenges. For example, developing countries have stepped up efforts to fight HIV/AIDS backed up by promises of significant increases in external funding. Adolescent reproductive health is considered to have emerged as a worldwide concern. Early marriage is said to be increasingly opposed as a risk to girls' health and a violation of their rights. The persistence of high maternal mortality has sparked an intensified examination of its causes and remedies. There is growing recognition of, and support for, women's reproductive health needs in emergency situations. And the UN Security Council unanimously adopted a resolution on 'Women, Peace and Security' in October 2000, which called for the incorporation of special needs of women and girls into all decisions related to post-conflict reconstruction.

But the UNFPA report also noted that there was still a long way to go to meet the goals set at the ICPD, and a number of daunting challenges remain. While some progress has been made in maternal and child health programmes, an infant born in Africa is 13 times more likely to die before one year of age than in Europe and the United States. With land and water in limited supply, population growth could have an adverse effect on future environmental and social stability. As people continued to seek better livelihoods, it was predicted that international migration would continue to remain high in the coming decades. About 2 million people a year were moving to the developed regions of the world, principally to the United States, which received an annual net average of 1.1 million immigrants. By 2050, it was estimated that international migration would add up to 55 million for the half century, nearly equal to the population of France. Migration to urban areas was resulting in population growth there about twice as fast as that in the countryside. By 2007, half the world's population was living in urban areas.

Over 350 million couples still lacked access to the full range of reproductive health and family planning services. Some 8 million women a year suffered from life-threatening pregnancy-related complications. Over 529,000 died as a consequence, almost all in developing countries. One-third of all pregnant women received no health care during pregnancy. Meeting the needs of 201 million women without access to a range of effective family planning services was estimated to cost $3.9 billion a year. This could avert 52 million pregnancies, of which about 22 million were ended by induced abortions. The report advocates that the most humane way to achieve low-level population growth was to improve health

Dimensions of Poverty and Food Insecurity 415

and social conditions and promote population stabilization through reduced birth rates, not to allow death rates to climb as a result of negligence. In 2003, some 3 million people died of AIDS, 2.5 million adults and 500,000 children under fifteen years. Five million new cases of HIV infection occurred during 2003, an average of 14,000 a day, 40 per cent of whom were women and nearly 20 per cent children. At the same time, the population was ageing, especially in the developed countries. Between 2005 and 2050, it was projected that the proportion of the world's population aged 65 years and older would double in most developed countries.

The UNFPA report concluded that the ICPD had given practical meaning to human-centred development. Its action programme had acknowledged that investing in people and broadening their opportunities and capabilities was indispensable for achieving sustained economic growth and alleviating poverty. As the world sought to achieve the MDGs, it advocated that political commitment and the dedication of adequate financial and human resources to implementing the ICPD action programme remained of central importance.

The income factor

The level of income has been recognized as a key factor in determining access to adequate essential basic needs, including food. A pivotal MDG is to halve the proportion of the world's population whose income is less than a dollar a day by 2015. The World Bank estimated that in the year 2000, at the start of a new millennium, of the world's 6 billion people, 1.2 billion – one-fifth – lived on less than one dollar a day, and 2.8 billion – almost half – lived on less than two dollars a day (World Bank, 2001). In 2002, the World Bank estimated that, by this standard, there were 200 million fewer poor in the world in 1998 than there were in 1980 (World Bank, 2002). This figure was contested, hence a new study by the Bank's Development Research Group (Chen and Ravallion, 2004). This involved constructing a new, internally consistent, data series over the 1980s and 1990s.

The results of the study give both encouraging and worrying signs. Over the twenty-year period 1981–2001, it was found that the percentage of the population of the developing countries living below a dollar a day almost halved, falling from 40 to 21 per cent. Expressed as a proportion of the world's population, the decline was from 33 to 18 per cent. This assumed that there was nobody living below a dollar a day in the developing world. The number of poor fell by 390 million from 1.5 billion in 1981. There was clearly more progress in some periods than in others. The late 1980s and early 1990s were difficult times for the world's poor, with low economic growth in both China and India, the countries with the largest number of people. Once economic growth was restored, the rate of poverty reduction in the 1990s returned to its long-term trend. The new study's estimates suggest less progress in overcoming the two dollar a day poverty line. The poverty rate by this standard fell from 67 per cent in 1981 to 53 per cent in 2001, insufficient to prevent a rise in the number of people below this standard from 2.4 to 2.7 billion. Thus, the number of people living on between one and two a day was estimated to have risen sharply over the two decades from about one to

416 *Assessment. The Graveyard of Aspirations*

1.6 billion. The conclusion was that the bunching up of poor people just above the dollar a day line suggested that 'a great many people in the world remained vulnerable to aggregate economic slowdowns'.

There have been marked regional differences in the performance against poverty, and notable changes in regional poverty rankings over the twenty-year period, with sub-Saharan Africa replacing East Asia as the region with the highest incidence of extreme poverty (see Table 41.4). The composition of world poverty has also changed noticeably over this period. The number of poor has fallen in Asia but has risen elsewhere. There has been what was described as 'dramatic progress' in East Asia, where the MDG target was said to have been already reached in 2001, with China's progress against absolute poverty a key factor.

While the overall situation reflected in the new World Bank study is regarded as good news, the authors conclude that 'it is no cause for complacency'. While the estimated fall in the number of abjectly poor living on a dollar a day by 390 million over the period 1981–2001 is good news, it should be remembered that this group is still very poor by the standards of middle-income and rich countries. At the same time, the number of people living on under two dollars a day is estimated to have actually risen. Nor has this aggregate progress for the poorest been shared by all regions. In the developing world outside China, the number of abjectly poor is estimated to have risen slightly. The situation in sub-Saharan Africa is particularly worrying. Not only has that region the highest incidence of poverty but the depth of poverty is also markedly higher than in other regions, suggesting that without lower inequality economic growth in Africa, the region will have a harder time reducing poverty in the future than elsewhere. The results of the new study suggest that if maintained over the period 2001–15, the trend rate of decline in the incidence of abject poverty will be sufficient to reach the MDG in only two parts of the developing world, South and East Asia. No doubt, this new study will be subject to close scrutiny by number crunchers who regard estimating the numbers of the world's poorest as an imperfect science.

A revised estimate published in April 2007 put the number of people living on less than $1 a day in 2004 at below one billion for the first time (Chen and Ravallion, 2007). The revised estimate showed that 969 million people, 18 per cent of the population, lived in absolute poverty in the developing world in 2004. At the same time, it was estimated that 2.8 million or 48 per cent of the population in developing countries in 2004 lived on less than $2 a day, reflecting the rising number of people living on between $1 and $2 a day. A major reason for the decrease in the number of people living in absolute poverty in the developing world was substantial poverty reduction in China. Excluding China, there was a 'fairly static' picture of the number of people living on under a $1 a day, with 'no clear trend', and 'a clear trend *increase*' (original emphasis) in the number of people living on under $2 a day. There was a clear indication of rising poverty in sub-Saharan Africa and, as urbanization increased, the rural poverty rate fell much more than the urban rate. In some countries, inequality had worsened as poor people had not benefited from the economic expansion because of lack of job opportunities, limited education, and bad health. At the current rate of decline, it

Table 41.4 Numbers of people living below $1 and $2 a day, 1981–2001

Region	1981	1984	1987	1990	1993	1996	1999	2001
Number of people living below $1.08 per day (million)								
East Asia	795.6	562.2	425.6	472.2	415.4	286.7	281.7	271.3
Of which China	633.7	425.0	308.4	374.8	334.2	211.6	222.8	211.6
Eastern Europe and Central Asia	3.1	2.4	1.7	2.3	17.5	20.1	30.1	17.0
Latin America and Caribbean	35.6	46.0	45.1	49.3	52.0	52.2	53.6	49.8
Middle East and North Africa	9.1	7.6	6.9	5.5	4.0	5.5	7.7	7.1
South Asia	474.8	460.3	473.3	462.3	476.2	461.3	428.5	431.1
Of which India	382.4	373.5	369.8	357.4	380.0	399.5	352.4	358.6
Sub-Saharan Africa	163.6	198.3	218.6	226.8	242.3	271.4	294.3	312.7
Total	1481.8	1276.8	1171.2	1218.5	1207.5	1097.2	1095.7	1089.0
Number of people living below $2.15 per day (million)								
East Asia	1169.8	1108.6	1028.3	1116.3	1079.3	922.2	899.6	864.3
Of which China	875.8	813.8	730.8	824.6	802.9	649.6	627.5	593.6
Eastern Europe and Central Asia	20.2	18.3	14.7	22.9	81.3	97.8	113.0	93.3
Latin America and Caribbean	98.9	118.9	115.4	124.6	136.1	117.2	127.4	128.2
Middle East and North Africa	51.9	49.8	52.5	50.9	51.8	60.9	70.4	69.8
South Asia	821.1	858.6	911.4	957.5	1004.8	1029.1	1039.0	1063.7
Of which India	630.0	661.4	697.1	731.4	769.5	805.7	804.4	826.0
Sub-Saharan Africa	287.9	326.0	355.2	381.6	410.4	446.8	489.3	516.0
Total	2450.0	2480.1	2477.5	2653.8	2763.6	2674.1	2738.8	2735.4

Source: Chen and Ravallion (2004).

418 *Assessment. The Graveyard of Aspirations*

is projected that there would still be over 800 million people living on under $1 a day in 2015, thereby missing the MDG target of halving the number of people at that level by that date, and 2.8 billion people living on less that $2 a day, reflecting the rising number of people living on between $1 and $2 a day.

Education for all

Education has been recognized as the gateway to development in the broadest sense and gender parity in education as particularly important in ensuring equitable and sustainable development, including food security. These basic truths were recognized in the two of the MDGs, which are to ensure that all children had access to primary education by 2015, and that gender disparity in primary and secondary education should be eliminated by 2005 and in all levels of education no later than 2015. The goal of extending a basic level of education to all was a major outcome of the *World Conference on Education for All* in 1990. It was reconfirmed in the series of UN conferences and summits throughout the 1990s and 're-specified' as six major goals at the *World Education Forum* (WEF) in Dakar, Senegal in 2000, two of which, as noted above, were included in the MDGs.[9] An important complementary resolution adopted at the WEF was that governments and international agencies should be held accountable for progress towards achieving these educational goals. For this purpose, UNESCO instituted an annual series of *EFA Global Monitoring Reports* starting in 2002. These reports are written by an independent international team based in UNESCO, supported by UNECSO staff and drawing from UNESCO's Institute for Statistics and commissioned studies by researchers and institutes around the world. Of the four reports so far published in the series: the first assesses whether the world is on track to meet the educational MDGs (UNESCO, 2002), the second examines the question of gender disparity in education (UNESCO, 2004), the third looks at the important question of the quality of education (UNESCO, 2005) and the fourth focuses on literacy for life (UNESCO, 2006).

According to these reports, 'steady progress' has been made since 1998, especially towards UPE and gender parity among the poorest countries but the overall conclusion is that 'the pace is insufficient' for the educational MDGs to be met by 2015. There have been some encouraging trends that show considerable achievements in many low-income countries. Primary school enrolment is up sharply in both sub-Saharan Africa and South and West Asia, with nearly 20 million new students in each region. Some 47 countries out of 163 for which data are available have achieved UPE, and another 90 are on track to achieve UPE by 2015: 44 countries are making good progress but are unlikely to achieve the goal. Enrolment of girls in primary schools has risen rapidly in some low-income countries in sub-Saharan Africa and South and West Asia. Gender and quality goals are increasingly more visible in national educational plans of developing countries, where public expenditure on education has increased as a share of national income in about 70 countries out of the 110 countries with available data. And aid for basic education more than doubled between 1999 and 2003 and could rise further to

$3.3 billion a year by 2010 following commitments made by major donors at the G8 summits. What is called the *Fast Track Initiative* (FTI) has emerged as a key co-ordinating mechanism for aid agencies. The FTI was established by the Development Committee of the IMF and World Bank in 2002 to accelerate progress towards universal completion of quality primary education by 2015. It is supported by a partnership of all the major education donors and UNESCO, UNICEF and the regional development banks. But by mid-2005, the FTI had resulted in pledged of only $298 million, well below what is required.

Despite these achievements, major EFA challenges remain. About 100 million children are estimated not to be enroled in primary schools, 55 per cent of them girls. As their net enrolment ratios are declining, 23 countries are at risk of not achieving UPE by 2015. Primary school fees, a major barrier to access, are still collected in 80 countries of the 103 countries surveyed. And high fertility rates, HIV/AIDS and armed conflict continue to exert pressure on and disrupt the education systems in many regions with the greatest EFA challenges. The MDG 2005 gender parity target was missed by 94 countries of the 194 for which data are available. Quality in education has been assessed as being too low, with too few primary school teachers and many of them lacking adequate qualifications.

Literacy remains neglected, with an estimated 771 million people aged 15 and above without basic literacy skills and insufficient priority and funding being given by governments and aid agencies to youth and adult literacy programmes. Aid for basic education is assessed to be still inadequate. Bilateral aid to education was $4.7 billion in 2003, well below the 1990 high of $5.7 billion, of which 60 per cent went to post-secondary education. Total aid to basic education accounts for only 2.6 per cent of ODA, with adult literacy receiving a miniscule share. It is estimated that aid to education would have to double to reach the $7 billion necessary just to achieve UPE and gender parity. As with aid to other sectors, the neediest people and countries miss out. A disproportionate amount goes to middle-income countries with relatively high primary school enrolment.

The EFA global monitoring reports published by UNESCO have been complemented by reports by UNICEF and the World Bank. UNICEF's annual report on *The State of the World's Children 2004* focused on gender disparity in education and its implications for development (UNICEF, 2004). In his foreword to the report, the UN secretary-general, Kofi Annan, paints a tragic picture of the human waste of uneducated, marginalized girls and women 'ill-prepared to participate fully in the political, social and economic development of their communities. They – and their children in turn – are at higher risk to poverty, HIV/AIDS, sexual exploitation, violence and abuse'. Conversely, 'to educate a girl is to educate a whole family, and what is true of families is also true of communities and, ultimately, whole countries'. Thus, 'there is no tool for development more effective than the education of girls'.

The UNICEF report points out that despite decades of attention to the importance of education for all, some 121 million children were out of school, 65 million of them girls. To focus attention on improving the quality and availability of girl's education, 13 UN agencies had formed a *UN Girls' Education Initiative*, with

UNICEF as its lead agency. UNICEF had also launched a *25 by 2005* initiative, with a special focus on 25 countries, 15 of them in sub-Saharan Africa, considered to be most at risk in failing to achieve the MDG of eliminating gender disparity in education. It was recognized that this 'acceleration strategy' would not be easy. UNICEF's role was to 'accompany governments on the road to gender equality in education'. This was defined as a new concept that sought to transcend the well-established framework of partnership by instituting long-term support with a total resource package, without being unduly obtrusive or trying to dictate and by being constructive with both support and advocacy for change where needed, graphically described as 'walking the distance with a country – and if necessary going the extra mile'.

The report explains why girls have been systematically left out of education as a series of failures in accountability, understanding and development theory, and a strategy focusing on the education sector alone. It points out that change would not be achieved by enrolment drives. UNICEF called for a 'concerted global push' that was a moral imperative, practical and catalytic. It called on all those concerned to embrace a human rights-based, multisectoral approach to development, which was described in detail in an annex to the report. The report argues that for too long girls' lack of education had been seen as a private matter for individual families. Integrated strategies were required at all levels – family, community, local and national government – to get and keep girls in school. Leaders from all levels of society were called upon to make seven steps forward to: include girls' education as an essential component of development efforts; create a national ethos for girls' education; allow no fees of any kind; think both outside and inside the 'education box'; establish schools as centres of community development; integrate strategies of investment, policy and institutional initiatives, service delivery and conceptual frameworks that combine economic and human rights principles; and increase international funding for education. Strategies are proposed for both within and outside the classroom to increase school attendance and completion by girls.

The Development Committee of the IMF and World Bank that established the FTI also called for a close monitoring of its impact. For this purpose, the World Bank developed a new database to track progress in achieving UPE by 2015, which showed that over the 1990s, the average rate of primary school completion on the developing world (on a country-weighted basis) improved only from 72 to 77 per cent, far short of the progress needed to reach the MDG education target (Bruns *et al.*, 2003). On a population-weighted basis, buoyed by China's high reported primary school completion rate, the global situation looked slightly better, rising from 73 to 81 per cent. But the global average masked large regional differences. Sub-Saharan Africa had the lowest completion rate by far, with barely half of all school-age children completing primary school, followed by South Asia with an average rate of about 70 per cent. The Middle East and North Africa showed a 'disturbing picture of stagnation' with an average completion rate of around 74 per cent. Europe and Central Asia came closest to the MDG education target with 92 per cent, followed by Latin America and the Caribbean (82 per cent) and Asia and the Pacific (84 per cent).

Dimensions of Poverty and Food Insecurity 421

Overall, the trends indicated that where political will was strong, effective reforms were adopted, and international support adequate, 'dramatic progress' in increasing primary completion rates was possible. But progress was 'fragile': 13 middle-income countries and 15 low-income countries saw their rates stagnate or decline over the 1990s; 37 out of 155 developing countries had achieved, or virtually achieved, universal primary school completion, and another 32 were on track; 86 countries risked not reaching the MDG target, unless progress was accelerated; and another 27 countries are seriously off track. Of the 70 countries lagging behind, 51 are in the low-income category.

An attempt is made to estimate what would be required to achieve the MDG in terms of both education reform and incremental domestic and international financing. Focusing on the 55 largest low-income countries (with gross national income per capita of $885 or less in 2000), where 75 per cent of all out-of-school children globally are located, the World Bank study confirmed an earlier conclusion that attainment depends more crucially on education reform than on incremental financing. Using a simulation model specially constructed for the study, it was estimated that $9.7 billion per year up to 2015 would be needed to achieve UPE in all low-income countries, of which about $3.7 billion a year would need to come from ODA. For all developing countries, it was estimated that $33–38 billion a year in additional spending would be needed if the MDGs were to be met, of which $5–7 billion, a small fraction of global annual military expenditure, would need to come through external aid.

The World Bank analysis suggests that a relatively small set of key parameters were important determinants of progress and provided core elements of a policy framework. Using indicative parameters to guide education planning could bring technical rigour, transparency and financial discipline and help ensure that new investment in school expansion, domestic resource mobilization and external assistance are measured against clear benchmarks. But it was stressed that this indicative framework was not sufficient for a credible EFA plan, for three reasons. First, the system-wide average values on which these parameters were based did not guarantee efficient or equitable distribution, particularly in large federal education systems, as in India or Nigeria. Second, while the indicative benchmarks could provide a useful point of reference for all countries, there may be cases where they are culturally, institutionally or financially inappropriate. Third, and most importantly, the indicative framework can help ensure that education systems have adequate overall resources but it cannot guarantee the effective management of those resources. The study emphasizes that education ministries should achieve greater equity and efficiency in allocating, financing and deploying personnel across different regions and schools as well as between administrative support services and school-level delivery. Management capacity at the school level was also crucial. And, ultimately, it was management in the classroom that transformed education resources into student learning.

Regarding donor support, the World Bank study identified six basic steps: significantly increasing funding for primary education; ensuring better targeting of EFA priority countries; shifting a larger share of external assistance to recurrent

422   *Assessment. The Graveyard of Aspirations*

budget support; improving the efficiency of aid transfers; assuring stability and predictability of external assistance; and more effective monitoring of progress, increased research and faster diffusion of knowledge about what works. The Development Committee of the IMF and World Bank endorsed a new compact for primary education, called the *EFA* FTI, in April 2002, as did the G8 in its *Action Plan for Education* at its June 2002 summit. In June 2002, a first set of 18 low-income countries and a second set of high-priority countries (Bangladesh, Democratic Republic of Congo, India, Nigeria and Pakistan) were invited to join the FTI. The study concludes that universal completion of primary education was crucial for national economic and social advancement, a goal to which all developing countries should be committed. But this goal would not be achieved without significant acceleration in current progress, which would require bridging substantial gaps in policy, capacity, financing and data.

Employment, productivity and poverty reduction

While the importance of employment in eradicating poverty and food insecurity had been appreciated for some time, the 1967 ILO World Employment Conference and the work of Amartya Sen, among others, served to re-emphasize the imperative of ensuring productive and remunerative work for the hungry poor as an essential part of a strategy to satisfy people's basic needs. It is surprising therefore that the call for full employment did not figure in the MDGs in addition to the call to develop and implement strategies for decent and productive work for youths as part of the global partnership for development.

The main aim of ILO's *World Employment Report 2004–05* was to explore the evidence regarding the impact of productivity performance on both employment growth and poverty reduction (ILO, 2005). Productive employment was described as the economic foundation for what was called 'decent work', which remained only an aspiration for many hundreds of millions of people, frustrated by a reality of rising unemployment or employment that did not provide the chance to escape poverty. The ILO report found that there were tradeoffs to be made in striking a balance between employment and income growth and between productivity growth and poverty reduction. But increased focus on the generation of what was called 'decent work' opportunities was regarded as central to achieving the MDGs. This echoed the call for the promotion of freely chosen productive employment in ILO Convention No 122 on Employment Policy. Much work was so poorly remunerated as to prevent those classified as employed from earning more than a dollar a day. Better as well as more jobs were therefore needed.

The report centred on poverty among the world's workers or on what was described as 'working poverty'. This concept of the working poor in the developing world added a new dimension to the study of labour markets by placing decent and productive employment at the forefront of the poverty discussion. It was estimated that in 2003, 1.39 billion people were unable to lift themselves and their families above the two dollars a day poverty line. Among them, 550 million could not rise above the dollar a day threshold. This meant that almost half (49.7 per cent) of the world's workers and over half (58.7 per cent) of the developing world's workers did not earn enough to lift themselves and their families above the two dollars a day poverty line. Almost one-quarter (19.7 per cent) of the employed persons in the world, and approaching a quarter (23.3 per cent) of the developing world's workers, were living on less than a dollar a day. In addition, it was estimated that there were 185.9 million unemployed people in the world.

The analysis of trends in labour productivity, labour markets, working poverty and total poverty showed that those regions that managed to increase productivity levels and create employment opportunities for their growing labour forces best managed to reduce working poverty and overall poverty. They were also on track to meet the MDG of halving the proportion of people living on less than a dollar a day. This included Southeast Asia, South Asia and the Transition economies, and the Middle East and North Africa. The region of Latin America and the Caribbean was said to be slightly off track, while sub-Saharan Africa was significantly off track. The outlook was described as being even bleaker when the goal was to halve the working poor living on less than two dollars a day, for which only East Asia was said to have a realistic chance. The report concluded that given the persistently high number of working poor, together with the high number of unemployed and the uncertain number of people who remain outside the labour force for involuntary reasons, there was a large and persistent deficit of decent work in the world, which constituted a great challenge in the fight against poverty. It argued that the focus needed to be on parts of the economy where the majority of people worked, such as agriculture, small-scale activities in the urban and rural informal economy and services as well as manufacturing.

International trade

The importance of fair and open international trade for economic development and the elimination of hunger and poverty, particularly in the developing countries, and the achievement of the MDGs, is now widely recognized. Yet the failure to implement the Doha development agenda and the insistence of the two most powerful trading forces, the United States and the EU, to maintain protectionist measures for their agricultural products and pursue regional trading policies over which they have more control, has thrown into serious question the continuing relevance the international organization that was set up to conduct multilateral trade negotiations. The creation of the World Trade Organization (WTO) in 1995 has been described as the most dramatic advance in multilateralism since the 1940s, when the UN and several of its specialized agencies were established (Croome, 1995). The WTO is the only multilateral institution created recently and explicitly for a global and wholly interdependent world market and trading economy, following the Uruguay Round of multilateral trade negotiations, which took over four to prepare and seven more to complete. It was even suggested that it might be viewed as an arena for the most far-reaching negotiations on any economic subject. Yet over a decade after its establishment, although the organization has achieved notable successes and enlarged its membership, it has

424 *Assessment. The Graveyard of Aspirations*

also been subjected to widespread criticism and violent public demonstrations. A key challenge confronting the WTO is in addressing perceptions that the organization, and the disciplines it embodies, is not supportive of fair and equitable development. And while multilateral discussions in the WTO remain mired in contentious debate, new bilateral and regional preferential trading arrangements are mushrooming around the world.

How did the early promise of WTO turn so sour? First, it is important to note that WTO differs substantially from the International Trade Organization (ITO), envisaged in the 1948 Havana Charter on Trade and Employment and Keynes' original vision, and the UN body concerned with trade and development, the United Nations Conference on Trade and Development (UNCTAD). WTO is not a UN body. The major industrialized countries, particularly the US and EU, did not want the trade organization to be part of the UN system. While UNCTAD explicitly links trade and development, WTO is only concerned with trade. Unlike the proposed ITO, WTO is not concerned with the stabilization of commodity prices and with controlling the activities of multinational corporations, which account for up to 70 per cent of international trade. WTO serves to facilitate export orientation, which is an essential component of the Washington Consensus and corporate expansion. Its mandate to co-operate with the IMF and the World Bank, 'with a view to achieving greater coherence in global economic policy making', is seen by many developing countries as another strike against their interests.

Criticism of the WTO emerged even before its first ministerial meeting in Singapore in 1996 (Krueger, 1998).[10] A conference held at Stanford University, California, two months before the Singapore meeting, the deliberations of which were designed to provide input for defining the agenda for the WTO ministers, called into question the ability of the WTO to carry out its mandate on account of: its size, budget and analytical capacity; its working relations with the Bretton Woods institutions and other UN bodies; its ability to influence domestic policies, particularly of the major developed countries, and to settle trade disputes among them; and the thorny issue of the relationship with the United States, given the historical record, including the refusal of the US Congress to ratify the Havana Charter to establish the ITO. Six major subjects were identified and discussed concerning challenges facing the WTO: reconciling domestic policy objectives and the multilateral trade order; the role, if any, of the WTO concerning the environment and labour standards; greater coherence on global economic policy-making; reaching effective agreements covering services; imposing multilateral discipline on administered protection; and regionalism. The special problems facing WTO of economies in transition and developing countries were also recognized. Four key issues were identified as difficulties facing WTO's future agenda: the tendency to pursue negotiations sector-by-sector and issue-by-issue; the emergence of preferential trading arrangements; efforts to link trade issues to a variety of other international concerned, such as the environment and labour standards; and the proliferation of anti-dumping regulations and enforcement.

An interesting US perspective shows that the initial years of the WTO were a time of hiatus and indecision for trade policy with the US preoccupied with domestic politics leading up to the 1996 presidential election (Preeg, 1998).[11] Further, trade liberalizing initiatives in the WTO were considered bad politics by both major political parties, the general assumption being that renewed US leadership would be forthcoming after the election of the US president in 1997 to formulate a post-Uruguay Round trade strategy, based partly on various elements of policy already in train and partly on new initiatives. But such a formulation was slow to materialize. Meanwhile, there was considerable unofficial strategizing among experts, private sector leaders and *ex-officio* government officials, leading to two separate tracks in the world trading system, the multilateral, for which the WTO was responsible, and the regional, which was fostered and controlled by the major industrialized powers.

How might these two tracks be integrated? Three scenarios were presented: first, to continue the two-track course, leaving the formal synthesis for later; second, what was called a WTO free trade 'grand bargain'; and third, an extension and integration of the regional free trade groupings. The last was judged to be preferable but was a complex scenario that required thorough analysis. During the period 1997–97, the 'striking irony' in US trade strategy was that regional free trade objectives were more comprehensive and far-reaching than the multilateral WTO agenda. The US is now committed to free trade and investment across the Pacific by 2010, to a similar agreement in the Americas much earlier, and to a sweeping yet still largely undefined 'new transatlantic market place' with Europe. In contrast, the US has resisted any grand design or even new round of multilateral negotiations in the WTO, preferring item-by-item negotiations, mostly old loose ends from the Uruguay Round agreement. A broader conceptual and operational focus on multilateral objectives is needed but this can only be done in conjunction with the already established regional free trade objectives.

Faced with increasing and hostile criticism, WTO's director-general, Supachai Panitchpakdi, requested WTO's Consultative Board, under the chairmanship of Peter Sutherland, the first WTO director-general, to 'examine the functioning of the institution [WTO] and consider how well equipped it is to carry out the weight of future responsibilities and demands' (WTO, 2004). The Board's report followed two tracks. The first concerned multilateralism and the essential role of the WTO. The authors believed strongly that political leaders and the WTO itself should go back to the basic arguments in favour of open trading and a rules-based trading system. The second track concerned many practical matters of institutional improvement. In reaching its conclusions and making its recommendations, the Board believed that the process of globalization and the role played by the WTO were 'widely misunderstood and seriously misrepresented' and that 'too many constituencies understand neither its benefits nor its limitations'. At the same time, it pointed to some serious shortcomings. The report concluded that it was time to respond to what was called 'the erosion of non-discrimination'. This had been done through the spread of preferential trade agreements and the 'spaghetti bowl' of discriminatory preferences by means of the effective reduction

426 Assessment. The Graveyard of Aspirations

of the most-favoured nation (MRN) tariffs and non-tariff measure in multilateral trade negotiations. In essence, the report recommended that preferential trade agreements should be subject to meaningful review and effective discipline in the WTO.

The report addressed the concern of some major members over the loss of sovereignty in ceding power to the WTO. It concluded that ultimately what counted was whether the balance was positive or negative between some loss of 'policy space' at the national level and the advantages of co-operation and the rule of law at the multilateral level. In the Board's view, the balance was already positive for all WTO members and would be increasingly so in the future. Co-operation with other intergovernmental agencies generally added value and legitimized to the activities of WTO, although the latter should be preserved from undue external interference. Observer status should be granted only on the basis of potential contribution to the WTO's role as a forum for trade negotiations. The report recommended that international development agencies, chiefly the World Bank, should fund trade policy-related adjustment assistance for developing countries. It also suggested that clear objectives should be developed for the WTO's relations with civil society and the public at large, and that no single set of organizations should be constituted to the exclusion of others. Contentiously, it expressed the view that the WTO secretariat should be under no obligation to engage seriously with groups whose expressed objective was to undermine or destroy the WTO. And a special effort should be made to assist local civil society organizations dealing with trade issues in least-developed countries, especially in Africa.

WTO's Dispute Settlement Understanding (DSU) was found to be a 'significant and positive step forward' in the general system of rules-based international trade diplomacy. A number of proposals were made in the belief that caution and experience were necessary before making any dramatic changes in WTO's rules and procedures. Any measures or ideas for reform that would create a sort of 'diplomatic veto' should be strongly resisted. The WTO secretariat should encourage and facilitate technical assistance to instil broader understanding of the role of 'rule orientation' in treaty implementation as well as the general approaches that virtually all juridical institutions take to their work. Critically, the report recommended that a member considering blocking a measure that would otherwise have broad consensus should declare its intentions in writing with reasons that would declare the matter one of vital national interest.

A number of recommendations were made to strengthen the organization of the WTO. These included: holding annual ministerial conferences; requiring the WTO director-general to make six-monthly written reports on trade policy developments to WTO ministers; holding a WTO summit of world leaders every five years; and giving the WTO director-general and secretariat the capacity and standing to be 'at the centre of negotiations' during WTO ministerial meetings. To further improve transparency and inclusiveness, the WTO director-general should explore with relevant groups the potential for increased co-ordination and group representation in restricted meetings. And to get the best out of the WTO director-general and secretariat, it was recommended that: the powers and duties of the director-general should be spelled out clearly by WTO's general council; a selection process for both the director-general and senior secretariat staff should be adopted to ensure that the best qualified were appointed; the 'management culture' in the secretariat should be strengthened, perhaps through the appointment of a chief executive officer, equivalent to a deputy to the director-general; a greater intellectual output and policy analysis should be required of the secretariat; and, to obtain these improvements, WTO's budget should be appropriately increased. The main rationale that permeated throughout the report was to establish a transparent and inclusive forum for multilateral trade negotiations that would produce commercial benefits for all and to avoid the public protests that had occurred at Seattle and Cancun and delayed and halted progress in the Doha Round of trade negotiations.

How different has been the history and record of the UN body most concerned with trade and development issues, UNCTAD. The first UN Conference on Trade and Development was held in 1964 with the specific aim of promoting the integration of developing countries into the world economy. The new UN agency was established on the basis of a report, and the lobbying skills, of Raul Prebisch, who became its first secretary-general (1964–69) and dominated its early years (Prebisch, 1964). He advocated the need for a fairer international trading system based on his work, and that of Hans Singer, that had shown the long-term deterioration in the terms of trade of the primary products of developing countries in comparison with the manufactures of industrialized countries. The Prebisch–Singer thesis as it became known had a major influence in shaping the demands of developing countries for a new international economic order (Shaw, 2002b; Toye and Toye, 2003, 2004). From the start, under Prebisch's leadership, UNCTAD was therefore seen by the developing countries as their champion against the economic power of the rich Western industrialized countries.

Within UNCTAD, set up with a permanent secretariat in Geneva, Switzerland, the Group of 77 (G77) developing countries (now comprising 131 members) was established to voice their concerns of market reforms that are seen by them to add to the economic advantage of the richer countries and threaten their nascent industries. They consider that the market-based liberalization foisted on developing countries since the 1980s has led to unsatisfactory outcomes. Criticism of market economics and deregulation mutedly voiced during the 1980s and 1990s are now being made more openly in UNCTAD publications, especially as recriminations following the collapse of the Doha round of trade negotiations have taken the gloss off the free traders and halted the momentum of trade liberalization. The organization's annual report for 2006, while rejecting the protectionism of major developed countries, argued that countries such as the Asian 'tiger economies' had been able to strengthen the creative power of their markets through pro-active industrial policies that provided some temporary protection, which should be considered a key element of a policy aimed at 'strategic trade integration' (UNCTAD, 2006). The call for subsidies, however temporary, comes at a fragile time for the efforts to bring down the tariff barriers of developed countries and open their markets to developing countries. The UNCTAD secretary-general explained that his organization was not recommending any anti-trade stance but to point to the need to strengthen the creative forces of the market. Free-market campaigners have attacked the UNCTAD report on grounds that its advice would lead to lower living standards and create inefficient industries that would ill-serve consumers in developing countries.

UNCTAD insists that it has close links with WTO, with which it signed a memorandum in 2003 providing for co-operation and joint studies. But WTO is seen by developing countries to have a very different aim and philosophy, which favour the rich countries. UNCTAD's call for a level playing field in trade and development harks back to the work of both Singer and Prebisch. But UNCTAD's powers of persuasion have been muted by the work of other UN bodies, particularly the IMF and the World Bank, and by the creation of WTO.

Human security

Human security was on the international agenda well before the *al-Qaeda* terrorists flew the passenger planes into the twin towers of the World Trade Center in New York and the Pentagon in Washington, DC on 11 September 2001, described as a 'defining moment' in the history of the modern world, and triggering the war on international terrorism. It also carried further the debate on redefining the concepts and relationship between human security and food security. Up to the late 1980s, the concept of security was more narrowly interpreted as security of territory from external aggression or global security from the threat of nuclear holocaust (Clay and Stokke, 2000). With the end of the Cold War and the break up of the imposed political structure of the former Soviet Union, a broadening of the concept occurred as the number of conflicts within, not between, states increased.

This process was taken further by the North–South Dialogue of the Society for International Development at a high-level meeting on 'The Economics of Peace', held in Costa Rica in 1990. The meeting called for a new concept of global security that focused not on military security but on 'the overall security of individuals from social violence, economic distressed and environmental degradation' and sought to focus attention on the obstacles to 'realization of the full potential of individuals' (MacFarlane and Khong, 2006). This transformation was captured and redefined further in the annual UNDP *Human Development Reports* (HDR) that began in 1990. The HDR for 1994 introduced a concept of human security that had two elements:

- safety from chronic threats such as hunger, disease and repression; and
- protection from sudden and hurtful disruptions in the pattern of daily life (UNDP, 1994).

This concept explicitly linked human security with the development process. It allowed people to exercise their expanded choices and develop their capabilities. Conversely, the absence of such security undermined the process of development

Dimensions of Poverty and Food Insecurity   429

and led to social disintegration and humanitarian catastrophes. Under this broadened concept, the threats to human security are wide, including: food security, health security, economic security, environmental security, personal and community security and political security. Human security is also seen to have four characteristics: as a universal concern; with a number of components, including food security, that are interdependent; encompassing prevention and protection, and most recently pre-emptive, measures; and essentially with a people-centred concern and solution.

On the initiative of Canada and Norway, and like-minded states, a Human Security Network (HSN) was founded in 1999 to define concrete policies in the area of human security as a basis for co-ordinated action and attempts to serve as a catalyst that raised awareness of new issues as they arose. The HSN considered it necessary to go beyond it original 'freedom from fear' focus to incorporate the 'freedom from want' issues emphasized in the HDR 1994. In May 2003, the UN Commission on Human Security (CHS) presented a report to the UN secretary-general in which it defined human security in the following terms:

> In essence, human security means safety for people from both violent and non-violent threats. It is a condition or state of being characterized by freedom from pervasive threats to people's rights, their safety, or even their lives. From a foreign policy perspective, human security is perhaps best understood as a shift in perspective or orientation. It is an alternative way of seeing the world, taking people as its point of reference, rather than focusing exclusively on the security of territory or governments.
>
> (CHS, 2003)

The CHS was established in 2000 with the remit of promoting public understanding of human security and developing the concept as an operational tool for policy formulation and implementation and to propose a concrete programme of action. The CHS report took a broad approach, bringing together physical protection, human rights and development. According to the CHS, human security necessitated policies that went beyond ensuring people's survival to policies that focused on people's livelihoods and dignity in good times and in bad. The UN secretary-general convened a high-level panel on threats, challenges and change to consider the best ways of implementing the recommendations of the CHS report (UN, 2005a).

Most recently, the Worldwatch Institute devoted its annual publication on the *State of the World* in 2005 to 'redefining global security' (Worldwatch Institute, 2005).[12] In his foreword to the publication, Mikhail Gorbachev, former president of the Soviet Union, Nobel Peace Prize holder, and now chairman of Green Cross International, identified three inter-related world challenges: security, including the risks associated with weapons of mass destruction and terrorism; poverty and underdevelopment; and environmental sustainability. He stated: 'We are the guests, not the masters, of nature and must develop a new paradigm for development and conflict resolution, based on the costs and benefits to all people and

430   *Assessment. The Graveyard of Aspirations*

bound by the limits of nature herself rather than the limits of technology and consumerism'.

Worldwatch emphasizes that the need for international co-operation has grown stronger even as the rifts and divides among nations have widened. It identifies four 'core insights' in examining the roots of global insecurity. Weapons do not necessarily provide security. Real security in a globalizing world cannot be provided on a purely national basis. The traditional focus on state or regime security is inadequate and needs to encompass the safety and well-being of those living there. And non-military dimensions have an important influence on security and stability. It observes that throughout history big powers have repeatedly intervened in resource-rich countries in order to control lucrative resources. Most worrisome in some ways is the vast reservoir of unemployed young people in many developing countries. Demographic forces can exert strong pressures on a society and its institutions and can have important implications for domestic stability and even international security.

Over the past few decades, the Worldwatch report points out that countries from every major political and religious background, and in virtually every region, have experienced momentous changes in the size and structure of their populations. Yet the global transformation from short lives and large families to longer lives with smaller families remains incomplete. Roughly, one-third of all countries are still in the early stages of transition, with fertility rates at about four children per woman. Studies have shown that these countries bear the highest risks of becoming embroiled in armed civil conflict. Many are bogged down by a debilitating demographic situation: a large and growing young population; low per capita availability of cropland or fresh water; a rising pandemic of HIV/AIDS; scarce economic opportunities; social challenges and political hazards. According to UN data, over 100 countries had what was called a 'youth bulge' in 2000, where people aged 15–29 years accounted for over 40 per cent of all adults.

Severe social, economic and environmental problems, particularly if mixed with 'festering political grievances', can radicalize societies and may even bring about state failures. Dysfunctional, fragile and violence-prone 'failed states' can be the breeding grounds of despair and chronic instability. Prior to the dramatic events of 11 September 2001, poverty, instability and warfare in poor countries were widely regarded as marginal to the interests and welfare of the rich countries. After the attacks on the World Trade Center in New York and the Pentagon in Washington, DC, it was quickly realized that conditions of political turmoil and social misery could not be confined to the periphery. But, Worldwatch points out, the war on international terrorism runs the risk of sidelining the struggle against hunger, health epidemics, poverty and environmental degradation.

Three 'core principles' are therefore identified for a more secure world. First, a new security policy needs to be 'transformative' in nature, strengthening the civil institutions that can address the root causes of insecurity. Second, it must be above all 'preventive' in nature, based on a clear understanding of the root causes of conflict and insecurity, which implies a far broader and earlier applicability, not merely a reaction that addresses symptoms. Lastly, it needs to be 'cross-cutting and integrative', bring together insights from a broad range of disciplines. As the Worldwatch report demonstrates, there are many social, economic and environmental policies that can help create a more just and sustainable world. It concludes that such policies offer the added bonus of creating real security in a way that the force of arms never can.

42
Future Action

Practical proposals

Two specific proposals have been made to end hunger and achieve the MDGs established in the UN *Millennium Declaration* in 2000. George McGovern, US congressman and senator, the first director of the US Food for Peace programme in the Kennedy Administration, and the candidate of the Democratic Party for US president in 1972, has been a constant and tireless proponent of the conquest of world hunger for over half a century. As this history has shown, he has made a number of proposals to end hunger in the world and took the personal initiative that led to the founding of the UN World Food Programme in 1961 (Shaw, 2001b). More recently, while US ambassador to the UN food and agriculture agencies in Rome, Italy, he advocated another strategy to defeat world hunger (McGovern, 2001). His strategy consists of a five-point initiative: a school lunch programme to reach every child in the world; a worldwide special nutrition programme for women, infants and children; the establishment of food reserves globally; an assistance programme to help developing countries improve their own food production, processing and distribution; and the dissemination of the results of high-yielding scientific agriculture, including genetically modified crops.

McGovern estimates the cost of this strategy to be $5 billion a year of which, he suggests, $1.2 billion could come from the United States. If correct, the cost would be well within the financial means of developing countries and the international community. He considers that if this annual allocation continued for 15 years (until 2015), the number of chronically undernourished people in the world would be cut by half, the goal set by the 1996 *World Food Summit*. Hunger among the remaining malnourished would disappear if roughly the same cost is invested for a further fifteen years, to the year 2030. McGovern informs us that the US Agency for International Development (USAID) puts the cost of his scheme at $2.6 billion annually and FAO at $6 billion a year. He correctly points out the cost of *not* ending world hunger would be much higher. The World Bank, for example, estimates that each year, malnutrition robs the world of 46 million years of productive living at a cost of $16 billion. He recognizes that the cost of hunger cannot be evaluated only in dollar terms. He asks, 'what is the value of a human life?' In the last half of the twentieth century, he estimated 450 million may have died from malnutrition or related causes. And the vicious circle of hunger, conflict and more hunger will continue unless decisive steps are taken to end it.

The *UN Millennium Project* is an independent advisory body commissioned by the UN secretary-general to propose the best strategy for achieving the MDGs (UNDP, 2005).[13] In its report, *Investing in Development: A Practical Plan to Achieve the Millennium Development Goals*, the MDGs are described as 'the most broadly supported, comprehensive, and specific poverty reduction targets the world has ever established'. For the international political system, they are regarded as the 'fulcrum' on which development policy should be based. For the people living in extreme poverty, they represent 'the means for a productive life'. And for everyone else, they are described as the 'linchpin' to the quest for a more secure and peaceful world. The report recognizes that there has been 'significant progress' in achieving many of the MDGs. But it also notes that progress has been 'far from uniform' across the world, or across the MDGs, and there remained 'huge disparities' across and within countries. Within countries, poverty is greatest in rural areas, though urban poverty is also 'extensive, growing and underreported'. Sub-Saharan Africa is described as the 'epicentre of crisis', with a widespread shortfall in most MDGs. Asia is the region with the 'fastest progress'; other regions had 'mixed records'.

In addressing the vexed question as to why progress has been so mixed, the report observes that, in the process of economic growth, the MDGs play two roles: as ends in themselves; and as inputs to economic growth and further development. But when the most basic infrastructure, health services and education are lacking, market forces alone could accomplish little. People, and whole economies, remained trapped in poverty, and failed to reap the benefits of globalization – and can even suffer from it through the adverse effects of the brain drain, environmental degradation, biodiversity loss, capital flight and terms-of-trade declines. The report identifies four main reasons for shortfalls in achieving the MDGs: failures of governance; poverty traps, where many well-governed countries are too poor to help themselves; pockets of poverty, most economies experiencing considerable variations in household incomes; and areas of specific policy neglect, some MDGs not being met simply because policy-makers are unaware of the challenges or of what to do, or are neglectful of core policy issues.

The report that makes 10 major recommendations:

- All countries should have what are termed 'MDG-based poverty reduction strategies' by 2006. These strategies should provide the 'anchor' and 'framework' for cohesive action concerning public investment, capacity building, domestic resource mobilization, and official development assistance, and for strengthening governance, promoting human rights, engaging civil society, and promoting the private sector.
- Governments in developing country should 'craft and implement' these strategies closely, in transparent and inclusive ways, with civil society organizations, the domestic private sector, and international partners.
- International donors should identify at least a dozen MDG 'fast-track' countries for a rapid scale-up of ODA.

434   *Assessment. The Graveyard of Aspirations*

- Developing and developed countries should jointly launch 'quick win actions' and 'massive training programmes' of community-based workers to save and improve millions of lives and promote economic growth.
- Developing country governments should align national strategies to regional initiatives, groups and projects.
- High-income countries should increase ODA from 0.25 per cent of donor GNP in 2003 to around 0.54 per cent in 2015 to support the MDGs, particularly in low-income countries, with improved ODA quality that was harmonized, predictable and largely in grant form, with debt relief more extensive and generous.
- High-income countries should open their markets to developing country exports and help the least-developed countries raise their export competitiveness through investments in critical trade infrastructure. The *Doha Development Agenda* should be fulfilled and the Doha round of multilateral trade negotiations completed.
- International donors should mobilize support for global scientific development to address special needs of the poor in areas of health, agriculture, natural resources and environmental management, and climate control, for which about $7 billion would be needed by 2015.
- The UN secretary-general and the UN Development Group should improve the co-ordination of UN agencies, funds and programmes. The UN country teams should be strengthened and should work closely with the international financial institutions to achieve the MDGs.

The costs of meeting the MDGs in all developing countries are estimated to be of the order of $121 billion in 2006, rising to $189 billion in 2015, taking into account co-financing increases at the country level. This is regarded as being well within the promises made by donors at the Monterrey conference to increase their aid. The requested doubling of annual ODA to $135 billion in 2006, rising to $195 billion in 2015 (0.44 per cent and 0.54 per cent of donor GNP, respectively) 'pales' when compared with the wealth of high-income countries and the world's military budget of $900 billion a year. It is estimated that the United States has spent $400 billion on the war in Iraq and that the final cost of the US involvement in Iraq could run as high as $2 trillion (Baker and Hamilton, 2006, p. 32). The increase in development assistance would make up only half of one per cent of rich countries' combined incomes.

The spirit of optimism that pervades the Millennium Project is conveyed by Jeffrey Sachs, the projects director, in his preface to the project's report. He writes:

The human spirit, we have seen on innumerable occasions, is truly remarkable. This triumph of the human spirit gives us the hope and confidence that extreme poverty can be cut by half by 2015, and indeed ended altogether within the coming years. The world community has at it disposal the proven technologies, policies, financial resources and most importantly the human courage and compassion to make it happen.

Sachs carries this optimistic outlook further in his own personal perspectives on development and prescriptions for ending poverty (Sachs, 2005b). He identifies what he calls the 'Big Five' development interventions, with investments in agricultural inputs, basic health and education, power, transport and communication services, and safe drinking water and sanitation. In his view, the key to ending poverty is 'to create a global network of connections that reach from impoverished communities to the very centers of world power and wealth and back again'. The starting point should be the poor themselves.

He outlines a strategy for scaling up investments and a system of governance that empowers the poor while holding them accountable. Six major kinds of capital required are identified: human capital, business capital, infrastructure, natural capital (the natural endowment of a country), public institutional capital and knowledge capital. Sachs explains how the poverty trap works and how foreign aid can help in overcoming it. He correctly argues that good investment comes in packages and maintains that one of the weaknesses of development thinking is the relentless drive for one magic bullet, 'one decisive investment that will turn the tide, which, alas, does not exist'. Each one of the six types of capital is needed for an effective, well-functioning economy, and to escape the poverty trap. But success in any single area depends on investments across the board.

Next in his perspective of development comes the need for a global compact to end poverty. Poor countries must take ending poverty seriously and devote a greater share of their national resources to it. Similarly, rich countries will need to move beyond platitudes and follow through on their repeated promises to deliver more help. A global compact therefore carries responsibilities on both sides. Sachs advocates an MDG-based poverty reduction strategy consisting of five parts: a 'differential diagnosis' that identifies the policies and investments that a country needs to achieve the MDGs; an investment plan; a financial plan; a donor plan giving multi-year aid commitments; and a public management plan. He recognizes that poor countries have critical needs that cannot be solved by national or regional investments or by domestic policy reforms. And there are concerns that must be addressed at the global level. He believes that the four most important are the debt crisis, global trade policy, science for development and environmental stewardship.

Sachs raises the question: who conducts the international system to implement the global compact? He observes that poor countries refer euphemistically to the UN agencies, including the Bretton Woods institutions, and to bilateral donors as their development partners but that often they are as much nuisance as help. Aid flows are often small and unpredictable, while many small-scale projects consume the time and attention of overstretched and impoverished governments. Harmonization of aid was vital, for which all those involved needed to do a better job. The key is to use the UN system to the best advantage. He considers that the UN secretary-general is the best-placed official in the world to help co-ordinate the various stakeholders who must contribute to the achievements of the MDGs. Following the lead of the UN secretary-general, he recommends that each low-income country should have an effective country team, under a single resident

436 Assessment. The Graveyard of Aspirations

co-ordinator, to organize the work of the UN specialized agencies, including the IMF and the World Bank.

Thus far, he has constructed a paradigm in which ending poverty can be achieved through targeted, tested and proved, investments and implemented as part of a global compact between poor and rich countries. He next raises the question whether the rich countries can afford to help the poor reach the MDGs. According to his calculations, and those of the *UN Millennium Project*, the task can be achieved within the limits to which the rich world is already committed: 0.7 per cent of the GNP of the donor countries, or seven cents out of every $10 in income. He advances five reasons to explain why the level of help needed is so modest. First, the numbers of extremely poor have declined to a relatively small proportion of the world's population. Second, the goal is to end *extreme*, not all, poverty, from which point the poor would be better able to help themselves. Third, the focus should be on specific, proven, low-cost interventions that can make a difference in living standards and economic growth. Fourth, the rich world today is vastly richer. (Sachs is particularly scathing about the United States for flunking on its commitments, with the lowest percentage of GNP as official development assistance of all the major donor countries, a mere fraction of its military expenditure.) And, finally, the tools for ending poverty are more powerful than ever before.

In a spirit of optimism that pervades Sachs' thinking, he calls on 'our generation, the heirs to two and a half centuries of economic progress', to respond to the challenge of ending poverty and secure global well-being. He believes that the time to end poverty has arrived, although hard work lies ahead. He identified nine steps to achieve that goal: commitment to the task, adoption of a plan of action to meet the MDGs, raising the voice of the poor, redeeming the role of the United Nations in the world, rescuing the IMF and the World Bank to play a decisive role in ending global poverty, strengthening the United Nations, harnessing global science, promoting sustainable development and making a personal commitment.

As might be expected, these concrete proposals have their supporters and detractors. Some have called the *UN Millennium Project* an impressive, even heroic, piece of work, with clear and attainable guidelines. Others are more sceptical, regarding the proliferation of goals and recommendations as hugely over-ambitious, tending towards a kind of utopian central planning by global bureaucrats that places far too great a strain on the puny resources of dysfunctional administrations in the elusive quest for growth (Easterly, 2006). Sachs' retort is to find where aid can work, spend it generously, and sustain it. Critics point to the difficulties of targeting the poor and involving them in their own development. They see a trade-off between an active pro-poor policy and higher economic growth, although there is evidence that such a trade-off, if it exists, is unlikely to be very significant (Rajan and Subramanian, 2005). Uneven progress has been made in achieving the MDGs: a number of countries, especially in Africa, now seem unlikely to reach the targets set by 2015 unless there is a major increase in the efforts of poor and rich countries alike. But the MDGs are the most broadly supported, comprehensive and specific poverty reduction targets ever established, and they can now be closely monitored. Most seem to agree that they call for a sea change in the attitudes and determination of national governments and sustained and adequate support from the international community.

Remaining conundrums

There remain three major issues that could have a profound effect on future food security, and economic and social advancement generally, on which opinion, particularly between the United States and Europe, remains dangerously divided: genetic modification (GM) of crops and food; climate change and its environmental effects; and globalization of the world economy.

GM crops and food

As the world population continues to grow, pressure on the earth's finite resources to produce more food has increased. In the past, agricultural production was able to keep ahead of increasing demand through advances in plant breeding, technological innovations and the expansion of the arable land base. The search for new technologies has intensified as the limits of these options and possibilities were seen to be rapidly approaching. Since the 1970s, a major breakthrough was seen to lie through advances in genetic engineering that has made it possible to modify the genetic information of living organisms in a new way, by transferring one or more gene-sized pieces of DNA directly between them. This GM of crops has been claimed by science and the food industry to be the answer to the future world food problem but sharp differences in perspectives on the need for GM crops and food, and what benefits and costs they bring, remain.

GM crops currently occupy only a relatively small proportion of the world's croplands. In 2002, they were cultivated on some 59 million hectares, almost entirely in four countries: the United States (66 per cent), Argentina (23 per cent), Canada (6 per cent) and China (4 per cent). Three crops dominate GM cultivation: soybean (62 per cent), maize (corn) (21 per cent) and cotton (12 per cent). Traits achieved by GM primarily involve herbicide tolerance (75 per cent) and insect pest resistance (15 per cent), or a combination of both in the same crop.

In July 2002, faced with growing interest and concern over the potential risks and dangers as well as the potential benefits of GM crops and food, the UK government took the unprecedented step of initiating what was called a 'GM Dialogue' consisting of three strands: a public debate; a study of the possible costs and benefits of GM by the Prime Minister's Strategy Unit in his Cabinet Office; and a review of GM science undertaken by an independent review panel. The GM national debate stemmed from the report, *Crops on Trial*, of the Agriculture and Environment Biotechnology Commission, published in September 2001, which stressed the importance of encouraging a broad national debate. The UK government funded the debate, which was organized by an independent steering board composed of individuals with diverse backgrounds and views on GM issues serving in their personal capacities.[14] The debate took place in June and July 2003, the first nationwide public discussion around GM issues to be held in the UK. Meetings were organized across the country by local authorities and network groups. The debate generated a great deal of voluntary activity that deepened and multiplied as it got under way. The number of local meetings increased each week of the debate, involving thousands of people across the country. By the end of the process, an estimated total of over 600 regional, county and local meetings were held. As expected, sharp differences emerged in perspectives on the need for GM and what benefits and costs it brought.[15]

Seven key messages about public attitudes to GM were reported to emanate from the national debate. First, participants expressed unease about GM not only on issues directly related to GM technology but on a range of broader social and political issues. The mood was said to range from caution and doubt, through suspicion and scepticism, to hostility and rejection. The belief was strongly expressed that GM technology and GM food carried potential risks. A majority rejected any suggested benefits from GM, except to the companies that promoted it. Participants felt uninformed about GM, were unable to express an opinion on particular GM issues, and thus had little confidence in their own power to influence decisions about GM.

The second key message was that the more people engaged in GM issues, and chose to discover more about them, the harder their attitudes and more intense their concerns. In particular, they were concerned that not enough was known about the long-term effects of GM on health. Thirdly, there was little support for the early commercialization of GM crops. Just over half of the participants never wanted to see GM crops grown in the UK 'under any circumstances'. Almost all the remainder wanted the potential risks to the environment and human health reduced to 'an acceptable level' before commercialization took place. Fourthly, there was widespread mistrust of government and multinational companies about their motives, intentions and behaviour in taking decisions about GM. Concern was expressed that government may not have adequate knowledge and advice to help take the right decisions and could be too close to producers' interests. Companies were motivated overwhelmingly by profit than meeting society's needs and had the power to make their interests prevail over the wider public interest.

Fifthly, there was a broad desire to know more, and be better informed, and for further research to be conducted. Sixthly, there was a 'debate within the debate' on the potential role of GM for developing countries. While there was an initial assumption that GM technology might help developing countries produce more food and offer them medical, social and economic benefits, there was a clear divergence between the majority, who felt that the potential benefits would not actually materialize and that there were better and more important ways to promote development, including fairer trade, better distribution of food, income and power, and better government, and the minority, who felt benefits would accrue especially after people got more engaged in GM issues. Finally, the debate was welcomed and valued. Participants expressed appreciation for the opportunity both to express their own views and to hear those of others.

The report of the Prime Minster's Strategy Unit[16] noted that GM crops represented just one application of GM technology and one approach to plant breeding. It pointed out that GM crops were widely grown across the world and had been available for human and animal consumption for almost a decade. GM crops were not an end in themselves but should be considered in the context of policy areas including agriculture and the environment, rural development, science, innovation and competition, food safety and quality, and international development. It recalled that a wide-ranging regulatory framework had been in place in the European Union (EU) since 1990 and that any new GM crop or food was subject to an approval process that looked in detail at potential impacts on the environment and health both of the crops and the food made with it. It recognized that public attitudes would be important in determining the future of GM crops and foods and that differences in approaches between EU and some other countries on GM policy was already causing trade tensions.

The report concluded that in the short term, negative consumer attitudes could be expected to limit the demand for products containing GM foods and therefore the economic value of the current generation of GM crops. But there was significant potential benefits from the future development of GM crop technology. However, the international implications could be significant and should not be underestimated. The ability of developing countries to choose whether or not to adopt GM crop technology may be affected by considerations about the possible impact on exports to the EU. And taking a significantly policy direction from other countries could cause serious trade tensions.

The GM Science Review was described as a review of published scientific literature and other sources of appropriate scientific evidence in the areas related to GM crops and foods.[17] The review panel included both specialists and non-specialist scientists and social scientists from a wide range of backgrounds. In the words of its chairman, 'the review endeavoured to take an open look at the science relevant to GM crops and food, and to do so in a way that recognized the interests and concerns of the public as well as the science community'. Many claims had been made about the potential benefits available from GM crops and food. At the same time, considerable reservations and concerns had been expressed. The first report of the review panel was published in July 2003 and attracted wide public and media interest in the UK and abroad, with over 20,000 copies downloaded from the review website. Comments were invited on the panel's report, which were taken into consideration along with the report of the GM public debate, *GM Nation*, in the publication of a second report by the panel in January 2004.

In its conclusion to the first report, the panel noted that new technologies in whatever field always brought uncertainties and generated new gaps in knowledge. Uncertainty and divergence of interpretation were a key part of scientific development. An essential part of science was the ability to be honest about uncertainty and to be able to judge the quality or strength of evidence in reaching a particular conclusion. Challenge was central to the scientific process – as was speculation. The way to resolve controversies, when they were amenable to scientific resolution, was to do better science by going back to the real world and examining it with better tools and better ideas to improve understanding. The panel recognized the difference between those who considered GM to be similar in many ways to conventional plant breeding and others who stress the differences between GM and non-GM, and that because the technology was relatively new, the uncertainties were too great to pursue it with safety. At the same time, absence of evidence of harm was not evidence of the absence of harm. Reliability of GM technology was a concern for many people.

In the opinion of the review panel, the current, and widely accepted view within the biological research and plant breeding communities was that the methods for evaluation of the current generation of GM crops for food and feed carried out within the European regulatory framework were robust *when consistently applied* (emphasis added). It was recognized, however, that there were those who were not so confident, and their challenge was an important factor in the improvement of the framework and that regulatory evaluation needed to keep pace with the challenges posed by developments in GM technology. For human health, there was no evidence that commercialized GM crop varieties or foods made from them were toxic, allergenic or nutritionally deleterious, although the review panel recognized that others were less convinced, pointing out that the assessment techniques used had limitations. With respect to GM-derived animal feeds, several research studies had been unable to find transgenic DNA (or its gene products) in meat, meat or eggs produced from animals fed on GM crops. Concerning the potential effects on the environment, detailed field experiments on several GM crops had demonstrated that they were 'very unlikely' to invade the countryside or become problematic plants, or be toxic to wildlife or significantly perturb soil structure. Field studies also indicated that there was very little gene flow from GM crops to wild relatives living in semi-natural habitats, although this was the subject of ongoing research. The few studies that had been conducted had been unable to detect evidence for horizontal gene flow between GM plants and either bacteria in the soil or viruses.

There was insufficient evidence to predict what the long-term impact of GM herbicide-tolerant crops would have on weeds and the wildlife that depended on weeds for food. In the review panel's opinion, this poses perhaps the most serious potential harm arising from these crops. Looking to the future, the panel recognized that complexity and uncertainty would increase as the range of plants and traits increased and it listed areas where gaps in current knowledge existed. A case-by-case approach was advocated as the appropriate approach in making assessments on environmental impact. The panel noted that there had been no reports of GM crops causing any significant environmental damage in countries that had grown them, but there should be caution in drawing this general conclusion as these observations were based on relatively few field experiments. In addition, the panel pointed to the difficulty in generalizing confidently from one country to another. What was appropriate for UK agriculture could not be fully determined, but it would clearly need to be sympathetic to wildlife and allow the co-existence of farming systems.

Political decisions, market forces and other pressures would ultimately decide whether co-existence of different farming systems was practical, and in particular what thresholds were set for GM presence in crops and food labelled non-GM. Ultimately, the impact (positive or negative) of GM plants would be largely dependent on how GM technology was deployed by farmers, and this in turn may depend in part upon incentives to optimize a combination of productivity and environmentally friendly usage. GM was not a homogeneous technology, and each GM application should be considered on a case-by-case basis. There was a clear need for the science community to do more research in a number of areas, for companies to make good choices in terms of transgene design and plant hosts, and to develop products that met wider societal wishes.

The second report of the review panel took account of the substantial range of comments and questions raised on the first report. It repeated the general conclusion of the first report that the panel found no scientific case for ruling out all GM crops and their products, but nor did it give them blanket approval. It emphasized that GM was not a single homogeneous technology and that its applications needed to be considered on a case-by-case basis.

The GM Science Review pointed to two of the most serious potential negative effects of GM: acceleration of the loss of agricultural biodiversity and what has been called 'biopiracy' (Shand, 1998). During the twentieth century, as much as three quarters of the genetic diversity of agricultural crops may have been lost (FAO, 1993). The greatest factor contributing to the loss of crop and livestock genetic diversity has been the spread of industrial agriculture and the displacement of more diverse, traditional agricultural systems. New, uniform plant varieties were replacing farmers' traditional varieties and their wild relatives were becoming extinct. Industrial agriculture favoured genetic uniformity, and the prospect of GM would accelerate that process. But a uniform GM crop would be a breeding ground for disaster because it would be more vulnerable to epidemics of pests and diseases with no fall-back position that biodiversity provides.

At the same time, the rights of farmers have eroded as plant and animal resources have become subject to monopoly control under evolving intellectual property rights systems. Plant breeders' rights and industrial patents increasingly denied farmers the right to save seed, prohibit researchers from using proprietary germplasm, and thus restrict access to and exchange of germplasm. This process could be taken further if GM crops and foods become the monopoly control of multinational food corporations. The *Convention on Biological Diversity* of 1995, the first legally binding framework for the conservation and sustainable use of biodiversity, recognizes the knowledge, innovation and practices of indigenous and local communities and specifically encourages the equitable sharing of benefits arising from their utilization. FAO has championed the rights of farmers and through the *International Undertaking on Plant Genetic Resources* of 1983 (amended in 1989), and other measures, has sought to strengthen intergovernmental control over crop germplasm, held in trust under the auspices of the United Nations and to prohibit intellectual property claims on this material.

FAO issued a statement on biotechnology in March 2000 in which it stated that the biotechnology provided powerful tools for the sustainable development of agriculture and the food industry (FAO, 2000b). When appropriately integrated with other technologies for the production of food, it could be of significant assistance in meeting the needs of an expanding and increasing urbanized population. But FAO also recognized that genetically modified organisms (GMOs) had become the target of very intensive and at time emotionally charged debate. FAO recognized that genetic engineering had the potential to help increase production and productivity in agriculture. However, FAO was also aware of the concern about the potential risks posed by certain aspects of biotechnology on human and animal health and on the environment. FAO therefore supported a science-based evaluation system that would objectively determine the benefits and risks of each GMO.

The subject was addressed again in 2002 when several governments in Southern Africa expressed reservations about accepting food aid containing GMOs and sought advice from the UN (FAO, 2002b). It was noted that no existing international agreements were in force regarding trade in food or food aid that dealt specifically with food containing GMOs. And that it was UN policy that the decision rested with the recipient country. It was WFP policy that all donated food met the food safety standards of both donor and recipient countries and all applicable international standards, guidelines and recommendations. The UN believed that governments must consider carefully the severe and immediate consequences of limiting the food aid available for citizens so desperately in need. Based on information available from a variety of sources and current scientific knowledge, FAO, WHO and WFP held the view that the consumption of food containing GMOs was not likely to present human health risk. The FAO/WHO Codex Alimentarius Commission had established an ad hoc Intergovernmental Task Force on Foods Derived from Biotechnology to consider the health and nutritional implications of such foods in 1999. Any potential risks to biological diversity and sustainable agriculture should be judged and managed by countries on a case-by-case basis.

The controversy over GM crops and food has been exacerbated by the criticism that in drawing up its 1992 policy, which remains in effect, the US Food and Drug Administration (FDA) 'responded to political pressure for a permissive regulatory approach by exploiting gaps in scientific knowledge, creatively interpreting existing food law and limiting public involvement in the policy's development' (Pelletiet, 2006). This has led to a situation which has been characterized as one of 'great uncertainty', and despite repeated recommendations that this issue be the topic of a major public research effort, no action has so far been taken. Thus, while FDA's policy settles questions as a legal matter, questions remain unsettled as a scientific matter. Equally disturbing are the implications for farmers in the developing world. Focusing on GM crop improvements and the development of seven GM crops (six food staples and cotton) over the past fifteen years in Africa, case studies revealed a number of unexpected scientific, legal, economic and political barriers to the development of GM crops and long delays in developing and implementing national biosafety regulations and guidelines (Eicher *et al*, 2006). It was concluded that most GM crops are at least ten to fifeteen years or longer from reaching smallholder farmers in Africa. It was proposed that during this time, special attention should be given to strengthening conventional plant breeding programmes into which biotechnology approaches should be 'nested and integrated'. Special attention should also be given to raising public awareness of biotechnology, mobilizing political support and commitment to strengthening African capacity in biotechnology, biosafety, food safety and intellectual property rights, and mounting long-term training programmes to train the next generation of African plant breeders and GM crop specialists.

Climate change and global warming

Climate change is now regarded as one of the greatest challenges facing humankind. Potentially, it could pose a serious threat not only to food security but to the existence of life on earth. Concern with the effects of climate change on world food security is not new. A major conference held on the issue by the NATO Scientific Affairs Division in Oxford, UK in 1993 concluded that while there was much uncertainty that remained to be resolved, climate change threatened the livelihoods of vulnerable populations in marginal areas already marked by serious food insecurity, resulting in subsequent increases in the number of hungry people (Downing, 1996). And yet the world is deeply divided both on an assessment of the dimensions of this global threat and on developing a common and united response to address it. Climate change and global warming have taken place in the past, caused by variations either in the angle of the earth's rotation or in its distance from the sun. There was even a period in the middle of the last century when temperatures fell slightly that led to predictions of a cooling world in which there could be a drastic decline on food production.

This time, the difference is that climate change is being induced by man-made greenhouse gases that are building up in the atmosphere and may remain there for many years to come. Nobody knows with certainty what is happening to the world's climate. The debate involves scientists, economists, politicians and anybody interested in the future of the planet. Ignorance, and perhaps fear, has divided those involved in the debate into three categories: those who challenge the evidence that climate change and global warming are happening; those who regard that it isn't worth trying to do anything about it; and those who argue that the process of climate change is speeding up and should be tackled now.

International concern about the possible negative interaction of human activity and climate change was voiced at the first *World Climate Conference* organized by the World Meteorological Organization (WMO) in 1979, which expressed the view that 'continued expansion of man's activities on earth may cause significant extended regional and even global changes in climate', and called for 'global co-operation in exploring the possible future course of global climate'. In 1985, the conference on *Assessment of the Role of Carbon Dioxide and other Greenhouse Gases on Climate Variations and Associated Inputs*, organized by WMO and UNEP, concluded that 'as a result of increasing greenhouse gases it is now believed that in the first half of the next century a rise of global mean temperatures could occur which is greater than in any in man's history'. The conference resulted in the setting up of

444 Assessment. The Graveyard of Aspirations

the Advisory Group on Greenhouse Gasses to ensure periodic assessments of the state of scientific knowledge on climate change and its implications. Recognizing the need for objective, balanced and internationally co-ordinated assessment of climate change, WMO and UNEP jointly agreed to set up an Intergovernmental Panel on Climate Change (IPCC) in 1988. The panel, a worldwide network of 2,500 leading scientists and experts, review scientific research in three working groups on the available scientific information on climate change, the environmental and socio-economic impacts and the formulation of response strategies.

The first IPCC assessment report of 1990 served as a basis for negotiating the *United Nations Framework Convention on Climate Change*, which aims 'to achieve . . . stabilization of greenhouse gas concentrations in the atmosphere at a level which would prevent dangerous anthropogenic interference with the climate system'. The convention entered into force in March 1994 and is now ratified by 189 of the 192 members of the UN (the United States has not yet ratified). It sets an overall framework for intergovernmental efforts to tackle the challenges posed by climate change. The convention recognizes that the climate system is a shared resource whose stability can be affected by industrial and other emissions of carbon dioxide and other greenhouse gases. Under the convention, developed countries agreed to reduce their emissions to 1990 levels by 2000 and to transfer to developing countries technology and information to help them respond to the challenges of climate change.

In 1997, the *Kyoto Protocol* was adopted, which strengthened the convention by committing parties to individual, legally binding, targets to limit or reduce their greenhouse gas emissions. The protocol entered into force in February 2005 and is ratified by 165 countries. Of these, 35 countries and the EU are required to reduce greenhouse gas emissions below levels specified for each of them in the treaty. Total cuts in emissions add up to at least 5 per cent from 1990 levels in the commitment period 2008–2012. Australia and the United States have declared their intention not to ratify the protocol and therefore will not adopt Kyoto emission reduction targets.

The third IPCC assessment report, issued in 2001, reviewed in depth the scientific, technical and socio-economic aspects of climate change. It concluded that there was strong evidence that climate change due to the emission of greenhouse gases was already occurring and that future emissions were likely to raise global temperatures by between 1.4 and 5.8 °C during this century, with a wide range of impacts on the natural world and human society. The report emphasized that the issue of climate change is part of the larger challenge of sustainable development. As a result, climate policies can be more effective when consistently embedded within broader strategies designed to make national and regional development paths more sustainable. The report noted that there was new and stronger evidence that most of the global warming observed over the past 50 years was attributable to human activities. Changes in sea level, snow cover, ice extent and precipitation were consistent with a warming climate. Yields of cereal crops in some temperate areas were expected to increase with small temperature changes but decrease if larger temperature changes took place. In most tropical and sub-tropical regions, potential crop yields were projected to decrease.

Climate change was also expected to exacerbate water shortages in many water-scarce areas. Overall, climate change was projected to increase threats to human health, particularly in lower income populations, predominantly within tropical and sub-tropical countries. Ecological productivity and biodiversity would be altered by climate change and sea-level rise, with an increased risk of extinction of some valuable species. The aggregate market sector effect, measured as changes in GDP, was estimated to be negative for many developing countries for all magnitudes of global mean temperature increases studied and estimated to be mixed for developed countries for up to a few degrees of warming and negative for warming beyond a few degrees. Populations inhabiting small islands and low-lying coastal areas would be particularly at risk of severe social and economic effects of sea-level rises and storm surges. In sum, the impact of climate change would fall disproportionately on developing countries, and the poor within all countries, thereby exacerbating inequalities in health status and access to adequate food, clean water and other resources.

Numerous possibilities existed for adaptive options to reduce the adverse and enhance the beneficial impacts of climate change, the report noted, but costs would have to be incurred. Greater and more rapid climate change would pose greater challenges for adaptation and greater risks of damage than would lesser and slower change. Inertia, doing nothing in the hope that the problem would go away, was the greatest danger. Many opportunities, including technological option, to reduce near-term emissions existed but barriers to their deployment remained to be overcome. Forests, agricultural lands and other terrestrial ecosystems offered significant carbon mitigation potential.

A scientific symposium on 'Avoiding Dangerous Climate Change', held in the UK in February 2005 and attended by over 200 participants from some 30 countries, mainly scientists and representatives from international organizations and national governments, focused on the key impacts of different levels of climate change for different regions and sectors and the world as a whole, and on options for achieving stabilization taking into account costs and uncertainties.[18] At the start of the symposium, Dr. Rajendra K. Pachauri of India, chairman of the IPCC, said that dangerous climate change requires a value judgement but that this should be based on the principles of universal human rights and the needs of future generations, as exemplified in sustainable development. However, science could provide essential information on impacts and damage, taking into account socio-economic dimensions.

The symposium noted that compared with the IPCC 2001 report, there was greater clarity and reduced uncertainty about the impacts of climate change. In many cases, the risks were more serious than previously thought. A global temperature increase of up to 1 °C could be beneficial for a few regions and sectors, such as high latitude areas and agriculture, but changes that were occurring in the acidity of the oceans was likely to reduce their capacity to absorb carbon dioxide from the atmosphere and affect the entire marine food chain. (A survey conducted in 2006 found that unless there were major changes in the managements and conservation of fish stock, commercial fishing could end by 2050.) In general, surveys of the

446 *Assessment. The Graveyard of Aspirations*

scientific literature suggested increasing damage if the earth warmed about 1–2 °C above current levels, resulting in the serious risks of large-scale, irreversible system disruption. Many climate impacts, particularly the most damaging ones, would be associated with an increased frequency or intensity of extreme events. Adaptive capacity in some sectors and systems may be sufficient to delay or avoid much potential damage; in others it was quite limited. Capacity to adapt was closely related to technological ability, income levels, and the form of governance in a country. Africa was particularly worrying.

Carbon dioxide emissions were predicted to increase by 63 per cent over the 2002 level by 2030. If this were to happen, in the absence of urgent and strenuous mitigation actions in the next 20 years, there would be a temperature rise of between 0.5 and 2.0 °C above current temperatures by 2050. Technological options for significantly reducing emissions over the long term already existed. Large reductions could be attained using a portfolio of options whose costs were likely to be smaller than previously considered. Sustainable development strategies could make low-level stabilization easier. But there were no 'magic bullets': a portfolio of options was needed and excluding any option would increase costs. Major investment was needed now in both mitigation, to minimize future impacts, and adaptation, to cope with impacts that cannot be avoided in the near and medium term.

Other predictions have pointed to the dangers of widespread drought, affecting one third of the earth by 2100, an increasing rate of climate change, and the importance of taking urgent and effective action now with the technology that is available and within manageable costs before effects spiralled out of control and became irreversible. They also underline that this global problem will require concerted and cohesive global action and the necessary level of investment and political will to carry out a common strategy and framework. Yet serious differences impede co-ordinated international action. A major impediment is the marked differences between the United States and other countries in participating in international agreements to tackle world issues. We saw that this applied to international cooperation regarding food security and human rights. But there have been other areas and critically it applies to measures to address climate change and related environmental issues. The United States has not ratified the *Kyoto Protocol* despite being the world's largest source of global greenhouse gas emissions. With 5 per cent of the world's population, the United States accounts for 24 per cent of global carbon dioxide emissions and for 36 per cent of 1990 global emissions.

It is important to understand both the implications of the lack of strong US involvement in global environmental agreements and institutions and the possible reasons for it (DeSombre, 2006, pp. 164–7). In the past, the US played a crucial, often leading, role in initiating and implementing international agreements. In the case of climate change, uncertainty and unacceptance of the scientific evidence and predictions of the severity of the problem, and the costs of proposed solutions, have been quoted as reasons for US reluctance. Aspects of domestic politics are likely to play an important role. Many attribute the US reluctance to take action on climate change to politically powerful industrial and energy interests and to the argument that imposing cuts in greenhouse gas emissions is a ploy to impose a tax on them, which would handicap their competitiveness in domestic and international markets and result in losses in economic growth and employment. Another factor is that the separation between the executive and legislative branches in the US domestic political process requires a super-majority of the Senate plus presidential approval to take on international obligations.

The former vice president of the United States, Al Gore, has played his part in turning public opinion against the sceptics in the United States and elsewhere with his commentary on the film, and his book, on *An Inconvenient Truth*, which sounds a strident alarm about global warming (Gore, 2006). Al Gore announced in February 2007 that a 24 hour 'Live Earth' event would take place simultaneously in major cities around the world at which leading names in music would appear in a series of concerts to highlight the threat of climate change. The latest twist is that in the absence of federal leadership to reduce greenhouse gas emissions, many US states and regions have begun taking action to address the issue of climate change, almost always with long-term economic well-being in mind. As the US Senate is particularly prone to pressure from special interest groups, with senators responsive to issues that affect their individual states rather than the country as a whole, the action of state governors, and most recently leading industrialists, to seriously address climate change issues may have a strong influence in eventually persuading domestic action leading to federally accepted international support.

The most comprehensive review ever carried out on the economics of climate change was published in October 2006 (Stern, 2006). The review, commissioned by the UK Treasury and submitted to the British Prime Minister and Chancellor of the Exchequer, was carried out by Sir Nicholas Stern, head of the UK Government Economic Service and formerly chief economist of the World Bank. At the launch of the review, the author said:

> The conclusion of the Review is essentially optimistic. There is still time to avoid the worst impacts of climate change, if we act now and act internationally. Governments, businesses and individuals all need to work together to respond to the challenge. Strong, deliberate policy choices by governments are essential to motivate change. But the task is urgent. Delaying action, even by a decade or two, will take us into dangerous territory. We must not let this window of opportunity close.

Climate change was described in the review as 'the greatest market failure the world has seen'. The review found that all countries will be affected by climate change but the poorest will suffer earliest and most. Climate change threatened the basic elements of life for people around the world – access to water, food production, health, the use of land and the environment – and the damage caused by climate change would accelerate as the world got warmer (Figure 42.1). But there was still time to avoid the worst impacts of climate change, is strong action was taken now. The benefits of strong, early action would outweigh the costs. To avoid the worst impacts of climate change, the review estimated that the costs

Figure 42.1 Possible impacts of climate change on growth and development

Temperature rise (°C)	Water	Food	Health	Land	Environment	Abrupt and large-scale impacts
1	Small glaciers in the Andes disappear completely, threatening water supplies for 50 million people	Modest increases in cereal yields rise in temperature regions	At least 300,000 people each year die from climate-related diseases (predominantly diarrhoea, malaria and malnutrition). Drop in winter mortality in higher latitudes (Northern Europe USA)	Permafrost thawing in Canada and Russia damages buildings and roads	At least 10% of land species face extinction (according to one estimate). 80% bleaching of coral reefs, including the Great Barrier Reef	Atlantic thermohaline circulation starts to weaken
2	Potentially 20–30% decrease in water available in some vulnerable regions, e.g. Southern Africa and Mediterranean	Sharp declines in crop yields in tropical regions (5–10% in Africa)	40–60 million more Africans exposed to malaria	Coastal flooding affects up to 10 million more people each year	15–40% species face extinction (according to one estimate). High risk of extinction of Artic species, including polar bear and caribou	Potential for Greenland ice sheet to begin melting irreversibly, accelerating sea levels rise to possible 7 m
3	Serious droughts in southern Europe occur once every 10 years. 1–4 billion more people suffer shortages, while 1–5 billion gain water, which may increase flood risk	150–550 million more people at risk of hunger (if carbon fertilization weakens). Agricultural yields in higher latitudes likely to peak	1–3 million more people die from malnutrition (if carbon fertilization weakens)	Coastal flooding affects 1–170 million more people each year	20–50% of species face extinction (according to one estimate). Onset of Amazon forest collapse (some models only)	Rising risk of abrupt changes to atmospheric circulations, e.g. the monsoon. Rising risk of collapse of West Antarctic ice sheet threatened with collapse

4	Potentially 30–50% decrease in water availability in Southern Africa and Mediterranean	Agricultural yields decline 15–35% in Africa, and entire regions out of production (e.g. parts of Australia)	Up to 80 million more Africans exposed to malaria	Coastal flooding affects 7–300 million more people each year	Loss of around half the Artic tundra. Around half of the world's nature reserves cannot fulfil their objectives	Rising risk of collapse of Atlantic thermohaline circulation.
5	Possible disappearance of large glaciers in the Himalayas, affecting one-quarter of China's population and hundreds of millions of people in India	Continued increase in ocean acidity seriously disrupting marine ecosystems and possibly fish stocks		Major cities such as London, New York and Tokyo and low-lying coastal areas such as Florida threatened by rising sea levels		
More than 5	This level of global temperature rise would be equivalent to the amount of warming that occurred between the last ice age and today – and is likely to lead to major disruptions and population movements. Such 'socially contingent' effects could be catastrophic but are currently very hard to capture with current models as temperatures are so far outside human experience.					
	Note: The table shows illustrative impacts of different degrees of warming. Temperatures represent increases relative to pre-industrial levels. The impacts are expressed for a 1 °C band around the central temperature, e.g. 1 °C represents the range 0.5–1.5 °C.					

Source: Adapted from N. Stern (2006) *The Economics of Climate Change* (Cambridge: Cambridge University Press).

450 *Assessment. The Graveyard of Aspirations*

could be limited to around 1 per cent of global GDP a year. Based on the assessment carried out in the IPCC 2001 report, the review calculated that the dangers of unabated climate change would be equivalent to at least 5 percent of global GDP each year. A range of options existed to cut greenhouse gas emissions. Climate change was a global threat that demanded a global response, based on a shared understanding of long-term goals and agreements on frameworks for action. And contrary to the views the opponents for early global action, steps could be taken without adversely affecting employment and economic growth in rich and poor countries.

The review identified a number of elements of policy required for an effective response to climate change, including carbon pricing through taxation, emissions trading or regulation; technology policy to drive the development and deployments of arrange of low-carbon and high-efficiency products; removing the barriers to energy efficiency and to inform, educate and persuade individuals about what can be done; reducing deforestation; integrating climate change concerns into development policy; and assisting the poorest countries to make the changes necessary in their development programmes. The review gained the support of Nobel Prize economists Amartya Sen, Robert Solow and Joseph Stiglitz. The president of the World Bank, Paul Wolfowitz, said that he was committed to addressing the dangers of climate change. The World Bank had developed an Investment Framework for Clean Energy and Development through which the private sector might become more involved in a partnership between the Bank, the World Economic Forum and the World Business Council on Sustainable Development.

The *United Nations Climate Change Conference* in Nairobi, Kenya in November 2006, which was the second meeting of parties to the *Kyoto Protocol* and the twelfth session of the parties to the UN Climate Change Convention, provided an opportunity for reconciling the differences between the US and other countries, for an assessment of the progress made in reaching the targets set, for reaching agreement on the necessary investments that must be made, and in declaring the political will to tackle the problem that threatens future existence. At the opening of the conference, the UN secretary-general, Kofi Annan, criticized a 'frightening lack of leadership' within the international community on tackling climate change. He said, 'the message is clear. Global climate change must take its place alongside those threats – conflict, poverty, the proliferation of deadly weapons – that have traditionally monopolized first order political attention'. He announced a new UN plan, called the 'Nairobi Framework'. Six UN agencies (including the UNDP, the World Bank group, the African Development Bank and the UN Framework Convention on Climate Change) launched an initiative to help developing countries, especially in Africa, participating in the Kyoto Protocol's Clean Development Mechanism. The UK government also announced that it will introduce legislation to reduce carbon emissions. Others advocate the setting of verifiable annual targets for which an independent authority should be responsible from monitoring progress. It is generally agreed that the involvement of the United States, China and India will be essential in any global agreement to tackle the problems arising from climate change and global warming, and that developing countries will require assistance from donor countries to help them implement the measures necessary to reduce the emission of greenhouse gasses.

FAO has provided an important reminder of another, hitherto overlooked, contributor to global warming (FAO, 2006). As the world's human population has grown, so too has its livestock population. At present, there are about 1.5 billion cattle and domestic buffalo and about 1.7 billion sheep and goats. With pigs and poultry, they form a critical part of what has been called our 'biological footprint' on this planet. Global livestock grazing and feed production use some 30 per cent of the earth's land surface. Livestock, which consume more food than they yield, also compete with humans for water, and the drive to expand grazing land destroys more biologically sensitive terrain, especially rain forest, than anything else. Livestock are also responsible for about 18 per cent of the global warming effect, more than the effect of transportation, through methane, the natural result of bovine digestion, and nitrogen emitted by manure. Deforestation of grazing land adds to this effect. There are no easy trade-offs and the human passion for meat is not likely to be curtailed very soon. But as the FAO report makes clear, our health and the health of our planet depend on pushing livestock production in more sustainable directions.

The IPCC fourth assessment report, released in March 2007, declared, for the first time, that warming of the world's climate system is 'unequivocal'. Eleven of the past twelve years (1995–2006) ranked among the twelve warmest years in the instrumental record (started in 1850) of global surface temperature. The linear warming trend over the past fifty years is nearly twice that for the last 100 years. The report paints a picture of a world of starvation, mass migration of people, rampant diseases and the extinction of many animal species. If unchecked, climate change could lead to 50 million people becoming refugees as soon as 2010. The worst effects would be felt in regions that are mainly poor and already face dangers from existing climate change and coastal hazards. About 250 million people would face hunger. Diseases such as malaria, dengue fever, yellow fever and Nile fever would spread. Billions of people in Asia would be at risk from flooding. Nearly a third of animal species would be put at risk of extinction. Adapting to climate change would cost at least 5–10 per cent of GDP in Africa. On the other hand, the wealthier countries in higher latitudes could benefit from higher temperatures leading to increased agricultural production, open Arctic seaways and fewer deaths from cold. The report warns that the world must begin to adapt or face a bill of many billions of dollars more and a heavy toll in human suffering within a few decades. It points out that most of the cost should be met by the private sector and business rather than governments.

Globalization

Globalization is now one of the most prominent and contentious issues in development economics, as seen from the burgeoning literature on the subject and public demonstrations at the sites of international meetings. It has become a major theme in many disciplines and a source of ongoing inquiry in academia

452   Assessment. The Graveyard of Aspirations

and industry. Depending on its definition, intent and projected outcomes, it has attracted passionate supporters and violent opponent. Given such a disarray, it is difficult to separate impartial analysis from rhetoric, or as one publication put its, the 'virtue' from the 'vice' (Shojai and Christopherson, 2004). The process of globalization has been conceived predominantly in economic terms with little linkage to politics, history, cultural, environment and society, but encompasses important non-economic processes (Singh, 2005).

While the protagonists see globalization as an inevitable process with benefits for all, the antagonists, particularly, although not exclusively, in the developing world, see the lack of tangible benefits to Third World countries, and particularly the poorest among them, from opening their economies to free trade. Despite the claims of exports and income gains, the economic losses and social dislocation caused by rapid financial trade liberalization, the growing inequalities of wealth and opportunities, and the perception that environmental, social and cultural problems are said to have been worse by the workings of the global free-market economy (Khor, 2001). Divergence, not convergence, is seen to be occurring between developed and developing countries because globalization is taking place in an unreformed world order, which is unequal, unsafe and unsustainable, that is already stacked against the poorer countries, and without the specific aim of reducing, then eradicating, world hunger and poverty. While globalization has been facilitated and influenced by technological development, especially modern information and communications technology, it is argued that the process is mainly driven and enabled by policy choices at the global and national levels that have led to the rapid liberalization of finance, trade and investment. Both forces have been mainly shaped and dominated by powerful developed countries and international institutions controlled by them.

The protagonists for globalization point to the superiority of the market economy over any other alternative. They start from the proposition that a world integrated through the market should be highly beneficial to the vast majority of the world's inhabitants, and that the market is the most powerful institution for raising living standards (Wolf, 2004). But markets need states, just as states need markets. In a proper marriage between the two, comes liberal democracy, regarded as the best way to manage a society. The problem is not that there is too much globalization, but there is too little. Much more could be achieved with the right mix of more liberal markets and more co-operative global governance, through a better understanding by states of their long-term interest in a co-operative global economic order that would extend opportunities to the world as a whole. Political fragmentation is seen as the chief obstacle to making the world better through globalization. The deep-seated differences in the institutional quality of states is seen as determining the persistence of inequality throughout the world. A key challenge is therefore to reconcile a world divided into states of highly unequal capacities with exploitation of the opportunities for convergence offered by international economic integration. A better world needed better politics, not different economies. Two other impediments are to remove the hypocrisy of the developed world on market liberalization (as revealed by the breakdown of the

Doha multilateral trade negotiations) and the performance of the institutions set up to manage the global economy.

Many of the antagonists see the problem not with globalization itself, which some regard as a necessary and inevitable process for one planet with finite resources, but the way in which globalization has so far been managed (Stiglitz, 2002, 2006). Economic forces have been driving globalization, especially through lowering communication and transportation costs. But politics has shaped it, and decisions are made because of ideology, pre-conceived ideas and denial, not impartial evidence. The rules of the game that govern globalization have been largely set by the advanced industrial countries, and particular interest groups (like agriculture and energy) in those countries to further their own interests. They have not sought to create a fair set of rules, let alone those that would promote the well-being of the poorest countries and people. Witness the contrasting views expressed at the meetings of the World Economic Forum with those of the World Social Forum. There is lack of consultation and effective representation in the world's key economic decision-making bodies that were set up in 1945 by the victorious Second World War powers. There is therefore what has been described as a 'democratic deficit' in the way globalization has been managed. This has lead to the view that globalization, as currently pursued, has caused or sustained hunger and poverty and inequalities in the distribution of benefits rather than remove them (Kaplinsky, 2005).

Faced with growing criticism, even resentment, the ILO established a World Commission on the Social Dimensions of Globalization in 2001.[19] The commission produced a highly sceptical report in 2004, which began, 'The dominant perspective on globalization must shift more from a narrow preoccupation with markets to a broader preoccupation with people'. The social dimension of globalization was not only about jobs, health and education but about democratic participation and national prosperity. In the view of the commission, 'A better globalization is the key to a better and secure life for people everywhere in the 21st century'. The report of the commission indicated what was generally felt about globalization at the time:

> The current process of globalization is generating outcomes, both between and within countries. Wealth is being created, but too many countries are not sharing in its benefits. They also have little or no voice in shaping the process. Seen through the eyes of the vast majority of women and men, globalization has not met their simple and legitimate aspirations for decent jobs and a better future for their children. Many of them live in the limbo of the informal economy without formal rights and in a swathe of poor countries that subsist on the margins of the global economy. Even in economically successful countries some workers and communities have been adversely affected by globalization. Meanwhile the revolution in global communications heightens awareness of these disparities... [which] are morally unacceptable and politically unsustainable.
>
> (ILO, 2004)

454 *Assessment. The Graveyard of Aspirations*

The commission surveyed 73 countries, which produced some startling conclusions. In every region of the world, except South Asia, the United States and the European Union, unemployment rates increased between 1990 and 2002. By 2004, global unemployment had reached a new high of 185.9 million people. Fifty-nine per cent of the world's population was living in countries with growing inequality; only 5 per cent in countries with declining inequality. Even in the most developed countries, the gap between rich and poor was widening. While there were no simple solutions, the commission called for a focus on people, a democratic and effective state, and sustainable development. The problem was not due to globalization as such but to deficiencies in its governance. Global markets had grown rapidly without the parallel development of economic and social institutions necessary for their smooth and equitable functioning.

At the same time, concern was expressed about the unfairness of key global rules on trade and finance and their asymmetric effects on rich and poor countries, and the failure of international policies to respond adequately to the challenges posed by globalization. Market opening measures and financial and economic considerations predominated over social ones. ODA fell far short of the minimum amounts required to achieve the MDGs and tackle growing global problems. The multilateral system responsible for designing and implementing international policies was 'under-performing'. It lacked policy coherence as a whole and was not sufficiently democratic, transparent and accountable. These rules and policies were the outcome of a system of global governance shaped largely by powerful countries and powerful people.

The commission made a number of proposals at the national and international levels for making globalization more fair and equitable. At the national level, a number of 'essentials' were identified, on which there was wide international agreement, including: good political governance; an effective state; and a vibrant civil society, including strong representative organizations of workers and employers for fruitful social dialogue. At the global level, parliamentary oversight of the multilateral system should be 'progressively expanded', which would include the creation of a 'Parliamentary Group' concerned with the coherence and consistency between global economic, social and environmental policies, to develop an integrated oversight of the major international organizations. Developing countries should have increased representation in the decision-making bodies of the Bretton Woods institutions and the working methods of the WTO should provide for their full and effective participation in its negotiations. The commission recognized that the multilateral system had to play a 'pivotal' role in carrying forward reforms at the global level. It proposed new 'operational tools' for upgrading the quality of policy co-ordination between international organizations on issues in which the implementation of their mandates intersected and their policies interacted, including 'policy coherence initiatives', 'policy development dialogues' and a 'global policy forum' to review on a regular and systematic basis the social impact of globalization and produce a periodic state of globalization report. Specific proposals were made to strengthen the role that ECOSOC could play to promote global policy co-ordination in the economic and social fields.[20]

In a major study on food and nutrition security in the process of globalization and urbanization, published in 2005, mainstream international thinking was summarized as follows (Kracht and Schulz, 2005).[21] Global economic integration had increased considerably over the past two decades, particularly in trade, investment and capital flow. In the process, the world had become much more prosperous and well fed. But absolute poverty and food insecurity persisted and was worsening in sub-Saharan Africa. Globalization and related technological advances offered growing possibilities for overcoming hunger and poverty, despite the slowdown in global trade since 2001. However, the slow opening of developing countries to agricultural markets had been a disappointment since the mid-1990s. Since 1980, contrary to the viewpoint frequently expressed by critics of globalization, human development had displayed positive signs. But the effects of globalization on the poor were as heterogeneous as the sources of income and resources at their disposal and the political and economic environment in which they lived. Nations were not at the mercy of globalization. They retained considerable manoeuvrability in relation to the extent they participated in the globalization process and market liberalization. New players in civil society, including the poor themselves, were of growing relevance, especially when they acted in concert. Strengthened international institutions, a further opening of the global rule-based trading system, increased regulation of the practices of multinational corporations, and the work of NGOs could help globalization serve the poor. National social and health policies, the promotion of rural development, and improved access to rights for poor people remained necessary preconditions for effective reduction of hunger and poverty.

The critics of globalization challenged this view. They argued that the focus of globalization was on neither food security nor food safety. Food security is an issue for people in the global South, while food safety was the concern of the global North. Such differences in perspective made it difficult for the critics of globalization to agree on a common agenda concerning food and nutrition security within the broader context of human security, the provision of basic needs, and fair and equitable economic and social advancement. The editors of the major study concluded in their observations on policy implications that 'Current trends for achieving food security contradict hopeful assertions that hunger and malnutrition can be eradicated in our lifetime and are not consistent with political commitments by the international community substantially to reduce food and nutrition insecurity by 2015'. In the 1990s, the net decrease in the number of the hungry poor in the developing world was barely 19 million when a decrease of over 100 million was achieved in the 1980s. The remaining over 800 million of undernourished people constituted 'the hard core of world poverty'. While globalization offered opportunities for economic growth essential for reduction in poverty and hunger, the world's poor have in many cases not been able to seize these opportunities for their own benefits. Social science had captured this phenomenon in the 'theory of fragmented development' which portrayed the benefits of globalization accruing to the few, while the costs were borne by many, and with an attendant tendency of increased marginalization. At the same time,

456 Assessment. The Graveyard of Aspirations

the concept of a 'globalization dividend' resulting from a more efficient use of world resources, and gains from globalization that would allow for the provision of more development aid to combat poverty in the developing world, had yet to materialize.

Economic growth generated by globalization on its own, while a necessary precondition, was not sufficient to overcome poverty. Strategic attention by national governments and the international community focused on the reduction of poverty, and specifically on the reduction and eventual eradication of hunger, remained central for meeting political commitments to globally agreed goals, including the MDGs. The broad contours of a global strategy to achieve those goals had been delineated at a series of global conferences and summits, ending in the *Millennium Summit* and *Declaration* in 2000. The challenge now was to muster the resolve, resources and know-how necessary to translate the declared political commitments into effective and co-ordinated action, focusing on that proportion of the world's population that was most food insecure. Five priority areas were identified for at the national level: increasing agricultural productivity among food-insecure, small farmers; restoring and conserving the environment; improving rural infrastructure and market access; increasing emphasis on programmes focused on access to food and nutrition; and investing in research, extension and nutrition education. At the international levels, the priorities included: establishing an open international trading system to achieve food security; strengthening international finance and technical cooperation; and harnessing the private sector and civil society. But the greatest challenge was now to build collective action through global partnership or alliance for development to keep the momentum for the action needed to realize the vision of an equitable, just and inclusive global community, free from hunger and poverty.

Leadership for effective, cohesive and co-ordinated action

The co-existence of poverty and food insecurity affecting large numbers of our fellow world citizens and the availability of the resources and capacity required to overcome these dehumanizing forces is one of the most critical paradoxes of our time. Not only is this situation morally and ethically unacceptable but it is also politically, economically and socially indefensible, and a threat to world peace. As we traverse the first decade of the twenty-first century, the quest for food security for all will assume even more critical dimensions for future generations (Delisle and Shaw, 1998).

The rationale for setting food security as a central development goal (at the household, local, national and global levels) is based on the fact that food is a fundamental human need – and a basic human right. Food security is both an important outcome of, and a vital contributor to, the development process and the achievements of the Millennium Development Goals that world leaders approved at the *Millennium Summit* in 2002. Access to adequate food at all times is a major factor in ensuring a healthy, productive and fulfilling life. Yet the complexity of food security as a multi-dimensional and multi-sectoral concept has been a major barrier in reaching consensus on how to define and achieve it, and lack of agreement on effective policy prescriptions has resulted in inadequate concerted and co-ordinated national and global action.

A number of general conclusions can be drawn from this history of the quest for world food security. One is the uneven progress by countries and regions to achieve the MDGs. It now seems unlikely that a number of countries, particularly in sub-Saharan Africa, will achieve the targets set by 2015, unless there is a major increase in the combined efforts of poor and rich nations above past trends. Furthermore, seen together, and not separately, progress, or the lack of it, in one of the dimensions of poverty can have significant effects on progress, or the lack of it, in the other dimensions of poverty. This particularly applies to the goals of eradicating hunger and poverty, which are key to achieving the other MDGs. A combined attack on all the dimensions of poverty will make the biggest and most sustainable advance in the conquest of hunger and poverty. For this, an incremental strategy, with carefully designated priorities and sequences, will be necessary at the national and international levels.

A major redirection of the resources that are available in the developing countries will be necessary in order to achieve the MDGs. Even then, they, especially the poorest, will require international co-operation to attain the targets set. As the *Millennium Project* has shown, the aid required is well within the resources of donor countries and would represent only a small fraction of their current military budgets. Promises have been made to increase aid expenditure to the levels required in what has aptly been called 'a confusion of good intentions'. But many questions remain unanswered. Will donors live up to their promises and actually deliver their aid commitments? Will the aid be provided as grants or loans? What will actually be done to settle the outstanding promises on debt relief? What conditions will be attached to the aid provided? What mechanisms will be put in place to ensure that there is co-ordination, and not conflict, in the aid provided? And what steps will be taken to ensure and monitor that donors provide the aid promised in the amounts and with the terms, consistency, and assurance necessary? Even then, international co-operation alone will not be enough. It will require the full and unreserved commitment of the developing countries themselves and their leaders.

The dimensions of hunger and poverty need to be fitted together like pieces of a jigsaw puzzle and dealt with holistically if progress towards their reduction and eventual elimination are to be achieved. However, as this history has shown, there are many actors involved, each with their own motivations, mandates, governing bodies and budgets. Some have seen a major impediment in institutional incoherence, the compartmentalization of the dimensions of hunger and poverty, institutionalized in the structure of the UN system, and in international co-operation generally. Other feel that the causes of hunger and poverty can best be understood and analyzed through separate specialist organizations. But there is gathering recognition that a central force is required to fit the pieces together, to agree on priorities and to monitor and evaluate progress at both the national and international levels.

458 *Assessment. The Graveyard of Aspirations*

The report of the UN secretary-general's *High Level Panel on Threats, Challenges and Change*, which addressed all the major threats to international peace and security around the world, is perhaps the most comprehensive and ambitious review undertaken since the UN was set up in 1945 (UN, 2004). A similar review is now needed of the structure of the UN system as a whole to align this sprawling, unfocused organization to focus on attacking the scourge of hunger and poverty through the implemention of the MDGs. In addition, an appraisal of the interconnections between the UN system and other major international institutions and NGOs concerned and involved in food security issues is required so that their activities can have compounded benefit. Without this, much of the seminal work of the UN and international bodies and institutions will be inconclusive as none of them alone has the competence and the capacity to address all the interrelated concerns that affect the achievement of food security. The reforms of the UN system introduced by the UN secretary-general Kofi Annan in 1997, which he described as 'the most extensive and far-reaching' in the history of the UN system for 'preparing the United Nations to meet the major challenges and needs of the world community for the 21st century', while making some progress did not go far enough (Annan, 1997). Confined to the UN secretariat and the UN funds and programmes, they did not address such system-wide problems as co-ordination and leadership of the UN specialized agencies and the policy and operational rift between the Bretton Woods institutions and the rest of the UN system as well as fundamental changes in process of appointing the UN secretary-general and providing adequate and stable resources for the UN system to carry out the ever-increasing tasks that are required successfully (Shaw, 1997).

Co-ordinated action is required at the national and international levels to achieve food and nutrition security for all (Shaw, 1999). At the national level, where responsibility lies first and foremost with national governments, development strategies should be formulated with clearly defined priorities for achieving the MDGs and for improving institutional and administrative capacities and to foster co-ordinated management of national action and international support. The international community can effectively support developing countries' efforts by adjusting their own management and co-ordinating procedures to the needs of developing countries, including improvements in their internal co-ordination of action within donor agencies, and providing management support and training to improve the capacities of developing countries to plan and manage their national policies and programmes and external aid.

At the international level, food and nutrition security are seen as issues of global dimensions. Their achievement will require cohesive global action; lack of achievement will have wide negative global consequences. This history has shown that solution of the food and nutrition security problem lies not only in the food and agricultural sphere but in other economic and social sectors, and in the maintenance of peace and security. Overcoming food and nutrition insecurity will require cohesive global political will and resources. To add to the complexity, world food and nutrition security is not a separate issue but is bound up with a series of impending and interlocking crises including food supplies, water resources, population growth, unemployment, international migration, money and debt, finite oil and energy resources, international trade, environment and sustainable development, and human security and the threat of international terrorism – to which has recently been added the threat of climate change and global warming, and the inequitable process of globalization. For this reason, various proposals have been made to adjust and strengthen the multilateral management of major global economic and social objectives, including food and nutrition security, set up at Bretton Woods in 1944 with the creation of the IMF and the IBRD, and at San Francisco in 1945 with the creation of the United Nations (Singer, 1995).

As this history has shown, the experience of the past sixty years confirms that a co-ordinating and supervisory authority for world food and nutrition security cannot be located in a single agency with a limited sectoral mandate and membership. The fate of the World Food Council suggest that the solution does not lie in setting up a separate institution without executive authority and with a mandate that cuts across that of other UN bodies. The proposals to create a World Food Authority or a World Food Security Council at the highest political level, with supporting subsidiary bodies attached to existing UN and FAO institutions, were not approved at the World Food Conference in 1974 (UN, 1975, p. 37).

Subsequently a number of other proposals have been made. One is for the creation of a UN Economic Security Council, 'a decision-making forum at the highest level to review the threats to global human security and agree on necessary action . . . including basic issues – such as global poverty, unemployment, food security, international migration and a new framework for sustainable human development' (ul Haq, 1995; UNDP, 1994, pp. 10–11). The report of Commission for Global Governance, *Our Global Neighbourhood* (1995), supported this proposal. The report of the Independent Working Group on the future of the United Nations, *The United Nations in its Second Half Century* (1995), recommended the establishment of two councils, an Economic Council and a Social Council, empowered to supervise and integrate the work of all UN activities in the economic and social fields. The creation of one UN Economic and Social Security Council, to replace ECOSOC, was also proposed to 'provide a structure to deal with issues of world economic governance and world action toward poverty and social needs in a systematic and politically realistic way' (Stewart and Daws, 1998).

The Group of Seven (G7) leading industrialized countries and the Group of Fifteen (G15) developing countries have been called upon to establish a joint high-level steering committee for sustainable food security. Other proposals have included extending the role of the UN Security Council to cover major economic and social issues and strengthening and modifying the role and structure of ECOSOC. Whatever decisions are taken on further UN reform, it is necessary to have a focal point on food and nutrition security at the highest political level to ensure that it is advocated and managed as a central issue embedded in national and world action for equitable and inclusive economic and social development and lasting peace, with cohesive and co-ordinated programmes of international development and humanitarian assistance.

460 *Assessment. The Graveyard of Aspirations*

An opportunity for decisive reform and action comes with the appointment of a new UN secretary-general, Ban Ki-moon, formerly Foreign Minister of South Korea, from the beginning of 2007. His immediate attention will no doubt be taken up with the threats of nuclear proliferation and international terrorism. But he would do well to recall that, as stated in its *Charter*, the UN was set up not only 'to save succeeding generations from the scourge of war' but also to promote 'social progress and better standards of life in larger freedoms', which is essential for sustainable peace. The G8 has also focused its attention on poverty reduction, especially in Africa, as necessary for global development and peace. But if history is to be a guide, two ingredients are necessary to provoke decisive action: a large-scale cataclysmic event and international leadership. The failed League of Nations was preceded by the First World War and resulted from the leadership of US President Woodrow Wilson. The UN was established after the Second World War and resulted from the leadership of US Presidents Franklin D. Roosevelt and Harry S. Truman and UK Prime Minister Winston Churchill. What world event and which leaders will galvanize the action required to eliminate world hunger and poverty? And what direction is that action likely to take? Important changes will take place in world leadership in the next few years not only in the United Nations but also in major developed and developing countries. Will the new leaders that emerge take up the challenge where their predecessors have patently failed? They would be encouraged, and helped considerably, in the task if a grand coalition was formed, in a planetary pact, of UN and international organizations, bilateral aid agencies, development institutes, civil society bodies, and NGOs, that have all professed to have concern. This would effectively link their resources, expertise and experience to the mutual advantage of all, and especially for the benefit of the hungry poor.

The rise of the human rights movement in the 1980s, led particularly by the Netherlands and Scandinavian countries, has resulted in a proposal to shift the focus from 'political will' towards establishing 'obligations' in addressing world hunger and poverty (Alison and Tomasevski, 1984; Eide and Kracht, 2005, 2007; Kent, 2005; Kolstad and Stokke, 2005). This would be in keeping with the right to adequate food as a basic human right for all people everywhere and the role of the United Nations, as stipulated in its *Charter*, 'to reaffirm faith in fundamental human rights, in the dignity and worth of the human person, in the equal rights of men and women and of nations large and small'. People have a right to adequate food, and to be free from hunger, as a matter of international law. This right is articulated in the *Universal Declaration of Human Rights* (1948), the *International Covenant on Economic, Social and Cultural Rights* (1966) and other international instruments. States and the governments that represent them, and other parties, have obligations to ensure that these rights are realized. States that are parties to these international agreements have made a commitment to ensure the realization of these rights. Yet malnutrition continues to lead to the death, illness and significant reduction in the quality of life of hundreds of millions of people.

What distinguishes a human rights approach to the elimination of hunger and poverty, and the realization of other basic socio-economic goals, is the focus on the dignity of human beings (as recognized in the UN *Charter*), their role as a subject and agent of change, and as a rights-holder. The argument in favour of the human rights approach is that policy objectives come and go with changing governments, and the numerous declarations of intent to end world hunger and poverty are not legally binding, but the imperative of human rights based on human dignity with consequent legal obligations would remain of constant value beyond the volatility of politics. Getting all countries to adopt this approach, particularly powerful nations like the United States that have shown aversion in the past, and translating the content of legal commitments into operational strategies and action, would still present formidable challenges. Several UN bodies have adopted a statement of common understanding regarding a rights-based approach to their co-operation and development programmes (UN, 2003). And the FAO Council has adopted a set of voluntary guidelines to support the progressive realization of the right to adequate food in the context of national food security (FAO, 2005a). It remains to be seen whether the human rights approach will prove to be more successful than the other commitments made over the past sixty years.

So ends this history of attempts to achieve world food security and the elimination of hunger and poverty since the Second World War. It is a story of good intentions, as can be seen in the graveyard of noble aspirations, depicting a civilization that now seems able to live with the ignominy and shame of knowing that a large number of its citizens continue to live in hunger and poverty, while the knowledge, resources and repeated commitment to end this scourge exist, and obesity in some parts of the world is becoming a major killer. It is to be hoped that this history as well as showing the lessons of the past will help to inspire a renewed determination to end this great paradox for the sake of sustainable and equitable world development and peace. For, as Santayana put it: 'Progress far from consisting of change, depends on retentiveness . . . those who will not learn from the past are doomed to repeat it' (Santayana, 1905).

Notes

Part I. 1945–70. Early attempts: FAO's pioneering work

1. This account is taken from Boyd Orr, with Lubbock, 1953, pp. 83–6 and Boyd Orr, 1966, pp. 118–20.
2. The words 'and ensuring humanity's freedom from hunger' were added to FAO's constitution in 1965 at the twentieth FAO Conference (resolution 12/65).
3. In 1950, first Hans Singer and then Raul Prebisch conclusively established, in what became known as the Prebisch–Singer thesis, that the net barter terms of trade between primary products and manufactures were subject to a long-term downward trend (Prebisch, 1950; Singer, 1950).
4. This proposal was first outlined in resolution 27 of the Hot Springs conference and further endorsed by the Marketing Committee at the Quebec conference.
5. The 16 member countries invited were: Australia, Belgium, Brazil, Canada, China, Cuba, Czechoslovakia, Denmark, Egypt, France, India, Netherlands, Philippines, Poland, United Kingdom and the USA. Argentina, the USSR and Siam were also invited to join as full members. Siam accepted the invitation and Argentina sent an observer.
6. The proposal to set up an FAO Council was approved at the third session of the FAO Conference, which was held in Geneva, Switzerland, in September 1947. Stanley Bruce of Australia, who had been elevated to a peerage as Viscount Bruce of Melbourne, was appointed as the Council's first independent chairman, not as a representative of his government, a practice that has been continued to the present.
7. Resolution 827 (IX) on the 'Establishment of a World Food Reserve'. Document A/2710. Ninth Session, United Nations General Assembly, December 1954, New York: United Nations.
8. Statement of the delegate for Costa Rica, United Nations General Assembly, Ninth Session, 328th Meeting, 2 December 1954. Document A/2710. New York: United Nations.
9. Senate Resolution 85, 84th Congress, 1st Session, March 1955, Washington, DC.
10. It was assumed that the use of the term 'chronic malnutrition' in the UN General Assembly resolution was intended to refer to 'diets inadequate for health', meaning either insufficient calories, that is, not enough food, or inadequate composition of diet, that is, the wrong kinds of food, or, more generally, a combination of deficiencies in regard to both quantity and quality. This interpretation of the term 'malnutrition' differs somewhat from the technical meaning of the term, said to be used by nutritionists for denoting 'the wrong kind of food' and 'under-nutrition' for 'denoting not enough food'.
11. A protracted debate took place in ECOSOC and the UN General Assembly for almost a decade (between 1950 and 1959) concerning an attempt to set up a Special United Nations Fund for Economic Development (SUNFED) to provide soft financing to assist developing countries achieve economic development. This attempt was not successful owing to opposition from some developed countries, notably the United States. Instead, the International Development Association (IDA) was created as the soft financing arm of the World Bank. An account of this turning point is given in Shaw, 2005a.
12. Chronic food insecurity involves a continuously inadequate diet caused by a persistent inability to acquire food by whatever means. Transitory food insecurity in a temporary decline in a household's access to enough food arising from instability of production,

prices or income. Policies and programmes for addressing both types of food insecurity differ. For chronic food insecurity they may include increasing food supply, subsidizing consumer prices and targeted income transfers. For transitory food insecurity, they may involve stabilizing supplies and prices, and assisting vulnerable groups directly through aid programmes (World Bank, 1986).

13. The causes of famine were subsequently revisited and redefined, particularly through the work of Amartya Sen (Sen, 1981).

14. These provisions were later extended and made more sophisticated, see, for example, Masefield, 1967.

15. The working party on an emergency famine reserve consisted of M. F. Louis Closon (France), director general of the National Institute of Statistics and Economic Studies; C. C. Farrington (United States), vice-president of the Archer Daniels Midland Company, Minneapolis, Minnesota and for many years economist at the US Department of Agriculture; R. S. Krishnaswamy (India), director-general of Food, Ministry of Food and Agriculture; H. M. Tomlinson (Australia), general manager of the Australian Barley Board; and J. E. Wall (United Kingdom), deputy head of the Finance Department, Unilever Limited, formerly of the Ministry of Food and chairman of the FAO Committee on Commodity Problems. Mr. Wall was elected chairman of the working group, which met at FAO headquarters in Rome, Italy, from 1 to 12 September 1952.

16. Under the provisions of the Indian Famine Code, the Indian Government tried to keep itself well informed about the condition of the Indian people and their reserves of food and money through information provided mainly by district administrative officials. This provided an early warning system of the threat of widespread hunger and famine and triggered government action, which could increase in intensity from the reduction or remission of land revenue, to the provision of relief employment and finally to various other relief measures, as conditions worsened.

17. It is important to distinguish clearly between the different types of funds and reserves referred to. The term 'International Relief Fund' is meant to denote an internationally owned pool of money, or credit, as distinct from an 'International Emergency Food Reserve' composed of stocks in kind. The distinction is in composition not purpose. In referring to the proposal for a 'World Food Capital Fund' (WCFC) and a 'Food Stabilization Reserve', the distinction is in purpose not composition. A WFCF would be non-self-liquidating and would be drawn on for grants or long-term low-interest loans in aid of development in developing countries. It would be a pool of stocks in kind as distinct from the proposed International Relief Fund, which would be a pool of money or credit.

18. The group of experts consisted of: M. J. L. Dols (Netherlands), State Adviser on Nutrition to the Netherlands Government; Sarda Bajpai (India), Commercial Counsellor, Indian Embassy, Rome, Italy; Maurice Equor (France), Chief of the Bureau of Economic Affairs, National Cereals Office; Juan B. Martose (Argentina), Economic Counsellor, Argentine Embassy, Rome, Italy; A. L. Senger (Australia), Commercial Counsellor, Australian Legation, Rome, Italy; Robert C. Tetro (United States), Agricultural Attache, American Embassy, Rome, Italy; and J. E. Wall (United Kingdom), Deputy Head of the Finance Department, Unilever Ltd, and former chairman of the Working Party on an Emergency Food Reserve, FAO Committee on Commodity Problems. Professor Dols was elected as chairman of the group, which met at FAO headquarters in Rome from 23 February to 6 March 1953.

19. In the biblical story of the seven fat years and the seven lean years (Genesis, Chapter 41), Joseph's storage equilibrium operations in Egypt, when a fifth of the crop in good years was stored to offset shortages in lean years, while not strictly speaking international, did have some elements of world scale. It would not have been possible during the lean years to relieve the shortages by supplies from outside because, as the bible, relates 'there was famine over all the face of the earth', and 'all countries came into Egypt to Joseph to buy corn, because the famine was so sore in all the lands'. It might be argued that

464 *Notes*

it was this very character of universality seen in relation to the concept of the universe at the time, which helped Joseph in achieving simultaneously at least three of the four main objectives usually associated with a world food reserve, namely: emergency famine relief, international price stabilization, and surplus disposal.

20. Although no reference is made to the work of Singer and Prebisch, which was published a few years earlier in 1950, its influence is felt in the FAO report. Much more use could have been made of the Prebisch–Singer thesis, which is generally taken to be the proposition that the net barter terms of trade between primary products and manufactures have been subject to a long-term downward trend (Prebisch, 1950; Singer, 1950).

21. Keynes was the originator of the proposal for an International Trade Organization (ITO). He was a strong believer in the stabilization of primary commodity prices, which was to be one of the main functions of the ITO. Keynes combined his proposals for a world central bank and world currency with his proposal for primary commodity price stabilization by suggesting a world currency based on 30 primary commodities, rather than gold, dollars or special drawing rights. This would have stabilized the average price of the 30 commodities included (Moggridge, 1992; Skidelsky, 2000).

22. For a review of the evolution and criticism of the two gap models, see Kruger, Michalopoulos and Ruttan (1989).

23. Of the 145 people who attended the conference, 41 were from 20 foreign countries. Ezekiel played a key role in the conference and presented three papers, one on 'The State of Food and Agriculture Today' (pp. 3–6), another on 'The Basic Economic Ideas of Using Surplus Food to Help Finance Economic Development' (pp. 126–30) and a third on 'FAO Studies on Results in Using Surplus Food for Economic Development' (pp. 131–5). See also his 'Apparent Results in Using Surplus Food for Financing Economic Development', *J. Farm Economics*, 40, November 1958, pp. 915–23.

24. The working party met in Washington, DC, from 23 February to 18 March 1854 and was composed of representatives of eight member countries: Argentina, Egypt, France, India, Netherlands, New Zealand, United Kingdom and the United States. The final text of its report was issued as FAO document CCP 54/2, 1954a.

25. The FAO *Principles of Surplus Disposal*, first published in 1954, were subsequently revised and expanded and renamed the FAO *Principles of Surplus Disposal and Consultative Obligations of Member Nations* and appeared in a number of reprints and editions, the last being in 2001.

26. ECOSOC resolution 621 (XXII), 950th Plenary Meeting, 6 August 1956.

27. UN General Assembly resolution 1025, 656th Plenary Meeting, Eleventh Session, 20 February 1957.

28. *Report of the Working Party on National Reserves.* Document CCP/CSD/57/61 Rev., 24 June 1957.

29. For this and other reasons, WFP found it particularly difficult to establish food reserves in developing countries with food aid donations.

30. For an account of the work of Hans Singer and Raul Prebisch in what became known as the Prebisch–Singer thesis, see Shaw (2002b, pp. 49–71) and Toye and Toye (2003; 2004). Subsequent studies have largely upheld their original work leading to the conclusion that 'There can be few hypotheses in economics which have stood the test of time, not to mention the onslaught of increasingly sophisticated statistical techniques' (Sapsford and Chen, 1998).

31. The UN committee of experts consisted of I. H. Abdel-Rahman, Antonio Carrillo Flores, Albert G. Hart, S. Posthuma, M. L. Qureshi and Sir John G. Crawford (chairman).

32. The original signatories of the 1967 FAC were Argentina, Australia, Canada, Denmark, the Commission of the European Communities (for EEC community aid), Finland, Japan, Norway, Sweden, Switzerland, the United Kingdom and the United States.

33. The Fourth World Food Survey, conducted in 1978 with even more sophisticated statistical tools, estimated that the number of undernourished people in the world was

Notes 465

496 million, close to the estimate of the 1962 survey. The 1962 survey was not without its critics, notably Colin Clark, who accused Sen of manipulating the results to gain support for the FFHC.

34. McGovern Papers, Box TK-2, Seeley G. Mudd Manuscript Library, Princeton University.

35. *Agricultural Policy for the New Frontier* by Senator John F. Kennedy (p. 5), Kennedy's agricultural policy platform for the 1960 presidential campaign (McGovern Papers, Box TK-7, Accession No. 67A1881, Seeley G. Mudd Manuscript Library, Princeton University).

36. Press release, 31 October 1960 (Meyer Feldman Papers, Food for Peace Program (10/60-1/3/61) File, Box 9, John Fitzgerald Kennedy Library, Boston).

37. Presidential Office Files, File 1T6/Food Conference, John Fitzgerald Kennedy Library, Boston.

38. The expert group consisted of Dr. M. R. Benedict, Professor of Agricultural Economics, University of California at Berkeley, USA; Dr. J. Figueres, ex-President of the Republic of Costa Rica; Dr. V. K. R. V. Rao, ex-Vice-Chancellor, University of Delhi, India; Dr. P. N. Rosenstein-Roden, Professor of Economics, Massachusetts Institute of Technology, USA; and Dr. H. W. Singer, Principal Officer, Office of the Under-Secretary for Economic and Social Affairs, New York, USA. Dr. Singer, who was appointed as chairman of the group, enjoyed the confidence of the executive heads of both the UN and FAO. He brought to the group the unique and profound experience he had gained in working at the United Nations, including the proposal for a Special United Nations Fund for Economic Development and a UN Expanded Program of Technical Assistance, and had a special interest in a multilateral form of the US food aid programme (PL 480).

39. *The Papers of Adlai Stevenson: Vol. VIII. Ambassador to the United Nations 1961–1965* (Boston: Little, Brown and Co., 1979, p. 149).

40. Memorandum to the United States Secretary for Agriculture, Orville Freeman, 21 June 1961 (Secretary's Records Section, Food for Peace Program, File IX, US Department of Agriculture, National Agricultural Library, Beltsville, Maryland, United States).

41. Executive Order 10914 'Providing for an Expanded Program of Food Distribution to Needy Families' and Executive Order 10915 'Amending Prior Executive Orders to Provide for the Responsibilities of the Director of the Food-for-Peace Program', in *Code of Federal Regulations Title 3 – The President. 1959-1963 Compilation* (Washington, DC: Office of the Federal Registrar, National Archives and Records Service, General Services Administration, pp. 443–4). See also, 'Memorandum to the Federal Agencies on the Duties of the Director of the Food-for-Peace Program' in *Public Papers of the Presidents of the United States. John F. Kennedy, 20 January to 31 December 1961* (Washington, DC: US Government Printing Office, 1962, p. 6).

42. President Kennedy's Speeches. Papers of President Kennedy. Presidential Office Files (1/19/61-5/25/61), Box 34, John Fitzgerald Kennedy Library, Boston.

43. McGovern Papers, Food for Peace Proposals and Correspondence File, Box TK-2, Seeley G. Mudd Manuscript Library, Princeton University.

44. Kennedy had gone to South Dakota to support McGovern in his bid to become senator of that State. When McGovern lost by a small margin, it was interpreted that this was due to the 'religious factor'. Kennedy was a Catholic and South Dakota was predominately a Protestant state. Kennedy, feeling that he was responsible for McGovern's defeat, offered him a post in his new administration. McGovern expressed an interest in the position of Secretary of Agriculture. When that post was given to Orville Freeman, McGovern accepted the directorship of the newly created Office of Food for Peace and special assistant to the president in the White House (McGovern, 1977).

45. Memorandum to President Kennedy from McGovern of 28 March 1961 and attached report on 'Recommendations for Improvements in the Food for Peace Program', pp. 35–6 (McGovern Papers, Box TK-5, Seeley G. Mudd Manuscripts Library, Princeton University).

46. McGovern was accompanied to Rome by Raymond A. Ioanes of the US Department of Agriculture and Sidney Jacques of the US State Department.

466   *Notes*

47. For what transpired during the Intergovernmental Advisory Committee in Rome in April 1961, I have drawn from a number of sources including: the statement by McGovern at the meeting (reproduced in FAO, 1961c, pp. 121–2); an interview with George McGovern by John Newhouse on 24 April 1964 for the Oral History Program of the John Fitzgerald Kennedy Library, Boston; the address of McGovern at WFP's Twenty-fifth Anniversary Commemorative Meeting in Rome on 30 May 1988, which is recorded in WFP, 1988, pp. 64–8; McGovern, 1964, pp. 107–10; Sen, 1982, p. 202; personal correspondence from Raymond A. Ioanes, 16 February 1995; personal correspondence from George McGovern, 23 August 1994; and personal interview with George McGovern at the Middle East Policy Council, Washington, DC, on 22 April 1997.
48. Memorandum to President Kennedy from McGovern, 11 February 1961. Presidential Office Files, Box 78, Food for Peace Program 1/61-3/61, John Fitzgerald Kennedy Library, Boston.
49. Personal interview with McGovern in Washington, DC on 22 April 1997.
50. Personal communication from McGovern, 21 July 1997.
51. Memorandum to President Kennedy from Adlai E. Stevenson, United States Ambassador to the United Nations, 13 November 1961 in *The Papers of Adlai E. Stevenson: Volume VIII. Ambassador to the United Nations 1961–1965* (Boston: Little, Brown and Co., 1979, pp. 148–50) and Memorandum from the President's Special Assistant (Arthur M. Schlesinger Jr.) to the President's Special Assistant for National Security Affairs (McGeorge Bundy), 6 December 1961 in *Foreign Relations of the United States 1961–63. Volume IX. Foreign Economic Policy. Department of State, Washington, DC. International Investment and Development Policy* (Washington, DC: US Government Printing Office, 1995, pp. 422–3).
52. 'Annotated Agenda for the Meeting on Use of Surplus Food for Emergency and Development Purposes through Multilateral Channels (FAO and UN)' (with annexes on the two food aid proposals of McGovern and the US representatives at the UN) at the State Department, Washington, DC, on 25 October 1961. Copy in the McGovern Papers, Box TK-3, Seeley G. Mudd Manuscript Library, Princeton University.
53. During its first forty years of operations, WFP has grown to become the largest international humanitarian organization. Since 1963, WFP has invested $27.8 billion and more than 43 million tons of food to combat hunger, promote economic and social development and provide relief assistance in emergencies throughout the developing world. In 2006, WFP reached 88 million people, including 59 million children, 64 million through emergency operations and 24 million through development projects, in 78 countries with four million tons of food at an expenditure of $3 billion. WFP has a staff of over 10,500 over 90 per cent of whom serve in developing countries. WFP's administrative expenditure is about seven per cent of total expenditure. For details see www.wfp.org. For a histroy of WFP, see Shaw (2001b).
54. The study, entitled *A New Approach to the World Food Programme*, was prepared by E. L. Samuel, counsellor, Agrarian Affairs, at the Embassy of Israel in Rome, and distributed to WFP governing body members in March/April 1965 as document WM/IGC: 7/24.
55. The Argentine proposal to convert WFP into a 'World Food Fund' was submitted to the WFP governing body at its session in March/April 1965 in document WM/IGC: 7/1 Add. 2.
56. The proposal of Uruguay to establish a 'World Food Bank' was submitted to WFP's governing body in October 1971 in document WFP/IGC: 20/12 Add. 3.
57. The proposal of Lebanon was later withdrawn.
58. The proposal of the Netherlands to establish an 'Emergency Food Supply Scheme' was submitted to WFP's governing body in October 1971 in document WFP/IGC: 20/12 Add. 1.
59. Other relevant documents that were prepared at the time included: FAO, 1968a,b,c; UN, 1969 and WFP, 1969.
60. This form of emergency food reserve arrangement, which linked national food reserves globally, contained elements of the International Undertaking on World Food Security that was later adopted by the World Food Conference and the FAO Conference in 1974.

Notes   467

61. The 'group of seven' advisers who were appointed by the WFP executive director were: F. Deeleman, director, Agricultural Assistance to Developing Countries, Ministry of Agriculture and Fisheries, The Hague, The Netherlands; F. Ellis, deputy co-ordinator, Food for Peace, Agency for International Development, Department of State, Washington, DC, United States; J. M. Figuerero, director, International Co-operation Department, Ministry of Foreign Affairs, Buenos Aires, Argentina; H. J. Kristensen, counsellor, Ministry of Agriculture, Copenhagen, Denmark; A. A. Mourai, under-secretary, Ministry of Agriculture, Cairo, Egypt; S. R. Sen, vice-chairman, Irrigation Commission, Ministry of Irrigation and Power, New Delhi, India; and F. Shefrin, director, International Liaison Service, Department of Agriculture, Ottawa, Canada. The group met for three sessions in Rome, Italy, in July and October 1969 and February 1970 under the chairmanship of WFP's executive director. Assistance was also provided by the UN and FAO as well as the WFP secretariat.

62. This was similar to the proposal for country programming of UNDP projects contained in the UN study of the capacity of the UN system (UN, 1969b). The approach was adopted by UNDP but uncertainty about WFP resources precluded its involvement.

63. In the decade up to 2005, global food aid deliveries in cereals (in grain equivalent) fluctuated between over 15 million tons in 1999 to under 8 million tons in 2004. Over that period, emergency food aid, particularly to sub-Saharan Africa, more than doubled (WFP, 2006).

Part II. 1970–90. The world food crisis of the 1970s and its aftermath

1. See 'The Sixth Wave. The World Food Question and American Agriculture', *Foreign Agriculture*, October 28, 1974.

2. Details of the world food crisis of the 1970s are taken from the documents prepared of the 1974 World Food Conference (see UN, 1974a,b) and from personal correspondence and material from Sartaj Aziz. As deputy secretary-general of the conference, he was intimately involved in its preparations and deliberations (Aziz, 1975a,b).

3. These food aid data do not include the 'grey area' between statistically recorded food aid and outright commercial sales (Shaw and Singer, 1995).

4. Sayed Marei was elected to the presidency of the Egyptian Parliament shortly before the conference began. It was generally believed that he was appointed as secretary-general of the conference at least in part because his nationality facilitated negotiations with Arab countries whose oil wealth made them logical contributors to the proposed International Fund for Agricultural Development (Weiss and Jordan, 1976; Talbot, 1990, pp. 75–123; Marchisio and Di Blasé, 1992, pp. 74–86).

5. ECOSOC resolution 1840 (LVI), *Preparations for the World Food Conference, 15 May 1974*.

6. FAO (1974) *World Food Security: Evaluation of World Cereals Stock Situation*. Document CL 64/27 (Rome: FAO).

7. The eminent persons attending the Rome Forum were Sartaj Aziz, Henrik Beer, Norman E. Borlaug, Lester Brown, Jacques Chonchol, H. C. Coombs, Rene Dumont, Ma'moun El Beheiry, Erhard Eppler, Orville L. Freeman, Jens Hedegaard, Henry J. Heinz II, Guy Hunter, John H. Knowles, Thorkil Kristensen, Jean Mayer, Margaret Mead, Dom Moraes, Thomas R. Odhiambo, H. M. A. Onitiri, Escott Reid, Walter Orr Roberts, Ignacy Sachs, M. S. Swaminathan, Mahbub ul Haq, Auguste A. J. Vanistendael and Barbara Ward (Lady Jackson).

8. A precedent had been set after the Second World War. Boyd Orr, the first FAO director-general, recommended grain rationing in the United Kingdom in the winter of 1946–47 to release supplies to offset the risk of starvation in Asia, Eastern Europe and Germany. The British, who had been spared bread rationing throughout the war, complied, and food rationing continued to 1954. In the event, there was no great famine (Ward, 1974).

468 *Notes*

9. I was in Rome during the conference as a WFP staff member. I did not attend the conference sessions but met with delegates and followed its deliberations closely through discussions with delegates, the local press and the conference newspaper, PAN, which was published by the International Council of Voluntary Agencies. Its journalists were independent. Some had worked on ECO, the newspaper of the Stockholm Environment Conference and on PLANET, the newspaper of the World Population Conference in Bucharest. Eleven issues were produced. Each issue carried the reminder to conference participants, 'Remember. They can't eat your words'. The statements of many of the leading participants have been taken from UN, 1974c. I have also drawn from the clinical accounts of the conference in Martin (1974) and Weiss and Jordan (1976).

10. An additional interpretation was that three food ideologies contested for domination in US food policies at the time: the neo-Hamiltonian (the market economy); the neo-Jeffersonian (the public economy); and the neo-Madisonian (the pluralist interest-group economy) (Talbot, 1977).

11. After the conference, FAO director-general Boerma proposed that Sartaj Aziz become executive director of the World Food Council (WFC). Another suggestion was that he should run for the director-generalship of FAO in November 1975 at the end of Boerma's first term of office. Eventually, Aziz became WFC's deputy executive director of WFC (1975–76), president of the Society for International Development (1976–79) and assistant president of IFAD (1978–84). He then returned to Pakistan to become a member of the Pakistan senate in March 1985. He was appointed Minister of State for Food and Agriculture (1985–88), Minister for Finance and Economic Affairs (1990–93 and again in 1997–98) and Minister for Foreign Affairs (1998–99) (Dil, 2000).

12. The US delegation to the 29–30 September 1975 meeting at the International Wheat Council in London was led by Richard E. Bell, Assistant Secretary of Agriculture for International Affairs and Commodity Programs, seconded by Julius L. Katz, Deputy Secretary of State for Economic and Business Affairs. Katz headed the delegation following Bell's departure on 30 September for grain talks in Moscow. Also present at the meeting were representatives from Argentina, Australia, Canada, Egypt, El Salvador, the European Economic Community, Finland, India, Japan, South Africa, Sweden, Switzerland, Tunisia and the Soviet Union.

13. Intensive debate on the drafting of the modalities of the IEFR took up many hours in the drafting group of WFP's governing body, often into the early hours of the morning, before they were completed and later approved.

14. This formulation had its origins in the recommendation of a Panel of Experts on the Protein Problem Confronting Developing Countries, which stated: There is, however, a clear need for a political body or committee operating at the highest level within the United Nations system with responsibility for mobilizing international opinion and action . . . Such a body should be composed of representatives of Governments at the highest possible level, preferably cabinet ministers, so that nations concerned are closely identified with its efforts, and could be established by the General Assembly or the Economic and Social Council (UN, 1971b; Weiss and Jordan, 1976, p. 99).

15. The number of WFC members was agreed by the UN General Assembly in its resolution XXIX of 17 December 1974.

16. Of the 36 members of the WFC, nine were to come from African states, eight from Asian states, seven from Latin America and the Caribbean, four from the Socialist States of Eastern Europe and eight from Western Europe and other states.

17. In the 'Rules of Procedure' adopted by WFC at its second session in June 1976, the executive head was referred to as the 'executive secretary', whose appointment would be 'subject to the approval of the General Assembly'. This was amended at the third session of WFC in June 1977, in the light of UN General Assembly resolution 31/120, when the title 'executive secretary' was changed to 'executive director' and approval by the UN General Assembly was dropped. The post was established at the assistant director-general level, although attempts were made to raise it to the under-secretary level.

Notes 469

18. Of the 18 annual WFC ministerial session that were held, three were held in Rome, one at the UN headquarters in New York, nine in developing countries and five in developed countries.
19. One delegate objected to this description.
20. Some have interpreted the aggressive stance adopted by the G77 at the initial sessions of the Council as evidence that many of its members 'had been fascinated, if not mesmerized', by the power OPEC was exerting over oil prices and markets and that they might exert a similar control over food. But they found out that food and oil were radically different, and confrontational politics soon gave way to consensus policies (Talbot, 1982, pp. 211–12; 1990, p. 81).
21. The ACC is the highest administrative co-ordinating body in the UN system. Its sessions are chaired by the UN secretary-general and attended by the executive heads of the UN agencies and programmes.
22. $8.3 billion was a WFC secretariat re-evaluation in 1975 prices of the $5 billion for which there was board support at the World Food Conference. The concessional element was based on at least 86 per cent being provided as grants (WFC, 1977b).
23. A detailed review of the activities and assistance of the United Nations bodies and bilateral and other agencies for Africa was submitted in to the Council in a report by the executive director at its eighth session in 1982 (WFC, 1982c).
24. This pre-dated the publication of Amartya Sen's concept of food 'entitlements' (Sen, 1981).
25. Other terms such as 'national food security scheme' and 'national agricultural and nutrition plan' were used. The Mexican government launched its national plan for resolving its food problems under the title 'Mexican Food System'.
26. I am grateful to Uwe Kracht for this information. Personal correspondence, 14 and 26 June 2006.
27. A study of the implications for food aid showed diversion, not additionality, of food aid to eastern Europe (Benson and Clay, 1998).
28. The Government of Canada reserved its position regarding the FAO Plan of Action.
29. The members of the panel were: Walter P. Falcon, Food Research Institute, Stanford University, USA; C. T. Kurien, Madras Institute of Development Studies, India; Fernando Monckeberg, Institute of Nutrition and Food Technology, University of Chile, Chile; Achola P. Okeyo, University of Nairobi, Kenya; S. O. Olbyide, University of Ibadan, Nigeria; Ferenc Rabar, Institute of Planning Economy, Hungary; and Wouter Tims, Centre for World Food Studies, the Netherlands. The panel began its deliberations in New York in March 1983 and completed its work in Rome in December. The cost of the study was met by grants from the governments of Australia, Canada and the Netherlands. Their only requirement was that the assessment should be independent. The panel acknowledged the benefit it had from the 'vast flow' of analysis from the 'large community' of scholars, policy-makers and practitioners. Special appreciation was given to Sir W. Arthur Lewis and Professor Vernon Ruttan and the WFC staff for providing 'invaluable administrative services'.
30. The content of these 'declarations' are presented here in highly summarized form. The full details can be found in each statement separately.
31. A special working group composed of the WFC bureau and representatives from Bangladesh, Chad, Hungary, Indonesia, Japan, Nigeria, Trinidad and Tobago, the United Kingdom and the United States considered the text of the Communiqué on the basis of the report of the WFC Preparatory Meeting prepared by the WFC secretariat under the instruction of the WFC president.
32. The draft of the Mexico Declaration was first considered at the WFC Preparatory Meeting and redrafted by the WFC rapporteur on the basis of the WFC secretariat proposals and proposals from the floor. A working group was set up by the Preparatory Meeting to consider the rapporteur's draft composed of the WFC Bureau and representative from Bangladesh, Cuba, Denmark, German Democratic Republic, Indonesia, Ivory Coast,

470 *Notes*

Somalia, Soviet Union, Venezuela and the United States. The working group's draft was transmitted by the Preparatory Meeting to the ministerial session, where it was amended and adopted 'in the early hours of 15 June 1978.

33. The special session of the UN General Assembly devoted to disarmament took place simultaneously with the Council's fourth session at which the Mexico Declaration was approved.

34. The Beijing Declaration was drafted by a drafting group consisting of representatives of Argentina, Australia, China, Colombia, the German Democratic Republic, Germany (Federal Republic of), Guinea, Somalia, Thailand, the Union of Soviet Socialist Republics and the United States. After minor amendments, it was adopted by consensus.

35. Eleven development agencies and institutions attended the two-day consultation in Rome, Italy, in May 1987. The consultation filled an important information gap in the area of economic adjustment and efforts to protect the poor and clarified agencies policies regarding economic adjustment. Among its conclusions was recognition that the elimination of hunger, malnutrition and poverty required special policy attention that neither economic growth nor market forces could, by themselves, spread the burden of adjustment and equitable distribution of the benefits of development. UNICEF pioneered poverty-focused adjustment approaches under the title 'adjustment with a human face' (Cornia, Jolly and Stewart, 1987).

36. *The Cyprus Initiative*, together with the conclusions and recommendations of the fourteenth session of the Council, were prepared by a drafting group consisting of two representatives from each of the five WFC regional groups and were adopted by consensus in plenary. The members of the drafting group were Argentina, Canada, Colombia, China, Cyprus, the German Democratic Republic, the Federal Republic of Germany, Madagascar, the Union of Soviet Socialist Republics and Zambia. The group was chaired, on behalf of the WFC president, by a representative of Mexico.

37. The group was established at a meeting of Council members in New York in October 1988 with the following membership: Africa: Madagascar, Somalia, Zambia; Asia: China, Cyprus, Japan; Latin America: Colombia, Uruguay, Honduras (Guatemala from January 1989); Western Europe and Other States: Australia, France (with support from the Commission of the European Communities), United States; Socialist States of Eastern Europe: Bulgaria, Union of Soviet Socialist Republics. The group met first in Paris in December 1988 to discuss the overall approach to the preparation of the report and its policy thrust. A second meeting was held in Nicosia, Cyprus, in March 1989 at the invitation of the Cyprus government to examine a first draft of the report. The WFC president and executive director consulted with many governments, both Council members and non-members, and sought the support of international agencies and NGOs through direct consultations and an inter-agency meeting held in Geneva, Switzerland, in January 1989. The WFC president was responsible for the final report.

38. *The Cairo Declaration*, together with the conclusions and recommendations of the Council at its fifteenth session, was prepared by a drafting group consisting of 10 council members: Argentina, Colombia, Egypt, France, German Democratic Republic, Indonesia, Japan, Niger, Union of Soviet Socialist Republics and the United States, and were adopted unanimously by the plenary.

39. To give some idea of the workload carried by the WFC executive director, according to WFC records, Maurice Williams made 85 statements outside those he made at WFC meetings and wrote 47 progress reports, papers and articles, during his eight years as WFC executive director.

40. As an illustration of the Council's limited resources, it approved a budget of the order of $20,000 'to promote more effective dissemination of information about the World Food Council's effort' (sic) in 1980, and the preparatory meetings before ministerial sessions were discontinued in 1986 'because of the tight budgetary situation'. The WFC secretariat had about a dozen professional officers and an annual budget of $2 million.

Notes 471

41. The group was chaired by Margaret Joan Anstee, an assistant director-general with a long and distinguished career in the UN. The other members of the group were Sartaj Aziz, Minister of Agriculture of Pakistan, who, as deputy director-general of the 1974 World Food Conference, was closely involved in the creation of the WFC, and served as its deputy executive director and Abdellatif Ghissassi of Morocco. In her autobiography, *Never Learn to Type. A Woman at the United Nations* (Chichester, UK: Wiley, 2003, p. 394), Dame Anstee wrote: 'Our report was well received but with the financial situation of the UN worsening, no follow-up action was taken by the governments that had mandated the review'.
42. In common with ILO practice, the term 'tripartite' referred to the three parties concerned; governments, employers and workers.
43. I am grateful to Louis Emmerij, who, as director of ILO's World Employment Programme and secretary general of the World Employment Conference, was in charge of the preparations for the conference in ILO, for his personal recollections on the factors influencing the decisions on the focus of the conference, and for its outcomes and the legacy of the basic needs concept (Personal communications, 30 August and 1 and 1 September 2005).
44. The concept of 'redistribution from growth' was developed by Hans (later Sir Hans) Singer who was co-leader of the ILO employment mission to Kenya in 1972 (see Technical Paper No. 6 of the Kenya mission report, ILO, 1972, pp. 363–70). It was designed to redistribute gains in the incomes of the rich to investments which would raise the incomes of the poor. The concept, amended to become 'redistribution of growth', was adopted as the signature concept of the World Bank's approach to poverty alleviation during the McNamara presidency (Kapur, Lewis and Webb, 1997, vol. 1, p. 263).
45. Sen's seminal contributions to an understanding of the causes of food insecurity, famines and poverty were recognized when he was awarded the Nobel Prize for Economics in 1998. For an appreciation of his work, see Devereux and Singer, 1999; Cameron and Gasper, 2000; Corgridge, 2006 and Riskin, 2006.
46. For a detailed account of the origins of WFP's constitution and the struggle to gain autonomy, see Shaw (2001b), Chapter 8 and Ingram, 2006.
47. The study was prepared by Shlomo Reutlinger and Jack van Holst Pellekaan of the Bank's Agricultural and Rural Development Department with the assistance of Craig Lissner, Claudia Pendred and Colleen Roberts.

Part III. The 1990s and beyond

1. I am indebted to Andrew Cooper and Thomas Weiss for their insightful analyses of the roles and work of UN conferences during the 1990s (see Cooper, 2004; Weiss and Jordan, 1976; Weiss *et al.*, 1994).
2. It is instructive that Henry Kissinger makes no reference to multilateral diplomacy and the role of the UN world conferences in his substantial tome on *Diplomacy* (New York: Simon & Schuster, 1994), not even to the 1974 World Food Conference that was held through his initiative.
3. The *World Summit for Children* was attended by 71 heads of state and government and 88 other senior officials, mostly at ministerial level.
4. The World Bank historians concluded that 'the [UNICEF] book was well-timed politically and achieved rhetorical success. "Human face" became part of the adjustment language, discomforting the Bank' (Kapur, Lewis ad Webb, 1997, vol. 1, p. 352).
5. The Institute of International Environmental Affairs, founded by Robert Anderson, chief executive officer of the oil company, Atlantic Richfield, in 1971 became the International Institute for Environment and Development with Barbara Ward as its first president on condition that 'development' was included in its title and its headquarters relocated from New York to London.

472 *Notes*

6. At the United Nations Conference on Environment and Development in Rio de Janeiro, Brazil, in 1992, 'Developed countries reaffirmed their commitments to reach the accepted United Nations target of 0.7 per cent of GNP for ODA and, to the extent that they have not yet achieved that target, agree to augment their aid programmes in order to reach that target as soon as possible and to ensure prompt and effective implementation of Agenda 21. Some countries have agreed to reach the target by the year 2000 . . . Those countries that have already reached the target are to be commended and encouraged to continue to contribute to the common effort to make available the substantial additional resources that have to be mobilized. Other developed countries, in line with their support for reform efforts in developing countries, agree to make their best efforts to increase their level of ODA' (*Report of the United Nations Conference on Environment and Development*, Rio de Janeiro, 1992, paragraph 33.13).

7. Madame Simone Veil of France was elected chairperson of the conference with vice-chairpersons from Bangladesh, Chine, Italy, Japan, Lebanon and Nicaragua. The chairman of the Preparatory Committee, Ibrahim Adam of Ghana, was elected chairman of the Commission of the Whole to review drafts of the *World Declaration and Plan of Action for Nutrition*, assisted by a drafting committee comprised of representative of Indonesia (chair), Algeria, Czechoslovakia, Egypt, Germany, Iran, Nigeria, Norway, Panama, Philippines, Uruguay, and the United States.

8. The conferences and documents referred to in the *World Declaration on Nutrition* included: the World Food Conference (1974); the Alma Ata Conference on Primary Health Care (1978); the World Conference on Agrarian Reform and Rural Development (1979); the Convention on The Elimination of All Forms of Discrimination Against Women (1979); the Innocenti Declaration on the Protection, Promotion and Support of Breastfeeding (1990); the Montreal Policy Conference on Micronutritent Malnutrition (1991); and the Rio Declaration on Environment and Development (1992).

9. The *Plan of Action for Nutrition* provided detailed guidance for governments and others. It ran to 40 pages of the final report of the ICN (FAO and WHO, 1992b), While some considered that this was a considerable achievement, others thought it was overkill and a deterrent, rather than an aid, for governments.

10. Food security was defined 'in its most basic form as access by all people at all times to the food needed for a healthy life'.

11. Jose Ayala Lasso was named by the UN secretary-general as the first UN Commissioner for Human Rights, who assumed office in April 1994.

12. The conference was chaired by Ismail Serageldin, vice-president, Environmentally Sustainable Development, World Bank.

13. Congressman Tony Hall had dramatically drawn notice to the problem of hunger by going on hunger strike.

14. In referring to the 'new abolitionists', the conference had recalled the role of the abolitionists who had ended slavery.

15. Reference was made to the special section of the World Bank's *World Development Report, 1980* on 'Poverty and Human Development' and the 'seamless web' of concerns in a relationship of 'cumulative causation' between nutrition, health and education (World Bank, 1980).

16. During the two final plenary meetings in which agreement was reached on the *Programme of Action*, 13 countries (Afghanistan, Brunei Darussalem, El Salvadore, Honduras, Jordan, Kuwait, Libya, Nicaragua, Paraguay, the Philippines, Syria, United Arab Emirates and Yemen) expressed reservations or comments on specific chapters, paragraphs or phrases, which they requested to be recorded in the final report of the conference (A/CONF.171/13). Ten states (Argentina, Djibouti, the Dominican Republic, Ecuador, Egypt, Guatemala, the Holy See, Iran, Malta and Peru) submitted written statements for inclusion in the report.

17. Keith Bezanson subsequently became director of the Institute of Development Studies at the University of Sussex, UK.

18. Ester Boserup showed that with changes in technology associated with modernization and patterns of land use, the status of women was reduced on account of their marginalization in agricultural systems. She pointed out that injections of development funding for agriculture usually focused on cash crops and ignored subsistence farming that women typically engaged in. Boserup attended the first UN expert group on women and economic development in 1972 and was Denmark's representative to the UN Commission on the Status of Women.

19. The *World Survey on the Role of Women in Development* has been described as the 'flagship' publication of the UN Department of Economic and Social Affairs. In 1988, the UN General Assembly requested the UN secretary-general in close collaboration with appropriate UN organizations and agencies to prepare a multisectoral and interdisciplinary survey on the role of women in development. The following year, it requested the UN secretary-general to update the survey on a regular basis focusing on selected emerging development issues that had an impact on the role of women in the economy at the national and international levels. The survey submitted to the Beijing conference gave an overview of employment and displacement effects of economic trends associated with globalization from a gender point of view.

Part IV. Assessment. The graveyard of aspirations

1. The difference between halving the *number* (the WFS target) and the *proportion* (the MDG) of the world's hungry is some 180 million people. The first would imply a reduction from 816 to 408 million; the second would mean reducing the prevalence from 19.8 to 9.9 per cent (591 million) (Task Force on Hunger, 2003).
2. I am particularly indebted to Uwe Kracht for his work in this area (Kracht, 2005).
3. The SCN serves as a UN focal point for harmonizing nutrition policies and strategies throughout the UN system and for strengthening collaboration with other partners for accelerated and more effective action against malnutrition. The SCN membership consists of representatives of 18 UN bodies, IFPRI and the Asian Development Bank. Representatives of bilateral donor agencies and NGOs also actively participate in SCN activities. The SCN secretariat is located at WHO headquarters in Geneva, Switzerland. The SCN has played an important role in keeping its member organizations and the general public aware of the importance of nutrition security over its thirty years of operations (Longhurst, 2007).
4. The UNICEF/World Bank joint assessment is based on an analysis of policy change, country case studies in India, Madagascar, the Philippines and Tanzania, a review of the project experiences of the two organizations over two decades, and workshops between their staffs and external experts.
5. Peter Griffiths is an economic consultant who has worked in 30 countries with aid organizations, including the World Bank, the European Union, UNDP and FAO.
6. Joachim von Braun was formerly director of IFPRI's Food Consumption and Nutrition Division. Between 1993 and 1996, he held the Chair for World Food Issues at the University of Kiel, and later professor and director of the Centre for Development Research at the University of Bonn in Germany.
7. The essay was co-authored by IFPRI's director-general, Joachim von Braun, the co-ordinator of the Millennium Project's Task Force on Hunger, M. S. Swaminathan, and the director of IFPRI's Environment and Production Technology Division, Mark Rosegrant.
8. The medical literature classifies a person as obese if the body mass index (BMI), taking into account both weight and height, is 30 or higher.
9. The other four goals established at the *World Education Forum* were:

   (a) expanding and improving comprehensive early childhood care and education, especially for the most vulnerable and disadvantaged children;

474 *Notes*

    (b) ensuring that the learning needs of all young people and adults are met through equitable access to appropriate learning and life-skills programmes;

    (c) achieving a 50 per cent improvement in levels of adult literacy by 2015, especially for women, and equitable access to basic and continuing education for all adults and

    (d) improving all aspects of the quality of education and ensuring excellence for all so that recognized and measurable learning outcomes are achieved by all, especially in literacy, numeracy and essential life skills.

10. Anne Kruger, who edited the book on *The WTO as an International Organization*, which was the outcome of the conference at Stanford University on that subject, was professor in Humanities and Sciences and director of the Center for Research for Development and policy reform at Stanford University at the time. Previously, she was chief economist at the World Bank and later, first deputy managing director at the IMF in Washington, DC.

11. Ernest Preeg was a US trade negotiator in both the GATT Kennedy Round in the 1960s and the Uruguay Round in the 1980s. He subsequently became professor in International Business at the Center for Strategic and International Studies in Washington, DC.

12. The Worldwatch Institute was founded in Washington, DC, in 1974 by Lester Brown as an independent research organization that works for an environmentally sustainable and socially just society. Its *State of the World 2005* was the twenty-second edition of its annual report. The Worldwatch institute and Lester Brown, now president of the Earth Policy Institute, have created a special niche in the international debate concerning world food security, the environment and sustainable development and related issues. Their publications have provided a different, often controversial, and frequently influential view from that of other official UN and other bodies.

13. Jeffrey Sachs is the director of the *UN Millennium Project*, special adviser to the UN secretary-general on the MDGs and director of the Earth Institute at Colombia University in New York. The bulk of the analytical work of the *UN Millennium Project* was carried out by a number of thematic task forces comprising over 250 experts. In addition to the report of the project, *Investing in Development: A Practical Plan to Achieve the Millennium Development Goals*, 13 task-force reports were produced on hunger, universal primary education, gender equality in education and empowering women, child and maternal health, HIV/AIDS, malaria, TB, access to essential medicines, water and sanitation, improving the lives of slum dwellers, trade, environmental sustainability, and science, technology and innovation. The 14 volumes are published by Earthscan/James and James in a UN Millennium Development Library set.

14. The steering board of the GM national debate was chaired by Professor Malcolm Grant, Pro-Vice-Chancellor and Professor of Land Economic, University of Cambridge, UK.

15. The report of the GM national debate, *GM Nation*, can be seen at the website http://www.gmnation.org.uk.

16. The report of the Strategy Unit of the Prime Minister's Cabinet Office on *Fieldwork: Weighing up the Cost and Benefits of GM Crops* can be seen at the website http://www.strategy.gov.uk.

17. The two reports of the GM Science Review can be seen at the website http://www.gmsciencedebate.org.uk. The review panel was chaired by Sir David King, UK Government Chief Scientific Adviser.

18. The report on *Avoiding Dangerous Climate Change. Scientific Symposium on Stabilisation of Greenhouse Gases. February 1–3, 2005* held at the Met Office in Exeter, UK, can be seen at the website http://www.ipcc-wg2/metoffice.gov.uk.

19. The World Commission on the Social Dimensions of Globalization was co-chaired by President Benjamin W. Mkapa of Tanzania and President Tarja Kaarina Halonen of Finland. The report of the commission is available at www.ilo.org/public/english/fairglobalization/report/index.htm.

20. The report of the World Commission on the Social Dimensions of Globalization was followed up by resolution A/RES/59/79 adopted by the UN General Assembly without a vote at its 59th session on 2 December 2004. The resolution was tabled by Tanzania and Finland and supported by 74 other co-sponsoring states. The resolution requested the UN General Assembly to take note of the report 'as a contribution to the international dialogue towards a fully inclusive and equitable globalization', invited organizations of the UN system to provide information to the UN General Assembly on their activities to promote an inclusive and equitable globalization, and requested the UN secretary-general to take account of the report in his comprehensive report for the high-level review of 2005 at the 60th session of the UN General Assembly on the follow-up of the *Millennium Summit*.
21. This major study involved 62 contributors and has a total of 909 pages. It was preceded by another major study, also edited by Kracht and Schulz, on *Food Security and Nutrition. The Global Challenge* (1999), which has 33 contributions covering 692 pages.

Bibliography

Primary references

FAO documentation (Rome: Food and Agriculture Organization of the United Nations – unless otherwise stated)

FAO (1943) *United Nations Conference on Food and Agriculture. Hot Springs, Virginia, May 18–June 3. Final Act and Section Reports* (Washington, DC: United States Government Printing Office).

—— (1945) *Report of the First Conference of FAO held at Quebec City, October 16–November 1* (Ottawa: Dominion Department of Agriculture).

—— (1946a) *Proposal for a World Food Board. Prepared for submission to the Second Session of the Conference of the Food and Agriculture Organization, Copenhagen, Denmark, 2 September 1946* (Washington, DC: FAO).

—— (1946b) 'Proposals for a World Food Board', *Report of the Second FAO Conference, Copenhagen, September 1946*.

—— (1947) *Preparatory Commission on World Food Proposals* (Washington, DC: FAO).

—— (1951) *Study of an Emergency Food Reserve*. FAO Conference resolution 16/51.

—— (1952a) *Report of Working Party on an Emergency Famine Reserve*. Document CCP 52/55. Committee on Commodity Problems.

—— (1952b) *Report of Working Party on Emergency Famine Reserve*. FAO Council document 16/14.

—— (1952c) *Emergency Food Reserve*. FAO Council document CL 15/10.

—— (1952d) *A Reconsideration of the Economics of the International Wheat Agreement*. FAO Commodity Policy Study No. 1.

—— (1953) *Report of Group of Experts on an Emergency Food Reserve*. Document C 53/19.

—— (1954a) *Report of the Working Party on Surplus Disposal to the FAO Committee on Commodity Problems*. Document CCP 54/2.

—— (1954b) *Disposal of Agricultural Surpluses. Principles Recommended by FAO*. Subsequently revised and expanded in five versions and editions. Last edition (2001).

—— (1955a) *Uses of Agricultural Surpluses to Finance Economic Development in Under-Developed Countries: A Pilot Study in India*. Commodity Policy Studies No. 6.

—— (1955b) *Report of the Eighth Session of the Conference*. Document C/55.

—— (1956) *Functions of a World Food Reserve. Scope and Limitations*. FAO Commodity Policy Studies No. 10.

—— (1958a) *Report of the Third Session of the FAO Group on Grains*.

—— (1958b) *National Food Reserve Policies in Underdeveloped Countries*. Policy Studies No. 11.

—— (1960a) *Freedom from Hunger Campaign*. FAO Conference Resolution No. 13/59. 27 October 1960.

—— (1960b) *Review of the World Wheat Situation*. FAO Group on Grains. Third Report. April.

—— (1960c) *Report of the 10th Session of the Conference: 31 October–20 November 1959*.

—— (1961a) National Price Stabilization and Support Policies: Guiding Principles. Recommendations by FAO.

—— (1961b) *Utilization of Food Surpluses. World Food Programme*. FAO Conference resolution 1/61, adopted on 24 November 1961.

—— (1961c) 'Expanded Program of Surplus Food Utilization'. Report by the Expert Group to the Director-General of FAO, in *Development Through Food: A Strategy for Surplus Utilization*. FFHC Basic Study No. 2, pp. 69–117. Republished in FAO (1985) pp. 223–343.

—— (1961d) *Utilization of Food Surpluses. World Food Programme.* FAO Conference resolution 1/61, adopted on 24 November 1961.

—— (1962a) 'Agricultural Commodities – Projections for 1970', *FAO Commodity Review.* Special Supplement.

—— (1962b) *Nutrition and Working Efficiency.* FFHC Basic Studies No.5.

—— (1962c) *Education and Training in Nutrition.* FFHC Basic Studies No. 6.

—— (1962d) *State of Food and Agriculture 1962.*

—— (1962e) 'Agricultural Commodities – Projections for 1970', *FAO Commodity Review.* Special Supplement.

—— (1963a) *Third World Food Survey.* FFHC Basic Studies No. 11.

—— (1963b) *Possibilities of Increasing World Food Production.* FFHC Basic Studies No. 10.

—— (1963c) 'Changing Attitudes Toward Agricultural Surpluses', Document CCP/CSD 63/27, 12 April, *Consultative Sub-Committee on Surplus Disposal, Committee on Commodity Problems.*

—— (1964) *Food Aid and Other Forms of Utilization of Agricultural Surpluses. A Review of Programs, Principles and Consultations.* FAO Commodity Policy Studies No. 15.

—— (1965a) *Report of the World Food Congress. Washington, DC, 4 to 18 June 1963 Volume 1.*

—— (1965b) *Report of the World Food Congress. Washington, DC, 4 to 18 June 1963 Volume 2. Major Addresses and Speeches.*

—— (1968a) *Milk Products as Food Aid.* Document CCP OF 68/5/4.

—— (1968b) *Internationally Financed Food Aid.*

—— (1968c) *The Possible Role of Rice in Food Aid. A Technical Feasibility Study.* Document CCP: RI68/4.

—— (1969) *Towards a Strategy for Agricultural Development.* FFHC Basic Studies No. 21.

—— (1970) 'Speech delivered at the Closing Ceremony by the Chairman, H. E. P. J. Lardinois', in *Report of the Second World Food Congress, Volume 1.*

—— (1973) *Index. FAO Conference and Council Decisions 1945–1972.*

—— (1974) 'An Estimation of the Desirable Minimum Safe Level of Global Stocks for World Food Security', *Intergovernmental Group on Grains.* Document CCP: GR 74/11.

—— (1975) 'International Approaches to Food Stocks 1945–75', *FAO Commodity Review and Outlook 1974–75.*

—— (1977) *The Fourth World Food Survey.*

—— (1978–81) *Reports of the Agro-Ecological Zones Project. World Soils Resources Report 48, Volumes 1–4.*

—— (1979a) *World Food Security: The Need for Balance of Payments Support to meet Exceptional Variations in Food Import Bills.* Document prepared jointly by the FAO and World Food Council secretariats for submission to the International Monetary Fund.

—— (1979b) *Plan of Action on World Food Security.* FAO Council Resolution 1/75.

—— (1980a) *Objective Indicators to Signal Acute and Large-Scale Food Shortages.* Document CFS: WP/80/4.

—— (1980b) *Ways of Improving National Preparedness to meet Acute and Large-Scale Food Shortages, Including Improvements in Internal Distribution Networks.* Document CFS: WP/80/5.

—— (1981) *Requirements of Developing Countries for Food Security Assistance: Storage Needs for Cereals.* Document CFS:81/5.

—— (1982a) *Regional and Sub-Regional Food Security Schemes aimed at Strengthening the Collective Self-Reliance of Developing Countries.* Document CFS: 82/4.

—— (1982b) *Director General's Report on World Food Security: A Reappraisal of the Concepts and Approaches.* Document CFS: 83/4.

—— (1983a) *World Food Security Compact.* Document CFS/8. Eighth Session, Committee on World Food Security.

—— (1983b) *Assessing Food Aid Requirements: A Revised Approach.* FAO Economic and Social Development Paper No. 39.

—— (1984a) *Food Security Assistance Scheme.*

—— (1984b) *World Food Security: Selected Issues and Approaches.* Document CFS: 84/4.

—— (1985a) *Food for Development.* Economic and Social Development Paper No. 34.

478 *Bibliography*

—— (1985b) *Food Aid and Food Security: Past Performance and Future Potential.* FAO Economic and Social Development Paper No. 55.

—— (1985c) *World Food Security: Selected Themes and Issues.* FAO Economic and Social Development Paper No. 53.

—— (1986) *African Agriculture. The Next 25 Years. 7 Volumes.*

—— (1987a) *Fifth World Food Survey.*

—— (1987b) *Evaluation of the Food Security Assistance Scheme.* Document C 87/8-Sup. 3.

—— (1987c) *Impact on World Food Security of Agricultural Policies in Industrialized Countries.* Document CFS 87/3.

—— (1989) *Effects of Stabilization and Structural Adjustment Programmes on Food Security.* Economic and Social Development Paper 89.

—— (1992) *FAO Principles of Surplus Disposal and Consultative Obligations of Member Nations.* Third Edition.

—— (1993) 'Plant Genetic Resources' in *Development Education Exchange Papers.*

—— (1994a) *Director-General's Statement to the One Hundred and Sixth Session of the Council.* Document CL106/INF5.

—— (1994b) *Assessment of the Current World Food Situation and Recent Policy Developments.* Document CFS: 94/2.

—— (1996) *World Food Summit. Rome Declaration on World Food Security and World Food Summit Plan of Action.*

—— (1997) *Report of the World Food Summit.*

—— (1999) *The State of Food Insecurity in the World 1999.*

—— (2000a) *Guidelines for National FIVIMS. Background and Principles.*

—— (2000b) *Statement on Biodiversity.*

—— (2002a) *Report of the World Food Summit: Five Years On.*

—— (2002b) *UN Statement on the use of GM Food as Food Aid in Southern Africa.*

—— (2002c) *The State of Food Insecurity in the World 2002.*

—— (2003) *The State of Food Insecurity in the World 2003.*

—— (2004) *The State of Food Insecurity in the World 2004.*

—— (2005a) *Voluntary Guidelines to Support the Progressive Realization of the Right to Adequate Food in the Context of National Food Security.* Adopted by the 127th Session of the FAO Council, November 2004.

—— (2005b) *The State of Food Insecurity in the World 2005.*

—— (2006a) *The State of Food Insecurity in the World 2006.*

—— (2006b) *Livestock's Long Shadow.*

FAO/IFAD/WFP (2002) *Reducing Poverty and Hunger: The Critical Role of Financing for Food, Agriculture and Rural Development.* Paper prepared for the *International Conference on Financing for Development,* Monterrey, Mexico, March 2002 (Rome: FAO/IFAD/WFP).

FAO and WHO (1992a) *International Conference on Nutrition. Nutrition and Development – A Global Assessment.*

FAO and WHO (1992b) *International Conference on Nutrition. Final Report of the Conference.*

United Nations documentation (New York: United Nations – unless otherwise stated)

UN (1945) *Charter of the United Nations.* Signed in San Francisco on 26 June 1945.

—— (1948a) *Universal Declaration of Human Rights.* Adopted by the General Assembly of the United Nations on 10 December 1948.

—— (1948b) *United Nations Conference on Trade and Employment held at Havana, Cuba 21 November 1947 to 24 March 1948. Final Act and Related Documents.*

—— (1951) *Measures for International Economic Stability. Report by a Group of Experts Appointed by the Secretary-General.*

—— (1952a) *Food and Famine.* United Nations General Assembly resolution 525 (VI) of 26 January.

Bibliography   479

—— (1952b) *Food and Famine: Procedures for International Action in the Event of Emergency Famines Arising from Natural Causes*. Document E/2220, 14 May.

—— (1953) *Commodity Trade and Economic Development*. Document E/2519.

—— (1960a) *868th Plenary Meeting. United Nations General Assembly. Fifteenth Session. Official Records (Part1). Plenary Meetings Volume 1. Verbatim Records of Meeting 20 September–17 October 1960*.

—— (1960b) 'Economic Development Of Under-Developed. Food Surpluses; Distribution to Under-Developed Countries'. Second Committee 649th Meeting, 18 October 1960. *General Assembly – Fifteenth Session – Second Committee. Summary Records of Meetings, 21 September – 14 December 1960*.

—— (1960c) *Provision of Food Surpluses to Food-Deficit People through the United Nations System*. United Nations General Assembly resolution 1496 (XV) adopted at the 908th Plenary Meeting, 27 October 1960.

—— (1961a) *World Food Programme*. General Assembly resolution 1714 (XVI), adopted on 19 December 1961.

—— (1961b) *United Nations Development Decade*. UN General Assembly Resolution 17 (XVI), 19 December.

—— (1961c) *International Compensation for Fluctuations in Commodity Trade*.

—— (1962a) *The United Nations Development Decade: Proposals for Action*.

—— (1962b) *Population and Food Supplies*. FFHC Basic Studies No. 7.

—— (1963) *Official Records of the General Assembly. Eighteenth Session. Plenary Meetings. Volume 1. Verbatim Record of Meetings 17 September–14 October 1963*.

—— (1965a) *Programme of Studies of Multilateral Food Aid*. General Assembly Resolution 2096 (XX) adopted on 20 December 1965.

—— (1965b) *Continuation of the World Food Programme*. General Assembly Resolution 2096 (XX) adopted on 20 December 1965.

—— (1967) *A Guide to Food and Health Relief Operations for Disasters*.

—— (1968a) *Multilateral Food Aid*. General Assembly Resolution 2462 (XXIII) adopted on 23 December 1968.

—— (1968b) *Inter-Agency Study on Multilateral Food Aid*. Document E/4538.

—— (1969a) *International Action to Avert the Impending Protein Crisis*. Report of the UN Advisory Committee on the Application of Science and Technology to Development. Document E.68.XII.2.

—— (1969b) *A Study of the Capacity of the United Nations Development System* (Geneva, Switzerland: United nations).

—— (1971a) *Comprehensive Report of the Secretary-General on Assistance in Cases of Natural Disasters*. Document E/4994.

—— (1971b) *Strategy Statement on Action to Avert the Protein Crisis in Developing Countries*. UN Sales No. E.71 H.A.17.

—— (1972) *Report of the United Nations Conference on the Human Environment, Stockholm 5–16 June 1972*.

—— (1974a) *United Nations World Food Conference. Assessment of the World Food Situation, Present and Future*. Document E/CONF. 65/3.

—— (1974b) *United Nations World Food Conference. The World Food Problem. Proposals for National and International Action*. Document E/CONF. 65/4.

—— (1974c) *World Food Conference. Note by the Secretary-General*. Document E/5587.

—— (1974d) *World Food Conference*. United Nations General Assembly Resolution 3348 (XXIX) adopted 17 December 1974.

—— (1975) *Report of the World Food Conference, Rome 5–16 November 1974* Document E/CONF. 65/20.

—— (1976) *Development and International Economic Co-operation*. Resolution 3362 (S-VII) adopted by the UN General Assembly During its Seventh Special Session, 1–16 September. UN General Assembly Official Records, Supplement No. 1 (A/10301).

—— (1977) *Terms of Reference and Rules of Procedure of the World Food Council*.

480 *Bibliography*

—— (1980) *International Development Strategy for the Third United Nations Development Decade.* UN General Assembly resolution 35/56 adopted on 3 December 1980.

—— (1987a) *Food 2000. Global Policies for Sustainable Agriculture. Report of the World Commission on Environment and Development* (London and New Jersey: Zed Books Ltd).

—— (1987b) *Environmental Perspectives to the Year 2000 and Beyond.* UN General Assembly Resolution 42/186 adopted on 11 December.

—— (1987c) *Co-ordination in the United Nations and the United Nations System.* Report by the United Nations Secretary-General. Document A/42/232.

—— (1989) *Operational Activities for Development.* Document A/C.2/44/L.87.

—— (1990) *International Development Strategy for the Fourth United Nations Development Decade.* UN General Assembly Resolution 45/199 adopted on 21 December 1990.

—— (1991) *Implementation of the International Development Strategy – Role of the United Nations System.* Joint Meetings of the Committee for Programme and Coordination and the Administrative Committee on Coordination. Conference Room Paper No. 1.

—— (1993a) *Earth Summit. The Final Text of Agreements Negotiated at the United Nations Conference on Environment and Development (UNCED), 3–14 June 1992, Rio de Janeiro, Brazil.*

—— (1993b) *Vienna Declaration and Programme of Section. Note by the Secretariat.*

—— (1994) *Report of the International Conference on Population and Development.* Document A/CON.171/13.

—— (1995a) *Report of the World Summit for Social Development, Copenhagen, 6–12 March.* Sales No. E.96.IV.8.

—— (1995b) *Report of the Fourth World Conference on Women. Beijing 4–15 September 1995.*

—— (1997) *UN Briefing Papers. The World Conferences. Developing Priorities for the 21st Century.*

—— (1999) *World Survey on the Role of Women in Development: Globalization, Gender and Work.*

—— (2000a) *Further Actions and Initiatives to Implement the Beijing Declaration and Platform for Action. UN General Assembly Resolution S-23/3.*

—— (2000b) *United Nations Millennium Declaration. UN General Assembly Resolution 55/2.*

—— (2001) *World Population Prospect: The 2000 Revision, Volume 1.*

—— (2002) *International Conference on Financing for Development, Monterrey, Mexico, March 2002.*

—— (2003) *The Human Rights Based Approach to Development Cooperation. Towards a Common Understanding Among the UN Agencies.* Report of the Second Interagency Workshop on Implementing a Human Rights-based Approach in the Context of UN Reform Stanford, USA, 5–7 May 2003.

—— (2004) *A More Secure World: Our Shared Responsibility.* Report of the High-Level Panel on Threats, Challenges and Change. Document A/59/565.

—— (2005a) *2005 World Summit Outcome.* Document A/RES/60/1.

—— (2005b) *World Population Prospects.*

—— (2006) *Coherence, Coordination and Cooperation in the Context of the Monterrey Consensus and the 2005 World Summit Outcome.* Note by the Secretary-General.

World Food Council documentation (Rome: World Food Council – unless otherwise stated)

WFC (1975a) *Programme of Work on the Council.* Note by the Executive Director. Document WFC/4.

—— (1975b) *Report of the World Food Council on its First Session.* Official Record of the General Assembly, Thirteenth Session. Supplement No. 19 (A/10019) (New York: United Nations).

—— (1976a) *International System of Food Security.* Report by the Executive Director. Document WFC/22.

—— (1976b) *Report of the World Food Council on its Second Session.* Official Record of the General Assembly, Thirty-First Session. Supplement No. 19 (A/31/19) (New York: United Nations).

—— (1977a) *Progress Towards Increasing Food Production in Developing Countries.* Document WFC/36.

Bibliography 481

—— (1977b) *Report of the World Food Council on the Work of its Third Session*. Official Record of the General Assembly, Thirty-Second Session. Supplement No. 19 (A/32/19) (New York: United Nations).

—— (1978) *Report of the World Food Council on the Work of its Fourth Session*. Official Records of the General Assembly, Thirty-Third Session. Supplement No. 19 (A/33/19) (New York: United Nations).

—— (1979a) *World Food Security for the 1980s*. Report by the Executive Director. Document WFC/1879/5.

—— (1979b) *World Food Security for the 1980s. Plan of Action on World Food Security*. Document WFC/1979/5/Add.1.

—— (1979c) *World Food Security for the 1980s. International Trade*. Document WFC/1979/5/Add.2.

—— (1979d) *Report of the World Food Council on the Work of its Fifth Session*. General Assembly. Official Records. Thirty-Fourth Session. Supplement No. 19 (A/34/19) (New York: United Nations).

—— (1980) *Report of the World Food Council on the Work of its Sixth Session*. General Assembly. Official Records: Thirty-Fifth Session. Supplement No. 19 (A/35/19) (New York: United Nations).

—— (1981) *Report of the World Food Council on the Work of its Seventh Session*. General Assembly. Official Records: Thirty-Sixth Session. Supplement No. 19 (A/36/19) (New York: United Nations).

—— (1982a) *National Food Strategies to Eradicate Hunger*.

—— (1982b) *Report of the World Food Council on the Work of its Eighth Session*. General Assembly Records. Thirty-Seventh Session. Supplement No. 19 (A/37/19) (New York: United Nations).

—— (1982c) *The African Food Problem and the Role of International Agencies*. Document WFC/1982/4 (Part II).

—— (1982d) *World Food Security and Market Stability. A Developing Country-Owned Reserve*. Report by the Executive Director. Document WFC/1982/5.

—— (1982e) *Food Security for People – Direct Measures to Reduce Hunger*. Report by the Executive Director. Document WFC/1982/6.

—— (1984a) *Food Strategies in Africa – Progress and Critical Issues*. Report by the Executive Director. Document WFC/1984/4 (Part I).

—— (1984b) *Global Assessment of Resources Through the United Nations System to the Food and Agriculture Sector*. Document WFC/1984/9.

—— (1984c) *The World Food and Hunger Problem: Changing Perspectives and Possibilities 1974–1984. An Independent Assessment Presented to the World Food Council*. Document EFC/1984/6.

—— (1984d) *Towards Redoubled Efforts to End Hunger and Malnutrition. Some Non-Governmental Organization Recommendations. A Report Prepared by North American Non-Governmental Organizations for Consideration at the Tenth Session of the World Food Council*. Document WFC/1984/NGO/1.

—— (1984e) *Statement by Non-Governmental Organizations on the Issues Facing the Tenth Ministerial Session of the World Food Council*. In WFC (1984f) Annex II.

—— (1984f) *Report of the World Food Council on the Work of Its Tenth Session*. General Assembly. Official Records: Thirty-Ninth Session. Supplement No. 19 (A/39/19) (New York: United Nations).

—— (1985a) *African Women and Food Strategies. A Guide for Policy and Implementation Measures relating to the Role of African Women in Food Systems*.

—— (1985b) *Report of the World Food Council on the Work of its Eleventh Session*. General Assembly. Official Records: Fortieth Session. Supplement No. 19 (A/40/19) (New York: United Nations).

—— (1986a) *Programme for Recovery in Africa: The Importance of Food-Centred Development*. Report by the Executive Director. Document WFC/1986/4.

—— (1986b) *The World Food Council. Recommendations and Suggestions for the Future. Report of the Advisory Group*. Document WFC/1986/5.

482 Bibliography

—— (1986c) *Report of the World Food Council on the Work of its Twelfth Session*. General Assembly. Official Record: Forty-First Session. Supplement No. 19 (A/41/19) (New York: United Nations).

—— (1987a) *Report of the World Food Council on the Work of its Thirteenth Session*. Supplement No. 19 to the Official Records of the General Assembly, Forty-Second Session (A/42/19) (New York: United Nations).

—— (1987b) *Consultation on the Impact of Economic Adjustment on People's Food Food Security and Nutritional Level in Developing Countries*. Document WFC/1987/2/Add.1.

—— (1987c) *Future Programme of the Council and Other Business*. Document WFC/1987/10.

—— (1988a) *International Food Trade*. Document WFC/1980/5.

—— (1988b) *Growing Hunger Amidst Food Surpluses. The Potential for Hunger Reduction Through Food-Surplus Based Development*. Report by the Secretariat. Document WFC/1988/2.

—— (1988c) *Towards Sustained Food Security: Critical Issues*. Report by the Secretariat. Document WFC/1988/5.

—— (1988d) *Sustainable Food Security: Action for Environmental Management of Agriculture*. Report prepared by the United Nations Environment Programme in consultation with the World Food Council Secretariat. Document WFC/1988/5 Add.1.

—— (1988e) *Report of the World Food Council on the Work of its Fourteenth Session*. General Assembly. Official Records: Forty-Third Session. Supplement No. 19 (A/43/19) (New York: United Nations).

—— (1989a) *The Cyprus Initiative Against Hunger in the World. President's Report to the Fifteenth Ministerial Session. Introduction and Part One. World Hunger Fifteen Years After the World Food Conference: The Challenges Ahead*. Document WFC/1989/2/Part One.

—— (1989b) *Part II. Assessment of Selected Policies and Instruments to Combat Hunger and Malnutrition*. Document WFC/1989/2(Part II).

—— (1989c) *Approaches to Targeted Food, Nutrition and Health Programmes. Assessment of Country Experiences. Addendum to Part II*. Document WFC/1989/2/(Part II/Add. 1).

—— (1989d) *The Impact of Economic Adjustment on the Poor and Measures to Protect and Improve their Nutritional Levels. Addendum 2 to Part II*. Document WFC/1989/2(Part II/Add.2).

—— (1989e) *Part III. A Programme of Co-operative Action*. Document WFC/1989/2(Part III).

—— (1989f) *Report of the World Food Council on the Work of its Fifteenth Session*. General Assembly. Official Records: Forty-Fourth Session. Supplement No. 19 (A/44/19) (New York: United Nations).

—— (1990a) *Additional and More Effective Measures by Governments to Alleviate Hunger and Poverty*. Report by the Executive Director. Document WFC/1990/3.

—— (1990b) *Improving Co-ordination of National and International Action Towards A More Concerted Attack on Hunger*. Document WFC/1990/5.

—— (1990c) *Report of the World Food Council on the Work of its Sixteenth Session*. General Assembly. Official Records: Forty-Fifth Session. Supplement No. 19 (A/45/19) (New York: United Nations).

—— (1991a) *Focusing Development Assistance on Hunger and Poverty Alleviation*. Report by the Secretariat. Document WFC/1991/5.

—— (1991b) *Report of the World Food Council on the Work of its Seventeenth Session*. General Assembly. Official Records: Forty-Sixth Session. Supplement No. 19 (A/46/19) (New York: United Nations).

—— (1991c) *Migration and Food Security. A Background Note*. Prepared by the Food Security Unit, Institute of Development Studies, University of Sussex, UK. Conference Paper No. 1.

—— (1992a) *Implications of the Changes in Eastern Europe and the Commonwealth of Independent States for Food Security in Developing Countries*. Progress Report by the Executive Director. Document WFC/1992/3/Add.1.

—— (1992b) *The Importance of Greater Political Leadership and Co-ordination by a Stronger Council in the Fight Against Hunger*. Document WFC/1994/4.

—— (1992c) *Report of the World Food Council on the Work of its Eighteenth Session*. General Assembly. Official Records: Forty-Seventh Session. Supplement No. 19 (A/47/19) (New York: United Nations).

Bibliography 483

—— (1992d) *The Mandate, Functions and Future Role of the World Food Council. Statements and Member-Country Submissions to the Ad Hoc Committee on the Review of the World Food Council.* Document WFC/G/1992/3.

—— (1993) *Sustainable Agriculture and a New Green Revolution.* Paper prepared by the World Food Council Secretariat for the International Symposium on Sustainable Agriculture and Rural Development, Beijing, China, May 1993.

World Food Programme documentation (Rome: World Food Programme)

WFP (1965) *Recommendations by the Intergovernmental Committee to the Economic and Social Council of the United Nations and to the Council of FAO on the Future of the World Food Program.* MO/IGC: 7/19, 30 April.

—— (1969) *Inclusion of Non-Food Items in WFP Resources.* Document WFP/IGC: 15/14 Rev. 1.

—— (1970) *Food Aid and Related Issues during the Second Development Decade.* Report of the Intergovernmental Committee of the World Food Programme in response to resolution 2462 (XXIII) of the United Nations General Assembly. Document WFP/IGC: 17/5 Rev. 1.

—— (1971) *Proposal of the Delegation of the Kingdom of the Netherlands to the Intergovernmental-Committee of the World Food Programme to Establish an Emergency Food Supply Scheme.* Document WFP/IGC: 20/12 Add.1.

WFP (1978) *Modalities of Operation of the International Emergency Food Reserve.* Report of the Sixth Session of the United Nations/FAO Committee on Food Aid Policies and Programmes. Document WFP/CFA: 6/21, Annex IV.

—— (1979) *Guidelines and Criteria for Food Aid.* Report of the Seventh Session of the United Nations/FAO Committee on Food Aid Policies and Programmes. Annex IV.

WFP (1981) *Study of WFP Emergency Operations and Improvements of All Aspects related to such Matters.* Document WFP/CFA: 12/5-B.

—— (1982) *Further Review of Proposals and Recommendations to Improve the Effectiveness of Emergency Operations.* Document WFP/CFA: 13/P/5-B.

—— (1987) *Roles of Food Aid in Structural and Sector Adjustment* Document WFP/CFA: 23/5 Add. 1.

—— (1988) *Report of the Twenty-Fifth Session of the Committee on Food Aid Policies and Programmes.* WFP/CFA: 25/18.

—— (1995) *Food Aid for Humanitarian Assistance.* Proceedings of the United Nations World Food Programme African Regional Seminar. Addis Ababa, Ethiopia, February 1995.

—— (2004) *Vulnerability Analysis and Mapping – VAM.*

—— (2006) *2005 Food Aid Flows. The Food Aid Monitor, June.*

Other references

Abbott, J. (1992) *Politics and Poverty: A Critique of the Food and Agricultural Organization of the United Nations* (London: Routledge).

AJAE (1990) 'Invited Papers Session on Food Insecurity of the American Agricultural Economics Association', *American Journal of Agricultural Economics*, vol. 72, no. 5, pp. 1304–24.

Alexandratos, N. (ed.) (1988) *World Agriculture: Towards 2000. An FAO Study.* (Rome and London: Published by arrangement with FAO by Belhaven Press).

Alexandratos, N. (ed.) (1990) *European Agriculture: Policy Issues and Options to 2000. An FAO Study* (Rome and London: Published by arrangement with FAO by Belhaven Press).

Allen, R. (1974) 'Why you are here', PAN, No. 1, 5 November, pp. 4–5.

Alston, P. and K. Tomasevski (eds.) (1984) *The Right to Food: From Soft to Hard Law* (Utrecht, the Netherlands: Martinus Nijhoff Publishers and SIM Netherlands Institute of Huamn Rights).

484 Bibliography

Annan, K. A. (1997) *Renewing the United Nations: A Programme of Reform* (New York: United Nations).

Annan, K. A. (2000) *We the People: The Role of the United Nations in the Twenty-First Century.* Document A/54/2000 (New York: United Nations).

Annan, K. A. (2005) *In Larger Freedom: Towards Development, Security and Human Rights for All.* Document A/59/2005 (New York: United Nations).

Attiga, A., L. Glover and R. L. Kristjanson (eds.) (1958) *Proceedings of the International Wheat Surplus Utilization Conference* (Brookings, SD: Department of Economics, South Dakota State Collage).

Austin, J. E. and M. B. Wallerstein (1978) *Toward a Development Food Aid Policy* (Cambridge, MA: MIT INP Discussion Paper).

Aziz, S. (1974) 'The Real Issues in the Food Crisis'. Unpublished article (private papers).

Aziz, S. (1975a) 'A World Grain Reserve: History and Prognosis', in S. Aziz (ed.) (1975b).

Aziz, S. (ed.) (1975b) *Hunger, Politics and Markets. The Real Issues in the World Food Crisis* (New York: New York University Press).

Baker, J. E. (1979) *Food for Peace, 1954–1978. Major Changes in Legislation* (Washington, DC: Congressional Research Service, Library of Congress).

Baker, J. A. and L. H. Hamilton (2006) *The Iraq Study Group Report. The Way Forward – A New Approach* (New York: Vintage Books).

Barraclough, S. (2002) *Toward Integrated and Sustainable Development?* UNRISD Overarching Concerns Paper No. 1 (Geneva: United Nations Research Institute for Social Development).

Barrett, C. B. and D. G. Macwell (2006) 'Towards a Global Food Aid Compact', *Food Policy*, vol. 31, pp. 105–118.

Benedict, M. and E. Bauer (1960) *Farm Surpluses: U.S. Burden or World Asset?* Berkeley: University of California Press.

Benson, C. (2000) 'The Food Aid Convention: An Effective Safety Net?' in Clay and Stokke (2000).

Benson, C. and E. Clay (1998) 'Additionality or Diversion? Food Aid to Eastern Europe and the Former Soviet Republics', *World Development*, vol. 26, no. 1, pp. 31–44.

Berridge, G. R. (1991) *Return to the UN: UN Diplomacy in Regional Conflicts* (London: Macmillan).

Bertrand, M. (1985) *Some Reflections on Reform of the United Nations* (Geneva, Switzerland: UN Joint Inspection Unit).

Blau, G. (1954) *Disposal of Agricultural Surpluses.* FAO Commodity Policy Studies No. 5 (Rome: FAO).

Blau, G. (1963) 'International Commodity Agreements and Policies', *Monthly Bulletin of Agricultural Economics and Statistics*, vol. 12, no. 9, September, pp. 1–9.

Boerma, A. H. (1968) *FAO and the World Food Problem: Past, Present and Future* (Rome: FAO).

Boerma, A. H. (1975) *The Thirty Years War Against World Hunger.* Inaugural Lecture of the Boyd Orr Memorial Trust delivered at Aberdeen, Scotland, April 10 (mimeographed).

Boerma, A. H. (1976) *A Right to Food. A Selection of Speeches* (Rome: FAO).

Bohlen, C. (1996) 'Pope Agrees to Meet Castro', *The New York Times*, November 17.

Borgstrom, G. (1969) *Too Many* (London: Macmillan).

Boserup, E. (1970) *Women's Role in Economic Development* (New York: Praeger).

Bouet, A. (2006) *How Much Will Trade Liberalization Help the Poor? Comparing Global Trade Models.* Research Brief No. 5 (Washington, DC: International Food Policy Research Institute).

Boutros-Ghali, B. (1995) 'A New Departure on Development', *Foreign Policy*, No. 98, Spring, pp. 44–9.

Bowbrick, P. (1986) 'The Causes of Famine: A Refutation of Professor Sen's theory', *Food Policy*, May, pp. 105–24. A. K. Sen (1986) 'The Causes of Famine: a reply', *Food Policy*, May, pp. 125–32. Bowrick, P. (1987) 'Rejoinder: an untentable hypothesis on the causes of famine', *Food Policy*, February, pp. 5–9. A.K. Sen (1987) 'Reply: Famine and Mr Bowbrick', *Food Policy*, February, pp. 10–14.

Boyd Orr, J. (1936) *Food, Health and Income: Report on a Survey of Adequacy of Diet in Relation to Income* (London: Macmillan).

Boyd Orr, J. (1949) *Science, Politics and Peace*. Lecture delivered on the occasion of the award of the Nobel Peace Prize of 1949 (London: National Peace Council).

Boyd Orr, J. and D. Lubbock (1953) *The White Man's Dilemma* (London: Unwin Books).

Boyd Orr, L. (1966) *As I Recall* (London: MacGibbon and Kee).

Brown, L. R. (1970) *Seeds of Change. The Green Revolution and Development in the 1970s* (New York and London: Published for the Overseas Development Council by Praeger Publishers).

Brown, L. R. (1975) *The Politics and Responsibility of the North American Breadbasket*. Worldwatch Paper No. 2 (Washington, DC: Worldwatch Institute).

Brown, L. R. (1997) *Who Will Feed China? Wake-Up Call for a Small Planet* Worldwatch Environmental Alert Series (London: Earthscan Publications Ltd).

Brown, L. R. (2004) *Outgrowing the Earth: The Food Security Challenge in an Age of Falling Water Tables and Rising Temperatures* (New York and London: W. W. Norton).

Brown, L. R. and E. P. Eckholm (1974) *By Bread Alone* (New York and Washington, DC: Published for the Overseas Development Council by Praeger Publishers).

Brown, L. A., G. Gardner and B. Halweil (2000) *Beyond Malthus. Nineteen Dimensions of the Population Challenge* (London: Earthscan Publications Ltd).

Brownell, K. D. and K. B. Horgen (2004) *Food Fights: The Inside Story of the Food Industry, America's Obesity Crisis and What We Can Do About It* (New York and London: Contemporary Books McGraw-Hill).

Bruns, B., A. Mingat and R. Rakotomalala (2003) *Achieving Universal Primary Education by 2015: A Chance for Every Child* (Washington, DC: World Bank).

Buckingham, D. E. (1998) 'Food Rights and Food Fights: A Preliminary Legal Analysis of the Results of the World Food Summit', *Canadian Journal of Development Studies*, vol. XIX, special issue, pp. 209–36.

Cameron, J. and D. Gasper (eds.) (2000) 'Policy Arena: Amartya Sen on Inequality, Human Well-Being, and Development as Freedom', *Journal of International Development*, vol. 12, no. 7, pp. 985–1045.

Cathie, J. (1997) *European Food Aid Policy* (Aldershot: Ashgate).

Chen, S. and M. Ravallion (2004) 'How Have the World's Poorest Fared Since the Early 1980s?', *Policy Research Working Paper 3341* (Washington, DC: World Bank).

Chen, S. and M. Ravallion (2007) 'Absolute Poverty Measures for the Developing World, 1981–2004', *Development Research Group Report* (Washington, DC: World Bank).

CHS (2003) *Human Security Now* (New York: UN Commission on Human Security).

Clark, I. (2001) *The Post-Cold War Order: The Spoils of Piece* (Oxford: Oxford University Press).

Clay, E. (1991) 'Famine, Food Insecurity, Poverty and Public Action', *Development Policy Review*, vol. 9, pp. 307–12.

Clay, E. (2005) *The Development Effectiveness of Food Aid* (Paris: OECD Publishing).

Clay, E. and O. Stokke (eds.) (1991) *Food Aid Reconsidered: Assessing the Impact on Third World Countries* (London: Frank Cass).

Clay, E. and O. Stokke (eds.) (2000) *Food Aid and Human Security* (London: Frank Cass).

Clay, E., N. Pillai and C. Benson (1998) *The Future of Food Aid: A Policy Review* (London: Overseas Development Institute).

Cleveland, H. (1975) 'The U.S. vs the UN', *The New York Times Magazine*, 4 May.

Conway, G. (2003) 'Sustainable Agriculture' in N. Cross (ed.) *Evidence for Hope: The Search for Sustainable Development – The Story of the International Institute for Environment and Development* (London and Sterling, VA: Earthscan).

Cooper, A. F. (2004) *Tests of Global Governance. Canadian Diplomacy and United Nations World Conferences* (New York: United Nations University Press).

Corgridge, S. (2006) *Amartya Kumar Sen*, in D. Simon (ed.) *Fifty Key Thinkers on Development* (London and New York: Routledge), pp. 230–36.

Cornia, G. A., R. Jolly and F. Stewart (eds.) (1987) *Adjustment with a Human Face. Protecting the Vulnerable and Promoting Growth. A Study by UNICEF* (Oxford: Clarendon Press).

486 *Bibliography*

Croome, J. (1995) *Reshaping the World Trading System* (Geneva: World Trade Organization).

Currey, B. (1978) 'The Famine Syndrome: Its Definition for Relief and Rehabilitation in Bangladesh', *Ecology of Food and Nutrition*, vol. 7, no. 2, pp. 87–97.

Delisle, H. and D. J. Shaw (eds.) (1998) 'The Quest for Food Security in the Twenty-First Century', *Canadian Journal of Development Studies*, vol. XIX, special issue.

DeSombre, E. R. (2006) *Global Environmental Institutions* (London and New York: Routledge).

Devereux, S. and H. W. Singer (1999) 'A Tribute to Professor Amartya Sen on the Occasion of His Receiving the 1998 Nobel Prize for Economics', *Food Policy*, vol. 24, pp. 1–6.

Devereux, S. and S. Maxwell (2001) *Food Security in Sub-Saharan Africa* (London: ITGD Publishing).

de Waal, A. (1990) 'A Re-Assessment of Entitlement Theory in the Light of Recent Famines in Africa', *Development and Change*, vol. 21, no. 3, pp. 489–90.

Dil, A. (2000) *Hunger, Poverty and Development: Life and Work of Sartaj Aziz* (San Diego, CA and Islamabad, Pakistan: Intercultural Forum and Ferozsons (Pvt) Ltd).

Downing, T. E. (ed.) (1996) *Climate Change and World Food Security* (Berlin: Springer-Verlag in cooperation with NATO Scientific Affairs Division).

Dreze, J. and A. K. Sen (1989) *Hunger and Public Action* (Oxford: Clarendon Press).

DSE (1987) *Food Security in Africa*. Report of a Ministers' Round Table organized by the Development Policy Forum of the German Foundation for International Development in co-operation with the President of the World Food Council (Berlin, Germany: German Foundation for International Development).

Easterly, W. (2006) *The White Man's Burden. Why the West's Efforts to Aid the Rest Have Done so Much Ill and so Little Good* (Oxford and New York: Oxford University Press).

Egerstrom, L. (1983) '74 World Food Conference Resembled a Roman Circus', *St. Paul Pioneer Press Dispatch*, 4 December. Quoted in Ruttan, 1996, p. 572.

Ehrlich, P. R. (1968) *The Population Bomb* (New York: Ballantine Books).

Eicher, C. K., K. Maredia and I. Sithole-Niang (2006) 'Crop Biotechnology and the African Farmer', *Food Policy*, vol. 31, no. 6, December, pp. 504–27.

Eide, W. B. and U. Kracht (eds.) (2005) *Food and Human Rights in Development. Volume 1. Legal and Institutional Dimensions and Selected Topics* (Antwerp and Oxford: Intersentia).

Eide, W. B. and U. Kracht (2007) *Food and Human Rights. Volume II. Evolving Issues and Emerging Applications* (Mortsel, Begium: Intersentia).

Emmerij, L., R. Jolly and T. G. Weiss (2001) *Ahead of the Curve. UN Ideas and Global Challenges* (Bloomington and Indianapolis, IN: Indiana University Press).

Epstein, S. B. (1987) *Food for Peace, 1954–1986: Major Changes in Legislation* (Washington, DC: Congressional Research Service, The Library of Congress).

Evans, G. (2006) 'Foreword' in J. Ingram, *Bread and Stones. Leadership and the Struggle to Reform the United Nations World Food Programme* (North Charleston, SC: BookSurge).

Falk, R. A. (2000) 'The Quest for Humane Governance in the Era of Globalization', in D. Kald *et al.* (eds.) *The Ends of Globalization: Bringing Society Back* (Lanham, MD: Brown and Littlefield).

Freidel, F. (1990) *Franklin D. Roosevelt. Rendezvous with Destiny* (New York and London: Little, Brown & Co.).

Gardner, R. A. (1974) *The Role of International Organizations* (New York: Institute of Man and Science).

Gelb, L. H. and A. Lake (1974–75) 'Less Food, More Politics', *Foreign Policy*, 17 Winter, pp. 176–89.

George, S. (1987) *Food Strategies for Tomorrow*. The Hunger Project Papers, No. 6, December.

Gillespie, S., M. McLachlan and R. Shrimpton (eds.) (2003) *Combating Malnutrition: Time to Act* (Washington, DC: World Bank).

Goodwin, G. and J. Mayall (eds.) (1979) *A New International Commodity Regime* (London: Croom Helm).

Gordon-Ashworth, F. (1984) *International Commodity Control. A Contemporary History and Appraisal* (London: Croom Helm).

Gore A. (2006) *An Inconvenient Truth* (New York: Rodale).

Grant, J. P. (1973) 'Development: The End of Trickle Down?', *Foreign Policy*, No. 12.

Griffiths, P. (2003) *The Economist's Tale: A Consultant Encounters Hunger and the World Bank* (London and New York: Zed Books).

Haas, E. B. (1969) *Tangle of Hopes. American Commitments and World Order* (Englewood Cliffs, NJ: Prentice-Hall, Inc.).

Hall, J. A. (1996) *International Orders* (Cambridge: Polity Press).

Hambridge, G. (1955) *The Story of FAO* (New York: D. Van Nostrand Co., Inc.).

Hanrahan, C. E. (1996) *The World Food Summit. CRS Report for Congress* (Washington, DC: Congressional Research Service, The Library of Congress).

Holmes, P. (1996) 'At Forum. U.S. Rejects Food Rights', *The Washington Post* November, 18.

Holt, J. (1995) 'Prevention, Preparedness and Mitigation: The Ethiopian Experience' in WFP (1995), pp. 12–31.

Howe, J. W. (1974) *The U.S. and the Developing World. Agenda for Action 1974* (Washington, DC: Overseas Development Council).

Huang, J., S. Rozelle and M. Rosegrant (1997) *China's Food Economy to the Twenty-First Century: Supply, Demand and Trade* (Washington, DC: International Food Policy Research Institute).

Hudson, S. C. (1960) 'The Role of Commodity Agreements in International Trade', *Journal of Agricultural Economics*, vol. XIV, no. 4, December, pp. 507–30.

Humphrey, H. H. (1958) *Food and Fiber as a Force for Freedom.* Report to the Committee on Agriculture and Forestry, United States Senate (Washington, DC: US Government Printing Office).

ICFTU (1978) *Towards a New Economic and Social Order: The ICFTU Development Charter* (Brussels, Belgium: International Federation of Free Trade Unions).

IFAD (2001) *Rural Poverty Report 2001: The Challenge of Ending Rural Poverty* (Oxford University Press for the International Fund for Agricultural Development).

IFPRI (1995a) *A 2020 Vision for Food, Agriculture, and the Environment. Speeches Made at an International Conference, June 13–15, 1995* (Washington, DC: International Food Policy Research Institute).

IFPRI (1995b) *A 2020 Vision for Food, Agriculture, and the Environment. The Vision, Challenge, and Recommended Action* (Washington, DC: International Food Policy Research Institute).

IFPRI (2002) *Reaching Sustainable Food Security for All by 2020: Getting the Priorities and Responsibilities Right* (Washington, DC: International Food Policy Research Institute).

IFPRI (2004a) *Assuring Food and Nutrition Security in Africa by 2020: Prioritizing Actions, Strengthening Actors, and Facilitating Partnerships – Proceedings of an All-Africa Conference, Kampala, Uganda, 1–3 April* (Washington, DC: International Food Policy Research Institute).

IFPRI (2004b) *Annual Report 2003–04* (Washington, DC: International Food Policy Research Institute).

IJAA (1949) 'International Wheat Agreements', *International Journal of Agrarian Affairs* vol. 1, no. 3, September.

ILO (1943) *Intergovernmental Commodity Control Agreements* (Montreal, Canada: International Labour Office).

ILO (1963) *Hunger and Social Policy.* FFHC Basic Studies No. 14 (Geneva: International Labour Office).

ILO (1976) *Tripartite World Conference on Employment, Income Distribution and Social Progress and the International Division of Labour* (Geneva, Switzerland: International Labour Office).

ILO (1979) *Follow-Up of the World Employment Conference: Basic Needs* (Geneva, Switzerland: International Labour Office).

ILO (1998) *Declaration on Fundamental Principles And Rights at Work.* Adopted by the ILO Conference, 18 June 1998 (Geneva, Switzerland: International Labour Office.

ILO (2004) *A Fairer Globalization: Creating Opportunities for All.* Report of the World Commission on the Social Dimensions of Globalization (Geneva: International Labour Office).

ILO (2005) *World Employment Report 2004–05: Employment, Productivity and Poverty Reduction* (Geneva: International Labour Office).

488   *Bibliography*

Ingram, J. (2006) *Bread and Stones. Leadership and the Struggle to Reform the United Nations World Food Programme* (North Charleston, South Carolina, USA: BookSurge).

IWC (1974) *International Wheat Agreements. A Historical and Critical Background.* Document CL71/8 (London: International Wheat Council).

IWC (1988) *The Food Aid Convention and the International Wheat Agreement. History.* (London: International Wheat Council).

Jolly, R., L. Emmerij, D. Ghai and F. Lapeyre (2004) *UN Contributions to Development Thinking and Practice* (Bloomington and Indianapolis, IN: Indiana University Press).

Kaibni, N. M. (1988) 'Financial Facilities of the IMF and the Food Deficit Countries', in Shaw and Singer (1988), pp. 73–82.

Kaplinsky, R. (2005) *Globalization, Poverty and Inequality. Between a Rock and A Hard Place* (Cambridge, UK and Malden, MA: Polity Press).

Kapur, D., J. P. Lewis and R. Webb (1997) *The World Bank. Its First Half Century. Volume 1. History* (Washington, DC: The Brookings Institution).

Kent, G. (2005) *Freedom from Want. The Human Right to Adequate Food* (Washington, DC: Georgetown University Press).

Khor, M. (2001) *Rethinking Globalization. Critical Issues and Policy Choices* (London and New York: Zed Books).

Kissinger, H. (1973) *A Just Consensus. A Durable Peace.* Address to the 28th Session of the United Nations General Assembly, 24 September (Washington, DC: Department of State).

Kissinger, H. (1994) *Diplomacy* (New York: Simon & Schuster).

Knock, T. J. (1992) ' "Food for Peace": George McGovern and the New Frontier's Endeavours to Preclude "Inevitable Revolutions" '. Paper presented to the Organization of American Historians Annual Convention, April (typescript). State Publication 8742, p. 8.

Kolstad, I. and H. Stokke (eds.) (2005) *Writing Rights. Human Rights Research at the Chr. Michelsen Institute 1984–2004* (Bergen, Norway: Fagbokforlaget).

Kracht, U. (2005) 'Whose Right to Food? Vulnerable Groups and the Hungry Poor', in Eide and Kracht (2005), pp. 119–39.

Kracht, U. and M. Schulz (eds.) (1999) *Food Security and Nutrition. The Global Challenge* (Munster and New York: Lit verlag and St. Martin's Press).

Kracht, U. and M. Schulz (eds.) (2005) *Food and Nutrition Security in the Process of Globalization and Urbanization* (Munster: Lit verlag).

Kruger, A. O. (ed.) (1998) *The WTO as an International Organization* (Chicago and London: University of Chicago Press).

Kruger, A. O., C. Michalopoulos and V. W. Ruttan (1989) *Aid and Development.* (Baltimore, MA: The Johns Hopkins University Press).

League of Nations (1937) *The Relation of Health to Nutrition, Agriculture and Economic Policy. Final Report of the Mixed Committee of the League of Nations* (Geneva: League of Nations).

Leisinger, K. M., K. Schmitt and R. Pandya-Lorch (2002) *Six Billion and Counting. Population Growth and Food Security in the 21st Century* (Washington, DC: International Food Policy Research Institute).

Lipton, M. and C. Heald (1985) *African Food Strategies and the EEC's Role: An Interim Review.* Commissioned Study No. 6 (Brighton, UK: Institute of Development Studies at the University of Sussex).

Longhurst, R. (2007) *SCN. The First 30 Years* (draft).

MacFarlane, S. N. and Y. F. Khong (2006) *Human Security and the UN. A Critical History* (Bloomington and Indianapolis: Indiana University Press).

Malthus, T. R. (1817) *An Essay on the Principle of Population.* Reprinted from the original publication (London: J. Murray).

Marchisio, S. and A. Di Blasé (1992) *The Food and Agriculture Organization* (Dordrecht, The Netherlands: Martinus Nijhoff).

Martin, E. M. (1974) *Hunger and Diplomacy: A Perspective on the U.S. Role at the World Food Conference* (Washington, DC: Government Printing Office).

Masefield, G. (1967) *Food and Nutrition Procedures in Times of Disaster.* FAO Nutritional Studies No. 21 (Rome: FAO).

Maxwell, S. (1990) 'Introduction', *IDS Bulletin*, vol. 21, no. 3, July.

Maxwell, S. (1996a) 'Review Article. Perspectives on a New World Food Crisis', *Journal of International Development*, vol. 8, no. 6, pp. 859–67.

Maxwell, S. (1996b) 'Food Security: A Post-Modern Perspective', *Food Policy*, vol. 21, no. 2, pp. 155–70.

Maxwell, S. (2001) 'The Evolution of Thinking About Food Security' in S. Devereux and S. Maxwell *Food Security in Sub-Saharan Africa* (London: ITGD Publishing).

Maxwell, S. and D. J. Shaw (1995) 'Food, Food Security and UN Reform', *IDS Bulletin*, vol. 26, no. 4, pp. 41–53.

Maxwell, S. and R. Slater (eds.) (2004) *Food Policy Old and New* (Oxford: Blackwell Publishing).

McGovern, G. S. (1961) *Statement of the Delegate of the United States of America at the Intergovernmental Advisory Committee*, 10 April 1961. In FAO (1961c), p. 121. Republished in FAO (1985), pp. 315–16.

McGovern, G. S. (1964) *War Against Want. America's Food for Peace Program* (New York: Walkers and Co.).

McGovern, G. S. (ed.) (1967a) *Agricultural Thought in the Twentieth Century* (New York: Bobbs-Merrill).

McGovern, G. S. (1967b) *That None Shall Want. Food for Freedom*. McGovern Papers, Box TK-5. Seeley G. Mudd Manuscript Library, Princeton University.

McGovern, G. S. (1977) *Grassroots. The Autobiography of George McGovern* (New York: Random House).

McGovern, G. S. (2001) *The Third Freedom. Ending Hunger in Our Time* (New York: Simon & Schuster). Also published in paperback in 2002 by Rowman & Littlefield.

McNamara, R. (1973) *Address to the Board of Governors of the World Bank*. Nairobi, Kenya, September 24 (Washington, DC: World Bank).

Meadows (1972) *The Limits to Growth: A Report for the Rome's Project on the Predicament of Mankind* (New York: Universe Books).

Moggridge, D. E. (1992) *Maynard Keynes. An Economist's Biography* (London and New York: Routledge).

Morgan, D. (1979) *Merchants of Grain* (New York: The Viking Press).

Murray, P. E. (1989) *Paradox and Narrative: The Social Construction of Reality Within International Secretariats*. Ph.D. dissertation (Washington, DC: Catholic University of America).

Nestle, M. (2003) *Food Politics: How the Food Industry Influences Nutrition and Health* (Berkeley and Los Angeles, CA and London: University of California Press).

ODI (1997) 'Global Hunger and Food Security after the World Food Summit', *Briefing Paper 1997* (1) (London: Overseas Development Institute).

OECD (1973) *Development Co-operation, 1973 Review. Report by the Chairman of the Development Assistance Committee* (Paris: Organisation for Economic Co-operation and Development).

OECD (1978) *Development Co-operation, 1978 Review. Report by the Chirman of the Chairman of the Development Assistance Committee* (Paris: Organisation of Economic Co-operation and Development).

PAN (1974) 'Post-mortems and postscripts'. Newspaper of the World Food Conference, November 16, no. 11, p. 4.

Parotte, J. H. (1983) 'The Food Aid Convention: Its History and Scope', *IDS Bulletin*, vol. 14, no. 2, pp. 10–15.

Pearson, L. (1969) *Partners in Development. Report of the Commission on International Development* (New York: Praeger).

Pelletiet, D. L. (2006) 'FDA's Regulation of Genetically Engineered Foods: Scientific, legal and Political Dimensions', *Food Policy*, vol. 31, no. 6, December, pp. 570–91.

Peterson, T. H. (1975) *The Agricultural Trade Policy of the Eisenhower Administration*. Ph.D. dissertation (Ames, IA: Iowa).

Phillips, R. W. (1981) *FAO: Its Origins, Formation and Evolution 1945–1981* (Rome: Food and Agriculture Organization of the United Nations).

Pilon, J. G. (1988) 'The UN's Food and Agriculture Organization: Becoming Part of the Problem', *Society*, vol. 25, no. 6, pp. 6–10.

490 *Bibliography*

Pinstrup-Andersen, P. (ed.) (1988) *Food Subsidies in Developing Countries. Costs, Benefits and Policy Options* (Baltimore, MD and London: Published for the International Food Policy Research Institute by The Johns Hopkins University Press).

Pinstrup-Andersen, P., D. Nygaard and A. Ratta (1995) *The Right to Food: Widely Acknowledged and Poorly Protected.* 2020 Brief No. 22 (Washington, DC: International Food Policy Research Institute).

Pollan, M. (2007) 'Unhappy Meals. Thirty Years of Nutritional Science has Made Americans Sicker, Fatter and Less Well Nourished. A Plea for a Return to Plain Old Food', *The New York Times Magazine*, January 28, pp. 40–70.

Power, J. (1976) 'A New "Joseph" in Food Diplomacy', *International Herald Tribune*, May 7.

Power, J. (1979) 'The Distant Goal of Ending Hunger', *International Herald Tribune*, May 3.

Prebisch, R. (1950) *The Economic Development of Latin America and its Principal Problems* (Santiago, Chile: United Nations Commission for Latin America).

Prebisch, R. (1964) *Towards a New Trade Policy for Development: Report by the Secretary-General of the United Nations Conference on Trade and Development* (New York: United Nations).

Preeg, E. H. (1998) *From Here to Free Trade. Essays in Post-Uruguay Round Trade Strategy* (Chicago and London: University of Chicago Press).

Quisumbling, A. R., L. R. Brown, H. S. Feldstein, L. Haddad and C. Pena (1995) *Women: The Key to Food Security. Food Policy Report* (Washington, DC: International Food Policy Research Institute).

Rahe, D. H. (1974) 'US Farm Exports Hit $21.3 Billion Record in Fiscal Year 1974', *Foreign Agricultural Trade of the United States*, August, pp. 5–19.

Rajan, R. and A. Subramanian (2005) 'What Undermines Aid's Impact on Growth?' IMF Working Paper No. 05/126 (Washington, DC: International Monetary Fund).

Riches, G. (ed.) (1997) *First World Hunger. Food Security and Welfare Politics* (Basingstoke, UK and New York: Macmillan Press).

Riskin, C. (2006) *Sen, Amartya Kumar* in D. A. Clark (ed.) *The Elgar Companion to Development Studies* (Cheltenham, UK and Northampton, MA, USA: Edward Elgar), pp. 540–45.

Rosegrant, M., S. Rozelle and R. V. Gerpacio (eds.) (1997) 'China and the World Economy', *Food Policy* (Special issue), vol. 21, no. 4/5, September/October.

Rosenman, S. I. (ed.) (1950) *Public Papers and Addresses of Franklin D. Roosevelt 1941–45.* 4 vols (New York: Harper).

RTI (1984) *Food Strategies in Four African Countries.* Amsterdam, The Netherlands: Royal Tropical Institute for the Commission of European Communities.

Ringe, C. F., B. Senauer, P. G. Pardey and M. Roegrant (2003) *Ending Hunger in Our Lifetime: Food Security and Globalization* (Baltimore, MD and London: Johns Hopkins University Press for the International Food Policy Research Institute).

Ruttan, V. W. (1996) *United States Development Assistance Policy. The Domestic Politics of Foreign Aid* (Baltimore, MD: The Johns Hopkins University Press).

Sachs, J. D. (2005) *The End of Poverty. Economic Possibilities for Our Time* (New York: The Penguin Press).

Santayana, G. (1905) *The Life of Reason; or, The Phases of Human Progress*, vol. 1, chapter XII, 'Flux and Constancy in Human Nature' (New York and London: Charles Scribner's Sons and Constable).

Saouma, E. (1993) *FAO in the Front Line of Development* (Rome: Food and Agriculture Organization of the United Nations).

Sapsford, D. and J. Chen (1998) 'The Prebisch-Singer Terms of Trade Hypothesis: Some (Very) New Evidence', in D. Sapsford and J. Chen (eds.) *Development Economics and Policy. The Conference Volume to Celebrate the 85th Birthday of Professor Sir Hans Singer* (Basingstoke and London: Macmillan), pp. 27–38.

Schechter, M. G. (2005) *United Nation Conference* (London and New York: Routledge).

Schlosser, E. (2002) *Fast Food Nation: The Dark Side of the All-American Meal* (New York: Perennial).

SCN (1995) *Estimates of External Flows related to Nutrition*, Document SCN 95, Resources (Geneva: Administrative Committee on Co-ordination/Subcommittee on Nutrition).

SCN (2004) *Fifth Report on the World Nutrition Situation: Nutrition for Improved Development Outcomes* (Geneva: United Nations System Standing Committee on Nutrition).

Sen, A. K. (1976) 'Famines as Failures of Exchange Entitlement'. *Economic and Political Weekly*, vol. 11, special number, pp. 1–10.

Sen, A. K. (1977) 'Starvation and Exchange Entitlements: A General Approach and it Application to the Great Bengal Famine'. *Cambridge Journal of Economics*, vol. 1, pp. 22–37.

Sen, A. K. (1981) *Poverty and Famines: An Essay on Entitlements and Deprivation* (Oxford: Clarendon Press).

Sen, A. K. (1982) *Choice, Welfare and Measurement* (Oxford and Cambridge, Mass: Blackwell and MIT Press).

Sen, A. K. (1984) *Resources, Values and Development* (Cambridge, MA: Harvard University Press).

Sen, A. K. (1999) *Development as Freedom* (New York: Alfred Knopf).

Sen, B. R. (1982) *Towards a Newer World* (Dublin: Tycooly).

Sen, S. R. (1965) *Implications of the UNCTAD and Argentine Proposals for the Modification of the World Food Program*. Document WFP/IGC: 8/15 (Rome: WFP).

Serageldin, I. and P. Landell-Mills (eds.) (1994) *Overcoming Global Hunger. Proceedings of a Conference on Actions to Reduce Hunger Worldwide hosted by the World Bank and held at The American University, Washington, DC, November 30–December 1, 1993*. (Washington, DC: Environmentally Sustainable Development Proceedings Series No. 3, World Bank).

Shand, H. J. 'Agricultural Biodiversity, Biopiracy and Food Security' in Delisle, H. and D. J. Shaw (eds.) (1998), pp. 161–83.

Shapouri, S., M. Missiaen and S. Rosu (1992) *Food Strategies and Market Liberalization* (Washington, DC: United States Department of Agriculture).

Shaw, D. J. (1997a) 'World Food Security: The Impending Crisis? *Development Policy Review*, vol. 15, no. 4, pp. 413–20.

Shaw, D. J. (1997b) 'UN reform', *The Times*, October 7.

Shaw, D. J. (1999) 'Multilateral Development Co-operation for Improved Food Security and Nutrition', in U. Kracht and M. Schulz (eds.) *Food Security and Nutrition. The Global Challenge* (Munster and New York: Lit Verlag and St. Martin's Press), pp. 555–80.

Shaw, D. J. (2001a) 'The Opportunity and the Challenge: H. W. Singer's Contribution to the International Debate on Food Aid' in D. J. Shaw (ed) *International Development Co-operation. Selected Essays by H. W. Singer on Aid and the United Nations System* (Basingstoke, UK and New York: Palgrave Macmillan), pp. 199–244.

Shaw, D. J. (2001b) *UN World Food Programme and the Development of Food Aid* (Basingstoke and New York: Palgrave Macmillan).

Shaw, D. J. (2002a) 'Food Aid in Sub-Saharan Africa: Policy Lessons for the Future', *Canadian Journal of Development Studies*, vol. XXIII, no. 3, pp. 571–99.

Shaw, D. J. (2002b) *Sir Hans Singer. The Life and Work of a Development Economist* (Basingstoke and New York: Palgrave Macmillan). Also published in paperback in New Delhi, India by BRPC (India), 2004.

Shaw, D. J. (2004a) 'Darfur: We Can Take Four Immediate Steps to Handle the Next Humanitarian Catastrophe', *Financial Times*, July 24/25.

Shaw, D. J. (2004b) 'Food for Thought: Malnutrition and Obesity', *Development Policy Review*, vol. 22, no. 3, pp. 343–55.

Shaw, D. J. (2005a) 'Turning Point in the Evolution of Soft Financing: The United Nations and the World Bank', *Canadian Journal of Development Studies*, vol. XXVI, no. 1, pp. 43–61.

Shaw, D. J. (2005b) 'Dimensions of Poverty: Status and Solutions Towards the Millennium Development Goals', *Development Policy Review*, vol. 23, no. 4, pp. 497–523.

Shaw, D. J. and E. J. Clay (1998) 'Global Hunger and Food Security after the World Food Summit', *Canadian Journal of Development Studies*, vol. XIX, pp. 55–76.

Shaw, D. J. and H. W. Singer (1995) 'A Future Food Aid Regime: Implications of the Final Act of the GATT Uruguay Round', *IDS Discussion Paper* No. 352 (Brighton: Institute of Development Studies). See different versions of this paper in *Food Policy*, vol. 21,

492 Bibliography

no. 4, 1996, pp. 447–60; and in H. O'Neil and J. Toye (eds.) *A World Without Hunger* (Basingstoke and London: Macmillan for the UK Development Studies Association, 1996), pp. 305–34.

Shaw, D. J. and H. W. Singer (eds.) (1988) 'Food Policy, Food Aid and Economic Adjustment', *Food Policy*, vol. 13, no. 1, February.

Shojai, S. and R. Christopherson (eds.) (2004) *The Virtuous Vice: Globalization* Westport, CT and London: Praeger.

Singer, H. W. (1950) 'The Distribution of Gains between Investing and Borrowing Countries', *American Economic Review*, XL, 2.

Singer, H. W. (1995) 'Revitalizing the United Nations: Five Proposals', *IDS Bulletin*, vol. 26, no. 4, pp. 350–40.

Singer, H. W., J. Wood and T. Jennings (1987) *Food Aid: The Challenge and the Opportunity* (Oxford: Clarendon Press).

Sinha, R. P. (1976) 'World Food Security', *Journal of Agricultural Economics*, XXVII, 1, pp. 121–35.

Singh, K. (2005) *Questioning Globalization* (London and New York: Zed Books).

SIPRI (2004) *SIPRI Yearbook 2004: Armaments, Disarmaments and International Security* (Stockholm, Sweden: Stockholm International Peace Research Institute).

Sivard, R. (1991) *World Military and Social Expenditure 1991* (Washington, DC: World Priorities, Inc.).

Skidelsky, R. (2000) *John Maynard Keynes. Volume 3. Fighting for Britain 1937–1946* (Basingstoke and London: Macmillan).

Smith, M., J. Pointing, and S. Maxwell (1993) *Household Food Security, Concepts and Definitions: An Annotated Bibliography*. Development Bibliography No. 8. (Brighton, UK: Institute of Development Studies).

Snow, C. P. (1968) *The State of Siege*. Address at Westminster College, Fulton, Missouri, USA, 12 November. Reproduced by the Office of the War on Hunger, Agency for International Development. Washington, DC.

Sorensen. T. C. (1965) *Kennedy* (New York: Harper and Row).

Srinivasan, T. N. (1983) 'Review of A. K. Sen's *Poverty and Famines*', *American Journal of Agricultural Economics*, vol. 65, no. 1, February.

Stern, N. (2006) *Review on the Economics of Climate Change* (Cambridge: Cambridge University Press). Also available at www.sternreview.org.uk.

Stewart, F. (1982) 'Review of A. K. Sen's *Poverty and Famines*', *Disasters*, vol. 6, no. 2, pp. 145–6.

Stewart, F. and S. Daws (1998) 'An Economic and Social Security Council at the United Nations', in D. Sapsford and J. Chen (eds.) *Development Economics and Policy. The Conference Volume to Celebrate the 85th Birthday of Sir Hans Singer*. Basingstoke, UK: Macmillan, pp. 389–417.

Stiglitz, J. (2002) *Globalization and Its Discontents* (London: Penguin Books).

Stiglitz, J. (2006) *Making Globalization Work. The Next Steps to Global Justice* (London: Allen Lane).

Stratton, C., J. Green and M. Elia (2003) *Disease-Related Malnutrition: An Evidence-Based Approach to Treatment* (Wallingford, UK: CABI Publishing).

Talbot, R. B. (1977) 'The Three US Food Policies. An Ideological Interpretation', *Food Policy*, vol. 2, February, pp. 3–16.

Talbot, R. B. (1982) 'The Four World Food Organizations. Influence of the Group of 77', *Food Policy*, August, pp. 207–21.

Talbot, R. B. (1990) *The Four World Food Agencies in Rome* (Ames, IW: Iowa State University Press, pp. 75–129).

Task Force Hunger (2005) *Halving Hunger: It Can Be Done* (London and Sterling, VA: Earthscan, James and James).

Taylor, L. (1975) 'The Misconstrued Crisis: Lester Brown and World Food', *World Development*, vol. 3, nos. 11 & 12, pp. 827–37.

The Economist (2003) 'A Survey of Food', December 13.

The New York Times (1961) 'Friend of Farmers. George Stanley McGovern', March 31.

The New York Times (1974) 'Food: A Crisis for All', September 19.

The Report of the Commission on Global Governance (1995) *Our Global Neighbourhood* (Oxford: Oxford University Press).

The Report of the Independent Working Group on the Future of the United Nations (1995) *The United Nations in Its Second Half Century* (New York: Ford Foundation).

The Washington Post (1961) 'Food for Development', April 1.

Toye, J. and R. Toye (2003) 'The Origin and Interpretation of the Prebisch-Singer Thesis', *History of Political Economy*, vol. 35, no. 3, pp. 437–67. Also in J. Toye and R. Toye (2004) *The UN and Global Political Economy. Trade, Finance, and Development*. United Nations Intellectual History Project Series (Bloomington and Indianapolis, IN: Indiana University Press), pp. 111–34.

Trueheart, C. (1996) 'Food Summit Paints Picture of Crisis. Conference Cites Hunger, But Can Do Little but Talk About It', *The Washington Post*, November 14.

UK (1996) *Food Security and the World Food Summit. United Kingdom Policy Paper* (London: Overseas Development Administration).

ul Haq, M. (1995) 'An Economic Security Council', *IDS Bulletin*, vol. 26, no. 4, pp. 20–27.

UNCTAD (1964) *United Nations Conference on Trade and Development. Final Act* and Report, Proceedings, vol. 1. Recommendation World Food Program. No. A. II. 6. Sales No. 64.II.B. 11 (New York: United Nations).

UNCTAD (1977) *United Nations: New Directions and New structures for Trade and Development. Report of the Secretary-General of UNCTAD to UNCTAD IV* (Geneva, Switzerland: United Nations Conference on Trade and Development).

UNCTAD (2006) *Trade and Development Report, 2006* (Geneva: United Nations Conference on Trade and Development).

UNDP (1994) *Human Development Report 1994* (New York: Oxford University Press for the United Nations Development Programme).

UNDP (2005) *UN Millennium Project 2005. Investing in Development: A Practical* Plan to Achieve the Millennium Development Goals. Overview (New York: United Nations Development Programme).

UNDP (2006) *Human Development Report 2006. Beyond Scarcity: Power, Poverty and the Global Water Crisis* (New York: United Nations Development Programme).

UNEP (1987) *Our Common Future. Report of the World Commission on Environment and Development*. Nairobi, Kenya: United Nations Environment Programme.

UNESCO (1963) *Education and Agricultural Development*. FFHC Basic Studies No. 15 (Paris: United Nation Educational, Scientific and Cultural Organization).

UNESCO (2002) *EFA Global Monitoring Report 2002. Education for All – Is the World on Track?* (Paris: United Nations Educational, Scientific and Cultural Organization).

UNESCO (2004) *EFA Global Monitoring Report 2003/4. Gender and Education for All – The Leap to Equality* (Paris: United Nations Educational, Scientific and Cultural Organization).

UNESCO (2005) *EFA Global Monitoring Report. Education for All – The Quality Imperative* (Paris: United Nations Educational, Scientific and Cultural Organization).

UNESCO (2006) *EFA Global Monitoring Report. Education for All. Literacy for Life* (Paris: United Nations Educational, Scientific and Cultural Organization).

UNFPA (2004) *State of the World Population2004: The Cairo Consensus at Ten – Population, Reproductive Health and the Global Effort to End Poverty* (New York: United Nations Population Fund).

UNICEF (1984) 'The Impact of Recession on Children. A UNICEF Special Study' in *The State of the World's Children 1984* (New York: Published by Oxford University Press for the United Nations Children's Fund, pp. 137–72).

UNICEF (1991) 'World Declaration on the Survival. Protection and Development of Children in the 1990s and Plan of Action adopted at the World Summit for Children' in *State of the World's Children 1991* (New York: Published by Oxford University Press for the United Nations Children's Fund).

494 *Bibliography*

UNICEF (2004) *The State of the World's Children 2004. Girls, Education and Development* (New York: United Nations Children's Fund).

UNICEF (2005) *The State of the World's Children 2005: Childhood Under Threat* (New York: United Nations Children's Fund). US (1962) *Public Papers of the Presidents of the United States. John F. Kennedy, 20 January to 31 December 1961* (Washington, DC: US Government Printing Office).

US (1963) *President Kennedy Speeches*. Papers of the President's Office Files. Box 34. John Fitzgerald Kennedy Library, Boston.

US (1964a) *Political Interest in Agricultural Export Surplus Disposal Through Public Law 480*. Technical Bulletin 161 (Tucson, AR: Agricultural Experiment Station, The University of Arizona).

US (1964b) *Sixteenth Semi-Annual Report on Activities Carried Out Under Public Law 480* (Washington, DC: United States Agency for International Development, Office of Material Resources).

US (1973) *The Impact of an International Food Bank*. Report by a Task Force of the Council for Agricultural Science and Technology (Washington, DC: Council for Agricultural Science and Technology).

US (1974a) *Report on Nutrition and the International Situation. Prepared by the Staff of the Select Committee on Nutrition and Human Needs, United States Senate* (Washington, DC: US Government Printing Office).

US (1974b) *Report on the World Food Conference. Hearings before the Committee on Foreign Affairs, House of Representatives, Ninety-Third Congress, Second Session,* November 26 (Washington, DC: US Government Printing Office).

US (1975a) *Implementation of the World Food Conference Recommendations. Hearing Before the Subcommittee on Foreign Agricultural Policy of the Committee on Agriculture and Forestry, United States Senate, Ninety-Fourth Congress, First Session,* November 6 (Washington, DC: US Government Printing Office).

US (1975b) *The US Proposal for an International Grain Reserves System*. Report of a Staff Study Mission to the September 29–30, 1975, Meeting of the International Wheat Council Preparatory Group (Washington, DC: US Government Printing Office).

US (1976) *A Basic Human Needs Strategy of Development. Staff Report on the World Employment Conference* (Washington, DC: US Government Printing Office).

US (1980) *Evolution of the Basic Needs Concept*. Development Coordination Committee Policy Paper (Washington, DC: Agency for International Development).

US (1996) *The U.S. Contribution to World Food Security. The U.S. Position Paper Prepared for the World Food Summit* (Washington, DC: US Department of Agriculture).

Uvin, P. (1994) *The International Organization of Hunger* (London and New York: Kegan Paul International).

von Braun, J. (ed.) (1995) *Employment for Poverty Reduction and Food Security* (Washington, DC: International Food Policy Research Institute).

von Braun, J. (2003) 'Berlin Statement on Food Aid for Sustainable Food Security' in *International Workshop on Food Aid – Contributions and Risks to Sustainable Food Security, September 2–4, Berlin, Germany* (Washington, DC: International Food Policy Research Institute).

von Braun, J., T. Teklu and P. Webb (1991) *Labour-Intensive Public Works for Food Security: Experience in Africa*. Working Papers on Food Security No. 6 (Washington, DC: International Food Policy Research Institute).

Wallerstein, M. B. (1980) *Food for War – Food for Peace. United States Food Aid in a Global Context* (Cambridge, MA: The MIT Press).

Ward, B. (1972) *Only One World* (Stockholm: UN Environment Conference).

Ward, B. (1974) 'The Fat Years and the Lean', *The Economist*, November 2, pp. 19–25.

Watson, A. (1982) *Diplomacy: The Dialogue Between States* (London: Methuen Eyre).

Webb, P. and J. von Braun (1994) *Famine and Food Security in Ethiopia: Lessons for Africa*. (Chichester, UK and New York: Wiley and Sons).

Weiss T. G. and R. S. Jordan (1976) *The World Food Conference and Global Problem Solving* (New York: Praeger).

Weiss, T. G., D. P. Forsythe and R. A. Coate (1994) *The United Nations and Changing World Politics* (Boulder, CO: Westview).

WHO (1962) *Weather and Food*. FFHC Basic Studies No. 1 (Geneva: World Health Organization).

WHO (1963) *Malnutrition and Disease*. FFHC Basic Studies No. 12 (Geneva: World Health Organization).

Williams, A. (1998) *Failed Imagination? New World Order of the Twentieth Century* (Manchester: Manchester University Press).

Williams, M. J. (1978) *Statement by Maurice J. Williams, Executive Director of the World Food Council to the Second Committee of the General Assembly*. New York, 20 October 1978 (Rome: World Food Council documents).

Williams, M. J. (1982) 'Prospects for Eliminating Hunger in the face of World-Wide Economic Recession', *International Labour Review*, vol. 121, no. 6, pp. 657–69.

Williams, M. J. (1984) 'National Food Strategies: Focal Point for Food Policy Action', *The Courier*, No. 84, March–April, pp. 48–50.

Williams, M. J. (1986) 'Developing Political Support for Food Policy Planning' in C. K. Mann and B. Huddlestone (eds.) *Food Policy: Framework for Analysis and Action* (Bloomington: Indiana University Press).

Williams, M. J. and T. W. Stephens (1984) 'Resource flows through the multilateral system for food and agriculture. Trends of the decade', *Food Policy*, vol. 9, no. 4, pp. 331–41.

Wilson, Jr., T. W. (1974) *World Food: The Political Dimension* (Washington, DC: The Aspen Institute for Humanitarian Studies).

Winter, L. A., N. McCulloch and A. McKay (2004) 'Trade Liberalization and Poverty: The Evidence so Far', *Journal of Economic Literature*, 42 (March), pp. 72–115.

Wolf, M. (2004) *Why Globalization Works* (New Haven, CT and London: Yale University Press).

Woodbridge, G. (1950) *UNRRA: The History of the United Nations Relief and Rehabilitation Administration* (New York: Columbia University Press).

Woodham-Smith, C. (1962) *The Great Hunger. Ireland 1845* (London: Hamish Hamilton).

World Bank (1978) *World Development Report, 1978* (Washington, DC: World Bank).

World Bank (1980) *World Development Report, 1980*. Part II. Poverty and Human Development (New York: Published for the World Bank by Oxford University Press).

World Bank (1985) *Ensuring Food Security in the Developing World: Issues and Options*. Agricultural and Rural Development Department. Report No. 5926 (Washington, DC: World Bank).

World Bank (1986) *Poverty and Hunger. Issues and Options for Food Security in Developing Countries. A World Bank Policy Study* (Washington, DC: World Bank).

World Bank (2001) *World Development Report 2000/2001: Attacking Poverty* (New York: Oxford University Press for the World Bank).

World Bank (2002) *World Development Report 2002* (New York: Oxford University Press for the World Bank).

Worldwatch Institute (2005) *State of the World 2005: Redefining Global Security* (New York and London: W. W. Norton).

WTO (2001) *Ministerial Declaration of the Doha Multilateral Negotiations* (Geneva: World Trade Organization).

WTO (2004) *The Future of the WTO: Addressing Institutional Challenges in the New Millennium* (Geneva: Consultative Board of the World Trade Organization).

Yates, P. L. (1955) *So Bold An Aim. Ten Years of International Co-operation Toward Freedom from Want* (Rome: FAO).

Index

A 2020 Vision for Food, Agriculture and the Environment, *see* International Food Policy Research Institute (IFPRI)

Adam, Ibrahim (Chair, Preparatory Committee, International Nutrition Conference, 1992), 305, 472 n7

Adjustment with a Human Face (UNICEF study, 1987), 279, 385

Africa, increased aid to, 374

'Agriculture, Food Security, Nutrition and the Millennium Development Goals', 2005 article, 404–5

Ahmed, Salahuddin (Bangladesh Permanent Representative to FAO, Deputy Executive Director, World Food Council, (1978–82) Deputy Executive Director, World Food Programme (1982–94), 182–4

al-Qaeda terrorist attacks on New York and Washington, DC, 11 September 2001, 428

Annan, Kofi A. (United Nations Secretary-General, 1997–2006), 283, 292, 297, 356–7, 370, 450

Anstee, Margaret Joan (United Nations Assistant Secretary-General), 471 n41

Armstrong, Anne (President Ford's adviser and leading member of US delegation to 1974 World Food Conference), 135

Atlantic Charter (signed by US President Roosevelt and British Prime Minister Churchill, August 1941), 16, 25

Atwood, Brian (Administrator, United States International Aid Department), 318

Avoiding Dangerous Climate Change, scientific symposium, UK, February 2005, 445–6

Aykroyd, Dr. D. (co-author, League of Nations report on *Nutrition and Public Health* (1935), 6

Aziz, Sartaj (Director, FAO Commodities and Trade Division, Deputy Secretary-General, 1974 World Food Conference, first Deputy Executive Director, World Food Council, Deputy

President, International Fund for Agricultural Development, Pakistan Minister of Agriculture and Foreign Minister)

assessment of 1974 World Food Conference, 146

career, 144, 471 n41

contributions to 1974 World Food Conference, xvi, 123–5, 144–5

proposal for an international system of food security (1976), 180

proposal for Rome Forum (1974), 128

Ban, Ki-moon (present United Nations Secretary-General, 2007–), 460

Bariloche Foundation, 222

basic needs concept, *see* International Labour Organization (ILO), World Employment Conference, 1976

Baumgartner, M. (French Minister of Finance), 86

Beckmann, David (President, Bread for the World), 403

Bennet, Dr Paul (co-author, League of Nations report on *Nutrition and Public Health* 1935), 6

Benson, Ezra Taft (US Secretary of Agriculture), 87, 472 n17

Berlusconi, Silvio (President, Italian Council of Ministers and Chair, World Food Summit +5, 2002), 356

Bevin, Ernest (member of PM Winston Churchill's war cabinet), 25

Bezanson, Keith (President, Canadian International Development Research Council, later Director, Institute for Development Studies, University of Sussex, UK), 337–8

Blau, Gerda (Director, FAO Commodities and Trade Division), 35

Boerma, Addeke (FAO Director-General 1968–75), 29, 121, 137, 219

Address to 1974 World Food Conference, 135–6

Boserup, Ester (author of *Women's Role in Economic Development* (1970) Danish representative to the UN Commission on the Status of Women), 341, 473 n18

Boudreau, Dr Frank (Head, League of Nations Health Division), 6

Boumedienne, Houari (President of Algeria), 122

Boutros-Ghali, Boutros (United Nations Secretary-General, 1992–6), 215, 218, 318–19, 331–2, 351

Brandt, Willy (Chancellor of West Germany), 122

Broadley, Herbert (member of UK delegation and chairman of committee that discussed the World Food Board proposal, Second FAO Conference, 1946), 26

Brown, Lester (Founder, President, Worldwatch Institute (1974) and Founder, President, Earth Policy Institute (2001), 286, 407–8, 467 n7

Brownell, Kelly (co-author,*Food Fights*, Director, Yale Center for Eating and Weight Disorders), 411

Bruce, Stanley (later Viscount Bruce of Melbourne), 7, 27

Brundland, Mrs Gro Harlem (Norwegian Prime Minister and Head, World Commission on Environment and Development), 286

Buffer stock financing facility (IMF), 240–1

Butz, Earl (US Secretary of Agriculture and leader of the US delegation to the 1974 World Food Conference)
views at conference, 132–3
views on international grains reserves proposal, 157

Calder, Richie (Introduction to Boyd Orr autobiography *As I Recall*, 1966), 304

Canadian food surpluses, 14

Canadian Wheat Board, 14

Carter, Jimmy (US President), 227, 319

Castro, Fidel (Cuban President), 351

Chavez, Hugo (Venezuelan President, Chairman,), 298

China, effects on world food security, 407

chronic food insecurity, concept of, 40

Churchill, Winston (later Sir Winston) (UK Prime Minister), 16, 25

Clayton, Will (US government official charged with trying to organize the International Trade Organization), 27

climate change and global warming, 443–51
An Inconvenient Truth, film and book on global warming, 447
Convention on Biodiversity (1972), 290
Convention to Combat Desertification (1995), 290
Kyoto Protocol (1997), 444
livestock and global warming, 451
Montreal Protocol on climate change (1987), 290
Multilateral Fund for implementing the Montreal Protocol (1991), 291
Nairobi Framework to help developing countries reduce carbon emissions, 450–1
Stern report on the economics of climate change, 447–8
UN Framework Convention on Climate Change, 1992, 290, 296
US objections, 446–7
Vienna Convention for the Protection of the Ozone Layer (1997), 290

Cochrane, Willard (Director, US Department of Agriculture's Economic Service), 93

Codex Alimentarius Commission (FAO/WHO), 304

Colombia [University] Declaration on a broad concept of economic and social development (1970), 144

Commission for International Commodity Trade, 30

Commonwealth of Independent States (CIS), former Soviet Union, 192

Compensatory Financing Facility (IMF), 194, 210, 240–1

Comprehensive Africa Agricultural Development Programme, 360

Conliffe, John B. (University of California, chairman of the expert group that proposed an International Commodities Clearing House), 32

Consultative Group on International Agricultural Research (CGIAR), 208, 334, 349

consumer food subsidies programmes, 364–8

Convention on the Elimination of All forms of Discrimination against Women, *see* United Nations (UN)

498 *Index*

Convention on the Rights of the Child (1989), 280, 284
Copenhagen Declaration on Social Development (1995), *see* United Nations (UN)
Copenhagen Seminars for Social Progress, 331
Costa Rican government proposal for a World Food Reserve, 38
Crookes, Sir William (predictor of worldwide starvation in the 1890s), 115

Dag Hammarskjold Foundation, 222
De Cuellar, Perez (United Nation Secretary-General), 215
de la Warr, Earl (UK Under-Secretary for Agriculture), 8
Declaration of the United Nations, 1942, 23
Declaration on the Right to Development, 315
Desai, Nitin (Chief, UN Department on Sustainable Development and Secretary-General, World Summit on Sustainable Development, 2002), 293–4
Diouf, Jacques (present FAO Director General, 1996), 347, 357–8
Disability-adjusted life years (DALYs), concept of, 396
Dodd, Norris, E. (US Undersecretary of Agriculture and FAO Director-General, 1948–53), 26, 32
Doha Development Agenda/Round, *see* World Trade Organization (WTO)
Donne, John (English poet), 79
Dublin Statement on Water and the Environment, 1992, 300

Education for All, global monitoring reports (UNESCO), 418
aid for, 419
gender disparities, 418
literacy, 419
meeting the Millennium Development Goals for education, 421
Eisenhower, Dwight D. (US President)
food for peace proposal, 87
multilateral food aid facility proposal, 89
Elliot, Walter (UK Minister of Agriculture), 8
Emmerij, Louis (Director, ILO World Employment Programme, Rector, Institute for Social Studies, The Hague, The Netherlands, President, OECD Development Centre, Special Adviser to the President, Inter-American

Development Banks, Co-Director, United Nations Intellectual History Project), xvi, 471 n43
employment, importance of, 422–3
concept of working poverty, 422
extent of unemployment, 423
Ending Hunger in our Lifetime (IFPRI publication, 2003), 403–4
European Union (EU), formerly EEC
agricultural surpluses, 86
Common Agricultural Policy, 86
views at 1974 World Food Conference, 136
Ezekiel, Mordecai (Director, FAO Economic Division), 35–6, 464 n23

Fall, Ibrahim (UN Assistant Secretary-General for Human Rights, Secretary-General, World Conference on Human Rights, 1993), 314
famine in biblical times (seven fat and seven lean years in Egypt), 44, 115, 463 n19
fast food industry, growth of, 409–10
Fast Track Initiative for aid to education (IMF/World Bank), 419
Food Aid Conventions, 75–6, 194
Food aid, development of, 85–109
concept of food entitlement, 230–1
criticisms of concept, 233–4
entitlement protection, 231–2
an expanded programme of surplus food utilization, *see* World Food Programme (WFP)
famines and entitlement, 231
food aid during the second UN development decade study, *see* World Food Programme (WFP)
food aid for food security, *see* Food and Agriculture Organization of the United Nations (FAO)
food aid in sub-Saharan Africa, 393
food entitlement concept of Amartya Sen, 230–4
future of food aid, 109
global food aid compact proposal, 109
guidelines and criteria for food aid, *see* World Food Programme (WFP)
improved food aid policy resolution of 1974 World Food Conference, 141
international emergency food reserve modalities, *see* World Food Programme (WFP)
multilateral food aid study (1968), 103–5

Index 499

Food and Agriculture Organization of the United Nations (FAO)
Committee on Commodity Problems (CCP), 35
Committee on World Food Security (CFS), 142
Constitution and functions, 9–10, 23
Consultative Subcommittee on Surplus Disposal (CSD), 35
counteracting excessive food price fluctuations, 44–8
creation of FAO, 3–4, 9–10
disposal of agricultural surpluses study (1954), 51
effects on 1974 World Food Conference on FAO, 146
European Agriculture: Policy Issues and Options to 2000 (1990), 250–1
famine reserve proposal, 28
FAO Charter for the Soil (1981), 286
FAO Council, 29
FAO Group on Grains, 74
FAO motto, 'Fiat Panis', 31
FAO *Trust Fund for Food Security and Food Safety*, 359
financing of FAO, 10
First FAO (Founding)Conference, Quebec, Canada, 1945, 9–10, 11
food aid and food security paper (1985), 251–5
food financing facility proposal, 240–1
Food Insecurity and Vulnerability Information and Mapping System (FIVIMS), 394
Food Security Assistance Scheme, 238–40
Freedom from Hunger Campaign (1960–70), 77–84, 305; *Man's Right to Freedom from Hunger Manifesto* (1963), 81–2; publications, 80; Special Assembly on Man's Right to Freedom from Hunger, 14 March 1963, 81–2; World Food Congress (1963), 81–3; World Freedom from Hunger Week, March 1963, 82; Young World Assembly (1965), 83
Global Information and Early Warning System on Food and Agriculture, 163–4, 202
impact of economic adjustment on food security and nutrition in developing countries study, 201
Indian pilot study on agricultural surpluses to finance economic development (1955), 52–4

Indicative World Plan for Agricultural Development, 244–6
infrastructure and storage needs of developing countries study, 194, 239
Interim Commission for detailed plan of FAO (1943–5), 4
International Alliance Against Hunger, 358. 360
international commodity agreements, 65–76; objectives, 66–8; types of agreements, 68–73
International Commodity Clearing House proposal, 32–4
International Conference on Nutrition, with WHO (1992), 304–12, 347; FAO/WFO collaboration, 304; Plan of Action on Nutrition (1992), 311–12; World Declaration on Nutrition (1992), 309–11
International Emergency Council (later FAO Distribution Division), 11
international price stabilization reserve proposal, 29
international trade, stability, and agricultural adjustment, 165–6
International Treaty on Plant Genetic Resources for Food and Agriculture, 359
International Undertaking on World Food Security, 150–4
location of FAO, 10
medium-term projections for agricultural commodities, 1962–70
minimum safe level of global food stocks for world food security, estimate of, 152–4
national food reserves in developing countries report, 58–64; commodity composition, storage, rotation and costs, 63–4; definition of roles, 61–3
Plan of Action on World Food Security, 194, 255–6
Preparatory Commission on World Food Proposals (1946), 27–30
Preparedness for large-scale and acute food shortages, 237–8
Principles of Surplus Disposal (1954), 54–7
regional and sub-regional food security schemes, 243–4
revised concept of World Food Security, 241–3
Second FAO Conference, Copenhagen, Denmark (1946), 11, 25–7

500 *Index*

Food and Agriculture Organization of the
United Nations (FAO) – *continued*
Soil Map of the World (with UNESCO)
(1961–78), 249
Special Action Programme for the
Prevention of Food Losses, 239
Special Meeting on Urgent Food
Problems, Washington, DC (1946),
15
Special Programme for Food Security,
launched 2002, 35
UN Conference on Food and Agriculture,
Hot Springs, Virginia, USA, May/June
1943, 3–4, 8–9, 10
voluntary guidelines to the right to food
security, 461
World Agriculture: Toward 2000 (1988),
248–50
world emergency food reserve study,
37–57; Plan of the Three Circles, 44
World Food Board Proposal, 15–31
World Food Capital Fund proposal, 54
World Food Reserve study, 37–57
World Food Security Compact, 256–8,
308
world food security, revised concept of,
241–3
World Food Summit (1996), 347–56
World Food Summit +5 (2002), 356–60
World Food Surveys: first (1946); second
(1952); third (1962); fourth (1977);
fifth (1987), sixth (1996), 246–8
food security
a central development goal, 456
definitions of, 383
difference between food and nutrition
security, 397
*Food and Nutrition Security in the Process of
Globalization and Urbanization* (2005),
455, 475 n21
*Food Security and Nutrition : The Global
Challenge* (1993), 381, 475 n21
food security for children: effects of
poverty, armed conflicts and
HIV/AIDS, 398–401
human right approach to, 460–1
international conventions, declarations,
compacts and resolutions, 388
redefinition of the concept, 383–6
food surpluses, historical background,
12–14
changing attitudes towards food
surpluses, 85–6
possible uses, 48–57

Principles of Surplus Disposal, see Food and
Agriculture Organization of the
United Nations (FAO)
Ford, Gerald (US President), 121
Address to the UN General Assembly
(1974), 130, 134
Fourth World Conference on Women
(1995), *see* United Nations (UN)
Freedom from Hunger Campaign, *see* Food
and Agriculture Organization of the
United Nations (FAO)
Further Actions and Initiatives to
Implement the Beijing Platform of
Action [for Women] (2000), 344–6

G77, 121, 138
see also non-aligned countries (G77)
G8 Summit, Gleneagles, Scotland (2005),
374
GATT (General Agreement on Tariffs and
Trade), 30
gender-in-development, concept of,
341–2
gender mainstreaming, 342
genetically modified (GM) crops and food,
437–43
criticism of US Food and Drug
Administration policy on, 443
FAO statement on biotechnology,
441–2
FAO, WHO and WFP statement on,
442
future prospects for Africa, 442–3
GM Science Review, UK, 439–41
report of UK Prime Minister's Strategy
Unit on, 439
UK public debate on, 437–8
German Foundation for International
Development, 181
Ghissassi, Abdellatif (member of World
Food Council review group), 471 n41
Glickman, Dan (US Secretary of Agriculture,
head of US delegation to 1996 World
Food Summit), 351
Global Burden of Disease Study (WHO and
World Bank sponsors), 392
*Global Conference on the Sustainable
Development of Small Island Developing
Countries* (1994), 290
Global Consultation on Safe Water and
Sanitation for the 1990s, New Delhi,
India (1990), 299
Global Environment Facility (GEF), *see*
United Nations (UN)

Global Information and Early Warning System for Food and Agriculture, *see* Food and Agriculture Organization of the United Nations (FAO)

globalization, 451–6
  antagonists views of, 453–6
  protagonists views of, 452–3

Gorbachev, Mikhail (former President, Soviet Union, Nobel Peace Prize, and chairman, Green Cross International), 429–30

Gore, Al (US Vice President, presenters of documentary, and author of book, on *An Inconvenient Truth* on global warming), 447

Grant, James. P. (UNICEF Executive Director), 279

Grant, Malcolm (Pro-Vice-Chancellor and Professor of Land Economics, University of Cambridge, UK), 474 n14

Green Revolution, 115

Griffiths, Peter (author of *The Economist's Tale*, 2003), 473 n5

Hall, Tony (US Congressman), 318, 472 n13

Halonen, Tarja Kaarina (President of Finland and Co-Chair, World Commission on the Social Dimensions of Globalization), 474 n19

Hammarskjold, Dag (United Nations Secretary-General, 1953–61), 381

Hannah, John (Deputy Secretary-General, 1974 World Food Conference, first Executive Director, World Food Council), 123, 169

Hao, Chung-Shih (Chinese Vice-Minister for Agriculture), 136

Hoffman, Paul (US Administrator of the Marshall Plan, Managing Director, UN Special Fund, and first Administrator, UNDP), 100

Hoover, J. Edgar (US President), 13

Horgen, Katherine (co-author, *Food Fights,* Consultant, Yale Center for Eating and Weight Disorders, 411

human rights approach to food and nutrition security, 460–1

human rights movement in the 1980s, 460

human security
  concept of, 428–9
  Human Security Network (founded 1999), 429

UN Commission on Human Security, *see* United Nations (UN)

Worldwatch Institute report on, 430–1

Humphrey, Hubert H. (US Senator and Vice President in the Johnson Administration), 86–7

hunger and malnutrition
  causes of, 387–8
  classification of hungry poor, 391–4
  costs of, 394–7
  effects of IMF/World Bank structural adjustment programmes on, 385–6
  effects on children, 397–400
  food emergency 'hotspots', 392
  hunger, malnutrition and poverty linkages, 387
  scientific study of disease-related malnutrition, 402
  special problems of sub-Saharan Africa, 392–3
  Task Force Hunger report on *Halving Hunger: It Can Be Done* (2005), 406–7
  UNICEF/World Bank joint study on, 400–2

Hunger and Public Action (Dreze and Sen,1989), 230

IMPACT (IFPRI's research and global food model), *see* International Food Policy Research Institute (IFPRI)

income factor: number of people living on $1 and $2 a day, 415–18

Indian Famine Code, 42

institutional incoherence, 349

Inter-American Coffee Agreement (1940), 22

Intergovernmental Panel on Climate Change (IPPC), 444, 451

International Alliance Against Hunger, see Food and Agriculture Organization of the United Nations (FAO)

International Bank for Reconstruction and Development (IBRD), *see* World Bank

International Bill of Rights (1966), 314

international commodity agreements, *see* Food and Agriculture Organization of the United Nations (FAO)

International Confederation of Free Trade Unions (ICFTU), 229

International Conference of Financing for Development (2002), 369–74
  The Monterrey Consensus, 372–3

International Conference on Human Rights (1968), 314

502 *Index*

International Conference on Population and Development (ICPD) (1994), 321–7
Programme of Action, 322–4
targets, 324–6
ten years later, report on, 413–15
UN Special Session (ICPD +5), 327
International Conference on Water and the Environment (1992), 299–303
international conferences (1990–2005), 274–8
international conferences on population issues, 321
International Convention to Combat Desertification (1995), *see* climate change and global warming
International Covenant on Civil and Political Rights (1966), 314
International Covenant on Economic, Social and Cultural Rights (1966), 314, 460
International Development Association (IDA), *see* World Bank
International Development Strategy for the 1990s, 271–3
International Drinking Water and Sanitation Decade (1980s), 299
International Emergency Food Reserve (IEFR), *see* World Food Programme (WFP)
International Finance Facility, launched 2005, 377
International Food Policy Research Institute (IFPRI)
A 2020 Vision for Food, Agriculture and the Environment, 334–9
All Africa Conference on Food and Nutrition Security (2004), 406
annual report 2003–4, 404–5
IMPACT (IFPRI's research and global food model), 338
International Fund for Agricultural Development (IFAD), 141. 142, 145, 202, 264–8
International Institute for Environment and Development, 286, 471 n5
International Labour Organization (ILO)
intergovernmentally controlled commodity agreements, report on (1943), 6
World Employment Conference (1976), 222–9; basic needs concept, 223; criticism of basic needs concept, 226–7; Declaration of Principles, 223;

defence of basic needs concept, 228; Programme of Action, 223–4
World Employment Programme, 222
international migration and food security, concern about, 193
International Monetary Conference, Bretton Woods, New Hampshire, USA (1944), 29
International Monetary Fund (IMF), 11, 23, 29, 72, 194
International Nutrition Conference (1992), *see* Food and Agriculture Organization of the United Nations (FAO)
International Organization of Hunger (P. Uvin, 1994), 386
International Rice Commission, 30
International Trade Organization (ITO), 23, 25, 29, 30
Draft Havana Charter of ITO (1948), 30, 66–9, 69
international trade, stability and agricultural adjustment, *see* Food and Agriculture Organization of the United Nations (FAO)
International Treaty on Plant Genetic Resources for Food and Agriculture (2002), *see* Food and Agriculture Organization of the United Nations (FAO)
International Undertaking of World Food Security, *see* Food and Agriculture Organization of the United Nations (FAO)
International Wheat Agreement, 73–5, 189
International Wheat Council (later International Grains Council), 22, 29

Japan, agricultural surpluses, 14
Johannesburg Declaration on Sustainable Development (2002), *see* United Nations (UN)
Johnson, Lyndon B. (US President), 86
Joint Organization for marketing wool surpluses (1946), 23
Jolly, Richard (Director, Institute of Development Studies (IDS), University of Sussex, UK, Deputy Executive Director, UNICEF, Architect, UNDP *Human Development Report*, Chair, UN Standing Committee on Nutrition, Chair, Water Supply and Sanitation Collaborative Council, Co-Director, United Nations Intellectual History Project, Honorary Professorial Fellow, IDS), xv, 279

Index 503

Kalantari, Issa (Iranian Agricultural Minister, President, World Food Council), 215

Kennedy, John F. (US President 1961–3)
address to UN General Assembly, 11 January 1962, 102
executive order on an expanded programme of food distribution to needy families in the United States (21 January 1966), 94
executive order on responsibilities of director, US Food for Peace Programme (22 January 1961), 94
inaugural address (20 January 1961), 94
last address to the UN General Assembly (20 September 1963), 103
presidential election campaign speeches, 88
proposal for an international conference to establish a world food agency, 88
proposal to establish an American Food for Peace Council (1960), 94
special message to Congress on agriculture (1961), 95
special message to Congress on foreign aid (1961), 95
State of the Union address, 11 January 1962, 94–5
UN decade for development (1960s) proposal, 71, 99
World Food Congress address (March 1963), 81

Keynes, John Maynard (famous British economist, leader of the UK delegation to the Bretton Woods conference 1944, originator of the International Trade Organization proposal), 29

Kissinger, Henry (US Secretary of States, Nixon and Ford Administrations), 121–2, 471 n2
Keynote address at 1974 World Food Conference, 131–2
national security study memorandum on food (1972), 131
proposal for a world food conference, 121–2, 130
statement to UN General Assembly (24 September 1973), 121
views on an international grains reserve system, 121–2, 130

Koehler, Horst (Managing Director IMF), 371

Kracht, Uwe (Senior Economist (1976–86) and Chief, Policy Development and Economic Analysis (1986–93), World Food Council secretariat, Coordinator, World Alliance for Nutrition and Human Rights), xvi, xvii, 469 n26, 473 n2

Kruger, Anne (Chief Economist, World Bank, First Deputy Managing Director, IMF, Director, Centre for Research for Development and Policy, Stanford University, USA), 474 n10

Kyoto Protocol (1997), *see* climate change and global warming

Lasso, Jose Ayala (first UN Commissioner for Human Rights), 472 n11

Latimer, Hugh, 7

leadership, national and international, 456–7

League of Nations
International Standards of Food Requirements (1937), 7
Nutrition and Public Health report (1935), 6
The Relation of Health to Agriculture and Economic Policy report (1937), 8
Study of the Problems of Raw Materials (1937), 6

Lima Declaration and Plan of Action on Industrial Development and Cooperation (1975), 222

locating food insecure people, 394

Long, Carolyn (President, InterAction), 320

'Make Poverty History' speech of Nelson Mandela, London, 3 February 2005, 387

Malthus, Thomas (author of population growth outstripping food production prediction), 115

Mandela, Nelson (former South African President and Nobel Peace Prize 1993), 387

Marei, Sayed Ahmed (Secretary-General, 1974 World Food Conference and first President, World Food Council), 123, 128, 130–1, 137, 138–9, 144, 169, 467 n4

marriage of health and agriculture concept, 7

Marshall, George C. (US Secretary of State, Truman Administration and originator of the Marshall Plan for European recovery after World War II), 13

Marshall Plan (European Recovery Programme), *see* United States (US)

504 *Index*

Maxwell, Simon, (Director, Overseas Development Institute, London), xv
Mbeki, Thabo (South African President, President, World Summit on Sustainable Development), 292–3
McCarthy, Joseph (US senator leading the communist witch-hunt in the 1950s), 30
McDougall, Frank (FAO founding father), 8
McGovern, George S. (US Congressman and Senator, first Director of the US Food for Peace programme), xv, 95–6, 131, 465 n46, 466 n47
 Food for Peace programme achievements, 101
 initiative to establish a multilateral food aid programme, *see* World Food Programme (WFP)
 proposal at 1974 World Food Conference, 133, 135, 141
 proposal to end world hunger, 432–3
 US Senate Select Committee report on *Nutrition and Human Needs* (1974), 133
McNamara, Robert (President, World Bank), 227
Millennium Development Goals (MDGs), *see* United Nations (UN)
Mkapa, Benjamin W. (Tanzanian President, Co-Chair, World Commission on the Social Dimensions of Globalization), 474 n19
Mongella, Gertrude (UN Assistant Secretary-General for the Advancement of Women, Secretary-General, Fourth UN Women's Conference, 1995), 342
Monroe, Charles (President, International Federation of Agricultural Producers), 137
Montreal Protocol [on climate change] (1987), *see* climate change and global warming
Moore, Mike (WTO Director-General), 371–2
Mubarak, Mohamed Hosni (Egyptian President, President, International Conference on Population and Development, 1993), 322
Multilateral Debt Relief Initiative, 380
Multilateral fund for implementing obligations under the Montreal Protocol (1991), *see* climate change and global warming

Nakajima, Hiroshi (WHO Direct-General), 308–9
national food reserves in developing countries, *see* Food and Agriculture Organization of the United Nations (FAO)
Nestle, Marion (author of *Food Politics*, Professor and Chair, Department of Nutrition, Food Studies and Public Health, New York University), 410
New International Economic Order (UN General Assembly resolution 1974), 129
New Partnership for Africa's Development, 360
Nixon, Richard M. (US Vice President in the Eisenhower Administration, later US President), 88, 121
 proposal for a multilateral food aid facility, 88–9
non-aligned countries (G77), 121, 138, 173, 469 n20

obesity, 408–13
 contributing factors, 409–12
 definition, 473 n8
 WHO International Task Force on Obesity, 412
OPEC (Oil Producing and Exporting Countries) and fund, 117, 176, 469 n20
Orr, Sir (later Lord) John Boyd (first FAO Director-General, 1945–48)
 address at Hot Springs conference after election in 1945, 4–5
 autobiography *As I Recall* (1966), 16
 cable by Stanley Bruce from the League of Nations Assembly, 7
 FAO takeover of UNRRA responsibility, 11
 Food, Health and Income report (1936), 16–17
 human nutrition work in Scotland, 16
 League of Nations committee on standard diet for health, 7
 Nobel Peace Prize, 1949, 31
 UK peerage, 31
 World Food Board proposal, 15–31

Paarlberg, Don (US Food for Peace Coordinator), 87
Panitchpakdi, Supachai (Director-General, World Trade Organization), 425
Patton, James G. (President, US National Farmers Union), world food agency proposal, 88

Pearson, Lester (Canadian Prime Minister), proposal to the UN General Assembly for a world food bank (1959), 100

Pinstrup-Andersen, Per (IFPRI Director General), 334–6, 402

Pisani, M. (French Minster of Agriculture), 86

Plan of Implementation, World Summit for Sustainable Development, 2002, *see* United Nations (UN)

Pope John Paul II
address at 1996 World Food Summit, 350–1
inaugural address, 1992 International Nutrition Conference, 307

Pope Paul VI, views at 1974 World Food Conference, 136–7

Powell, Colin (US Secretary of State), 298

Prebisch, Raul (Executive Secretary, UN Economic Commission for Latin America, first Secretary-General, United Nations Conference on Trade and Development secretariat), 66, 68, 462 n1, 462 n3, 464 n3, 464 n20, 464 n30

Preeg, Ernest (US trade negotiator), 474 n11

Preston, Lewis T. (World Bank President), 318

Principle of Surplus Disposal, *see* Food and Agriculture Organization of the United Nations (FAO)

Quesada, Vicente Fox (Mexican President), opening statement at International Conference on Financing of Development (2002), 370

Rasmussen, Anders Fosh (Danish Prime Minister and EU President), 298

Rasmussen, Poul Nyrup (Danish Prime Minister, President, Social Summit, 1995), 329

Redistribution from/with growth concept, 471 n44

right to food, US objections, 354–5, 358–9

Roosevelt, Franklin D. (US President), 3, 8, 23, 25
four freedoms address, January 1941, 3, 355, 365

Rosegrant, Mark (Director, IFPRI Environment and Production Technology Division), 374 n7

Roslov, Aleksei (Soviet Union Deputy Secretary-General, 1974 World Food Conference), 123

Runov, B. (Soviet Deputy Agriculture Minister), 136

Sachs, Jeffrey (Director, Earth Institute, Columbia University, New York, Director, UN Millennium Project), 434–6, 474 n13

Sadat, Anwar (Egyptian President), 123

Sadik, Nafis (Executive Direct, UNFPA, Secretary-General, International Conference on Population and Development, 1993), 322, 326–7

Santayana, George (author of *The Phases of Human Progress*, 1905), 461

Saouma, Eduoard (FAO Director-General 1976–84), 219–20, 235–7, 251, 255, 256–8, 307–8

Schlosser, Eric (author of *Fat Food Nation*, 2002), 409

Second World Food Congress (1970), 159

Sen, Amartya (Nobel Prize for Economics, 1998), 230–4, 404, 450, 463 n13, 472 n12

Sen, Binay Ranjan (FAO Director-General 1956–67), 77–80, 87, 93–4, 96–7, 304, 308

Sen, S. R. (Indian Planning Commission), 103–4

Serageldin, Ismail (Vice President, Environmentally Sustainable Development World Bank, Chair, World Conference on Overcoming Global Hunger, 1999), 320, 472 n12

Singer, Hans (later Sir Hans), v, xv, 66, 68. 462 n1, 462 n3, 464 n20, 464 n30, 465 n38, 471 n24

Snow, C. P. (British scientist and author)
address at Westminster College, Fulton, Missouri, USA on 12 November 1968 on the threat of widespread famine, 163, 388

Solow, Robert (Nobel Prize for Economics), 450

Soviet Union record grain imports (1972–3), 116, 120

Stern, Sir Nicholas (Chief Economist, World Bank, Head, UK Government Economic Service), author of *The Economics of Climate Change* (2006), 447–50

Stevenson, Adlai (US Ambassador to the UN), 465 n39

Stiglitz, Joseph (Chief Economist, World Bank, Nobel Prize for Economics), 399, 450

506 *Index*

Strachey, John (UK Minister of Food), 26
Strong, Maurice (Secretary-General, Earth
Summit 1992), 289–90
Sub-Saharan Africa, improving the response
to food insecurity, 392–3
Sutherland, Peter (first WTO
Director-General), 425
Swaminathan, M. S. (Co-Coordinator,
Millennium Project Task Force on
Hunger), 473 n7
Swift, Jonathan (British author of *Gulliver's
Travels*), 1

Tanco Jr., Arturo R. (Philippines
Agricultural Minister, President, World
Food Council), 211
trade, importance of, 363
transitory food insecurity, concept of, 40
Trant, Gerald I. (Executive Director, World
Food Council, 1986–92), 214, 221
Truman, Harry S. (US President), 13

UN bodies with interests in food and
nutrition security, 207–8, 349
UN Conference on Food and Agriculture,
Hot Springs, Virginia, USA May/June
1943, *see* Food and Agriculture
Organization of the United Nations
(FAO)
    UN Conference on the Human
    Environment, Stockholm, Sweden,
    1972, 129, 286
    UN Conference on Trade and
    Employment, Havana, Cuba, 1948,
    66–7
    UN Conference on Water, Mar del Plata,
    Argentina, 1977, 299
    UN Convention of the Elimination of All
    Forms of Discrimination against
    Women, 345
    UN Decade for Human Rights Education,
    1995–2004, 316
    UN Decade for Women, 1976–85, 340
    UN Decade on the Eradication of Poverty
    (1997–2006), 331
    UN Declaration on Human Rights (1948),
    314, 360
    UN Development Decades: first (1960s);
    second (1970s); third (1980s); fourth
    (1990s), 271, 341
    UN Development Fund for Women, 341
    UN Division for the Advancement of
    Women, 341, 342
    UN Emergency Operation, 1974, 130

UN four world conferences on women,
340
UN Fourth World Conference on Women
(1995), 340–6; Beijing Declaration
and Platform for Action, 342–3;
Implement the Beijing Platform of
Action (2002), 344–6; UN General
Assembly resolution on Further
Action and Initiatives to Implement
the Beijing Platform for Action, 344;
UN Special Session on progress in
implementing the Beijing
Declaration (2002), 343–4
UN Framework Convention on Climate
Change, 1994, *see* climate change
and global warming
UN Girls' Education Initiative (UNICEF
lead agency), 419
UN High-level Committee on
Programmes, 298
UN High-level Dialogue on Financing for
Development (2005), 373
UN High-level Forum on Aid
Effectiveness (2005), 377
UN High-level Panel on Threats,
Challenges and Change (2003), 375,
378
UN Inter-Agency Task Force on
Employment and Sustainable
Livelihoods (chaired by ILO), 290
UN International Resources and Training
Institute for the Advancement of
Women, 341
UN Millennium Declaration (2000),
365–6, 372
UN Millennium Development Goals and
Targets, 360, 366–7
UN Millennium Project for Achieving the
UN Millennium Development Goals,
360, 376, 433–4, 436; Task Force on
Hunger report, 406–7
UN Population Conference, Bucharest,
Romania (1974), 129, 321
UN Population Division, 322, 413
UN Programme of Action for African
Economic Recovery and
Development, 1986–90, 180
UN Security Council, reform of, 364, 378
UN Special Session on Children (2002),
282–5; A World Fit for Children,
declaration and plan of action, 283–5
UN Special Session on Population and
Development, 1999

UN Special Session on the Social Summit (2000), 332–3
UN Standing Committee on Nutrition (SCN), 208, 397
UN Sudano-Sahelian Office (UNSO), 286
UN System Chief Executive Board (CEB), 298
UN World Food Conference (1974), 121–49; conference impact, 143–8; conference proceedings, 129–39; conference resolutions: on food production, 104–1; on food aid, 141; on food security, 141; on follow-up measures, 141–2; national and international action proposals, 125–7; NGO declaration, 142–3; preparations for, 123–5; Rome Forum, 128–9; Universal Declaration on the Eradication of Hunger and Malnutrition, 139–40; World Food Authority proposal, 137–8; World Food Security proposal, 146
UN World Summit (2005), 375–80
United Nations reform, 364, 458
Universal Declaration of Human Rights, 1948
Women, Peace and Security. UN Security Council resolution (2000), 346
World Charter for Nature (1982), 286
World Commission on Environment and Development (1983), 286–7
World Conference on Human Rights (1993), 313–17; Vienna Declaration and Programme of Action on Human Rights (1993), 314–16
World Summit for Social Development (Social Summit) (1995), 328–33; Copenhagen Declaration on Social Development, 329–31
World Summit on Sustainable Development (2002), 291–8
UN Economic and Social Security Council proposal, 221
UN Economic Security Council proposal, 220
United Nations (UN)
Administrative Coordination Committee (ACC), 208
Advisory Committee on Administrative and Budgetary Questions (ACABQ), 208
Charter of the United Nations (1945), 16, 313–14, 315, 372, 460

Economic and Social Council (ECOSOC), 23, 30
Expanded Programme of Technical Assistance (EPTA), 10
Special Fund (SF), 10
Special United Nations Fund for Economic Development (SUNFED), 369, 462 n11
UN Central Emergency Revolving Fund, 379
UN Climate Change Conference, Nairobi, Kenya, November 2006, 450
UN Commission for Human Rights (converted to UN Human Rights Council), 316–17, 379
UN Commission for Social Development, 331
UN Commission on Sustainable Development, 290
UN Commission on the Status of Women, 341–2
UN Committee on Programme and Coordination, 208
UN Committee on the Elimination of Discrimination against Women, 341
UN Conference on Environment and Development (Earth Summit) (1992), 286–91, 296–7, 321; Agenda, 21. Programme of Action for Sustained Development, 288–9; Rio Declaration on Environment and Development, 288; Statement of Forest Principles, 289
United Nations Children's Fund (UNICEF), 206, 279, 398–403
United Nations Conference on Trade and Development (UNCTAD), 194, 229, 427–8
United Nations Development Programme (UNDP), 10, 208, 229
United Nations Educational, Scientific and Cultural Organization (UNESCO), 23, 249
United Nations Environment Programme (UNEP), 191, 290
United Nations Joint Inspection Programme (JIU), 208, 210
United Nations Relief and Rehabilitation Agency (UNRRA), 11, 26
United Nations World Food Conference, 1974, *see* Food and Agriculture Organization of the United Nations (FAO)

508 *Index*

United States (US)
  Agricultural Adjustment Act, 1933, 13
  Agricultural Adjustment Act, 1935, 13
  Agricultural Trade Development and
    Assistance Act (PL 480), 1954,
    49–51
  Agriculture Act, 1949, 34
  Centers for Disease Control and
    Prevention, 409
  Commodity Credit Corporation (CCC),
    13, 34
  European Recovery Programme (Marshall
    Plan), 1948–53, 13, 34
  Export-Import Bank, 1934, 34
  Federal Farm Board (established 1929),
    12
  food aid programme, 86, 133
  Grain Stabilization Board, 1933, 13, 34
  International Food and Nutrition Act,
    1965, 102
  International Grains Reserves System
    proposal, 1974, 155–8; House of
    Representatives resolution, 1974,
    155
  Lend-Lease Act, 1941, 13, 34
  Mutual Security Act, 1951, 34, 49
  Overseas Development Council, 119
  Public Law (PL) 480 Food Aid
    (Food-for-Peace) Programme record
    cereals exports 1974, 116
  Surgeon General's Report on Nutrition
    and Health, 1988, 411
  Surplus Act, 1944, 34
  US reservations concerning the right to
    food: at the 1996 World Food
    Summit, 354–5; at the 2002 World
    Food Summit +5, 358–9
  US views expressed at the 1974 World
    Food Conference, 133–5, 147

Veil, Simone (Chair, International Nutrition
  Conference, 1992), 472 n7
Vienna Convention for the Protection of
  the Ozone Layer, 1985, *see* climate
  change and global warming
Voluntary Guidelines to Achieve the
  Progressive Realization of the Right to
  Adequate Food, *see* Food and
  Agriculture Organization of the United
  Nations (FAO)
von Braun, Joachim (IFPRI Director
  General), 402, 473 n6, 473 n7
Vulnerability Analysis and Mapping (VAM),
  see World Food Programme (WFP)

Waldheim, Kurt (UN Secretary General,
  1972–81), 130
Wallace, Henry (US Vice President in the
  Roosevelt Administration), 8
Ward, Barbara (Lady Jackson), 128, 144,
  147–8, 279, 286, 467 n7, 471 n5
Water Supply and Sanitation Collaborative
  Council (WSSCC), 299, 302
Whelan, Eugene (Canadian Agriculture
  Minister, President World Food
  Council), 211
Williams, Maurice (Chairman, OECD
  Development Assistance Committee,
  second World Food Council Executive
  Director 1978–86), 182–3, 185, 198–9,
  470 n39
Wilson, Woodrow (US President and
  founder of the League of Nations), 460
Wolfensohn, James D. (President, World
  Bank), 371
Wolfowitz, Paul (President, World Bank),
  450
women in development concept, 341
Women, Peace and Security, UN Security
  Council resolution 2000, *see* United
  Nations (UN)
Women's Role in Economic Development
  (1970), 341
World Bank
  International Bank for Reconstruction
    and Development (IBRD), 11,
    23, 29
  International Development Association
    (IDA), 320, 462 n11
  perspective on hunger and malnutrition,
    259–63
  World Conference on Overcoming Global
    Hunger (1993), 318–20
World Campaign against Hunger, Disease
  and Ignorance proposal, 83–4
World Charter for Nature, 1992, *see* United
  Nations (UN)
World Commission on the Social
  Dimensions of Globalization
  (established by ILO in 2001), 453–4
World Conference on Overcoming Global
  Hunger (1993), *see* World Bank
World Declaration and Plan of Action on
  Nutrition, 1992, *see* Food and
  Agriculture Organization of the United
  Nations (FAO)
World Economic Forum, 453

Index 509

World Food Board proposal, *see* Food and Agriculture Organization of the United Nations (FAO)

World Food Congress, June 1963, *see* Food and Agriculture Organization of the United Nations (FAO)

World Food Council (WFC)
  assessment of effectiveness, 210–21; advisory group report on, 212–13
  coordination mechanism, 206–10
  establishment, 146–7, 167
  functions and responsibilities, 167–8, 170
  major food and hunger issues, 174–7
  membership, 167
  modus operandi, 168–74
  presidents and executive directors, 167, 168, 221; World Food Conference resolutions, implementation of, 175–6; World food situation, 174–5
  strategic perspectives on world hunger and poverty, 193–7
  WFC declarations: Beijing Declaration, 1987, 200–2; Beijing Proposal on Sustainable Agriculture and Rural Development,1993, 205–6; Cairo Declaration, 1989, 188, 203–5; Cyprus Initiative, 1988, 188, 202–3; Manila Communiqué, 1977, 197–8; Mexico Declaration, 1978, 198–200
  WFC initiatives: Africa's food problems, 180–1; developing countries food security and changes in eastern Europe and the CIS, 192; developing country-owned reserves, 190–1; eradicating hunger and malnutrition, 184–9; food crisis contingency planning, 189–90; food priority countries, 177–9; food security and environmental management, 191–2; international food security system, 179–80; international hunger initiative, 187, 202; migration and food security, 193; national food strategies, 182–4

World Food Conference 1974 resolution establishing WFC, 175–6

world food crisis, 1972–4, 115–20

World Food Programme (WFP)
  An Expanded Programme of Surplus Food Utilization proposal, 89–93
  Food aid during the Second UN Development Decade report, 106–9

governing bodies, changing roles and responsibilities, 141–2
growth and status, 109
guidelines and criteria for food aid, 109–11
International Emergency Food Reserve (IEFR), 159–62, 194
McGovern initiative to establish a multilateral food aid programme, 97–9, 100–1
multilateral food aid study, 103–5
proposals to change WFP: Argentine proposal for a 'World Food Fund', 103; Israeli proposal for increased food production, 103; Lebanon proposal to establish a 'World Commodity Organization', 103; Netherlands proposal to create an 'Emergency Food Supply Scheme', 103; Uruguayan proposal for a 'World Food Bank', 103
UNCTAD recommendation for a future WFP, 103
Vulnerability Analysis and Mapping (VAS), 394

World Food Reserve study, *see* Food and Agriculture Organization of the United Nations (FAO)

world food security, alternative views, 407–8

World Food Summit +5, 2002, *see* Food and Agriculture Organization of the United Nations (FAO)

World Food Summit 1996, *see* Food and Agriculture Organization of the United Nations (FAO)

world food system, evolution of, 385–6

World Health Organization (WHO), 23, 304, 308

World Meteorological Organization (WMO), 164

World Monetary and Economic Conference, London, 1932–3, 7

world population growth, 413
  effects of HIV/AIDS, 413

World Social Forum, 453

World Summit for Social Development (Social Summit), 1995, *see* United Nations (UN)

World Summit on Children, 1990, *see* United Nations (UN)

World Survey on the Role of Women in Development (1995), 343

510 *Index*

World Trade Organization (WTO), 208, 361, 423
  criticism of, 424
  proposals for reform, 425–7
  WTO Working Group for Trade and Food Security, 354
world water forums, 302

World Water Week, Stockholm, Sweden, 2006, 302
World Weather Watch System, 164
Worldwatch Institute (founded 1974), 286

Yugoslavia proposal for a world food report, League of Nations, 1933, 6